KT-463-296

British Politics in Focus

AS Level

Roy Bentley

Alan Dobson

Peter Dorey

David Roberts

Edited by
Steve Lancaster
& David Roberts

Causeway Press

Editor at Causeway Press - Steve Lancaster
Cover design by Tim Button (Waring Collins Limited)
Graphic origination by Derek Baker (Waring Collins Limited)
Reader - Wendy Janes
Original artwork by Tim Button and Derek Baker (Waring Collins Limited)

Acknowledgements

The publishers wish to thank the following for permission to reproduce photographs, cartoons and other illustrations:

Brick 23, 92, 210 (b), 214, 215, 228, 329; Commission for Racial Equality 33; Conservative Party 259; Countryside Alliance 197 (t); Crossley, Neil 53; Equal Opportunities Commission 25, 195 (r); Gibbard 124, 300 (t), 306; Hulton Getty 43 (bl), 211; Liberal Democrats 260; Lucas, Caroline 184; Mary Evans Picture Library 39, 50, 121 (both), 122, 125, 126, 130, 153, 156 (top), 167 (all 3), 173 (top 8); Museum of London 43 (r); Newman, Nick 300 (b); Ormskirk Advertiser 282; Oxfam 195 (l); PA Photos 4, 10, 30, 31, 80 (all), 102, 104, 111, 123, 127, 129, 134 (b), 154 (r), 156 (b), 164, 165, 166, 173 (bottom 4), 175, 178 (both), 197 (b), 198, 238, 242 (bottom 2), 243 (both), 256 (b), 264 (both), 266, 268, 289, 304, 305, 308 (both), 374 (both), 379, 380, 384; Peter Newark's Historical Pictures 45; Rex Features 73 (3); Riddel, Chris 256 (t), 294 (t), 301 (t & bl); Rowson, Martin 56; Simmonds, Posy 28; Simonds, David 236, 294 (b), 301 (br); Topham Picturepoint 73 (1&2); 132, 152, 154 (l), 156 (middle 3), 237 (both), 239, 242 (top), 353, 385; Winterbottom, Tony 338; Wright, Andrew 1, 2, 6 (both), 15, 101, 106, 182, 207, 221

Every effort has been made to locate the copyright owners of material used in this book. Any omissions brought to the attention of the publisher are regretted and will be credited in subsequent printings.

British Library Cataloguing in Publication Data
A catalogue record for this book is available from the British Library.

ISBN 1 902796 78 0

Causeway Press Limited
PO Box 13, Ormskirk, Lancs, L39 5HP

© Roy Bentley, Alan Dobson, Peter Dorey, David Roberts
1st impression, 2004

Printed and bound by Scotprint, Haddington, East Lothian

Contents

Contents

Unit 7   *Political ideology*   117

Unit 8   *The party system*   142

Unit 9   *Political parties in the UK*   152

1 *What is politics?*

1.1 *The origins of politics*

The need for politics arises because people are social animals. This means that they choose to live together in groups. Because they live together in groups, it is necessary to make decisions about matters affecting the group. People have to decide, for example, about how the resources available to the group are to be shared out and how conflicts between members of the group are to be resolved. The study of politics is the study of how such decisions are made and how people believe they should be made.

Since the resources available to any group are limited, questions arise about how the resources which are available should be distributed. Should everybody have a fair share, for example, or do some individuals or groups deserve a bigger share? Questions might also arise as to whether and how the available resources should be increased. There is no single correct answer to these questions and so people often differ about the principles which are to be used to resolve these questions and the arrangements which are to be employed to do so. According to some political commentators, the differences that arise as people in social groups try to resolve their problems are at the heart of politics. The study of politics is the study of conflict resolution (see Box 1.1).

1.2 *Politics as the study of conflict resolution*

Modern society is highly complex. Individuals argue over many different interests, values and beliefs. Conflict does not just take place between individuals, however. It also exists between larger groups - between countries as well as within them. According to one viewpoint, the aim of politics is to remove conflict so that people can live in reasonable harmony with each other. In other words, the aim of politics is to produce consensus - a general agreement over what people want and what they believe is right.

In general terms, it can be argued that conflict arises for two main reasons. First, it arises because of conflicting interests. And second, it arises because of conflicting values or beliefs.

Conflicting interests

In a country such as Britain there is a complex web of interests which people want to expand and protect. Many of these interests are economic and financial. People want a job with good pay, a comfortable house, holidays and so on. They want a good education for their children, health care and security against poverty. Farmers and agricultural workers want a prosperous farming industry. Publishers want people to buy lots of books.

Although many of the interests, such as the desire for a good health system, are common to all people, difficulties and disagreement emerge because resources are limited and different people have different priorities. Some people might want more money to be spent on high-tech machinery in hospitals, for example, while others want more nurses to be employed at a better rate of pay. Since there may not be the resources to take both approaches, choices have to be made. It is the necessity of making such choices which leads to conflict.

Conflicting values and beliefs

When people defend their interests, it does not necessarily mean that they are being selfish. Opponents of a new open cast mine, for example, might be furious that it is close to their homes, but they might also claim, with some justification, that to open the mine would be an ecological disaster because of the damage it would cause to the wildlife living on the site. Such arguments might produce support from people living miles away who are not personally affected by the project. Political activity, in other words, can spring from a set of values and beliefs as well as from self-interest. Equally, the way in which a conflict is resolved might owe more to the values and beliefs of the decision-makers than to their personal interest in the matter.

Box 1.1 Politics as conflict resolution

1.3 Politics as the study of power

The sociologists Dowse & Hughes (1972) argue that politics is about power, claiming that 'politics occurs when there are differentials in power' (see Box 1.2). This suggests that:

> 'Any social relationship which involves power differentials is political. Political relationships would extend from parents assigning domestic chores to their children to teachers enforcing discipline in the classroom; from a manager organising a workforce to a general ordering troops into battle.' (Haralambos & Holborn 1995, p.501)

If people have power, it means that they are able to make other people do what they want them to do, even if the other people do not want to do it. Power is, therefore, the ability to influence the behaviour of another either by threat, sanctions or through manipulation. In all political situations, those who have power are able to reward those who conform and punish those who do not.

Power cannot be exercised unless there is some way of backing it up. This may be the direct threat of or the use of force, but it does not have to be. Power that is based on the direct threat of or the use of force is usually described as 'coercion'. But individuals (or governments) often do not have to resort to coercion to get their own way. Rather, some forms of power are accepted as 'legitimate' (as fair and right) and people are obedient because of that. In Britain, for example, most people obey the laws made by the government even if they themselves do not agree with them. They do this because they accept that the government is legitimate. Power which is regarded as legitimate is usually described as 'authority'.

Box 1.2 Politics as the study of power

Weber's three ideal types of authority

The German sociologist, Max Weber (1864-1920), identified three ideal types of how authority might be established. No person or group in authority is likely to be exactly like any one of these types, but, Weber believed, they are useful tools for analysing any given example of authority.

A. Traditional authority

Traditional authority arises where people choose to obey because of established customs and traditions. One reason people obey the government in the UK, for example, is because it commands a majority in the House of Commons and, by tradition, the political party (or parties) holding such a majority forms a government.

B. Charismatic authority

Charismatic authority arises from the personality and qualities of a leader. People obey because they believe the leader should be obeyed as a consequence of the qualities they display. Winston Churchill was held by many to have displayed such qualities during the Second World War. Similarly, some people believe that Margaret Thatcher displayed special charismatic qualities when she was Prime Minister. Such authority can command strong loyalty, but it may not last. Churchill and his party lost the post-war election because many who thought his qualities were suited to war did not believe they were suited to times of peace. Similarly, Thatcher's charismatic power ebbed away, leading members of her own party to reject her.

C. Rational-legal authority

Rational-legal authority is such that obedience is secured as a result of those in power following a set of rules. In the UK, for example, the governing party (or parties) has, by following electoral rules, secured a majority in the House of Commons and been invited to form a government by the monarch. Because the government has followed this set of rules, it expects UK citizens to obey it, provided it exercises itself lawfully. This form of authority can be seen at work even more clearly in the USA where government authority comes from obedience to the US constitution - a set of rules which is the source of all federal and state authority in that country (see Goodwin 1997, pp.311-12).

Main points Sections 1.1 - 1.3

- **Politics is about how decisions are made and how people believe they should be made.**
- **Some people argue that politics is mainly about resolving conflicts. They claim that the aim of politics is to produce a consensus by resolving conflicts in an acceptable way.**
- **Other writers claim politics is about the exercise of power. There are two ways of exercising power - by threatening or using force (coercion) or by making decisions which people regard as legitimate, even if they don't agree with them (authority).**
- **The German sociologist Max Weber identified three types of authority - traditional, charismatic and rational-legal authority.**

Activity 1.1 What is politics?

Item A What is politics?

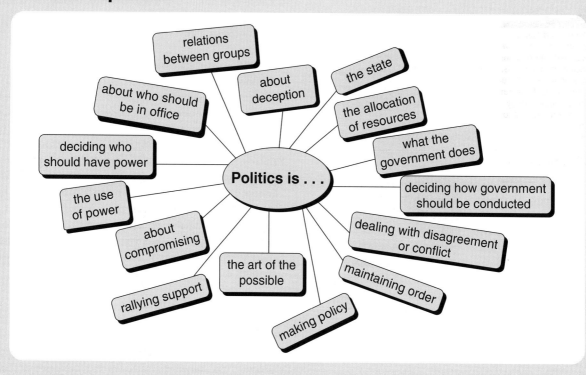

Item B Weber's three types of authority

Max Weber, a German sociologist who lived in the 19th century, distinguished between three different types of authority:

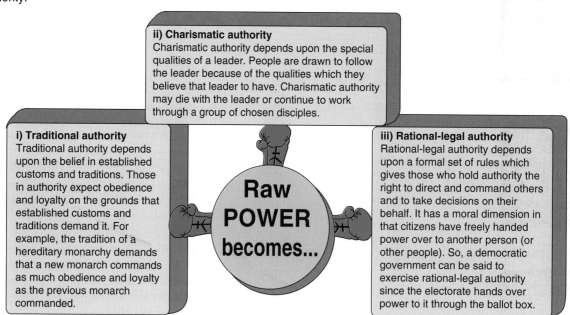

ii) Charismatic authority
Charismatic authority depends upon the special qualities of a leader. People are drawn to follow the leader because of the qualities which they believe that leader to have. Charismatic authority may die with the leader or continue to work through a group of chosen disciples.

i) Traditional authority
Traditional authority depends upon the belief in established customs and traditions. Those in authority expect obedience and loyalty on the grounds that established customs and traditions demand it. For example, the tradition of a hereditary monarchy demands that a new monarch commands as much obedience and loyalty as the previous monarch commanded.

Raw POWER becomes...

iii) Rational-legal authority
Rational-legal authority depends upon a formal set of rules which gives those who hold authority the right to direct and command others and to take decisions on their behalf. It has a moral dimension in that citizens have freely handed power over to another person (or other people). So, a democratic government can be said to exercise rational-legal authority since the electorate hands over power to it through the ballot box.

It should be noted that Weber regarded these three categories as 'ideal types'. In the real world, authority might come from two or more of the three sources. Second, Weber believed that there was a fixed amount of power in any society. Since the amount of power is constant, power held by any individual or group is power not available to any other individual or group. And third, Weber suggested that power is always used to further the interests of those who hold it.

Item C **Lukes' three faces of power**

In a book published in 1974, Steven Lukes argued that power has three faces or dimensions.

i) Decision-making
The first face of power is its open face - the power that can be seen to be exercised when a decision is taken. Suppose the government proposed a law in Britain. This proposal would be debated in Cabinet and in Parliament. Interest groups would lobby MPs. There might be demonstrations for or against the proposal. Eventually, the proposal might pass through Parliament, gain Royal Assent and become law. In this decision-making process, it would be relatively straightforward to identify where power lies.

iii) Manipulating desires
The third face of power goes one step further. Lukes suggests that power can be exercised through manipulation. People with power can persuade others that what is being offered is what is desired. For example, some feminists would argue that men exercise power over women in contemporary Britain by persuading them that being a mother and a housewife are the most desirable roles for women. In reality, feminists claim, women who occupy these roles are exploited by, and for the benefit of, men.

ii) Non-decision-making
The second face of power is its secretive face. Power is exercised behind closed doors. Those who have the power to set the political agenda have the power to determine not only what can be discussed, but, more important, what cannot be discussed. Power is, therefore, not just about making decisions. It is also about preventing decisions being taken or about narrowing the choices which are considered. For example, a teacher might offer students the opportunity to decide whether to do a piece of homework that week or the following week. The class appears to have been given the opportunity to reach a decision. In reality, however, power still rests with the teacher who has limited the options open to the students. The students are not free to decide whether or not they do this particular piece of work, nor can they choose to reject doing homework altogether.

Item D **Demonstrators against the war against Iraq in London, February 2003**

Questions

1. Using Item A, write a paragraph explaining what is meant by 'politics'.

2. a) Which of Weber's three types of authority in Item B best describes the British political system today? Give reasons for your answer.

   b) Can you think of examples to illustrate the other two types of authority?

3. What does Item C tell us about the way in which politics works in Britain today?

4. a) Explain why what is happening in Item D is political.

   b) What does this picture tell us about the British political system?

1.4 Political activity - voting

Voting is the most common form of political activity in Britain, as in many other countries. Turnout in general elections is higher than in other elections, but the 2001 general election saw the lowest level of turnout since the right to vote was extended to all adults over the age of 21 in 1928. In 2001, only 59.4% of those eligible to vote actually voted. This was down from 71.4% in 1997 (Lancaster 2002, p.30). Turnout in local elections is generally lower. It stood at 34% in the May 2003 local elections. In 1999, only 28% of the electorate voted at the European elections. Despite these figures, however, elections involve far more people in the political process than do any other types of political activity.

1.5 Other types of political activity

Apart from voting, people have the opportunity of participating in the political process in a number of other ways. Writing to a local councillor, Member of Parliament (MP) or Member of the European Parliament (MEP), or to a local or national newspaper is one way of participating in the political process. Joining a pressure group or political party is another. But, while some people feel that paying their membership fee to a pressure group or political party is enough, others are prepared to spend a great deal of their spare time campaigning. There is, in other words, a scale of political participation. This scale ranges from complete inactivity at one end to full-time activity at the other end.

1.6 Activism and apathy

During election campaigns, activists from the political parties telephone potential voters, email them or go round from house to house, knocking on doors and canvassing support. On the doorstep or via emails, people are often prepared to air their views. When asked what sort of people, in their opinion, are involved in politics, most mention councillors, MPs and MEPs, but few mention themselves. Many say that they are disillusioned with politics and that it is not even worth voting since 'they're all the same'. The fact that they refer to politicians as 'they' rather than 'we' shows that they feel removed from the political process.

In reality, however, political activity covers a much wider area than many people realise. People are involved in political activity whenever they interact with others in any form of social activity. This is because any group, however large or small, involves an element of decision-making - and, therefore, involves political activity.

If politics is about decision-making, then everybody can be said to be involved in politics through their everyday participation with others. All members of society, after all, are members of groups - either because they are born into them (such as their family or ethnic group) or because they choose to join them (such as a sports club or religious group).

Although everybody participates in political activity in this broad sense, far fewer people choose to participate in political activity in the narrower sense of working for a

political party or group, or of standing for office. The fall in turnout suggests that people are even becoming more reluctant to participate by voting - see Box 1.3.

Box 1.3 Public apathy

'I like it! It's a blatant appeal to public apathy.'

Why participate?

Those who do choose to get involved in politics in the narrower sense may do so for a number of reasons. First, they may hold a set of beliefs strongly and hope to persuade others to accept them. Second, they may want to bring about change and feel that participation in the political process is the best way to achieve this. Third, they may want to help others. Fourth, they may want to promote their own interests or the interests of their group. And fifth, they may enjoy exercising power over others and want to hold power for its own sake.

1.7 Where political activity takes place

If politics is taken in its broadest sense, then it is possible to argue that:

> 'Politics is at the heart of all collective human activity, formal and informal, public and private, in all human groups, institutions and societies, not just some of them, and it always has been and always will be.' (Leftwich 1984, p.63)

In this sense, political activity can be said to take place wherever one person tries to influence or change the behaviour of another. It takes place in any situation in which decisions have to be made or disagreements sorted out. It takes place wherever there is a power relationship between the participants. It takes place, therefore, at both the micro (small) level and at the macro (large) level.

The small picture

At the micro level, political activity can be identified, for example, within the family - see Box 1.4 on page 6. Take the traditional 'nuclear' family, made up of two parents and two children. In such a family, the roles are clearly defined. The father goes out to work to support the family, while the

Box 1.4 Politics at the micro level

mother stays at home to look after the children and the house. The children are expected to obey the wishes of the parents without question. What the father says, goes. There is, in other words, a power relationship in which the children are at the bottom and the father is at the top. When important decisions have to be made, it is the father who has the final say. But, families do not have to work like this, and, indeed, many do not. Many families, for example, have a single parent or, if there are two parents, make decisions jointly rather than allowing the father to have all the power. The point is that, in every family (whether it works as a traditional nuclear family or not), there is a power relationship which determines how decisions are made and disputes are settled. Activity within the family, therefore, can be described as 'political' at the micro level. The same is true of activity which takes place in the workplace or in school or college.

The big picture

At the macro level, political activity is, perhaps, easier to identify. The work of government ministers, the civil service, opposition MPs or MEPs and local councillors, for example, all comes under the heading of political activity at the macro level - see Box 1.5. Political activity takes place, therefore, where these people work - at Number 10 Downing Street, in Whitehall, in the British and European Parliaments or in the local council chamber.

It is not only in these places, however, that political activity takes place at the macro level. Since the position of most politicians is dependent on their election to office, it is necessary for them to gain and maintain their electors' support. To do this, they need to communicate with the electorate. As a result, the media is also the centre of a great deal of political activity at the macro level. It is on television or radio, or in the newspapers that politicians try to persuade their electors of the validity of their views. Politicians and political activists, therefore, attempt to gain positive exposure of their views in the media and they often stage events for the benefit of the media.

The fact that the media is the focus of a great deal of political activity does not mean, however, that political activity at the macro level is something which only takes place in public. On the contrary, most important decisions are made behind closed doors. Take, for example, the decisions made by the Cabinet. During a parliamentary session, the Cabinet meets each week to discuss what the Prime Minister decides are the key political issues of the day. What is discussed in Cabinet and many of the decisions which are reached, however, remain secret. Since part, or even the whole, of the decision-making process goes on in secret, it is sometimes difficult to find out exactly how a decision came to be made. It is, therefore, sometimes difficult to be sure exactly where political activity takes place.

Box 1.5 Politics at the macro level

1.8 How political participation has changed

Since the 1950s, the nature of political participation has changed in two main ways. First, there has been a decline in the number of people participating in the formal political process. Membership of the main political parties has, for example, dropped dramatically. In the 1950s, well over 2 million people were members of the Conservative Party. This had dropped to 330,000 by 2002. In the same year, Labour had 280,000 members - down from over 1 million in the 1950s (Lancaster 2002). Similarly, the proportion of the working population belonging to a trade union has dropped considerably since the unions' heyday in the 1970s. In 1978, 53% of workers were trade union members. By 1996, that figure had dropped to 31%. It has remained fairly static since then. When combined with the low figures for voter turnout at elections, these figures on party and trade union membership suggest a clear trend toward decreased involvement in the formal and traditional political process.

At the same time, a second trend has become evident. Participation in less formal forms of politics has risen. Membership of pressure groups has risen dramatically (see Unit 10) and large numbers of people have become involved in protests - at various levels:

- at local level - such as protests against the building of particular roads or airport runways
- at national level - such as the demonstration against war in Iraq in February 2003 which brought well over a million people to London or the march organised by the Countryside Alliance in 1998 which mobilised around 250,000 supporters
- at international level - such as annual May Day rallies and the demonstrations round the world organised by the anti-globalisation movement.

Recourse to unconventional politics is by no means confined to demonstrators marching through the streets. During the fuel blockade of September 2000, for example, protestors who were angry at high fuel duty blockaded oil distribution depots in an attempt to starve the country of fuel (see McNaughton 2001). Within five days, the protestors nearly brought Britain to a standstill as garages ran out of fuel and panic-buying emptied supermarket shelves. The protestors called off the protest, giving the government a 60-day ultimatum. They demanded the government either to announce a cut in fuel duty in the November pre-Budget speech or to face renewed blockades. In November, the Chancellor of the Exchequer offered just enough concessions and initiatives to avert a repeat performance.

Main points Sections 1.4 - 1.8

- **Voting is the most common form of political activity in the UK.**
- **Although the number of political activists is small, everyone participates in politics to some extent.**
- **Political activity takes place whenever one person tries to influence another. At the micro level this might take place within the family, at the macro level at Whitehall or in Parliament or in Brussels.**
- **Two dominant trends can be identified in terms of political activity since the 1950s - the decline in traditional forms of political activity and the rise of less conventional forms of political activity.**

Activity 1.2 Political activity in the UK

Item A Turnout

(i) Turnout in general elections 1945-2001

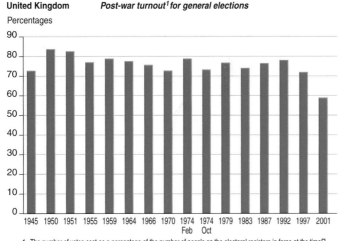

United Kingdom   *Post-war turnout¹ for general elections*

Percentages (chart with bars for years: 1945, 1950, 1951, 1955, 1959, 1964, 1966, 1970, 1974 Feb, 1974 Oct, 1979, 1983, 1987, 1992, 1997, 2001)

1 The number of votes cast as a percentage of the number of people on the electoral registers in force at the time of the elections.

This chart shows the turnout in general elections held between 1945 and 2001.

(ii) Turnout in European elections 1979-99

Country	1979	1984	1989	1994	1999
Belgium	91.6	92.2	90.7	90.7	91.0
Denmark	47.1	52.3	46.1	52.5	50.5
France	60.7	56.7	48.7	53.5	46.7
Germany	65.0	56.8	62.4	58.0	45.2
Greece	78.6	77.2	79.9	71.1	75.3
Ireland	63.6	47.6	68.3	44.0	50.2
Italy	85.5	83.9	81.5	74.8	70.8
Luxembourg	88.9	87.0	87.4	90.0	87.3
Netherlands	57.8	50.5	47.2	35.6	30.0
Portugal	-	72.2	51.1	35.7	40.0
Spain	-	68.9	54.8	59.6	63.4
UK	31.6	32.6	36.2	36.2	23.1
Total EU	63.0	61.0	58.5	56.4	

This chart shows the turnout in European elections held between 1979 and 1999.

Source: Social Trends 2003 and Coxall, Robins & Leach 2003.

Item B Political activism

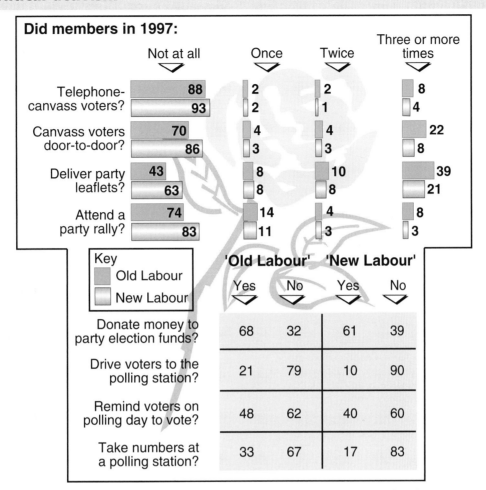

Did members in 1997:

	Not at all	Once	Twice	Three or more times
Telephone-canvass voters? (Old)	88	2	2	8
Telephone-canvass voters? (New)	93	2	1	4
Canvass voters door-to-door? (Old)	70	4	4	22
Canvass voters door-to-door? (New)	86	3	3	8
Deliver party leaflets? (Old)	43	8	10	39
Deliver party leaflets? (New)	63	8	8	21
Attend a party rally? (Old)	74	14	4	8
Attend a party rally? (New)	83	11	3	3

Key
- Old Labour
- New Labour

	'Old Labour'		'New Labour'	
	Yes	No	Yes	No
Donate money to party election funds?	68	32	61	39
Drive voters to the polling station?	21	79	10	90
Remind voters on polling day to vote?	48	62	40	60
Take numbers at a polling station?	33	67	17	83

This chart examines the extent to which members of the Labour Party took part in political activity in 1997. Those who joined the Labour Party before 1994 are described as 'Old Labour'. Those who joined the Labour Party after 1994 are described as 'New Labour'.

Source: Whiteley & Seyd 1998.

Item C Views on the political system in 1973 and 2003

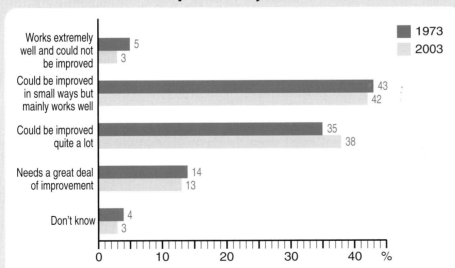

- 1973
- 2003

	1973	2003
Works extremely well and could not be improved	5	3
Could be improved in small ways but mainly works well	43	42
Could be improved quite a lot	35	38
Needs a great deal of improvement	14	13
Don't know	4	3

This chart shows the results of a survey carried out in 1973 and repeated in 2003. People were asked to give their opinion about the system of governing Britain. The figures are percentages.

Source: *Politics Review*, Vol.13.1, Sepotember 2003.

Questions

1. What does Item A tell us about political activity in the UK?

2. Using the evidence in Item B:
   a) what were the main political activities of members of the Labour Party in 1997?
   b) how politically active were members of the Labour Party?

3. Using Item C and your own knowledge, discuss the view that the level of political activity has not decreased but has shifted its focus.

1.9 *The state and sovereignty*

The institution which exercises power over a defined area is usually described as the 'state'. Sovereignty (that is, supreme power) normally lies with the state. All states have certain characteristics in common - see Box 1.6.

Box 1.6 Characteristics states have in common

States have five main characteristics in common. These can be summarised as follows:

- states have territory with clearly defined geographical boundaries
- membership is compulsory - all members of the population become citizens at birth
- since the state is a sovereign body, it holds the ultimate legal power over its members
- the state delegates its power to certain institutions
- all states have some kind of constitution (a set of rules) and a pattern of offices which have to be filled.

Notes

A. Since the state is a sovereign body which holds the ultimate legal power over its members, it controls coercive bodies such as the military and the police and it can decide who may use force and to what extent it should be used. Laws made by the state can result in a citizen's imprisonment or even a citizen's death.

B. In some countries, such as the USA, a state's constitution is written down in a document ('codified'). In the UK, it is not. It is uncodified.

Liberal democracies

The UK, like the USA and the other members of the EU, is a 'liberal democracy'. Three basic types of power are involved in the running of liberal democracies. These are outlined in Box 1.7.

Box 1.7 Three basic types of power in liberal democracies

The three basic types of power involved in the running of liberal democracies are as follows:

1. Legislative power
Legislative power is the power to make laws. In the UK, this power has been granted to Parliament. It is the role of Parliament to make new laws and to reform those already in existence.

2. Executive power
Executive power is the power to suggest new laws and to implement existing laws. In the UK, this power has been granted to the government and its departments. The government is helped to fulfil its role by the civil service, a permanent body of supposedly impartial state employees.

3. Judicial power
Judicial power is the power to interpret laws and to make judgements about whether they have been broken or not. This power is exercised by the courts. In the UK, these range from the House of Lords, the highest appeal court, to local courts presided over by magistrates.

The location of sovereignty

In the UK, it is possible to talk of 'parliamentary sovereignty' - the idea that power rests with Parliament. This is because Parliament has the power to make laws which cannot be challenged. Since, however, at regular intervals Parliament (or, at least the House of Commons) must submit itself to the people in elections, it could be argued that the people are sovereign because they have the power to decide who will rule them.

1.10 *The institutional framework*

The UK's institutional framework has five key elements.

A. The monarchy

The UK is a constitutional monarchy. In former times, the monarch possessed a great deal of political power, but this has now been eroded. While the monarch remains the nominal head of state, the political role played by monarchs in the past is now undertaken by the Prime Minister and other members of government.

B. The executive

The political power once exercised by the monarch, is now, therefore, exercised by the executive - by the Cabinet which is chaired by the Prime Minister and by the government departments. Most government departments are headed by a Cabinet minister chosen by the Prime Minister. The Cabinet meets once a week at the Cabinet Room in Number Ten Downing Street, the Prime Minister's official residence.

Most Cabinet ministers are in charge of a government department - such as the Department of Health, the Department of Transport and so on. These ministers are responsible for a particular area of the government's work. Occasionally, however, a Cabinet minister is appointed 'without portfolio'.

As well as choosing Cabinet ministers, the Prime Minister also chooses the junior ministers who work in government departments. At any one time, there are around 100 ministers in total. Periodically, the Prime Minister has a 'reshuffle' and sacks, promotes or moves ministers. Whilst ministers are, therefore, political appointees, they work in tandem with permanent civil servants who are state employees.

C. The legislature

Legislative power is exercised by Parliament which consists of two Houses, the House of Commons and the House of Lords (see Box 1.8 on page 10). Each member of the House of Commons is elected by people living in a constituency (a geographical area). General elections must take place every five years, but they can be called before the five-year term has been completed. The vast majority of candidates in general elections belong to a political party and they stand on behalf of that party. The political party which gains the largest number of seats in the House of Commons is usually invited to form a government (it is possible that the combined number of seats held by two or more parties might outnumber the largest party and, by making a coalition, these smaller parties might then be in a position to form a government). The Leader of the party invited to form the

Box 1.8 The Houses of Parliament

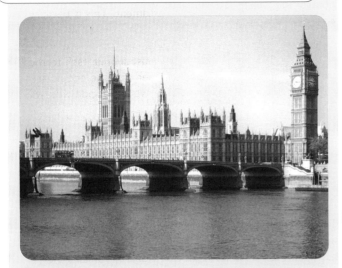

This photograph shows the Houses of Parliament in Westminster, London.

government becomes Prime Minister. The largest party outside government forms the official Opposition. The Leader of the Opposition normally chooses a 'shadow Cabinet'. All proposed legislation must pass through a number of stages before it becomes law. Most proposals ('Bills') are first put forward in the House of Commons. They must pass through both the Houses of Parliament, however, before they can be sent to the monarch for Royal Assent. Once a Bill has received Royal Assent, it becomes law.

D. An adversarial system

When a party wins an election and forms a government, it is generally regarded as having a mandate (the authorisation) to put into practice the promises it made in its election manifesto. The British system of government, however, is **adversarial** - it relies on two sides being taken on any issue. It is, therefore, the job of the Opposition to oppose proposals made by the government and to criticise them. Since the government usually commands a majority in the House of Commons, it can usually rely on its supporters to pass its proposals regardless of the criticism made by the Opposition.

E. The House of Lords

Members of the House of Lords or 'peers' are not elected. Until November 1999, the majority of members of the House of Lords were hereditary - they acquired their right to sit in the Lords by accident of birth. The remainder were:

- Life Peers (peers appointed by the Prime Minister to sit in the House for their lifetime only)
- Lords Spiritual (the two archbishops and other bishops of the Church of England)
- Lords Pastoral (Law Lords who sit in judgement when the House of Lords is used as a court of appeal).

The House of Lords Act passed in November 1999 removed the right of all but 92 hereditary peers to sit in the Lords. In September 2003, it was announced that the right of the 92 remaining hereditary peers to sit in the Lords would be withdrawn (for further details on Lords reform see Unit 14).

1.11 Who exercises power in the UK?

Three main models have been developed to explain who exercises power in the UK - the pluralist model, the élite model and the Marxist model.

A. The pluralist model

According to the pluralist model, power is exercised by the mass of the population, rather than by a small, élite group. This conclusion is derived from two main arguments - see Box 1.9.

Box 1.9 The pluralist model - key arguments

1. **Voters can throw out representatives at the next election**
   Pluralists note that, if a majority of people do not like what their representatives are doing, they can vote them out of office at the next election. Representatives, therefore, have to act in a way that is pleasing to the majority.

2. **People can exercise power between elections**
   Pluralists claim that people are able to exercise power between elections by joining groups (such as political parties, trade unions and other pressure groups). Group activity, they argue, is vital to the successful functioning of the political system. Groups constantly compete to gain the attention of decision-makers and it is the job of the decision-maker to decide between the competing claims made by different groups.

It follows from this, therefore, that what matters to pluralists about the distribution of power in society is not that it is uneven, but that it is widely dispersed rather than concentrated into the hands of the few. It also follows that, according to the pluralist model, the state acts impartially, responding to the demands of different popular pressures. No single group can possibly dominate in society since, for every force exerted by one group, there is an equal and opposite force exerted by other groups.

Pluralists argue that such a system is healthy because it encourages political participation, it ensures that people can exert influence over decision-makers, it ensures that power is dispersed rather than concentrated into the hands of a few and, at the same time, it allows the view of minority groups to be voiced.

B. The élite model

Élite theorists suggest that power in the UK is held by a small minority of people who use it for their own ends. The unequal distribution of power in society, the model suggests, is not necessarily in the best interests of the majority of people. Rather, it benefits a ruling élite.

Classical élite theorists argued that all states are governed by an élite or conflicting élites and that the majority of the population is basically passive and uninterested in politics.

Schumpeter, for example, defined the role of elections in liberal democracies as:

'That institutional arrangement for arriving at political decisions in which individuals acquire the power to decide by means of a competitive struggle for the people's vote.' (Schumpeter 1974, p.269)

The élite model differs from the pluralist model in a number of ways. These are outlined in Box 1.10.

Box 1.10 The élite model contrasted with the pluralist model

1. Political parties stifle debate
Unlike pluralists, élite theorists argue that political parties do not act as a route through which different interests can be expressed. They point out that political parties often prevent views and opinions being aired if they do not coincide with the particular party's stance.

2. Those in power narrow the range of choices on offer
Élite theorists argue that a process of non-decision-making can operate to prevent certain interests reaching the political agenda. To put this in terms used by Lukes (1974), pluralists concentrate on the first face of power only, whilst élite theorists also consider the second face of power (see above Activity 1.1, Item C).

3. Interest groups are not equal in status
Élite theorists point out that interest groups are not equal in status. Some are more powerful than others and any dispute or disagreement is likely to favour the more powerful group. Those with more economic clout or a well-educated and articulate membership, for example, are more likely to shape the political agenda than those representing groups like the homeless, the poor or the elderly. Pluralists imply that interest groups compete on a level playing field.

The Establishment
Studies of the British political system have led some élite theorists to suggest that there is a cohesive political class which monopolises power. This is sometimes described as the 'Establishment'. Members of the Establishment share the same sort of social and educational background and have a distinct set of values:

'A number of researchers have found that the majority of those who occupy élite positions in Britain are recruited from a minority of the population with highly privileged backgrounds. This appears to apply to a wide range of British élites including politicians, judges, higher civil servants, senior military officers and the directors of large companies and major banks...There is also evidence that there may be some degree of cohesion within and between the various élites.' (Haralambos & Holborn 1995, pp.518-19)

C. The Marxist model
Like most other liberal democracies, the UK is a capitalist

country. The vast bulk of its wealth is owned by individuals rather than by the state. In simple terms, those who own and control the wealth are capitalists while the people they employ are workers. Although the capitalists are fewer in number than the workers, they tend to acquire political as well as economic power.

Marxists are fundamentally opposed to the capitalist system. They argue that it is responsible for the inequalities in British society and the unevenness of the distribution of power. Marxist studies of the British political system are, therefore, (unlike some pluralist or élitist studies) necessarily critical of the system (see Miliband 1994, Chapter 1).

The Marxist model is closer to the élite model than to the pluralist model. Like élite theorists, Marxists argue that a cohesive political élite exists in the UK. Also like some élite theorists, Marxists agree that the democratic institutions in the UK are a sham. It is not, therefore, in their conclusions that élite theorists and Marxists disagree. Rather, it is in the arguments they use to reach these conclusions. Marxists argue that the élite - the ruling class - has power because it controls and owns capital. The source of power lies, therefore, in the economic infrastructure (in the way in which the economic system works). Élite theorists, on the other hand, argue that the explanation for the domination of élites is psychological.

Marxists are particularly critical of the pluralist idea that the state is, in some way, neutral. On the contrary, Marxists argue, the capitalist system developed to protect the interests of those with economic power. Power is distributed in the state to ensure that this happens. One way in which the state does this is to manipulate people's views. The Marxist model, therefore, incorporates Lukes' third face of power (see above, Activity 1.1, Item C).

Main points Sections 1.9 - 1.11

- The institution which exercises power over a defined area is usually described as the state. Sovereignty (that is, supreme power) normally lies with the state.
- Britain is a liberal democracy. Legislative power is exercised by Parliament. Executive power is exercised by the government. Judicial power is exercised by the courts.
- It is debatable whether Parliament or the people are sovereign.
- The monarch is the nominal head of state. The political power once exercised by the monarch is now exercised by the government (executive).
- The British system is adversarial.
- Three main models have been developed to explain who exercises power in the UK: (1) the pluralist model - the mass of the population exercises power; (2) the élite model - a small minority of people exercise power; and (3) the Marxist model - the system is flawed because capitalists exercise power.

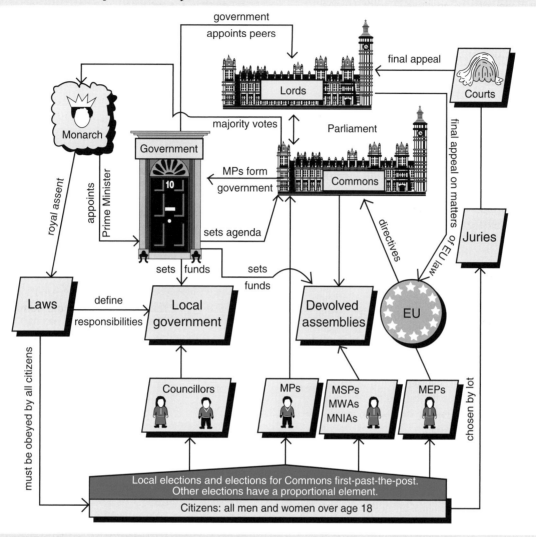

Activity 1.3 *The British political system*

Item A **The British political system**

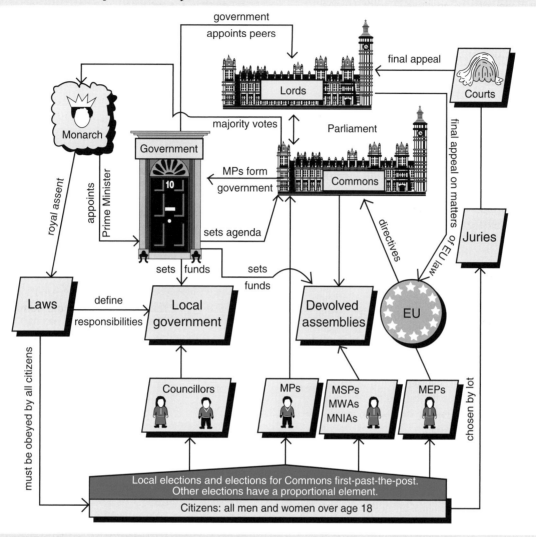

government
appoints peers

Lords

final appeal

Courts

Monarch

majority votes

Parliament

Government

10

MPs form
government

Commons

final appeal on matters of EU law

royal assent

appoints
Prime Minister

sets agenda

Juries

Laws

define
responsibilities

sets funds

Local
government

sets
funds

Devolved
assemblies

directives

EU

must be obeyed by all citizens

Councillors

MPs

MSPs
MWAs
MNIAs

MEPs

chosen by lot

Local elections and elections for Commons first-past-the-post.
Other elections have a proportional element.

Citizens: all men and women over age 18

Item B **Political decision-making in the UK**

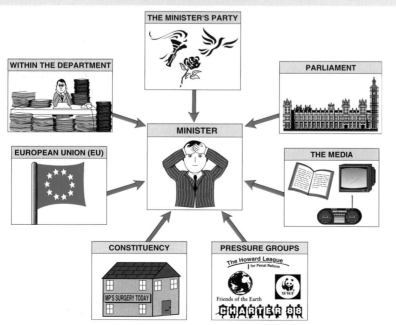

THE MINISTER'S PARTY

WITHIN THE DEPARTMENT

PARLIAMENT

MINISTER

EUROPEAN UNION (EU)

THE MEDIA

CONSTITUENCY

MP'S SURGERY TODAY

PRESSURE GROUPS

The Howard League
for Penal Reform

Friends of the Earth

WWF

Questions

1. Use Item A to write a short passage explaining where power is exercised in the UK.

2. a) Which of the three models described in Section 1.11 above is illustrated by Item B? Explain how you know.

   b) Design a similar diagram to illustrate one of the other two models.

3. Where does political activity take place in the UK? Use Items A and B and your own diagram from 2b in your answer.

1.12 *Political culture*

'"Political culture" has been defined as 'the set of values within which the political system operates'. (Kavanagh 1983, p.49)

Since the values within which a political system operates vary from country to country, each country has its own political culture. For example, the USA's political system does not just differ from the British system institutionally, it also differs culturally. American citizens have different expectations of their government from British citizens. They expect their politicians to behave in ways which would seem alien to British citizens. In other words, there is a different set of values in the USA and it is this different set of values which distinguishes political life there culturally from political life in Britain. In any country, political culture is passed on from generation to generation but it is not static. The political culture changes as society changes.

Traditionally the UK's political culture was seen to be a product of the elements listed in Box 1.11.

Box 1.11 The UK's political culture

Traditionally the UK's political culture was seen to be a product of the following elements:

- history - a strong sense of continuity with the past and the gradual evolution of democracy
- geography - a small island nation mainly urbanised
- gradual political change rather than sharp revolution
- a tradition of tolerance and broad support for the political system
- a Christian tradition
- a post-1945 consensus between the major parties on the role of the state, support for the mixed economy (a mixture of private and public) and the Welfare State.

Subcultures

Of course, not all citizens can be expected to accept the same set of values and so, within a single country, it is possible for different political cultures to co-exist. For example, in the UK today, there are different attitudes towards the settlement of political disputes by the use of violence. The vast majority of people oppose the use of violence to settle disputes, but a small minority disagree with this view. In some cases, a dissenting minority whose members share similar values may be said to belong to a 'subculture'.

1.13 *Civic culture*

Almond & Verba (1963) classified differences in political involvement and awareness in different countries and found three broad types of political culture - see Box 1.12.

Definition of a civic culture

Almond & Verba argued that Britain was an example of a fourth type of political culture - a 'civic culture'. A civic culture is a mixture of elements of a subject culture and

Box 1.12 Three types of political culture

1. Parochial cultures
These are cultures where people only have a limited awareness of government and do not feel affected by its policies.

2. Subject cultures
These are cultures where individuals know about government and might even express strong support for it, but do not expect to have any influence over it.

3. Participant cultures
These are cultures where people know about government and expect to be able to influence it.

elements of a participant culture. It is, they argued, because it is such a mixture that it is the most appropriate culture for a stable democracy.

In a country with a civic culture, ordinary citizens allow decision-makers the freedom to make any decisions they feel appropriate so long as these decisions take into account public opinion. Supporters of Almond and Verba argue that, historically, the UK's political culture has had the three key features outlined in Box 1.13.

Box 1.13 Key features of a civic culture

1. Deference
Central to this view of British political culture is the notion of 'deference' (accepting that others are superior and that their lead should be followed). This notion of deference is used to explain why the British people are law-abiding and why there has been little support for radical change. Almond & Verba argue that the British people have a tendency to accept decisions made by those in authority (ie they are deferential) and this tendency has resulted in peace and stability.

2. Consensus
'Consensus' suggests that there is broad agreement about fundamental issues in society and, as important, agreement on the means to solve any potential disputes. These means include peaceful resolution of conflict through the democratic system.

3. Homogeneity (uniformity)
Homogeneity means uniformity. The idea here is that people in the UK are very alike and have a common sense of forming a community.

Criticism of Almond and Verba's model

Critics of Almond and Verba's model argue that it is outdated because deference, consensus or homogeneity - or all three - do not exist any longer. Kavanagh, for example, argued that, by 1981, civic culture was in decline:

'There is no great confidence in the political institutions, though there is also no desire for radical changes...
[There is] more dissatisfaction with the specific performance of government than the system as a whole.

The recent years of slow economic growth have led to greater social tensions, group rivalries and growing dissatisfaction with the authorities...What does seem clear is that the traditional bonds of social class, party and common nationality are waning and with them the restraints of hierarchy and deference.' (Kavanagh 1981, p.73)

Since 1981, there is evidence that dissatisfaction with government and politicians has grown and that the traditional bonds of class, party and nationality have broken down still further. Also, lower turnouts in recent elections and support for fundamental constitutional reform (as indicated by Scottish and Welsh devolution, for example) suggest that dissatisfaction with the system and not just with the specific performance of government has developed since the 1980s.

1.14 The Marxist view

There is a disagreement about how the political culture emerges. Marxists argue that when people talk of the 'political culture', what they usually mean is the **dominant** political culture (see Miliband 1972). They argue that the ruling class, which has economic and political power, successfully promotes a dominant value system which consolidates the position of the rich and powerful. This promotion of dominant values takes place through institutions such as the education system, the mass media and the main political parties. So, while consensus may be a feature of political life, it is a consensus imposed by the ruling class (whose aim is to protect its own interests). While the ruling class may appear to be successful in imposing its view of the world, however, there is always the potential for the working class to resist and for class conflict to break out.

1.15 A cultural revolution?

During the 1980s, the Thatcher governments set out to alter the political culture in a fundamental way. The dominant political culture of the 1970s was regarded as a reason for Britain's poor economic performance and the Thatcher governments aimed to create a new culture of self-reliance, enterprise and market values. There is little evidence, however, to suggest that the Thatcher governments achieved this aim. The 14th British Social Attitudes Survey, subtitled *The End of Conservative Values*, published in 1997, reviewed the whole 18 years of Conservative rule from 1979 to 1997. It claimed that the period failed to produce the revolution in the nation's political attitudes that the Thatcherites had hoped for. Box 1.14 summarises the report.

Cultural diversity and change
While the Thatcher revolution might not have succeeded, other changes were taking place. Research suggests that there is now a fragmentation in society and a cultural diversity which pervades all aspects of social and political life (Taylor 1997). This diversity has developed as traditional class divisions have changed and new important divisions in society based on gender, ethnicity, nationality and region have emerged. For example, in the UK, the Christian tradition has been challenged both by the growth of minority religions, for

Box 1.14 The 14th British Social Attitudes Survey

People remained attached to state provision in health. Those who bought their own homes did not, as the Conservatives hoped, take on Tory allegiances too. They continued to doubt the much advertised benefits of a flexible jobs market. Attitudes hardened on welfare and people liked the tougher line on law and order but they also increasingly backed the cases for sweeping constitutional change which both Thatcher and Major fiercely opposed.

Source: The *Guardian*, 19 November 1997.

example Islam, and by the growth of atheism. Similarly, the authority of tradition has evaporated and the social hierarchies and class structures of the past have gone. Barnett (1997) argues that the death of Diana, Princess of Wales, was a particular turning point in this regard. Since then, the UK has become more inclusive, more expressive and more emotional.

New Labour and the Third Way
New Labour has sought to 'modernise' the political culture (Denver & Fisher 2003). This has mainly come through:
- the notion of the 'Third Way' (a political position between traditional socialism and Conservative individualism - see Unit 7)
- measures of constitutional reform
- an emphasis on the importance of responsibilities as well as rights.

This new focus has been described by some as the 'new politics' (Fielding 2000). However, critics argue that there is 'only limited evidence of a sharp break with the past' (Denver & Fisher 2003, p.16).

1.16 Post-modernism and political culture

Post-modernists argue that we are living through a period of change and diversity. They argue that we live in post-materialist age where the population is used to economic security and material well-being. Traditional political attitudes and allegiances, they claim, have been weakened and there has been a growth of individualism. The post-modernists' views are summarised in Box 1.15 on page 15.

1.17 Political socialisation

The term 'socialisation' refers to the way in which people, through interaction with members of their family and other social groups, learn how to become members of society. Political socialisation, therefore, is the process through which people develop their attitudes towards politics. People are not born with a particular political outlook. As children and then as adults, their attitudes are shaped by their experiences and what they are taught from others. Two models have been developed to explain the process of political socialisation - the primacy and recency models.

Box 1.15 Post-modernist views on political culture

Post-modernists argue that the new political culture that is developing has the following features:

- traditional distinctions between the left in politics and the right are in decline
- class is no longer as important in shaping political behaviour
- the politics of today reflects a society which is more culturally diverse and pluralist than it used to be
- globalisation affects political life and decisions and there is a compression of time and space
- new issues like environmentalism cut across traditional boundaries
- new technologies, for example the internet, play a more significant part in political communication and change the relationships between the people and the government.

The primacy model

Some studies of political socialisation focus on childhood on the grounds that this is a time when people are particularly open to the influence of others. This emphasis on childhood has been described as the 'primacy model'. Research has found that children develop political attitudes early on in their lives, mainly from their parents. There is, for example, some continuity of voting patterns between parents and children. Research suggests that by the age of ten or 11 children have acquired party loyalties, a sense of national identity and a basic knowledge of their country's main political institutions.

The recency model

Other studies have suggested that political socialisation is a lifelong process. This idea has been described as the 'recency model'. According to this model:

'Socialisation experiences have a greater impact the closer in time they are to the political context.' (Kavanagh 1983, p.45)

So, as people get older, experiences in adulthood are likely to be more important than childhood experiences because they are closer in time to the present. The recency model also examines how the impact of personalities, issues and events associated with certain periods in adults' lives affect people's political attitudes. For example, the 1960s is often seen as a period which affected a whole generation.

1.18 Agencies of socialisation

According to Rush (1992), the main agencies of political socialisation are those outlined in Box 1.16 below. Only political parties within the list in Box 1.16 are openly and consciously intent on political socialisation as a main aim. The other items on the list can be defined as agencies of political socialisation for the following reasons.

The family

The family is a small, intimate group that, in the early years, has a near monopoly of a child's development. Through socialisation, the child learns attitudes, values and ways of looking at the world. Also, the family is located within the class and social structure of this country and this influences the life of the child in profound ways. The family can be seen

Box 1.16 The main agencies of political socialisation

Education system
Peer groups
Religion
The family
Political parties

The main agencies of political socialisation are:
- the family • peer groups • organised religion • the education system • the mass media • political parties.

as a power structure in miniature. Families can operate in authoritarian or democratic styles and, in so doing, can influence the way in which children think.

Peer groups

Peer groups are people who associate with each other on the basis of equal status. Children's peers are usually thought to have a particular significance. Friendship groups and work groups, however, are important throughout people's lives. Peer groups act as reference points for individuals and, in so doing, influence the attitudes and behaviour of individuals.

Organised religion

As Britain has become increasingly secular (ie non-religious), the influence of organised religion has declined. Nevertheless, organised religion does still play an important role in the social and political life of many people and organised religions do seek to influence the attitudes and behaviour of people.

The education system

The education system provides a place in school for all children aged five to 16. So, for around 15,000 hours in a child's life, the education system is responsible for that child's development. Ironically, little (and in some schools none) of that time is spent learning about contemporary politics. Yet, schools play an important part in political socialisation since children learn how to survive in a hierarchical, bureaucratic organisation which provides a framework for the bulk of their waking lives.

The mass media

The mass media provides a view of the world beyond an individual's immediate experience. Newspapers, radio, film and television reach millions of people and they undoubtedly make some impact on people's attitudes and behaviour. Precisely what impact they make is the subject of debate.

Imitation, instruction and motivation

Political scientists argue that socialisation takes place through imitation, instruction and motivation. According to Rush, these terms can be defined as follows:

'[Imitation is] the copying of the behaviour of other individuals or groups of individuals and is generally most important in childhood...[Instruction is] the more or less intended learning of appropriate behaviour through formal education and less formally through discussion groups and other activities such as vocational training...[Motivation is] the learning of appropriate behaviour by experience, by a process of trial and error.' (Rush 1992, p.104)

1.19 Political socialisation - problems

One problem with political socialisation is that no satisfactory way has been devised to find out how far early experiences in a child's life compare with later experiences as an adult when it comes to determining political attitudes and behaviour. Attitudes and behaviour are not just determined by socialisation alone. Personal and situational factors operating at the time affect how an individual responds to events. A second difficulty is that no satisfactory way has been devised to judge the effects of socialisation, particularly when much socialisation is simply part of a pattern of everyday assumptions. Even when socialisation definitely takes place, individuals can appear not to respond to the process. In other words, it is necessary to devise a sophisticated model of political socialisation or there is a danger of ending up with an 'over-socialised' view which simply regards people as puppets waiting to be manipulated.

Main points   Sections 1.12 - 1.19

- The term 'political culture' is a shorthand way of describing the dominant set of values within which a society operates. Political culture can change according to place and time.
- The idea that Britain has a 'civic culture' (where ordinary citizens allow decision-makers to make any decisions they think appropriate as long as public opinion is taken into account) has been criticised for exaggerating consensus and uniformity.
- There is evidence today of greater cultural diversity and fragmentation than there used to be.
- Political socialisation is the process through which people develop their attitudes towards politics.
- The main agencies of socialisation are the family, peer groups, organised religions, the education system, the mass media and political parties.
- It is difficult to measure the impact made by the main agencies of socialisation and it is difficult to judge the effects of socialisation.

Activity 1.4 Political socialisation & political culture

Item A Political socialisation

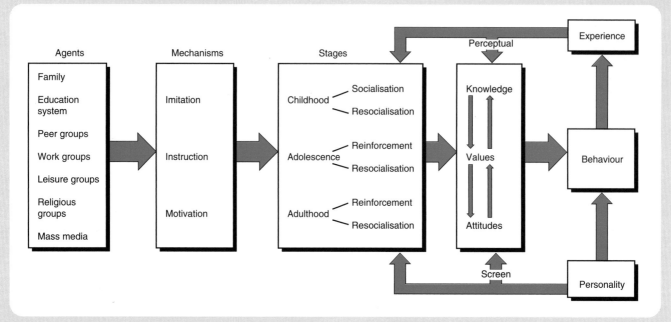

Source: Rush 1992.

Item B The Floral Revolution

One of the great puzzles of public life until 1997 was the extraordinary gulf between the institutions of government - Westminster, Whitehall, Buckingham Palace, the judiciary - and the culture of most people. Government institutions were dominated by the Great and the Good, by tradition, suits, solemnity, emotionless behaviour, protocol, formality, deference and hypocrisy. In contrast, from the 1960s onwards, the culture of the people came to embrace a different set of values - feelings, honesty, informality, humour, meritocracy, the personal, the admission of weakness and vulnerability, the casual and the female. There were many representatives of the people's culture in entertainment and television, in business and in sport. But, until Tony Blair, it is impossible to think of a major public figure in politics or royalty who embraced the new culture - with one remarkable exception, Princess Diana. Diana redefined the nation, enfranchising groups that had previously felt disenfranchised. The Floral Revolution is a new kind of revolution. There are more traditional components - the defeat of the old Establishment, the demise of the old-style Royal family, possibly even the end of the monarchy. But, above all, the Floral Revolution heralds the victory of the new culture over the old, the legitimacy and authority of the self, the embrace of new social groups, the support for diversity. Diana, in redefining a nation, redefined each and every one of us.

Source: The *Observer*, 7 September 1997.

Item C A shifting culture

The old Establishment was caught on the hop. There was no trickle-down effect in the grief for Diana. Rather this was a movement from the bottom up that did not so much proclaim the birth of a new order as illustrate how unconcerned we were with the old one. What I am suggesting is that a culture can shift. A mood can change. New forms can emerge and yet many old structures can stay in place. The mistake is to presume that cultural shifts are somehow less 'real' or less 'meaningful' than the traditional manifestations of political power. The strength of the dominant culture is precarious because it rests on assumptions about the way we live which are no longer tenable. The people on the streets felt at home, at ease and that they belonged together. They did not need an official sanctioning and those whose job it is to give it may well feel redundant. Something that was perceived as only going on at the edge has moved inwards and the centre cannot hold because it suddenly appears as one little sub-culture jostling alongside the others for our attentions.

Source: The *Independent*, 19 September 1997.

Item D Trends in political trust 1974-2000

% who trust the following 'just about always' or 'most of the time'	1974	1987	1991	1994	1996	1998	2000
British governments of any party to place the needs of the nation above the interests of their own political party	39	37	33	24	22	29	16
Politicians of any party to tell the truth when they are in a tight corner	-	-	-	9	9	9	11
British police not to bend the rules in trying to get a conviction	-	52	49	47	51	48	59
Top civil servants to stand firm against a minister who wants to provide false information to Parliament	-	46	-	27	28	-	35

Source: Park 2001.

Questions

1. a) Using Item A, make a list of people, groups and institutions that have helped to shape your attitudes towards politics.

   b) Put the items on the list in order of priority.

   c) Why is it difficult to produce an adequate model of political socialisation? Use Item A in your answer.

2. a) What do Items B and C tell us about British political culture in the late 1990s?

   b) Explain why political culture is a difficult term to define.

3. Using Items B-D, give arguments for and against the view that Almond and Verba's civic culture model is an adequate explanation of political culture in Britain at the end of the 20th century.

References

Almond & Verba (1963) Almond, G. & Verba, S., *The Civic Culture: Political Attitudes and Democracy in Five Nations*, Princeton University Press, 1963.

Almond & Verba (1981) Almond, G. & Verba, S., *The Civic Culture Revisited*, Little Brown (Boston, USA), 1981.

Barnett (1997) Barnett, A., *This Time. Our Constitutional Revolution*, Vintage, 1997.

Bromley, Curtice & Seyd (2001) Bromley, C., Curtice, J. & Seyd, B., 'Political engagement, trust and constitutional reform' in *Park (2001)*.

Coxall, Robins & Leach (2003) Coxall, B., Robins, L. & Leach, R., *Contemporary British Politics*, Palgrave, 2003.

Denver & Fisher (2003) Denver, D. & Fisher, J., 'The Contexts of British Politics' in *Fisher, Denver & Benyon (2003)*.

Dowse & Hughes (1972) Dowse, R.E. & Hughes, J.A., *Political Sociology*, John Willey and Sons, 1972.

Dunleavy et al. (2000) Dunleavy, P., Gamble, A., Holliday, I. & Peele, G., *Developments in British Politics 6*, Macmillan, 2000.

Fielding (2000) Fielding, S., 'A New Politics' in *Dunleavy et al. (2000)*.

Fisher, Denver & Benyon (2003) Fisher J., Denver, D. & Benyon, J., *Central Debates in British Politics*, Longman, 2003.

Goodwin (1997) Goodwin, B., *Using Political Ideas*, John Wiley and sons, 2003.

Haralambos & Holborn (1995) Haralambos, M. & Holborn, M., *Sociology: Themes and Perspectives*, HarperCollins, 1995.

Kavanagh (1981) Kavanagh, D., 'Political Culture in Great Britain: the decline of the civic culture' in *Almond & Verba (1981)*.

Kavanagh (1983) Kavanagh, D., *British Politics, Continuities and Change*, Oxford University Press, 1983.

Lancaster (2002) Lancaster, S. (ed.), *British Politics Update*, Causeway Press, 2002.

Leftwich (1984) Leftwich, A., *What is Politics?*, Blackwell, 1984.

Lukes (1974) Lukes, S., *Power*, Macmillan, 1974.

McNaughton (2001) McNaughton, N., 'Populist Movements – a new development in the politics of pressure', *Talking Politics*, Vol.14.1, September 2001.

Miliband (1989) Miliband, R., *Divided Societies*, Oxford University Press, 1989.

Miliband (1994) Miliband, R., *Socialism in a Sceptical Age*, Polity Press, 1994.

Park (2001) Park, A. (ed.) British Social Attitudes, 18th Report, Sage 2001.

Rush (1992) Rush, M., *Politics and Society. An Introduction to Political Sociology*, Harvester Wheatsheaf, 1992.

Schumpeter (1974) Schumpeter, J.A., *Capitalism, Socialism and Democracy*, Urwin, 1974.

Social Trends (2003) National Statistics, *Social Trends, No.33*, HMSO, 2003.

Taylor (1997) Taylor, P., *Investigating Culture and Identity*, Collins Educational, 1997.

Whiteley & Seyd (1998) Whiteley, P. & Seyd, P., *New Labour, New Grass Roots Party?* Paper presented at Keele University, April 1998.

2 The social context

2.1 A changing society

Politics in the United Kingdom does not function in a vacuum. It operates in a context which is the product of historical, geographical, demographic, social and economic factors. Since 1945 British society has changed in many important ways. Take gender, for example. Not only have there been objective changes since the 1940s (for example, it is now illegal to pay a woman less than a man for the same work), attitudes have changed, too. People in public positions now talk the language of equal opportunities, even if their actions do not always live up to their rhetoric.

The pattern of migration since the 1950s has changed the ethnic make-up of the country. Greater longevity of life has changed the age distribution of the country. Religion has declined in significance. Social changes are closely intertwined with economic changes. Since 1945 Britain's industrial base has changed dramatically. While the old manufacturing industries have declined, service industries and new industries have grown up. The growth of service industries and new industries has meant that class relationships have changed. Because of all these changes, the contemporary way of life is very different from that which existed after the Second World War and this, in turn, has affected political life.

2.2 Social class - definitions

The trouble with the term 'social class' is that it can be defined in many different ways. Income, wealth, education, accent, dress, work, lifestyle, and housing may all be taken into account when deciding which class a person belongs to. Most definitions of social class, though, are economic in origin. The job a person does determines, to a large extent, the class they belong to. Over the years, writers have used a variety of occupational classifications to identify social classes. Today, two main classifications are used - the Office of National Statistics (ONS) classification and the Institute of Practitioners in Advertising (IPA)'s classification.

The Office of National Statistics (ONS) classification

Until 2000, government reports and surveys used the Registrar General's occupational definition of social class. This divided the British population into five classes according to occupation. The scale made a distinction between manual occupations (working with your hands) and non-manual occupations (working with your brains).

Criticism of the Registrar General's classification, however, resulted in it being replaced, in 2000, by the Office of National Statistics (ONS) classification which is outlined in Box 2.1. The scale has been expanded to eight classes and is also based on employment. But there are three criteria:
- employment relations (whether people are employers, self-employed, employed)
- whether they exercise authority at work
- employment or market conditions (salary scales,

promotion prospects, sick pay, how much control people have over hours worked or how work is done).
The scale no longer makes the distinction between manual occupations and non-manual occupations.

Box 2.1 The ONS classification

Class 1 Higher managerial and professional occupations
    1.1 Employers in large organisations (eg corporate managers)
    1.2 Higher professionals (eg doctors or barristers).
Class 2 Lower managerial and professional occupations (eg journalists, actors, nurses).
Class 3 Intermediate occupations (eg secretary, driving instructor).
Class 4 Small employers and own account workers (eg publican, taxi driver).
Class 5 Lower supervisory, craft and related occupations (eg plumber, butcher, train driver).
Class 6 Semi-routine occupations (eg shop assistant, traffic warden).
Class 7 Routine occupations (eg waiter, road sweeper).
Class 8 Never worked/long-term unemployed.

The IPA's classification

The IPA's classification is commonly used by the media. In this classification, society is divided into six classes. Advertisers use the sixfold division to work out where to place an advert and which groups to target when selling a particular product. The IPA's definition has been adopted by political commentators not least because political parties have to 'sell' their image and polices in much the same way that a company has to sell its brand name and products. The six classes are shown in Box 2.2.

Box 2.2 The IPA's definition of class

Class A Higher managerial, administrative or professional
Class B Intermediate managerial, administrative, or professional
Class C1 Supervisory or clerical, and junior managerial, administrative or professional
Class C2 Skilled manual workers
Class D Semi-skilled and unskilled manual workers
Class E State pensioners or widows (no other earnings), casual or lowest grade workers, or long-term unemployed.

2.3 Class and politics in Britain

The class structure 1945 to c.1970

For the first 25 years after the Second World War, most political commentators agreed that social class was the driving force behind British politics. Studies were conducted to show that people voted on a class basis. The two-party system was seen as a reflection of the British class system - the Conservative Party represented the capitalist class while the Labour Party represented the working class. This attitude was summed up by Butler & Stokes in 1971:

> 'Our findings on the strength of links between class and partisanship [support for political parties] in Britain echo broadly those of every other opinion poll or voting study...the pre-eminent role [of class] can hardly be questioned.' (Butler & Stokes 1971, p.102)

The class structure since c.1970

More recently, however, the claim has been made that the class structure has changed fundamentally. These changes include the following:

1. Social mobility between the classes has increased and divisions between the classes are more fluid.
2. Inequalities in income and wealth are thought to be less marked than used to be the case and there has been a major expansion of middle-class occupations.
3. There has been the spread of share ownership and house ownership and the growing consumption of consumer durables.
4. It is argued that ownership and control of industry are no longer in the hands of a small élite, but in the hands of millions of shareholders and professional managers.
5. The upper class no longer has the power and privileges that it once had and the middle class has expanded.
6. Traditional working-class communities have disappeared as heavy industries, such as shipbuilding and mining, have declined.
7. New industries have developed which no longer have organisations which reflect class differences.

It is also argued that Britain's industrial structure has changed dramatically. There has been a shift away from the mass production of standardised products to flexible specialisation in production and products. There has also been a shift away from the old centres of capitalism (in Europe) to a new, global system of capitalism. One result of these changes is a decline of traditional class-based politics and institutions, such as the trade unions, and, in the opinion of some writers, the emergence of new class groupings. According to some writers, one of these new class groupings is the 'underclass'.

2.4 The 'underclass'

Since the 1980s, there has been a debate about whether or not an 'underclass' has come into existence in the UK. According to those writers who support the theory, members of this 'underclass' are so poor and disadvantaged that they are 'under' the normal class structure. They suffer poverty, long-term unemployment, bad housing, ill health and poor educational opportunities. Some writers see them as more or less permanently trapped at the bottom. They say

that there is a 'cycle of deprivation' (see Box 2.3 below) which ensures that the values and lifestyles of the underclass are passed on from one generation to another.

Box 2.3 The cycle of deprivation

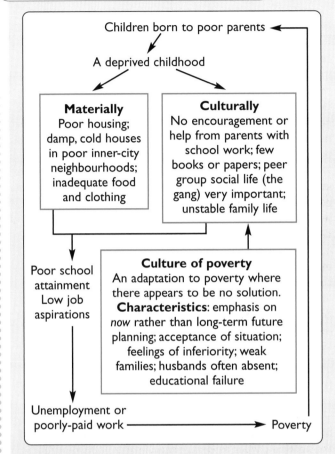

This diagram illustrates the cycle of deprivation which, some authors argue, is responsible for the development of an underclass.

There are four main arguments against the view that an underclass has come into existence in the UK.

1. Those who support the underclass theory do not agree on either who belongs to the underclass or how many people belong to it. This suggests there is a major flaw in the argument.
2. Those who support the underclass theory make links between groups of people and types of behaviour that do not necessarily stand up to scrutiny. For example, there is not necessarily a link between single parenthood and crime.
3. Some of those who support the underclass theory argue that members of the underclass have a separate culture - a different set of values - from the rest of the population. Research for the Policy Studies Institute, however, shows that the very poor generally have the same beliefs as the rest of the population - for example, wanting the best for their children. In addition, studies have shown that many in the so-called 'underclass' move in and out of work at different points in their lives and are just as likely to vote as the rest of the population.
4. By blaming the poor for their own condition, supporters of the underclass theory divert attention away from the

real causes of poverty - unemployment or low-paid work and the low rates at which benefits are paid.

2.5 Post-modernism and globalisation

In contrast to those who have promoted the idea of an underclass, post-modernists argue that class no longer has any real significance. They argue, for example, that it no longer makes sense to generalise about the middle class because there is a huge range of different experiences that middle-class people have. Instead of class, post-modernists emphasise that people have very different lifestyles and that these are a matter of choice. An individual's identity is not based on class but on a range of factors including age, ethnicity, gender, as well as personal choices such as musical taste, clothes or even support for a particular football team. Furthermore, in recent years, a process of globalisation has taken place so that the wider world is more open to us. People soak up the images of different cultures around the world that are offered continuously through media advertising, news and entertainment. In other words, globalisation also diminishes class identity.

2.6 Class dealignment?

The decline in class-based politics, it is claimed, is reflected in changing voting patterns (see also Unit 6). Proportionally fewer working-class people vote Labour than used to be the case and a growing number of members of the middle class vote for third parties like the Nationalists or Greens rather than for the Conservative Party. This, it is argued, has forced the political parties to change their image. The Labour leadership has worked hard to rid itself of its 'cloth cap' image and the Conservative leadership has worked equally hard to rid itself of its 'hunting, shooting and fishing' image. Nearly all the parties now claim to represent the national interest rather than a particular section of society. Some commentators argue that political behaviour can be better explained by reference to new social movements - such as feminism or environmentalism - rather than to class.

Classlessness

In 1990, John Major argued that Britain was becoming a classless society in which everybody would have opportunities to fulfil their ambitions, regardless of their class background. Adonis & Pollard (1997) point out that this view of classlessness did not mean that class differences would entirely disappear. Instead, it meant that the class structure would be a meritocracy - people would advance by ability regardless of their class origins.

Major's view is not far from that expressed by Tony Blair. This is explored in Box 2.4 (above right).

Changing patterns of employment

Over the past two decades, it would be hard to argue that there have not been changes in the class structure, especially the growth of the middle class and decline in the working class. There has been a big increase in the number of professional jobs - for example, a big growth in the number of

Box 2.4 New Labour and classlessness

When he was still in Opposition, Tony Blair said:

'Our task is to allow more people to become middle class. The Labour Party did not come into being to celebrate working-class people having a lack of opportunity and poverty, but to take them out of it.' (*Sunday Times*, 1 September 1996)

Blair said something similar in 1999 when he argued that New Labour's role was to replace the old Establishment with a new, larger, more meritocratic middle class that would include millions of people who, in the past, might have seen themselves as working class.

In the mid-1990s, commentators noted the marked reluctance of New Labour politicians to use the word 'class' in their speeches. In part, this was a matter of image. One way of appearing to be new and modern was to drop the sort of dialogue used in the past (especially the 'class warrior' rhetoric employed by the left). In part, it was a tactical device. By appealing to society as a whole rather than to a single class, New Labour could hope for votes from society as a whole. And, in part, it was evidence of an ideological shift - an admission that there had been a decline in class-based politics.

accountants. In contrast, the number of miners has fallen from 750,000 after the Second World War to fewer than 10,000 today. In general, primary industries (agriculture, fishing, and mining) and secondary industry (manufacturing) have declined whereas the service sector has expanded. Within these overall changes, the proportion of female employees has risen, many of them working in low-paid jobs and often working part time.

However, important class divisions remain, for example in access to higher education. The Education and Child Poverty Report, published in 2003, revealed that young people from unskilled backgrounds are five times less likely to enter higher education than those from professional backgrounds.

In addition, income inequality exists and has actually grown under New Labour since 1997 (ONS 2003). In July 2003, Michael Meacher, then Environment Minister, pointed out that, from 1997 to 2002, the post-tax income of the bottom tenth of the population rose by 13% but the income of the top tenth of the population increased by 39% (*Guardian*, 15 July 2003). Box 2.5 on page 22 shows the highest and lowest-paid occupations.

In 2003, concern about income inequality resulted in a row about 'fat cat' directors' salaries. For example, it emerged that Jean-Pierre Garnier, Chief Executive of GlaxoSmithKline, earned £7 million in 2002 and was due to receive a £22 million pay off if the company was taken over. In this case, shareholders rejected the arrangement. But, in many other cases, top directors continued to receive huge salaries, bonuses and fringe benefits. Meacher noted:

'The company car benefit amounts to £7,800 on average, nearly twice what a pensioner has to live on... While the average-paid have had pay increases of 3-4% in recent years, Britain's highest paid salary executives had salary increases of 23% in 2000, 19% in 2001, 16% in 2002.' (*Guardian*, 15 July 2003)

Such vast income and wealth inequalities provide a strong argument for suggesting that little has changed in the class structure.

Box 2.5 Highest and lowest paid occupations

Great Britain; April 2002 **Highest paid**	Average gross weekly pay (£)*
1 General managers; large companies and organisations	2,079
2 Treasurers and company financial managers	1,235
3 Medical practitioners	1,160
4 Management consultants, business analysts	933
5 Underwriters, claim assessors, brokers, investment analysts	924
6 Solicitors	899
7 Computer systems and data processing managers	865
8 Police officers (inspector and above)	840
9 Marketing and sales managers	808
10 Purchasing managers	794

Great Britain; April 2002 **Lowest paid**	Average gross weekly pay (£)*
1 Retail cash desk and check-out operators	205
2 Launderers, dry cleaners, pressers	207
3 Kitchen porters, hands	210
4 Waiters, waitresses	211
5 Petrol pump forecourt attendants	212
6 Bar staff	217
7 Counterhands, catering assistants	218
8 Educational assistants	225
9 Hotel porters	234
10 Cleaners, domestics	234

*Full-time employees on adult rates, whose pay for the survey period was unaffected by absence.

Source: New Earnings Survey 2002.

Main points Sections 2.1 - 2.6

- 'Class' is a difficult term to define. Today, the two main classifications are the ONS which divides the population into eight classes and the IPA which divides it into six classes.
- Most writers agree that class was the driving force behind British politics during the period 1945-c.1970.
- Some writers argue that the class structure has changed since c.1970 and that class is a less significant factor than it used to be. Some people have even argued that Britain is becoming a 'classless' society.
- Other writers argue that inequalities, together with disparities in educational opportunities and housing patterns, mean that society is still shaped by class.

Activity 2.1 A classless society?

Item A Distribution of wealth

United Kingdom	1976	1981	1986	1991	1996	1999	2000
Marketable wealth							
Percentage of wealth owned by:							
Most wealthy 1%	21	18	18	17	20	23	22
Most wealthy 5%	38	36	36	35	40	43	42
Most wealthy 10%	50	50	50	47	52	54	54
Most wealthy 25%	71	73	73	71	74	74	74
Most wealthy 50%	92	92	90	92	93	94	94
Total marketable wealth (£ billion)	280	565	955	1,711	2,092	2,861	2,968
Marketable wealth less value of dwelling							
Percentage of wealth owned by:							
Most wealthy 1%	29	26	25	29	26	34	32
Most wealthy 5%	47	45	46	51	49	59	57
Most wealthy 10%	57	56	58	64	63	72	72
Most wealthy 25%	73	74	75	80	81	87	88
Most wealthy 50%	88	87	89	93	94	97	99

This table shows how wealth was distributed in the UK between 1976 and 2000. The figures in italics are percentages.

Source: Social Trends 2003.

Item B **The classless society?**

Britain cannot be understood without understanding its class system which separates its people as clinically today as it did half a century ago when George Orwell described it as 'the most class-ridden country under the sun'. The classes have changed, but the barriers between them remain the same - money, education, family and occupation (or the lack of them). Class divisions are intensifying as the distance between the top and bottom widens and the classes at both extremes grow in size and identity. This growing division is obvious to everyone - except crucially to most of the nation's élite which for reasons of fear and self-interest is struggling to eliminate class from the realm of respectable debate. To achieve this, the élite has developed two tactics. The first is the use of the term 'underclass' to denote a minority isolated from the mainstream majority. The second is the transformation of this mainstream into a 'classless society'. This is a myth and distortion in equal measure. Almost every visible and saleable aspect of modern life betrays the class hierarchy from Harrow to Hackney, sushi to sausages, sharp suit to shell suit, *FT* to *Sun*, Porsche to Escort, Channel Four to Radio One.

The man on the left represents the upper class, the man in the middle the middle class and the man on the right the working class.

Source: Adonis & Pollard 1997.

Item C **The equality gap**

Inequality rose sharply under Thatcher, fell slightly under Major and has risen to, and remains at, new heights under Labour. So, although the poorest have seen big rises in their income since 1997, the richest 20% have jumped up and away from the middle, and the top 1% distort the whole picture. Put it another way, over two-thirds of people now earn below-average income and soon it will be 70% according to Income Data Services, as the numbers of low-paid grow and pay at the top swells. Does the widening gap matter? The old 'Third Way' of Blair and Clinton always said that it didn't - all that matters is improving the lot of the poorest. The trouble is that, in the end, the two things are intimately related. The US-UK view that what happens among the rich does not matter has led to the widest and fastest growing equality gaps in these low-tax countries.

Source: Polly Toynbee, *Guardian*, 11 July 2003.

Item D **Poll taken in July 2002**

	1994 %	1997 %	1999 %	2002 %
Strongly agree	14	19	17	28
Tend to agree	37	39	35	40
Tend to disagree	29	29	30	21
Strongly disagree	15	9	9	6
Don't know	4	3	10	5
Agree	51	58	52	68
Disagree	44	38	39	27
Net agree	+7	+20	+13	+41

This table shows the results of a poll carried out in July 2002. The polling organisation MORI asked the question: 'To what extent do you agree or disagree with the statement - "At the end of the day, I'm working class and proud of it"?'

Source: MORI, August 2002.

Questions

1. a) Suppose you had been asked to conduct a survey to find out the class background of the students in your school or college. Write down the criteria you would use. Devise a questionnaire. Conduct the survey and write a report.

   b) Describe your own class using (i) the ONS classification and (ii) the IPA's definition. Give reasons for your choices.

2. Give the arguments for and against the view that Britain is becoming a classless society. Use Items A-C in your answer.

3. Consider the figures for wealth distribution in Item A.

   a) What percentage of marketable wealth did the most wealthy own in 1976? How had this changed by 2000?

   b) What percentage of wealth did the bottom 50% of the population own in 2000?

   c) How much did wealth increase between 1976 and 2000?

4. How accurate are the class differences portrayed in the cartoon in Item B?

5. a) What does Item D tell us about attitudes towards class in the UK?

   b) To what extent have attitudes changed?

2.7 Gender - an important social factor

It is not just class that determines the position and role of people in British society. Other social factors are important. Take gender, for example. Masculinity and femininity are crucial parts of our identity and, to some extent, the lives we lead are dependent on our gender. For example, although there is some evidence to suggest that in the UK there is less discrimination against women today than was once the case, there is overwhelming evidence that women have less chance of achieving high status and high earnings than men. Women may have won equality in the eyes of the law, but they have yet to win equality of opportunity.

Supporters of and campaigners for equality between women and men are called feminists. The ideas behind feminism are examined in Unit 7.

2.8 Women's legal status

The Prime Minister, Stanley Baldwin, argued in 1928, after the Electoral Reform Bill allowing women - like men - to vote at the age of 21 was passed, that:

'The inequality of women, if there be such a thing, will not now depend on any creation of the law. It will never again be possible to blame the state for any position of inequality. Women will have, with us, the fullest rights.' (Speech in the House of Commons, 29 March 1928)

But it was not until 1975 that the Equal Pay Act 1970 came into force. Before then, the law allowed employers to pay women a lower rate of pay for doing the same job as a man. Similarly, it was not until 1975 that the Sexual Discrimination Act was passed. Before then the law did not allow the idea that a woman might be discriminated against because of her sex. Although the Equal Pay Act and Sexual Discrimination Act mean that, in theory, men and women are now equal before the law, in reality this legislation has lacked teeth and legal loopholes have allowed inequality to continue. In addition, there is a lack of knowledge about the provisions of the legislation and there is a reluctance by employees to pursue cases through industrial tribunals. Once at industrial tribunal, many sex discrimination cases fail compared to other cases - see Box 2.6.

Box 2.6 Success rate at industrial tribunal hearings 2001-02

Type of hearing	% success
Redundancy	65%
Wages Act	60%
Working Time	56%
Breach of Contract	49%
Unfair Dismissal	31%
Sex Discrimination	28%

This table shows success rates at industrial tribunal hearings in 2001-02.

Figures from *Labour Research*, April 2002.

2.9 Women at work

The number of women in work is growing while the number of working men is declining. Women now amount to almost half the labour force in the UK. West argues:

'However, shifts in the division of labour do not amount to fundamental transformations. Women's integration into employment has largely been through part-time work. Job segregation actually remains very marked, despite women's inroads into some male-dominated occupations. Masculine, sexist cultures persist in many workplace environments, despite formal commitments to equal opportunities. And, there is little evidence of change in the domestic division of labour. Motherhood still depresses women's lifetime earnings and, other things being equal, tends to be associated with downward occupational mobility (as many women re-enter the workforce at a lower level than when they left it).' (West 1997, p.127)

Consequences of these changes

Women often find that employers assume that, because they are women, they are suited to particular kinds of work (usually caring, non-competitive roles) and not suited to other kinds of work (such as management, engineering or scientific research). Because an invisible barrier (sexual discrimination) prevents women breaking into these areas of work, commentators have talked of a 'glass wall' blocking women's way forward. The statistics in Box 2.7 support this theory.

Box 2.7 Employees jobs by sex and industry

United Kingdom	Males			Females			Percentages
	1982	1992	2002	1982	1992	2002	
Manufacturing	30	24	21	17	11	8	
Distribution, hotels, catering and repairs	17	20	22	26	26	26	
Financial and business services	12	16	20	13	17	19	
Transport and communication	10	10	9	2	2	3	
Construction	8	8	8	2	2	1	
Agriculture	2	2	1	1	1	1	
Energy and water supply	4	2	1	1	1	0	
Other services	16	18	19	39	41	41	
All employee jobs (millions)	12.7	11.6	13.0	10.0	11.6	12.7	

This table shows the percentage of men and women working in particular jobs between 1982 and 2002.

Source: Social Trends 2003.

Even when women are allowed into what were previously regarded as male occupations, they often find that they are not promoted as often as men or that they are not promoted at all. Again, an invisible barrier - a 'glass ceiling' - blocks their way upwards. For example, while women's access to the higher grades of management has improved in the last 20 years, the change still leaves women in a tiny minority. Out of the 600 plus senior executive jobs in Britain's boardrooms in the largest listed 100 companies, only ten are filled by women which is less than 2% of the total (*Guardian*, 5 October 2002). The figures underline what has been called the 'golf club culture' of British management which encourages only white Anglo-Saxon men.

Pay and discrimination

According to a survey conducted by the London School of Economics in 2000, during the course of a typical woman's working life she can expect to earn £250,000 less than a man. Contrary to popular belief, this gender gap in earnings is not primarily caused by taking time off work to have children. According to the report, the main reasons are that women are concentrated in lower-paid sectors of the job market and they are paid less than men while doing the same work as men (even 25 years after the Equal Pay Act). At the highest level, Britain's top-paid male executive earned £9 million a year in 2003 compared to the £1.2 million for the top-paid female executive (*Guardian*, 1 August 2003). The survey also reveals that there is a greater pay gap for women working part time. Full-time women workers earn on average 84% of men's wages but female part-time workers only receive 58% of the rate per hour for male full-time workers.

The Equal Opportunities Commission (EOC) has blamed employers for the pay inequality and discrimination women face in the workplace - see Box 2.8. An EOC survey found that women were commonly denied access to bonuses and performance-related pay. In addition, 10% of part-time employees, mainly women, were illegally excluded from pension schemes. However, the Confederation of British Industry (CBI - the main employers' organisation) rejected these findings, claiming that there was little evidence that employers were operating unfair pay structures. The CBI argued that the main cause of pay inequalities is occupational segregation - women are more likely to work in lower-paying sectors of the labour market.

Box 2.8 Poster produced by the EOC

This poster was produced in 1999 as part of the Equal Opportunity Commission's Valuing Women campaign for equal pay with men.

The EOC's annual report for 2001 highlighted the disparity between the high performance of women in school and university compared to the chances of reaching the top in their field of work. In addition, the EOC reported on 8,900 complaints of possible discrimination at work, including 1,800 cases on pregnancy and maternity issues, 1,500 on working hours, 1,400 on equal pay for like work and 700 on sexual harassment. These figures are likely to be an underestimate of the gender inequalities in the workplace as many workers are not aware of their rights and may be reluctant to pursue legal cases even if they are.

2.10 Women at home

Although the traditional attitude that women (especially married women) should stay at home and tend to the needs of their children and husband is changing, women still do most of the domestic work in Britain. This was graphically illustrated by research carried out by Xavier Ramos on the British Household Survey panel - a long-term survey panel of some 5,500 households which reported in 2003. Ramos discovered that, when it comes to housework, on average, women do almost four times as much as their partners - men averaging five and a half hours a week, compared to women's 19:

> 'If the woman is in part-time employment, and the man is working full-time, she ends up with a much higher total workload than her male partner - 13 hours more, most of it housework.' (*Guardian*, 30 July 2003)

Feminists have argued that women experience the triple shift. This means they still have the main responsibility for domestic work, while increasingly working either full or part time. In addition, they generally also have responsibility for the 'emotion work' (care for individual family members, remembering birthdays and so on) in the home. Madeleine Leonard argues, having reviewed the literature and carried out her own research, that children in the home actually do as much domestic work as their fathers (Leonard 2000).

A major reason why 80% of part-time jobs are taken by women is that women are expected to combine work with their domestic responsibilities. Since few employers make any provision for childcare, it is women who generally break their careers to look after their family. Until recently, this expectation was reflected in law. Companies had a statutory obligation to provide maternity leave but not paternity leave. As a result of the Labour government's decision to sign the Social Chapter, however, this changed in June 1998. From that month, all companies were obliged to provide all employees (men and women) with a minimum of three months' unpaid leave. As Peter Baker pointed out:

> 'This is a significant step towards recognising the importance of family-friendly employment practice and the role of fathers.' (*Observer*, 7 December 1997)

Since then, further employment rights have been extended to men and women. From April 2003, fathers have had the right to two consecutive weeks' paternity leave and parents with children under the age of six have the right to ask for flexible working practices. Despite these legal changes, there is still a tendency for women to be regarded as the ones who have the main domestic responsibilities. For example, it is telling to see which parent takes time off work if their child is sick.

2.11 *Women and education*

Some writers argue that girls are disadvantaged at school because of the sexist attitudes of some teachers and because of the different socialisation of boys and girls - boys are encouraged to be assertive and competitive while girls are encouraged to be quiet and non-competitive. It is argued that this has affected educational performance and the choice of subjects (girls are less inclined to take science and technology-based subjects). But, even if girls do have to overcome such obstacles, figures compiled by the government show that girls are increasingly outclassing boys at every level up to and including degree level. At Key Stage 3 in the 2002 National Curriculum assessments for example, 75% of girls but only 59% of boys reached the expected standard in English. Girls also outperformed boys in Maths and Science (EOC 2003). In 2001, 33% of males obtained two or more A levels compared to 42% of females (Social Trends 2003).

In higher education, the number of female students has increased dramatically in the last 30 years. In 2003, 53% of university undergraduates were women. At university, however, differences in subject choice remain, with women being more likely to opt for arts and men dominating the sciences - see Box 2.9. Also, women are still more likely to be found in the less prestigious educational institutions. For young people who do not go to university, major differences in the job market remain, reflecting both subject choice at school and expectations of gender roles. Men account for 99% of modern apprenticeships in construction and 96% in engineering while 97% of apprenticeships in childcare are taken by women (*Guardian*, 8 July 2003).

Box 2.9 Students in Higher Education Institutions 2001-02

Great Britain		Thousands
Subject Area	**Women**	**Men**
Medicine & dentistry	15.8	13.1
Subjects allied to medicine	40.0	12.5
Biological sciences	39.9	23.9
Agriculture & related subjects	4.1	2.8
Physical sciences	16.9	27.2
Mathematical sciences	5.8	9.4
Computer science	11.0	45.0
Engineering & technology	11.1	60.2
Architecture, building & planning	5.4	13.8
Social, economic & political studies	44.6	30.1
Law	21.0	13.1
Librarianship & information science	10.9	6.6
Languages	40.0	15.4
Creative arts & design	46.8	31.6
Education	32.2	9.6
All subjects	473.1	419.5

This table shows the number of men and women who were full-time first degree undergraduates in 2001-02 for selected subjects. The figures are in thousands.
Source: *Students in Higher Education Institutions 2000/01*, Higher Education Statistics Agency.

2.12 *Women and politics*

Although women have been able to stand as candidates in parliamentary elections since 1918, women are still under-represented in Parliament and on local councils. Following the 2001 general election, there were only 118 women MPs in Parliament, representing 17% of the total. The UK has 'slid down the international league table of the representation of women in the lower or single chambers of national Parliaments from 27th place in 1999 to 47th place in 2002, and to tenth (rather than eighth) place in the EU' (Longmate 2003, p.92).

Although, in 2003, there were six women in the Cabinet out of a total of 22, overall there are only 29 women in government out of 92 posts (Women and Equality Unit 2003). All the main parties now have mechanisms to encourage more women to stand as candidates, but only the Labour Party has introduced all-women shortlists in some constituencies (*Guardian*, 29 January 2003). In 2003, women only held 34% of national public appointments though this represented a rise of 10% since 1991. There have been a number of initiatives to try to encourage more women to become involved in political life. Some successes have been achieved, the best example coming from the Welsh Assembly elections in 2003. Half of the members of the Welsh Assembly elected were women. However, The Liberal Democrats have claimed that at the current rate of progress it will take more than 30 years to achieve a 50% ratio of male and female for all public appointments (*Guardian*, 13 February 2002).

2.13 *Recent trends*

Some feminist writers have criticised what they have termed Western feminism's 'dirty little secret' which is that, for some successful middle-class career women, there is now a tendency to employ female domestic servants, often migrant workers, who become responsible for cleaning, cooking and care of the children (Ehrenreich & Hochschild 2003). Middle-class women may have gained from feminism, these writers suggest, but many ordinary women have not.

Some writers have argued that young women are 'articulating a new strand of feminism which is marking a departure from previous ones' (Jowett 2000, p.12). For example, Natasha Walters in *The New Feminism* acknowledges that some inequality exists but makes the following claims:
- the central argument that women's lives are filled with politics and oppression is no longer true
- New Feminists are using new tools to gain equality
- New Feminists run their own businesses rather than campaigning groups
- there is a generational change which means that old feminist ideas and forms of action are no longer appropriate for young women.

Crisis in masculinity

Critics of feminism have argued that there is now a 'crisis of masculinity' with men uncertain of their role and confused about what women really want (Coward 2000). Men come to see themselves as redundant as they fail in education, find that their skills are no longer valued at work and they are no longer needed in the home as their wives divorce them in ever increasing numbers.

Post-feminism

Post-feminist writers have expressed concern at the tendency of feminism to 'demonise men' and 'implicitly idealise women' (Coward 2000, p.239). Post-modern feminism has gone even further, arguing that:

'The meaning of being a woman (or a man) is never fixed...This means that we cannot talk about "women" or "men" as stable political entities. We can however, analyse and challenge the ways in which gender identities are constructed.' (Bryson 2003, p.9) Gender identities are then seen as free-floating and fluid and the final goal of equality is rejected.

Main points Sections 2.7 - 2.13

- Like class, gender is an important social factor.
- Although the Equal Pay Act (1970) and Sexual Discrimination Act (1975) mean that men and women are equal before the law, overall, women are still paid less than men and are expected to do more domestic work as well.
- Girls are outperforming boys in education at every level up to university level, but women are

still reluctant to pursue degrees and careers in traditionally male areas such as science and engineering.
- While there are now more women MPs, women are still under-represented in Parliament and in public life in general.
- Although gender inequality remains, traditional forms of feminism are under challenge.

Activity 2.2 Gender

Item A Women in 1952 and 2002

This chart compares the position of women in 1952 with their position in 2002.

Source: EOC 2002.

Item B The glass ceiling

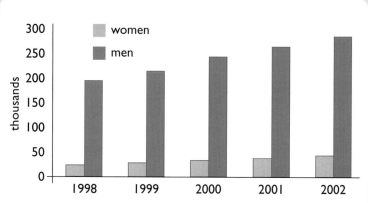

This chart shows the number of men and women earning over £100,000 in the years 1998-2002.

Source: Inland Revenue/*Guardian* 13 June 2002.

Working women have largely won the battle for equality with men on pay but should be provided with help to crack the so-called glass ceiling at work according to the government Equal Pay Tsar, Denise Kingsmill. Her words will anger some campaigners who regard the struggle for a fair wage as far from over, with women still earning 82 pence for every pound a man takes home. But her early findings suggest that the key to the pay gap is not so much women earning less than a man for the same job, but female workers being denied the most senior, most lucrative posts. Her research repeatedly found women clustered at middling ranks, unable to reach the higher-paid jobs. Women have to prove themselves repeatedly to get promoted while men get the benefit of the doubt.

Source: The *Observer*, 19 August 2001.

Item C Superwoman

Item D Domestic chores

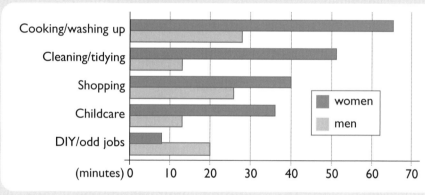

This chart shows the average time per day that men and women spend doing unpaid work in the UK.

Source: Office for National Statistics, October 2000.

Item E Women elected in British general elections 1945-2001

Year	Conservative	Labour	Liberal	SNP	Others	Total	% MPs
1945	1	21	1	0	1	23	3.8
1950	6	14	1	0	0	21	3.4
1951	6	11	0	0	0	17	2.7
1955	10	14	0	0	0	24	3.8
1959	12	13	0	0	0	25	4.0
1964	11	18	0	0	0	29	4.6
1966	7	19	0	0	0	26	4.1
1970	15	10	0	0	1	26	4.1
1974 Feb.	9	13	0	1	0	23	3.6
1974 Oct.	7	18	0	2	0	27	4.3
1979	8	11	0	0	0	23	3.5
1987	17	21	2	1	0	41	6.3
1992	20	37	2	1	0	60	9.2
1997	13	101	3	2	1	120	18.2
2001	14	95	5	1	4	118	17.9

Source: Childs 2002.

Questions

1. Using Items A-D, explain why gender is a useful tool to use when analysing what kind of society exists in Britain.

2. Consider the figures in Item A.

   a) Judging from Items A, B and E what evidence is there to suggest that women lack equal opportunities in the workplace and in public life?

   b) Is there any evidence to suggest that old prejudices are being broken down?

3. What does Item C tell us about the pressures women face in contemporary Britain?

4. What conclusions can be drawn from Item D?

2.14 *What is 'ethnicity'?*

Along with class and gender, sociologists argue that ethnicity is a key social factor. 'Ethnicity', however, is a difficult term to define. One definition is provided in Box 2.10.

Box 2.10   A definition of ethnicity

According to a House of Lords ruling in 1983, an ethnic group is a group in society which has:

● a distinct cultural identity
● a long, shared history
● a common geographical origin or common descent
● a common language
● a common literature peculiar to the group
● a common religion.

Using these criteria, it is possible to divide the British population into a number of ethnic groups. The majority of the population belongs to a single, dominant ethnic group (white Britons descended from white Britons) whilst the remainder of the population belongs to a number of ethnic minority groups - for example, white Britons descended from Irish immigrants, black Britons descended from West Indian immigrants. Although, as these examples indicate, some ethnic minority groups are white, all black and Asian Britons belong to ethnic minority groups. As a result, the issues of skin colour (race) and racism (prejudice against people because of their skin colour) are closely linked to any discussion of ethnicity.

The term 'black'

In the past, many studies failed to distinguish between different ethnic groups, lumping people together as 'blacks' and 'whites'. There were a number of problems with this. First, 'black' took on a dual meaning, sometimes referring to all black people and sometimes referring only to African-Caribbean groups. Second, this classification did not take account of the way in which ethnic minorities see themselves. Modood (1988), for example, argues that people from or descended from the Indian subcontinent do not define themselves as 'black'. Third, some critics argue that the black-white distinction is unlikely to improve race relations since it encourages polarisation. As a result, it is difficult to find a suitable shorthand to describe non-white members of ethnic minority groups. In this book, either specific ethnic groups are named or the term 'black and Asian' is generally used. Quotations using other terms have not been altered, however.

2.15 *Why is ethnicity important?*

By dividing up society along ethnic lines, sociologists are able to target groups in society and find out how different ethnic backgrounds affect the life chances of different groups of people. This means of classification includes consideration of cultural factors as well as skin colour and, therefore, provides a more complex model than that based simply on skin colour

alone. For example, a study showing that Indian Britons do better at school than both Bangladeshi Britons and African-Caribbean Britons, but not as well as Chinese Britons, may be of greater use than a study which simply shows that, overall, white Britons do better at school than black Britons since it allows politicians to target resources to areas which need it (areas where Bangladeshi Britons live, for example). Having said this, however, it should not be assumed that each ethnic culture is uniform. Gilroy (1987) warns against 'ethnic absolutism' - the idea that once a researcher has identified which ethnic group a person belongs to, then that person's behaviour can be predicted. Ethnicity is dynamic and flexible. It is not fixed - see Box 2.11.

Box 2.11   PSI survey, 1997

The idea that ethnicity is dynamic and flexible is supported by the Policy Studies Institute in a national survey of ethnic minorities which discovered that mixed marriages and partnerships were increasing (PSI 1997). Half of the African-Caribbean men born in Britain and a third of African-Caribbean women have a white partner. Mixed marriages have become so common that nearly half of 'African-Caribbean' children have one white parent. Also, about one in five British-born Indians has a white partner.

2.16 *Britain's black and Asian population*

The 2002 Labour Force Survey revealed that, out of a total population in this country of 58.8 million, 4.5 million people were black or Asian. This amounted to 7.6% of the total UK population. The three largest groups of black and Asian Britons were Indian Britons (1.7%), Caribbean Britons (1%) and Pakistani Britons (1.3%). In 1950, less than 1% of the total UK population was black or Asian. This figure gradually increased to 2.3% in 1971, 3.9% in 1981 and 5.5% in 1991. To put the current figures another way, in 2002, one person in 14 living in the UK was black or Asian (Sociology Update 2003).

2.17 *Ethnicity and disadvantage*

Black and Asian people from certain ethnic minority groups have a greater chance both of poverty and disadvantage (Rowntree 2003). This can be illustrated by examining ethnicity in relation to employment and educational achievement.

Employment

There are wide variations in employment patterns for different black and Asian groups. Indians and Chinese are, on average, doing well. For example, one in 20 Indian men is a doctor compared to one in 200 white men. However, other groups are doing less well. Pakistanis, Bangladeshis and African Caribbeans experience, on average, significantly lower earnings than whites (see Box 2.12 on page 30) and are more likely to be found in lower-paid working-class jobs. Yet, even for the groups doing relatively well, they 'are not doing as well as they should, given their education and other characteristics' (Cabinet Office 2003).

While there has been a certain movement of black and Asian people into non-manual employment, especially self-employment, black and Asian people are generally unlikely to find high-status jobs.

Box 2.12 Pay differences by ethnic group and sex

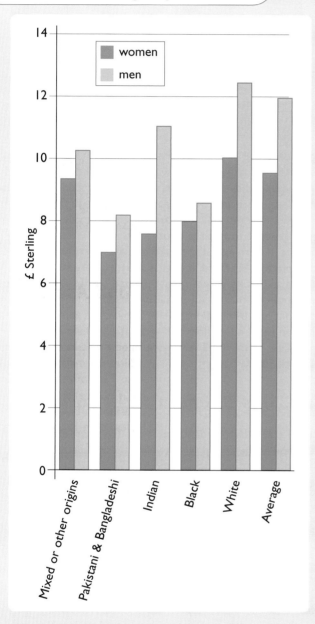

This chart compares the hourly rates of pay for full-time employees in Great Britain (excluding London) by ethnic group and sex.
Source: The Labour Force Survey 2000.

Ethnicity and education

One reason why black and Asian people are under-represented in the professions is because they have been educationally disadvantaged. The statistics for GCSE performance in 2002 reveal significant differences between different groups of black and Asian people. On average, only

30% of African-Caribbean pupils, 40% of Pakistani pupils and 45% of Bangladeshi pupils achieved five or more good GCSEs. This compares with the 51% for white pupils, 65% for Indian pupils and 80% for Chinese pupils. A significant problem for some groups is the rate of exclusion from school. This is four times higher for African-Caribbean males than their peers (*Times Educational Supplement*, 7 March 2003).

There are some signs, however, that the educational position is changing. Black and Asian people are now much more likely than white people to continue their education after the age of 16. Also, apart from African-Caribbean men and Bangladeshi women, black and Asian people are now more likely to go to university (PSI 1997).

2.18 Racism and the police

Relations between the police and black and Asian people have become strained over many years. Black and Asian communities have complained that they have been harassed by the police. In turn, the police have claimed that black and Asian people are disproportionately involved in street crime and so it is inevitable that arrest rates for young blacks and Asians are high. Figures from the Home Office in 2002 show that black and Asian people are eight times more likely than white people to be stopped and searched by the police and, once arrested, are more likely to be remanded in custody than other offenders charged with similar offences (*Observer*, 29 February 2002).

The Stephen Lawrence case

Police attitudes came under scrutiny following the murder of black teenager Stephen Lawrence in 1993 (see Box 2.13). When the police attended the crime scene, they failed to appreciate that Stephen was the victim of a racist attack and, instead of looking for his (white) attackers, took his (black) companion in for questioning (Pilkington 2003). The failure to undertake a rigorous investigation became a focus of public concern as Stephen's parents campaigned to discover the truth.

Box 2.13 Stephen Lawrence

A tribute to Stephen Lawrence.

The Macpherson Inquiry

The Macpherson Inquiry was set up to discover the truth in the Lawrence case and, in 1999, it reported that the police were guilty of 'institutional racism'. The report defined institutional racism as:

'The collective failure of an organisation to provide an appropriate and professional level of service to people because of their colour, culture or ethnic origin. It can be seen or detected in processes, attitudes and behaviour which amount to discrimination through unwitting prejudice, ignorance, thoughtlessness and racist stereotyping which disadvantages minority ethnic people.'

While this conclusion was controversial, the police accepted that change was needed.

Race Relations Amendment Act 2000

Following the Macpherson Inquiry, the 1976 Race Relations Act was amended in 2000 and, for the first time, the police were included under the provisions of the Act. In addition, the Race Relations Amendment Act required all 43,000 public bodies in the UK, including the police, to promote good race relations and equality of opportunity. A Commission for Racial Equality (CRE) survey of progress in 2003, however, revealed that a third of all public bodies had yet to implement their race equality duties (*Guardian*, 4 July 2003). In addition, the Chair of the CRE, Trevor Phillips, has argued that public services are now hiding behind the concept of institutional racism to avoid tackling cases of discrimination head-on (*Guardian*, 1 September 2003).

2.19 Race riots in Oldham and other northern towns

Labour's 2001 election manifesto claimed that:

'Labour believes that Britain can be a model of a multicultural, multi-racial society, now is the time to build the inclusive society in tune with British values'.

Events in some northern towns and cities just before and just after the 2001 general election, however, cast doubt on whether such hopes could be realised. In April 2001, rioting took place in Bradford after rumours of racist attacks on Asians. This was followed by violence in Oldham in May - see Box 2.14 - after a British National Party (BNP) march in the town which was ostensibly held to protest against alleged attacks on whites by Asians (the BNP supports the voluntary repatriation of non-white immigrants to their lands of ethnic origin). There were also media reports that Asian youths had established 'no go' areas for whites in parts of Oldham. The tension in the town increased when the BNP fielded candidates in the June 2001 general election. In Oldham West and Royton, Nick Griffin, the Leader of the BNP, achieved 16.4% of the vote and in Oldham East and Saddleworth, the BNP achieved 11.2% of the vote.

Burnley and Bradford

The second area where racial tension erupted was in Burnley in July 2001. After a number of racial attacks, over 200 white youths marched on a predominantly Asian area of the town. They were met by more than 100 Asian youths who threw bricks and set alight a local pub. Such events were

Box 2.14   Race riots in Oldham, May 2001

This photo shows police officers arresting one of the rioters in Oldham in May 2001.

unprecedented in Burnley. The town had no history of racial violence on a large scale. However, the racial divide that had opened up led to the election of eight BNP councillors in the 2003 local elections (with the result that the BNP became the second largest political party on the council). Sporadic racial violence took place in other northern cities following the riot in Burnley, but the third and most serious rioting took place in Bradford in August 2001. Hundreds of Asian youths and white youths fought pitched battles as the police attempted to control the situation. In subsequent local elections and by-elections, the BNP managed to secure the election of 17 councillors and were able to field 221 candidates in the 2003 local government elections (*Guardian*, 29 April 2003).

2.20 Is Britain a racist society?

There is abundant evidence to show that racist attitudes are common in the UK. In recent years, these racist attitudes have led to serious consequences. In 2000-01 the police recorded 25,100 racially aggravated offences in England and Wales including 3,176 cases of racially aggravated wounding. The 2000 British Crime survey estimated the number of racially motivated offences in England and Wales was 280,000, which, although high, was a fall from 390,000 in 1995.

A report on race relations in Bradford, written by a panel headed by Herman Ouseley, the former head of the Commission for Racial Equality and published in July 2001 after the riots there, found that:

'Relations between different cultural communities should be improving, but instead they are deteriorating. There are signs that communities are fragmenting along racial, cultural and faith lines. Segregation in schools is one indicator of this trend. Rather than seeing the emergence of a confident multicultural district where people are respectful, people's attitudes are hardening and intolerance is growing.'

Reports on the riots in Burnley and Oldham painted a similar picture of segregated communities and 'white flight' from inner-city areas. In addition, the report on Oldham noted that, although Asians made up 11% of Oldham's population, they only made up 2% of the council's workforce. In Burnley, extreme poverty, drugs, squalid housing and criminal gang activity had been seized on by white racists who blamed the black and Asian population. This picture of disadvantage and discrimination is not confined to a small number of northern cities. The Cabinet Office's own research notes that there are problems throughout the country (Cabinet Office 2003).

Among the white population, the 2000 British Social Attitudes Survey found 'a sharp increase in the numbers of "Little Englanders" who do not identify themselves as British and tend towards racist and xenophobic views'. These figures are reflected in a negative approach to asylum seekers (who are often black) and concern expressed about immigration by voters in a MORI poll held on 17 May, just before the 2001 general election. This poll revealed that asylum/immigration was one of the few areas where voters preferred the Conservatives' policy to Labour's and the issue ranked above transport in terms of importance to the electorate. A MORI poll for the Commission for Racial Equality in 2002 found that 47% of those questioned thought that there was more racial prejudice in Britain now than ten years ago.

2.21 Ethnicity and parliamentary representation

Despite all the political parties claiming that they wished to see an increase in the number of black and Asian MPs, in fact only 12 were elected in the 2001 general election, all from the Labour Party. This was an increase of two on the 1997 general election, but well below the numbers that should have been elected if the black and Asian population is to be represented proportionately in the House of Commons. The actual figure should be closer to 60 black and Asian MPs,

according to Trevor Phillips, the Chair of the Commission of Racial Equality (*Guardian*, 24 June 2003). One of the main reasons why 57 black and Asian candidates in the general election were not elected was that most were fighting 'unwinnable' seats (Rowe 2002). This may have reflected the fears of the main parties that votes would be lost if they selected ethnic minority candidates in safe seats.

Main points   Sections 2.14 - 2.21

- **Like class and gender, ethnicity is an important social factor.**
- **Since all black and Asian Britons belong to ethnic minority groups, the issues of race and racism are closely linked to any discussion of ethnicity.**
- **The 2002 Labour Force Survey revealed that, out of a total population in this country of 58.8 million, 4.5 million people were black or Asian. This amounted to 7.6% of the total UK population.**
- **Black and Asian people are, on average, poorer than whites and under-represented in high-status jobs. Some are educationally disadvantaged.**
- **Since Labour came to power in 1997, there have been race riots in northern towns and the Macpherson Report found that the Metropolitan Police Force was institutionally racist.**
- **Studies show not only that many white Britons are racists, but also that many violent attacks are racially motivated.**

Activity 2.3 *Ethnicity*

Item A **Ethnicity and educational achievement**

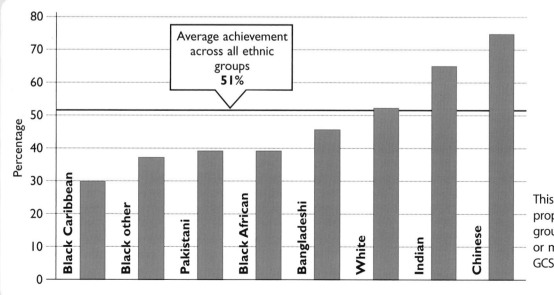

This chart shows the proportion of various groups achieving five or more A* to C GCSEs in 2002.

Source: The *Times Educational Supplement*, 7 March 2003.

Item B **Racism in Britain (1)**

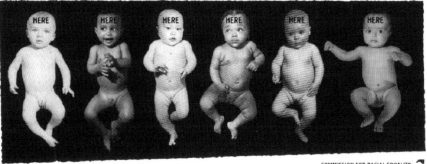

This poster was produced by the Commission for Racial Equality (CRE) as part of a three-year campaign to combat racism.

Item C **Racism in Britain (2)**

More or less discrimination? *Question: Do you think there is generally more, less or about the same amount of racial prejudice in Britain now than there was ten years ago?*

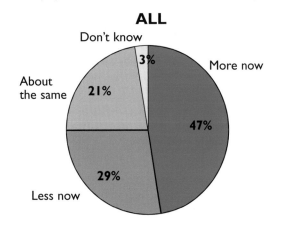

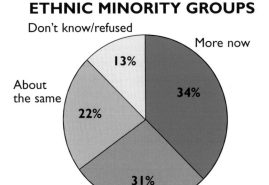

Source: MORI/Commission for Racial Equality Poll April/May 2002.

Item D **Corporate Britain and black and Asian consumers**

Corporate Britain is coming to grips with the complex realities of a multi-ethnic society. Needless to say, its motives are not exactly altruistic. It wants a bigger share of the c.£15 billion in after-tax income said to be in the hands of black and Asian consumers. Some big companies have realised that they need to change recruitment policies to attract the new customers they are seeking. HSBC, for example, set out to woo the South Asian business community with a banking service specifically tailored to their needs. Coincidentally or not, almost 50% of the staff on the bank's 12 special teams have South Asian backgrounds. Similarly, Lloyds TSB increased its intake of graduates with ethnic minority backgrounds from 4% to 19% in three years. Recent figures reveal intriguing trends in spending power. On a household to household basis, Indians, Chinese and African Asians all have average incomes higher than the white population. It is true that Pakistanis and African-Caribbeans have lower incomes, but young black Brits are seen as style gurus. Over the last three years there has been a sea change in attitudes within the advertising industry. Recent TV advertising campaigns for washing powder, washing up liquid, even sanitary towels have used blacks and Asians. Everyday products are seen to be promoted by black women and their families. Not icons or sports stars and not just background faces in a crowd. Bruce Haines, President of the Institute of Practitioners in Advertising, points out that: 'One of the powers of advertising is to normalise things. The fact that it has embraced multiculturalism, particularly through the TV, means that viewers soon won't even think about it as being unusual'.

Source: The *Guardian*, 31 October 2001.

Questions

1. Using Items A-D and your own knowledge, give arguments for and against the view that Britain is moving towards racial harmony.

2. a) 'Ethnicity is an important social factor'. Explain this statement using Items A and C.

   b) What use should politicians make of the information in Item C?

3. a) What is the point being made by the poster in Item B?

   b) Explain why a three-year campaign was necessary.

4. What does Item D tell us about attitudes towards black and Asian people in the UK?

2.22 Other social factors (1) - age

The distribution of different age groups varies over time and from country to country. The UK has an increasingly aging population as life expectancy has increased for both men and women while the birth rate has remained low - see Box 2.15.

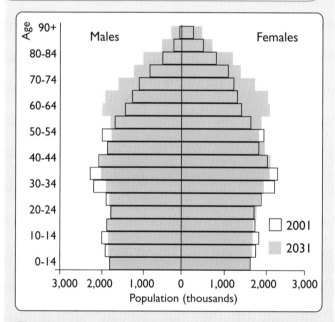

Box 2.15 Population projection pyramid for the UK 2001- 2031

The chart shows the distribution of the UK's population in 2001. The shaded area shows the projected population in 2031.

Source: The Government Actuary Department 2003 (Demos).

Babies born in 1997 can expect to live, on average, until nearly 80 if they are female and until their mid-70s if male. The number of pensioners is increasing and now stands at 11 million. The 2001 census found that, for the first time, there were more people over the age of 60 than under 16. In 1951, those under 16 made up 24% of the population - a proportion that had fallen to 20% in 2001. Those over 60, on the other hand, increased from 16% to 21% over the same period.

The 'grey vote'

Some commentators have argued that there will be a growth in the 'grey vote' as pensioners decide to vote collectively on issues that concern them. However, pensioners cannot be lumped together as a single group any more than teenagers can. Important differences exist between them. For example, working-class pensioners have a much greater reliance on the state pension than middle-class pensioners.

Other commentators have argued that different generations have different life experiences and different attitudes to issues, including politics, determined by the era in which they grew up. For example, older people are much more likely to vote in elections, regarding it as their civic duty, whereas young people generally do not take that view and are less likely to vote. There is evidence to support this view from the 2001 British Election Study which considered the age of those voting. Each higher age category was more likely to vote than lower age categories. For example, 76% of the 65+ age group voted compared to 40% of the 25 to 34 age group. Kelly (2002) identifies four post-war generations all crucially affected by the spirit of the times as they reached maturity. These groups are outlined in Box 2.16.

Box 2.16 Kelly's four post-war generations

1. The baby boomers
This group was born between 1945 and 1957 and reached maturity between 1963 and 1975. This group is seen as liberal and egalitarian.

2. The 'lost generation'
This group was born between 1958 and 1962 and reached maturity between 1976 and 1979. This group is seen as depressed, nihilistic and anarchic.

3. Thatcher's children
This group was born between 1962 and 1972 and reached maturity between 1980 and 1990. This group is seen as favouring freedom, individualism and materialism.

4. Touchy feelies
This group was born between 1973 and 1983 and reached maturity between 1991 and 2001. This group is seen as less combative and abrasive than Thatcher's children with more emphasis on tolerance and empathy.

Source: Kelly 2002.

Recent post-modernist writers have argued that age boundaries are breaking down and that 'stages on the life course are becoming increasingly blurred' (Kidd 2001, p.5). Examples in support of this idea include recent proposals to raise the age at which people can claim pensions and medical advances, including cosmetic surgery, which mask aging. Age affects behaviour and is, therefore, one of the variables that affect an individual's political behaviour.

2.23 Other social factors (2) - religion

Although religions deal with spiritual matters, they also have an influence on social attitudes and behaviour. This influence works at a number of levels.

First, a religion offers a set of moral values and, over time, these values become part of the culture of a society. For many centuries, Britain was a predominantly Christian country and, as a result, its mainstream culture was shaped by Christian values. For the past century, however, Christianity has been in decline and British culture has become more secular (non-religious). At the same time, there has been a growth in multiculturalism - a willingness to tolerate and celebrate the values of many faiths.

Second, religious rituals and ceremonies have traditionally been seen as a force for social unity. Collective acts of worship - such as at marriages, baptisms and funerals - bring people together and remind them of their common bonds and shared values.

Third, religions prescribe a moral code (eg the Ten Commandments) which is supposed to guide people's behaviour. It is significant, for example that, in 2001, Tony Blair called for a new style of politics 'where the church would be the bedrock of local communities'. In the same speech, he made what he saw as the link between religion and politics very clear when he suggested.

'Moral values expounded by religious teaching had important lessons for politicians.' (*Guardian*, 4 June 2003) Although religion continues to influence political debate and political activity in the UK, religion (as suggested above) is declining in significance. In a survey carried out in 2000, 60% of people claimed to belong to a religion, with 55% saying that they were Christians. However, 'half of all adults aged 18 and over who belonged to a religion have never attended a religious service' (Social Trends 2002) and real levels of active involvement in religious activities remain low. At peak times, only 7% of the population (at most) attends church and the Church of England only attracts an average weekly attendance figure of around 1 million (Sociology Update 2003). In addition, 40% of people do not claim any religious membership at all (Social Trends 2002).

Main points Sections 2.22 - 2.23

- Like class and gender and ethnicity, age and religion are important social factors.
- The UK has an aging population. This is likely to affect political developments.
- Kelly has identified four post-war generations - (1) the baby boomers; (2) the lost generation; (3) Thatcher's children; and (4) touchy feelies.
- Although religion continues to influence political debate and political activity in the UK, religion is declining in significance.

Activity 2.4 Age and religion

Item A Baby boomers come of age

The British political landscape is about to be rocked by changes caused by the aging of the baby boomers, the generation that has consistently challenged conventional behaviour patterns, the think tank Demos warns today. They are the first generation to have grown up in a strong consumer society, bombarded with advertising all their lives and led to expect satisfaction of their needs. A view of this group - in general more affluent than the previous generation - is that a significant number within it backed movements such as anti-racism, women's liberation and environmentalism, and had a disrespect for authority and conservative values. It is assumed that they will not respond as placidly as their parents and grandparents to being sidelined after retirement into possible poverty and a sense of powerlessness. In the first detailed exploration of this age group's likely response to aging, Demos says: 'The government is risking a baby boomer backlash, if it doesn't deal with the demands of a generation who plan to grow older very differently from their parents.'

Source: The *Guardian*, 1 September 2003.

Item B The young and old in the UK population

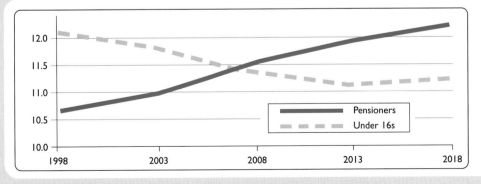

This graph shows the number of pensioners and under 16s expected to live in the UK by 2018, given current trends.

The figures are millions.

Source: Denscombe 2001.

Item C Religion

Belonging to a religion *Percentages*

(UK)	1996	2000		1996	2000		1996	2000
Church of England/Anglican	29.3	29.8	Other Protestant/other Christian	2.2	2.5	Sikh	0.2	0.4
Roman Catholic	8.9	9.2	United Reform Church	0.8	0.5	Other non-Christian	0.4	0.4
Christian - no denomination	4.7	6.3	Brethren	0.1	-	Buddhist	0.5	0.1
Presbyterian/Free-Presbyterian/			Islam/Muslim	1.8	2.0			
Church of Scotland	3.8	3.5	Hindu	0.6	1.0	Refusal/not answered/didn't know	0.8	0.6
Baptist or Methodist	3.0	3.4	Jewish	0.3	0.8	None	42.6	39.5

This table compares the percentage of people belonging to various religions in 1996 and 2000.

Source: Social Trends 2002.

Questions

1. Using Items A-C, explain why age and religion are important social factors.

2. Judging from Items A and B, how is the changing age profile of the British population likely to affect political developments?

3. a) What does Item C tell us about the UK?

   b) What are the political implications of this?

References

Adonis & Pollard (1997) Adonis, A. & Pollard, D., *A Class Act*, Hamish Hamilton, 1997.

Bryson (2003) Bryson, V., ' Feminism', *Politics Review*, Vol.12.4, April 2003.

Butler & Stokes (1971) Butler, D. & Stokes, D., *Political Change in Britain*, Penguin 1971.

Cabinet Office (2003) *Ethnic minorities and the Labour Market Strategy Unit*, Cabinet Office 2003.

Childs (2002) Childs, S., 'Parliament, women and representation', *Talking Politics*, Vol.14.3, April 2002.

Coward (2000) Coward, R., *Sacred Cows*, HarperCollins, 2000.

Denscombe (2001) Denscombe, M., *Sociology Update 2001*, Olympus Books, 2001.

Ehrenreich & Hochschild (2003) Ehrenreich, B. & Hochschild R., *Global Women: Nannies, Maids and Sex Workers in the New Economy*, Granta, 2003.

EOC (2003) *Facts about Women and Men in Great Britain 2003*, Equal Opportunities Commission, 2003.

Gilroy (1987) Gilroy, P., *There Ain't No Black In The Union Jack*, Hutchinson, 1987.

Haralambos (1997) Haralambos, M. (ed.), *Developments in Sociology*, Vol.13, Causeway Press, 1997.

Jowett (2000) Jowett, M., 'New feminism in contemporary Britain', *Politics Review*, Vol.9.3, February 2000.

Kelly (2002) Kelly. R., 'Talking 'bout my generation? Post war political culture and the shifting zeitgeist', *Talking Politics*, Vol. 14.3., April 2002.

Kidd (2001) Kidd, W., 'Time to think about age?', *Sociology Review*, Vol.10.3, 2001.

Lancaster (2003) Lancaster, S. (ed.), *Developments in Politics*, Vol.14, Causeway Press, 2003.

Leonard (2000) Leonard, M., 'Back to the future? The domestic division of labour', *Sociology Review*, November 2000.

Lister (1996) Lister, R. (ed.), *Charles Murray and the Underclass: the Developing Debate*, Institute of Economic Affairs, 1996.

Longmate (2003) Longmate, J., 'Women and politics' in *Lancaster (2003)*.

Modood (1988) Modood, T., 'Black, racial equality and Asian identity', *New Community*, Vol.14.3, 1988.

MORI (2002) *The Voice of Britain - Britain beyond Rhetoric*, MORI/Commission for Racial Equality, 2002.

ONS (2003) Office for National Statistics, *Income Inequality Gap Widens Slightly from the Mid-1990s*, ONS, 2003.

Pilkington (2003) Pilkington, A., *Racial Disadvantage and Ethnic Diversity in Britain*, Palgrave, 2003.

PSI (1997) Policy Studies Institute, *Ethnic Minorities in Britain*, Policy Studies Institute, 1997.

Rowe (2002) Rowe, M., 'The changing politics of race and ethnicity', *Politics Review*, Vol.12.1, September 2002.

Rowntree (2003) Joseph Rowntree Foundation, *Tackling Disadvantage*, Joseph Rowntree Foundation, 2003.

Social Trends (2002) Government Statistical Service, *Social Trends*, Vol.26, HMSO, 2002.

Social Trends (2003) Government Statistical Service, *Social Trends*, Vol. 27, HMSO, 2003.

Sociology Update (2003) *Sociology Update*, Olympus Books, 2003.

West (1997) West, J., 'Gender and work: continuity and change in the sexual division of labour' in *Haralambos (1997)*.

Women and Equality Unit (2003) *Women in Public Life: Key facts*, Department of Trade and Industry, 2003.

3 Democracy, political participation and citizenship

3.1 What is democracy?

The distinction between democracy and other political systems had already been established by the 4th century BC when the Greek philosopher Aristotle distinguished between:

- democracy (rule by the many)
- oligarchy (rule by the few)
- monarchy (rule by one).

Aristotle was aware that there is an important difference between how political systems work ideally and how they work in practice. He claimed that all existing political systems were imperfect because their rulers aimed at their own interests rather than at the interests of all. Oligarchs, for example, promoted their own interests (the interests of the rich) at the expense of poor. Democrats promoted their own interests (the interests of the poor) at the expense of the rich.

Defining 'democracy'

Aristotle's line of argument indicates that a simple definition of democracy as 'rule by the many' is not sufficient. Most modern political scientists would agree with this conclusion. Robertson argues:

> 'Democracy is the most valued and also the vaguest of political terms in the modern world...The ancient Greek word "democracy" means rule by the demos which can be translated as either rule by "the people" or by "the mob", depending upon one's ideological preference. By itself, democracy means little more than that, in some undefined sense, political power is ultimately in the hands of the whole adult population and that no smaller group has the right to rule. Democracy only takes on a more useful meaning when qualified by one of the other words with which it is associated, for example liberal democracy, representative democracy...or direct democracy.' (Robertson 1986, p.8)

3.2 Direct democracy

According to the traditional view, the birthplace of democracy was ancient Athens. By the 5th century BC, a form of 'direct democracy' had developed in Athens. This meant that every Athenian citizen had the right to attend meetings of the Assembly, a meeting of the citizen body which was called more than 40 times per year (see Box 3.1). Decisions at the Assembly were taken on the basis of a majority vote and any proposals which were passed by a majority became law. Because every citizen had the right to speak and to vote at the Assembly, every citizen had the chance of directly determining what the laws should be. It is

because of this that the system is known as **'direct democracy'**.

Box 3.1 The Athenian system

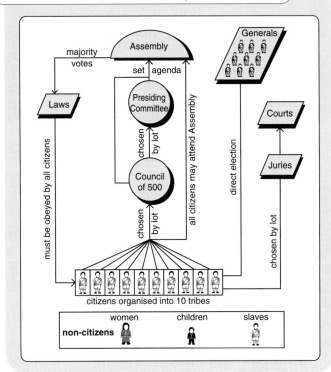

The Athenian system established a number of democratic principles or ideals, some of which have survived in modern democracies:

- one of the basic principles behind the Athenian system was that every citizen should have the right to vote and to hold office
- a second principle was that it was the duty of all citizens to participate actively in the system
- a third principle was that decisions should be made by majority vote.

Elements of direct democracy are practised today. For example, the Swiss constitution allows frequent referendums. Many states in the USA also frequently hold referendums and, in recent years, increasing use has been made of 'initiatives' - devices through which an individual or group can propose legislation by securing the signatures of a required number of voters and then having the issue put to the electorate to accept or reject (see Watts 1997, p.45 and Unit 5). Unlike initiatives, it should be noted, referendums are organised by the government. It is the government (not the public) which decides whether to hold the referendum, the wording of the question and the timing of the event.

There is an argument that, given the rapid development of communications technology, direct democracy is now possible in a large society today (every citizen could vote for or against a new law by pressing a button on a home computer, for example). Since 1997, the Labour government has moved a little way in this direction by setting up an on-line consultation on key issues and by allowing members of the public to e-mail questions to ministers directly. In addition, as an experiment, the government set up a 'People's Panel' in conjunction with MORI, the polling organisation, to test reaction to its policies. There was also a 'Citizen Space' experiment on the e-government portal 'UKOnline'. In Scotland, the Scottish Parliament has introduced new technology to assist the interaction between Parliament members and the public. This technology is examined in Box 3.2.

Box 3.2 Innovations for the Scottish parliament

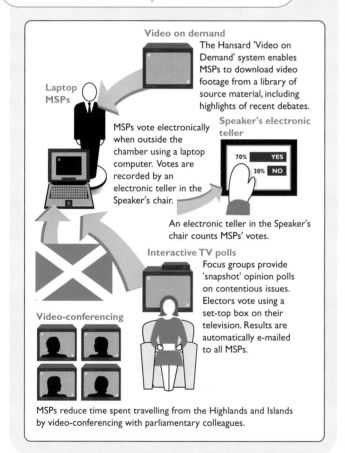

Video on demand
The Hansard 'Video on Demand' system enables MSPs to download video footage from a library of source material, including highlights of recent debates.

Laptop MSPs

MSPs vote electronically when outside the chamber using a laptop computer. Votes are recorded by an electronic teller in the Speaker's chair.

Speaker's electronic teller

70% YES
30% NO

An electronic teller in the Speaker's chair counts MSPs' votes.

Interactive TV polls
Focus groups provide 'snapshot' opinion polls on contentious issues. Electors vote using a set-top box on their television. Results are automatically e-mailed to all MSPs.

Video-conferencing

MSPs reduce time spent travelling from the Highlands and Islands by video-conferencing with parliamentary colleagues.

In addition to the innovations described above, citizens' juries have been set up to consider local issues and informal referendums pioneered by individual MPs have been held to give views on key issues like the introduction of identity cards (*Guardian*, 5 November 2003). Supporters of such developments suggest that as people become more involved in the process of decision-making, so they will become better informed about issues (see, for example, Batchelor 2002). But critics - such as Stephen Coleman, first Professor of e-democracy at Oxford University - see these developments as a gimmick rather than genuine consultation. Coleman argues that they give the illusion of public participation rather than

genuine public involvement in decision-making (*Guardian*, 27 February 2003).

It is important not to exaggerate the steps taken in the direction of direct democracy. In general, representative democracy is very much the norm and is likely to remain so at least in the near future.

3.3 *Representative democracy*

Whereas in a direct democracy every citizen is able to participate directly in decision-making, in a representative democracy citizens elect representatives to make decisions for them. In Britain, for example, voters elect Members of Parliament (MPs) to represent them. These MPs meet in an assembly (the House of Commons) which is responsible for making laws. Every MP has the right to speak and vote for or against proposed laws. Proposals become law if a majority of MPs vote in favour of them.

By voting for a representative, citizens hand over the responsibility for making decisions to someone else. This has important implications.

Representatives and accountability

Although the voters have handed over responsibility for making decisions to their representative, that does not necessarily mean that they have no further part to play in the political process. A key to representative government is that the representatives are, in some way, accountable to the electorate or, to put it the other way round, the electorate, in some way, exercises control over the representatives. Unless representatives act in a way that meets with the approval of the majority of the electorate, for example, they (or their party) will not be re-elected. The fear of this affects the representatives' behaviour. On the other hand, by handing over responsibility for making decisions to someone else, citizens hand over the opportunity of making a personal contribution to the formation of legislation.

Representatives and constituents

The exact role played by the representative is crucially important. Whereas some representatives argue that it is their duty only to do what their electors or their party have instructed them to do, others argue that, once elected, it is their duty to act according to their conscience. It is the latter view which was famously put forward by Edmund Burke in a speech to his constituents in Bristol in 1774 - see Box 3.3 on page 39.

Problems with representative democracy

Burke's view has made a lasting impression on British politicians and it is often used by MPs to justify their behaviour. The problem is that it is a licence for MPs to ignore the wishes of their constituents and their party leadership. On the other hand, the view that representatives should only do what they are instructed to do by their constituents (or party) is equally difficult to sustain. How can representatives know what the majority of their constituents think about a particular issue? And even if they do know, sticking only to the wishes of the majority can, on occasion, lead to tyranny for the minority (something which democracy is supposed to prevent). There are two other key problems

Box 3.3 Edmund Burke and the role of representatives

In a speech to his constituents in Bristol in 1774, Edmund Burke (above) said: 'Your representative owes you not his industry only but his judgements; and he betrays, instead of serving you, if he sacrifices to your opinion.'

with representative democracy. First, it can lead to low rates of turnout and participation since members of the public feel removed and disengaged from the political process. And second, representatives can lose touch with the voters and are only directly accountable at election times.

3.4 Participatory democracy

To combat the problems with representative democracy, another type of democracy - 'participatory democracy' - has

been suggested as a compromise. Hancock (1996) suggests that:

'[Participatory democracy] combines the pragmatic advantages of representative democracy with the theoretical attractions of direct democracy. It allows all citizens a greater say in policy issues through such mechanisms as public enquiries, advisory referendums and consultative bodies.' (Hancock 1996, p.7)

The steps towards direct democracy described above may suggest that the Labour government is moving in the direction of participatory government.

3.5 Liberal democracy

Britain and other industrialised countries in the West are often described as 'liberal democracies'. According to Heywood:

'The liberal element in liberal democracy is a belief in limited government, the idea that the individual should enjoy some protection from arbitrary government. The second element, democratic government, reflects the idea that government should in some way be tied to the will of the people.' (Heywood 1991, p.57)

Ideas about liberal democracy evolved in the 19th century in Britain. In the 20th century, liberal democracies have come to have a number of defining characteristics. Box 3.4 describes these characteristics and contrasts them with those of dictatorships.

Civil liberties

Central to a liberal democracy is the existence of civil liberties - for example, freedom of speech, freedom of assembly and freedom to protest. In Britain, these civil liberties are safeguarded by the 'rule of law' (a 19th-century concept) and the separation of the powers (the maintenance of a separate executive and judiciary). The rule of law guarantees equality before the law and ensures that the powers of rulers can be curtailed by laws enforceable in courts. The separation of the powers ensures that independence is maintained and that power is fragmented.

Box 3.4 Characteristics of liberal democracies

Liberal Democracies	Dictatorships
1. They are representative democracies. Political authority is based on popular consent.	1. Leaders are in power because they have seized power or held onto power unfairly. There is lack of popular consent.
2. Popular consent must be given by the whole adult population, with no groups excluded.	2. Either there is no system of voting or voting is restricted to a minority.
3. Elections are free and fair.	3. Elections, if they happen, are rigged.
4. There is an open competition for power and a real choice between the individuals, groups and parties which put up candidates for election.	4. There is a one-party state and no opposition parties are allowed.
5. There is freedom of expression and a free media.	5. There is no freedom of expression and the media is state controlled.
6. There is the rule of law and government is bound by it.	6. Legal rights are non-existent or not protected. The government can act without legal checks.

Using the criteria above, the UK would be defined as a liberal democracy whereas China or Saudi Arabia would not.

3.6 Parliamentary democracy

Liberal democracies work in different ways. The two main ways are through a parliamentary system or through a presidential system. According to Norton:

> '[The term "parliamentary democracy"] distinguishes the system from those in which the executive and legislature are elected independently of one another and in which one does not depend for its continuance in office on the confidence of the other.' (Norton 1991, p.22)

So, in the USA which has a presidential form of democracy, the elections for President and for Congress are held separately and the President forms a separate administration. By contrast, the UK is a parliamentary democracy and the government is formed from whichever party can command a majority in the House of Commons.

The main characteristics of parliamentary democracies are given in Box 3.5.

Box 3.5 Parliamentary democracy - main characteristics

Parliamentary democracy has the following characteristics:

- parliamentary authority is unlimited and is the highest source of political authority
- the authority of the government of the day comes from Parliament
- members of the government are drawn from Parliament and are not elected separately from it
- the government is usually created from whichever party wins an overall majority in a general election
- the Prime Minister is the Leader of the majority party
- between general elections, a government relies upon its majority to survive and to ensure that its legislative programme is implemented.

Marxist criticisms of parliamentary democracy

Marxists are critical of parliamentary democracy on the grounds that it is a sham in which the democratic parliamentary institutions provide a smokescreen for the exploitation of the majority of the population. For Marxists, parliamentary elections merely serve to permit competing political élites, all of which fundamentally represent ruling-class interests, to alternate in positions of power. Parliamentary democracy conceals the location of real power which is based on wealth and capital. This is true when the Labour Party forms the government since the power of capital still predominates. In support of this argument, Marxists point to the growth in power of capitalist organisations outside and beyond the state - such as multinational companies, the International Monetary Fund and the EU. The growing power of these institutions, they argue, exposes the limitations of parliamentary democracy.

Right-wing criticisms of parliamentary democracy

Criticism of parliamentary democracy also comes from the right. For example, Lord Hailsham, a former Conservative minister, suggested in 1976 that parliamentary democracy brought the danger of an 'elective dictatorship'. Writing in 1978 when Labour was in power, he said:

> 'It is only now that men and women are beginning to realise that representative institutions are not necessarily guardians of freedom but can themselves become engines of tyranny. They can be manipulated by minorities, taken over by extremists, motivated by the self-interest of organised millions. We need to be protected from our representatives no less than our former masters.' (Hailsham 1978, p.13)

Hailsham's main criticism was that elected governments have too few checks on their power.

Other criticisms

Other criticisms include the following. First, the political process in a parliamentary democracy is slow. In times of war, for example, this can be a problem (since there might be a need to respond to events at speed). Second, there are times when open debate (which is permitted in Parliament) is dangerous. One reason why the Labour government refused to hold a debate in Parliament over war with Iraq in 2002 was the fear that vital defence information would be made public and national security would be undermined. Third, parliamentary democracy can be expensive and cumbersome. And fourth, parliamentary democracy can result in 'sheer apathy' as members of the public lose interest in politics (Grant 2003).

Finally, it should be noted that Parliament itself has only one democratic element - the House of Commons. The House of Lords is an appointed second chamber and the monarch retains certain prerogative powers.

Main points Sections 3.1 - 3.6

- **In a democracy, power is ultimately in the hands of the whole population and no smaller group has the right to rule.**

- **When citizens make political decisions themselves and do not rely on representatives, this is known as 'direct democracy'.**

- **In a representative democracy, citizens elect representatives to make decisions for them. By doing this, citizens hand over the responsibility for making decisions to someone else.**

- **Representatives are, in some way, accountable to the electorate, but it is unclear whether they can or should take into account their voters' wishes when making decisions.**

- **Today, liberal democracies are representative democracies whose authority stems from the whole adult population voting in fair and free elections where there is open competition.**

- **In a parliamentary democracy, the legislature and executive are elected at the same time. This form of democracy has come under attack from both left and right.**

Activity 3.1 Different forms of democracy

Item A What is democracy? (1)

Democracy is a simple idea based on two principles - popular control and political equality. Democracy requires that the rules and policies of any group should be subject to control by all its members. Also, the members of the group should have equal influence over the framing of its rules and policies. In a small group, these two principles can be realised directly. In a larger group, they can only be realised indirectly through the agency of chosen representatives. In a representative democracy, popular control means exercising control over the decision-makers. It should be noted that democracy is not an all or nothing affair. It is a matter of degree - of the extent to which the two principles of popular control and political equality are realised in practice. The answer to the following four questions can be used to measure the level of democracy in a country. First, what kind of electoral system is used - is it free and fair? Second, how open and accountable is the government? Third, what civil and political rights exist (for example, is there freedom of speech)? And fourth, does the political and social culture encourage democracy to flourish at all levels in society?

Source: Beetham 1993.

Item B What is democracy? (2)

Quality	%
Living in a free country	64
An equal society	38
Voting for a government in elections	31
Strong and effective government	27
Popular control over government	17
A free-market economy	13

A survey carried out in 1994 asked people to choose two qualities out of a list of six that they felt were 'most important about democracy'. The results of this survey are shown above.

Source: Weir 1994.

Item C Direct and representative democracy

Representatives are always different from us and in a democracy we need to be able to control them. It is here that the question of direct democracy is important. Direct democracy involves the citizen in policy-making. People can vote not simply on whom they want to represent them, but, for example, in referendums which are put to them. The communications' revolution has facilitated direct involvement. There is no doubt that the individual can and should be involved. The right to demonstrate is being more widely exercised and direct interventions like these make representatives aware of grass-roots feeling. People do not have the time, energy or expertise to replace representatives. It is a question of how we are able to control our representatives, not whether we have them. As for these representatives, they can only act on behalf of those they represent if they understand their problems and way of life. The 'mirror' theory of representation suggests that exact percentages of groups within a population should be represented proportionally. So, if the population of Leicester, say, has 40% black people, then 40% of local councillors should be black. The trouble with this is that black people in Leicester are divided ethnically, regionally, along class and gender lines and so on. It would be wrong to assume one black person is the same as another. It does not follow that black representatives will necessarily represent the interests of black constituents. The mirror theory suggests there should be no differences between ourselves and those who represent us. But everyone is different. The reason some people put themselves forward for election and others don't is that they have resources and interests that set them apart. On the other hand, this difference must not become a justification for élitism. Representatives should be accountable. They should take account of what we say. We need to feel comfortable with our representatives, that they 'speak our language', understand our problems and are sensible people. This is only possible if they include significant numbers who are the same gender, colour and so on as the population at large.

Source: Hoffman 2003.

Item D **Teledemocracy**

On 26 February 1998, the *Guardian* reported that a ground-breaking exercise in teledemocracy had been launched in Minnesota, USA, when an on-line debate began between the people and the candidates for the state's governorship. The idea was that, for two weeks, 14 candidates would participate in an on-line debate on six key topics selected by the non-profit making organisation Minnesota E-Democracy. Candidates (who were campaigning for selection within their own parties before the final run-off for Governor in November) were allowed 300-word responses to each issue and subsequent rebuttals of any accusations made by their opponents. Media commentators then posted instant analyses of the debate on-line, and a public e-mail forum, open to anyone, scrutinised the issues and politicians' responses in parallel. On hearing about this project, one *Guardian* reader argued that this was yet another scientific advance that was not progress. First, it reduced politics to the level of a game show. Second, it removed the need for a Parliament and handed control of decision-making to the media and to those who control the media. And third, it set up every choice as a calculation of material benefit, removing consistency of values from the reckoning and making policy options merely a product to be marketed. 'We do actually still need representational politics', the reader concluded.

Source: The *Guardian*, 26 February and 5 March 1998.

Questions

1. a) Compare the criteria outlined in Item A with Item B. Give reasons why Britain could be described as a democratic country.
   b) Are there elements in Britain that could be described as undemocratic? Explain your answer.
2. In Item B, only 17% of respondents thought that 'popular control over government' was crucial in a democracy.
   a) Make a list of ways in which control is exercised over decision makers in Britain.
   b) What does the list tell us about democracy in Britain?
   c) Why do you think only 17% of respondents in 1994 chose this quality?
3. a) Using Item C and your own knowledge, describe the problems with representative democracy.
   b) How can these problems be solved?
   c) What role should direct democracy play today?
4. What view do you take of the advantages and disadvantages of so-called 'teledemocracy', as outlined in Item D? Give reasons for your answer.

3.7 *The evolution of democracy in the UK before 1832*

In Britain, the evolution from absolute monarchy to representative democracy was a slow and complex process. Gradually, the power of the monarchy was handed over to elected representatives and democratic mechanisms and controls developed. Unlike in France where the revolution of 1789 swept away the monarchy for good, in Britain civil war in the 17th century was followed by the restoration of the monarchy. It is the lack of a decisive break in the past which explains the survival of undemocratic elements (such as the unelected monarchy and House of Lords) in the British political system today.

Although Parliament's control of public finance and law-making has been guaranteed since 1688, other democratic elements are much more recent. In 1688, for example, less than 5% of the adult population had the right to vote. This was still the case in 1830. Given that the provision of fair and free elections is a basic component of representative democracy, it seems reasonable to argue that Britain should not be regarded as a legitimate democracy until fair and free elections were established. The struggle for the universal right to vote (also known as the 'franchise' or 'suffrage') and the development of fair electoral practice occurred during the 19th and early 20th centuries.

3.8 *The electoral system in the 19th century*

At the beginning of the 19th century, the British electoral system was far from democratic. It was not just that less than 5% of adults had the right to vote or that bribery and corruption were prevalent. The electoral system did not provide the means for fair and equal representation. The right to vote (and to stand for election) was restricted to men and was dependent on a property qualification - only those who owned property worth a certain value were eligible to vote.

Electoral procedures

Elections at the beginning of the 19th century were not conducted by secret ballot. They were 'open'. When an election was announced, a large wooden platform (the 'hustings') was built in a public place. Candidates made speeches from the platform and then the voters were asked to vote by a show of hands. If the vote between two candidates was close then a 'poll' could be demanded. Each voter would have to go up onto the platform and prove that he had a vote. He would then have to state publicly which candidate he supported. This system was a recipe for corruption. Intimidation and bribery were common.

Reform of the electoral system

Reform of the electoral system was gradual, but gained a

momentum of its own. The first Reform Act was passed in 1832, but it was not until 1928 that universal suffrage was achieved. During the 19th century legislation affecting electoral procedure was passed which provided for the elements described in Box 3.6.

Box 3.6 Development of electoral procedure in the 19th century

Reform in the 19th century resulted in the following:

- the provision of an electoral register
- the gradual broadening of the vote to men with property
- the introduction of the secret ballot
- control over election expenses and other measures to prevent bribery.

By the end of the 19th century, therefore, some progress had been made towards free and fair elections. But the majority of the adult population still could not vote.

3.9 Women and the vote

In the second half of the 19th century, women began to campaign for the vote. While their campaign in the 19th century was conventional and muted, at the beginning of the 20th century it boiled up into a major confrontation with the patriarchal (male-dominated) state.

The suffragists

The term 'suffragist' is usually used of those women who were members of the National Union of Women's Suffrage Societies (NUWSS) - see Box 3.7. The NUWSS was founded in 1897 when suffragist groups from all over Britain joined together to form a single campaigning organisation. The NUWSS used peaceful, moderate, law-abiding tactics. By 1914, over 600 local groups had joined the NUWSS and it had over 100,000 members. Throughout the period 1897 to 1914, the NUWSS continued to lobby MPs, gather petitions and organise peaceful rallies.

Box 3.7 Millicent Fawcett

Millicent Garrett Fawcett, the first President of the NUWSS.

Suffragettes

The term 'suffragette' is usually used of those women who were members of the Women's Social and Political Union (WSPU). The WSPU was set up by Emmeline Pankhurst and her daughters (see Box 3.8) in 1903. Unlike the NUWSS, the WSPU believed that, because peaceful, law-abiding tactics had not won women the vote, more forceful action was necessary. Members of the WSPU began a campaign of direct action to draw attention to their cause. Suffragettes made public protests and, if arrested, always chose prison rather than paying a fine. From 1909, imprisoned suffragettes began to go on hunger strike and were subsequently force-fed by the authorities. These tactics certainly brought great publicity but opponents argued that the publicity was damaging to the cause.

Box 3.8 Emmeline, Christabel and Sylvia Pankhurst

Emmeline Pankhurst (left) with her daughters Christabel and Sylvia in October 1911.

The First World War to 1928

During the First World War, women made an important contribution by taking over the work that had previously been done by men, allowing men to go and fight. When the war was over, the government promised to support the extension of the franchise to women. In Parliament, MPs argued that it was wrong that men who had served in the British army during the First World War should not have the vote. They also agreed that women should be rewarded for their contribution to the war effort. As a result, all men over the age of 21 and all women over the age of 30 were given the right to vote. A separate Act in 1918 gave women over the age of 30 the right to stand for election as MPs. By the mid-1920s, most people agreed that it was ridiculous to allow men aged 21 the vote but not women. The Equal Franchise Act of 1928 at last gave women the vote on the same terms as men at the age of 21. The historian A.J.P. Taylor notes:

'The British electoral system reached theoretical democracy only in April 1928... The Act of 1928 added about five million new voters to the register.' (Taylor 1965, p.332)

3.10 Acts since 1928

Since 1928 several further electoral reform Acts have been passed. These are outlined in Box 3.9.

Box 3.9 Electoral reform Acts passed 1928-2003

1. The **Representation of the People Act 1949** abolished additional votes for university graduates and for those owning business premises and land in constituencies other than those in which they lived. It also removed the six-month residence qualification.

2. In 1969 the minimum voting age was lowered from 21 to 18.

3. The **Representation of the People Act 1985** gave British citizens living abroad the right to vote for a period of five years after they had left Britain.

4. In 1989, this period was extended to 20 years and those who were too young to register as voters before they left Britain became eligible to vote.

Main points Sections 3.7 - 3.10

- Before the 19th century, less than 5% of British adults had the right to vote and bribery and corruption were rife. The electoral system did not provide the means for fair and equal representation.
- During the 19th century, a number of electoral reform Acts were passed, gradually broadening the electorate.
- In the second half of the 19th century, women began to agitate for the vote. At first they used peaceful means, but, in the early 20th century, suffragettes used direct action.
- After the First World War, the Representation of the People Act was passed, giving all men over 21 and women over 30 the vote.
- Since 1928 the voting age of men and women has been the same (age 18 since 1969).

Activity 3.2 The evolution of democracy in Britain

Item A The six points of the people's charter

The Chartist movement in the 1830s and 1840s was the first nationwide protest movement. It attracted the support of many thousands of people, but the government refused to listen to Chartist demands. Although the Chartists failed to achieve their demands in the short term, five out of the six points were achieved in the long term. The second point refers to the introduction of a secret ballot. The fourth point - the payment of MPs - was introduced in 1911. Before 1911, MPs were unpaid and this made it very difficult for the working class to gain representation in Parliament. The sixth point (electing a new Parliament each year) is the only one not to have been put into practice.

Item B Patriarchy

The channels of democracy in our society - trade unions, political parties, local councils, Parliament - were set up by men, for men. They are not designed to allow women's participation. They ignore important areas of women's lives. They must be forced to change. We have grown used to the idea that we are living in a democracy. But, we women are still, in effect, fighting for the franchise. We will not be the silent majority.

Source: Coote & Campbell 1982.

The Six Points
OF THE
PEOPLE'S
CHARTER.

1. A VOTE for every man twenty-one years of age, of sound mind, and not undergoing punishment for crime.

2. THE BALLOT.—To protect the elector in the exercise of his vote.

3. NO PROPERTY QUALIFICATION for Members of Parliament —thus enabling the constituencies to return the man of their choice, be he rich or poor.

4. PAYMENT OF MEMBERS, thus enabling an honest tradesman, working man, or other person, to serve a constituency, when taken from his business to attend to the interests of the country.

5. EQUAL CONSTITUENCIES, securing the same amount of representation for the same number of electors, instead of allowing small constituencies to swamp the votes of large ones.

6. ANNUAL PARLIAMENTS, thus presenting the most effectual check to bribery and intimidation, since though a constituency might be bought once in seven years (even with the ballot), no purse could buy a constituency (under a system of universal suffrage) in each ensuing twelvemonth; and since members, when elected for a year only, would not be able to defy and betray their constituents as now.

Item C **Extension of the franchise**

(i) Electorate and population.

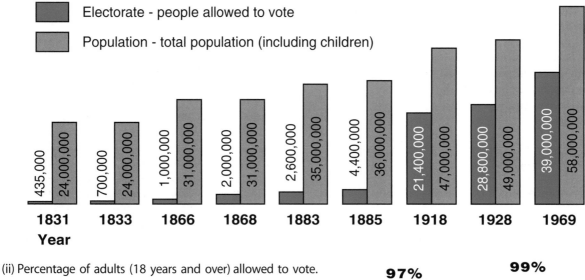

████ Electorate - people allowed to vote

░░░░ Population - total population (including children)

	1831	1833	1866	1868	1883	1885	1918	1928	1969
Electorate	435,000	700,000	1,000,000	2,000,000	2,600,000	4,400,000	21,400,000	28,800,000	39,000,000
Population	24,000,000	24,000,000	31,000,000	31,000,000	35,000,000	36,000,000	47,000,000	49,000,000	58,000,000

Year

(ii) Percentage of adults (18 years and over) allowed to vote.

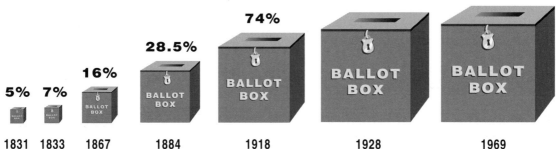

1831	1833	1867	1884	1918	1928	1969
5%	7%	16%	28.5%	74%	97%	99%

Year

Item D **Suffragette banner**

What a Woman may be, and yet not have the Vote

MAYOR NURSE MOTHER DOCTOR or TEACHER FACTORY HAND

What a Man may have been, & yet not lose the Vote

CONVICT LUNATIC Proprietor of white Slaves Unfit for Service DRUNKARD

This banner was produced in the early 20th century.

Questions

1. 'Britain has a long tradition of democratic government.' Give arguments for and against this statement.

2. a) What does Item A tell us about democracy in Britain in the 1830s?

   b) Give arguments for and against the view that annual elections (point 6) would strengthen democracy in Britain.

3. What do Items C and D tell us about the development of democracy in Britain?

4. a) Explain why the extension of the franchise, on its own, is not sufficient to guarantee democracy. Use Item B in your answer.

   b) How might the extension of the franchise lead to greater democracy?

3.11 Direct democracy and political participation

In a direct democracy, every citizen has the chance to make an impact on every decision put before the citizen body. There is, therefore, a great deal of incentive to participate in political decision-making. By participating, citizens make sure that their views are heard and taken into account. If they do not participate, those citizens with opposing views may be able to gain a majority. Citizens, therefore, have a direct and vested interest in participating.

3.12 Representative democracy and political participation
(see also Unit 1, Sections 1.4 to 1.8)

In a representative democracy, the mass of citizens does not have a direct input into political decision-making. Representatives are elected to make decisions on their behalf. As a result, some people argue that there is no need for people to become involved in politics, other than to vote at elections. After all, those who are elected as representatives have the time, the skills and the access to information that ordinary people do not have and are, therefore, in a far better position to make decisions. Others, however, argue that a high level of political participation is important because it ensures that popular control is exerted on decision-makers. Decision-makers, supporters of this viewpoint claim, take into account the views of those who are politically active. Activists constantly monitor the work of decision-makers and hold them accountable for their action.

Participation and representation
The debate over participation is, therefore, similar to that about representation. Those who agree with Burke's view that representatives should act according to their conscience, rather than in response to the wishes of their constituents or party, imply that, once representatives are elected, they have no obligation to listen to anyone else. As a result, ordinary citizens should leave their representatives alone so that they can get on with decision-making without interference.

By contrast, those who argue that representatives should act in accordance with the wishes of the majority of their constituents imply that political participation should be encouraged. Ordinary citizens should be constantly informing their representatives of their views so that the representative has firm guidance about what view is held by the majority. Similarly, those who argue that it is the duty of representatives to ensure that a party's manifesto commitments are carried out encourage people to join political parties to ensure that their manifestos prioritise the issues they feel strongly about.

3.13 Participation and democracy

The level of political participation can determine, to some extent, the behaviour of decision-makers. In states with low levels of political participation, decision-makers have greater leeway to impose their will than they do in states with high levels of political participation. But, this does not necessarily mean that a state with a high level of political participation is more democratic than a state with a low level. This idea is explored in Box 3.10.

Box 3.10 Political participation and democracy

It is important to take care not to confuse democracy with participation, or to define democracy in terms of the level of citizen participation. To do this would produce the bizarre conclusion that the societies under Communist rule were the most democratic because they had the highest levels of voter turnout and the most active and widespread involvement of citizens in party life and public affairs. The problem with such 'participation' from a democratic point of view is that the mass of people exercised very little control over the political agenda or over personnel of government because they were largely subject to control by the government itself.

Source: Beetham 1993.

3.14 Participation and collective action

Since political participation in a representative democracy is a means by which popular control can be exerted on decision-makers, it is understandable that people should act collectively. By demonstrating that a large number of people have the same viewpoint, individual supporters of that viewpoint increase the pressure on decision-makers to act in their favour. That is why activities such as collecting and signing petitions, mass lobbies of MPs at Westminster and marches and rallies are organised. Linked to this type of activity are the publicity stunts and other forms of direct action that are reported in the media. People and groups are well aware that the mass media play a part in setting the political agenda and they design their political activity accordingly.

3.15 Why have levels of participation changed?

It was noted in Unit 1, Section 1.8 that, over the past 50 years, levels of political participation have declined. Evans lists five explanations for changing levels of political participation. These are summarised in Box 3.11 on page 47.

3.16 Measuring participation - elections

It is easy to measure the level of participation in elections since the turnout is measured as a matter of course. In general elections, the tendency has been for the large majority to participate - though recently there has been a significant decline (see Unit 6, Section 6.25).

Low levels of voting have been the cause of much concern as they seem to suggest a rejection of the political process.

Box 3.11   Why levels of political participation have changed

Evans argues that levels of political participation have changed for five main reasons:

1. The impact of globalisation

Globalisation has shifted the focus of power, moving it away from Westminster. The new political structures which are emerging as a result of globalisation encourage people to participate in new ways.

2. The impact of de-industrialisation

De-industrialisation has loosened the old social controls which had developed during industrialisation. As a result, there has been a shift in culture which is manifested, in part, in new forms of political participation.

3. The statist thesis

Britain is a strong, centralised state and the growth in unconventional political participation is a response to the fact that opportunities for success using conventional channels are limited.

4. The new class thesis

While political protest used to be the preserve of the working class, changes in the class structure mean that it is now a middle-class phenomenon. This explains why political activity has changed its nature.

5. The party dealignment thesis

Since people are less loyal to a single party than they used to be, they are more open to the appeal of single-issue groups. Conversely, the growth of single-issue groups has encouraged party dealignment.

Source: Evans 2003.

3.17 *Measuring participation - parties and pressure groups*

Membership of political parties and pressure groups can also be measured both in terms of numbers of members and activity levels.

Party membership has been in decline. For example, at the end of 2003, the Labour Party was thought to have only 250,000 members, down from 400,000 in 1997. Furthermore, studies of party membership activity levels suggest that even party members are not particularly active. Broughton notes:

> 'Offered a range of activities, the majority of Labour Party members had chosen to display an election poster or to deliver party leaflets during an election. Far fewer had stood for office, canvassed votes or donated money to party funds.' (Broughton 2000, p.14)

There have been complaints from members of both Labour and the Conservatives that their parties do not want their active engagement in policy- and decision-making. Instead, the parties just want their money and their willingness to knock on doors at election time.

Pressure group membership has varied from group to group but organisations like Friends of the Earth have continued to grow.

3.18 *Other forms of participation*

It is more difficult to measure the other ways in which people participate in the political process. Survey research is often undertaken and respondents are asked to say in which political activity they have participated. One of the main annual research surveys, the British Social Attitudes Survey suggests that there is not a declining level of participation for other forms of political activity.

> 'In our most recent survey, just over half say they have undertaken at least one action in response to a government action they considered unjust and harmful. In 1994, when we last asked this question, the figure was a little under a half, as it was in 1986 when we first asked it. Indeed the proportions who claim to have taken three or more actions has slowly but consistently risen from five per cent to nine per cent now.' (18th British Social Attitudes Survey 2001-02, p.202)

Box 3.12 examines political action between 1986 and 2000.

Box 3.12   Actual political action 1986-2000

% saying they had	1986	1989	1991	1994	2000
Signed a petition	34	41	53	39	42
Contacted their MP	11	15	17	14	16
Contacted radio, TV or newspaper	3	4	4	5	6
Gone on a protest or demonstration	6	8	9	9	10
Spoken to an influential person	1	3	5	3	4
Contacted a government department	3	3	4	3	4
Formed a group of like-minded people	2	3	2	3	2
Raised the issue in an organisation they already belong to	5	4	5	4	5
None of these	56	48	37	53	47

Source: 18th British Social Attitudes Survey 2001-02.

Petitions and demonstrations

By far the most common form of political activism in 2001 was signing a petition (42%). Few people take part in time-consuming political activity. Unorthodox activities, for example taking part in a demonstration, have increased, with 10% claiming to have taken part in such activity in 2001 compared to 6% in 1986. Recent examples of mass demonstrations include:

● the fuel protests of 2000 which brought farmers and lorry drivers to the streets

● the Countryside Alliance's 400,000-strong march in London in September 2002

● the demonstrations against the war in Iraq in February 2003 which included a march of over 1 million people in London.

It is not the case that people are going on protests instead of voting. The British Social Attitudes Survey 2001-02 shows that those attending protests and demonstrations are actually more likely to vote than those who do not go on protests and demonstrations.

3.19 *Political inactivity*

The British Social Attitudes Survey 2001-02 discovered that 47% of the population takes no part in any form of political action. However, this figure is actually lower than most earlier years. The conclusion of the survey is that:

> 'Recent low election turnouts do not appear to be symptomatic of a wider malaise. There is little evidence that other forms of political participation are in decline or that people are resorting to such activities instead of voting.' (18th British Social Attitudes Survey 2001-02, p.203)

Political apathy amongst the young

Young people, in particular, seem alienated from traditional forms of participation. Electoral turnout fell among 18 to 24 year olds to 35% in the 2001 general election. Membership of the youth wings of the main political parties is low and relatively few are involved in pressure group activity. The think tank Demos has claimed that only 6% of 15-34 year olds describe themselves as 'very interested in politics', and concluded that 'an entire generation has opted out of party politics' (Wilkinson & Mulgan 1995, p.99). However, there is the counter-argument - namely that:

> 'Age differences in participation are complex. The young are less likely to vote than the old and are more likely to be alienated from conventional forms of participation. However, they are more likely to engage in unconventional forms of participation, such as protest politics. In short, it is not that young people do not participate in politics, rather that they participate differently.' (Evans 1997, p.112 - slightly adapted)

This view is confirmed in the 2001 British Election Study which discovered that young people between 18 and 24 were the least likely to vote of any age group but had the highest level of participation of any age group. 'Participation' was defined in terms of having strong convictions and being likely to persuade others to vote, being helpers in the campaign and being active, committed party supporters.

3.20 *Who are the activists?*

Parry and his colleagues (1991) discovered that the minority of the population which is politically active is not typical of the nation as a whole. This conclusion was reached by examining four characteristics - class, gender, party identification (which political party a person supports) and political outlook (whether a person holds 'moderate' or 'extreme' views). The findings are discussed in Box 3.13.

3.21 *New Labour and political participation*

New methods of encouraging political participation are part of the Labour government's modernisation agenda. For

---

Box 3.13 The findings of Parry and colleagues 1991

Class

In terms of class, it was found that the majority of activists came from the 'salariat' - people who are relatively wealthy and who have professional and managerial occupations. Parry & Moyser argue that:

> 'This arises because class is associated with the possession of social and economic resources like education and wealth. These are the resources that ease the entry of the individual into the political arena.' (Parry & Moyser 1993, p.21)

Gender and party identification

Gender and party identification, however, seem to play little part in determining how active people are. Activists are no more likely to be men than women and, while people who support different political parties may differ in the type of activities they choose, there is little difference in the level of participation between supporters of the main parties.

Political outlook

Although party identification does not seem to determine how active people are, political outlook does. Those with more 'extreme' views on both the right and the left tend to be more active than those with more moderate views.

These findings suggest that, overall, the average activist is well educated, earns more than the average wage and holds views which are 'stronger' than the views of most people.

---

example, citizens' juries or panels are being increasingly used by local authorities and health authorities as a means of consulting the public. Focus groups, deliberative opinion polls, standing citizens, panels, user group forums and local referendums have also been recommended by the government. In some local authorities, 'People's Parliaments' have been set up. These are regular open meetings attended by local residents and councillors. In addition, all the major political parties have used focus groups as a way of testing out ideas.

By December 2003, the Labour government had become so concerned about the lack of interest in politics and so afraid that it was becoming remote from the electorate that it launched the 'Big Conversation' in Newport to engage directly with the public. The idea was that Blair and other ministers would tour the country over the year, listening to voters' concerns and hearing their ideas. Critics, however, claimed that, in reality, this was just a publicity stunt and that Labour had already made up its mind on the key issues.

New channels of communication

Both central and local government have increasingly promoted e-democracy through the internet. The Hansard Society has even produced a report *A Tale of Two Houses* which compares audience involvement in the TV series *Big Brother* with the lack of engagement of the public with the work of the House of Commons. The *Observer* pointed out:

'Both are televised houses in which a popularity contest takes place...But Parliament is failing to satisfy the demands of a generation raised on text messaging and e-mail.' (*Observer*, I June 2003)

Given the significant changes in methods of communication, it seems likely that:

'The development of interactive and virtual technologies will be bound to alter the methods of communication and the voters, producing both new opportunities and barriers to effective participation. The days of trudging around a windswept housing estate knocking on doors during an election campaign seem to be numbered.' (Broughton 2000, p.15)

This is already leading the government and local authorities to consider alternative avenues to encourage more public participation in politics.

Criticisms

Critics claim, however, that new techniques like those described above are:

- cosmetic
- top-down
- do not allow for real decision-making.

There are also warnings that:

'[The new technology could] undermine the democratic process by compounding existing biases in the distribution of knowledge and information; by fragmenting discourse between increasingly differentiated policy areas; and by reducing participation to a distanced and marginalised vote in a knee jerk reaction to a limited number of sound bite options.' (Horrocks & Wring 2001, p.32)

Despite these warnings, the fear of apathy in politics has led the chairpersons of both the Conservative Party and Labour Party, to agree to work together to promote e-democracy, among other new ideas, in order to restore respect for Parliament and politicians (*Guardian*, 11 February 2002).

Main points   Sections 3.11 - 3.21

- **Some people argue that, in a representative democracy, there is no need for people to participate in politics (except voting). Others argue that a high level of participation is important.**
- **Research shows that only a small minority of people in Britain are very politically active and, although most vote in general elections, turnout is declining.**
- **The nature of participation has changed over the last 30 years. People are more reluctant to join trade unions and political parties, but there has been a dramatic upsurge in single-issue protest activity.**
- **Levels of political participation and voting are particularly low among young people though a minority are very active.**
- **Political activists tend to be well educated, earn more than the average wage and to be more 'extreme' in their views than others.**

Activity 3.3 *Political participation in Britain*

Item A **The level of political activity in Britain**

The 2001 British Election Survey suggested seven categories of participants in the election campaign:

1. Apathetics
Apathetics have little or no interest in politics or the election and do not follow the campaign in the media.

2. Minimalists
Minimalists do not follow the campaign but say that they have some interest.

3. Spectators
Spectators, as the name implies, follow the campaign in the media.

4. Talkers
Talkers discuss the election campaign and/or politics with others.

5. Proselytisers
Proselytisers are talkers with strong convictions and are more likely to try to persuade others to vote in a certain way.

6. Helpers
Helpers are willing to give money to a party or candidate or help out in some way in a local campaign.

7. Gladiators
Gladiators are active and committed party supporters who work in campaigns.

Category	% in the population	% turnout in the election
Apathetics	12	29
Minimalists	8	54
Spectators	37	62
Talkers	27	68
Proselytisers	7	71
Helpers	8	73
Gladiators	2	91

Source: Denver 2002.

Item B Suggestions for improving electoral turnout:

- New ways of voting including postal voting and e-voting
- Compulsory voting
- Electoral reform so that all votes would really count
- More politics and citizenship classes
- Make the House of Commons and Lords more interesting
- Revive the civic culture especially through the mass media so that people are interested in political issues

Source: Game 2001.

Questions

1. Draw up a questionnaire and find out the level of political activity of your colleagues. Are the results above or below the average? Suggest reasons for the results.

2. Using Items A and B and your own knowledge, answer the following questions.

   a) Why is the level of political participation in Britain important?

   b) What factors would you say determine the level of political participation in the UK?

3. Look at the list in Item B. Re-order the list, ranking the factors in the order of likely effectiveness and explain why you have ranked them in this order.

3.22 *What is a citizen?*

A citizen is any member of a state who is formally recognised as a citizen by that state. The concept of citizenship is, therefore, legalistic. Citizens are individuals who have some sort of legal status within a state - they have been granted certain rights by the state and are expected to perform certain duties:

> 'The citizen should be understood in the first instance not as a type of person...but as a position in the set of formal relationships defined by democratic sovereignty.' (Donald 1996, p.174)

The precise range and balance between the rights granted to citizens and the duties they are expected to perform varies from time to time and from state to state. In times of warfare, for example, the duties a state expects its citizens to perform may be very great and the rights and liberties enjoyed by citizens may be very few. When peace returns, however, the situation may be reversed. The precise balance between rights, liberties and duties is a matter to be resolved, either by negotiation or through conflict, by the citizens living in a particular society at a particular time.

3.23 *Where exactly do political rights come from?*

The question of where political rights come from has concerned political philosophers for many centuries. While no single satisfactory answer has been found, the distinction is often made between natural rights and positive rights.

a) Natural rights

Political theorists who acknowledge that there are natural rights argue that certain rights are universally applicable to all societies. The origin of these rights, it is generally argued, is to be found in the essential nature of human beings or in laws given by God. The classic statement of this theory is to be found in the writing of John Locke (see Box 3.14) who argued in his Second Treatise on Government of 1690 that, before the creation of political societies, human beings existed in a state of nature in which God-given natural laws and rights existed. These laws and rights were to be the basis of

political societies when they were eventually created. Locke claimed that life, liberty and property were natural rights.

Box 3.14 John Locke

John Locke (1632-1704)

b) Positive rights

Despite the attraction of natural rights theories, a number of problems arise. It is difficult to prove that a state of nature ever existed, for example, or that rights are derived from God. It is also difficult to work out which rights are natural and which are not. As a result, some political philosophers have abandoned the idea of natural rights altogether in favour of a theory which asserts that the only rights which exist are positive rights granted by a state to its citizens. This avoids the problems associated with natural rights theories, but it raises questions about:

- why citizens should be given rights
- which rights (if any) they should be given
- how extensive these rights should be.

Also, if rights are not granted by God or nature, there is the problem of whether they are absolute or whether they can be taken away by the state in certain circumstances (for example, in a national emergency).

3.24 The development of rights and liberties in the UK

People living in the UK are both citizens and subjects. They are citizens because they have certain defined rights and liberties, but they are also subjects of the monarch. Unlike in the USA and many other states, the rights and liberties of British citizens are not set out in a single constitutional document. Rather, they are part of the British uncodified constitution (see Unit 11). Some of these rights and liberties are the product of custom and convention. Others are contained in written documents, namely Acts of Parliament. The rights and liberties contained in these Acts are the result of struggles waged by people and their representatives against the absolute power of their rulers. The key events are outlined in Box 3.15.

3.25 International agreements

In addition to the pieces of domestic legislation outlined in Box 3.15, three international agreements have a bearing on rights in the UK. The first is the United Nations Declaration of Human Rights, agreed in 1948. The Declaration sets out a number of general rights which governments are meant to grant to their citizens and more detailed guidelines stipulating specific rights and types of treatment. The second is the European Convention on Human Rights, signed in 1950. This treaty not only set out the rights which all citizens in Europe could expect, it also established a Commission of Human Rights and a European Court of Human Rights to enforce the treaty. And the third is the Maastricht Treaty which was ratified by all members of the EU by the end of 1993. This gave citizenship a new dimension since workers' rights and voting rights became guaranteed throughout the EU.

As a result of the above developments, British citizens enjoy the basic rights and liberties set out in Box 3.16.

Box 3.16 Basic rights and liberties

- Freedom of movement.
- Freedom from arbitrary arrest or unjustified police searches.
- Freedom of conscience in matters of religion and politics.
- Freedom of expression.
- Freedom of association, including the right to protest peacefully.
- Social freedoms - such as the right to marry, divorce, procure abortions or enjoy homosexual relations.
- The right to vote and to stand for election.
- The right to a fair trial.
- The right not to be coerced or tortured by agents of the state.
- The right not to be subjected to surveillance without due legal process.
- The right to own property.

3.26 Citizenship in the UK from the 1990s

Since the late 1980s, a debate about what citizenship is and what it should be has risen up the political agenda. There are three main reasons for this:
1. There was a campaign by the Conservative government under John Major to promote 'active citizenship'.
2. There was concern that legislation passed in the 1980s and early 1990s resulted in the erosion of many of the rights and liberties enjoyed by British citizens.

Box 3.15 Key events - rights and liberties

Magna Carta, 1215
In 1215, King John was forced to sign the Magna Carta. This was the first time in the UK that the power of an absolute ruler had been limited by law. The Magna Carta limited the monarch's scope to make law and to levy taxes. It also prevented people from being imprisoned except by a process of law involving the lawful judgement of the person's peers.

Habeas Corpus Act, 1679
The Habeas Corpus Act of 1679 insisted that people should be told the reason for their arrest and should be informed of the charges against them. A person who was arrested had to be brought before a court and charged with a specific offence within three days. This Act was particularly important since it limited the arbitrary power of rulers.

Bill of Rights, 1689
In 1689, the Bill of Rights was passed. Unlike such Bills in other countries, the British Bill of Rights had no special status. It was an ordinary Act of Parliament. Nonetheless, it did increase the rights enjoyed by citizens. The Bill guaranteed the supremacy of Parliament over the monarch and prevented the monarch from imposing taxation unless this was agreed by the House of Commons. The Bill also guaranteed freedom of speech and the right of citizens to petition both the monarch and Parliament.

Further Acts
Subsequently, a number of Acts were passed extending the rights and liberties of British citizens. The right to worship freely, for example, was established by a number of Acts such as the Catholic Emancipation Act of 1829 (which allowed Catholics to stand for Parliament for the first time). Slavery was abolished in 1833. Sex Discrimination Acts were passed in 1975 and 1987. The first Race Relations Act was passed in 1976. The Data Protection Act was passed in 1984.

3. The Labour government elected in 1997 promised to take the debate in a new direction:

'The millennium symbolises a new era opening up for Britain...Our aim is no less than to set British political life on a new course for the future.' (Labour 1997, p.1)

Active citizenship

The idea of active citizenship came out of the Conservatives' experience of government in the 1980s. According to Oliver:

'By the end of the 1980s, the Conservative government had itself become disillusioned with the potential for government to solve problems with any real or lasting success.' (Oliver 1993, p.26)

Since, Oliver argues, governmental policies had, for example, failed to solve the problem of rising crime and rising public spending levels, the government began to look for solutions to these problems which did not involve governmental intervention. One solution was to suggest that responsibility for society's problems did not lie with the government, but with the whole community. Every British citizen, in other words, had a duty to take an active part in solving society's problems:

'Active citizens, according to the Conservative view, would themselves take responsibilities for some of the things that needed doing in society, rather than expect the state to do them: charitable and voluntary work, housing associations, neighbourhood watch schemes and the like are seen as alternatives to expensive and often unsuccessful state provision.' (Oliver 1993, p.26)

Not only did this fit with the predominant ideology in the Conservative Party, it also presented the government with a means of deflecting criticism. Other features of the Conservative's approach to citizenship are outlined in Box 3.17.

Box 3.17 Active citizenship

- The promotion of the citizen as consumer
- Individual self reliance
- The need to take responsibility for your own family
- The need to be patriotic

Source: Frazer 2000.

The Citizen's Charter

To promote the idea of active citizenship, John Major launched the Citizen's Charter initiative in the summer of 1991. This contained three central provisions.

1. Public services had to set themselves performance targets which were then published as individual charters and made available to the public.
2. Provision was made for redress where services failed to achieve the standards laid out in a charter (an independent inspectorate was established to monitor the performance of public services against their charter standards and to make judgements in cases where citizens were seeking redress for failures).
3. A Charter Mark Scheme was set up to give recognition to those public services which performed well consistently.

The notion of active citizenship and the Citizen's Charter demonstrate the dual nature of citizenship - its concern both with the responsibilities of citizens towards each other and with what can be expected as a right from the state. McInnes notes, however, that:

'The Citizen's Charter uses the language of empowerment. However, it relies on redressing the grievances of the individual...There is little attempt to invite citizens to determine the optimum [best] level of services. It is paternalist [father-like] and reactive rather than pro-active. The citizen is consumer, not participant.' (McInnes 1996, p.25)

Liberties under attack

The second reason for the prominence of the debate over citizenship is the concern expressed by some pressure groups and opposition parties that, between 1979 and 1997, Conservative governments eroded and even destroyed basic rights which used to be enjoyed by citizens.

At heart, this concern is derived from the nature of the British constitution. Since Parliament is sovereign, Parliament can pass laws which take away (or add to) any or all of the rights enjoyed by citizens. This means that the rights and responsibilities enjoyed by British citizens are entirely dependent on the government of the day. Citizens have no right of appeal if the government chooses to take away a right or liberty which they hold dear. This, it is argued, is especially unsatisfactory when a single party holds onto power for a prolonged period, especially given that, in all the general elections held since 1945, no single party has won 50% of the vote.

There was a number of occasions in the 1980s and early 1990s when opponents of the Conservative government were outraged by the government's erosion of civil liberties. During the miners' strike of 1984-85, for example, the police prevented miners (or those suspected of being miners) from travelling freely around the country. In 1985, the government banned employees at the Government Communications Headquarters (GCHQ) from belonging to trade unions. And, in 1990, many protestors at an anti-poll tax demonstration in London complained that they were being denied their right to protest peacefully in public. According to the pressure group Liberty (which campaigns on a wide range of civil rights issues), however, the greatest threat to civil liberty since the Second World War was the Criminal Justice Act of 1994 - see Box 3.18.

The Criminal Justice Act (1994) placed considerable discretionary powers in the hands of the police and made it more difficult for people to protest or practise an unorthodox lifestyle.

Box 3.18 The Criminal Justice Act (1994)

The Criminal Justice Act (1994):
- removed the right of silence for suspects
- allowed the police powers to stop and search
- limited the right to protest by introducing the offence of 'aggravated trespass'
- restricted the rights of ravers and squatters.

Main points   Sections 3.22 - 3.26

- Citizens are individuals who have some sort of legal status within a state - they have been granted certain rights by the state and are expected to perform certain duties.
- Some theorists argue that rights are natural (granted by God or nature). Others argue that the only rights which exist are positive rights granted by a state to its citizens.

- In Britain, some rights and liberties are the product of custom and convention and others are granted by Acts of Parliament.
- Since the late 1980s, a debate about citizenship has developed because (i) Major's government promoted 'active citizenship' (ii) opponents argued that the 1979-97 Conservative governments eroded citizens' rights.

Activity 3.4 Citizenship

Item A A definition

Citizenship is a relationship between the individual and the state in which the two are bound together by rights (such as voting and the protection of the law) and duties (such as paying taxes and obeying the law). Citizens differ from subjects and aliens in that they are full members of their political community or state because they possess basic rights. Citizenship is viewed differently depending on whether it is shaped by individualism or communitarianism. Individualism emphasises individual rights. It places particular stress on what individuals are entitled to and on their freedom to act independently. Communitarianism emphasises duties. It places particular stress on the role of the state as a moral agency and the importance of community.

Source; Heywood 1997.

Item B Active citizenship (1)

Item C Active citizenship (2)

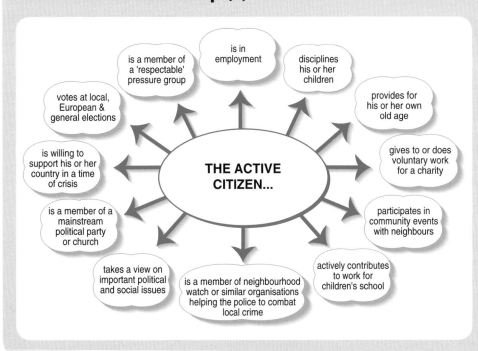

Questions

1. Using Item A, explain the differences between individual and communitarian approaches to citizenship.

2. a) Judging from Items B and C, what is an active citizen?

   b) What are the benefits and drawbacks of active citizenship?

3.27 New Labour and citizenship

It is clear from Labour's 1997 general election manifesto both that Labour had a new approach to citizenship and that citizenship was high on its agenda. In the manifesto, for example, a number of pledges were made which were clearly designed to strengthen the rights of British citizens. These are outlined in Box 3.19.

> **Box 3.19** Pledges made by New Labour in 1997
>
> - a Freedom of Information Act
> - the incorporation of the European Convention on Human Rights into British law
> - the promise of legal aid for those seeking to enforce their rights
> - improved rights for workers through a minimum wage and signing the Social Chapter of the Maastricht Treaty
> - statutory trade union recognition.

The fact that the Labour Party was committed to strengthening citizens' rights suggests that it might have a different approach from the previous Conservative administration. However, Labour was also concerned about the decline in civic engagement by ordinary people who were no longer involved in their communities - a trend which is not just a UK phenomenon (in the USA, Putman has noted the decline in engagement by citizens in the life of their communities in his book *Bowling Alone*). Research has suggested that the consequence of the decline in involvement would be a breakdown in solidarity and trust, a detachment from the political process and a decline in development and efficiency (Ashbee 2000). Labour intended to promote measures to re-engage members of the community through democratic citizenship.

Rights and responsibilities

At the same time as promising to strengthen citizens' rights, the Labour government has placed emphasis on the idea that citizens have responsibilities. For example, when the Welfare to Work legislation was proposed, ministers stressed that people had a responsibility to work since, by working, they would be able to make a valuable contribution to society as a whole. In May 2001, the government encouraged volunteering with a £130 million package of measures 'to tackle inequality and poverty through community action rather than direct state provision' (Faulks 2002 p. 9). In introducing the measures, Gordon Brown claimed that:

> 'All the measures accounted today will strengthen and empower local organisations to take a more active role in tacking the problems faced by local people...[This is] the start of a new era of active citizenship with an enabling state, and a renewal of civic duty at its core.' (Ten Downing Street Newsroom 2001 quoted in Faulks 2002)

Citizenship in schools

In July 1997, the government published a White Paper which gave the commitment to 'strengthen education for citizenship'. To investigate how this was to be achieved, the Advisory Group on Citizenship and Democracy in Schools was set up. This produced interim proposals that the education of pupils in the principles and practice of citizenship and democracy should be a statutory duty for schools. By accepting these proposals (and changing the school curriculum from 2002 to make citizenship compulsory), the government made it clear that it recognised that the goal of active citizenship could only be achieved if people know about, understand and are able to debate their rights and responsibilities (*Times Educational Supplement*, 27 March 1998). However, the practice of citizenship education in schools has been criticised by OFSTED inspectors who have also taken a negative view of much of the teaching material being sent to schools by businesses, charities and campaigning groups (*Times Educational Supplement*, 4 July 2003). The government's commitment to education for citizenship indicates that citizenship is still high on its agenda. David Blunkett, the Home Secretary, has maintained this concern with citizenship arguing that 'in a functioning democracy we should all be more active citizens, socially engaged even if it's over nothing grander than Neighbourhood Watch' (*Guardian*, 11 June 2003).

Citizenship and immigrants

Another area where Labour has promoted the idea of citizenship is the plan for a compulsory citizenship programme for the 110,000 immigrants each year who apply to become naturalised Britons. Immigrants can apply for citizenship after living legally in the UK for five years, or after three years if they are married to a British citizen. The intention is that all applicants for naturalisation will take classes to teach them how to cope with life in the UK, how to find a job and how to use the NHS and social services. The Home Office panel has also recommended that the 'values of toleration and fair play' are taught, along with etiquettes of everyday life and a political lesson on British national institutions. The Nationality, Immigration and Asylum Act 2002 requires that all applicants for naturalisation pledge loyalty to their new country. It also expects them to 'have sufficient knowledge of English' and 'sufficient knowledge of life in the UK'. Beverly Hughes, the Home Office Minister, has stated:

> 'We want to make acquiring British nationality a special and meaningful event. People acquiring the status of British citizenship should embrace the diversity of living in Britain and play an active role - both economically and as citizens - in our society.' (*Guardian*, 1 February 2003)

Trials for this new scheme began in eight areas in January 2004. The ceremony for the loyalty pledge is the responsibility of local authorities (*Guardian*, 26 July 2003). The Home Office issued a consultation paper in July 2003 to ask whether the flag and national anthem should be part of the ceremony.

While the citizenship programme is planned for those seeking naturalisation, other groups like asylum seekers and illegal immigrants are denied rights of citizenship and, in increasing numbers of cases, are returned to their homelands. The government's proposed national identity cards are being suggested partly to exercise greater control over immigration and asylum seekers. The proposed national identity cards will define very sharply who is a citizen and who is not.

The Human Rights Act

The European Convention on Human Rights, despite being accepted in this country since 1950, was not incorporated into British law for 50 years. Until 2000, therefore, British citizens had to seek redress from the European Court at Strasbourg rather than British courts - a process which was costly and time-consuming for the individual. As part of Labour's plans for active citizenship, Labour's 1997 election manifesto promised to incorporate the European Convention on Human Rights into UK law 'to bring these rights home and allow our people to access them in their national courts' (Labour Party 1997). The provisions of the Human Rights Act are outlined in Box 3.20.

Box 3.20 The Human Rights Act

The Human Rights Act was introduced in 1998, and became effective from 2000. It guarantees:
- the right to life
- prohibition of torture
- prohibition of slavery
- the right to liberty and security
- the right to a fair trial
- no punishment without law
- the right to respect for private and family life
- freedom of thought, conscience and religion
- freedom of expression
- freedom of association and assembly
- the right to marry and found a family
- the prohibition of discrimination.

There have been relatively few cases heard in the UK courts under the Human Rights Act, despite initial concerns that there would be a floodgate of actions.

Limitations of the Act

After 11 September 2001, the Home Secretary, David Blunkett, announced emergency powers to combat terrorism. The powers included the right to hold terrorist suspects without trial, and to search bank accounts and premises. This has led to individuals being held in detention without trial for two years. These measures would usually contradict Article 5 (the right to liberty) of the Human Rights Act. However, governments can suspend rights in emergency circumstances under Article 15. This indicates 'how frail the protection of human rights can be, especially while the British Parliament remains sovereign' (*Talking Politics* 2002, p.45).

Conclusion

Since 1997, there has been a move towards a new form of 'democratic citizenship'. Frazer argues:
> 'The language of citizenship, and the proposal that revitalised citizenship requires changes in political culture have been prominent in government policy discussions and proposals since May 1997.' (Frazer 2000, p.218)

Democratic citizenship involves cultural change, the promotion of 'community', the promotion of the active citizen who votes and is engaged in the whole political process and recognition of the ethnic and cultural diversity of our society.

Main points   Section 3.27

- **In the Labour Party's 1997 election manifesto, a number of pledges were made which were clearly designed to strengthen the rights of British citizens.**
- **At the same time as promising to strengthen citizens' rights, the Labour government has placed emphasis on the idea that citizens have responsibilities.**
- **The government has made the study of citizenship compulsory at school in an effort to promote active citizenship.**
- **Labour has made plans for a compulsory citizenship programme for immigrants who apply to become naturalised Britons.**
- **The Human Rights Act was introduced in 1998, and became effective from 2000. After 11 September 2001, however, some of the Act's provisions were suspended.**

Activity 3.5 New Labour and citizenship

Item A Education for citizenship

Bernard Crick, Chair of the Advisory Group on Citizenship and Democracy in Schools, argues that, since the time of Aristotle (4th century BC), most of the world has recognised that citizenship is a great educative force, and not something that can just be bolted on as an extra. The Advisory Group's terms of reference, he says, were precise - to provide advice on effective education for citizenship in schools. This should include:
- the nature and practices of participation in democracy
- the duties, responsibilities and rights of individuals as citizens
- the values to individuals and society of community activity.

As a result, Crick claimed, citizenship is by no means just political education. Education about the community and about community service is equally important. There are, in short, three strands of citizenship:
- social and moral responsibility
- community involvement
- political literacy.

Source: The *Times Educational Supplement*, 27 March 1998.

Item B **Identity cards**

The *Guardian*'s view of what an identity card might look like.

Chip
Will store many details such as DNA, blood group or whether the holder wants to donate organs. Could also store criminal records, relevant immigration status and religion.

Number
A unique number could be easily checked against other details, helping to combat welfare fraud. It would also contain your national insurance number.

Iris recognition
When swiped it could recognise holder's unique iris pattern.

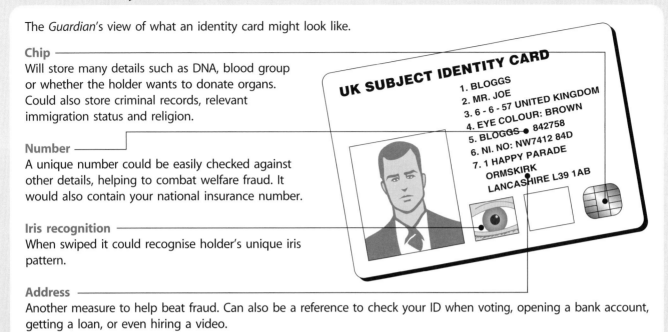

Address
Another measure to help beat fraud. Can also be a reference to check your ID when voting, opening a bank account, getting a loan, or even hiring a video.

Source: *Guardian*, 12 November 2003.

Item C **Citizenship and asylum seekers**

One government response to the growing public anxiety over asylum seekers was to call for ethnic minority groups to display greater sensitivity to traditional British norms and values. In December 2001, for example, the Home Secretary, David Blunkett, stated that the practice of enforced marriages for (some) Asian girls was incompatible with integration into British society. 'We don't tolerate the intolerable under the guise of cultural difference', he said, 'We have norms of acceptability, and those who come in…should accept those norms'. In the same speech, Blunkett picked up on an idea floated in August 2001 by Geoff Rooker, a Home Office Minister with special responsibility for immigration, and suggested that immigrants applying for British citizenship might be required to demonstrate proficiency in the English language, as well as other 'norms of acceptability'.

Such ideas were reflected in the White Paper *Secure Border Safe Haven* which the Home Office published in February 2002. This suggested that immigrants seeking permanent residency in Britain would be required to attend 'citizenship courses' at which they would be taught not just English language, but aspects of British culture, politics and traditions. The successful completion of such a course would be marked by a ceremony at which an oath would be sworn, pledging to 'respect the rights and freedoms of the United Kingdom…uphold its democratic values…observe its laws faithfully and fulfil my duties and obligations as a British citizen'.

Such initiatives were clearly intended to reflect New Labour's 'Third Way' emphasis on 'rights and responsibilities', the clear implication being that while the government was keen to tackle racism and associated socio-economic deprivation, black and Asian immigrants had to do more to help themselves, while, at the same time, avoiding behaviour or practices which alienated the indigenous or 'host' population.

Source: The *Observer*, 19 August 2001, the *Independent on Sunday*, 9 December 2001 and www.Homeoffice.gov.uk/rds/immigration.

Item D Citizenship oath and pledge for applicants for British citizenship

I..........................swear by almighty God that, on becoming a British citizen, I will be faithful and bear true allegiance to Her Majesty Queen Elizabeth II, her heirs and successors according to law. I will give my loyalty to the United Kingdom and respect its rights and freedoms. I will uphold its democratic values. I will observe its laws faithfully and fulfil my duties and obligations as a British citizen.

Applicants can choose an alternative opening - namely:
'I ... do solemnly, sincerely and truly declare and affirm that on becoming a British citizen...'

Source: *Guardian*, 26 July 2003.

Questions

1. What do Items A-D tell us about the Labour government's view of citizenship?

2. a) Give arguments for and against the view that every student should spend 5% of their time learning about citizenship. Use Item A in your answer.

b) What should be taught in citizenship lessons? Give some concrete examples.

3. Give arguments for and against the view that applicants for naturalisation should have to take the oath in Item D.

References

Almond & Verba (1963) Almond, G. & Verba, S., *The Civic Culture: Political Attitudes and Democracy in Five Nations*, Princeton University Press 1963.

Almond & Verba (1981) Almond, G. & Verba, S., *The Civic Culture Revisited*, Little Brown (Boston, USA), 1981.

Ashbee (2000) Ashbee, E., 'Bowling alone', *Politics Review*, Vol.10.1, September 2000.

Batchelor (2002) Batchelor, A., 'Direct democracy', *Talking Politics*, Vol. 14.2, January 2002.

Beetham (1993) Beetham, D., *Auditing Democracy In Britain*, The Charter 88 Trust, 1993.

British Social Attitudes (2001) Park, A. et al. (eds), British Social Attitudes 18th Report, Sage, 2001.

Broughton (2000) Broughton, D., 'Political participation in Britain', *Politics Review*, April 2000.

Butler & Kavanagh (2002) Butler, D. & Kavanagh, D., *The British General Election Of 2001*, Macmillan, 2002.

Coote & Campbell (1982) Coote, A. & Campbell, B., *Sweet Freedom: the Struggle for Women's Liberation*, Blackwell, 1982.

Denver (2002) Denver, D., 'Who voted in 2002', *Sociology Review*, November 2002.

Denver & Fisher (2003) Denver, D. & Fisher, J., 'The contexts of British Politics' in Fisher, *Denver & Benyon (2003)*.

Donald (1986) Donald, J., 'The citizen and the man about town' in *Hall & Dugary (1986)*.

Dunleavy et al. (1997) Dunleavy, P., Gamble, A., Holliday, I. & Peele, G., *Developments in British Politics 5*, Macmillan, 1997.

Dunleavy et al. (2000) Dunleavy, P., Gamble, A., Holliday, I. & Peele, G., *Developments in British Politics 6*, Macmillan, 2000.

Dunleavy et al. (2003) Dunleavy, P., Gamble, A., Holliday, I. & Peele, G., *Developments in British Politics 7*, Palgrave Macmillan, 2003.

Dunleavy & Weir (1997) Dunleavy, P. & Weir, S., 'The true aim of electoral reform', *New Statesman*, 5 December 1997.

Evans (1997) Evans, M., 'Political participation' in *Dunleavy et al. (1997)*.

Evans (2003) Evans, G., 'Political Culture and Voting Participation' in *Dunleavy et al. (2003)*.

Faulks (2002) Faulks K., 'Citizenship', *Politics Review*, Vol.12.3, November 2002.

Fisher, Denver & Benyon (2003) Fisher J., Denver, D. & Benyon, J., *Central Debates in British Politics*, Longman, 2003.

Frazer (2000) Frazer, E., 'Citizenship and culture' in *Dunleavy et al. (2000)*.

Game (2001) Game, C., 'Britain's changing and unchanging electoral systems' in *Lancaster (2001)*.

Grant (2003) Grant, W., *Key ideas in Politics*, Nelson Thornes, 2003.

Hailsham (1978) Hailsham, Lord, *The Dilemma of Democracy*, Collins, 1978.

Hall & Dugary (1996) Hall, S. & Dugary, P. (eds.), *Questions of Cultural Identity*, Sage, 1996.

Hancock (1996) Hancock, J., 'Democracy', *Politics Review*, Vol 5.4, September 1996.

Heywood (1991) Heywood, A., 'Liberal democracy', *Talking Politics*, Vol.3.2, Winter 1990-91.

Heywood (1997) Heywood, A., *Politics*, Macmillan, 1997.

Hoffman (2003) Hoffman, J., 'Direct and representative democracy', *Politics Review*, Vol.13.1, September 2003.

Labour (1997) *New Labour: Because Britain Deserves Better*, Labour Party manifesto, Labour Party, 1997.

Lancaster (2001) Lancaster, S. (ed.), *Developments in Politics*, Vol.12, Causeway Press, 2001.

Lib Dem (1997) *Make The Difference*, Liberal Democrat manifesto, Liberal Democrats, 1997.

McInnes (1996) McInnes, P., 'Citizenship', *Politics Review*, Vol.5.3, February 1996.

Norton (1991) Norton, P., 'Parliamentary democracy', *Modern History Review*, Vol.2.3, 1991.

Oliver (1993) Oliver, D., 'Citizenship in the 1990s', *Politics Review*, Vol.3.1, September 1993.

Parry & Moyser (1993) Parry, G. & Moyser, G., 'Political participation in Britain', *Politics Review*, Vol.3.2, November 1993.

Parry et al. (1991) Parry, G., Moyser, G. & Day, N., *Political Participation in Britain*, Cambridge University Press, 1991.

Robertson (1986) Robertson, D., *The Penguin Dictionary Of Politics*, Penguin, 1986.

Talking Politics (2002) Politics Association, News Briefing, *Talking Politics*, Vol.14.2, January 2002.

Taylor (1965) Taylor, A.J.P., *English History 1914-45*, Penguin, 1965.

Watts (1997) Watts, D., 'The growing attractions of direct democracy', *Talking Politics*, Vol. 10.1, Autumn 1997.

Weir (1994) Weir, S., 'Crisis of confidence' in *Bite the Ballot*, a supplement in *New Statesman and Society*, 29 April 1994.

4 Electoral systems and electoral reform

4.1 What are the different voting systems?

A Royal Commission appointed in 1911 to examine voting systems claimed that there were over 300 voting systems either actually in existence or potentially available. In other words, every country in the world could have a different voting system and there would still be systems that remained unused. The plurality voting system used for elections to the House of Commons in the UK (often called the 'first-past-the-post' system) is, then, only one voting system out of a very wide range of options available.

Despite this great diversity, many of these 300 or more voting systems have much in common - they differ in terms of practical details. For convenience, it is possible to distinguish between four main groups of electoral systems:

- plurality systems
- majority systems
- proportional systems
- mixed systems.

This unit will examine each group in turn.

4.2 Plurality systems

A plurality system is one in which the candidate who wins the largest number of votes in a constituency is elected regardless of whether or not a majority of the electors in that constituency voted for that candidate. An example of how this system works is given in Box 4.1.

The plurality system is used for elections to the House of Commons in the UK as well as for local government elections. It is often described as the 'first-past-the-post' system.

Box 4.1 The plurality system in practice

Name	Party	Votes
Jones, Carol	Labour	15,000
Smith, Bill	Conservative	12,000
Watkins, Jo	Liberal Democrat	7,000
Morley, Jan	Green Party	1,000

In this instance, Jones won the seat even though she failed to win a majority of the votes. A majority - 20,000 constituents - voted against Jones and only 15,000 voted for her. Despite this, Jones still won the seat as she won more votes than any other single candidate.

4.3 Majority systems

Majority systems include mechanisms to ensure that the winning candidate achieves more than 50% of the vote in a constituency. The three best known of these systems are:

- the Alternative Vote system
- the Supplementary Vote system
- the Second Ballot system.

All three systems assume that the country is divided into single-member constituencies. None of the systems is proportional because none ensures that, in the country as a whole, the results of general elections reflect the proportion of votes cast for each party.

A. The Alternative Vote system

Under the Alternative Vote system, voters have the opportunity of ranking all the candidates whose names appear on the ballot paper in order of preference. As in the British plurality system, candidates stand for election in a constituency and one member is elected in each constituency.

If any candidate receives more than 50% of first preferences in the initial ballot, then that candidate is elected. If, however, no candidate receives more than 50% of first preferences, then the candidate with the lowest number of first preferences is eliminated and that candidate's second preferences are redistributed to the other candidates. If no candidate has reached 50% of the vote after this redistribution, then the candidate with the lowest number of votes after the redistribution is eliminated and that candidate's second preferences are redistributed. This process is continued until a candidate gains more than 50% of the vote.

Voters are not obliged to indicate preferences on their ballot paper. They may vote for a single candidate because they do not want to support another candidate should their candidate be eliminated. In safe seats, there may be little point in indicating preferences since it is likely that a candidate will gain more than 50% of the vote without the need for any redistribution of votes. In marginal seats, however, second preferences might be crucial. Indeed, the system can encourage electoral pacts between two parties at the expense of a third since the two parties making the pact can then recommend to their supporters which party to nominate as their second preference.

Supporters of this system emphasise that it retains constituency representation and it ensures that the winning candidate has more than 50% of the vote. Critics argue that the system leads to disproportional support for the centre parties because, while they are not voters' first choice, they are nearly always voters' second choice. The Alternative Vote system is used in elections to the Australian House of Representatives.

B. The Supplementary Vote system

Under this system, which is a variation of the Alternative Vote system, voters have just two preference votes. They can mark a cross in the first preference column for one candidate and in the second preference column for a second candidate. Candidates who win more than 50% of first preferences in the initial ballot are automatically elected. But, if no candidate gains more than 50% of the vote, only two candidates remain in the race - the two candidates with the highest number of first preferences. The second preferences from the losing candidates are then redistributed. Second preferences for eliminated candidates are discarded and those for the two remaining candidates added to their total. After this, whichever of the two remaining candidates has the greatest number of votes wins the seat. The winning candidate, therefore, does not necessarily need to win more than 50% of the votes cast. The London Mayoral elections in 2000 were held using the Supplementary Vote system - see Box 4.2.

The Supplementary Vote system has several advantages. First, like the Alternative Vote system, it is constituency based and is likely to produce strong governments. Second, it is easy to understand. And third, since only the top two candidates remain after first preferences are counted, it does not allow a third-placed candidate to come through the middle.

C. The Second Ballot system

As the name implies, the Second Ballot system includes the provision for voting to take place on two separate occasions.

In the first ballot, voters vote for their favourite candidate. If any candidate wins more than 50% of the vote in a constituency, then that candidate is elected. But if no candidate wins more than 50%, a second ballot is held, usually a week or two later. In some variations of this system, only the two candidates with the highest number of votes in the first ballot are allowed to stand in the second ballot. This ensures that the successful candidate in the second ballot achieves an absolute majority. In other variations, either all the earlier candidates are allowed to stand or there is a threshold in the first ballot (10% of the vote, for example) and only those who crossed the threshold (by winning more than 10% of the vote, for example) are allowed to stand in the second ballot. Some variations even allow newcomers to stand in the second ballot.

This system is in no sense proportional and does nothing to ensure a fair representation for small parties. It does, however, allow genuine choice since voters can vote for their favourite party in the first ballot, knowing that their vote will not be wasted since they will probably be able to cast a second vote in the second ballot. The system also encourages pacts between parties - parties which put up candidates in the first ballot agree not to stand in the second ballot to ensure that their allies have a better chance of being elected.

A version of the Second Ballot system is used in France. Only those candidates who win more than 12.5% of the vote in the first ballot are allowed to stand in the second ballot.

Box 4.2 The London Mayoral elections of 2000

Table (i): Mayoral election, first preference votes

Candidate	Party	Votes	% Vote
Ken Livingstone	Independent	667,877	38.96
Steven Norris	Conservative	464,434	27.09
Frank Dobson	Labour	223,884	13.06
Susan Kramer	Liberal Democrat	203,452	11.87
Ram Gidoomal	Christian People's Party	42,060	2.45
Darren Johnson	Green	38,121	2.22
Michael Newland	British National Party	33,569	1.96
Damian Hockney	UK Independent	16,324	0.95
Geoffrey Ben-Nathan	Pro-Motor	9,956	0.58
Ashwinkumar Tanna	Independent	9,015	0.53
Geoffrey Clements	Natural Law Party	5,470	0.32

Table (ii): Mayoral election, final result

Candidate	Party	Votes	% Vote
Ken Livingstone	Independent	776,427	57.92
Steven Norris	Conservative	564,137	42.08
Majority		212,290	15.84

The Greater London Authority, comprising the Assembly and the Mayor, has responsibility for:

- economic development and regeneration
- fire and emergency planning
- culture and tourism
- public health
- environment
- transport
- planning
- police.

Table (iii): The GLA, election result

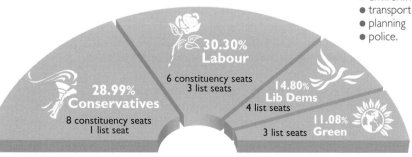

30.30% Labour — 6 constituency seats, 3 list seats

28.99% Conservatives — 8 constituency seats, 1 list seat

14.80% Lib Dems — 4 list seats

11.08% Green — 3 list seats

The GLA can only block the Mayor's budget by a two-thirds majority.

The 32 London boroughs continue to provide day-to-day services.

Although Ken Livingstone only won 38.96% of the votes on the first count, this was boosted to 57.92% of the votes after second preferences were counted, so he was elected Mayor. Stephen Norris, the Conservative candidate, came second in the first count with 27.09% of the votes but only had this boosted to 42.08% in the second count.

Source: D'Arcy & Maclean 2000.

4.4 Proportional systems

Majority voting systems do not ensure that, in the country as a whole, the results of general elections reflect the number of votes cast for each party. After all, a successful candidate in a majority system might have won just 51% of the vote. That means that, in a sense, 49% of votes in that constituency have been wasted. In the country as a whole, a party might have won many thousands of votes but not have won even one seat. This is what happened in the European elections in Britain in 1989. The Green Party won 15% of the vote nationally. But, it did not win a single seat. In a system which was truly proportional, the Green Party would have won 15% of the seats.

Proportional systems - systems of proportional representation (PR) - do not work on a single-member constituency basis. In fact, the bigger the number of representatives elected in a single constituency the more proportional the result because the election of a large number of representatives means that smaller parties have a greater chance of winning seats. Ideally (for those who support PR), a whole country should be a single multi-member constituency. The voters can then vote for their favourite party and seats can be allocated to the parties on the basis of the number of votes each has secured.

It can be argued that PR has two conflicting aims. First, it attempts to ensure that party representation mirrors as closely as possible the level of support for various parties over the country as a whole. Second, PR aims to provide voters with some degree of choice not only between the parties but also between individual candidates.

There are two main systems of PR - the List system and the Single Transferable Vote system. The List system comes closer to achieving the first aim while the Single Transferable Vote system comes closer to achieving the second aim.

A. The List system

The List system involves multi-member constituencies. In a Closed List system, each party submits a list of candidates for each constituency, but the ballot paper contains a list of political parties rather than a list of individual candidates. Seats are allocated to each party according to the proportion of votes won (a quota is calculated to determine how many votes are needed to win a seat). The number of seats allocated to a party is then filled by the requisite number of candidates from that party's list, starting with the candidate at the top of the list. The system is 'closed' because voters are not able to express a preference for a particular candidate. A version of the Closed List system was used for the 1999 European elections in Britain. In an Open List system, voters are able to vote for individual candidates and the party vote is determined by adding together all the votes cast for the different candidates in that party. Seats are then allocated to a party according to the proportion of votes won by that party. If a party wins one or more seats, candidates are elected according to the number of votes they won (with the candidate who won most votes for that party being elected first and so on). An example of how this system works is given in Box 4.3.

The List system is used in many countries including Sweden, Norway, Belgium, Spain and Finland. The exact details

Box 4.3 How the List system works

In its most basic form, a whole country is a single constituency (this is the case in Israel and the Netherlands). So, suppose that a country had 100 seats in its Parliament, it used a Closed List system with three parties 'A, B and C' putting up lists for an election and the result was as follows:

	Party A	Party B	Party C
% of the vote,	45	40	15

In this case, the top 45 candidates on Party A's list would be elected. Similarly, the top 40 candidates on Party B's list and the top 15 on Party C's list would be elected.

of how it works vary from country to country. In the UK, a version of the List system is used in elections to the European Parliament held every five years. Outhwaite (2001) explains:

'The idea of the regional party list is that the nation is divided into regions for which the party headquarters [based on ballots of the party membership] choose lists of candidates. This form of regional party list is 'closed' because voters vote for a party rather than a candidate. The parties then decide which candidates are elected because the higher up the list a candidate is the more chance of being elected.' (Outhwaite 2001, p.32)

Criticisms of the List system

Critics of the Closed List system argue that, since the lists of candidates are drawn up by party headquarters, voters have no real choice over individual candidates. In addition, the size of constituencies means that the links between a representative and the local community are broken. MPs do not individually have a constituency and so there is no sense of local MPs being accountable to their electors.

B. The Single Transferable Vote system

The Single Transferable Vote system (STV) was created in the 19th century and is based upon the idea that votes should be given to candidates rather than parties. The country is divided into multi-member constituencies and parties may put up as many candidates in each constituency as there are seats. Voters have the opportunity of ranking all the candidates whose names appear on the ballot paper in order of preference. Alternatively, they can vote for just one or two candidates if they choose to do so.

Seats are allocated according to a quota system (see Box 4.4 on page 62). If any candidate reaches the quota on first preferences, then that candidate is elected. If the candidate receives more first preferences than are required by the quota, then the surplus votes are redistributed to that candidate's second preferences on a proportional basis (in other words, all the candidate's second preferences are counted and the surplus votes redistributed proportionally amongst the other candidates). This redistribution may allow other candidates to reach the quota. If that happens and a candidate (or more than one candidate) gains more votes than are needed for the quota, the second preferences of that candidate (or candidates) are redistributed in the same way. If, however, seats still remain unfilled, the candidate with the least number of votes is eliminated and that candidate's second preferences are redistributed. This process is continued until all the seats are filled. As a result, third, fourth and even fifth placed preferences may be brought into the calculation.

> **Box 4.4** The formula used to calculate the quota under the STV system

The formula most often used for calculating the quota is as follows:

$$Q = \frac{\text{(number of votes cast)}}{\text{(number of seats in the constituency +1)}} + 1$$

It is difficult in a multi-member constituency to hold by-elections and different versions of STV use different methods. Some versions hold a ballot of the whole constituency using the Alternative Vote system since only one seat is to be filled. Some versions ballot only part of the constituency. And still others do not hold a ballot at all. They elect the candidate who, according to the original ballot, would have been next to win a seat.

The STV system is currently used in the Republic of Ireland, in Australia (for the Senate) and in Northern Ireland (for European elections). It is also the system chosen for the elections to the Northern Ireland Assembly. It has also been recommended for local government elections in Scotland and Wales.

4.5 *Hybrid systems*

A. The Additional Member system

After the Second World War, the Allies created the Additional Member system in West Germany. Of the four wartime Allies, Britain and the USA used a plurality system while France and the Soviet Union used proportional systems. As a result, the Additional Member system is a mixture (a hybrid) which combines a Regional List system with a single-member constituency plurality system.

The Additional Member system remains the system used in Germany and has been adopted in Hungary. Also, a version of the Additional Member system is used to elect members of the Welsh Assembly and Scottish Parliament (see Activity 4.1 below).

The country is divided into single-member constituencies and into regions. The same number of representatives is elected by each. Voters have two votes - one for a constituency candidate and one for a party. In each constituency, a candidate is elected by simple majority. The remaining seats are then allocated from regional party lists of candidates on a proportional basis. The share of seats won by a party in the constituency election is compared with the proportion of the vote won by the party overall. If there is a discrepancy, this is corrected by the allocation of seats from

the regional party lists. Parties which won fewer constituency seats than was merited by their proportion of the party vote gain extra regional seats and vice versa. By this means, the overall result is approximately proportional.

In some countries, to qualify for this redistribution of seats, parties need to cross a 'threshold'. In Germany, this means parties must win either at least three constituency seats or 5% of the party vote.

B. The Alternative Vote Plus system

The Alternative Vote Plus system is very similar to the Additional Member system. The only real difference is that the single-member seats are elected by the Alternative Vote system (see above) rather than by a simple majority. There is then a top-up of additional seats on a regional or area basis to provide a total number of MPs which is roughly proportional to the total votes cast for the different parties in the region or area as a whole. In both the Additional Member system and the Alternative Vote Plus system, a key decision is the proportion of seats which are top-up seats. If the proportion is as high as 50% (as in Germany, for example), then the overall result of the election is such that proportionality is achieved. If a lower proportion is chosen, then the degree of proportionality declines.

Advantages and disadvantages

Supporters of the Alternative Vote Plus system claim that it retains the best feature of plurality and majority systems, namely the fact that everyone has a local MP, and removes the worst feature, namely the fact that some parties are grossly over-represented in Parliament. Critics argue that two classes of representative are created - those who have to fight for re-election in their constituency and those whose re-election is ensured if they remain at the top of the party list. Also, since constituencies elect only half of the representatives, they are very large and representatives correspondingly more remote.

> ### Main points   Sections 4.1 - 4.5
>
> - **There are four main types of voting system - plurality, majority, proportional and mixed systems.**
>
> - **Unlike proportional and mixed systems, plurality and majority systems do not ensure that, overall, the results of elections reflect the number of votes cast for each party.**
>
> - **There are three main types of majority system - the Alternative Vote system, Supplementary Vote system and Second Ballot system.**
>
> - **There are two main types of proportional representation (PR) - the List system and the Single Transferable Vote system (STV).**
>
> - **The Additional Member system and Alternative Vote Plus system are hybrid systems - a mixture of a majority system and a proportional system.**

Activity 4.1 *Different voting systems*

Item A **The Alternative Vote system**

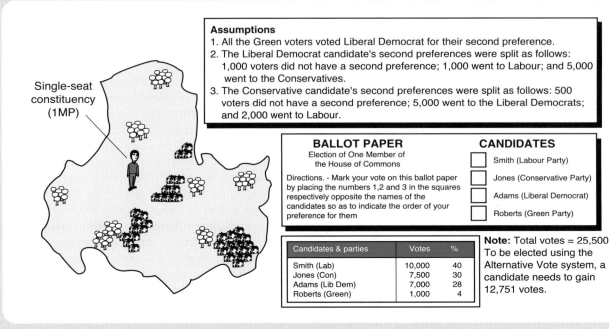

Single-seat constituency (1MP)

Assumptions
1. All the Green voters voted Liberal Democrat for their second preference.
2. The Liberal Democrat candidate's second preferences were split as follows: 1,000 voters did not have a second preference; 1,000 went to Labour; and 5,000 went to the Conservatives.
3. The Conservative candidate's second preferences were split as follows: 500 voters did not have a second preference; 5,000 went to the Liberal Democrats; and 2,000 went to Labour.

BALLOT PAPER
Election of One Member of the House of Commons

Directions. - Mark your vote on this ballot paper by placing the numbers 1,2 and 3 in the squares respectively opposite the names of the candidates so as to indicate the order of your preference for them

CANDIDATES
☐ Smith (Labour Party)
☐ Jones (Conservative Party)
☐ Adams (Liberal Democrat)
☐ Roberts (Green Party)

Candidates & parties	Votes	%
Smith (Lab)	10,000	40
Jones (Con)	7,500	30
Adams (Lib Dem)	7,000	28
Roberts (Green)	1,000	4

Note: Total votes = 25,500 To be elected using the Alternative Vote system, a candidate needs to gain 12,751 votes.

Item B **The Single Transferable Vote system**

Notes

Stage 1. This shows first preferences. Since Evans has 36 more than quota, she is elected and 36 of her votes need to be redistributed.

Stage 2. All of Evans' second preferences are counted (see bottom right). Since Evans received a surplus of 36 votes out of a total of 144, each second preference vote = 144/36 = 0.25 of a vote. So, Vine receives 0.25 x 80 = 20 votes and so on.

Stage 3. No other candidate has yet reached the quota and so Pearson is excluded. He received 30

| | Number of valid votes: 647 | Number of seats: 5 | Quota: $\frac{647}{5+1} = 108$ | | | | | |

Candidates		Stage 1	Stage 2	Stage 3	Stage 4	Stage 5	
Name	Party	First preferences	Transfer of Evan's surplus	Exclusion of Pearson	Exclusion of Lennon	Exclusion of Wilcocks	
Evans	B	144	- 36	108	108	108	108 Elected
Augustine	W	95		95	+ 1	96	96	+ 32	128 Elected
Harley	W	91	+ 1	92	+ 1	93	93	+ 15	108 Elected
Stewart	G	66	+ 2	68	+ 1	69	+ 46	115	115 Elected
Wilcocks	W	60		60		60	60	- 60	-
Lennon	G	58		58		58	- 58	-	
Cohen	B	55	+ 9	64	+ 5	69	+ 2	71	+ 1	72
Vine	B	48	+20	68	+23	91	+ 6	97	+ 7	104 Elected
Pearson	B	30	+ 4	34	- 34	-		-	
Non-transferable					+ 3	3	+ 4	7	+ 5	12
Total		647		647		647		647		647

first preferences and 16 second preferences. The first preferences are redistributed at face value (if anybody chose Evans as a second preference, their third preference is counted since Evans has already reached the quota). The second preferences are redistributed at 0.25 of a vote. If voters did not choose a second preference (or only chose Pearson and Evans), the vote is non-transferable (see relevant line).

Stage 4. No other candidate has yet reached the quota and so Lennon is excluded. The same procedure is followed as Stage 3.

Stage 5. Stewart has been elected and has seven votes more than the quota. Since this surplus is less than the difference between the two candidates with fewest votes, the surplus is not redistributed as it cannot affect the order. Rather, Wilcocks is excluded and the same procedure followed as Stage 3 (except that, if anybody chose Evans and Stewart as a second and third preference, their fourth preference is counted).Two further candidates are elected and two candidates now have surplus votes. Since the combined surplus (27 votes) is not enough to make any difference to the order of the bottom two candidates, Vine is elected even though she did not quite reach the quota.

Evans' 2nd prefs	
Vine	80
Cohen	36
Pearson	16
Stewart	8
Harley	4
Total	**144**

Source: ERS 1997.

Item C The Additional Member system

Table 1 Result of constituency election		
Party	Votes	Seats
A	184,000	5
B	116,000	3
C	55,000	1
D	50,000	0

Table 2 Final overall result			
Party	Constituency results	Additional seats	Total seats
A	5	1	6
B	3	1	4
C	1	0	1
D	0	1	1

ASSUMPTIONS

1. The region is made up of 9 single-seat constituencies and 3 additional seats. The electorate in the region, therefore, elects a total of 12 members.
2. Additional seats are allocated as follows:
a) The total number of votes for each party is divided by the number of single-seat constituencies already won, plus one. The first additional seat is allocated to the party which now has the highest number of votes (ie Party D) in Table 3).
b) The party's original total number of votes is re-divided by its new total number of seats plus one. The next additional seat is then allocated to the party with the highest total of votes (ie Party A) in Table 3).
c) The process is repeated until all additional seats are allocated (ie Party B) in Table 3 also receives an additional seat).

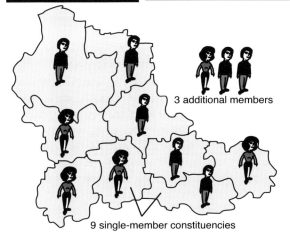

3 additional members

9 single-member constituencies

Table 3 Allocation of Additional Seats				
Party:	A	B	C	D
Directly elected seats	5	3	1	0
Number of votes	184,000	116,000	55,000	50,000
Divide by: 1				50,000
2			27,500	25,000
3				
4		29,000		
5				
6	30,667			
7	26,286			

The diagram above shows how the Additional Member system would work in an area divided into nine constituencies with three additional members. In Germany, a region with nine constituencies would elect nine additional members. It is assumed that four parties (A-D) won enough votes to cross the threshold and that each party in the region won the national average. Under the Jenkins Commission proposals, most areas would elect one additional member, but in some areas there would be two additional members.

Source: Watts 1994.

Questions

1. a) Using Item A explain which of the four candidates would have won under the Alternative Vote system.
   b) Explain how the election would have worked if the Supplementary Vote System had been used.
   c) What are the benefits and drawbacks of (i) the Alternative Vote system and (ii) the Supplementary Vote system?

2. Look at Item B.
   a) Explain why the five candidates with the highest number of first preferences are not the same five to be elected.

   b) What problems do you think the STV system is designed to solve?
   c) What are the benefits and drawbacks of the STV system?

3. a) Why do you think the Additional Member system (Item C) has been described as a 'hybrid' system?
   b) What are the benefits and drawbacks of the Additional Member system?

4.6 *Arguments in favour of the plurality system*

There are six main arguments in favour of the plurality (first-past-the-post) system currently used in general and local elections. These are outlined in Box 4.5 on page 65.

4.7 *Arguments against the current plurality system*

There are eight main arguments in support of the view that the current electoral system should be changed. These can be summarised as follows.

A. Wasted votes

Under the plurality (first-past-the-post) system, as many as 70% of the votes are wasted in each constituency because votes cast for the losing candidates are simply ignored in seat allocation and votes that add to the winning candidate's majority give no extra benefit to the party whose candidate has won. As a result, the number of seats won by each party nationally is in no way proportional to the number of votes cast for each party. For example, in the 2001 general election, the Liberal Democrats won 18% of the vote nationally but they won just 8% of the seats. Indeed, under the current system, it is possible for a party to win fewer votes than another party but more seats. This happened in February 1974 when Labour won 301 seats with 37.2% of the vote while the Conservatives won just 297 seats with 37.9% of the vote.

Box 4.5 Six arguments in favour of the status quo

A. Strong government
The plurality system produces strong single-party governments.

B. Links between MP and constituents
There are strong links between an MP and the local community. Small single-member constituencies mean that local people can air their grievances directly with their MP.

C. Easy to understand
The system is based on a readily understood principle - everyone has a vote and the candidate with the most votes is the winner. All a voter has to do is to mark an X on the ballot paper.

D. Provides a mandate
By providing an outright winner (most of the time), the current system ensures that a single party has a mandate to carry out its programme. There is (usually) no need for post-election trade-offs and coalitions. The party with the most seats normally has an overall majority. This maintains the principle that a party in government should be elected on the strength of its proposed programme and then judged on its actions.

E. Allows decisive political change
The system allows voters to hold governments to account and, if necessary, decisively vote them out of office (see Game 2001).

F. It works
The system works and has been proved to work over many years. All other electoral systems are flawed and so there is little point in replacing one flawed system with another.

B. A minority's choice

The winning party rarely wins an outright majority of votes cast. In fact, since 1900 there have only been two occasions when, nationally, a single party has won more than 50% of the vote in a general election - in 1900 when the Conservative and Liberal Unionists won 50.3% of the vote and in 1931 when the Conservatives won 55% of the vote. In 1935, candidates standing for the National government won a total of 53.3% of the vote but the National government was a coalition and the biggest party within the coalition (the Conservatives) won just 47.8% of the vote. The fact that the government is normally formed by a party which has only won a minority of the total vote means that more people voted against it rather than for it.

C. Regional imbalance

The current system results in regional imbalance. For example, in the 2001 general election, not a single Conservative MP was elected in Wales despite the fact that the party attracted 21% of the vote there. Britain's 'electoral geography' means that some parties gain an electoral advantage while others do not. Recently, this has been a particular problem for the Conservatives. Curtice and Steed (1997), for example, argue that the Conservative vote is

geographically relatively evenly spread from one part of the country to another. Compared to Labour and even the Liberal Democrats whose votes are more unevenly distributed, this places the Conservatives at a disadvantage when it comes to translating votes into seats. Curtice argues that the current plurality system now has an inbuilt bias to Labour. He claims that:

'If turnout remains low in Labour-held seats or if Labour's vote remains more efficiently distributed than that of the Conservatives...[there is] the potential to result in the party that comes first in votes failing to do so in terms of seats.' (Curtice 2001, p.249)

D. Over-importance of marginals

General elections are decided by what happens in a small number of marginal constituencies. Usually, around 500 seats are 'safe' seats. In these seats, the result is almost a foregone conclusion. The winning party gains many more votes than it needs to win. Votes for the other parties count for little. In marginal seats, however, every vote is important. The result in marginals determines the complexion of the government. In other words, the vote of a few hundred thousand voters in marginal seats can determine the fate of the country as a whole.

E. Link between MPs and constituents

The importance of the link between an MP and the local community is exaggerated. In reality, MPs cannot possibly represent all those who live in the area. Besides, it is possible to look at the concept of representation rather differently - see Box 4.6.

As Box 4.6 suggests, a system which divides the country into small single-seat constituencies is likely to produce a Parliament which is less representative than a system which divides the country into large multi-seat constituencies.

Box 4.6 Representation defined by Raymond Plant

Supporters of proportional representation believe that Parliament should not be made up of individuals who each claim to speak on behalf of all people in a particular area. Rather, Parliament should be seen as a 'microcosm of society'. In other words, Parliament should represent all sections of society so long as they are numerically significant. The result would be a Parliament which looked like a miniature version of the country as a whole. In such a Parliament, if 53% of people in the country as a whole were women, there would be (roughly) 53% women MPs. If there were 8% black and Asian people in the UK, then there would be (roughly) 8% black and Asian MPs. And so on.

Source: Plant 1992.

F. Electoral dictatorship

Under the current system, there is the danger of a single party becoming an 'electoral dictator' - good at winning overall majorities by capturing the vote of a minority of the electorate as a whole, but then ignoring the views of opponents. The Conservatives governed with large overall majorities between 1979 and 1992, having won only 43.9% of the vote or less (they won 43.9% in 1979). Labour has governed with huge Commons majorities since 1997, despite having won just 44.2% of the vote in 1997 and 42% in 2001.

G. Accountability
Coalition governments are not necessarily less accountable than single-party governments. Temple (1995) points out that:

> 'In systems where long-term coalitions are the norm, there is evidence to suggest that voters vote in anticipation of certain partnerships. In many systems, the parties announce their preferred coalition partner in advance so that voters can vote in anticipation of proposed governments.' (Temple 1995, p.54)

H. Complexity
Although systems such as the Single Transferable Vote are mathematically complex, all voters have to do on the ballot paper is to indicate their order of preference. It is the returning officer who is responsible for working out the result. There is, therefore, no reason why voters should not be able to cope with other voting systems.

For further information on this debate - see www.electoral-reform.org.uk.

4.8 Evaluating electoral systems

McNaughton (2000) has suggested that electoral systems have four principal objectives. These are:

Objective 1 - to meet the need for decisive government.
Objective 2 - to provide political representation that is fair, giving political parties seats in proportion to votes.
Objective 3 - to provide social representation so that representative chambers are typical of the electorate in terms of gender, ethnicity and other factors.
Objective 4 - to provide sufficient choice for voters so that they can choose between candidates and parties.

Using these criteria, McNaughton creates a scoring system with ten points allocated to each of these four aims. Ten points are awarded if the objective is totally acheived and nought if the aim is ignored altogether. Box 4.7 gives McNaughton's scoring for the different voting systems based on an analysis of the different voting systems in different countries.

4.9 Electoral reform since 1997

Until 1997, the Conservative grip on power ensured that electoral reform remained low on the political agenda. During their years in opposition, however, the Labour Party began to consider alternatives to the current system used to elect MPs and local councillors in Britain. In 1990, the Labour Party set up the Plant Commission to investigate electoral reform. It recommended a range of different voting systems and helped set an agenda for change.

Box 4.7 An evaluation of voting systems

SYSTEM	1	2	3	4	Total
FPTP	9	5	5	3	22
List	2	10	7	6	25
STV	5	8	8	9	30
AMS	6	7	7	7	27
SB	6	7	6	7	26
AV	7	7	6	7	27

Using these criteria, STV scores the highest total and the first-past-the-post system the lowest points. So, STV is the most successful in meeting the four criteria. The evaluation suggests one way of comparing the different systems and making a judgement on their relative worth. The problem is that all the objectives are weighted equally in this scheme but different individuals might well have different views on the weighting and the scoring.

By June 1998, six firm announcements had been made by the government concerning new electoral arrangements and, on each occasion, the decision was made to introduce a system which had at least an element of proportionality. The announcements were:

1. A regional Closed List system for the 1999 European elections.
2. A version of the Additional Member system for the new Scottish Parliament.
3. A version of the Additional Member system for the new Welsh Assembly.
4. A version of the Additional Member system for the new Greater London Assembly.
5. STV for the new Northern Ireland Assembly.
6. The Supplementary Vote system for the London Mayoral election.

In addition, a five-strong commission, headed by Lord Jenkins, the retiring Leader of the Liberal Democrats in the Lords, was set up in December 1997 to consider new voting arrangements for the House of Commons. The Jenkins Commission published its report in October 1998 and recommended the Alternative Vote Plus system for general elections. The recommendations of the Jenkins Commission are summarised in Box 4.8 on page 67.

4.10 Reaction to the Jenkins Report

A. The Labour Party
The Prime Minister, Tony Blair, 'warmly welcomed' the Jenkins Report and urged the Cabinet to help him manage the debate it was bound to provoke (*Guardian*, 31 October 1998). However, at the time the report was published, it was common knowledge that the Cabinet was divided on the issue of electoral reform - as was the Labour Party as a whole. Despite Blair's initially positive reaction to the report, the hostility it provoked both inside the Labour Party and

Box 4.8 The Jenkins Commission's recommendations

1. Constituency borders for elections to the House of Commons would be completely redrawn, reducing 659 constituencies to between 530 and 560.

2. Every voter would have two votes. One vote would go to a constituency candidate. The other would go to a top-up MP. Electors would number constituency candidates in order of preference. The ballot paper would look something like this:

Constituency vote
This vote will help decide who is the constituency MP. Rank the candidates in order of preference (1 for your preferred candidate, then 2, 3 etc). Rank as many candidates as you wish.

Second vote
This vote will help decide the total number of seats for each party in the county. You may vote either for one party or, if you wish, for one of the listed candidates. A vote for a listed candidate will also be counted as a vote for that candidate's party.

Collins *Conservative*	
Crosby *Liberal Democrat*	
Morgan *Labour*	
Newman *Green Party*	
Quine *Natural Law Party*	

Conservative — Anderson / Coleman / Smith
Labour — Baxter / Franklyn / Jones
Liberal Democrat — Newton / Hussain / Morison
Natural Law — Delaney / Shab

3. Any constituency candidate winning 50% or more of the vote would automatically be elected. If no candidate wins 50% of the vote, the least popular candidate would be eliminated and their second preferences redistributed. If necessary, other candidates would be eliminated until one candidate reached 50% of the vote.

4. The remaining 15-20% of MPs would be top-up MPs chosen on a city-wide or county basis depending on the overall vote of the party in the area as a whole and the number of seats a party had already won. The election of top-up MPs would ensure that parties were not under-represented to the extent that they are in the current plurality system.

Source: The *Guardian*, 30 October 1998.

Box 4.9 Reasons why the Labour government's enthusiasm for electoral reform has cooled

1. **Experience in Scotland and Wales**
Under the new (Additional Member) voting system, the Labour Party has been unable to win an overall majority. As a result, the party has been forced into coalition and power sharing. This has made it difficult for the party to implement its programme.

2. **Change might threaten Labour's majority**
The government is aware that any change will threaten Labour's majority at Westminster. Having won two terms with large overall majorities, the government is reluctant to introduce a reform which might make a third overall majority more difficult to achieve.

3. **The Labour Party is divided**
There are major differences of opinion within the Labour Party on the issue of electoral reform. The party is divided into three groups:
- those who favour change
- those who want to retain the plurality (first-past-the-post) system
- those who have been prepared to support the Alternative Vote system instead of the Jenkins Commission proposals (*Guardian*, 8 July 2000).

proportional representation (PR) for Westminster elections because it would undermine the fundamental principle of democratic accountability. 'PR is a system of unfair votes', he claimed, 'It takes political power away from the electorate and gives it to small political parties' (*Guardian*, 25 February 1998). Some commentators have argued that one of the Jenkins Commission's underlying objectives was to prevent the Conservatives from ever again being able to form a majority government. In their 2001 general election manifesto, the Conservatives claimed that they would 'restore balance to our vandalised democracy' (Conservative Party 2001, p. 45).

C. Attitude of the Liberal Democrats
The Liberal Democrats, on the other hand, are fervent supporters of proportional representation both because the party would gain considerably more seats if a proportional voting system was used for elections to the Commons and because they support it in principle. In its 2001 election manifesto, the following pledge was made:

'We need a voting system which accurately reflects the wishes of voters and fosters a more constructive approach to politics. Liberal Democrats will secure fair votes for all national and local elections. For Westminster, we support the system of AV+ as proposed by the Jenkins Commission as a first step. We will, therefore, put the Jenkins Commission's recommendations before the British people in a referendum at the earliest possible opportunity. Ultimately, we wish to see the Single Transferable Vote (STV) used for Westminster elections. We will introduce STV immediately for local government and European elections.' (Liberal Democrats 2001, p.14)

outside was sufficient to persuade the government not to take steps to implement the recommendations of the report. The 2001 Labour election manifesto argued that a referendum was the right way to agree to any future changes for Westminster. This statement was widely seen as a ploy to avoid making any progress on electoral reform for Westminster (*Guardian*, 24 March 2001).

There are three main reasons why the government's initial enthusiasm cooled. These are outlined in Box 4.9.

Curtice points out that any decision on the voting system for the House of Commons will be based on 'calculations of political advantage and not the lessons of dispassionate analysis of how Britain's alternative proportional electoral systems have worked in practice' (Curtice 2003, p.118).

B. Attitude of the Conservatives
In 1998, the Conservative Leader, William Hague, said that Conservatives would fight 'every inch of the way' to resist

Labour's refusal to advance the case for electoral reform for Westminster, however, provoked the Liberal Democrats' withdrawal from a joint Cabinet Committee on constitutional issues in September 2001. Since then, they have attacked Tony Blair on the ground that he has become 'actively hostile' to electoral reform for the Commons (*Guardian*, 21 January 2002).

D. Attitude of minor parties

Minor parties tend to be in favour of electoral reform as it would give them the opportunity to gain electoral representation. For example, the Scottish Socialist Party and the Green Party in Scotland have been able to win seats in the Scottish Parliament because of the Additional Member system. Dunleavy (2000a) suggests that one possible effect of electoral reform is to weaken traditional voting allegiances. Minor parties would, therefore, hope to make more progress than they have made in elections held under the first-past-the-post system.

E. Attitude of the public

Opinion polls reveal inconsistencies in the public's response to suggestions of electoral reform. When asked abstract questions about electoral reform, respondents in polls want both strong effective government and fair representation for the smaller parties. In Scotland and Wales, voters have actually experienced new systems of voting. In both cases, Margetts claims:

> 'Experience of proportional representation in action …appears to have pleased voters.' (Margetts 2003, p.78)

Main points Sections 4.6 - 4.10

- **The main arguments in support of the plurality system are: (1) it produces strong, single-party governments; (2) it ensures that there are strong links between an MP and the local community; (3) the system is easy to understand; (4) by producing an outright winner, it provides the government with a mandate; (5) it allows for decisive change; and (6) the system works.**

- **Opponents of the plurality system currently used to elect MPs and councillors use the following arguments against it: (1) many votes are wasted; (2) the winner is almost always the choice of a minority; (3) there are regional imbalances; (4) marginal constituencies become over-important; (5) it ensures that Parliament is not** representative of society as a whole; (6) there is a danger that a single party will become entrenched in power; (7) single-party governments are no more accountable than coalition governments; (8) other systems are not necessarily more difficult to use.

- **Since its election in May 1997, the Labour government has introduced four new electoral systems - a List system for the European elections; a version of the Additional Member system for the new Scottish and Welsh assemblies and the Greater London Assembly; STV for the new Northern Ireland Assembly; the Supplementary Vote for the London Mayoral election.**

Activity 4.2 *Electoral reform*

Item A **The 2001 general election**

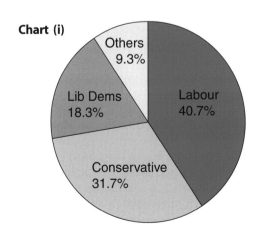

Chart (i)

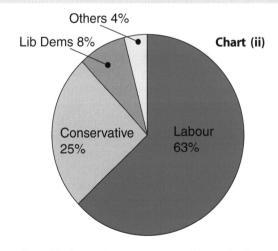

Chart (ii)

Chart (i) shows the percentage of the popular vote won in the 2001 general election.

Chart (ii) shows the percentage of seats in the Commons won in the 2001 general election.

Source; Butler & Kavanagh 2002.

Item B The relationship between seats and votes

This table shows the bias in the current electoral system. Using the 2001 election result, it shows what would happen to the number of seats won by each party if there were overall national percentage swings to the Conservatives ranging from 1% to 12%.

| Swing to Con | % Votes | | Seats | | | |
	Con	Lab	Con	Lab	LibDem	Others
0%	32.7	42.0	166	413	52	28
1%	33.7	41.0	177	407	48	27
2%	34.7	40.0	184	401	47	27
3%	35.7	39.0	199	388	44	28
4%	36.7	38.0	208	380	43	28
4.7%	37.4	37.4	224	364	43	28
5%	37.7	37.0	232	358	41	28
6%	38.7	36.0	249	342	40	28
6.5%	39.2	35.5	263	329	39	28
7%	39.7	35.0	274	318	39	28
8%	40.7	34.0	287	307	38	27
8.8%	41.5	33.2	297	297	38	27
9%	41.7	33.0	300	294	38	27
9.3%	42.0	32.7	305	290	37	27
10%	42.7	32.0	315	280	37	27
10.4%	43.1	31.6	330	269	35	25
11%	43.7	31.0	337	263	34	25
12%	44.7	30.0	351	249	33	26

Others include 18 seats in Northern Ireland.

Source; Butler & Kavanagh 2002.

Item C The case for PR

Britain's political system has changed for the better since 1997. We welcome the introduction of fairer votes for the Scottish Parliament, the National Assembly for Wales and the Northern Ireland Assembly. But the gap between the government and the governed is still too great. Public bodies are still not sufficiently accountable. Voters do not have a strong enough voice or choice. No wonder that more and more people feel alienated from politics.

Source: Liberal Democrats 2001.

Item D The case against PR

It is frequently assumed that, if proportional representation (PR) is achieved, this will solve most other political problems. Indeed, the usual argument in favour of a House of Commons elected according to PR principles is that the composition of the country's main legislative chamber should reflect the composition of views within the electorate, as expressed in party choice. What that case almost always fails to appreciate, however, is that proportional representation within the House will not necessarily be reflected in proportional bargaining power there. A party may get 10% of the votes cast and so be allocated 10% of the seats in the House, but does it get 10% of the political power ('power' being defined here as the ability to influence a government's legislative programme)? PR does not produce proportional power. For example, in assemblies where permanent coalitions are required, parties often bargain over the formation of a government after the election. In that bargaining process, some parties are more powerful than others because they are pivotal in more potential coalitions. Further, the distribution of bargaining power depends not just on each party's allocation of seats but also on the number of other parties and the distribution of seats among them. A small change, even in a three-party or a four-party assembly, can produce a major shift in bargaining power. A few by-election results, for example, could lead to some parties becoming much less powerful, while others find that their power increases (perhaps even without their own number of seats changing).

Source: Johnston 1995.

Questions

1. a) Using the items in this activity, give the arguments for and against reform of the voting system used in elections to the House of Commons.

   b) Why do you think the Leader of the Conservative Party is opposed to proposals to use PR in elections to the Commons when the Conservative Party appears to be so disadvantaged by the electoral system which is demonstrated by the data in Item B?

2. a) Write an analysis of the evidence which appears in Items A and B.

   b) Using Item B, what percentage swing will the Conservatives need to reach an overall majority in the House of Commons?

c) Using Item B, what would be the total number of seats won by Labour and Conservatives if both parties won 37.4% of the vote?

3. a) Using Item C and also your own ideas, why do you think that the Liberal Democrats favour electoral reform for the House of Commons?

   b) Judging from Item D, what problems might PR cause if it was used for elections to the Commons?

4. Who do you think should make decisions on the kind of voting system that is used in the different elections in the UK? Give reasons for your answer.

References

Butler & Kavanagh (1997) Butler, D. & Kavanagh, D., *The British General Election of 1997*, Macmillan, 1997.

Butler & Kavanagh (2002) Butler, D. & Kavanagh, D., *The British General Election of 2001*, Macmillan, 2002.

Conservative Party (2001) *Time for Common Sense*, election manifesto, Conservative Party, 2001.

Curtice (2001) Curtice, J., 'The Electoral System' in *Norris (2001)*.

Curtice (2003) Curtice, J., Changing Voting Systems' in *Dunleavy et al. (2003)*.

Curtice & Steed (1997) Curtice, J. & Steed, M., 'The results analysed' in *Butler & Kavanagh (1997)*, Appendix 2.

D'Arcy & Maclean (2000) D'Arcy, M. & Maclean, R., *The Race to Become London's Mayor*, Politicos, 2000.

Dunleavy (2000a) Dunleavy, P., 'Elections and Party Politics' in *Dunleavy et al. (2000)*.

Dunleavy et al. (2000) Dunleavy, P., Gamble., A, R., Peele, G., *Developments in British Politics*, Vol.6., Macmillan, 2000.

Dunleavy et al. (2003) Dunleavy, P., Gamble., A, Heffernan, R., Peele, G., *Developments in British Politics*, Vol.7., Palgrave, 2003.

ERS (1997) Electoral Reform Society, *What is STV?*, leaflet produced in 1997.

Fisher et al. (2003) Fisher, J., Denver, D. & Benyon, J., *Central Debates in British Politics*, Pearson Education, 2003.

Game (2001) Game, C., 'Britain's Changing and Unchanging electoral system' in *Lancaster (2001)*.

Johnston (1995) Johnston, R., 'Proportional representation and proportional power', *Politics Review*, April 1995.

Labour Party (2001) *Ambitions for Britain*, election manifesto, Labour Party 2001.

Lancaster (1995) Lancaster, S. (ed.), *Developments in Politics*, Vol.6, Causeway Press, 1995.

Lancaster (2001) Lancaster, S. (ed.), *Developments in Politics*, Vol. 12, Causeway Press, 2001.

Liberal Democrats (2001) *Freedom, Justice, Honesty*, election manifesto, Liberal Democrats, 2001.

Margetts (2003) Margetts, 'Electoral Reform' in *Fisher et al. (2003)*.

McNaughton (2000) McNaughton, N., 'Evaluating electoral systems', *Politics Review*, Vol. 10.1, September, 2000.

Norris (2001) Norris, P., *2001 Britain Votes*, OUP, 2001.

Outhwaite (2001) Outhwaite, D., 'UK electoral systems', *Politics Review*, Vol 11.2, November, 2001.

Plant (1992) Plant R., 'Electoral reform and electoral systems' in *Wale (1992)*.

Temple (1995) Temple, M., 'Electoral reform: the consequences of change' in *Lancaster (1995)*.

Wale (1992) Wale, W. (ed), *Developments in Politics*, Vol.3., Causeway Press, 1992.

Watts (1994) Watts, D., *Electoral Reform: Acheiving a Sense of Proportion*, PAVIC Publications, Sheffield Hallam University, 1994.

5.1 'First order' and 'second order' elections

'First order' elections are national parliamentary or presidential elections. In contrast, by-elections, local elections, the European election, the Scottish Parliament election, Welsh Assembly and Northern Ireland Assembly elections are termed 'second order' elections. The elections are 'second order' in two senses. First, they are regarded as less important than 'first order' elections. Second, the elections are used by national parties as barometers of their standing rather than of worth in their own right (Hix 2000). According to Rallings and Thrasher (2000), second order elections tend to have lower turnouts and the electorate may vote with 'their heart rather than their head' or make their vote a protest vote.

The mechanics for elections for the second order elections are similar to the mechanics for general elections. The main difference is that different voting systems are used:

- a version of the Additional Member system is used for the elections to the Welsh Assembly and Scottish Parliament
- a Closed List system is used for elections to the European Parliament (apart from in Northern Ireland where the Single Transferable Vote system is used)
- elections for the Northern Ireland Assembly use the Single Transferable Vote system.

The way in which these various systems work is explained in Unit 4.

A further difference between first order and second order elections is that second order elections are 'fixed term'. Elections must take place every four years in the case of Scotland and Wales and every five years in the case of the European elections.

5.2 The Boundary Commission

Since the movement of people within Britain results in some areas gaining and some areas losing population, the boundaries of constituencies are periodically altered so that the size of population within each constituency is roughly equal. The exact location of each constituency's borders is determined by the Boundary Commission - an independent body chaired by the Speaker of the House of Commons. The Boundary Commission makes its decisions after receiving representations from political parties. It recommends new general constituency boundaries every eight to 12 years. In between general reviews, it can also recommend minor changes for individual constituencies. These changes can have important political consequences and MPs monitor the work of the Boundary Commission closely. By the time of the 1997 general election, for example, decisions made by the Boundary Commission had resulted in:

- the creation of eight additional parliamentary seats (increasing the total from 651 to 659)
- significant changes in 418 existing seats
- minor changes in a further 76 seats.

As a result, only 157 seats remained completely unchanged. Before the new boundaries were settled, many commentators argued that the changes would prove beneficial to the Conservatives, giving them the advantage in around 20 seats. But, this did not happen:

> 'In the end, partly because Labour were more skilful in coordinating their submissions to the Boundary Commission, the final advantage to the Conservatives was negligible.' (Butler & Kavanagh 1997, p.22)

There were no major changes between 1997 and 2001. As a result, since the population figures used to set the boundaries were ten years out of date in the 2001 general election (since the last census had been held in 1991), Labour-held constituencies, on average, contained 6,400 fewer voters than Conservative-held constituencies (Curtice 2001).

Over-representation in Scotland and Wales

In addition to inequality of population between individual seats, there has historically been an over-representation of MPs from Scotland and Wales in the House of Commons. This is because the Redistribution of Seats Act (1944) guaranteed both countries a minimum number of seats. In 2003, the two countries combined had 19 more seats than their population strictly allowed. In recent general elections, this has been to Labour's advantage since Labour is stronger than the Conservatives in these areas. As part of the devolution process, though, the over-representation in Scotland is due to come to an end when the next general election is held.

5.3 General elections

The plurality system of voting for local and general elections in Britain (and for general elections in Northern Ireland) is often described as a 'first-past-the-post' system. The way in which this system works and arguments for and against it are discussed in Unit 4.

Electoral rules

All British citizens are entitled to vote in general elections provided that they are aged 18 or over and are not disqualified. Citizens of other Commonwealth countries and citizens of the Republic of Ireland who are resident in Britain are also eligible to vote so long as they are aged 18 or over and not disqualified. Further, British citizens living abroad are eligible to vote for up to 20 years after they have left Britain and those who were too young to vote when they left Britain are able to register when they reach the age of 18. Box 5.1 on page 72 lists the people who are disqualified from voting in parliamentary elections.

Those eligible to vote are only able to vote if they are registered in a constituency (British citizens living abroad register in the constituency in which they were living before they went abroad). There is a process of rolling registration so voters can register at any point in the year. Voting in elections in Britain is voluntary (in some countries it is compulsory and voters who fail to vote can be fined).

Box 5.1 Those disqualified from voting in parliamentary elections

The following people are disqualified from voting in parliamentary elections:

- members of the House of Lords
- patients detained under mental health legislation
- sentenced prisoners
- people convicted within the last five years of corrupt or illegal electoral practices.

Box 5.2 Those disqualified from standing for election

The following people are disqualified from standing for election:

- un-discharged bankrupts
- people sentenced to more than one year in prison
- clergy of the Church of England, Church of Scotland, Church of Ireland and Roman Catholic Church
- members of the House of Lords
- people holding offices listed in the House of Commons Disqualification Act 1975 - which includes judges, civil servants, some local government officers, members of the regular armed forces or the police service, some members of public corporations and government commissions and members of Parliaments or assemblies of countries outside the Commonwealth.

Source: HMSO 1991.

Electoral procedures

A government's term of office is subject to a five year maximum. However, the government can decide to call a general election at any time within that five-year period. That means that, unless the government loses a vote of confidence in the House of Commons or the full term has run, the Prime Minister can call a general election at the time when there is maximum party advantage to be gained.

Formally speaking, a general election is called when Parliament is dissolved by the monarch on the advice of the Prime Minister. Polling takes place within 17 days of the dissolution of Parliament, not including week-ends, bank holidays and days of public thanksgiving or mourning. If the monarch were to die after Parliament was dissolved, then polling would be delayed for two weeks. While the general election is in progress, senior civil servants take over the day-to-day running of the country - though the Cabinet can be reassembled if there is a crisis.

By convention, polling day is a Thursday. There is, however, nothing to prevent the Prime Minister choosing another day.

Candidates

Candidates for parliamentary elections must be aged 21 or over. They must be British citizens, citizens of another Commonwealth country or citizens of the Republic of Ireland. Those disqualified from standing for election are outlined in Box 5.2.

Candidates must return nomination papers to their local Returning Officer during the period between the publication of the notice of election and six days after the proclamation summoning the new Parliament. Nomination papers must be signed by ten electors from the constituency and must state the candidate's full name, address and description (six words maximum). Candidates must also put down a deposit of £500. This is returned to candidates who receive 5% or more of the votes cast.

Spending limits

There are strict limits on how much each candidate can spend in their constituency. Box 5.3 outlines the limits at the time of the 2001 general election.

5.4 By-elections

By-elections are called when a sitting MP dies or retires from the Commons before Parliament is dissolved. They may also take place if the High Court rules that election law has been broken, though this is a very unusual event.

Once a by-election has been called, the same procedural rules apply as in a general election with the exception that candidates are allowed a higher rate of expenses. National interest in by-elections tends to be high as they are regarded as barometers of public opinion between general elections. Because of this, there is a flat rate expenditure limit of £100,000 per candidate in by-elections, regulated by the Electoral Commission.

Box 5.3 Spending limits in 2001

In the 2001 general election, candidates could spend £5,483 plus 4.6p per elector in borough constituencies (the more densely populated urban areas) and 6.2p per elector in the county constituencies (less densely populated rural areas). This meant an average figure of approximately £9,000 maximum per constituency for each candidate. During the campaign, candidates could post one communication to each household free of charge. All other expenses were subject to the limit. After the election, every candidate's agent had to declare all election expenses within 35 days. The amount spent by national party organisations was also limited. The Political Parties, Elections and Referendums Act 2000 imposes limits on spending by parties in the 12 months prior to a general election. The maximum amount that a party can spend is determined by the number of constituencies it fights. Normally a party is allowed £30,000 expenditure for every seat it fights, so, if a party fights all 659 seats, the limit on its national expenditure for the 365 days leading up to polling day is £19.77 million. As the 2001 election was early in the year, the total national limit on spending for a party contesting all 659 seats was actually £15.4 million.

Main points   Sections 5.1 - 5.4

- The Boundary Commission ensures that roughly the same number of people is contained within the borders of every constituency.
- With a few exceptions, all British citizens over the age of 18 can vote in elections and stand as candidates.

- There are clear rules governing when elections can be held, the timetable to be followed, who can stand and how much they can spend. These rules vary according to the type of election that is being held.

Activity 5.1 General elections in the UK

Item A Electoral procedure

1

POLLING STATION

3

2

(1) A polling station
Most polling stations are in schools but other buildings are used. A presiding officer is responsible for ensuring that secrecy is maintained and there is no electoral malpractice.

(2) The count
Sealed ballot boxes are taken to the count together with unused and spoilt ballot papers. The count is presided over by the returning officer.

(3) Voting in the 1997 general election
Voters casting their votes on 1 May 1997.

Item B By-elections May 1997- September 2003

The 17 by-elections between the general elections in 1997 and 2001 were unusual in that the main opposition party - the Conservatives - failed to gain a single seat while Labour managed to hold all the seats it was defending. This was unusual because the normal assumption is that governments lose by-elections as their popularity declines. A second significant characteristic of the 17 by-elections between the general elections in 1997 and 2001 was their low turnout (the level fell back to that of the by-elections in the 1970s). Typical were the by-elections in November 2000 in West Bromwich East, Glasgow Anniesland and Preston, where Labour won each seat but on a turnout of 28%, 38% and 29% respectively. In the first by-election held after the 2001 general election, the same pattern continued. Labour held Ipswich with a turnout of 40% (down by nearly 17% from that in the general election five months earlier), though its majority was reduced from 8,081 to 4,087. However, the pattern in by-elections changed in September 2003 when Labour lost the Brent East by-election. The Liberal Democrats won the seat on a 29% swing against Labour and pushed the Conservatives into third place. The government admitted it had received a 'bloody nose' as voters turned against Labour in a protest vote. Many other voters stayed away from the polls as the turnout was only 36% even though there was a choice of 16 candidates.

Source: The *Guardian*, 20 September 2003.

Item C **The by-elections in Ipswich and Brent East**

IPSWICH **by-election, 22 November 2001**						Labour Hold
No. voting & % turnout		27,405	40.1%	**Nov. 2001**	38,873	57.0%	**June 2001**

Mole, C	**Lab**	**11,881**	**43.35**	-7.98	19,952	51.33	Lab
West, C	Con	7,794	28.44	-2.10	11,871	30.54	Con
Munt, T	LD	6,146	22.43	+7.24	5,904	15.19	LD
Cooper, D	CPA	581	2.12	-	-	-	-
Wright, J	UK Ind	276	1.01	-0.60	624	1.61	UK Ind
Slade, T	Green	255	0.93	-	-	-	-
Rameriz. J	LCA	236	0.86	-	-	-	-
Leech, P	Soc All	152	0.55	-0.23	305	0.78	Soc All
Winskill, N	Eng Ind	84	0.31	-	-	-	-

Labour majority	**4,087**	**(14.91%)**	**Labour majority**	**8,081**	**(20.79%)**

This table shows the result in Ipswich in the 2001 general election and in the by-election which was held on 22 November 2001.

BRENT							LibDem Gain
By-election, 18 September 2003				**General election, June 2001**			
Electorate & % turnout		57,558	36.23%	Electorate & % turnout		53,548	65.87%
Candidate	Party	Votes	%	Candidate	Party	Votes	%
Teather, S	**LibDem**	**8,158**	**39.1**	**Daisley, P**	**Lab**	**18,325**	**63.2**
Evans, R	Lab	7,040	33.8	Gauke, D	Con	5,278	18.2
Fernandes, U	Con	3,368	16.2	Bhatti, N	LibDem	3,065	10.6
Others (13)	-	2,286	11.0	Others (4)	-	2,324	8.0
LibDem majority		**1,118**	**(5.36%)**	**Labour majority**		**13,047**	**(45%)**

This table shows the result in Brent in the general election of 2001 and in the by-election which was held on 18 September 2003.

Source: *Guardian*, 23 November 2001 and 19 September 2003.

Questions

1. You have been given Item A as illustrations to accompany an article entitled, 'Electoral procedure at British general elections'. Write the article.

2. Using Items B and C, explain the difference between first order and second order elections.

3. Look at Item C. List ways in which electoral procedures and votes for the general election and by-election would (a) have differed and (b) stayed the same.

5.5 *Local elections*

Councillors are elected to serve four year terms. They are elected using the same plurality system that is used in parliamentary elections. But different councils (see Unit 18) elect councillors at different times. Some elect all the councillors in a clean sweep every few years. Others elect in a partial renewal system so that one council seat in a ward is elected each year. One advantage of the partial renewal system is that it means there is an election every year. This encourages participation and keeps local parties active. Local elections are usually held on the first Thursday in May. Turnout in local elections is generally much lower than in general elections. Candidates can spend up to £242 plus 4.7p per voter.

Elected mayors

In addition to electing councillors, a small number of councils have elected mayors (see Unit 18 for further details). In mayoral contests outside London, a 'first-past-the-post' system is used. In London, the Supplementary Voting system is used. This means that voters have two votes. They can choose their first preference and their second preference candidate. A candidate who wins more than 50% of first preferences is elected. If no candidate wins more than 50% of first preferences, the two candidates with the highest number of votes remain in the contest. All the others are eliminated and the second preference votes of the losers redistributed. The candidate with the highest number of votes after the redistribution is elected.

Local elections in 2003

Contests for 308 councils took place in May 2003. One feature of the local election campaign was the difficulty the parties had in finding candidates to fight the seats. The Conservative Party resorted to advertising for candidates in the local press (Guardian, 7 March 2003). The advertising paid dividends as the party was able to contest some 84% of the nearly 11,000 seats available. This was well ahead of Labour and Liberal Democrats.

The results of the local elections held in 2003 are given in Box 5.4.

Box 5.4 Local election results 2003

	Councils		Councillors	
	+/-	Total	+/-	Total
Labour	-28	66	-833	3,001
Conservative	+31	110	+566	4,423
LibDem	+5	28	+193	2,624
SNP	-1	1	-21	182
Independent	-2	10	-42	1,142
Other	0	2	-9	254
NOC	-5	123	n/a	n/a

This table shows the local election results in England and Scotland in May 2003. The figures show the number of councils or councillors gained or lost since local elections held the previous year.

5.6 European elections

Since 1979, voters have had the opportunity to vote in the elections for the European Parliament once every five years. The early elections used the first-past-the-post electoral system - apart from in Northern Ireland where the Single Transferable Vote (STV) system (see Unit 4) was used. In order to bring mainland Britain into line with other members of the EU, in March 1998 the House of Commons agreed to a system of proportional representation in mainland Britain for the 1999 Euro-elections. The system chosen by the government was a 'Closed List' system - voters have a choice of parties, not candidates, on their ballot papers. Also, instead of being divided into 87 separate constituencies as it was for the early Euro-elections, mainland Britain is divided into 12 regions, varying in size from North East England with 2 million voters and four MEPs to South East England (excluding London) with 5 million voters and 11 MEPs. In every case, seats are divided between the parties according to the proportion of the vote achieved in that region (a quota is calculated to determine how many votes are needed to win a seat). The seats are then allocated to candidates on the regional lists devised by the political parties. So, suppose a party won four seats in a region, the top four candidates on its regional list would be elected. In Northern Ireland, the STV system already in existence was retained.

Electoral rules

Those qualified to vote in parliamentary elections are qualified to vote in European elections. In addition, members of the House of Lords are allowed to vote in European elections. Similarly, those qualified to stand as candidates in parliamentary elections are qualified to stand in European elections. In addition, peers and members of the clergy of the Church of England, the Church of Scotland, the Church of Ireland and the Roman Catholic Church may stand. Candidates must be nominated by 30 electors and must put down a deposit of £5,000. This is returned if the candidate receives 5% of the vote in England, Scotland and Wales or one quarter of the electoral quota at any stage in the electoral process carried out in Northern Ireland. Candidates can stand in countries other than their home state but can only stand in one seat.

The results of the 1999 European election are shown in Box 5.5 on page 76.

5.7 Elections to the Scottish Parliament and Welsh Assembly

The Scottish Parliament

In Scotland, there is a unicameral (single chamber) body of 129 members. Voters have two votes - one for their local constituency (73 members are elected by the plurality system used in general elections) and one for the 56 additional members who are elected using a Closed List system. In order to elect these additional members, the electorate is divided into eight regions (with the same borders as the eight Euro-constituencies in Scotland which were in operation in 1994) and seven candidates are elected from each of the eight regions on a proportional basis.

The Welsh Assembly

In Wales, there are 40 single-member constituencies matching the 40 Westminster constituencies. The 20 additional members are elected from closed party lists - four additional members from each of five regions. As in Scotland, the borders of each region coincide with the borders of old Euro-constituencies.

The Northern Ireland Assembly

Elections to the Northern Ireland Assembly use the Single Transferable Vote (STV) system (see Unit 4). Northern Ireland is divided into 18 constituencies and 108 members are elected.

5.8 New electoral rules - the 2000 Representation of the People Act

Following the low turnout in a series of elections, the government introduced new forms of voting in an attempt to persuade more people to vote. In January 2001, Robin Cook, the then Leader of the House of Commons, described the traditional way of voting through a ballot box as 'astonishingly quaint'. The 2000 Representation of the People Act, allowed local councils to run a number of pilot schemes to make voting easier using electronic voting and counting, early voting, mobile polling stations, all-postal voting and more

Box 5.5 The 1999 European Election

	Conservative		Labour		LibDem		UKIP	Green
	%	Change	%	Change	%	Change	%	%
East Midlands	39.5	+4.6	28.6	-19.2	12.8	-0.8	7.6	5.4
Eastern	42.7	+3.2	25.2	-13.4	11.9	-5.2	8.9	6.2
London	32.7	+1.5	35.0	-14.5	11.7	-2.9	5.4	7.7
North East	27.4	+7.6	42.1	-21.9	13.5	+0.9	8.8	4.7
North West	35.4	+7.8	34.5	-19.1	11.7	-2.8	6.6	5.6
South East	44.4	+2.5	19.6	-9.5	15.3	-8.0	9.7	7.4
South West	41.7	+5.2	18.1	-8.3	16.5	-14.8	10.6	8.3
West Midlands	37.9	+4.2	28.0	-19.0	11.3	-2.5	5.9	5.8
Yorks & Humberside	36.6	+8.6	31.3	-20.6	14.4	-1.6	7.1	5.7
Scotland	19.8	+2.3	28.7	-16.8	9.8	-3.2	1.3	5.8
Wales	22.8	+3.2	31.9	-22.8	8.2	-4.1	3.2	2.6
Great Britain	35.8	+4.4	28.0	-16.4	12.7	-4.5	7.0	6.3
No. of seats won	36 (18)		29 (62)		10 (2)		3 (0)	2 (0)

Change = Percentage gain or loss in vote share since May 1997.

This table shows the results of the European election held in 1999. The figure in brackets in the column showing the number of seats won is the number of seats each party won in the previous election held in 1994 under a 'first-past-the-post' system.

Source: *Independent*, 15 June 1999.

postal voting. All the experiments assumed that:

'Voters were failing to exercise their democratic rights at elections because voting was a difficult or time-consuming process: not because of lack of trust in the political process or voter apathy.' (Lynch 2002, p.25)

Pilot schemes

The results of pilot schemes have varied. However, in the councils where polling stations were closed down and replaced with all-postal voting, turnout increased, in some cases substantially. Extended postal voting also attracted considerable interest. For example, in Milton Keynes the numbers of voters asking for postal votes rose from the usual 1,000 to 3,600. The 2000 Representation of the People Act made postal voting available on demand, with the result that any voter can now request a postal vote for a particular election or for an indefinite period. As a result, postal voting increased considerably in some parliamentary constituencies in the 2001 general election. For example, in Stevenage, some 25,000 of the 70,000 voters requested postal votes. More experiments were introduced in the 2002 and 2003 local elections. In the 2003 local elections, overall national turnout was 33% but all-postal ballots were held in 32 councils in the 2003 local elections:

'[This] boosted turnout to an average of 50%. Extended hours, mobile polling booths and telephone voting also encouraged people to vote. But e-voting, by digital television and internet, failed to catch on and in some pilots voting turnout was down.' (*Times*, 3 May 2003)

The Electoral Commission, which is analysing the results of

the experiments, has claimed that postal voting has substantially increased turnout. Yvette Cooper, the minister in charge of electoral law, argued that Labour should radically shake up the way in which Britain goes to the polls. Every voter, she says, should be encouraged to opt for postal voting (*Guardian*, 4 June 2003). The government has asked the Electoral Commission to introduce compulsory postal or e-voting in four of the ten regions in the 2004 European Parliament elections (*Guardian*, 29 March 2004). There are, however, some concerns that these changes could lead to more electoral fraud as it is relatively easy to forge another voter's signature. At least with voting in polling stations, the voter has to be there in person. Besides, this might not solve the problem of low voter turnout. Jackson has argued:

'There is no evidence that the physical process of voting in a polling booth puts a significant number of people off. The key issue that needs to be addressed is the nature of the relationship between the public, elected representatives and government' (Jackson 2003, p.182)

Compulsory voting

Compulsory voting for general and local elections has also been suggested as a solution to the problem of low voter turnout. Compulsory voting already exists, for at least some elections, in Australia, Luxembourg, Belgium, Singapore and Brazil. Where compulsory voting exists, penalties for non-voting include fines, withdrawal of certain government services or benefits and the 'naming and shaming' of those who do not vote. The arguments for and against compulsory voting are summarised in Box 5.6 on page 77.

Box 5.6 Arguments for and against compulsory voting

Arguments for:

- compulsory voting would solve the problem of low turnout
- as non-voting is higher among the working class than the middle class, compulsory voting would ensure that the needs of all voters were considered
- the role of money in elections would be less significant
- political literacy should increase
- this limited form of political participation is a minimum part of the public's political responsibilities.

Source: Faulks 2001.

Arguments against:

- compulsory voting would result in ill-considered judgements by those not interested in voting
- the political process would become devalued
- it would be impractical to implement
- it would favour established parties as it devalues new political activism
- voters have a right in a liberal democracy not to vote
- it would not deal with the root causes of political disaffection.

Main points   Sections 5.5 - 5.8

- **The system of voting for local elections in Britain is a plurality ('first-past-the-post') system.**
- **In the 1999 European elections, voters in England, Scotland and Wales used a system of proportional representation for the first time.**
- **Elections to the Scottish Parliament and Welsh Assembly use the Additional Member system. Elections to the Northern Ireland Assembly use the STV system.**

- **The 2000 Representation of the People Act allowed councils to run a number of pilot schemes to make voting easier using electronic voting and counting, early voting, mobile polling stations, all-postal voting and more postal voting.**
- **Extended postal voting appears to have been the most effective method of securing an increase in turnout.**

Activity 5.2 Elections in Wales and Scotland

Item A Elections to the Welsh Assembly (hypothetical region)

In Wales, the electors have two choices when they vote in the Assembly elections. There are 40 constituencies, each of which elects one Member of the Welsh Assembly (AM) using the first-past-the-post (FPTP) method. In addition, voters can also vote in five regional lists, based on the European electoral constituencies, for an additional 20 AMs. In the regional ballot, electors vote for the party rather than the candidate. Parties decide where to place their candidates on the regional list. After the seats are allocated through the first-past-the-post mechanism, the regional lists are used to top up the total number of seats won by each party to make the final count of AMs approximately proportional to the total votes cast.

Each party provides a list of candidates for the additional member seats in rank order.

The Additional Member System

The four additional members from each of the regions are identified by:

   counting the number of votes cast for each party on the electors' second ballot paper;

   dividing the number of each party's votes by the number of constituency seats won by that party under FPTP **plus** subsequent additional seats won **plus one**.

For example, using the statistics in the table on page 78, Party A won 116 votes under the party list votes of the electorate but had four constituency members elected. Therefore, divide 116 by four **plus one** giving a total of 23.2.

The party with the highest number after this calculation gains the first additional member. In this case it is Party B.

The table on page 78 shows how the first three additional members would be elected in Wales in a hypothetical region. In this example, Party A has four seats elected by the first-past-the-post system, Party B has none and Parties C and D have two each. There are four additional seats in total. To decide which party wins an additional seat, the number of votes cast for each party is divided by the number of constituency seats won by the first-past-the-post system **plus subsequent additional seats won plus one**. The party with the highest score after this calculation wins the additional seat.

Item A Elections to the Welsh Assembly (hypothetical region) (contd.)

	Party A	Party B	Party C	Party D
Total party votes cast	116	63	61	56
1st Additional Seat	÷5=23.2	÷1=63 **elected**	÷3=20.3	÷3=18.7
2nd Additional Seat	÷5=23.2	÷2=31.5 **elected**	÷3=20.3	÷3=18.7
3rd Additional Seat	÷5=23.2 **elected**	÷3=21.0	÷3=20.3	÷3=18.7
4th Additional Seat				
FPTP seats won	4	0	2	2
Total AMs				

Item B Scottish Parliament and Welsh Assembly election results in 1999 and 2003

(i) SCOTLAND	Constituencies		Regional Lists		
	Share of votes %	Seats won	Share of votes %	Seats won	Total seats
Conservative	16.6 (15.5)	3 (0)	15.5 (15.4)	15 (18)	**18 (18)**
Labour	34.6 (38.8)	46 (53)	29.3 (33.6)	4 (3)	**50 (56)**
Lib Dem	15.4 (14.2)	13 (12)	11.8 (12.4)	4 (5)	**17 (17)**
Scottish National	23.9 (18.7)	9 (7)	20.9 (27.3)	18 (28)	**27 (35)**
Scottish Socialist	6.2 (1.1)	0 (0)	6.7 (2.0)	6 (1)	**6 (1)**
Green	0 (0.0)	0 (0)	6.9 (3.6)	7 (1)	**7 (1)**
Others	3.4 (1.7)	2 (1)	9.0 (5.7)	2 (0)	**4 (1)**

(i) This table shows the election results in Scotland in 1999 *(in brackets)* and 2003. Turnout in 2003 was 49.4% - down from 58.7% in 1999.

(ii) WALES	Constituencies		Regional Lists		
	Share of votes %	Seats won	Share of votes %	Seats won	Total seats
Conservative	19.9 (15.9)	1 (1)	19.2 (16.3)	10 (8)	**11 (9)**
Labour	40.0 (37.6)	30 (27)	36.6 (35.4)	0 (1)	**30 (28)**
Lib Dem	14.1 (13.5)	3 (3)	12.7 (12.4)	3 (3)	**6 (6)**
Plaid Cymru	21.2 (28.4)	5 (9)	19.7 (30.3)	7 (8)	**12 (17)**
Others	4.8 (4.7)	0 (0)	11.8 (5.6)	0 (0)	**0 (0)**

(ii) This table shows the election results in Wales in 1999 *(in brackets)* and 2003. Turnout was 38.2% in 2003 - down from 46.6% in 1999.

Item C New ways of voting

Council	Nature of pilot(s)	No. of wards	No. of polling stations/ dates/hours	1999 % turnout	2000 % turnout	Impact turnout
Amber Valley	Postal votes on request	2		Up to 41	33.5 (av.)	-
Blackburn	Early voting	all	2 29/4 9-5	30.0	30.9	=
Bolton	All-postal ballot	3		25.5 (av.)	37.7 (av.)	+
Bury	Electronic voting + counting	1	5 (voting machines)	21.5	20.7	=
Coventry	Early voting	all	1 26-29/4 shop hours	26.7	26.5	=
Doncaster	All-postal ballot	1		24.5	44.0	+
Eastleigh	Postal votes on request	12		34.3	33.5	=
Gateshead	All-postal ballot - papers mailed to all voters	2		25.2 (av.)	53.7 (av.)	+
Gloucester	Postal votes on request	3		19.9 (av.)	25.6 (av.)	+
Manchester	Early voting	all	6 29-30/4 11-4	21.4	20.5	=
Milton Keynes	Postal votes on request	all		32.3	27.3	-
Mole Valley	Extended voting hours	all	7-10	40.6	42.7	+
Plymouth	Early voting	all	1 28/4 8-7; 29/4 8-6	40 ('95)	31.9	-
Redditch	Early (earliest) voting	all	1 25-28/4 8-9; 29/4 8-6	25.7	25.3	=
St. Helens	Early voting; extended hours	6	2 28-29/4 7-10	16.4 (av.)	18.3 (av.)	+
Salford	Electronic voting + counting - programmed voting cards	1	(voting machines)	24.9	22.2	-
Stoke on Trent	Early voting	all	1 8/4 office hours	22.3	24.8	+
Stratford on Avon	Electronic voting + counting	all		40.1	39.1	-
Sunderland	Early voting Mobile voting	all 8	3 28/4-2/5 10-6	19.5 20.6 (av.)	21.2 23.1 (av.)	+ +
Watford	Early voting Weekend voting Mobile voting Freepost communications	all all	1 27-29/4 8-9 6-7/5 8-6 (NOT 4/5) (1 delivery per candidate)	35.5	27.0	-
Wigan	All-postal ballot	3		17.6 (av.)	26.0 (av.)	+
Windsor & M'head	Early voting/mobile voting	2	(1 day per ward)	40.6 (av.)	35.4	-

If increased turnout was the main goal of these pilots, there can be no doubt about the most effective - all-postal balloting. Disappointingly for the authorities concerned, most of whom went to considerable lengths and expense to publicise their new arrangements, the several versions of early voting and extended voting hours produced little, if any, improvement on turnout figures. Nor did the electronic voting schemes. The all-postal ballots, though, did indisputably increase turnouts, by an average of some 14% compared with 1999. Gateshead took the headlines, with turnouts more than doubling in their two piloted wards:

- from 19% to 46% in Bensham, an inner-city Labour ward
- from 30% to a remarkable 62% in the more suburban and Liberal Democrat Whickham North.

Source: Game 2003 and Lancaster 2002.

Questions

1. a) Using Item A, calculate which party would have won the fourth additional seat. Then total the columns to provide the final number of Assembly Members for each party.

   b) How do elections to the Welsh Assembly differ from general elections in Wales?

2. Using Item B, explain how elections to the Scottish Parliament differ from general elections in Scotland.

3. a) What conclusions can you draw from the table in Item C?

   b) Will new ways of voting increase turnout? Explain your answer.

5.9 *General election campaigns*

Although some people claim that a fresh general election campaign begins the day after an election result is declared, it is only once the Prime Minister has asked the monarch to dissolve Parliament that the political parties begin to campaign in earnest. General election campaigns proper usually last for three or four weeks and are perhaps the most intense three or four weeks that politicians have to face in the political cycle. Before the development of the mass media, Party Leaders travelled round the country addressing election rallies and meeting ordinary voters. Today, they use the television and radio to communicate their ideas. They still make speeches and meet ordinary voters, but this is done in front of the cameras. As a result, their words and actions are not just designed to appeal to the audience at the meeting they are attending. They are intended to appeal to the wider audience at home.

Every general election campaign has its own characteristics, but there are some factors which all general election campaigns have in common.

First, all general election campaigns are run on two levels - the national level and the local level.

Second, at the national level, the party leadership decides upon the themes and tactics which it feels will project the best image for the party throughout the nation and it outlines the party's policies in a manifesto.

Third, leading members of the main parties become the focus of intense media coverage and they attempt to use this to persuade wavering voters to vote for their party. Box 5.7 shows just how intense media pressure is on the three main Party Leaders.

Box 5.7 Range of activity during an election campaign

Activity	Blair	Hague	Kennedy
Miles Travelled	9,693	6,000	15,600
Number of flights	6	45	75
Press Conferences	26	16	40
Interviews	400	660	340
Expenditure	£11,140,019	£12,769,028	£1,364,994

Source: The *Times*, 7 June 2003 and Electoral Commission 2001.

Fourth, the national parties organise nation-wide advertising campaigns and party election broadcasts and they may organise rallies or other political meetings or events.

Fifth, at the local level, parliamentary candidates and their agents run campaigns in their constituency. Again, a high

public profile is important and much time and effort is spent on generating publicity. All parties rely on volunteers to deliver leaflets and to knock on doors and canvass support. Box 5.8 shows the range of activity during an election campaign.

Box 5.8 Range of activity during an election campaign

The following questions were asked in MORI poll conducted on 24-30 May 2001 and compared with the results of a similar poll conducted during the 1997 general election campaign.

During the past few weeks have you:	2001 election	1997 election
Received leaflets?	69	89
Seen TV party election broadcasts?	58	73
Seen posters?	50	70
Seen Leaders on TV?	43	36
Seen press advertisements?	37	na
Heard radio Party election broadcasts?	16	15
Been called on?	14	24
Received letter?	12	20
Been telephoned?	5	7
Helped party?	3	4
Visited party website?	2	na
Used internet?	2	na
Attended meetings?	1	2
Received party video?	1	na
Received party e-mail?	1	na

Source: Butler & Kavanagh 2002.

5.10 *Party election broadcasts*

Although parties are permitted to pay for political adverts in the press or on billboards, they are not allowed to pay for political adverts on television or radio. Instead, free airtime is allocated to parties by broadcasters who follow the rules laid down in the Broadcasting Act (see Butler & Kavanagh 1997, p.155). These rules have remained fundamentally the same since 1947. The amount of time each party is allowed is determined, in part, by the number of candidates it puts up for election and, in part, by its strength in the previous Parliament. Parties which lack parliamentary representation (such as the Green Party) are allocated a five-minute broadcast if they contest at least 50 seats.

Between 1964 and 1979, party election broadcasts were allocated to the Conservatives, Labour and Liberal parties on a ratio of 5:5:3. The creation of the Alliance brought a revision to 5:5:4 in 1983 and 5:5:5 in 1987. From 1992, the ratio reverted to 5:5:4. A new rule, which came into force in time for the 2001 general election, meant that parties had to contest more than 106 seats nationally (or one sixth of seats in Scotland and Wales) to have party election broadcasts. An innovation in the party election broadcasts in 2001 was the 'sound bite' party political broadcast. During the election campaign, no broadcast lasted longer then five minutes and many only lasted for three minutes or less (Harrison 2002). The parties assumed that the electorate would not want to concentrate for too long on an official party political broadcast.

5.11 An overview of the general election campaign in 2001

The main events in the general election campaign in 2001 are outlined in Box 5.9 below.

5.12 Labour's campaign in 2001

Although the Prime Minister was not obliged to call an election until 2002, Labour strategists had always anticipated an early election, if the polls indicated that support for the party remained high.

In preparing for the election, Labour had developed three long-term objectives and, therefore, key aspects of their long term campaign (Seyd 2001). These were:

- to establish a governing reputation for economic competence
- to maintain an electoral strategy of appealing to middle England
- to manage a single minded and united party.

Labour targeted three groups of voters:

- voters who had voted Labour in 1997 for the first time
- other Labour voters whose support was lukewarm
- Labour voters who lived in low turnout areas.

In addition, Labour focused on 148 seats, nearly all of them gains in 1997. Labour Party members were encouraged to concentrate their activities in these constituencies. The Labour Party's campaign, during the election, focused mainly on two general themes, namely 'prudent' economic management and stability, and improved public services. The two themes were often linked, with continued economic growth to provide the basis of increasing investment in education and health, without raising income tax. Three other features of Labour's campaign are worth noting briefly. First, Labour gave little attention to the twin issues of the European Union and Britain's possible membership of the euro. Second, there were no significant attacks on the Liberal Democrats at national level. And third, the party issued a late warning about the danger of complacency or apathy. In view of the depressingly low turnout, it seems that the fears of the Labour leadership in this respect were entirely justified.

5.13 The Conservatives' campaign in 2001

The Conservatives began the election with a low opinion poll rating of 30% against Labour on 54% (MORI/*Times*, 8 May 2001). In addition, William Hague was seen as a poor Leader. Butler and Kavanagh argue:

'In projecting himself [William Hague] and his team as a credible alternative government and in challenging Labour's huge lead in the opinion polls…Hague's efforts made little impact. He had failed to communicate a clear image of modern Conservatism or to establish its relevance to the country he sought to govern.' (Butler & Kavanagh 2002, pp. 62-63)

Commentators agree that the Conservatives fought a poor campaign. The Conservative leadership focused heavily on three issues:

Box 5.9 Chronology of the campaign

2001 election campaign diary

May 8	Blair announces election.
9	Last PM's Questions. Labour issues Pledge card.
10	Conservative manifesto.
12	Hague suggests Labour means £6 a gallon petrol.
13	Blair at Sedgefield. Woodward selected at St. Helens.
14	Parliament dissolved. UKIP manifesto. Labour claims business vote.
15	Liberal Democrats manifesto. Letwin's £20 billion cuts.
16	Labour manifesto. Straw heckled. Prescott punch.
18	SNP manifesto. Green manifesto. Hague on asylum seekers.
19	Labour woos pensioners.
20	Heath on need for Conservative defeat.
22	Thatcher speech saying UK should never join the Euro.
23	EU document on tax-harmonisation.

May 24	MORI: 25% Labour lead
25	Nominations close. Archbishops ask for moral campaigning.
26	Hague's 12 days to save pound.
27	Oldham riots.
30	ICM puts labour 19% ahead. Last day for claiming postal votes.
31	MORI: 16% Labour lead.
June 1	Conservatives raise landslide fears.
2	Peerages for retiring MPs.
3	Polls show increasing Liberal Democrat support.
4	Hague's plans for office. Ladbrokes close books.
5	Final rallies. 11% labour lead.
6	ICM: 11% Labour lead.
7	Polling day MORI: 15% Labour lead; Gallup: 17% Labour lead.

Source: Butler and Kavanagh 2002.

- tax-and-spend
- asylum seekers
- saving the pound from the euro.

The problem was that Labour had a good reputation for economic competence and so it was difficult to make headway with the first issue, while the other two were low on the voters' list of priorities. A further problem was tension within the Conservative Party over Europe. The leadership ruled out Britain's membership of the euro for the next Parliament, but some candidates publicly declared that they were opposed to Britain ever joining the euro.

5.14 The Liberal Democrats' campaign in 2001

The Liberal Democrats decided to campaign on a small number of policy themes and to avoid major disagreements with the other main parties except on Europe and asylum. The Liberal Democrats claimed to be the only party genuinely committed to freedom and fairness, as well as decentralisation. Most commentators agree that the party's campaign enhanced the reputation of the party's Leader, Charles Kennedy, who decided to 'project himself as the new Leader, to advocate spending more to provide quality public services and to convey an approach of honesty and openness' (Times, 7 June 2001).

5.15 The cost of the campaign

According to figures from the Election Commission, the Conservatives spent nearly 2 million pounds more than Labour in the general election national campaign. In contrast, the Liberal Democrats spent significantly less than both main parties. Box 5.10 shows how the money was spent by each party.

Box 5.10 Spending in the 2001 general election campaign

This table shows the proportion of total party expenditure spent on different categories of campaign activity during the 2001 general election.

Expenditure by type	Con	Lab	Lib Dem
Party political broadcasts	4.45%	2.49%	4.07%
Advertising	34.58%	45.90%	14.45%
Unsolicited material to electors	9.53%	13.36%	3.99%
Manifesto/party policy documents	8.04%	4.73%	6.69%
Market research/canvassing	13.47%	7.94%	4.85%
Media	2.80%	6.88%	16.95%
Transport	11.66%	7.07%	43.58%
Rallies and other events	15.47%	11.73%	5.42%
Total expenditure	£12,751,813	£10,945,119	£1,361,377

Figures from the Electoral Commission Register of Election Expenditure Returns 2001.

In terms of returns on the money spent, the Conservatives only managed to increase their total number of seats by one while the Liberal Democrats increased their total by six. Fisher and colleagues argue that it is doubtful whether the new spending caps made any decisive difference to party success and that 'the principal impact is likely to have been in changing the proportions spent on [different] campaign items' (Fisher et al. 2003, p.31). Separate rules determine what individual candidates, as opposed to national parties, can spend. Conservative candidates spent £4.1 million compared to £3.7 million spent by Labour (Guardian, 27 November 2002).

5.16 Mass media and the 2001 election campaign

The Communications Research Centre at Loughborough University has claimed that 'media coverage of the 2001 general election was 'presidentialised', post-partisan and narrow in focus' (Guardian, 12 June 2001). This means that there was a focus during the campaign on the main political players, especially Tony Blair. Newspapers avoided taking a strong line in support of any of the main parties even though most newspapers supported a Labour victory. In addition, the media only focused on a limited number of issues, focusing on:

- the election campaign itself
- Europe
- the health service
- taxation.

While most people followed the campaign through television, the Electoral Commission found that 40% of television viewers changed channels to avoid programmes devoted to the election (Electoral Commission 2001). A MORI poll shows, however, that television was the most persuasive medium - see Box 5.11.

Box 5.11 MORI poll conducted in June 2001

	Great deal	Fair amount	Not v. much	None at all	Don't know
Election coverage on TV	13	36	20	30	1
Election coverage in the papers	8	30	22	39	1
Parties' leaflets or letters	4	22	25	49	<1
PEBs on TV?	6	16	20	57	1
Election coverage on radio	5	17	18	58	3
Views of friends or family	6	14	20	60	<1
Opinion polls	2	11	21	65	1
Billboard advertisements	2	8	17	72	1
Personal calls from the parties	2	6	9	80	3
Election coverage on the internet	1	3	5	87	4

The table above shows the responses of interviewees to the following question: Please tell me how much influence, if any, each of the following had on your decision about what you would do on the day of the general election. The poll was conducted on 9-18 June 2001.

The internet and the campaign

All the parties used modern technology in the election campaign. Telephone canvassing became much more widespread, replacing door-to-door canvassing. E-mails and text messages were used by the major parties and websites were also developed for the campaign. Coleman claims:

'2001 was for the Internet what 1959 had been for television: both were elections in which a new medium found its way on to the political stage and was tested.' (Coleman 2001, p.122)

5.17 Opinion polls

It is during election campaigns that opinion polls attract the greatest attention and interest. The first British general election campaign in which opinion polls were conducted was in 1945. At that time, only one polling organisation existed. Since then their numbers have grown and then declined. In the 2001 general election, there were five main polling organisations, producing 32 national polls mainly for newspapers and television companies.

What are opinion polls?

Strictly speaking, questions designed to discover how people will vote are not polls of public opinion but surveys of intended behaviour. Nor are poll results predictions of election results. What they provide is a snapshot of voting intentions on a certain day. Exit polls are conducted as people leave the polling stations so, in theory, they should be the more accurate. That is not necessarily the case, though, since people might not tell pollsters the truth about how they have just voted. Polling organisations have changed their methods of polling to try to increase accuracy but critics are dubious about some changes, for example the growth of telephone polling.

Forecasts

The media often do present poll data as forecasts (as do polling organisations when they present their final pre-election day polls - see Box 5.12). As a result, comparisons are made to assess the polls' accuracy. In fact, in 2001 all the polls predicted the outcome of the election with a fair degree of accuracy. The Association of Professional Polling Organisations claimed that the final polls were the 'most accurate since 1987...despite the record low turnout which made the forecast more difficult' (quoted in Watts 2001, p.11). Crewe (2002) is more critical, claiming that the polls were 'disappointing' as they overestimated the Labour vote and underestimated the Conservative vote.

Do polls influence voting behaviour?
(see also Unit 6)

There is a long-running debate about whether or not the publication of opinion polls influences voting behaviour. One view is that polls have a 'bandwagon' effect and encourage some voters to vote for the party which appears to be most popular. An opposite view is the 'boomerang' effect – a party trailing in the polls picks up sympathy votes as the 'underdog'. There is also the theory that, when one party has a big lead in the polls, supporters of that party become complacent and

---

Box 5.12 Final polls

This table shows the final polls taken just before the 2001 general election. All figures are percentages.

	Lab %	Con %	LibDem %	Lab Lead %	Error on Lab Lead %
MORI *Times* 7 June	45	30	18	15	+6
Gallup *D. Tel* 7 June	47	30	18	17	+8
ICM *Guardian* 6 June	43	32	19	11	+2
NOP *S. Times* 4 June	47	30	18	17	+8
Rasmussen 6 June	44	33	16	11	+2
Average	45	31	18	14	+5
Actual Result	42	33	19	9	

Source: Butler & Kavanagh 2002.

---

fail to turn up to vote. Butler and Kavanagh (2002) argue that this partly explains the low turnout in the 2001 general election.

There are two other ways in which opinion polls may influence voting behaviour. First, people who intend to vote tactically may be influenced by the polls. Since, however, effective tactical voting at a general election needs to be based on accurate information about relative party strength at constituency level, the publication of national opinion polls is not much of a guide. Second, whatever they say in public, opinion polls are taken seriously by politicians. Not only do parties commission private polls, to some extent they base their campaigns on information gained from the polls.

Because of fears about their effects, polls are banned just before a general election in some countries - for example, Germany.

5.18 A post-modern campaign?

Recent changes in election campaigning have been described as a move from the pre-modern to the modern, to the post-modern campaign - see Box 5.13 on page 84.

The pre-modern campaign involved direct communication between voters and candidates, local campaigns and voluntary party workers canvassing the streets.

The modern campaign was characterised by greater professionalism, coordination and centralisation.

The post-modern campaign, on the other hand, involves:

'The emergence of a more autonomous and less partisan press, following its own "media logic", the growing fragmentation and diversification of electronic media outlets, programmes and audiences, and, in reaction to all these developments, the attempts by the parties to reassert control through strategic communications and media management during the permanent campaign.' (Norris 1997, p.117)

Box 5.13 Pre-modern, modern and post-modern election campaign

	Pre-modern	Modern	Post-modern
Campaign organisation	Local and decentralised	Nationally coordinated	Nationally coordinated but decentralised operations
Preparations	Short-term and ad-hoc campaign	Long campaign	Permanent campaign
Central coordination	Party leaders	Central headquarters, more specialist consultants and party officials	More outside consultants, pollsters and specialist campaign departments
Feedback	Local canvassing	Opinion polls	Opinion polls, focus groups, internet websites
Media	National and local press, local handbills, posters and pamphlets. Radio leadership speeches	Television broadcasting through major territorial channels	Television narrow casting through fragmented channels, selective mailshots, selective advertisements
Campaign events	Local public meetings. Limited whistle-stop leadership tours	Media mangement. Daily press conferences. Themed photo opportunities. TV party political broadcasts. Billboard wars	Extension of media management to 'routine' politics, leadership speeches, policy launches etc.
Costs	Low budget and local costs	Higher costs for producing television party political broadcasts	Higher costs for consultants, research and television advertisements

Source: Norris 1997.

Main points Sections 5.9 - 5.18

- Parties are allowed election broadcasts if they have parliamentary representation or if they contest at least 106 seats.
- Labour entered the 2001 general election standing high in the opinion polls whereas the Conservatives, and especially William Hague, had a low rating.

- Labour managed to set the policy agenda in 2001. The Conservatives became demoralised and suffered divisions over Europe.
- Some argued there was a post-modern election campaign in 2001.
- Labour, Conservatives and the Liberal Democrats spent over £25 million, in total, on the campaign in 2001.

Activity 5.3 The 2001 general election campaign

Item A Campaign experiences in 2001

	All (1997)	Con	Lab	Lib Dem
Received leaflets	69 (89)	43	40	23
Saw TV PEBs	58 (73)	39	43	28
Saw posters	50 (70)	31	35	7
Saw leaders on TV	43 (36)	32	32	23
Saw press advertisements	37 (na)	23	25	11
Heard radio PEBs	16 (15)	10	10	7
Was called on	14 (24)	6	7	2
Received letter	12 (20)	6	6	2
Was telephoned	5 (7)	2	3	0
Helped party	3 (4)	1	1	1
Visited party website	2 (na)	1	1	0
Used internet	2 (na)	1	2	0
Attended meeting	1 (2)	0	1	1
Received party video	1 (na)	0	1	0
Received party e-mail	1 (na)	<1	<1	0

This table shows the response to a survey carried out between the 24 and 30 May 2001. Respondents were asked 'During the past few weeks have you...? If yes, which party was that?'

Source: www.mori.com

Item B Newspaper support in 2001

Labour	Conservative
Express	Daily Telegraph
Financial Times	Mail on Sunday
Guardian	Sunday Telegraph
Mirror	
News of the World	
Observer	**Not a Tory victory**
Star	Independent
Sun	
Sunday Express	
Sunday Mirror	**Not a Labour landslide**
Sunday People	Daily Mail
Sunday Times	Independent on Sunday
The Times	

This table shows which party national newspapers supported in the 2001 general election campaign.

Item C The internet and the 2001 general election

A survey conducted by MORI found that:

- 11% visited a media election website
- 7% used e-mail or websites to find out information about the election or parties
- 5% sent or received e-mails about the election
- 4% sent or received e-mails or visited websites that were humorous election-related sites
- 2% responded to a web-based opinion poll
- 1% volunteered to work for a party online
- 0% participated in a live chat or web-based discussion forum about the election
- 82% did none of these.

All adults 18+ with access to the internet/e-mail. Figures add up to more than 100% because some respondents used more than one form of the internet/e-mail.

Source: www.mori.com

Item D Issues in the election

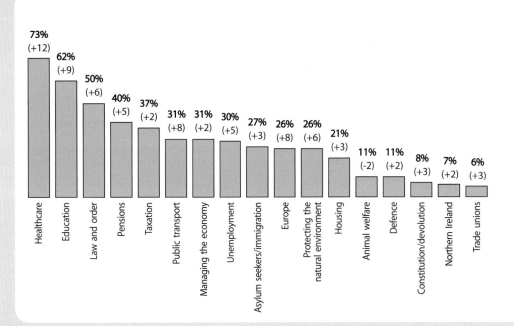

This chart shows the results of a survey carried out by MORI on 5-6 June 2001. The question that was asked was: *'At this general election, which, if any, of these issues do you think will be very important to you in helping you to decide which party to vote for?'* The figure in brackets shows the change since 10-14 May 2001.

Bar chart data:
- Healthcare: 73% (+12)
- Education: 62% (+9)
- Law and order: 50% (+6)
- Pensions: 40% (+5)
- Taxation: 37% (+2)
- Public transport: 31% (+8)
- Managing the economy: 31% (+2)
- Unemployment: 30% (+5)
- Asylum seekers/immigration: 27% (+3)
- Europe: 26% (+8)
- Protecting the natural environment: 26% (+6)
- Housing: 21% (+3)
- Animal welfare: 11% (-2)
- Defence: 11% (+2)
- Constitution/devolution: 8% (+3)
- Northern Ireland: 7% (+2)
- Trade unions: 6% (+3)

Questions

1. Using Items A-D and your own knowledge, write a short article summarising the main features of the 2001 general election.

2. What do Items A and B tell us about the nature of the 2001 general election campaign?

3. Judging from Item C, how important was the internet/e-mail in the 2001 general election campaign?

4. To what extent does Item D help explain Labour's success in the 2001 general election and the Conservative Party's failure?

5.19 What are referendums?

One of the problems with representative democracy is that when a party is elected to govern the country, there is no way of knowing whether the electorate supported all, or only some parts, of the party's programme. It is possible, for example, that voters for a particular party liked that party's economic policies but did not like its policies on education. Elections are not fought on a single question and so it is never clear which parts of a government's programme have popular support.

One way of finding out whether voters support a particular policy is to ask them to vote Yes or No to a single question on that policy. A vote on a single issue is known as a referendum (the plural is either 'referendums' or 'referenda'). Since the electorate is asked to vote directly on a particular issue, holding a referendum is a way of exercising direct democracy within a system of representative democracy.

Another form of direct democracy, which is similar to a referendum, is the 'initiative'. This is:

> '[A device] through which an individual or group may propose legislation by securing the signatures of a required number of qualified voters, and then having the issue put to the people to accept or reject.'
> (Watts 1997, p.45)

5.20 The use of referendums

Although referendums have not been held very often in Britain, they are common in some European countries as well as in Australia and the USA. Referendums are commonly held to answer questions of a constitutional or moral nature. Indeed, Bogdanor argues that:

> 'The main function of the referendum is to offer constitutional protection, to prevent laws being changed without the consent of the people.' (Guardian, 22 November 1991)

However, it has been argued that:

> 'This form of direct democracy (where the people are asked to vote on a single issue) sits uneasily alongside the form of representative democracy which exists in Britain.' (Magee & Outhwaite, 2001)

The arguments for and against the holding of referendums are summarised in Box 5.14.

5.21 Referendums held before 1997

Northern Ireland, 1973
In the UK, just four referendums were held before 1997. The

Box 5.14 Arguments for and against the holding of referendums

Eight main arguments are put forward in support of the holding of referendums:

- They encourage political participation, act as an educational device, mobilise consent and act as a form of direct democracy.
- They provide a single clear answer to a specific question.
- They increase the legitimacy of major measures of government.
- They are needed where a party system is either too rigid or no longer delivers the policy choices voters are seeking.*
- Referendums can strengthen the constitution when they are used as a means of confirming changes in the way we are governed.
- Referendums can help legislators keep in touch with the public mood and they can provide legislators with the justification for introducing key reforms.
- They can provide a mandate from the voters for controversial measures.
- They can be used to provide a clear and final answer to a political question.

*This was the argument put forward by the Referendum Party in the 1997 general election in Britain - namely, that a referendum was needed on Britain's future relationship with Europe because all the main parties were in favour of further European integration.

Ten main arguments are put forward against the holding of referendums:

- Their use undermines the sovereignty of Parliament. By voting at elections, people pass responsibility for decision-making on to these representatives. Since consent is given to government at election time, there is no need to hold referendums.
- If the government alone decides whether or not to hold a referendum, it is likely that referendums will essentially be a conservative weapon.*
- The phrasing of the question is very important. If the government chooses the wording, it might well be able to determine the outcome it desires.
- Voters may lack sufficient information to give a considered judgement. The question of who provides information before a referendum and how it is provided is a thorny one.**
- It is possible that an issue may be too complex to allow a Yes or No answer to a simple question.
- The result may not be decisive and there are alternative means of finding out what the wishes of the electorate are.
- There may be an imbalance in the funding provided for those campaigning on both sides in the referendum.
- There is the problem of public apathy. Low turnout might mean that the result of a referendum lacks credibility. The more referendums that are held, the lower the turnout is likely to be due to voting fatigue.
- Decisions may not always be final as governments can go back to the electorate again and again until they get what they want.
- Referendums can undermine Collective Cabinet Responsibility if ministers take different sides in the argument.

*Initiatives are different from referendums since, with an initiative, it is the voters themselves who decide to seek change, not the government.

** This became apparent in the build-up to the referendum in Northern Ireland in 1998. A leaked government document stated that 'government officials will be used to manipulate the media/public' (Guardian, 28 March 1998).

first was held on 8 March 1973 and involved only people living in Northern Ireland. Voters were asked in this referendum whether they wished to remain in the UK or to join the Republic of Ireland. The result was a large majority in favour of remaining in the UK. But, the referendum was boycotted by all shades of nationalist opinion, including supporters of Sinn Fein and the SDLP (nationalists want Northern Ireland to break away from the UK and become part of a united Ireland). The government hoped that the referendum would show that a large majority of people were in favour of remaining part of the UK. This would then encourage politicians on all sides to discuss, in a constructive manner, how best to resolve conflict in Northern Ireland. Because of the boycott, however, the voting figures became rather meaningless and government intentions were undermined.

UK, 1975

The second referendum was held on 5 June 1975. Voters throughout the UK were asked whether Britain - which had joined the European Economic Community (EEC) when the Conservatives were in power in 1973 - should remain a member (the Labour Party which had gained power in 1974 was divided on the issue). It should be noted that, in the run-up to the referendum, the pro-EEC campaigning group collected ten times as much money in donations as the anti-EEC group. Also, most of the press supported the pro-EEC campaign. The following question appeared on ballot papers:

'The government have announced the results of re-negotiation of the UK's terms of membership of the European Community. Do you think that the UK should remain in the EEC?'

A large majority of voters voted in favour of remaining in the EEC.

Scotland and Wales, 1979

The other two referendums which were held in the UK before 1997 were both held on 1 March 1979. On that day, the people of Scotland and the people of Wales voted on whether or not they wished to accept the devolution proposals passed by Parliament in the Scotland Act 1978 and the Wales Act 1978. The vote was complicated by the fact that Labour backbenchers managed to secure in the Acts the need for 40% of the electorate to vote in favour of devolution.

In Scotland, a majority of those voting voted in favour of the devolution proposals. But, because there was a relatively low turnout, the total voting in favour of devolution was less than 40% of the electorate as a whole. As a result, the Scotland Act 1978 was repealed. In Wales, there was little support for devolution and the Wales Act 1978 was also repealed.

It should be noted that, even if large enough majorities had been obtained in favour of devolution, there was no guarantee that the provisions of the two Acts would be implemented. Bruce Millan, Secretary of State for Scotland at the time when the referendums were held, said:

'Obviously the House, as well as the Secretary of State, will take full account of the referendum. Nevertheless, it is ultimately an advisory referendum in the sense that the House will make the final decision.' (Hansard, 20 April 1979)

Although no other referendums were held before 1997, in 1993 there were calls - notably from former Prime Minister Margaret Thatcher - for a referendum to be held before the Maastricht Treaty was ratified. The Leaders of the two main parties, however, opposed a referendum. Although the Maastricht Treaty was ratified without a referendum, both Labour and the Conservatives gave guarantees in their 1997 general election manifestos that there would be a referendum on membership of the single European currency.

5.22 Referendums held since 1997

Referendums have been widely held since 1997 both at regional and local level. Between 1997 and 2003, however, no referendums were held at national level.

Just four months after its election in May 1997, the Labour government carried out its manifesto commitment to hold referendums in Scotland and Wales on its devolution proposals (see Unit 18 for a detailed examination of devolution). The referendums held in September 1997 are examined in Box 5.15 on page 88.

Northern Ireland 1998

Following the 1998 Northern Ireland peace settlement (see Unit 18 for details on this), a referendum took place there in May 1998. While, formally speaking, the point of the referendum was to permit the people of Northern Ireland to vote on the peace settlement, the political intention of the referendum was to marginalise the paramilitaries and others who opposed the deal. All the main parties in Northern Ireland and in the UK supported a Yes vote. Opposition to the settlement was led by Ian Paisley's Democratic Unionists. They received support from some dissident Ulster Unionists.

When the referendum was held on 22 May 1998, a large majority voted Yes (71%). The legitimacy of the referendum, however, did not only depend on a simple majority. A high turnout and a significant Yes vote from the Unionist population were also required. After the referendum, most commentators agreed that a majority of Unionists had indeed voted Yes, though this was disputed by Ian Paisley (Observer, 24 May 1998).

Mayor of London 1998

The Labour government followed the referendum success over devolution with a referendum in May 1998 on proposals that Londoners should be able to elect a mayor and a Greater London Authority. The government was so concerned about voter apathy that:

'It instructed returning officers to count as valid as many ballot papers as possible, including ones marked with smiley faces...Papers bearing no crosses but marked with the words "I agree" or "OK" will also be considered valid.' (Times, 6 May 1998)

The vote took place on the same day as the local council elections (see Box 5.19), but this did little to enhance interest in the referendum. Only one-third of Londoners voted, with voting as low as 25% in some boroughs. Voter apathy was partly attributed to the fact that all the main parties were urging a Yes vote and partly to the perception that the mayor and new authority would have little real power.

Box 5.15 Devolution referendums, September 1997

Scotland

The Labour leadership decided to include two questions in the referendum for Scotland. The first asked whether the voter supported the setting up of a new assembly. The second asked whether voters supported tax-varying powers. Unlike in 1979, a simple majority of those voting in both referendums determined the outcome. An energetic 'Yes Yes' campaign (so-called because there were two questions) was launched with the support of the Labour Party, Liberal Democrats and Scottish Nationalist Party (SNP). The SNP's support was conditional since the party's position was that devolution should be considered only as a first step towards independence. The Conservative Party opposed devolution. From the start, opinion polls indicated a broad level of support for the 'Yes Yes' campaign.

Wales

In Wales, a low-key Yes campaign was fought, again with the Liberal Democrats and Nationalists supporting Labour's proposals and the Conservatives opposing them. Labour arranged matters so that the two referendums were held a week apart in September 1997 with the Scottish event held first in the hope that this would build up support in Wales where the outcome was uncertain.

Results

The result in Scotland was decisively Yes, Yes, with 74.3% for a Scottish Assembly and 63.5% in favour of tax-raising powers, on a turnout of 60.1%. In Wales, the result was much closer to call with the majority for devolution a mere 6,721 on a turnout of 50.1%.

Unlike the devolution referendums in 1979, the 1997 referendums can be considered as a more fundamental exercise in direct democracy because they were pre-legislative. Lynch (1998) argues that:

> 'Rather than relying solely on a general election mandate to institute major reforms, Labour has utilised the referendum as a device to deliver change through "popular consent", not change through "elective dictatorship".' (Lynch 1998, p.96)

Other mayoral referendums

The Local Government Act 2000 required local authorities with a population of over 85,000 to change their policy-making machinery. Local authorities were given three options, one of which was to have a directly elected mayor. Any local authority choosing this option had to ratify the choice by holding a local referendum. Also, a local authority is required to hold a referendum to decide whether to opt for a directly elected mayor if more than 5% of local voters petition for the change.

In a small minority of local authorities, the issue has been put to the voters in local referendums. The outcomes of these referendums have been mixed. For example, in Middlesborough, 84% of voters were in favour of a directly elected mayor whereas in Brighton 62% voted against. Turnout in these referendums has also varied, with only 18% voting in Lewisham and 36% voting in North Tyneside. In some local authority areas, there has been a grassroots campaign to win support for a referendum against the wishes of the local council. This happened in Oxford, in part because of a campaign by the local paper. However, when the referendum was held, 18,690 voted against a directly elected mayor and only 14,692 voted in favour.

Local referendums

Since 1997, central government has promoted the use of referendums as a way of involving local people in local decisions. In 1997, a government paper, *Local Democracy and Community Leadership*, suggested a large range of ways of seeking and responding to the views of the citizen, including the use of local referendums. Since then, some local referendums have been held on local issues. Box 5.16 on page 89 provides a case study of one such referendum in Bristol. Referendums are also to be held to decide whether elected regional assemblies should be set up in England.

Proposed referendum on the European constitution

In April 2004, Tony Blair proposed holding the first national referendum since the referendum on membership of the European Union. The referendum will be held on the proposed European constitution. Commentators doubt whether it will be held before the expected general election in 2005. This new policy represents a major U-turn as Labour opposed the idea of a referendum before April 2004.

5.23 Referendums - an overview

The use of referendums has grown since the 1970s with eight major referendums having taken place. McCartney argues that:

> 'The referendum can [now] be seen as an accepted part of Britain's constitutional furniture, called into play by politicians to confirm changes to the British governmental framework' (McCartney 2003 p.19)

Referendums are used when:

- there are major constitutional questions to be settled
- there is a division within the governing party on an issue
- there is a significant division of opinion between parties and tactical political advantage may be gained by the governing party by their use.

Box 5.16 Local referendum in Bristol, February 2001

Faced with a shortfall in their budget, the Labour-controlled council in Bristol decided to allow the electors to make the decision about future finances for the city in a referendum. George Micklewright, the Labour Council Leader, said that the referendum would be an important step for local democracy in Britain: 'We have been looking for ways to give Bristol people more say over important council decisions'.

Critics, however, argued that the referendum was an abdication of responsibility by the council leaders and that the referendum was being held to prevent a split in the ranks of the ruling Labour group, which only had a majority of two on the council. Several Labour councillors had earlier rebelled against their own party and voted against plans to close two primary schools.

In the event, the turnout for the referendum was 40%, compared to a turnout of 30% in recent local elections. However, of the 270,000 electors who voted, only 18% supported the council's preferred option for a 4% tax increase. Over half of the electorate backed the no increase option, even though the Labour council had warned that this would lead to cuts of £4.5 million in the education budget.

The Labour councillors described the vote as a useful exercise in local democracy, but admitted that the result was not one that they had wanted. The local *Bristol Evening Post* suggested that it was 'now left to the city council to pick up the pieces of a vote which had badly misfired'.

Main points Sections 5.19 - 5.23

- A referendum is a vote on a single question designed to find out whether voters support a particular policy or not.
- Referendums are usually held to answer questions of constitutional or moral nature.
- Labour managed to set the policy agenda in 2001. The Conservatives became demoralised and suffered divisions over Europe.
- Supporters argue refesendums encourage participation,!increase legitimacy, make the system more flexible, strengthen the constitution and keep legislators in touch.

- Opponents argue referendums undermine the sovereignty of Parliament, are conservative and weighted in favour of the government, oversimplify complex issues and threaten legitimacy if turnout is low.
- In Britain, referendums have been held on Northern Ireland (1973 and 1998), the EEC (1975), devolution (1979 and 1997), the Mayor of London (1998) and other mayoral elections. There have also been a small number of local referendums on local issues.
- The next national referendum is likely to be on membership of the single European currency.

Activity 5.4 Referendums in the UK

Item A Referendums in the UK

Date	Electorate	Issue	Yes vote	%	No vote	%	Turnout (%)
8 March 1973	Northern Ireland	Should Northern Ireland remain part of the UK?	591,820	98.9	6,463	1.1	58.1
5 June 1975	United Kingdom	Do you think that the UK should remain in the EEC?	17,378,581	67.2	8,470,073	32.8	63.2
1 March 1979	Scotland	Devolution for Scotland	1,230,937	51.5	1,153,500	48.3	62.9
1 March 1979	Wales	Devolution for Wales	243,048	20.3	956,330	79.7	58.3
11 September 1997	Scotland	Devolution for Scotland	1,775,045	74.3	614,400	25.7	60.1
		Tax-varying powers	1,512,889	63.5	870,263	36.5	60.1
18 September 1997	Wales	Devolution for Wales	559,419	50.3	552,698	49.7	50.1
7 May 1998	London	Mayor and Greater London Assembly	1,230,715	72.0	47,8413	28.0	33.0
22 May 1998	Northern Ireland	Support for the peace settlement	676,966	71.1	274,879	28.9	81.0

This table shows the results of the eight major referendums held in the UK between 1973 and 1998. Although 51.5% of voters in the referendum in Scotland in 1979 voted for devolution, this came to just 32.8% of the total electorate. The Scotland Act 1978 was therefore repealed. In Wales, the 20.3% who voted in favour of devolution came to just 11.9% of the total electorate and so the Wales Act 1978 was repealed. In 1997, the decisions on devolution in Scotland and Wales were based on a simple majority of those voting.

Item B Referendums - arguments for

Undoubtedly, direct democracy can play an important part in helping to make Britain more governable. Increasingly, governments seem to lack a mandate (decreasing turnout means that they are elected by fewer and fewer people and correspondingly have less and less credibility). At the same time, the party system and the electoral system produce huge majorities in Parliament which allow the government to steamroll its Bills through, undermining the concept of parliamentary sovereignty. Combine all this with declining levels of political interest and the result is rising levels of discontent. Direct democracy can re-engage people. Nobody doubts for a moment that sooner or later there will be a referendum on whether Britain should join the euro and probably other constitutional changes too - such as an elected House of Lords, the establishment of English regional assemblies and changing the local and parliamentary voting system. Then there are the alternative ways in which future governments will be able to have direct access to the public. These methods will allow the government better access to the electorate and, in turn, allow the electorate better access to government. There is no doubt that the internet has already made some inroads here. The scope and opportunity for direct democracy is increasing, and it is likely that people will be participating in more referendums and initiatives in the future.

Source: Batchelor 2002 and Magee & Outhwaite 2001.

Item C The referendum in Northern Ireland, 1998

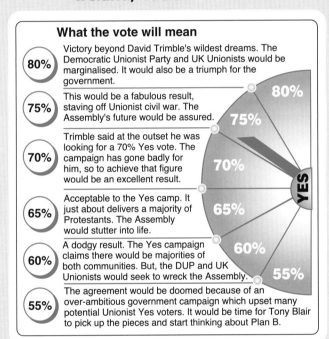

What the vote will mean

80% Victory beyond David Trimble's wildest dreams. The Democratic Unionist Party and UK Unionists would be marginalised. It would also be a triumph for the government.

75% This would be a fabulous result, staving off Unionist civil war. The Assembly's future would be assured.

70% Trimble said at the outset he was looking for a 70% Yes vote. The campaign has gone badly for him, so to achieve that figure would be an excellent result.

65% Acceptable to the Yes camp. It just about delivers a majority of Protestants. The Assembly would stutter into life.

60% A dodgy result. The Yes campaign claims there would be majorities of both communities. But, the DUP and UK Unionists would seek to wreck the Assembly.

55% The agreement would be doomed because of an over-ambitious government campaign which upset many potential Unionist Yes voters. It would be time for Tony Blair to pick up the pieces and start thinking about Plan B.

Source: The *Guardian*, 23 May 1998.

Item E Referendums - arguments against

People power is becoming the rage, as politicians fall further into disrepute. Yet, people power can be a manipulative sham. Representative democracy is being challenged by a referendum culture which may or may not make this a better governed country. Hanging over representative democracy are new money pressures (the question of finances available in referendum campaigns) that mirror those soon to be made available by technology (the use of the internet and e-mail). A million e-mails may be worth more than a majority in the House of Commons. There are British politicians who want to expand the referendum culture. It's a long time since any of them stood for democratic election. Already one sees the thin veil of high principles, to which referendum addicts appeal, failing to conceal motives of straightforward partisanship.

Source: The *Guardian*, 1 June 2000.

Item D Choosing a directly elected mayor

Council consults widely with local people and other stakeholders on the options available.

5% or more of voters petition their council to hold a referendum on whether a new form of local governance involving a directly elected mayor should be adopted.

Council decides which form of local governance it thinks is appropriate in the light of that consultation and further develops that into a formal detailed proposal for a directly elected mayor.

The council must draw up a formal detailed proposal for a form of local governance involving a directly elected mayor.

Proposal includes the new constitution (ie. the roles and duties of the directly elected mayor and council, in particular who takes what decisions and how they are held to account), any transitional arrangements necessary, any key standing orders underpinning the "new constitution", and a timetable for implementation.

Council holds referendum.

If referendum supports proposal, full council must adopt the proposal according to its timetable, copy it to the government, make it available to the public and make an announcement in the local press describing the new form of local governance and when it will come into force.

A mayor is elected and the new form of local governance comes into force.

Source: *Local Leadership, Local Choice*, HMSO, March 1999, Cn 4298.

Questions

1. Look at Item A.

   a) Why do you think these referendums were held?

   b) Would you agree that these referendums were a useful exercise in democracy? Give reasons for your answer.

2. Using Items A and C, analyse the results of the 1998 referendum in Northern Ireland.

3. Look at Item D.

   a) What are the two different ways in which a choice may be made in a local authority to have a directly elected mayor?

   b) Which method do you think is preferable? Give reasons for your answer.

4. a) In what circumstances, if at all, do you think referendums should be held? Use Items B and E in your answer.

   b) What would be the advantages and disadvantages of using the new technology (outlined in Item B) for referendums and initiatives in the future?

References

Batchelor (2002) Batchelor, A., 'Direct Democracy', *Talking Politics*, Vol.14.2, January 2002.

Butler & Kavanagh (1997) Butler, D. & Kavanagh, D., *The British General Election of 1997*, Macmillan, 1997.

Butler & Kavanagh (2002) Butler, D. & Kavanagh, D., *The British General Election of 2001*, Macmillan, 2002.

Coleman (2001) Coleman, S., 'Online campaigning' in *Norris (2001)*.

Conservative Party (2001) *Time for Common Sense*, election manifesto, Conservative Party, 2001.

Crewe (2002) Crewe, I., 'The opinion polls: still biased to Labour' in *Norris (2002)*.

Curtice (2001) Curtice, J., 'The Electoral System - biased to Blair?' in *Norris (2001)*.

Dunleavy et al. (1997) Dunleavy, P., Gamble, A., Holliday, I. & Peele, G., *Developments in British Politics 5*, Macmillan, 1997.

Dunleavy et al. (2000) Dunleavy, P., Gamble, A., Holliday, I. & Peele, G. (eds), *Developments in British Politics 6*, Macmillan, 2000.

Electoral Commission (2001) *Election 2001: The Official Results*, Electoral Commission, 2001.

Faulks (2001) Faulks, K., 'Should voting be compulsory?', *Politics Review*, Vol.10.3, February 2001.

Fisher et al. (2003) Fisher, J., Denver, D. & Benyon, J., *Central Debates in British Politics*, Pearson Education, 2003.

Game (2003) Game, C., 'Local government in Labour's second term: plenty of more modernisation and a few elected mayors' in *Lancaster (2003)*.

Harrison (2002) Harrison, M., 'Politics on the Air' in *Butler & Kavanagh (2002)*.

Hix (2000) Hix. S., 'Britain, the EU and the Euro' in *Dunleavy et al. (2000)*.

HMSO (1991) HMSO, 'Parliamentary Elections' in the *Aspects of Britain* series, HMSO, 1991.

Jackson (2003) Jackson, N., 'E-Democracy: the internet - changing British politics forever or an interesting sideshow?', *Talking Politics*, Vol.15.3, April 2003.

Labour (1997) *New Labour: Because Britain Deserves Better*, election manifesto, Labour Party, 1997.

Labour (2001) *Ambitions for Britain*, election manifesto, Labour Party, 2001.

Lancaster (2002) Lancaster, S. (ed.), *British Politics Update: 1999-2002*, Causeway Press, 2002.

Lancaster (2003) Lancaster, S. (ed.), *Developments in Politics*, Volume 14, Causeway Press, 2003.

Lib Dem (1997) *Make the Difference*, election manifesto, Liberal Democrats, 1997.

Liberal Democrats (2001) *Freedom, Justice, Honesty*, election manifesto, Liberal Democrats, 2001.

Lynch (1998) Lynch, P., 'Devolution and a new British political system', *Talking Politics*, Vol.10.2, Winter 1997-8.

Lynch (2002) Lynch, P., 'Goodbye ballot box, hello post box', *Talking Politics*, Vol.15.1, September 2002.

Magee & Outhwaite (2001) Magee, E. & Outhwaite, D., 'Referendums and Initiatives', *Politics Review*, Vol.10.3, February 2001.

McCartney (2003) McCartney, M., 'Oh referendum, where art thou?', *Talking Politics*, Vol. 16.1, September 2003.

Norris (1997) Norris, P., 'Political communications' in *Dunleavy et al. (1997)*.

Norris (2001) Norris, P., *Britain Votes 2001*, Oxford University Press, 2001.

Rallings & Thrasher (2000) Rallings, C. & Thrasher, M., 'Assessing the significance of election in 1999', *Talking Politics*, Vol.12.2, Winter 2000.

Seyd (2001) Seyd, P., 'The Labour campaign' in *Norris (2001)*.

Watts (1997) Watts, D., 'The growing attractions of direct democracy', *Talking Politics*, Vol.10.1, Autumn 1997.

Watts (2001) Watts, D., 'The record of opinion polls in 2001', *Talking Politics*, Vol.14.1, 2001.

6.1 *The social structures model - an overview*

According to the social structures model of voting behaviour, social factors - such as people's class, where they live, their age, their gender, their ethnicity and their religious affiliation - largely determine how they vote. Of course, not everyone from a certain class votes the same way in every election. Nevertheless, the social structures model suggests that, in general terms, people who share certain characteristics will vote in certain ways.

6.2 *Social factor (1) - class alignment and dealignment*

One explanation of voting behaviour is that people tend to vote according to their occupational class. Traditionally, it was thought that those in manual jobs - the working class - are more likely to vote for the Labour Party while those in non-manual jobs were more likely to vote for the Conservatives - see Box 6.1.

Box 6.1 The traditional view of class and voting

This cartoon shows the stereotypical way in which the British class system is sometimes viewed. Traditionally, it was thought that the man on the left (representing the upper class) and the man in the middle (representing the middle class) would vote Conservative while the man on the right (representing the working class) would vote Labour.

Class alignment

Between 1945 and 1970, the evidence supported the theory that people's class largely determined how they voted. Although there was always a degree of cross-class voting (particularly a proportion of the working class voting Conservative), nearly two-thirds of all voters voted for their 'natural' class party. In other words, most working-class voters did vote Labour and most non-working-class voters voted Conservative. There was quite strong class alignment.

Class dealignment

Since 1970, however, some political scientists, such as Ivor Crewe (Crewe et al. 1977) and John Benyon and David Denver (1990), have claimed that a process of class dealignment has been taking place. They argue that the link between class and voting has been reduced. Particularly noticeable was the big increase in the working-class Conservative vote from 1979.

Other writers have been less convinced about the theory of class dealignment. Anthony Heath and his colleagues, for example, denied that, in the 1980s, there was a fall in working-class loyalty to the Labour Party or that the proportion of members of the working class voting Labour fell (Heath et al. 1985, 1991). Instead, the overall decline in the Labour vote merely reflected a reduction in the size of the working class as a whole. There were simply fewer working-class people than there used to be.

6.3 *Class and the 1997 general election*

At the 1992 general election, the Labour Party won 34% of the vote. In 1997, it won 43%. One explanation for this increase could be that class dealignment had gone into reverse, with the working class returning in large numbers to Labour. John Curtice (1997), however, rejected this interpretation because survey data indicated that increases in support for Labour were fairly evenly spread across the different classes. Similarly, Pippa Norris argued:

'New Labour has triumphed by maintaining its traditional base and yet simultaneously widening its appeal to Middle England...[The] explanation lies in the changing pattern of party competition, notably New Labour's shift towards the ideological middle ground with a classless appeal.' (Norris 1997, pp.15-16)

6.4 *Class and the 2001 general election*

At the 2001 general election, the overall picture appears not to have changed much since 1997. The net change in votes was the smallest for any election after a full Parliament for almost 50 years (Crewe 2002). The party distribution of votes according to class does reveal some differences from 1997, however. In 2001, the Conservative Party lost ground among the middle classes (the A, B and C1s) while Labour increased its middle-class support. Dorey (2002) argues that the Labour gains among middle-class voters reflect the Labour government's strategy of targeting Middle England.

By targeting Middle England, Labour lost some support from working-class voters (the C2, D and Es). Its lead over the Conservatives within the working class overall fell from 31% to 21% (Kellner 2001). Compared to 1997, Labour's share of the D and E vote (the semi-skilled and unskilled working class) decreased from 57% to 50%, votes being lost in almost equal measure to the Conservatives and the Liberal

Democrats. The loss of support for Labour among the Ds and Es, did not, however, translate into a great loss of seats. It merely reduced the size of Labour's majorities in some of its safe seats.

6.5 Class and voting: conclusion

Overall, the statistical relationship between voting and class appears to be weakening and is probably weaker now than at any time since 1945. Curtice (2001) argues, however, that this does not necessarily endorse the dealignment thesis. He suggests that voters are changing their behaviour not because their motivations have altered but rather because the choices on offer from the parties have changed. In any case, there is still a relatively clear relationship between class and voting behaviour in British elections, with Labour still more popular among working-class voters and the Conservatives (just) with middle-class voters. It can be argued that class is still the most important social factor influencing voting behaviour.

Main points Sections 6.1 - 6.5

- According to the social structures model of voting behaviour, social factors - such as people's class, where they live, their age, their gender, their ethnicity and their religious affiliation - largely determine how they vote.
- Between 1945 and 1970, the evidence supported the theory that people's social class largely determined how they voted.
- Since 1970, however, some political scientists have claimed that a process of class dealignment has been taking place - the link between class and voting has been reduced.
- Overall, the statistical relationship between voting and class appears to be weakening and is probably weaker now than at any time since 1945.

Activity 6.1 Class and voting behaviour

Item A Class and voting 1964-2001

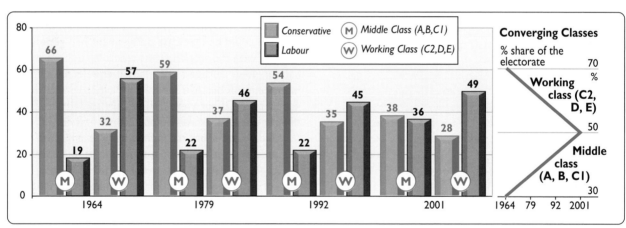

This chart shows how the relationship between class and voting for the two main parties has changed between 1964 and 2001.

Source: Kellner 2001.

Item B Class and voting in 1997 and 2001

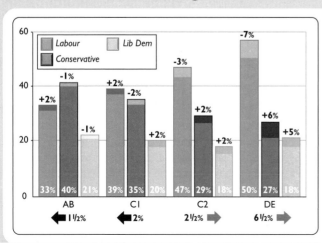

This chart shows how voting according to class differed in 1997 and 2001. Each column shows the percentage voting for one of the three main parties in 2001 and the rise or fall in the percentage compared to 1997.

Questions

1. a) Judging from Items A and B, what is the evidence that class dealignment has taken place?

   b) Does the information in Item B cast any doubts about the theory of class dealignment?

2. a) Using Item A, describe the changing relationship between class and voting between 1964 and 2001.

   b) What evidence is there to suggest that class is still an important factor in determining voting behaviour?

6.6 *Social factor (2) - regional differences*

During the 1980s, political commentators increasingly used the term 'North-South divide' to describe broad geographical differences in support for the Labour Party and Conservative Party. Support for the Conservatives appeared to be declining in the North of England, Scotland and Wales while support for Labour declined in the South of England.

In the two general elections held in the 1990s, the North-South divide began to narrow mainly because Conservative support fell most sharply in areas where the party had been very strong in the 1980s (notably London, the South East, East Anglia and the East Midlands - see Norris 1997, pp.9-10). This trend continued at the 2001 general election and, according to Norris (2001), was critical to the outcome. Labour's support in the South (nearly 6 million votes) continued to strengthen, relative to their vote in the North (almost 5 million). Although the Conservative vote in the South was similar in volume to Labour's, it was only 2.4 million in the North.

For the second successive election, the Conservative Party failed to win any seats in Cardiff, Glasgow, Leeds, Liverpool, Newcastle, Sheffield and Sunderland. Although it picked up one seat in Scotland, the Conservatives were relegated to the fourth party in Scottish politics (achieving only 15.6% of the votes there) and 'appear to be in a state of terminal decline in Scotland' (Bartle 2002, p.171).

The change in the North-South balance can be related to Labour's strategy of targeting Middle England. In 2001, the party made some further gains in southern constituencies with significant middle-class electorates. And, although it lost some support in its traditional working-class constituencies (mainly through low turnout), these were Labour safe seats. Since Labour held on to them, the drop in support did not, therefore, affect the overall electoral outcome. The Conservatives did not benefit from the change in the North-South balance. They remained, in 2001, 'a predominantly rural and suburban party' (Bartle 2002, p.171).

6.7 *Social factor (3) - age*

In 2001, the theory that younger voters tend to vote Labour and older voters tend to vote Conservative held true. Box 6.2 shows that 47% of voters aged 18-34 chose Labour, while 29% chose the Conservatives. Conversely, only in the 65+ age group did support for the Conservative Party exceed that for Labour. Support for the Liberal Democrats was fairly evenly distributed over all age groups.

It used to be thought that as people got older they became more inclined to vote Conservative. This assumption, however, was challenged by Butler and Stokes in 1969, when they put forward their 'generational cohorts' theory. As Dorey (2002) explains, they suggested that many of the Conservative-voting elderly in the 1960s would have acquired their political views and values from their parents in the early part of the 20th century when the Labour Party had not fully established itself as a credible party of government and before the marked decline of the Liberal Party had set in. Since many of the parents of those who were elderly in 1969

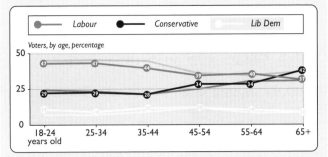

Box 6.2 Age and voting in 2001

This graph shows the way in which different age groups voted in the 2001 general election.

Source: Kellner 2001.

were Conservatives and would have transmitted their Conservative views to their children, this would explain why many of the elderly in the 1960s were Conservatives. It was not that they had become Conservative when they grew older. They had always been Conservatives. If that was the case, later generations which had been brought up when Labour was seen as a credible party of government (those, for example, who were young adults at the time of the Attlee government or those who were young adults at the time of the Wilson governments in the 1970s) would continue to support Labour in their old age. Evidence to test this theory can be found by examining voting behaviour over the past two decades.

Among the very youngest voters (the 18-22 age group), however, there is normally a greater volatility in voting behaviour and no party can afford to take the support of first-time voters for granted. They tend to be less interested in politics, less committed to any political party and less likely to turn out to vote.

6.8 *Social factor (4) - gender*

Writing in 1967, one political scientist stated:
> 'There is overwhelming evidence that women are more conservatively inclined than men.' (Pulzer 1967, p.107)

Pulzer argued that, between 1945 and 1966, while men had given the Labour Party a victory at every general election, women had done so only twice. Similarly, in the four general elections held between 1979 and 1992, more women voted for the Conservatives than for the other parties. By 1997, however, gender differences in party choice had all but disappeared and, in 2001, men and women voted for the two main parties in identical proportions - see Box 6.3 on page 95.

Three factors may account for this disappearance of gender differences in voting behaviour.

1. Labour's election tactics
The Labour Party has made a concerted effort to win over women voters. As well as emphasising improvements in childcare and education, for example, the party has increased women's representation in Parliament.

2. A changing workforce
It was only in the mid-1990s that the number of women in

Box 6.3 Gender and voting

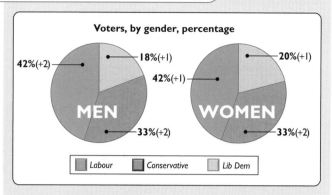

Voters, by gender, percentage

MEN: 42%(+2), 18%(+1), 33%(+2)

WOMEN: 20%(+1), 42%(+1), 33%(+2)

Labour | Conservative | Lib Dem

These pie charts show how men and women voted in the 2001 general election.

Box 6.4 Religion and party choice in 2001

	Con (%)	Labour (%)	LibDem (%)
No religion	21	48	23
Anglican	39	41	18
Scots Presbyterian	25	44	14
Roman Catholic	25	60	13
Non-conformist	31	42	21
Non-Christian	7	82	8

Rows do not total 100 because votes for other parties are not shown.

This table shows how religious affiliation affected voting in the general election of 2001.

Source: Denver 2002 which uses data from the British Election Study.

paid employment reached a similar level to that of men. Because more women are now working outside of the home, family and household roles are changing. Fewer women consider it to be their role to stay at home. As a result, there is a theory that traditional values relating to the family and domestic life (which used to be emphasised in Conservative election campaigns) now have less impact.

3. Gender and age

Since women's life expectancy is higher than men's, there are always more older women than older men in the population - and older people have been more likely than younger people to vote Conservative. But more recent evidence indicates that older voters are becoming less likely to vote Conservative.

6.9 *Social factor (5) - religion*

Historically, there have been close links between religion and politics in Britain. In the 19th century, for example, the Church of England was described as 'the Tory Party at prayer' and was closely identified with the political Establishment. Non-conformist sects such as Methodists and Baptists, on the other hand, were associated with support for the Liberal Party. Today it is often thought that politico-religious links in Britain are far less significant, although they are still important determinants of party choice in some parts of Western Europe (including Northern Ireland).

Box 6.4, however, reveals that - despite the apparent general decline of religion in Britain - religious denomination or identification continues to bear some relationship to party choice. Non-Christians, those with no religion and Roman Catholics appear to support Labour in much greater numbers than the other parties, while the Conservative Party receives more support from Anglicans than from other groups.

The reasons for any connections between religious groups and party choice, however, might not be due to religion itself. For example, the high Labour vote among British Catholics, many of whom are of Irish descent, might be related historically to the policies of the main parties on the 'Irish question'. Similarly, the voting preferences of Sikhs, Muslims and other 'non-Christian' groups in Britain may have more to do with ethnicity than with religion.

6.10 *Social factor (6) - ethnicity*

The more recent analyses of the relationship between voting behaviour and ethnicity have focused on the voting patterns of different black and Asian groups. Although studies show that the majority of black and Asian people vote Labour, different levels of party support have been noted between black and Asian voters as well as differences within each of these groups. For example, in 1997, there was a 16% difference between Asian (70%) and black (86%) support for the Labour Party (Saggar 1998, p.27). In an earlier study, Fitzgerald (1988), using data from the 1987 general election, noted markedly higher levels of support for the Conservative Party among East African Asians than among those from the Indian sub-continent.

Three main factors have been suggested to explain why the Labour Party attracts the votes of immigrants and their descendants.

1. Class

The most common reason given by black and Asian respondents to survey questions about why they vote for the Labour Party is that Labour is for the working class. But, by itself, a simple class explanation would not explain why the black and Asian working-class Labour vote is much higher than the working-class Labour vote in general. Fitzgerald (1988), for example, claims there is no clear evidence that black and Asian people especially perceive themselves to be working class.

2. Race

The Labour Party is usually seen as more liberal than the Conservatives on issues related to race and immigration. According to Denver (1994), this is one reason for the high black and Asian labour vote. But the majority of evidence suggests that black and Asian voters are not predominantly concerned with 'race' issues. Most surveys reveal a high similarity between black and Asian groups and whites. Differences among black voters are likely to be as significant as differences between black and Asian groups and whites.

3. Political geography

Although black and Asian voters make up a small proportion of the electorate, residential concentration of some black and Asian communities means that, in some constituencies, the black and Asian vote is large enough to make a significant impact. Some of these constituencies have become Labour strongholds and have been historically significant in forging the close two-way relationship between black and Asian communities and Labour (a link which has not developed with other political parties). Fitzgerald (1988) points out that, from the early days of post-war black and Asian immigration, black and Asian people have relied on their local Labour MPs for political support.

At the same time, the most obvious and accessible route for black and Asian people who wish to play a role in public life has been through the Labour Party. And, although still under-represented in the House of Commons, the 2001 general election saw the return of 12 black or Asian Labour MPs (most of whom represent constituencies with large minority populations - see Saggar 2001). Electoral geography has, therefore, functioned to strengthen the links between black and Asian people and the Labour Party.

Main points Sections 6.6 - 6.10

- Since 1990, the North-South divide has narrowed mainly because Conservative support has fallen most sharply in areas where the party had been very strong in the 1980s.
- In 2001, the theory that younger voters tend to vote Labour and older voters tend to vote Conservative held true. But, the generational cohorts theory suggests that it is not true that people become more inclined to vote Conservative the older they become.
- Gender differences have almost disappeared in the past two general elections.
- Despite the apparent general decline of religion in Britain, religious denomination or identification continues to bear some relationship to party choice.
- The majority of black and Asian people vote Labour, but different levels of party support have been noted between black and Asian voters as well as differences within each of these groups.

Activity 6.2 Social factors other than class

Item A The North-South divide

Year	Conservative vote (%)			Labour vote (%)		
	North	South		North	South	
1992	30.7	69.2	100%	50.6	49.4	100%
1997	29.0	70.9	100%	46.5	53.4	100%
2001	28.3	71.6	100%	45.0	54.9	100%

Note: The figures measure the proportion of Conservative and Labour votes from the South and the North. The South is defined as Greater London, the South East, South West, East Anglia and Midlands. The North is defined as the remainder of Britain.

Source: Norris 2001, p.13.

Item B Age and voting

How people aged 65+ voted, 1983-2001 (%)					
	1983	1987	1992	1997	2001
Conservative	53	50	49	44	42
Labour	28	27	36	34	37
Lib/Lib Dems	19	23	14	16	18

This table shows how people aged over 65 voted in elections between 1983 and 2001.

Source: Dorey 2002.

Item C Voting and ethnicity

	Oct 1974 %	1979 %	1983 %	1987 %	1992 %	1997 %	2001 %
Labour	81	86	83	72	81	78	75
Conservative	9	8	7	18	10	17	16

This table shows the percentage of black and Asian voters who voted for the Labour Party and Conservative Party between 1974 and 2001. The figures are percentages.

Source: Saggar 1997 and 2001.

Questions

1. a) Judging from Item A, what is the evidence of a
   North-South divide in voting behaviour?
   b) How did this divide affect the outcome of the 2001
   general election?
2. To what extent does the evidence in Item B support

the 'generational cohorts theory' of explaining the
voting behaviour of older voters?

3. What conclusions can you draw from Item C about
the trends in the voting behaviour of black and Asian
voters?

6.11 The party identification model - an overview

'Party identification' (or 'partisanship') refers to the
attachment, over a period of time, to a particular political
party. The party identification model is derived from studies
in the USA in the 1950s. In Britain, it became widely accepted
as an explanation of voting behaviour in the 1960s when
party identification was seen as a key long-term influence on
the way people vote (see Denver 2002).

By 'party identification', political scientists mean that people
vote for a party because they have a psychological attachment
to it rather than making a rational choice of who to vote for
through an assessment of the party's aims, promises or
practices. Box 6.5 outlines the key claims of the party
identification model.

Box 6.5 Key claims of the party identification model

According to Miller (1990), the basic claims of the party
identification model are that:

- many voters identify themselves as supporters of a
  particular party
- party identification is relatively stable and long-lasting
- party identification influences voters' attitudes towards
  issues, personalities, and government performance
- party identification directly affects voters' voting
  behaviour.

6.12 Political socialisation

Work on the party identification model in Britain in the
1960s stressed the effects of 'political socialisation' - the
process by which people acquire their political attitudes,
values and ways of behaving. Most theories of political
socialisation assumed that most people retain the party
preferences and voting habits formed when they first become
politically aware. The influences of childhood and early
adulthood were, therefore, considered important. Family
(especially parents), friends and work colleagues and the
social class to which voters belong were regarded as the main
agencies of political socialisation. Today, however, political
socialisation has become less central to most explanations of
voting behaviour.

Extent, direction, intensity

Research using the model has focused on three aspects of
party identification:

- **its extent (or incidence)** - what proportion of the
  electorate identifies with a particular political party and
  has this proportion increased or decreased over time?
- **its direction** - do some parties attract higher numbers
  of identifiers than others and how has this changed over
  time?
- **its intensity** - how strongly do people support their
  party and why do some people feel strongly attached to
  a party and others do not?

If the extent and intensity of party identification are high then
political scientists speak of high degrees of party alignment. If
the extent and/or the intensity of party identification are low
or falling then a process of party dealignment is said to be
taking place.

Variations in the extent and intensity of party identification
may affect the degree of electoral stability and volatility. High
levels of strong party identification are likely to mean that few
people switch their vote from one election to another -
producing a period of electoral stability. Weak or low levels
of party identification are likely to mean that voters are less
predictable in their party choices and so voting behaviour is
more volatile. When this is the case, short-term factors (such
as current issues, the personalities of the Party Leaders and
the role of the media) tend to have more influence on
electoral outcomes since party loyalty has less of a role to
play.

6.13 Party dealignment

Section 6.2 above shows that there has been a debate about
the extent or even the existence of class dealignment. There
is more general agreement, however, that party (or partisan)
dealignment (a drop in the number of voters identifying
strongly with the main parties) has been taking place since
the early 1970s.

Before 1970, the post-war period had seen extensive and
intensive party identification with the Conservative Party and
Labour Party. In the 1950s and 1960s, although there had
been changes of government, the outcome of elections (in
terms of votes cast and seats won by these two parties) had
not varied greatly. Party (and class) alignment supported a
stable two-party system. This electoral stability then started
to give way to greater volatility as the two-party system came
under attack from other parties (notably the growing support
for the Liberal Party but also the SNP in Scotland and Plaid
Cymru in Wales).

But to what extent have Labour and the Conservatives lost
support? Have they suffered equally? These questions can be
answered in two ways - by examining the changes in the
parties' share of the actual vote at election times and by
analysing the survey data related to party identification.

Share of the vote

Between 1951 and 1983, there was a marked decline in the share of the actual vote won by Labour and the Conservatives combined. This trend showed signs of reversal in 1987 and 1992 but has since dipped again - see Box 6.6.

Box 6.6 Votes for the two main parties

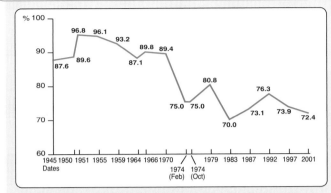

This graph shows the combined share of the vote for the Conservative Party and Labour Party in general elections held in the period 1945-2001.

The fall in the combined Conservative-Labour share of the vote can be explained by the growth in fortunes of other parties, especially the Liberals and, since its formation in the late 1980s, the Liberal Democrats. It is significant, for example, that the Liberal Party put up just 109 candidates at the 1951 general election, but 523 in 1979. In 2001, the Liberal Democrats contested 639 seats. Moran (1989) has argued that the willingness of third parties to field more candidates is itself a reflection of the decline in support for the two major parties. Until 1997, Labour suffered more than the Conservatives from the drop in voting support at general elections.

Survey data on party identification

Voting for a party is not the same thing as identifying with it. It is, therefore, necessary to add other information about party support to knowledge of the actual share of the vote. Survey data has revealed, for example, that the percentage of Conservative identifiers held up better than Labour's in the early 1990s. If, among the identifiers, however, intensity of identification is measured, then it can be seen that both major parties have suffered from party dealignment since the 1960s. Denver (1994) reported that, in 1964, 48% of Conservatives and 51% of Labour voters identified 'very strongly' with their party. By 1992, this had declined to 21% and 24% respectively.

Denver also found that, over the same period, the number of very strong Liberal Party identifiers had fallen from 32% to 8%. This suggested that partisan dealignment was not confined to the two main parties. It also suggested that the electoral fortunes of the Liberal Democrats could be expected to fluctuate more than the other parties since it had fewer identifiers. One explanation for this was that the Liberal Democrats tend to gain the votes of disaffected voters from the Conservative Party and Labour Party. The Liberal Democrats' record at by-elections would seem to confirm this. Their by-election gains are frequently wiped out in general elections.

The extent of party dealignment

Some political scientists, such as David Denver (see Activity 6.3 below), have concluded that the party identification model of voting behaviour is now of very limited value. Yet, almost three-quarters of voters at general elections still vote for one of the two main parties. Writing after the 1983 general election - at which the combined Labour-Conservative vote fell to its lowest level - Ivor Crewe nevertheless warned against over-emphasising the extent of the decline in party identification - see Box 6.7.

Box 6.7 Ivor Crewe on party dealignment

Long-term allegiance to the Conservative Party and Labour Party remains the dominant fact about the British electorate, the psychological anchor of a stable, slow-moving party system.

Source: Crewe 1988, p.3.

Indeed, a survey carried out after the 1992 general election (Sanders 1997) revealed a noticeable increase in respondents identifying 'very' or 'fairly' strongly with political parties. Nevertheless, the drastic reduction in voting support for the Conservatives in 1997 (which barely increased at the 2001 election) meant that any such increase is not reflected in the overall picture of combined Labour-Conservative support shown in Box 6.6 above.

The causes of party dealignment

Political scientists have suggested a number of factors which may have contributed to party dealignment. Taken individually, it is unlikely that any single factor could provide a definitive and undisputed case. Taken together, however, they provide an explanation for the trend.

1. Class dealignment (see Section 6.2 above)

Most commentators recognise a connection between party dealignment and class dealigment. A decline in the links between class and party may have helped to weaken party identification.

This theory could help to explain why Labour won such large victories in the 1997 and 2001 general elections. The party put a great deal of effort into attracting and retaining the support of people outside its 'natural' class (the working class). By appealing to Middle England, the Labour Party may have made it easier for voters who did not belong to the working class to vote for it.

2. The generational effect

The electorate does change from one general election to the next. New (usually young) voters enter the register while others (usually older) die in between elections. Research evidence suggests, however, that a decrease in party identification is not confined to younger voters. It has spanned the whole range of age groups in the electorate.

3. Education

There is an argument that partisan dealignment has followed a period during which the electorate became better educated. A better-educated electorate, it is said, is more able to make rational political decisions. Voters are therefore less reliant on an unthinking psychological attachment to a particular party.

4. Television

This argument is linked to the growing and changing television coverage of political events. It was not until the 1960s that the majority of households in Britain had a television set. Since then, coverage has changed. Interviews with politicians are now far less deferential, for example. Satirical programmes such as *Spitting Image* and *Have I Got News for You* may have contributed to, as well as merely reflected, a greater cynicism about politics. Developments in television broadcasting, together with a more educated electorate, therefore might well have heightened political awareness and led to the questioning of traditional political loyalties.

5. Ideological disjuncture

Party loyalty is likely to be reduced if the attitudes, beliefs or wishes of a party's supporters become out of step with some of the basic principles or policies of the party. Such an 'ideological disjuncture' may have affected the Labour Party in the 1960s and 1970s. More recently, the Conservative Party has suffered from ideological and policy splits - especially over Europe. In addition, there is growing evidence that, since the 2001 election, a sizeable proportion of Labour voters has become unhappy about the Labour government's policies - such as those on foundation hospitals and university tuition fees. Many Labour supporters also opposed the government's decision to invade Iraq in 2003.

6.14 *Performance of the parties*

It is sometimes argued that voters have become increasingly dissatisfied with the performance of their preferred party, particularly when that party has formed the government. High levels of satisfaction with party performance tend to go together with high levels of party identification. A decreasing faith in parties and politicians, on the other hand, is likely to accompany falling levels of party loyalty. What is debatable is whether growing dissatisfaction in the performance of parties is a cause or an effect of party dealignment.

Main points   Sections 6.11 - 6.14

- The 'party identification' model examines the psychological attachment to a political party and how this can directly influence voting behaviour.
- Party dealignment has been taking place since the early 1970s. Since then, there has been a fall in the share of the vote going to the two main parties and fewer voters now identify strongly with a party.
- Causes of party dealignment include: class dealignment, the generation effect, education, changing television presentation, ideological disjuncture and the performance of the parties.
- There is a debate about whether party dealignment has caused greater electoral volatility.

Activity 6.3 *The party identification model of voting behaviour*

Item A **Party identification**

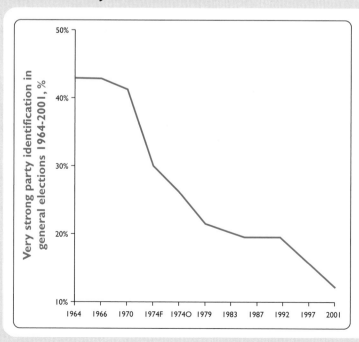

Doubts have been growing among electoral analysts about the value of the party identification approach in explaining party choice. Some of these doubters have suggested that not as many people have had a stable commitment to a party as was originally believed. Others have criticised the survey questions used to gain information about party identification. In any event, the graph shows that the strength in party identification in Britain has sharply declined and reached an all-time low in 2001. Of course, there are still some strong party identifiers around, for whom supporting their party at an election is more or less automatic, but they are thinner on the ground than they used to be. As an explanation for party choice in elections, the party identification model has less value than it used to and looks set to have even less value in the future.

Source: Denver 2002.

Item B Party dealignment and electoral volatility

A common argument is that party dealignment produces greater volatility in voting behaviour. Not all political scientists accept this argument, however. Some argue that, although party dealignment has taken place, volatility has increased very little. The different conclusions reflect, to some extent, the ways in which electoral volatility is measured. Measurements of electoral volatility distinguish between 'overall' and 'net' volatility. 'Net volatility' refers to the changes in the parties' share of the vote from one election to another. 'Overall volatility' refers to the total amount of vote-switching which takes place in a single election campaign. It is possible to have high overall volatility and low net volatility if, for instance, votes which have switched from Conservative to Labour are matched in number by votes switching from Labour to Conservative. The changes cancel themselves out in terms of their net effect. In 1992, David Denver drew attention to the example of the Conservative share of the vote from 1979 to 1992. The relatively small decline in the Conservative vote from 43.9% to 41.9% over this period appeared to indicate stability rather than volatility. But these figures showed only the net effect of switches in the vote between parties. According to Denver, the figures concealed a degree of overall volatility which indicated that the Conservatives as well as Labour had suffered from party dealignment. Chris Game showed that as many as 11 million voters changed their minds in both the 1992 and the 1997 general elections. By way of contrast, at the 2001 general election, electoral volatility was not a significant factor (other than a switch between voting and non-voting). In terms of net volatility, the change in votes was the smallest for any election following a full Parliament for almost 50 years (and the net turnover of seats was the lowest for 100 years.

Source: Denver 1992, Game 1995 and 1998 and Crewe 2002.

Questions

1. Using the party identification model, write a short passage describing the major trends in voting behaviour between 1960 and 2001.

2. a) To what extent to you agree with Denver (Item A) that the party identification model is now of little value in accounting for voting behaviour?

b) What do you think are the chief reasons for a decline in party identification?

3. a) Judging from Item B, what is the difference between 'net volatility' and 'overall volatility'?

b) What does the low volatility in the 2001 general election tell us about the nature of that election?

6.15 The rational choice model – an overview

Some political scientists argue that political parties in Britain can no longer rely simply on the loyalty of their supporters or on particular social classes to win elections. They say that parties now have to compete for votes on the basis of their policies, their past records and the credibility of their Leaders. These are the important features of the rational choice model of voting behaviour.

This model focuses on the connection between voters' attitudes and their decisions about which party to vote for. It is sometimes referred to as a 'supermarket' or 'consumer choice' view of voting behaviour. David Sanders argues that voters are now more likely to compare the 'policy and leadership packages' that the various parties offer and then vote 'according to which appears...to promise them the best deal' (Sanders 1997, p.73).

The rational choice model stresses the importance of instrumental voting (making rational decisions) rather than emotional voting (voting according to class or party loyalties).

6.16 Issue voting

Some political scientists believe that people are increasingly likely to decide which party to vote for after making a

rational analysis of the parties' positions on a range of issues and policies. Dorey (2002, pp.23-24) argues that, since 1970, issue voting has increased in importance both in terms of 'saliency' (the issues thought by electors to be most important) and in terms of which party is judged to have the best policies (or thought to be the most competent) on the salient issues.

Before 1997, opinion polls showed Labour to be popular on a number of salient social policy issues (including jobs, health and education). This popularity, however, was outweighed by the feeling of many voters that the Labour Party was not competent to handle the economy properly.

By the time of the 1997 general election, things had changed. Labour seemed to be far more in tune with the views of the electorate than were the Conservatives. The issues which Labour chose to highlight during their campaign (health, law and order, unemployment and pensions) were also those that most concerned the voters. The Conservatives, on the other hand, were out of touch with the voters. They emphasised issues (such as trade unions and devolution) which were not considered important by voters.

Box 6.8 on page 101 shows the issues cited by voters as important in the run-up to the general election of 2001. They are quite similar to those found in the same sort of exercise carried out at the 1997 election. This could be one reason why the election outcomes were very much the same in terms of the extent of Labour's victory.

Box 6.8 Votes for the two main parties

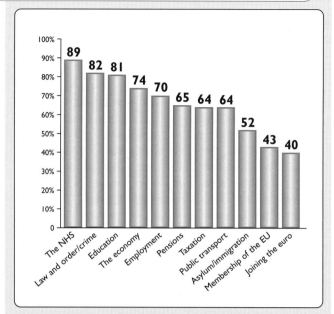

This chart shows the percentage of voters who said that particular issues were important in deciding how to vote.
Adapted from Dorey 2002.

Box 6.8 shows that the National Health Service and education, traditionally seen as 'Labour issues', rated very highly in terms of voter saliency in 2001. Other issues which at pre-1997 elections had been high on the list of voter concerns - law and order, the economy and taxation - still featured at the 2001 election. But, more significantly, they were not now seen as 'Conservative issues':

'Voters were concerned about crime and social disorder, but they no longer assumed that only the Conservatives had the answers.' (Dorey 2002, p.24)

While Labour seemed to benefit from voters' issue priorities at the 2001 election, the Conservatives did not. Two of the main policy areas on which the Tories concentrated in their campaign (Europe and asylum seekers) were low on voters' saliency list (see Box 6.8). Dorey argues that, to some extent, the Conservatives were restricted in their selection of campaign issues because Labour had already stolen policies that had, at one time, been seen as Conservative vote-winners - such as privatisation, tight control of public expenditure and low rates of income tax (Dorey 2002, p.3).

On the other hand, by promising a referendum some time after the election on the issue of Britain joining the single European currency, Labour managed successfully to sidestep the one issue which could have caused it some difficulty.

Although the official Conservative policy on the euro was supported by 70% of the public, voters did not regard it as a salient issue for the 2001 election. In any case, for an issue to cause large numbers of voters to change from one party to another, voters have to see clear differences between the parties on the issue. Yet, it was found that:

'Extraordinarily...at the end of the campaign after heavy media coverage of the [euro] issue, a majority of Conservative voters still did not recognise the official Conservative line.' (Butler & Kavanagh 2002, p.246)

Problems with the issue voting model

There are four main problems with the issue voting model.

First, it is difficult to disentangle the exact links between particular issues and voting behaviour. For example:

'Does the voter pick the party because of its policies or choose the policy positions because they are favoured by the party he or she supports?' (Benyon & Denver 1990, p.93)

Second, it is doubtful if voters normally decide their vote on a single issue, even if it is seen as a salient one, though there are occasional exceptions to this at a local level - see Item A in Activity 6.4 below for an example.

Third, even though certain issues may be of particular concern to voters, their final voting decisions are likely to be filtered through a wider set of values and their overall perception of what the parties stand for.

'Voting is not simply an instrumental act ("what's good for me?"). It is also often in part expressive ("how do I feel about voting for this party?").' (Butler & Kavanagh 2002, p.247)

Finally, the issue voting model ignores the way in which the choices confronting voters are limited or manipulated by the mass media - see Box 6.9. Media effects can produce contradictory opinions within the same voter. If this occurs, then the vote itself may not be the outcome of careful, rationally thought out decision-making.

Box 6.9 Issue voting and the media

'The issue voting model ignores how the media can manipulate voter choice.'

6.17 Perceptions of party competence

Some political scientists link issue voting to a further element of the rational choice model of voting - voter perceptions of competence. The relevant question here is:

To what extent do people cast their vote on how competent they judge the parties to be?

The answer to this question depends on how voters evaluate two factors:

- the past performance of the parties (the retrospective model)
- parties' likely future performance (the prospective model).

The prospective model

According to the prospective model, people vote for the party which they judge most likely to raise (or at least to protect) their standard of living. For some voters, this judgement depends not just on how they consider their own personal economic well-being. It also depends on a wider perception of the competence of a party to manage the economy in general.

The prospective model fits with what political commentator Stuart Hall has called 'the sociology of aspirations' (Hall 1992). According to this theory, the electorate thinks in terms of images rather than policies. And it is through these images that voters make judgements about how well each party might, in future, be able to meet the economic goals to which they aspire. If a party manages to project the image of economic competence, this theory suggests, then it will attract votes regardless of the existing economic circumstances.

There is also a reverse side to the prospective model. Not only do voters choose parties because they believe they will be competent in the future, they also reject parties because they believe they will be incompetent in the future. The change in fortune of the Labour Party in the 1990s provides an example of how both sides of the prospective model may come into play.

At the time of the 1992 general election, the economy was in recession. To deflect criticisms of its economic record, the Conservative government mounted a relentless attack on Labour's taxation plans, making it difficult for Labour to shake off its image as the party of high taxation. This strategy was adopted on the grounds that people tend to calculate how much they will be paying in tax not so much on their current earnings, but on the income they hope to earn in the near future. The strategy worked; the Conservatives won the election. Significantly, polls showed that, during the campaign, voters judged the Conservatives more competent (or, at least, less incompetent) to manage the economy than Labour.

By the time of the 1997 election, however, perceptions of competence had changed considerably. The Conservatives were no longer perceived by many voters to be competent and Labour had managed to banish the 'fear factor' which the Conservatives had exploited so skilfully in 1992. A key factor in this turnaround was thought to be an event which came to be known as 'Black Wednesday' - see Box 6.10.

Box 6.10 Black Wednesday

Norman Lamont, Chancellor of the Exchequer at the time of Black Wednesday.

In September 1992, the pound was forced out of the European Union's exchange rate mechanism. Almost overnight the Conservatives' reputation as a strong, competent government that knew how to run the economy and defend Britain's interests abroad was destroyed. As a result, the Conservatives' opinion poll ratings slumped by more than 10 points within a matter of weeks, and they never recovered. The impressions of incompetence and division caused by Black Wednesday were then simply reinforced by subsequent tax rises, sleaze and squabbling over Europe.

Source: Curtice 1997.

The retrospective model

Whereas the prospective model examines how forecasts of party performance affect voting behaviour, the retrospective model focuses on voters' perceptions of the parties' past records. The retrospective model, therefore, fits more closely into a purely rational choice model since voters can base their decisions on concrete evidence (especially on how well or badly the party in power has managed the economy).

The example of the turnaround in voter perceptions during the 1990s, described above, showed that, by the time of the 1997 election, the Conservative Party had lost its reputation for economic competence. Although the economy was in better shape than it had been five years earlier, a major opinion poll indicated that three-quarters of voters believed that their standard of living was either worse or no better than it had been in 1992. The political commentator Peter Kellner suggested that people may have understood the phrase 'standard of living' to mean more than just their level of earnings:

> '"Standard of living" embraces not just the purse or wallet but a wider sense of the quality of life, including the quality of the health and education services, public transport and so on...Surveys have shown that large majorities of people feel that the public services have deteriorated since 1992.' (Kellner 1997, p.112)

At the time of the 1997 general election, therefore, the record of the Conservative government counted against it, while Labour's new image had reduced any lingering doubts about the record of previous Labour governments.

Perceptions of competence at the 2001 election

In 2001, Labour entered the election campaign, having been the party of government for the previous four years. Voters could therefore judge the party on its record in office as well as its likely future competence. An analysis of relevant polling questions at the 2001 general election reveals that Labour fared measurably better than the Conservatives on both prospective and retrospective voter evaluations over a range of issues. Crucially, as Box 6.11 shows, Labour was trusted significantly more than the Conservatives on the issue of economic competence.

Box 6.11 Response to questions about which party could be most trusted to:

	Con (%)	Lab (%)	LibDem (%)
Run the NHS most efficiently?	22	41	16
Run state schools most effectively?	23	42	17
Manage the economy?	29	49	8
Tackle crime?	32	34	11
Protect Britain's interests in the EU?	35	36	11
Provide the best transport policies?	12	32	19

Source: Dorey 2002.

6.18 Leadership and personality

Between 1945 and the end of 2003, the Conservative Party chose ten Leaders and Labour eight, an average of a new Leader every six or seven years. Although some Party Leaders retained their position for considerably longer than the average (notably Margaret Thatcher for 15 years and Harold Wilson for 11), in general they changed fairly frequently. Consequently, voter perceptions of the personality or competence of a Party Leader can be classed as a short-term factor in accounting for voting behaviour. If developments such as a change in the class structure and party dealignment have led to long-term factors becoming less important in affecting voting behaviour, then perceptions of party leadership may have come to play a greater role in party choice at election times.

Although party leadership has long been recognised as a possible factor affecting voting behaviour, it can be argued that its potential influence has grown as the extent and style of media coverage of election campaigns has changed. Media attention on personalities, rather than policies, is not new. But, in elections from the mid-1970s onwards, the media has focused attention on the Party Leaders much more than previously.

Leadership and the 1997 election

In 1997, the overall public opinion poll ratings closely reflected the division of the vote between the parties at the election itself (Kellner 1997, p.117). Tony Blair's rating, however, was considerably higher than Neil Kinnock's had been in 1992 when he was Labour Leader, and this may have given a significant boost to Labour's performance:

'There is no doubt that his relative youth, dynamism, manner and televisual qualities enabled Blair to transform the negative image of the Labour leadership...into something more popular. This, together with [the Conservative] John Major's...image as a weak leader, meant that the deficit experienced by Kinnock in relation to Major in 1992 was transformed into a significant credit by Blair in 1997...The importance of this turnaround should not be underestimated.' (Dobson 1998, p.9)

Leadership and the 2001 election

During his first term as Prime Minister, the assessments of Tony Blair's personality and style of leadership were somewhat contradictory. On the one hand, he was described as weak and indecisive, while on the other, he was criticised for being arrogant and autocratic. He nonetheless 'remained the most popular Party Leader...by a wide margin' (Dorey 2002, p.28) - see Box 6.12.

Box 6.12 Who is the best Party Leader?

Best Leader	1992	1997	2001	Change 1992-2001
Conservative	40	21	13	- 27
Labour	30	34	47	+17
Liberal Democrats	9	8	5	- 4

This table shows which of the Leaders of the three main parties were chosen as 'the best' between 1992 and 2001.

Source: MORI (Butler & Kavanagh 2002, p.243).

A poll published a few days before the 2001 election showed that, when asked 'Who do you think would make the best Prime Minister?', 54% chose Blair and only 18% chose William Hague the then Leader of the Conservative Party (*Observer*/ICM, 3 June 2001). Hague fared slightly better in another poll which asked people to rate how well he was doing his job. But, while 25% chose 'good' or 'excellent', this was still a long way behind Blair's 56% rating (Butler & Kavanagh 2002, p.241). In general, the Conservative Leader lacked credibility with the electorate. According to Dorey (2002, p.29), Hague's popularity rating rarely rose above 20%.

These findings and observations, however, raise further questions.

First, if the personalities of Party Leaders do have some effect on party choice, is the impact positive or negative? In other words, do voters tend to vote for parties whose Leaders they like most or dislike least?

Second, can voters' attitudes towards Party Leaders be separated successfully from their views of the parties in general?

It is difficult to answer these questions because it is not possible to separate voters' attitudes towards Party Leaders from a whole range of other variables such as the images of the parties, perceptions of party competence and voter preference on particular issues and policies. Furthermore, as with many of the other possible factors influencing voting behaviour, it is also important to consider how such questions are presented through the mass media (see Sections 6.19 to 6.24 below).

Main points Sections 6.15 - 6.18

- **The rational choice model suggests that parties cannot rely simply on loyalty or social factors to win elections. It emphasises the importance of instrumental, rather than emotional, voting.**
- **The issue voting model suggests that voters' analysis of issues affects their voting behaviour. It is difficult, however, to find an exact link.**

- **The prospective model suggests that people vote for the party which they judge most likely to protect or raise their standard of living. The retrospective model focuses on voters' perceptions of the parties' past records.**
- **Voter perceptions of Party Leaders may have some effect on party choice, but it is difficult to discover the extent of the connection.**

Activity 6.4 *The rational choice model*

Item A **The Wyre Forest constituency at the 2001 general election**

Richard Taylor MP

Source: Dorey 2002.

In Wyre Forest, a retired consultant, Richard Taylor, stood in the 2001 general election as the Kidderminster Hospital and Health Concern candidate, his main concern being to highlight local anxiety and anger over the closure of Kidderminster Hospital's Accident and Emergency Unit. Such was the local concern that Taylor transformed a Labour majority of 6,946 into a majority of 17,630, having polled more than 28,000 votes. For an independent candidate to poll so many votes and defeat the sitting MP is nothing short of phenomenal. His success confirmed opinion poll evidence concerning issue saliency and the priority which voters ascribed to the NHS.

Item B **Voters' overall 'retrospective' and 'prospective' judgements, 2001**

Q. Do you think the government's policies have made things...?:		Q. If Labour wins, do you think their policies will make things...?:		Q. If the Conservatives win, do you think their policies will make things...?:	
A lot better	9%	A little better	48%	A little better	34%
A little better	56%	A lot better	12%	A lot better	6%
No difference	20%	No difference	13%	No difference	13%
A little worse	16%	A little worse	16%	A little worse	24%
A lot worse	26%	A lot worse	11%	A lot worse	23%

Source: Dorey 2002, p.27.

Questions

1. a) With the help of Item A, explain the importance of 'issue saliency' to the issue voting model.

   b) In what ways should the 2001 election outcome in the Wyre Forest constituency be seen as exceptional?

2. What do Items A and B tell us about the nature of the 2001 general election campaign?

3. a) From Item B, identify which parts of the table refer to the 'prospective' model and which to the 'retrospective' model.

   b) Explain how the data in Item B can be used to suggest that Labour fared better than the Conservatives in terms of voter perceptions of party competence during the 2001 general election campaign.

6.19 The dominant ideology model - an overview

The central claim of the dominant ideology model is that powerful groups in society (collectively the 'Establishment') influence the attitudes and behaviour (including the voting behaviour) of the public. This influence is exerted by the control that these groups exercise over and through the key institutions of society such as the mass media, the government, business interests, political parties and political leaders.

Together, these institutions are structured in such a way that they provide an advantage to mainstream (Establishment) political parties (which, in turn, serve or support the interests of the dominant groups in society). Supporters of the dominant ideology model have paid particular attention to the role of the mass media, especially the press and broadcasting, in influencing voting behaviour. It is through the mass media, according to this model, that groups attempt to set the political agenda and influence public opinion.

6.20 The party bias of the press

Most adults in Britain read a national daily and a Sunday newspaper. Until the mid-1990s, the vast majority of these newspapers actively supported the Conservative Party and urged their readers, on election days, to vote Conservative.

The tabloid newspapers, in particular, tend to be highly partisan. At the 1992 general election, most of the tabloids openly campaigned for the Conservatives. The *Sun* even boasted that it was single-handedly responsible for that party's victory. According to one study (Linton 1996), at that election, 70% of the press favoured the Conservatives compared to 27% preferring Labour. Linton also noticed that the Labour Party had never won an election when its press share was more than 18% behind the Conservatives.

By the time of the 1997 general election campaign, however, the position had changed considerably. By then, 11 national newspapers (dailies and Sundays) came out in support of Labour, at least three more than for the Conservatives. And the most notable shift in party allegiance came from the *Sun*. During the election campaign, the paper regularly gave the Labour Leader, Tony Blair, space 'for his unedited views'. Blair later thanked the *Sun* for 'its magnificent support' which 'really did make the difference' (Scammell & Harrop 1997, pp.160, 183). Earlier speculation - that Blair and Murdoch (owner of the *Sun*) had arranged a deal on cross-media ownership policy - received little in the way of renewed comment.

As in 1997, the Labour Party again had the support of a significant part of the press at the time of the 2001 general election. Indeed, in 2001, this support had reached record levels including, for the first time, endorsements from the *Times* and *Daily Express*. Although most newspapers supported Labour, much of the support was lukewarm or had 'conditions' attached to it. There was a notable increase in negative stories about Labour compared to 1997 and press coverage in the early stages of the campaign was not favourable to the party. Despite Labour's efforts to gain and keep as many newspapers as possible on its side, it seems

that the switch to Labour of some newspapers may not necessarily have been a permanent one. As one commentary concludes:

'Labour had disarmed and contained the press but not converted it.' (Scammell & Harrop 2002, p.156)

It should also be noted that press support for Labour in 2001 may have reflected the fact that the outcome of the election was seen as a foregone conclusion. The increasingly consumer-oriented press did not want to be seen to be on the losing side.

Yet, if many of the newspapers offered less than wholehearted support for Labour in 2001, the picture for the Conservative Party was far worse. Only two of the national dailies supported the party - the *Daily Telegraph* and the *Daily Mail*. And, not only did the *Mail* noticeably limit its front-page coverage of the election campaign (Scammell & Harrop 2002, p.163), it could not bring itself to endorse William Hague (the then Conservative Leader) as a possible future Prime Minister (MacArthur 2001, p.47).

6.21 Broadcasting

Unlike the press, news and current affairs broadcasts on television and radio are supposed to be neutral on party political matters. They are under legal obligations to be so. Broadcasters go to great lengths at election times to attempt an almost arithmetic balance in their coverage of the three main parties. For the 2001 general election campaign, however, revised guidelines allowed for this to be achieved on a weekly, rather than a daily, basis (Harrison 2002, p.133).

Since most voters gain most of their political information from television rather than from newspapers, it could be argued that such a balance is a political necessity because:

'Television (in contrast to the press) is commonly found to be the most important and trusted source of political information for the public.' (Gavin & Sanders 1997, p.128)

Can balance really be achieved?

As Box 6.13 shows, balance does not necessarily result in complete equality of air time for the main parties. At the 2001 general election, Labour had, marginally, the larger share, with the Liberal Democrats significantly behind.

Box 6.13 Parties' share of new coverage at the 2001 general election

	Con %	Lab %	LibDem %	Others %
BBC1	36.1	35.0	19.9	9.2
ITV	34.7	36.5	24.3	4.5
Channel 4	33.9	36.1	19.6	10.5
Channel 5	26.2	36.1	28.1	9.6
Radio 4	32.2	37.0	20.9	9.9
All 2001	34.3	36.1	21.1	8.6
All 1997	35.3	31.3	25.0	8.4

Source: Harrison 2002, p.134.

In any case, whether a genuine balance could ever really be achieved is debatable. One argument is that the attempt to be balanced restricts the extent and nature of election coverage. Another is that newspapers play a significant role in setting the agenda for television news coverage. The argument goes as follows. If most of the newspapers concentrate on issues which are more favourable to one party rather than another and ignore those less favourable to that party, then television might well reflect this in its coverage of the issues. Different studies suggest that the Conservatives and Labour have each benefited from this bias but at different elections.

Government advantage?

The apparent neutrality of radio and television broadcasting might also conceal another factor contributing to what Miller and his colleagues described as 'a massive bias towards the government' (Miller et al. 1990, p.57). Although the parties might well receive equal campaign coverage, the party in power can get a good deal of additional attention through the reporting of the activities and statements of the government of the day.

This seeming advantage can, of course, rebound on a governing party if news reports focus on government failures and problems as well as any successes. So, for example, although the Conservative Party benefited from this extra exposure at the 1992 election, it suffered from it in 1997 because of the prominent portrayal on television of the party's internal divisions over its European policies.

Perhaps with this in mind, in 2001 the Labour Party (which was fighting the election as the governing party) was not above attempting to put considerable pressure on the broadcasting media - see below.

6.22 *Does bias matter?*

It is one thing to show that the mass media is biased. It is quite another to show that this bias does, in fact, influence voters. The traditional view is that, while newspapers probably do not actually convert many people from one party to another, they may have a reinforcing effect on voting behaviour. At most, they play a role in persuading the previously uncommitted to vote for a particular party.

Nevertheless, in a period of party dealignment and electoral volatility (see Section 6.13 above), this role may be a growing one. Since dealignment means that there are fewer committed voters, more voters should be open to persuasion and there should, therefore, be more scope for media influence.

The problem facing all social scientists in trying to assess the degree of media influence on any aspect of behaviour, however, is how to isolate the effects of all the other possible variables - family, class, age and a whole range of other factors. Attempts to do this, though (for example, Miller 1991), have suggested that newspapers do exert some influence on the outcome of elections.

Short-term and long-term effects of bias

When Neil Kinnock resigned as Labour Leader following his party's defeat at the 1992 general election, he blamed the result on the anti-Labour bias, during the campaign, of the Conservative-dominated tabloid newspapers. Although short-term effects of media bias cannot be ruled out, the evidence for Kinnock's claim is ambiguous.

The conventional view that the media has limited influence, however, is challenged more strongly by studies that take a longer-term view. The traditional claim was that people's choice of newspaper depends on their political preference rather than the other way round and so newspapers reinforce rather than convert. But, the continual reinforcement over a long period may well be significant. The long-term drip by drip effect of the media may be more important than any short-term campaign or story run by a newspaper (see Box 6.14). A study by Miller attempted to look beyond the short-term effects of newspaper coverage during election campaigns by interviewing the same people on a number of occasions over a 12-month period in the run-up to an election (Miller 1991). The results of this survey indicated that newspapers do influence their readers over the long term.

At the 2001 general election, there is little evidence that the media had much direct or short-term influence on the people's voting behaviour. From the outset, there was not much doubt about the outcome of the election in terms of the eventual winner. Looking at media influence over the longer term, however, political scientists are still divided about the extent to which it reinforces people's outlooks or determines the way they vote.

Box 6.14 The constant drip drip drip of the media

'The long-term drip by drip effect of the media may be important in influencing voting behaviour.'

6.23 *The media effect on parties*

Perhaps more significant in recent years is the role played by the media in influencing the positions taken by the parties themselves. There is evidence to suggest that the Labour leadership repositioned itself, in part at least, to win the support of sections of the press. It has been argued that, in the 1990s, a Conservative-inclined press forced the Labour Party to be extra cautious and to abandon its socialist policies in order to become re-electable. According to this view, the changes in organisation, image and policies that accompanied the emergence of New Labour was a direct reaction to the activities of a right-wing media.

The manipulation of news

The relationship between the media and the political parties is not a one-way affair. All political parties attempt to manipulate the ways in which political affairs are reported and presented in the media. When most of the press supported the Conservative Party, that party found the process of manipulation easier to manage (at least, as far as newspapers were concerned). There was evidence, for example, of close collaboration at election times between leading Conservatives and the editors of some major newspapers.

During the 1997 election campaign, however, it was the Labour Party which appeared to be more successful in using such tactics. A combination of sophisticated organisation, skilful 'spin-doctoring' and a much more sympathetic press gave a clear advantage to Labour at that election.

By 2001, however, Labour had been in government for four years and felt that it could not expect the same degree of sympathy at the forthcoming general election. Its strategy at the 2001 election was, therefore, somewhat different. As Box 6.15 shows, Labour's press office tried hard to influence the way in which broadcast journalists reported their news stories. It wanted to ensure that its own slant or bias was put over and was prepared to push for this aggressively.

6.24 *Media manipulation and the dominant ideology model*

Supporters of the dominant ideology model do not view some of the activities described above merely as isolated attempts to secure support for or against particular policies. They see it as part of a wider network of control through which powerful groups, with the aid of the mass media, are able to influence the attitudes and behaviour of the public.

For example, rising economic optimism was thought to have been a significant factor in maintaining the Conservative Party in power throughout the 1980s. This could be explained using the rational choice model - economic optimism increased and those who were optimistic voted Conservative. But why did voters become optimistic? One explanation, using the dominant ideology model, is that Conservative governments successfully managed to manipulate the media and the economy. Before the 1987 election, for instance, Miller (1990) provides evidence to suggest that the government adjusted calculations of economic statistics, paid for political advertising out of public funds, pressurised the BBC in an attempt to manage and

Box 6.15 'On message'

During the 2001 general election campaign New Labour was determined that those responsible for coverage of political events should be 'on message'. The government would decide what the 'message' was, and everyone would follow it. The political agenda and its interpretation would then follow the New Labour line. Alastair Campbell, the Prime Minister's Press Secretary, and the other New Labour spin doctors put journalists - especially broadcast journalists - and news executives under a great deal of pressure. They would explain that a particular story should be treated in a certain way and complained if it was not. The political editor of the *Today* programme received almost daily complaints from Campbell or other Labour spin doctors. Reporters experienced most of the abuse. Where Bernard Ingham (Conservative Press Secretary during the Thatcher era) used the language of 'bunkum and balderdash', Campbell talked of 'bollocks' and 'crap'. Senior broadcasters, such as *Newsnight*'s Jeremy Paxman and the foreign correspondent John Simpson, were rubbished. BBC managers received long letters of complaint. 'The objective', one spin doctor was reported as saying, 'is to grind the BBC down, to shake journalists' confidence, implanting a self-censor in every BBC brain.'

Source: Seymore-Ure 2002, pp.124-26.

manipulate the news and manipulated the 'real economy' to stimulate a consumer boom in time for the election.

In the 1980s and 1990s, the dominant ideology model was sometimes employed to explain the apparent invincibility of the Conservatives. But the change to a Labour government in 1997 does not necessarily affect the validity of the model. It can be argued that the change in government was due less to a fundamental shift in the attitudes and behaviour of the voting public and more to shifts within the main parties themselves. In other words, supporters of the dominant ideology model would argue that it has been the Labour Party that has changed its politics, rather than the *Sun*.

In addition, since its return to power and, especially during the run-up to the 2001 general election, Labour has been accused of employing at least some of the manipulative tactics which Miller accused the Conservative Party of using at the 1987 election. These included using government funds to promote the party's pre-election campaign (Fisher 2001, p.128) and placing the BBC under undue pressure to try to manage the presentation of news (see Box 6.15 above).

Main points Sections 6.19 - 6.24

- **The central claim of the dominant ideology model is that powerful groups in society influence voting behaviour. A key role is played by the mass media through which attempts are made to set the political agenda and influence public opinion.**
- **Until the mid-1990s, the vast majority of these newspapers actively supported the Conservative Party. Since then, however, the majority have supported Labour.**
- **The media may have influenced parties to change their policies and image. But the relationship is not all one-way. Parties also attempt to manipulate the media.**

Activity 6.5 *The dominant ideology model*

Item A The press and the 2001 general election

Newspaper	Circulation (000s)		Preferred winner	
	2001	1997	2001	1997
Dailies				
Sun	3,288	3,935	Lab	Lab
Daily Mail	2,337	2,127	Con	Con
Mirror	2,056	2,390	Lab	Lab
Daily Telegraph	989	1,126	Con	Con
Express	929	1,208	Lab	Con
Times	667	772	Lab	Eurosceptic
Daily Star	585	660	Lab	Lab
Guardian	362	402	Lab	Lab
Independent	197	256	Not Con	Lab
Financial Times	176	304	Lab	Lab
Sundays				
News of the World	3,675	4,365	Lab	Lab
Mail on Sunday	2,238	2,112	Con	Con
Sunday Mirror	1,761	2,238	Lab	Lab
Sunday People	1,277	1,978	Lab	Lab
Sunday Times	1,206	1,310	Lab	Con
Sunday Express	870	1,159	Lab	Con
Sunday Telegraph	767	909	Con	Con
Observer	408	454	Lab	Lab
Independent on Sunday	211	276	Lab	Lab
Sunday Business	53	-	Lab	-

This table shows that, as in 1997, the Labour Party had the support of a significant section of the press at the time of the 2001 general election.

Source: Seymore-Ure 1997, MacArthur 2001 and Scammell & Harrop 2002.

Item B Did the press set the agenda in the 2001?

Topic	Front-page lead stories		Editorials	
	Number	%	Number	%
European Union	21	18	33	12
Party strategies/prospects	16	14	18	7
Prescott (punch)	16	14	11	4
Opinion polls	11	9	3	1
Taxation/public spending	7	6	14	5
Public services	6	5	12	4
Asylum/race	5	4	21	8
Exhortation to vote/advice on voting	4	3	17	6
Health	3	2	18	7
Party Leaders	3	2	15	6
Manifestos	2	2	14	5
Thatcher	-	-	6	2
Northern Ireland	-	-	6	2
Tactical voting/strong opposition needed	-	-	5	2
Constitutional reforms	-	-	5	2
Other	24	20	73	27
Total	118	99	271	100

This table shows the issues that the press focused on during the 2001 general election campaign.

The 1997 general election was the first occasion when Labour enjoyed the majority support of the national daily press in a general election. As far as the political history of the press is concerned, this was an historic moment every bit as significant as the size of Labour's majority.

Source: MacArthur 2001, Scammell & Harrop 2002 and Seymore-Ure 1997.

Questions

1. a) How does the dominant ideology model differ from the other models described in this unit?

   b) Explain why the work of the mass media is an important component in the dominant ideology model.

2. To what extent do the mass media influence the outcome of general elections? Use Items A and B in your answer.

3. How might a political scientist use Items A and B as evidence to support the view that the dominant ideology model helps us to understand why people voted as they did in 2001?

6.25 The voting context model - an overview

Miller (1990) uses the term 'voting context' to refer to voters' perceptions about the range of options available to them. These options may be influenced by what the voter perceives to be the purpose of the election - whether it is a 'first order' election (general election) or a 'second order' election (local, regional, European election or by-election). Unit 5, Section 5.1 defines these terms in more detail.

By emphasising the context, Miller suggests that voting is not always limited to a straightforward expression of personal preference. Voters are also weighing up the likely consequences of their vote.

6.26 Turnout and abstention

Turnout is an important factor in explaining voting behaviour since it is, in a sense, a measure of abstention (see Box 6.16 on page 109). The number of people turning out to vote at an election is expressed as a percentage of those whose names appear on the electoral register. Although it is a legal requirement for all people of or near voting age to be registered, not everyone appears on the register - and the number of those not appearing is believed to be increasing. A study at the time of the 1997 general election suggested that as many as 6 million people were not registered to vote (*Guardian*, 24 June 1998).

Box 6.16 Active and passive abstention

Abstainers
Abstainers are people who do not cast their vote in elections. They can be divided into two groups.

1. Passive abstainers
Passive abstainers are sometimes called 'accidental', 'negative' or 'apathetic' non-voters. They have no or very little interest in politics.

2. Active abstainers
Active abstainers refuse to vote on principle or as a protest. They may disagree with the electoral system (or with the entire political system) or they may simply not be attracted to any of the parties or candidates standing in their constituency.

Turnout trends

Turnout rates at UK general elections remained fairly consistent between 1966 and 1997. The level of 73-75% in the 1980s was lower than that in the early 1950s (84% in 1950 and 82.5% in 1951), but the elections in 1950 and 1951 can be seen as a high point. The average turnout between 1922 and 1945 was 74%.

Turnout at the 1992 general election was 77.7%. This was 2.4% up on the 1987 general election and was also the highest since 1974. Butler & Kavanagh (1992) suggest that this was because the 1992 general election was the first election since 1974 whose outcome, according to the opinion polls, was in doubt. Turnout in 1997, however, dropped to 71.4%, the lowest since 1935.

In 2001, turnout was even lower than it had been in 1997. At 59.4%, it was the lowest turnout for 83 years - since 1918 (see Box 6.17). In 1918, however:

'There was much post-war confusion. The electorate had jumped from the 8 million of 1910 to 21 million. Women had the [vote] for the first time. The register was compiled in a new way by unpractised hands and there was some administrative chaos over the forces' vote.' (Butler & Kavanagh 2002, p.259)

Obviously, the explanation for the low turnout in 2001 is very different.

Reasons for low turnout in 2001

Curtice and Steed (2002, pp.307-10) examine various possible reasons for the dramatic fall in turnout in 2001. These explanations fall into three categories:

- long-term changes such as a decline in party identification
- shorter-term changes
- dissatisfaction among Labour supporters.

Box 6.17 The 2001 general election - key turnout statistics

- 59.4% was the lowest recorded turnout since 1918
- Lowest turnout: 34.1% - Liverpool Riverside
- Highest turnout in UK: 80.5% - Ulster Mid
- Highest turnout in Great Britain: 72.3% - Winchester
- Number of constituencies where turnout was under 50% - 68 (none in 1997)
- Fall in turnout, from 1997, was fairly uniform across every region in UK (except for Northern Ireland) at between 11.6% and 13.1% (in Northern Ireland turnout increased by 0.6%)
- A far higher proportion of the electorate abstained (41%) than voted for the winning party (25%)
- Turnout was twice as high among older voters (65 and over) than it was among younger voters (18-24) - 79% to 38%.

1. Long-term changes

As might be expected, the stronger that people identify with a party, the more likely they are to vote. For some writers, the decline in party identification that has occurred since the early 1970s (see Section 6.13 above) has produced an electorate that is less motivated, more disillusioned and less trustful of politics and politicians. Young people and the less well-educated are particularly likely not to vote. Curtice and Steed claim that in 2001 there was some evidence of this:

'To some degree…turnout fell least in those constituencies with a relatively old age profile and a relatively well-educated population.' (Curtice & Steed 2002, p.307)

The variations, however, are not great and there is some doubt about whether a lack of trust can account for such a large drop in turnout between 1997 and 2001 (Curtice 2001).

Allegations of sleaze, dishonesty and insincerity may well have led to politicians being held in lower regard than ever before (Dorey 2002, p.12). But these allegations have been around for some time. On their own, they cannot account for the steep fall in turnout in 2001.

2. Shorter-term changes

It has been argued that turnout in 2001 was low because, first, many people could see very little difference between the main parties and, second, the result of the election was never in doubt.

One ICM poll carried out shortly before the election found that 57% of the electorate agreed (39% disagreed) with the statement: 'It won't make much difference to my daily life who wins the coming election' (Kellner 2001b). Another found that of those 'unlikely to vote', 77% did not mind which party won (Butler & Kavanagh 2002, p.258). The fact that the turnout in Northern Ireland increased, rather than fell, may be significant to this line of reasoning. Here, there were clear differences between the parties and the election was seen to matter (for many unionist voters it was seen as a referendum on the future of the Good Friday Agreement).

On its own, however, the perceived absence of significant differences between the main parties in Britain cannot satisfactorily account for the drastic fall in turnout. Turnout was considerably higher during the 'post-war consensus' period (ie between 1945 and 1979) when there was thought to be little difference between the Conservative Party and Labour Party (Dorey 2002, p.12).

There is also little evidence to support the argument that turnout was low because the result of the election was a foregone conclusion. It is true that Labour was well ahead in the opinion polls at the start of the campaign and remained so throughout. As a result, some people may well have thought that there was little point in bothering to vote. But opinion polls presented a similar picture in 1997 when turnout was 12% higher. It has also been noticed that there were elections in the 1950s and 1980s when the outcome was not in doubt but at which voters turned out in much higher numbers than in 2001 (Cohen 2001) - see Box 6.18. After reviewing the evidence, Curtice concludes:

'The perception that the election was a one-horse race was certainly not the main reason why people were reluctant to go to the polls.' (Curtice 2001)

Box 6.18 Turnout in UK general elections since 1945

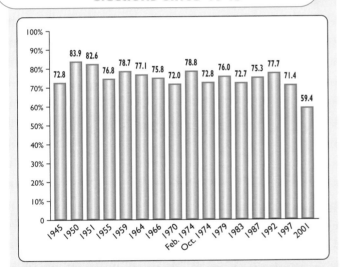

This chart shows the percentage of the electorate who voted in the general elections held between 1945 and 2001.

Source: Jones 2003.

3. Dissatisfaction among Labour supporters

One theory is that many Labour supporters, especially those in the older industrial 'heartlands', were alienated by New Labour's appeal to the middle classes and its courting of Big Business. If this was so, the drop in turnout would need to be greatest in those constituencies where the Labour vote had previously been highest. And there is some evidence to support this. Electors were particularly likely to stay at home in Labour's safer seats. Of course, precisely because the drop in turnout was higher in Labour safe seats, this abstention did not translate into a corresponding loss of seats for Labour.

It should also be pointed out, however, that turnout in safe seats is normally lower than in marginals. Nevertheless, the

'alienated Labour supporter' argument looks strong when the evidence for the 2001 election shows that 96 of the 100 lowest turnout constituencies were safe Labour seats (Dorey 2002, p.19).

Falling turnouts not confined to UK

Whatever the reasons for the low turnout in 2001, it should be noted that the UK is not alone in experiencing a fall in the rates of turnout at elections. Similar trends are occurring elsewhere and some commentators have linked this to broader cultural changes in an increasingly individualistic and post-modern world.

6.27 Tactical voting

Tactical voting occurs when voters, rather than choosing their preferred party, vote instead for another party in order to prevent the party they least like from winning the seat. Tactical voting is known to have been particularly significant at by-elections for a long time. But, in recent years, it has become increasingly influential in helping to determine the outcome of other elections, too.

Butler & Kavanagh (1992) claim that tactical voting at the 1992 general election reduced the Conservative majority by half. The evidence suggested, in particular, anti-Conservative tactical voting by Liberal Democrat supporters.

Tactical voting was also seen to play a particularly important role in 1997. It helps to explain why, at that election, Labour and the Liberal Democrats won more seats than the percentage of the vote they won nationally would suggest they should have won:

'There appears to have been more anti-Conservative tactical voting than ever before. Labour's vote rose by more than the national average in those seats where it started off second to the Conservatives, while the Liberal Democrats' support fell by above the average. In contrast, the Liberal Democrats' vote usually rose against the national trend in those seats where they were best placed, while Labour's rose considerably less than the average.' (Butler & Kavanagh 1997, pp.251-52)

Tactical voting at the 2001 general election

During the run-up to the 2001 election, there was speculation that tactical voting would be substantially higher than at previous general elections. In the event, this was not the case. Where it did take place, however, it was once again the Conservatives who were more often than not the targets.

There is evidence that tactical voting (Labour supporters voting Liberal Democrat) probably helped the Liberal Democrats to defeat Conservative candidates in Ludlow, North Norfolk and Teignbridge. There were also other seats - notably Kingston & Surbiton - where narrow Liberal Democrat wins in 1997 were converted into substantial majorities for the party, strongly suggesting tactical voting (Dorey 2002, p.16).

In most other Conservative/Liberal Democrat marginals, however, Labour voters do not appear to have voted tactically in significant numbers (Denver 2001, p.84; Norris 2001, p.8). Tactical voting was, though, thought to be significant in helping Labour to win some crucial marginal seats.

The vote swap campaign

At the 2001 general election, the musician and political campaigner Billy Bragg (see Box 6.19) achieved a certain amount of national publicity for his 'vote swap' campaign. Bragg claimed that the object of the campaign was wider than just tactical voting, describing it as 'spontaneous electoral reform' and as a way of encouraging proportional representation 'by the back door'.

Box 6.19 Billy Bragg

Billy Bragg.

Bragg launched a website from Dorset in which he urged Labour and Liberal Democrat supporters to 'swap' votes. The idea was that Liberal Democrats would agree to vote Labour in one Dorset constituency, in return for Labour supporters switching to the Liberal Democrats in three neighbouring constituencies. The success of the campaign appears to have been mixed, however. The Liberal Democrats and Labour won one seat each, but the Conservatives held on to the other two (see Dorey 2002, p.16 and Ferguson 2001).

What makes tactical voting effective?

To be effective, tactical voting needs to be based on good information about likely voting support for the different parties in that constituency. This is not always readily available and decisions about whether or not to vote tactically may in some cases be made on the basis of the standing of the parties nationally - a poor guide to the standing of the parties locally.

Alternatively, voter perceptions about party support in their own constituency may be based on the results of recent local elections. These can also be misleading since constituency and local government boundaries often do not coincide, and voter turnout is normally considerably lower at local elections.

6.28 Protest voting

A protest vote is a negative vote. It is a vote against a policy or against the current direction of a government, rather than a vote for one of the opposition parties. Tactical voting can

be seen as a form of protest voting in that it is based on voters' dislikes rather than on what they like.

Protest voting is more common in by-elections and in local or Euro-elections than in general elections. Since 1979, especially, protest voting has produced some spectacular results. No matter how large the government majority at the previous general election, the majority can be eroded at a by-election.

For example, in September 2003 the Liberal Democrats overthrew a Labour majority of 13,047 in the Brent East by-election (see Box 6.20). The party's share of the vote went down from 63.2% at the 2001 general election to 33.8% - a clear sign that the voters there wanted to protest about the government's recent behaviour.

Box 6.20 Brent East in 2001 and 2003

General election, June 2001

Candidate	Party	Votes	%
Paul Daisley	Labour	18,325	63.2
David Gauke	Conservative	5,278	18.2
Nowsheen Bhatti	Lib Dem	3,065	10.6
Others (4)		2,324	8.0

Electorate 53,548
Turnout 65.87%
Majority 13,047 (45.0%)

By-election, 18 September 2003

Candidate	Party	Votes	%
Sarah Teather	Lib Dem	8,158	39.1
Robert Evans	Labour	7,040	33.8
Uma Fernandes	Conservative	3,368	16.2
Others (13)		2,286	11.0

Electorate 57,558
Turnout 36.23%
Majority   1,118 (5.36%)

Governments can normally afford not to be too worried by protest voting, however. It is often short-lived and voters typically revert to their usual preferences at the next general election. In the 1992 general election, for example, the Liberal Democrats did not retain any of the seats which they had won in by-elections during the course of the previous Parliament.

6.29 Electoral campaigns and events

It is difficult to measure exactly how much of an impact the election campaign makes on voting behaviour. What is clear, however, is that politicians and party workers from all parties behave as if election results are solely determined by the success or failure of the campaign.

One argument is that, if class and party dealignment has taken place, then fewer voters should have made firm voting choices before the election date is announced. So, more voters should be open to persuasion and, therefore, influenced by the election campaign. Such reasoning could help explain why the main parties are prepared to spend so much money and effort ensuring that their campaigns are run professionally.

General election campaigns 1992-2001

The 1992 general election campaign came under intense scrutiny because, although the opinion polls showed Labour and the Conservatives to be neck and neck, the Conservatives ended up with a 7.6% lead. The immediate reaction of some commentators was to suggest that the campaign was decisive. Others, however, believed that it was unlikely that Labour could have done much else during the campaign to give them victory.

In both 1997 and 2001, the Labour Party was so far ahead in the opinion polls that there was probably nothing at all that the Conservative Party could have done in its campaign to give it any chance of winning.

Most general elections are won or lost in the marginal seats. It appears that the parties have become increasingly aware of this when planning their campaign strategies (see Box 6.21).

Box 6.21 Targeting the marginals at the 2001 general election

During the 2001 general election campaign, more than ever before, the parties concentrated their campaign resources on target voters in marginal seats. As a result, the campaign by-passed much of the electorate. Modern campaigners pride themselves on running campaigns like scientific marketing operations. Winning sufficient numbers of target voters in the hundred or so key seats, which will decide the overall result, is more important than maximising total vote across the country. The stage has been reached where it appears that more and more effort is precisely targeted at less and less of the electorate.

Source: Butler & Kavanagh 2002.

The overall outcome of the 2001 general election showed very little change on 1997. There was a small swing to the Conservatives of 1.8% but it resulted in a net gain for the party of just one seat. Only 21 of the 641 seats in Great Britain changed hands (Butler & Kavanagh 2002, p.251).

Main points   Sections 6.25 - 6.29

- 'Voting context' refers to perceptions that voters have about the purpose of an election and the options available to them.
- Turnout is a measure of abstention. In the 2001 general election, turnout was the lowest since 1918. Falling turnout, however, is not confined to Britain.
- Rather than voting for their preferred party, tactical voters vote for another party to help prevent their least favoured party from winning. Tactical voting has made an impact in recent general elections.

- A protest vote is a negative vote against a policy or the government, rather than a positive vote for a party. It is more common in by-elections, local elections and Euro-elections.
- It is difficult to measure exactly how much impact election campaigns make on voting behaviour. It is likely, however, that they have more influence in marginal constituencies and at close-run, rather than at one-horse, elections.

Activity 6.6 The voting context model

Item A Turnout at the 2001 general election (1)

(i) Sex	%
Male	58
Female	59

(ii) Age	%
18-24	35
25-34	40
35-44	53
45-54	64
55-64	67
65+	76

(iii) Occupation, education, income

Occupation	%	Income	%
Professional & managerial	66	Lowest third	56
Other non-manual	61	Middle third	59
Manual	54	Top third	62
Educational qualification	%		
None	63		
CSE	53		
A-Level	61		
Degree	70		

Source: Denver 2002b using data from a BES cross-section survey.

Item B Turnout at the 2001 general election (2)

(i) 'Voters were particularly likely to stay at home in Labour's safe seats where the party also lost ground to the Liberal Democrats and candidates of the far left. The party may be unwise to assume that its more left-wing supporters will always feel that they have nowhere else to go.' (Curtice & Steed 2002, pp.332-33)

(ii) 'The obvious fact of the 2001 election is that all the mainstream parties have given up on the working class, and therefore the working class has given up on them. There has been malingering in all constituencies, but the working-class constituencies have seen the sharpest falls.' (Cohen 2001)

(iii) 'Half the electorate, and 40% of Labour supporters, agree that "Labour has become too right-wing in recent years". Among people who voted Labour in 1997, but who would not do so now, the figure rises to 60%.' (Kellner 2001b)

(iv) 'Labour, instead of being a working-class party of the centre-left, seems on course to become a "catch-all" party of the centre and may well have made some voters doubt whether it is worth voting at all.' (Curtice 2001)

Item C Changes in turnout at national elections since the 1950s

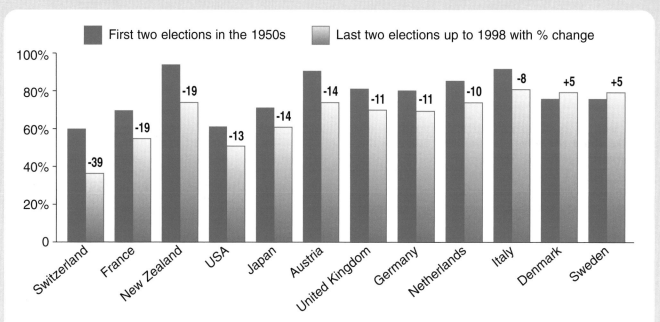

This chart compares turnout in a variety of countries. It shows the level of turnout in the early 1950s and late 1990s.

Questions

1. Using Items A and B and your own knowledge, explain why turnout was so low in the 2001 general election.
2. a) Which group of data in Item A shows the widest variation?
   b) How would you account for this?
3. a) What does Item C tell us about turnout rates?
   b) Suggest reasons for the trend shown in Item C.

6.30 *A general model of voting*

Each of the five models of voting behaviour discussed in this chapter provides an explanation of why people vote as they do. Political scientists disagree about which are the most useful or appropriate. However, not all the models necessarily compete with each other, nor do the different models necessarily claim to provide a full or exhaustive explanation of why people vote as they do. On the contrary, it is possible to find links between the different models and elements within them which complement each other.

Short-term and long-term factors

Some political scientists make a distinction between short-term and long-term influences on how people vote. Long-term influences include factors such as class, age, gender, occupation and region. Short-term factors may be those which determine the result of a single election - specific events, issues or policies, the style of Party Leaders or the attitude of the media during the campaign, for example. It has been suggested that if long-term factors predominate, then changes in voting patterns from one election to another are likely to be slight. If short-term factors predominate, electoral outcomes are likely to be less predictable and more volatile. Such a distinction, however, should not be exaggerated. Policies and issues do not occur in a political vacuum. They may well be related to longer-term party strategy or ideology. Similarly, changes in the class or age structure of the population may occur over time and result in significant alterations in the distribution of votes to the main parties. Also, the voting system is bound to affect voting behaviour. Euro-elections and elections to the Scottish Parliament and Northern Ireland and Welsh assemblies have a proportional element not found in the 'first-past-the-post' system used for Westminster and local elections.

A general model of voting

William Miller (1990) has constructed a general model of voting which summarises and synthesises the models of voting behaviour discussed earlier in this chapter. His model suggests some of the possible links between the different models. It also suggests a way in which political scientists might attempt a full explanation of why people vote as they do. This model is explored in Activity 6.7.

> ## Main points   Section 6.30
>
> - **Each of the five models provides an explanation of why people vote as they do. Political scientists disagree about which are the most useful.**
> - **But not all of the models necessarily compete with each other. Nor do each of the different models necessarily claim to provide a complete explanation of why people vote as they do. On the contrary, it is possible to find links between the different models and join the models together to make a single general model of voting behaviour. This model is shown in diagram form in Activity 6.7 below.**

Activity 6.7 The general model of voting

Item A A general model of voting

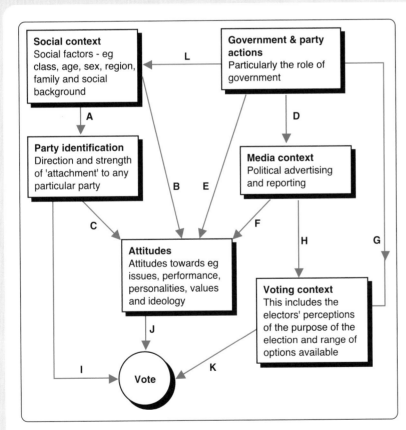

Arrow A says that voters' social and family backgrounds influence their sense of party identification. For example, working-class children with working-class, Labour-voting parents who grow up in a working-class neighbourhood are more likely to identify themselves with the Labour Party than those who come from a different background.

Arrows B and C suggest that voters' attitudes are influenced by their background and by any pre-existing sense of party identification.

Arrow D suggests that the content and style of the mass media is influenced by the actions of government and the parties.

The actions of government and parties influence voters' attitudes directly through personal experience (eg of inflation or unemployment) shown by Arrow E and indirectly through mass media reports (eg about defence policy) represented by Arrow F.

Voters' perceptions of party credibility are influenced by direct experience (eg the availability of candidates, whether they have been leafleted or canvassed) shown by Arrow G and by media reports (eg forecasts of the parties' chances) represented by Arrow H.

The voter's ultimate decision about which way to vote is based upon a mix of influences from party loyalty (Arrow I), political attitudes (Arrow J) and the voting context (Arrow K).

Governments can also influence social background (Arrow L). Obviously, nothing can be done to change family backgrounds but it is quite easy to change people's social circumstances - for example, by selling them council houses or privatising their employers.

Source: Miller 1990.

Item B Why a Labour voter switched to the Lib Dems

I have always voted Labour in the 30 years I have lived in Brent East. So why did I vote Lib Dem at the September 2003 by-election? Here are a few reasons. First, the illegal war in Iraq and all the lies from the government surrounding it. Second, the uncritical adulation for President Bush, whose policies make the world a more dangerous place politically, environmentally and economically. Third, the imposition of a mayor for London and the appalling treatment of Ken Livingstone as Labour's candidate. Fourth, foundation hospitals and top-up fees. Fifth, failure to reform the Lords into an elected second chamber with teeth. Sixth, the sell-off of the tube against the wishes of almost everyone. Seventh, endless PFIs that are not good value. Eighth, continued 'reform' and bullying from the top in health and education. Will I vote Lib Dem in the next general election? Possibly, although I am totally opposed to going into the euro. My vote is up for grabs, and I am not alone. But, Tories, don't bother to call.

Source: The *Guardian*, 20 September 2003.

Questions

1. Using Item A, explain the voting behaviour of the author of Item B?

2. You have been asked to explain why the 2001 general election resulted in a second successive convincing victory for the Labour Party. Go back through the unit and collect information relevant to each element in the general model in Item A. Use this information to write a newspaper article entitled: 'How Labour won again'.

References

Austin & Hames (2001) Austin, T. & Hames, T., *The Times Guide to the House of Commons June 2001*, Times Books, 2001.

Bartle (2002) Bartle, J., 'Why Labour won - again' in *King (2002)*.

Benyon & Denver (1990) Benyon, J. & Denver, D., 'Mrs Thatcher's Electoral Success', *Social Studies Review*, Vol.5.3, January 1990.

Butler & Kavanagh (1992) Butler, D. & Kavanagh, D., *The British General Election of 1992*, MacMillan, 1992.

Butler & Kavanagh (1997) Butler, D. & Kavanagh, D., *The British General Election of 1997*, MacMillan, 1997.

Butler & Kavanagh (2002) Butler, D. & Kavanagh, D., *The British General Election of 2001*, Palgrave, 2002.

Cohen (2001) Cohen, N., 'Democracy is dead. Now what?', *New Statesman*, 11 June 2001.

Crewe (1988) Crewe, I., 'Voting patterns since 1959', *Contemporary Record*, Vol.4.2, Winter 1988.

Crewe (2002) Crewe, I., 'A new political hegemony?' in *King (2002)*.

Crewe et al. (1977) Crewe, I., Sarlik, B. & Alt, J., 'Partisan dealignment in Britain 1964-1974', *British Journal of Political Science*, Vol.7.2, 1977.

Curtice (1997) Curtice, J., 'Anatomy of a non-landslide', *Politics Review*, Vol.7.1, September1997.

Curtice (2001) Curtice, J., 'General election 2001: repeat or revolution?', *Politics Review*, Vol.11.1, September 2001.

Curtice & Steed (2002) Curtice, J. & Steed, M., 'An analysis of the results' in *Butler & Kavanagh (2002)*.

Denver (1992) Denver, D., 'The 1992 general election: in defence of psephology', *Talking Politics*, Vol.5.1, Autumn 1992.

Denver (1994) Denver, D., *Elections and Voting in Britain* (2nd edition), Harvester Wheatsheaf, 1994.

Denver (2001) Denver, D., 'The Liberal Democrat campaign' in *Norris (2001b)*.

Denver (2002) Denver, D. 'Making the choice: explaining how people vote', *Politics Review*, Vol.12.1, September 2002.

Denver (2002b) Denver, D., 'Who voted in 2001?', *Sociology Review*, Vol.12.2, November 2002.

Dobson (1998) Dobson, A., 'The 1997 general election: explaining a landslide' in *Lancaster (1998)*.

Dorey (2002) Dorey, P., 'A languid landslide: the 2001 general election' in *Lancaster (2002)*.

Dunleavy et al. (1990) Dunleavy, P., Gamble, A., & Peele, G. (eds), *Developments in British Politics 3*, Macmillan, 1990.

Dunleavy et al. (1997) Dunleavy, P., Gamble, A., Holliday, I. & Peele, G., (eds), *Developments in British Politics 5*, Macmillan, 1997.

Ferguson (2001) Ferguson, E., 'King Billy assumes tactical mantle', *Observer*, 3 June 2001.

Fisher (2001) Fisher, J., 'Campaign finance: elections under new rules' in *Norris (2001b)*.

Fitzgerald (1988) Fitzgerald, M., 'There is no alternative...black people and the Labour Party', *Social Studies Review*, Vol.4.1, September 1988.

Game (1995) Game, C., 'Opinion polls: the lessons of 1992' in *Lancaster (1995)*.

Game (1998) Game, C., 'Opinion polls and the 1997 general election' in *Lancaster (1998)*.

Gavin & Sanders (1997) Gavin N.T. & Sanders, D., 'The economy and voting' in *Norris & Gavin (1997)*.

Hall (1992) Hall, S., 'No new vision, no new votes', *New Statesman & Society*, 17 April 1992.

Harrison (2002) Harrison, M., 'Politics on the air' in *Butler & Kavanagh (2002)*.

Heath et al. (1985) Heath, A., Jowell, R. & Curtice, J., *How Britain Votes*, Pergamon, 1985.

Heath et al. (1991) Heath, A., Jowell, R., Curtice, J., Evans, G., Field, J. & Witherspoon, S., *Understanding Political Change: The British Voter 1964-1987*, Pergamon, 1991.

Jones (2003) Jones, B., 'Apathy: why don't people want to vote?', *Politics Review*, Vol.12.4, April 2003.

Kellner (1997) Kellner, P., 'Why the Tories were trounced' in *Norris & Gavin (1997)*.

Kellner (2001) Kellner, P., 'It was always mission impossible for Hague', *Observer* (Election 2001 Supplement), 10 June, 2001.

Kellner (2001b) Kellner, P., 'Voters signal a political earthquake', *Observer*, 3 June 2001.

King (2002) King, A. (ed.), *Britain At The Polls 2001*, Chatham House, 2002.

Lancaster (1995) Lancaster, S. (ed.), *Developments in British Politics*, Vol.6, Causeway Press, 1995.

Lancaster (1998) Lancaster, S. (ed.), *Developments in British Politics*, Vol.9, Causeway Press, 1998.

Lancaster (2002) Lancaster, S. (ed.), *Developments in Politics*, Vol.13, Causeway Press, 2002.

Linton (1996) Linton, M., *Was it the Sun Wot Won It?*, Nuffield College, Oxford, 1996.

MacArthur (2001) MacArthur, B., 'Fleet Street avalanche to back the landslide' in *Austin & Hames (2001)*.

Miller (1990) Miller, W.L., 'Voting and the electorate' in *Dunleavy et al. (1990)*.

Miller (1991) Miller, W.L., *Media and Voters: the Audience, Content and Influence of press and television at the 1997 General Election*, Clarendon Press, 1991.

Miller et al. (1990) Miller, W.L., Clarke, H.D., Harrop, M., Leduc, L. & Whiteley, P.F., *How Voters Change: the 1987 British Election Campaign in Perspective*, Clarendon Press, 1990.

Moran (1989) Moran, M., *Politics and Society in Britain* (2nd edn), MacMillan, 1989.

Norris (1997) Norris, P., 'Anatomy of a Labour landslide' in *Norris & Gavin (1997)*.

Norris (2001) Norris, P., 'Apathetic landslide: the 2001 British general election' in *Norris (2001b)*.

Norris (2001b) Norris, P. (ed.), *Britain Votes 2001*, Oxford University Press, 2001.

Norris & Gavin (1997) Norris, P. & Gavin, N.T., *Britain Votes 1997*, Oxford University Press, 1997.

Pulzer (1967) Pulzer, P.G.J., *Political Representation and Elections in Britain*, Allen & Unwin, 1967.

Saggar (1997) Saggar, S., 'Racial politics' in *Norris & Gavin (1997)*.

Saggar (1998) Saggar, S., 'Party strategy and ethnic politics in the 1997 general election campaign', *Politics Review*, Vol.7.4, April 1998.

Saggar (2001) Saggar, S., 'The race card, again' in *Norris (2001b)*.

Sanders (1997) Sanders, D., 'Voting and the electorate' in *Dunleavy et al. (1997)*.

Scammell & Harrop (1997) Scammell, M. & Harrop, M., 'The press' in *Butler & Kavanagh (1997)*.

Scammell & Harrop (2002) Scammell, M. & Harrop, M., 'The press disarmed' in *Butler & Kavanagh (2002)*.

Seymore-Ure (1997) Seymore-Ure, C., 'Editorial opinion in the national press' in *Norris & Gavin (1997)*.

Seymore-Ure (2002) Seymore-Ure, C., 'New Labour and the media' in *King (2002)*.

7 Political ideology

7.1 The origins of the term 'ideology'

The term 'ideology' was first used by the French writer Antoine Destutt de Tracy in his *Elements d'Ideologie*, written between 1801 and 1805. The new term referred to a 'science of ideas' which was to be the basis of a new and better way of conducting politics. This science of ideas was to be free from the kind of prejudice and bias often associated with the intolerance of religious beliefs. In this sense, ideology was not just concerned with ideas but was also a hunt for an objective, scientific and truthful approach to politics.

The problems with defining the term

Since then the term 'ideology' has been used in a number of ways. Eagleton (1991), for example, provides 16 separate definitions of the term and suggests that:

> 'Nobody has yet come up with a single adequate definition of ideology...This is not because workers in this field are remarkable for their low intelligence but because the term "ideology" has a whole range of useful meanings, not all of which are compatible with each other. To try to compress this wealth of meaning into a single comprehensive definition would thus be unhelpful even if it were possible.' (Eagleton 1991, p.1)

While it may not be possible to come up with a single, suitable definition, it is possible to identify four distinct ways in which the term 'ideology' has been used. These are outlined in Box 7.1.

The descriptive meaning of ideology

The term 'ideology' is most often used by political scientists in this way:

An ideology is a reasonably coherent structure of thought shared by a group of people. It is a means of explaining how society works and of explaining how it ought to work.

Dobson (1992) describes this as the 'descriptive' meaning of ideology and argues that an ideology in this sense has five elements - see Box 7.2.

Box 7.2 The 'descriptive' meaning of ideology

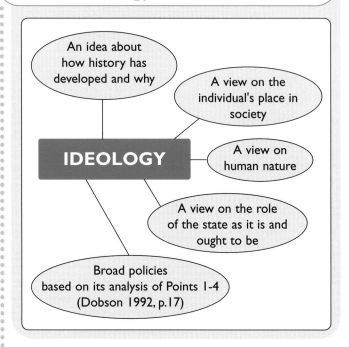

7.2 Ideology and human nature

What is the real nature of human beings? Should people be optimists and regard others as essentially trustworthy and able to make their own decisions with a minimum of interference or should they be pessimists who believe that

Box 7.1 Four uses of the term 'ideology'

1. The Marxist definition
Karl Marx and Friedrich Engels (1846) suggested that ideology was a set of false and misleading beliefs. These false and misleading beliefs helped to keep the ruling class in power because they prevented ordinary people from realising the true nature of the society in which they lived.

2. Karl Popper's definition
The philosopher Karl Popper used the term 'ideology' in a negative sense. He argued that ideologies were 'closed' systems of political thought:

> 'Ideologies claim a monopoly of truth, they seek to explain everything and in so doing refuse to tolerate rival views or opposing theories. An ideology is thus a "secular religion", which leads to intolerance, censorship and political repression.' (Heywood 1992, p.7)

3. The way the term is used in ordinary conversation
When people use the term 'ideology' in ordinary conversation they often use it as a term of abuse. A person who acts 'ideologically' is characterised as a person who is extreme, inflexible and intransigent. The implication is that people whose actions are motivated by ideology are completely committed to a set of beliefs which they follow blindly with their minds closed to alternative views. Those who are guided by ideology have a hidden agenda and are, therefore, not to be trusted.

4. Seliger's definition
According to Seliger (1976), an ideology is a way of explaining and justifying political action, regardless of what the actual aims were behind that particular action.

people are flawed and in need of control? How important are people's backgrounds? Does experience shape people's behaviour or is character predetermined?

Such questions may seem to be a long way from what is usually thought of as politics. But that is not so. Take the issue of censorship for example. Those 'optimists' who regard people as essentially trustworthy are likely to oppose censorship because, in their view, people are capable of making up their own minds about what they see, listen to or read. 'Pessimists', on the other hand, believe that people are essentially flawed and so, to them, censorship is necessary to ensure control.

Similarly, different views about human nature are often the basis of disputes about policy towards crime and punishment. Those who believe that experience shapes people's behaviour are likely to argue that crime is caused by poor social conditions and that improving these conditions would reduce crime. But those who believe that people's characters are predetermined are likely to argue that some people are born criminals and it is in society's interest to keep these criminals locked up.

7.3 Ideology and the past

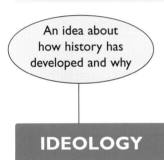

An idea about how history has developed and why

IDEOLOGY

How strong a role should tradition play in our lives? Should changes in society be cautious and build on what we know about the past? Or, should changes mean a radical break with the past? The answer to these questions depends on how what happened in the past is interpreted. History is not simply a collection of facts or objective truths, it is a matter of judgement. For example, although all historians would agree that it was the Labour government elected in 1945 which set up the welfare state, not all historians would agree that this was a good thing. Indeed, some historians have argued that the setting up of the welfare state exacerbated Britain's economic and political decline while others have argued that it was a positive development which led to several decades of social stability. There is no correct answer here. Historians on both sides use the same evidence. The difference lies in their approach and their attitude towards that evidence. In other words, the way in which they interpret the past is determined by their ideological stance. And, this is not just the case with professional historians. It is also the case with anyone who formulates an argument which expresses a view of the past or cites an historical precedent.

7.4 The individual and the group

A view on the individual's place in society

IDEOLOGY

What kind of identity do we have or should we have? Should we see ourselves as individuals, members of a class, a community, a nation, a race? People need a sense of place in the world. But what should be the basis for this? Given that people are all members of different groups, which one (if any) should be paramount? The position of an individual in society can cause particular disagreement. Some believe, for example, that the crucial unit is the individual and that individuals should be encouraged to pursue their own self-interest because, in this way, everybody would benefit. Others argue that this simply encourages selfishness and works against the wider interests of the community or against society as a whole. Still others argue that the nation or the race is the supreme unit and individuals only have any importance as part of such a group.

7.5 Ideology and the state

Given that the state

IDEOLOGY

A view on the role of the state as it is and ought to be

consists of the government, civil service, police, judiciary, armed forces and so on, it is bound to be of primary significance to all ideologies even though there is considerable disagreement about what its role ought to be. Do we need a strong state or are our interests best served by a much more limited structure with fewer powers? Does the power of the state pose a threat to our freedom or enhance it? What should be the main priority of the state - order, greater equality, freedom? Is 'big government' a positive benefit because it can improve our lives through planning and the provision of social services or does this produce a 'nanny state' where people are reluctant to look after themselves and expect everything to be done for them from the cradle to the grave?

7.6 Conclusions

It is useful to unpick an ideology so that the component parts can be identified. But these parts are also interrelated. Views about human nature, for example, influence attitudes towards the role of the state. Those who believe that individuals are capable of managing their own affairs are likely to regard a powerful state as unnecessary and perhaps even a danger to individual freedom. Those who are more dubious about human nature probably prefer a strong state, if only to maintain order. It is this kind of interrelationship which helps to provide coherence and consistency to an ideology and therefore, gives it a clearer identity.

It should be noted, however, that just because an ideology is called 'liberalism' or 'conservatism' that does not mean that it can only apply to the Liberal Party or the Conservative Party. It is true that ideologies are often heavily associated with a particular party, but the relationship is not entirely straightforward. Key liberal ideas, for example, have influenced both the Conservative Party and the Labour Party. Similarly, it could be argued that Margaret Thatcher was not really conservative at all when she was Leader of the Conservative Party. The activity which follows looks at a number of models which have been used to classify ideologies.

Main points Sections 7.1 - 7.6

- The term 'ideology' was first used at the beginning of the 19th century. Today, it is a difficult term to define because it is used in different ways.
- A definition accepted by most political commentators is: 'an ideology is a reasonably coherent structure of thought shared by a group of people. It is a means of explaining how society works and of explaining how it ought to work.'
- An ideology defined in this way has five main

elements: (1) a view of human nature; (2) a view of history; (3) a view on the place of the individual within society; (4) a view on the role of the state; and (5) broad policies based on its analysis of the Points 1-4.
- Political parties are often influenced by more than one ideology. Key liberal ideas, for example, have not just influenced the Liberal Democrats. They have influenced the Conservative Party and Labour Party too.

Activity 7.1 Classifying ideologies

Item A The linear model

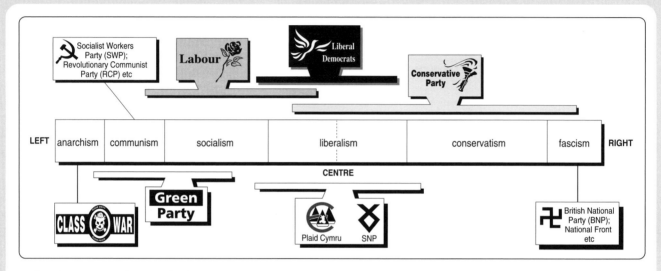

Political scientists who use the left/right linear model of the political spectrum argue that it reflects different political values about economic policy and different attitudes towards equality. Left wingers aim for greater equality and this is reflected in their economic policies. Those on the far left argue for a state-planned economy while socialists and liberals support a mixed economy. Right wingers claim that equality is either undesirable or impossible and support free-market capitalism and privately owned property. But the model is inconsistent. Some fascist regimes practised state ownership, for example, and anarchists are usually located on the left but they do not support state control.

Source: Heywood 1992.

Item B The political spectrum

The origin of the terms 'left' and 'right' dates back to the French Revolution. Different groups sat in different positions at the first meeting of the Estates-General in 1789. Aristocrats who supported the king sat on his right while radicals sat on his left. As a result 'right' was used of reactionaries (people who opposed change or wanted the old system to remain) while 'left' was used of revolutionaries (people who wanted radical change). Today the left/right divide still exists but it no longer simply distinguishes between reactionaries and revolutionaries. Although some right wingers are reactionaries, others are not. Similarly, although some left wingers are revolutionaries, others resist change.

Source: Heywood 1992.

Item C Eysenck's model

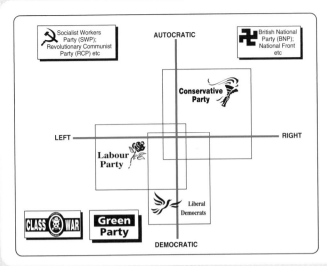

This diagram (left) is based on the model first suggested by Eysenck (1957). He accepted the left/right spectrum as the horizontal axis of his spectrum, but added a vertical axis. This vertical axis measured political attitudes which were, at one end, democratic (open and accountable) and, at the other end, autocratic (closed and not accountable). This model makes clear the similarities between extreme groups (for example, the fascists and communists) but also indicates the difference between them (for example, by placing the fascists on the extreme right and the communists on the extreme left).

Source: Heywood 1992.

Item D The 'horseshoe' model

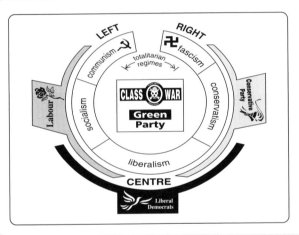

The 'horseshoe' model attempts to overcome the problems of the linear model by emphasising the similarities between the extremes. Both communist and fascist regimes have been described as repressive and authoritarian and so, in this model, they appear side by side. Critics argue that this overplays the similarities. In some respects, for example, Nazi Germany (a fascist state) was very different from the Soviet Union under Stalin (a communist state). For example, capitalism thrived under Nazism while it was eradicated by Stalin.

Source: Heywood, 1992.

Questions

1. Using the items in this activity give the arguments for and against pinpointing a person's ideological stance using the terms 'left' and 'right'.

2. Devise a questionnaire that could be used to find out where people fit on the political spectrum.

3. a) What do Items A, C and D tell us about the ideological stance of the three major political parties in Britain?

   b) In your view, which of the three models gives the most realistic account of political debate in Britain today? Give reasons for your answer.

7.7 The political roots of liberalism

Liberalism in the UK has clear political and economic roots. Its political roots lay in the reaction to the English Civil War of the 1640s and the execution of Charles I. It was in the context of the short-lived Republic, the restoration of the Monarchy in 1660 and the 'Glorious Revolution' of 1688 that the writings of John Locke (see Box 7.3 on page 121) became important. Locke argued that people had certain natural rights, in particular to life, liberty and property. Limits on these rights, he suggested, can only be set if the people

themselves agree. This idea led to principles which were to be central to liberalism as it developed in the 19th century. Locke believed that, because limits to people's natural rights could only be established by their agreement, government should be based on the consent of the governed. He also argued that the role of government should be limited to defending these natural rights. As a result, two principles of liberalism emerged in the writings of Locke:

- government can only exist with the agreement of the governed
- government must be limited to a small number of tasks - in other areas, it has no business interfering in people's affairs.

7.8 The economic roots of liberalism

The economic roots of liberalism are to be found in the industrial revolution of the 18th and 19th centuries and in the writings of economists who championed the new ways of manufacturing that were established during this period. Most important of the early supporters of industrialisation was Adam Smith (1723-90). Smith argued that mass production, freedom and competition were the best conditions for economic progress. As a result, he argued, the government should have no direct role in regulating the economy. Individuals and businesses should be left free to succeed or fail according to the laws of competition. The outcome of such a process, Smith believed, would be more prosperity for all.

The conclusions drawn from the writings of thinkers such as Locke and Smith were that government must be based on consent, that it should allow individuals as much freedom as possible and that the role of the state in the personal and economic lives of individuals should be very restricted. These ideas formed the core of what became known as classical liberalism and was an important part of the other two types of liberal thought, progressive liberalism and neo-liberalism.

Box 7.3 Locke and Smith

(i)   (ii)

(i) John Locke (1632-1704)   (ii) Adam Smith (1723-90)

7.9 Classical Liberalism

Locke, Smith and other writers who challenged the old order and emphasised the importance of freedom, choice and the needs of emerging capitalism helped to create and develop classical liberalism. Classical liberalism became enormously influential in British politics in the 19th century. Its core ideas can be identified as follows.

Classical liberals are guardedly optimistic about human nature. They believe that human beings are rational and reasonable and so are capable of making wise decisions for themselves. This means people should be subjected to the least amount of interference possible by the state. The free individual is at the heart of classical liberal philosophy.

Since they are guardedly optimistic about human nature, classical liberals see history as the consequence of individual

human choices and actions. Historical progress occurs when more people have more freedom to pursue their goals and desires. The classical liberal view of history is that there is a steady progression towards a more just and fair society.

As for the state, the classical liberal position can best be summed up in a statement of the American President Thomas Jefferson who said 'that which governs best governs least'. Classical liberals accept that the state has the legitimate function of preserving law and order, enforcing contracts and providing protection from external threats. However, the stress on the importance of the freedom of the individual makes them alert to the threat posed to the exercise of this individualism by the state and its functionaries.

In addition to its commitment to a minimal state, classical liberalism holds three principles to be central to policy-making and the attempt to create a liberal society. These are outlined in Box 7.4.

Box 7.4 Three principles held by classical liberals

1. Freedom

Classical liberals are committed to securing the freedom necessary to allow individuals to fulfil themselves as best they can. The problem with maximising freedom is that decisions have to be made about what limits on freedom are justified and when to apply such limits.

2. Equality

Classical liberals support equality before the law and equal political rights, the idea being that every individual has an equal (though restricted) level of freedom. Classical liberals also accept equality of opportunity, even though they realise that people might use the same opportunities in unequal ways - which could then lead to inequality.

3. Toleration

Classical liberals' emphasis on the individual and on personal freedom produces tolerance. Classical liberals are willing to accept the rights of others to live in ways different to them and for them to hold beliefs they do not hold. As a result, liberals have been at the forefront of campaigns against religious bigotry and in support of equal rights for minority ethnic groups and homosexuals.

7.10 Progressive liberalism

Classical liberalism developed in the 18th and early 19th centuries as Britain began the process of industrialisation. Later in the 19th century, the effects of this industrialisation on ordinary working people and upon the environment began to be felt. This led some liberals to review one of the key principles of classical liberalism - namely, their commitment to a minimal state. Classical liberalism had regarded a minimal state as the best way to secure individual freedom. Those who became progressive liberals saw that industrialisation posed threats to the freedom of the individual which came from sources other than the state. Long working hours, poor working conditions, a lack of health care, the threat of unemployment and a lack of educational facilities made a mockery of the idea of individual freedom for the majority of the population. Progressive liberals came to accept that the state must act to provide regulation of working hours and conditions, basic universal health care, some security in unemployment and a universal education system. In addition, they argued the state should intervene in other ways - by drawing up regulations to reduce the pollution coming from the new factories, for example.

Progressive liberalism inspired the Liberal government of 1906 to 1914 to intervene in areas of life previously untouched by government. For example, the government introduced old age pensions, national health insurance and unemployment insurance. Progressive liberalism also had a huge influence on British politics after 1945. Both the economist J.M. Keynes (see Box 7.5) and the man whose report inspired the creation of the welfare state, William Beveridge (see also Box 7.5), were progressive liberals.

Box 7.5 Progressive liberals

John Maynard Keynes (1883-1946)

For much of the post-war period, British economic policy was based on the theories put forward by Keynes. He rejected 'laissez-faire' policies which left the market to regulate wages and prices by itself. He argued that, to avoid damaging recessions, the government should

J.M. Keynes

be prepared to take steps - such as investing in new projects and lowering taxation - which would achieve full employment and planned economic growth.

William Beveridge (1879-1963)

Although the post-war Labour government was responsible for setting up the welfare state, the principles which underlay it were laid down by Beveridge. In the report he published in 1942, Beveridge argued that social problems could not be treated in isolation because they were all linked. For the first time, it was conceded that poverty and underachievement might be the result of material, social conditions rather than individual failings. As a result, the ground was cleared for the government to set up institutions designed to help all, regardless of their ability to pay.

7.11 *Neo-liberalism*

Although progressive liberalism was the dominant ideology during the period of post-war consensus (1945-c.1975), Keynesian economics and the welfare state have increasingly come under attack. Since Margaret Thatcher's election as Conservative Party Leader (in 1975) and certainly since her election as Prime Minister (in 1979), a new and distinctive type of liberalism has emerged - neo-liberalism. Neo-liberalism is usually associated with the New Right (see Section 7.15 below) and can be characterised as follows:

'Economic liberalism or neo-liberalism, often seen as the dominant theme within the New Right, draws heavily upon classical liberalism; it advocates that the frontiers of the state be rolled back and proclaims the virtues of private enterprise, the free market and individual responsibility. As such, neo-liberalism can be seen as a backlash against the steady growth of state power perpetrated [put into place] through much of the 20th century by liberal, socialist and conservative governments. Neo-liberals support an extreme form of individualism which leaves little room for public services or the provision of social welfare.' (Heywood 1994, p.11)

7.12 *Liberalism since March 1988*

Historically, liberalism was the ideology promoted by the Liberal Party - though, as noted above, liberal values have, on occasion, been promoted by politicians in other political parties. In March 1988, however, the Liberal Party merged with the Social Democratic Party, forming the Liberal Democrats. According to Robert Leach, the new party owed much more to the Liberals than to the Social Democrats:

'The Liberal Democrats were little more than the old Liberal Party with a few former Labour politicians.' (Leach 2002, p.30)

The new party retained a commitment to key liberal values, especially those in the progressive liberal tradition. In particular, it was committed to:
- civil liberties and the freedom of the individual
- the incorporation of European human rights legislation into British law
- support for the European Union.

Liberal Democrats have consistently supported devolution and constitutional reform, especially a change in the system of electing MPs to the House of Commons. They have made a progressive liberal commitment to raising taxes to fund welfare and education policy and placed an emphasis on community politics and participation.

Between 1988 and 1997, with the Conservatives in power and Labour revising its ideological and policy positions in the wake of successive electoral defeats, the Liberal Democrats had a clear and distinct position which marked them out as the heirs of the progressive liberal tradition. After Labour's victory in 1997, however, the Liberal Democrats' position, under Paddy Ashdown, became less clear and distinct. The new Labour government invited leading Liberal Democrats to sit on a Cabinet committee set up to discuss constitutional reform and there was even behind-the-scenes discussion of a coalition.

After Charles Kennedy was elected Leader of the Liberal Democrats in August 1999, he began to move the party away from New Labour both in terms of ideas and policy. This shift was most evident in the opposition to the war in Iraq mounted by the Liberal Democrats in 2003 which distanced them from both of the other main parties and drew upon a long anti-war tradition in British liberalism. It has been suggested by some political observers that Kennedy is trying to move the Liberal Democrats back to a position of 'equidistance' - to an ideological stance which is just as removed (or as close) from Labour as from the Conservatives, the idea being to attract support from disaffected elements in both parties.

Main points Sections 7.7 - 7.12

- The political roots of liberalism are to be found in the 17th century, especially in the work of John Locke. The economic roots are to be found in the 19th century, especially in the work of Adam Smith who argued for free markets and a minimal state.
- The concepts of the individual, freedom, equality and toleration are at the heart of liberalism.
- Liberalism has taken three forms: (1) classical liberalism which emphasised the freedom of the individual and a minimal state; (2) progressive liberalism which called for state intervention; and (3) neo-liberalism which refocused attention on the individual.
- The Liberal Democrats' ideological stance is closest to that of the progressive liberals.

Activity 7.2 Liberalism

Item A Classical and progressive liberalism

(i) The spirit of self-help is the root of all genuine growth in the individual. Help from others is often weakening while self-help is strengthening. Whatever is done for men or groups takes away the incentive (encouragement) and necessity of doing it themselves. And where people are over-guided and over-governed, the inevitable tendency is for them to become comparatively helpless.

Source: Smiles 1859.

(ii) The working classes have done their best during the past 50 years to make provision without the aid of the state. But it is insufficient. The old man has to bear his own burden while in the case of a young man who is broken down and who has a wife and family to maintain, the suffering is increased and multiplied to that extent. These problems of the sick, of the ill, of the men who cannot find means of earning a living are problems with which it is the business of the state to deal. They are problems which the state has neglected for too long.

Part of a speech made to Parliament by David Lloyd George on 15 June 1908.

Item B Liberalism and the Liberal Democrats

Three simple words. Freedom, justice, honesty. These sum up what the Liberal Democrats stand for. Freedom - because everybody should have the opportunity to make the most of their life. Justice - because freedom depends on fairness. Honesty - because where fairness has a cost, we explain how it will be paid for. The UK has huge potential. Unlock the energies and skills of its people and there is nothing that cannot be achieved. But we do not want government always telling people how to develop those assets. Government works best as an enabler. Its task is not to curb but to stimulate. To enjoy true freedom people must have good education, decent healthcare, reliable public transport, safety on the streets and a secure income in old age. The state must provide these basic public services to allow all citizens to achieve their full potential.

Source: Lib Dem 2001.

Item C Neo-liberalism

In 1979, the Conservatives came to power under the leadership of Margaret Thatcher with a clear and consistent neo-liberal programme. This was quite different from the consensus policies all the main parties had offered for the previous 30 years. The overall aim of the Thatcher governments from 1979 was to restore the UK's prosperity. This was to be achieved by relying on the free market, minimal government interference, and individual liberty and responsibility. The strategy was to create the conditions in which free enterprise could flourish. Policies can be grouped into four closely related areas:

* the conquest of inflation
* reducing the size and cost of the state
* providing incentives for hard work and enterprise
* removing restrictions on the operation of the free market.

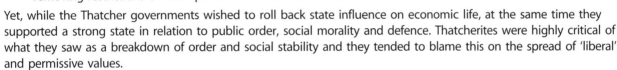

This cartoon pokes fun at the faith which Prime Minister Margaret Thatcher (right) and her Chancellor Nigel Lawson (centre) placed in a free market. It was published in March 1985.

Yet, while the Thatcher governments wished to roll back state influence on economic life, at the same time they supported a strong state in relation to public order, social morality and defence. Thatcherites were highly critical of what they saw as a breakdown of order and social stability and they tended to blame this on the spread of 'liberal' and permissive values.

Source: Adams 1993 and Heywood 1994.

Questions

1. Using the passages in Item A, write an article explaining what classical liberalism and progressive liberalism have in common and how they differ.

2. To what extent do liberal principles guide the ideas outlined in Item B? Give reasons for your answer.

3. a) Judging from Item C, what is neo-liberalism and how does it differ from other forms of liberalism?

   b) 'Thatcherites not Liberal Democrats are the real heirs of classical liberalism.' Using Items A-C, give arguments for and against this view.

7.13 *The main characteristics of conservatism*

The term 'conservative' is used in ordinary conversation to describe a particular state of mind. To be a conservative is to be suspicious of change, to be cautious and to prefer to keep things as they are. An extreme conservative might not want any change at all.

To be conservative in a political sense involves holding a more specific set of attitudes than is suggested by this general meaning. Like other ideologies, conservatism involves views on human nature, the past, the state and on policy. Despite this, some conservatives deny that conservatism is an ideology at all, preferring to see it as an attitude or disposition with certain common characteristics rather than a coherent ideological position (see Oakeshott 1962).

Some conservatives, particularly those influenced by Christian notions of original sin, take an especially pessimistic view of human nature. They hold that humans are driven by powerful and often wicked passions that lead them into conflict with each other. Less pessimistic conservatives still

lack the liberal belief in human reason and goodness and maintain that human beings are often driven by emotion, self-interest and greed rather than by rational considerations. Conservatives also believe that talent, drive and ability are unequally distributed and that any attempt to create an equal society will be doomed to failure, disaster or both.

Conservatives believe that people gain order and meaning in their lives from being part of a social organism. As a result, they value the ideas and institutions which have helped to create and preserve this social organism. This explains the conservative stress on the value of family life and the nation. It also explains their belief in a powerful state. Unlike liberals who believe that a minimal state provides the best opportunity for rational individuals to pursue their ends, conservatives hold that a strong state is required to discipline people to prevent their greedy and selfish natures running out of control. Conservatives also believe in strong leadership by a privileged élite, since the unreliability of human nature makes mass participation in decision-making undesirable, at worst, or in need of control, at best.

The conservative view of the past was first set out by Edmund Burke - see Box 7.6 on page 125 - in his *Reflections on the Revolution in France*, published in 1790, two years after the French Revolution began. Burke argued that the events in France were a threat to order and stability and so completely undesirable. Burke believed that societies develop slowly over time and are the product of the wisdom of the past. As a result, they cannot be improved by rapid and violent change. Burke believed that any plan for social change based upon a blueprint of what was to happen was doomed to failure and that, when change was necessary, it should be gradual and should look to preserve the best of the past. Failure to observe this advice, Burke believed, would result in chaos.

Box 7.6 Edmund Burke

Edmund Burke (1729-97) was born in Ireland in 1729. He became a writer and an active politician, serving as an MP. He died in 1797.

Burke's writings retain their influence on conservative thought. In particular they are the basis of three important conservative principles:
- a love of tradition
- a cautious support for change
- an opposition to idealistic blueprints.

Love of tradition

Burke's arguments are still highly relevant. Modern conservatism emphasises that society should be allowed to develop naturally so that it can reflect the deep needs, values and beliefs which have stood the test of time. Institutions which have evolved (such as Parliament) deserve respect precisely because they have this historic seal of approval. They have proved their worth.

Similar arguments can be used to justify the importance of the ownership of property. Ownership is a reflection of the established rights of individuals and it is a source of stability.

Cautious support for change

If change is necessary, the conservative approach would be to base it on experience and to proceed cautiously. Take the British monarchy for example. This still remains intact, though

the monarchy today is very different from the monarchy in 1900 (for example, it is less remote than it used to be). Conservatives would argue that it is by responding to changing values and attitudes that the British monarchy has managed to survive in a period when many other monarchies have been discarded.

Opposition to idealistic blueprints

It is the conservatives' respect for tradition which makes idealistic blueprints for social reform a particular target for criticism. According to conservatives, these are flawed in two ways. They are likely to be based on a lack of understanding of what people really want and, more dangerously, they can destroy something which works. Such a view can be illustrated by the rush to build tower blocks in the 1950s and 1960s. More accommodation was needed at the time, but it can be argued that many of the schemes subsequently failed because they did not take into account the long-established tradition of British people living in houses rather than flats. The result is that, 40 years later, many of these tower blocks are being pulled down.

7.14 *Different strands of conservatism*

Just as liberalism contains two distinct strands (classical liberalism and progressive liberalism), it is possible to distinguish between a number of different strands of conservatism. In their analysis of the Conservative Party, Whiteley and his colleagues (1994) suggest that there are three distinct ideological tendencies within the Conservative Party. All three tendencies can be described as variations of conservatism.

1. Traditional conservatism

Whiteley and his colleagues (1994) suggest that traditional conservatism is derived from the values and attitudes traditionally held by the land-owning aristocracy. The main characteristics of traditional conservatism are described in Box 7.7.

Box 7.7 Traditional conservatism

On the one hand, traditional conservatism stresses patriotism and authority. On the other, it often opposes social and political changes such as the emancipation of women, racial integration, the legalisation of abortion and easier divorce. It tends to oppose Britain's closer integration with Europe and is secretly, if not occasionally openly, racist. Traditional conservatives are also strong supporters of the idea of social discipline and law and order. They strongly favour capital punishment and emphasise the importance of punishment as a means of dealing with crime. They tend to oppose constitutional reform, preferring to retain old forms of government. They are strongly attached to the monarchy and to institutions like the House of Lords.

Source: Whiteley et al. 1994.

2. 'One nation' conservatism

One nation conservatism was developed in the mid-19th century. This brand of conservatism was first outlined by Benjamin Disraeli - see Box 7.8. Keen to broaden support for the Conservative Party, Disraeli argued that, despite class differences, the interests uniting the British people were of far greater significance than those dividing them. It was true that some were more privileged than others, but it was the duty of the more privileged to look after those in need. Heywood (1992) notes that Disraeli's argument had both a pragmatic and a moral strand. On the one hand, Disraeli realised that growing social inequality in Britain had the potential to lead to violent uprising like those that had taken place in Europe in 1789, 1830 and 1848. Reform was, therefore, necessary on practical grounds because it would protect the long-term interests of the wealthy by ensuring that revolution was avoided. On the other hand, Disraeli argued that reform was necessary on moral grounds. This argument was based on the traditional conservative belief that society was naturally arranged in a hierarchy. Since those at the top of the hierarchy had more wealth and privileges than those at the bottom, those at the top had a greater responsibility to consider the needs of those less fortunate than themselves. In other words, in return for their privileged position, those at the top of the hierarchy had a moral obligation to alleviate the suffering of those at the bottom of the hierarchy. The slogan 'one nation' was given to this type of conservatism because of Disraeli's emphasis on the unity between classes. The British people, the term suggested, all belonged to one happy family, each with a particular role to play and each with a particular place within the family hierarchy.

The main characteristics of one nation conservatism are described in Box 7.8.

3. 'Liberal' conservatism

While one nation conservatives accept that the government should play a positive role in economic management and the provision of welfare, 'liberal' conservatives disagree. Liberal conservatism (also called 'libertarian' conservatism) draws on classical liberalism and places it within a conservative framework.

Liberal conservatism is nothing new. Heywood (1992) notes that liberal ideas, especially liberal economic ideas about the free market, have been put forward by conservatives since the 18th century. These ideas are liberal because they support the greatest possible economic liberty and the least possible government regulation of the economy. Liberal conservatism, however, differs from liberalism because liberal conservatives argue that economic liberty is compatible with traditional conservative values such as the belief in authority and duty. Liberal conservatives, therefore, support free-market economics and regard state intervention in economic matters as unnecessary and a hindrance. On the other hand, unlike liberals, liberal conservatives do not believe that moral decisions can be left to the individual. They argue that a strong state is required to maintain public order and to ensure that traditional values are upheld.

Whiteley and his colleagues (1994) describe liberal conservatives as 'individualists'. Box 7.9 shows how they are categorised.

Box 7.8 One nation conservatism

Benjamin Disraeli (1804-81) was Prime Minister in 1868 and 1874-80. He is closely associated with the one nation brand of conservatism.

Whiteley and his colleagues describe one nation conservatives as 'progressives'. One nation conservatives are those conservatives who, following the Conservatives' election defeat in 1945, accepted and supported the welfare state and Keynesian methods of economic management introduced by the post-war Labour government. Today, one nation conservatives accept the importance of a safety net to deal with poverty. They also support a limited redistribution of income and wealth and they favour government intervention in the economy to regulate markets.

Source: Whiteley et al. 1994.

Box 7.9 Liberal conservatives

Liberal conservatism is preoccupied with concerns over private property and the interests of small businesspeople. It supports the idea of reduced government intervention in the economy. The most enthusiastic supporters of the Conservative government's privatisation programme in the 1980s/1990s can be found among this group. Individualists believe that the welfare state undermines self-reliance and enterprise and that the government should cut taxes and deregulate business. They also tend to oppose extensions to the welfare state, fearing that this will promote idleness and they are inclined to blame the victim when it comes to explaining the origins of poverty or unemployment.

Source: Whiteley et al. 1994.

7.15 The New Right

Liberal conservatism has made an important impact on British politics since the mid-1970s. The key event was the election of Margaret Thatcher as Leader of the Conservative Party in 1975. Much of Thatcher's thinking was informed by liberal conservatism and, in government, she appointed colleagues with views similar to her own. As a result, liberal conservatism replaced one nation conservatism as the mainstream ideology in the Conservative Party. Since much of liberal conservative thinking fits with attitudes that are generally regarded as being 'right wing' and since the revival of liberal conservatism is a relatively new phenomenon, those who subscribe to liberal conservative ideas are often said to belong to the 'New Right'. Like many political movements, the New Right is a loose coalition of writers, politicians and political activists whose views coincide on many, but by no means all, issues. Since the mid-1970s, the New Right has made its mark throughout the world. It was, for example, a major influence on American Presidents Ronald Reagan and George Bush during the 1980s.

7.16 *Conservative ideology since 1990*

The influence of New Right ideology was at its greatest between 1984 and 1990 as Prime Minister Margaret Thatcher and a like-minded Cabinet attempted to encourage individual responsibility, the acquisition of personal wealth and a reduced role for the state. Following Thatcher's resignation in 1990, a conflict developed between those who wished to implement a more radical New Right agenda - the 'revolutionaries' - and those who wished to move back towards the centre - the 'consolidator'.

This ideological conflict was a key theme of John Major's premiership. It has also been cited by the political commentator John Gray (1997) as a crucial cause of the Conservatives' 'cataclysmic defeat' on 1 May 1997 since ideological divisions meant that, unlike when Thatcher was Leader, the party no longer had a programme with a single vision.

After the Conservatives' defeat in 1997, Major resigned as Leader and there was a leadership contest. The candidates in this contest reflected the ideological divisions within the party. John Redwood was a 'revolutionary' who wished to move the party further to the right, while Kenneth Clarke was a 'consolidator'. With an agenda somewhere between the two was William Hague. To the surprise of many, it was Hague who won the leadership and who proceeded to launch what he described as a 'Fresh Approach'. Hague's 'Fresh Approach' had three elements. These are described in Box 7.10.

Electorally, this ideological position was designed to appeal to several groups who had deserted the Conservatives in 1997, namely the young, single parents, black voters, gays and lesbians. Unfortunately for Hague, however, his 'Fresh Approach' appealed neither to the public in general nor to Conservative Party activists in particular.

After the launch of the 'Fresh Approach', the polls continued to paint a dismal picture for the Conservatives. Moreover, their 1998 and 1999 'Listening to Britain' exercise in which they held 1,400 open meetings around the country failed to catch the imagination of the party or the public. Party members proved wholly opposed to both multiculturalism and moral relativism (the view that all moral positions are equally valid) and they reaffirmed Conservative commitments to 'normal family values' and 'the centrality of marriage' (Kelly 2001).

As a result, the new socially liberal conservatism promoted by Hague did not last long. After March 1998, Hague made a number of statements indicating a return to the Conservative Party's position that existed before the 'Fresh Approach'. This

Box 7.10 William Hague's 'Fresh Approach'

William Hague's 'Fresh Approach' had three main elements. The first two elements were scarcely 'fresh', however. It was the third element that was a major departure.

Element 1 - Defend and extend Thatcherite economic principles
Thatcherite economic principles were defended and extended, with a further commitment to privatisation and reductions in the role of the state.

Element 2 - Strengthen opposition to the European monetary union
Hague made 'euroscepticism' party policy by voicing a more single-minded opposition to European monetary union.

Element 3 - Extend neo-liberal individualism to the social sphere
Under Thatcher, neo-liberal individualism had been confined to economics, but Hague extended it. Individual choice was to be the theme not only economically but in moral and cultural spheres also. As a result, the Conservative Party's preference for Anglican Christianity, two-parent families and heterosexual relationships were to be replaced with an acceptance that, in the areas of faith, family life and sexuality, there was no norm and that all life-style choices were equally valid.

Source: Kelly 2001.

was insufficient to save Hague from electoral defeat in 2001 and, like his predecessor, Hague resigned as Leader shortly after the election.

Ideologically, the contest which followed mirrored that of 1997. The main contenders appeared, at first, to be Michael Portillo, a 'revolutionary' and Kenneth Clarke, a 'consolidator'. But Portillo lost out, meaning that the two candidates whose names went to the party membership in the final ballot were Clarke and a lesser known figure, Iain Duncan Smith. It was Duncan Smith's sceptical stance on Europe which did most to secure him the leadership. Clarke was keenly pro-European, a position shared by few of the Conservative rank and file. After becoming Leader, Duncan Smith maintained the traditionalist stance of the later years of Hague's leadership, imposing, for example, a three-line whip on a Commons vote over the right of unmarried couples to adopt. His failure to heal the ideological divisions in the party, however, resulted in the challenge to his leadership in October 2003 and his replacement by Michael Howard (see Dorey 2004).

The irony is that, since the mid-1990s, ideological division has been at the root of the electoral difficulties faced by a party which once claimed it had no ideology.

Main points Sections 7.13 - 7.16

- In general terms, to be conservative is to be cautious, suspicious of change and to prefer to keep things roughly as they are. Conservatives tend to have few idealistic hopes about people.
- Many conservative ideas come from Edmund Burke. He opposed rapid change, arguing in support of tradition and gradual reform. For conservatives, the family and the nation are the key units. They stress the importance of rule of law, duty and hierarchy.
- There are three main strands of conservatism : (1) traditional conservatism (which stresses patriotism and authority but opposes social reform and other threats to the status quo);

(2) one nation conservatism (which argues that, despite class differences, the interests uniting British people are far greater than those dividing them); and (3) liberal conservatism (which supports the greatest possible economic liberty and the least possible government regulation and intervention).
- In the 1980s, the Conservative Party was dominated by liberal conservatives. After the resignation of Margaret Thatcher, ideological divisions emerged between those intent on extending the neo-liberal approach and those wishing to maintain traditional conservative values.

Activity 7.3 Conservatism

Item A The Conservative decline since 1992

Conservative decline 1992-2001

MPs by party	1992	1997	2001
Labour	271	418	412
Conservative	336	165	166
Liberal Democrats	46	20	52

Votes cast			
Labour	11.6 million (34.4%)	13.5 million (43.4%)	10.7 million (40.7%)
Conservative	14.1 million (41.9%)	9.6 million (30.8%)	8.4 million (31.2%)
Liberal Democrats	6 million (17.8%)	5.2 million (16.8%)	4.8 million (18.3%)

Source: Wild 2002.

Tracing Conservative decline 1986-2001

1986 Michael Heseltine resigns from the Cabinet, criticising Thatcher's leadership style.

1988 Poll tax introduced in Scotland early, causing resentment.

1989 Poll Tax proves hugely unpopular in England.

1989 First challenge to Thatcher's leadership by Anthony Meyer.

1989 Geoffrey Howe resigns from the Cabinet and delivers a withering criticism of Thatcher's leadership.

1990 Thatcher defeated by Major in leadership election.

1992 Conservatives win a narrow victory in the general election.

1992 Britain humiliated in falling out of the European Exchange Rate Mechanism. Lamont removed as Chancellor of the Exchequer.

1992 Party splits over the EU Maastricht Treaty.

1995 Major submits himself to party leadership re-election following internal criticism. He wins but is fatally damaged.

1997 Landslide defeat in the general election. Major resigns and is replaced by Hague.

1999 Party moves to anti-EU position. Fails to make an impact in opinion polls.

2001 Second huge electoral defeat. Hague resigns and is replaced by Duncan Smith.

2003 Duncan Smith resigns and is replaced by Michael Howard.

Source: Wild 2002.

Item B Conservative values (1)

Conserving Conservatism implies conserving, keeping things as they are, as in the old adage, 'If it ain't broke, don't fix it.'

Tradition Conservatives have generally stressed the limitations of human reason, or rationalism, preferring to rely on tradition and the wisdom of the past.

Pragmatism Conservatives often claim to deal with issues on a practical common-sense basis (pragmatism) rather than through fixed preconceived ideas (or dogma).

Gradualism Pragmatism implies flexibility. While Conservatives are, almost by definition, opposed to radical change, following Edmund Burke, they have often favoured gradual reform which grows out of the past.

Inequality As compared with liberals or socialists, conservatives have generally seen inequality as natural and inevitable (although they have stressed equality of opportunity or 'the opportunity to be unequal').

Leadership and authority Conservatives have often stressed the need for leadership and strong authoritative government to restrain human weakness and maintain law and order.

Property Conservatives have justified the right of individuals to acquire property and use it and bequeath it as they please.

Paternalism However, property involved obligations to look after the well-being of those less fortunate, through voluntary action (preferably), but also through state action (sometimes referred to as 'Tory collectivism').

Nationalism Conservatives have stressed the unity of the nation which they see as transcending class or other interests. They have emphasised the defence of Britain's national interests in foreign affairs.

Source: Leach 2003.

Item C Conservative values (2)

We will free entrepreneurs to build businesses and to create prosperity, free those who use public services to choose what is best for them and free those who work in our schools and hospitals and police service from endless political interference. I value those aspects of our national life which are bigger than individuals and families. That is why we will nurture our towns and cities, our countryside, our local institutions, our charities, our democracy - for they make us who we are as a nation. Our programme is rooted in common sense. It shouldn't be necessary to make an appeal to common sense. Yet the common-sense wisdom of the mainstream majority, on crime or on taxes, or the family, or on Europe is under threat as never before.

Source: Conservative 2001.

Questions

1. Using Items A-C, explain how conservatism differs from liberalism.

2. Look at Item A and explain the Conservative Party's electoral decline since 1992 in ideological terms.

3. Read Item B and then write a definition of conservatism in a single paragraph.

4. (a) 'The principles which lie behind the Conservative Party are conservative principles'. Explain this statement using Item C.

   (b) What strand of conservatism is illustrated in Item C. Explain your answer.

7.17 *The origins of socialism*

The changes to British society brought about by the industrial revolution did not just result in the adaptation of existing ideologies such as liberalism and conservatism, they also led to the development of a new ideology - socialism. But while liberalism and conservatism accepted and embraced the new capitalist economic order, socialism opposed it, aimed to change it and provided an alternative to it.

Capitalism

An industrial country whose wealth is owned mainly by individuals rather than by the state is a capitalist country. In simple terms, those who own and control the wealth are 'capitalists' (they have capital which they invest in businesses). Those who have no capital of their own but rely on being paid for their labour are 'workers'. Although the capitalists are fewer in number than the workers, they tend to acquire political power and social privileges as well as economic power.

Industrialisation in Britain was piecemeal. It relied upon individual initiative. New industrial enterprises were set up and owned by private individuals. On the whole, central government did not encourage or attempt to organise economic development. It certainly did not attempt to gain ownership of the new industrial enterprises. As a result, it was left to the owners of businesses to decide what conditions their workers should work in and how much they should be paid. Since the aim of these businesses was to make a profit, working conditions were often poor and wages low. In fact, during the early years of the industrial revolution, many working people had to endure appalling working and living conditions.

Marx and Engels

Writers such as Karl Marx and Friedrich Engels (see Box 7.11) criticised capitalism. They argued that the workers were being exploited by the capitalists. Once the workers realised the extent to which they were being exploited, they would rise up and overthrow the capitalists in a revolution. This revolution would lead to a new way of organising society - socialism. In a socialist society, people would share property and work cooperatively.

Capitalism in the late 19th century

By the late 19th century, the character of capitalism in Britain had changed. Although there was still a huge divide between rich and poor, living and working conditions had begun to improve. In part, this was due to the more active role taken by government - laws banning child labour and restricting the length of the working week were passed by Parliament, for example, and local councils were given powers to raise local taxes which could be spent on improving local living conditions. But other factors also played a part. The growth and recognition of trade unions provided the workers with the machinery to take collective action. The campaign for greater democracy led to the gradual extension of the franchise and, therefore, wider participation in politics. As a result, there was less alienation among the workers. While groups of revolutionary socialists survived, the number of their supporters remained small. More and more socialists

Box 7.11 Marx and Engels

Karl Marx (1818-83) and Friedrich Engels (1820-95) were both born in Germany, but lived and wrote in Britain. It was Marx's work criticising capitalism, in particular, that led to the development of socialism.

supported the idea that socialism could be achieved by peaceful means and by working within the existing system. This split between revolutionary socialists (usually referred to as 'communists') and reformist socialists intensified after the Bolsheviks (Russian communists) seized power in Russia in the revolution of October 1917. In Britain, the influence of revolutionary socialism has remained slight while reformist socialism has managed to enter the political mainstream.

7.18 *What is socialism?*

Socialism has two elements. It is both a criticism of capitalism and a blueprint for an alternative way of organising society. But these two elements are intertwined. It is through the criticism of capitalism that the alternative way of organising society becomes apparent. This criticism of capitalism can be divided into four areas. These are outlined in Box 7.12 on page 131.

Socialism and human nature

To socialists, people are social beings who thrive best in a close relationship with one another. People are not just motivated by selfish interests, but are capable of living harmoniously and cooperatively together as part of a community with a compassionate attitude towards all. Socialists do not agree that people are flawed. Rather, they emphasise that people are largely the product of their upbringing and their environment. If people are selfish, greedy or uncaring it is because these are the dominant values in society. It follows from this that, if human capacities are to be developed, then the right environment must be created. This requires a decisive change in the nature of society.

Socialists argue that anti-social behaviour (including crime), to a large extent, results from material conditions such as unemployment and poverty rather than from weaknesses in human nature. Eliminating material problems would, therefore, be a major step towards solving many social problems.

Box 7.12 Four criticisms of capitalism

1. Workers are exploited

The toll on workers in a capitalist system is immense since capitalists compete with each other in the fight for the highest possible profits. Workers are exploited and dehumanised, becoming no more than numbers on a balance sheet. In such circumstances, work has no meaning other than as drudgery which keeps together body and soul.

2. Capitalism produces vast inequalities

Capitalism produces vast inequalities in society. There is a huge gap between the 'super rich' at the top and the poor at the bottom. The mass of people reap little reward for their labour. Yet, it is their labour which actually creates the wealth in the first place. Capitalism by its very nature perpetuates inequalities.

3. 'Freedom' is a sham

The so-called 'freedoms' which both conservatism and liberalism purport to support are merely a sham and an illusion. 'Freedom' in the conservative or liberal sense is only meaningful for the rich.

4. Capitalism is inefficient

Capitalism is not even an efficient system since it wastes all kinds of limited resources. The emphasis on the market place and the scramble for profits means that little attention is paid to the interests of society as a whole. The rich, for example, are more likely to spend their money on building a large house for themselves than on building a hospital for the good of the community.

Socialist aims

The socialist view of human nature indicates that human happiness depends on reshaping society according to socialist values. There are two main aims:

- the promotion of greater equality by means of a redistribution of resources from the wealthy to the rest
- the organisation of society through rational planning rather than by relying on market forces.

Socialism, the individual and the group

If the key unit in liberalism is the individual and in conservatism it is the family and the nation, the key unit in socialism is the group (or class). At the heart of socialism is the belief that people should join together and work collectively - see Box 7.13.

Box 7.13 Socialism means working together

Socialists see human beings as social creatures, capable of overcoming social and economic problems by drawing upon the power of the community rather than simply individual effort. Socialists stress the capacity of human beings for collective action, their willingness and ability to pursue goals by working together, as opposed to striving for personal self-interest.

Source: Heywood 1992.

Competition

Socialists differ from both liberals and conservatives in their attitude towards competition. Liberals and conservatives not only regard competition between people as natural, they also regard it as desirable. Socialists, on the other hand, believe that, by its very nature, competition turns people against each other and forces them to suppress or ignore their desire to cooperate. In simple terms, competition encourages selfishness and aggression while cooperation makes moral and economic sense. By working together rather than competing, the argument goes, people develop bonds between each other and are able to achieve more than could be achieved by working alone.

Responding to criticism

This belief in collective action has led to a great deal of criticism from non-socialists. Socialists have been accused, for example, of ignoring or suppressing individual freedom (by emphasising the needs of the group rather than the individual) and of lacking economic realism (since, it is claimed, economic success relies on competition). It should be noted, however, that socialism, like other ideologies, is ultimately no more than a framework upon which practical policies are based. Since Britain is a capitalist rather than a socialist state, it is perhaps understandable that the policies supported by most British socialists fall short of the ideal.

Socialism and the past

Some socialist historians still believe that:

> 'The history of all hitherto existing societies is the history of class struggles.' (Marx & Engels 1848, p.79)

But most accept that:

> 'Capitalism has not appeared to develop as Marx had predicted. Far from becoming more intense, class conflict has gradually been diluted by growing affluence.' (Heywood 1992, p.101)

Despite this, socialist historians are less likely to analyse developments in terms of individuals than are historians who subscribe to other ideologies. Socialists tend to argue that a 'great man' approach to history (an emphasis on the role of prominent individuals) is not very helpful. What matters is the changing relationship between different groups (classes) in society. By examining the past, socialists are able to understand how capitalism has been able to survive and to suggest ways in which a more just and fairer society, based on rational principles, can be established (it should be noted, however, that 'more just and fairer' has a different meaning for a socialist than it does for a liberal or a conservative).

Socialism and the state

Socialists aim to transform society. Gaining control of the state is, therefore, crucial. Once office has been won, the state becomes the main vehicle of change. A socialist government might introduce a system of progressive taxation so that the rich pay a larger proportion of their income in taxation than the poor. The money collected by the state in taxation could then be used to combat poverty and disadvantages. State power might also be used to defend the civil liberties of individuals and groups.

7.19 Different strands of socialism

Like liberalism and conservatism, it is possible to identify different ways in which socialism has been adapted. In general terms, it is necessary to distinguish between revolutionary socialism and reformist socialism.

Revolutionary socialism

One strand of British socialism is derived from the writing of Marx and Engels. This strand is known as 'revolutionary socialism' because its supporters believe that class conflict will inevitably result in the revolutionary overthrow of the capitalist system. Revolutionary socialists are also described as 'Marxists'. In the UK, revolutionary socialism or Marxism is regarded as an ideology on the extreme of the political spectrum (see Section 7.23 on page 136).

Reformist socialism

While some Marxists argue that the irresistible forces of class conflict mean that the revolutionary overthrow of the capitalist system is inevitable, other socialists argue for a more gradual approach. Reformist socialists suggest that, even without a revolution, socialist parties can gain election to government and then introduce reforms which will gradually transform society. Traditionally, reformist socialists have aimed to use the British Labour Party as a vehicle to achieve this goal.

Some political commentators distinguish between 'democratic socialism' and 'social democracy'. While both take the reformist rather than the revolutionary path towards socialism, each has rather different aims. Box 7.14 shows how they differ.

Box 7.14 Democratic socialism and social democracy

Democratic socialism

Democratic socialists hope to use the existing democratic mechanisms in society to gain power and then to introduce a hardline socialist programme which transforms the state. Their aim, in effect, is to alter the balance of power in society to such an extent that the capitalist system ceases to exist. They differ from revolutionary socialists, therefore, in terms of tactics, but not in terms of aims.

Social democracy

Social democrats, on the other hand, accept that they are living in a capitalist society and do not expect to change the fundamental nature of this society. Rather, they hope to introduce reforms which redistribute resources in such a way that the majority benefit rather than just the few. While social democrats might have similar ideals to democratic socialists, their views about what policies should be pursued are often quite different.

7.20 Socialism and the Labour Party

Early in its history, the Labour Party abandoned any traces of revolutionary socialist ideology (the Labour Party came into existence in 1906 - see Box 7.15). From the early days, however, there have been ideological battles between democratic socialists and those who support social democracy. A particularly serious battle was fought between these two groups after Labour's election defeat of 1979. This resulted in a period of ascendancy for the democratic socialists within the party and a radical manifesto for the 1983 general election. A heavy defeat for the party at this election, however, led the party to reconsider its ideological position and, by the time Tony Blair became Leader in 1994, his predecessors John Smith and Neil Kinnock had marginalised the democratic socialists.

Box 7.15 The birth of the Labour Party

In 1892, Keir Hardie (above) became the first independent labour (ie working-class) MP to be elected to Parliament. The following year, the Independent Labour Party was set up. This party campaigned hard to win the backing of trade unions. In 1900, the unions finally agreed to set up the 'Labour Representative Committee' (LRC). After winning 29 seats in the 1906 general election, the LRC officially became the Labour Party.

It is important to note that, throughout the Labour Party's history, periods of dominance by democratic socialists have been short-lived and they have not resulted in socialist governments. As Milliband (1972, p.13) points out, a commitment to capitalism, parliamentary procedures and constitutionalism has always been characteristic of the British Labour Party. Leach argues that the radicalism of the 1983 election manifesto was highly uncharacteristic and that the party's ideas and policies have been influenced far more by trade unionism and radical liberalism than it has by democratic socialism (see Leach 2002, pp.74-75). Despite Labour's reputation for being a 'socialist party', therefore, the relationship between the party and socialism is ambiguous.

Socialism and New Labour

Before Tony Blair was elected Leader of the Labour Party in 1994, the context within which changes to party procedure and party policy took place remained broadly within the social democratic tradition. During and after Tony Blair's successful leadership election campaign, however, it became clear that he stood outside this tradition. To signify this ideological shift, Tony Blair and his supporters made increasing use of the term 'New Labour' and one of Blair's first acts as Leader was to replace the old Clause IV of the Labour Party constitution (which committed the party to clear socialist goals) with a new clause (which did not) - see Box 7.16.

Box 7.16 Clause IV

(i) The old clause IV

The Labour Party's object is...to secure for the workers by hand or by brain the full fruits of their industry and the most equitable distribution thereof that may be possible upon the basis of common ownership of the means of production, distribution and exchange, and the best obtainable system of popular administration and control of each industry or service.

Source: Labour 1993.

(ii) The new clause IV

The Labour Party...believes that by the strength of our common endeavour we achieve more than we achieve alone, so as to create for each of us the means to realise our true potential and for all of us a community in which power, wealth and opportunity are in the hands of the many not the few, where the rights we enjoy reflect the duties we owe, and where we live together, freely, in a spirit of solidarity, tolerance and respect.

Source: Labour 1998.

The ideological position of Blair and his supporters has been described as the 'Third Way' - a path which supposedly runs through the middle ground between the left and the right. Whether or not this Third Way can be described as 'socialist' in any sense has been much debated - as Box 7.17 shows.

Box 7.17 The Third Way

For some, the term 'Third Way' is vacuous, a matter of style rather than substance. For others, it is a thin veil for the virtual acceptance of the principles and practice of neo-liberalism or Thatcherism. Others, again, see it as social democracy in another guise, or an attempt to revive social democracy. Freeden locates it somewhere between the three great Western ideological traditions - liberalism, conservatism and socialism - borrowing elements from all three. This rather implies that the Third Way is essentially a 'middle way' between left and right, or between state socialist planning and free-market capitalism. As such, it appeals to moderate social democrats and progressives in the political centre. Yet, the notion of a middle way was also embraced by Harold Macmillan for his brand of one nation conservatism. More damagingly, fascists once proclaimed a third or middle way between communism and capitalism. Anthony Giddens (1998) contrasts what he calls classical or old-style social democracy (which might be loosely identified with mainstream Old Labour) with the ideas of Thatcherism, neo-liberalism or the New Right. He argues that both doctrines are in trouble - and that is why there is a need for a Third Way. He argues that the Third Way involves a restatement of the traditional social democratic ideals of social justice and equality, coupled with a new relationship between the individual and the community, a redefinition of rights and obligations.

Source: Leach 2001.

Main points Sections 7.17 - 7.20

- Socialism provides a critique of capitalism and offers an alternative to liberalism and conservatism.
- At the heart of socialism is the belief that people should join together and work collectively. Socialists have two main aims: (1) the redistribution of resources from the wealthy to the rest in order to gain greater equality; and (2) the organisation of society through planning rather than by relying on market forces.
- Revolutionary socialists argue that class conflict will bring the revolution which overthrows the capitalist system and transforms society. Reformist socialists argue that, without a revolution, socialist parties can form governments which gradually transform society.

- Reformist socialists can be divided into: (1) democratic socialists who hope to gain power and then to introduce a socialist programme which transforms the state; and (2) social democrats who do not expect to change the nature of society, but hope to give the majority a fairer deal.
- Throughout the Labour Party's history, there have been ideological battles between those who support democratic socialism and those who support social democracy.
- When Tony Blair became Leader of the Labour Party there was an ideological shift away from socialism and there is a debate about whether the 'Third Way' can be described, in any way, as 'socialist'.

Activity 7.4 Socialism

Item A Socialism (1)

Item B Socialism (2)

Socialism is the collective ownership by all the people of the factories, mills, mines, railways, land and all other instruments of production. Socialism means production to satisfy human needs and it means direct control and management of the industries and social services by the workers through a democratic government. Under socialism, all authority will originate from the workers who will be integrally united in socialist trade unions. All persons elected to any post in the socialist government, from the lowest to the highest level, will be directly accountable to the rank and file. Such a system would make possible the fullest democracy and freedom. It would be a system based on the most primary freedom - economic freedom. For individuals, socialism means an end to economic insecurity and exploitation. It means workers cease to be commodities bought and sold on the labour market. It means a chance to develop all individual capacities and potentials within a free community of free individuals. It means a classless society.

Source: Levin 1976.

Item C Socialism and New Labour (1)

The daily worries that people face are my concerns too. But while there is always a market for people who say we are doomed, I am an optimist. For too long, our strengths have been undermined by weaknesses of élitism and snobbery, vested interests and social division, complacency bred by harking back to the past. In the 20th century, it was as if a glass ceiling has stopped us fulfilling our potential. Today, we can break through that glass ceiling. We can do this by putting power, wealth and opportunity in the hands of the many, not the few. Countries only prosper on the basis of partnership - between government, employers and their employees, and the voluntary sector. What Britain needs is an active, enabling state, not a nanny state. We know the power and value of markets, but we also know their limits.

Source: Labour 2001.

Item D Socialism and New Labour (2)

In 1983, the Labour Party was committed to increased public spending and state ownership, unilateral nuclear disarmament and leaving the European Community. All these policy positions have since been reversed, suggesting the betrayal of the party's former socialism. Yet, it is the Labour Party of the early 1980s which is untypical, not the Labour Party of today. Blair's leadership has much in common with that of earlier Leaders like Callaghan and Wilson. Blair describes his ideology as the 'Third Way'. This draws on some familiar Labour themes. Talk of social justice, community and responsibility draws on Labour's ethical socialist tradition. Blair's use of religious language reflects his debt to Christian socialism, a strand of socialism as old as the Labour Party. At the same time, the Third Way can also be related back to the progressive liberal quest for a middle way between a completely free market and state control. Once again, this is very much in the Labour tradition. Where Blair breaks with tradition is in distancing the party from the trade unions. Trade unions have lost members and their influence has weakened. The old manual working class is smaller and more fragmented. The Labour Party has become progressively less working class at every level. Blair's appeal to 'Middle England' may smack of betrayal of Labour's traditional core constituency, but it is electorally inevitable. The Third Way contains no positive role for unions.

Source: Leach 2002.

Questions

1. How does socialism differ from (a) liberalism and (b) conservatism? Use Items A and B in your answer.

2. Judging from Item C, would you describe Labour's 2001 election manifesto as 'socialist'? Explain your answer.

3. Judging from Items C and D and your own knowledge, is it accurate to describe the Third Way as 'a new form of socialism'?

4. Herbert Morrison, Labour's Deputy Leader after the Second World War, said that socialism is whatever the Labour Party happens to be doing at any one time.

a) What do you think he meant by this?

b) Do you think this is a sufficient definition of socialism? Give reasons for your answer.

7.21 'Extreme' ideologies

Liberalism, conservatism and socialism are all mainstream ideologies. It is these ideologies which determine the parameters of political argument in Britain. Any ideas that fall outside the ideological framework constructed by them are regarded as 'extreme' and unacceptable. In other words, despite their differences liberals, conservatives and reformist socialists have much in common. Take the system of parliamentary democracy which exists in Britain for example. Most liberals, conservatives and reformist socialists agree that Britain should have a system of parliamentary democracy even if they disagree over exactly how this parliamentary democracy should be organised.

Those who support ideologies on the extreme of the political spectrum, however, reject mainstream politics and support political systems which are fundamentally different. There are three main ideologies on the extreme of the political spectrum - anarchism, Marxism and fascism.

7.22 Anarchism

The word anarchy comes from the ancient Greek for 'no rule'. Anarchists are people who oppose all forms of authority. An anarchist state would be a state without any form of government or any laws. People would make decisions among themselves within their community without compulsion.

Since anarchists oppose all forms of government,

governments and people in authority are bound to feel threatened by the idea of anarchy, especially if (as has sometimes happened) anarchists are prepared to take violent action against them. The result is that in everyday language the term 'anarchy' is often used to mean chaos, disorder and mindless violence. This, most anarchists would argue, is an ugly distortion of the true meaning of the term.

While all anarchists believe that all forms of government and authority should be abolished, there are two distinct types of anarchism.

Anarcho-capitalism

One type can be characterised as an ultra-extreme form of liberalism. It is sometimes called 'anarcho-capitalism'. Anarcho-capitalists take free-market economics to their logical conclusion. If a market is to be truly free, they argue, then there is no need for government. People should be free to do anything they like. The success or failure of their actions will be determined by the market. The market will be self-regulatory and so there is no need for regulations to be imposed from outside (by government). Turner suggests that:

'In concrete terms this would translate into the modern era as meaning, for example, no taxation, no compulsory education, no protection of minimum rights for workers in areas such as health and safety or redundancy, no regulation of what could or could not be used in the preparation of food or medicines. It is 19th century liberalism pushed to its logical extreme.' (Turner 1993, p.29)

Left-wing anarchism

The second type of anarchism is known as 'left-wing anarchism'. This can be characterised as an ultra-extreme form of socialism in that it is based on the premise that people are naturally able and willing to cooperate and work together collectively. If this is the case, then there is no need for government. Left to their own devices, people are perfectly capable of working together and resolving any differences between them. Turner suggests that there is a series of core principles which are shared by left-wing anarchists:

> 'The right to complete individual freedom, a complete rejection of authority of all forms, the establishment of a non-hierarchical society and an abiding belief that human nature is always essentially good. Where it is evidently bad, this is always a consequence of the deleterious [damaging] impact on humans of state exploitation and capitalist influences.' (Turner 1993, p.29)

Drawbacks

Unlike the other major ideologies, anarchism has not been put into practice on a large scale. Heywood suggests that this is because anarchism suffers from three drawbacks. These are outlined in Box 7.18.

Box 7.18 Anarchism's drawbacks

Andrew Heywood argues that anarchism has three main drawbacks. These are as follows.

1. It is unrealistic

The goal of anarchism - the overthrow of the state and all forms of political authority - is often considered to be simply unrealistic. Certainly the evidence of modern history from most parts of the world suggests that economic and social development is usually accompanied by a growth in the role of government, rather than its reduction or complete abolition.

2. It relies on unorthodox methods

In opposing the state and all forms of political authority, anarchists have rejected the conventional means of exercising political influence, forming political parties, standing for elections, seeking public office and so on. Anarchists have, therefore, been forced to rely upon less orthodox methods, often based upon a faith in mass spontaneity rather than political organisation.

3. It is incoherent

Anarchism is not a single, coherent set of political ideas. Although anarchists are united in their opposition to the institutions of the state and, indeed, other forms of coercive authority, they arrive at this conclusion from many different philosophical paths.

Source: Heywood 1992.

7.23 Marxism

It has already been noted in Section 7.19 that socialism can be divided into two strands. While reformist socialists are able and willing to work within the existing capitalist system, revolutionary socialists (Marxists) hope to overthrow this system. Marxists may want the same end goal as reformist socialists, but their analysis of the current political situation and their tactics differ from them. For example, many Marxists are internationalists - they believe that a truly socialist society cannot be achieved until the working classes in countries all over the world rise up and overthrow capitalism. Because they are internationalists, they are not interested in existing state boundaries. As a result, they discourage patriotism. Because they believe that a revolution is a necessary precondition of socialism, they try to undermine the existing government by encouraging class conflict.

Marxist tactics

Tactics include educating the workers (revealing to them the true nature of their exploitation) and participating in political action designed to alienate workers from the existing political system (in the hope that this will lead the workers to rise up and overthrow the government). Such an analysis and such tactics are not shared by reformist socialists. As a result, Marxists are often branded as the 'enemy within' and tend to be marginalised by mainstream politicians.

7.24 Fascism

While Marxism is associated with the extreme left of the political spectrum, fascism is associated with the extreme right. Fascism is notoriously difficult to define. One definition is given in Box 7.19 on page 137.

7.25 What are 'new ideologies'?

Just as liberalism, conservatism and socialism were all shaped by the industrial revolution, two new ideologies have emerged out of the profound socio-economic changes which have taken place since 1945 - feminism and environmentalism. Although the roots of both lie in the pre-war world, it is only in recent years that political scientists have begun to accept that they are distinct ideologies rather than tendencies within other ideologies. Significantly, neither ideology fits neatly on the left/right model of the political spectrum. Both aim to influence people on both the left and the right.

7.26 Feminism

As with most ideologies, it is difficult to provide a simple, succinct definition of feminism. Bryson, however, argues that:

> 'A starting point for all feminism is the belief that women and men are not equal in society and that women are systematically disadvantaged, subordinated or oppressed. Unlike traditional political thinking which has either defended or ignored gender inequality, feminism sees this as a central issue. As a political theory, feminism tries to understand the nature and causes of women's disadvantage and as a political movement it tries to change it.' (Bryson 1994, p.31)

Although the term 'feminism' was first used over 100 years ago and the origins of modern feminism can be traced back to the 18th century, it is only since the 1960s that political scientists have begun to take feminism seriously - see Box 7.20 on page 137.

Box 7.19 A definition of fascism

Hunt (1992) suggests that fascism is made up of eight separate elements. These are:

1. Aggressive nationalism

Fascists are aggressive nationalists. They believe that their nation is the best, that all citizens should be enthusiastically patriotic and, if necessary, military conquest should be embarked upon to solve struggles between nations.

2. Militarism

Fascists are militarists. They admire organised violence and the military way of life.

3. Racism

Fascists are racists. This is a particularly important part of modern fascism. Contemporary British fascists, for example, argue that only white people should be allowed to live in Britain.

4. Leadership

Fascists believe in charismatic leadership. Fascists place their Leader on a pedestal and allow their Leader to have absolute authority. They prefer dictatorial rule to democratic rule.

5. The state is the key unit

The key unit to fascists is not the individual or the family but the state. The state is more important than the individual and, therefore, individuals should be prepared to sacrifice themselves for the good of the state.

6. Anti-Marxist

Fascists despise Marxism. They despise it because it is internationalist (the opposite of nationalist) and because Marxists encourage class conflict. Class conflict damages the unity of the state.

7. Anti-Parliament

Fascists are opposed to parliamentary government on the grounds that this type of government's fundamental concern is with the freedom of the individual rather than with the unity of the nation.

8. Belief in the irrational and mystical

Fascism revels in the irrational and mystical. Fascists assume that people are irrational and appeal to their irrationality. Fascists also construct myths which are used to bind their supporters together through rituals. For example, fascism often emphasises the idea of rebirth - the idea that fascism will bring economic, political and spiritual renewal. In this sense, fascism has much in common with religion.

Source: Hunt 1992.

Since the 1960s, three distinct strands of feminism have been identified - liberal feminism, socialist (or Marxist) feminism and radical feminism.

Box 7.20 The birth of feminism

'Until the 1960s, sexual divisions were rarely considered to be politically interesting or important. If the very different social, economic and political roles of men and women were considered at all, they were usually regarded as "natural" and, therefore, as inevitable. For example, men, and probably most women, accepted that some kind of sexual division of labour was dictated by the simple facts of biology: women were suited to a domestic and household existence by the fact that they could bear and suckle children, while the greater physical strength of men suited them to the outdoor and public world of work...The growth of the women's movement and feminist thought since the 1960s, however, has severely tested such complacency.'

Source: Heywood 1992, p.216.

Liberal feminism

Liberal feminists argue that women and men have equal moral worth and deserve equal treatment. Women, therefore, should have the same rights as men and the same opportunities. Forbes summarises the key elements of liberal feminism as follows:

'Liberal feminists dismiss any talk of essential differences between women and men and are happy to propose changes that introduce formal and legal equality into the relations between the sexes. There is a stress on equal civil and economic rights, the need for education for women (and to change men), full partnership in work and an equal share in the information of laws.' (Forbes 1991, p.63)

Socialist feminism

According to socialist feminists, however, it is the capitalist system which is responsible for women's oppression. Capitalism ensures that women are exploited either as unpaid workers in the home or as part-time workers on low wages. To combat this, structural change is required:

'Socialist feminists believe that the relationship between the sexes is rooted in the social and economic structure itself and that nothing short of profound social change, some would say social revolution, can offer women the prospect of genuine emancipation.' (Heywood 1992, p.232)

Radical feminism

While liberal and socialist feminism owe something to existing ideologies, radical feminism goes beyond them. Radical feminism is defined in Box 7.21 on page 138.

7.27 Environmentalism

Worldwide population growth, industrial growth and scientific advance are three factors which, combined, have led to a growing concern about the relationship between human beings and the environment. Until the 1960s, politicians did not really concern themselves with the environment except

Box 7.21 Radical feminism

'Radical feminism claims that the oppression of women by men is the oldest and most universal form of inequality that there is. It also argues that male domination or "patriarchy" is not confined to the public worlds of politics and economic life but that it is based upon the most intimate areas of our lives...Many radical feminists reject the idea that women should try to compete with men by becoming like them. They argue instead that women are in many ways better than men...For some this means that "womanly values" should be more powerfully expressed in society as a whole. For others, it leads to the claim that all men are to be seen as "the enemy" and that lesbian separatism is the only solution. Many, however, reject this conclusion and are careful to distinguish between male power (which they oppose) and individual men (who may be good friends or husbands).'

Source: Bryson 1994, pp.31-32.

Box 7.22 Sustainability - a definition

'The capacity of a system, in this case the biosphere [world] itself, to maintain its health and continue in existence. Sustainability sets clear limits upon human ambitions and material dreams because it requires that production does as little damage as possible to the fragile global ecosystem.'

Source: Heywood 1992, p.267.

to consider it as a resource bank to be exploited. Since then, however, there has been a realisation that many of the world's resources are finite and that current practices may be causing long-term, perhaps even irreversible, damage.

The impact of environmentalism

The growing concern about the damage that people are or may be doing to the environment is at the heart of the new ideology that has been called 'environmentalism'. The impact of this new ideology is great. Since the late 1980s, for example, all three major political parties in Britain have claimed that they have taken 'Green' issues on board. In other words, all three parties admit to having been influenced by environmentalism.

The main principle

Environmentalism is based upon the principle that there should be a balanced relationship between people and their environment. Whereas other ideologies are only or mainly concerned with the relationship between people,

environmentalists are concerned about the relationship between people and the natural world. Environmentalists emphasise that people are just one species within a complex ecosystem and that (because of people's ability to manipulate the environment) their behaviour will determine whether or not that ecosystem survives. The implication of this is that people should consider long-term environmental consequences when making political decisions.

Sustainability

Central to environmentalism is the notion of sustainability. Sustainability is defined in Box 7.23.

Take timber for example. In the world as a whole, an enormous amount of timber is being collected and used. At present, more trees are being cut down than are being planted. As a result, the total number of trees in the world is diminishing. Environmentalists argue that this is shortsighted. To carry on cutting down trees at the present rate is unsustainable since there will come a time when there are no trees left. In the long term, current practice will lead to an ecological disaster. To prevent this happening there should be a policy of sustainability - for every tree that is chopped down, for example, a new tree should be planted.

This idea has important implications. While other ideologies assume that economic growth is a fundamental aim, environmentalists question whether economic growth is in people's long-term interest. As a result, some environmentalists argue that people should be taught to reject materialism and to look for personal fulfilment in a lifestyle based only on sustainable resources.

Main points Sections 7.21 - 7.27

- There are three ideologies on the extreme of the political spectrum - anarchism, Marxism and fascism - and two new ideologies - feminism and environmentalism.
- Anarchists are opposed to all forms of authority. An anarchist state would have no government or laws.
- Marxists share the same goal as many reformist socialists, but they differ in their tactics.
- Fascism has eight main elements - nationalism, militarism, racism, love of leadership, belief in the

state as the key unit, hatred of Marxism and democracy, a belief in the irrational.
- The starting point for feminism is that women are disadvantaged. There are three main strands - liberal feminism, socialist feminism and radical feminism.
- The starting point for environmentalism is that there should be a balanced relationship between people and their environment. A key term is 'sustainability' - the capacity of a system to maintain its health.

Activity 7.5 New and non-mainstream ideologies

Item A Making assumptions

(i) Every language reflects the prejudices of the society in which it evolved and English evolved through most of its history in a male-centred, patriarchal (male-dominated) society. We shouldn't be surprised, therefore, that its vocabulary and grammar reflect attitudes that exclude or demean women. Once we begin looking at what the English language has to say at a subliminal level, some things become obvious. What standard usage says about males, for example, is that they are a species while females are a sub-species. From this flows a thousand other enhancing and degrading messages all encoded in the language which we, in English speaking countries, learn when we are born.

(ii) A British Rail advertisement aimed at company executives included the following passage:

'Consider the effects long distance driving can have on an executive. Chances are when he arrives at his meeting he'll be feeling every inch of that journey. Worse, his tiredness may make him unresponsive and irritable. Would you feel happy about doing business with a man like that?'

(iii) Bill's attempts to interest XYZ company in his products had finally paid off. He was invited to make a presentation and was offered the use of a conference room in a letter signed John Liveridge, assistant to the president. When Bill signalled that he was set up, a woman and a man entered the room. The woman said to Bill, 'I'm Virginia Hancock and this is John Liveridge, my...'. Bill enthusiastically broke in, drowning her last word. 'I'm delighted to meet you, Mr Liveridge, and you too, Ginny.' Ms Hancock owned the company, Mr Liveridge was her assistant and Bill lost a customer.

Source: Miller & Swift, 1989.

Item B Direct Action

Item C Socialist Worker

Item D British Nationalist

Item E The three main political parties and the environment

(i) The Labour Party
The Environmental Challenge*

The healthy future of our environment is one of the world's greatest challenges. We must make substantial changes in the way we work and live to safeguard all our futures. We must make the market work for the environment. We will support hybrid and fuel cell vehicles. It is imperative that we use natural resources more efficiently and recycle more. Water management is a vital challenge for the future. Environmental protection and sustainability go hand-in-hand. We cannot protect the environment without addressing the development needs of the poor.

*This is the only section of the manifesto to deal explicitly with the environment. The full section takes up one page out of a total of 44 pages.

Source: Labour 2001.

(ii) The Conservative Party
The Wider Environment*

Conservatives believe that each of us should act as a steward preserving and enhancing the natural world and the built environment for future generations. The biggest global challenge is to prevent climate change causing long-term damage though extreme weather conditions. We will meet the commitments made by successive British governments by a comprehensive package of emission permit trading, energy conservation measures, tax incentives, greater encouragement of renewable energy and cleaner energy generation.

*This is the only section of the manifesto to deal explicitly with the environment. The section takes up quarter of a page out of a total of 46 pages.

Source: Conservative 2001.

(iii) The Liberal Democrats

Green Action*

- Our National Recycling Programme will provide a doorstep recycling collection for every household by the end of the next Parliament. We will seek to recycle 60% of household waste within ten years.
- We will immediately set up a National Task Force to review arrangements for flood defence management and response.
- We will seek a moratorium at EU level on commercial growing of genetically modified crops.
- We will develop a national oceans and coasts policy to provide sustainable livelihoods and prosperity for coastal communities, improved health of the seas for wildlife and a safer environment for marine activities.
- We will protect the environment and create 'green jobs' in urban, rural and marine habitats.
- We will ensure that local authority structure plans incorporate targets for CO_2 emission reductions.
- We will protect green spaces.

*This is an extract from one 'Green Action' section in the manifesto - there are 'Green Action' sections on every page.

Source: Liberal Democrat 2001.

Questions

1. Look at Item A.

   a) What evidence is there in passage (ii) to support the view expressed in passage (i)?

   b) Why do you think some feminists argue that the way in which people use language is important?

   c) What does passage (iii) tell us about the impact of feminism?

2. a) Using Items B-D and your own knowledge, explain the main differences between anarchism, Marxism and fascism.

   b) The major chains of newsagents refuse to stock *Direct Action*, *Socialist Worker* and *British Nationalist*. Why do you think this is so?

3. a) What is the evidence in Item E that the main political parties have been influenced by environmentalism?

   b) How would you rate each party's commitment to environmentalism? Give reasons for your answer.

References

Adams (1993) Adams, I., *Political Ideology Today*, MUP, 1993.

Bryson (1994) Bryson, V., 'Feminism', *Politics Review*, Vol.4.1, September 1994.

Conservative (2001) *Time for Common Sense*, Conservative Party manifesto, Conservative Party, 2001.

Dobson (1992) Dobson, A., 'Ideology', *Politics Review*, Vol.1.4, 1992.

Dorey (2004) Dorey, P., 'The Conservatives under Iain Duncan Smith' in *Lancaster (2004)*.

Eagleton (1991) Eagleton, T., *Ideology*, Verso, 1991.

Eynsech (1957) Eynsech, H., *Sense and Nonsense in Psychology*, Penguin, 1957.

Forbes (1991) Forbes, I., 'The politics of gender' in *Wale (1991)*.

Giddens (1998) Giddens, A., *The Third Way: the Renewal of Social Democracy*, Cambridge, Polity Press 1998.

Gray (1997) Gray, J., 'Conservatism RIP', *New Statesman*, 12 September 1997.

Heywood (1992) Heywood, A., *Political Ideologies: an introduction*, Macmillan, 1992.

Heywood (1994) Heywood, A., *Political Ideas and Concepts: an introduction*, Macmillan, 1994.

Hunt (1992) Hunt, S., 'Fascism and the race issue in Britain', *Talking Politics*, Vol.5.1, Autumn 1992.

Kelly (2001) Kelly, R., 'British political parties; developments since 1997' in *Lancaster (2001)*.

Labour (1993) *Labour Party Rule Book 1993-94*, Labour Party, 1993.

Labour (1998) *Labour Party Rule Book 1998*, Labour Party, 1998.

Labour (2001) *Ambitions for Britain*, Labour Party election manifesto, Labour Party, 2001.

Lancaster (2001) Lancaster, S. (ed.), *Developments in Politics*, Vol.12, Causeway Press, 2001.

Lancaster (2002) Lancaster, S. (ed.), *Developments in Politics*, Vol.13, Causeway Press, 2002.

Lancaster (2004) Lancaster, S. (ed.), *Developments in Politics*, Vol.15, Causeway Press, 2004.

Leach (2001) Leach, R., Political ideas' in *Lancaster (2001)*.

Leach (2002) Leach, R. 'From Old Labour to the 'Third Way', *Talking Politics*, Vol.14.2, January 2002.

Leach (2003) Leach R., 'Whither Conservatism', *Talking Politics*, Vol.15.2, January 2003.

Levin (1976) Levin, J., 'Levin speaks for socialism', *Weekly People*, 9 October 1976.

Lib Dem (2001) *Freedom, Justice, Honesty*, Liberal Democrat general election manifesto, Liberal Democrats, 2001.

Marx & Engels (1846) Marx, K. & Engels F., *The German Ideology in McLellan (1977)*.

Marx & Engels (1848) Marx, K. & Engels, F., *The Communist Manifesto*, Pelican, 1967.

Mclellan (1977) Mclellan, D., *Karl Marx - Selected Writings*, OUP, 1977.

Miller & Swift (1989) Miller, C. & Swift, K., *The Handbook of Non-sexist Writing*, The Women's Press, 1989.

Milliband (1972) Milliband, R., *Parliamentary Socialism*, Merlin, 1972.

Oakeshott (1962) Oakeshott, M., *On Rationalism in Politics*, Methuen, 1962.

Seliger (1976) Seliger, M., *Politics and Ideology*, Allen & Unwin, 1976.

Smiles (1859) Smiles S., *Self Help*, Penguin, 1986.

Turner (1983) Turner, R. 'Anarchism: what is it?' *Politics Review*, Vol.3.1, 1993.

Wale (1991) Wale, W. (ed.), *Developments in Politics*, Vol.2, Causeway Press, 1991.

Whiteley et al. (1994) Whiteley, P., Seyd, P. & Richardson, J., *True Blues: the Politics of Conservative Party Membership*, Oxford University Press, 1994.

Wild (2002) Wild, E., 'The Recent history of the Conservative Party', *Talking Politics*, Vol.15.1, September 2002.

8.1 *The development of political parties*

Before the 19th century, political parties did exist but they were very different from modern political parties. The first political parties - the Whigs and the Tories - existed only within Parliament. These parties were rather loose groups of MPs who were drawn together by family ties or who shared similar views. It was not until the mid-19th century that mass political parties with organisations and members outside Parliament began to develop.

The key to the growth of mass political parties was the extension of the franchise (see Unit 3). Before there was a mass electorate, participation in politics was confined to a small and wealthy élite. As a result, political parties were unnecessary outside Parliament. There were so few voters that candidates could canvass their vote individually - they did not need a party machine behind them.

Impact of the Great Reform Act

The Great Reform Act of 1832 was the catalyst for change. Although the electorate remained tiny after 1832, one of the requirements of the Act was that voters must be registered. The political parties quickly realised that it was essential to get their supporters registered. To ensure that the registration process was carried out efficiently, the parties saw the need for some central control over the activities of groups of local supporters. The Tories, therefore, set up the Carlton Club as their headquarters in 1832 and the Whigs established the Reform Club as their headquarters in 1836.

The impact of further electoral reform

Further electoral reform between 1867 and 1918 led to a truly mass electorate and to the establishment of more rigorously democratic electoral procedures. For a party to win the support of a mass electorate, it is necessary for the party to have a reasonably clear set of policies and ideas which can be presented to the electorate. It is also necessary for a party which hopes to govern the country to have representatives and supporters in every constituency. So, the growth of the mass electorate led directly to the growth of the mass party. To survive, parties had to adapt to the new conditions. Not only did they have to ensure that party supporters actually went to the polls and voted on election day, they had to ensure that the government (when they formed it) was able to remain in office and implement its programme. This required discipline and tight organisation both in Parliament and in the constituencies.

By the early 20th century the fundamental features of modern political parties were in place. By then, the two main parties - the Liberal Party (which evolved from the Whigs) and the Conservative Party (which evolved from the Tories) - worked in a similar fashion to political parties today.

8.2 *The functions of political parties*

As Ball (1987) and Garner & Kelly (1998) point out, political parties exist because they perform functions which are essential for the working of the political system. It is possible to classify these functions in a number of ways. One way is shown in Box 8.1.

Box 8.1 The functions of political parties

A. The governing function
The British government is formed by the political party with an overall majority in the House of Commons or (more rarely) by the largest single party or (very rarely) by a coalition of parties. The Prime Minister is the Leader of the governing party and the Cabinet is drawn from its senior members (or, in a coalition government, from the senior members of the governing parties).

B. The electoral function
The electoral process is dependent upon political parties. Parties choose candidates at local and national elections. They provide funds and facilities for election campaigns. They devise policies which the electorate is asked to support. They provide a label with which voters can identify. They provide a means of accountability since the electorate is able to hold them responsible for policy successes or failures.

C. The representative function
Political parties enable the views of people to be heard and they ensure that matters of public concern reach the political agenda. Some parties allow the views of key sections of the population to be heard. For example, the Labour Party has traditionally represented the views of trade unions and members of the working class. To be successful nationally, however, parties have to show that they represent the interests of the nation as a whole, not just those of particular sections of the population.

D. The policy function
In performing their representative function, political parties are led to formulate policies. By formulating policies, they ensure that the electorate has a choice between different approaches at election time. This brings clarity to the political process. Parties are supposed to implement these policies if they form the government and they are held responsible by the electorate at the next election for their successes or failures.

E. The recruitment and participation function
Political parties play a key role in encouraging people to become political activists. Most political activists are members of political parties. Once people have joined a political party, the party provides a continuing means of political participation.

F. The communicative and ideological function
Political parties provide their leaders with the means to communicate with their members and vice versa. It is through political parties that debate takes place between competing ideologies (see Unit 7 for a definition of ideology).

8.3 Common criticisms of parties

Political parties are often criticised for a number of reasons. First, parties are accused of imposing a uniformity of views upon their members. Since party members are encouraged to 'toe the party line', important debate can be stifled. Second, it is argued that the existence of parties creates artificial divides in society. The essence of the party system is that the different parties compete against each other. As a result, it is necessary for them to emphasise their differences and, sometimes, to maintain them artificially. And third, it is claimed that parties prevent new ideas from emerging. As the British political system is dominated by the three main parties, it is very hard for new ideas to break through into the mainstream.

8.4 Political parties and the democratic process

In a representative democracy with a mass electorate (see Unit 3 for a definition of the term 'representative democracy'), it is important that political parties function effectively. If they do not, the sort of problems outlined in Box 8.2 can arise.

Some commentators argue that a decline in party membership since 1997 and the tendency of all three main political parties to occupy the same middle ground help to explain a decline in turnout in elections and an increase in the public's lack of trust in politicians and the political process, as

Box 8.2 Problems that arise when parties do not function properly

1. Elections become uncompetitive enough because parties lack funds or members.
2. Parties with a membership which is small and unrepresentative of the population as a whole become unresponsive to the public.
3. A genuine choice between policies becomes limited when parties share ideas in key areas.
4. Minority interests go unrepresented when no party champions them.
5. The quality of people involved in political life declines when able, new members are not recruited.
6. Debate becomes stale and limited when the political system is dominated by a very small number of parties.
7. When parties are funded by wealthy individuals or corporations, there is the possibility that such individuals or corporations will gain an unhealthy influence over the formulation of policy.

Source: McNaughton 2003.

measured in numerous opinion polls. In short, they argue, all seven of the problems outlined in Box 8.2 now need to be addressed if the democratic process in the UK is to regain its credibility.

Main points   Sections 8.1 - 8.4

- **Before the 19th century, political parties did exist but they were very different from modern political parties.**
- **The Great Reform Act of 1832 was the catalyst for change. But it was the development of a mass electorate between 1867 and 1918 that brought the need for mass parties.**
- **The functions of political parties can be divided as follows: (1) the governing function; (2) the electoral function; (3) the representative function; (4) the policy function; (5) the**

recruitment and participation function; and (6) the communicative and ideological function.
- **Political parties are often criticised because: (1) they impose a uniformity of views; (2) they perpetuate social divisions; and (3) they prevent new ideas from emerging.**
- **Some commentators argue that, because political parties in the UK are not functioning effectively, this is damaging the democratic process.**

Activity 8.1 Political parties in the early 21st century

Item A Party membership (1)

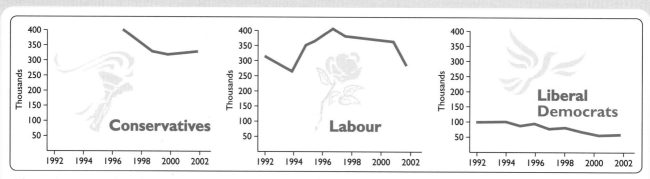

These charts provide information on the membership levels of the three main parties.

Item B Party membership (2)

Organisation	2002	2001	2000	Earlier
Labour	280,000	×	311,000	400,465 (1996)
Lib Dems	76,023	74,176	71,641	98,611 (1996)
Conservatives	330,000	×	318,000	350,000-400,000
Greens	5,000	4,000	×	3,500 (1996)
SNP	*Figures are confidential*			
Plaid Cymru	11,000	×	×	*no previous figures*
TUC	×	69 unions 6.7m members	76 unions 6.8m members	73 unions (1996) 6.7m members
Amnesty International	×	154,611	136,348	125,362 (1998)
Greenpeace	×	193,500	176,000	194,309 (1998)
Friends of the Earth	×	110,248	105,185	94,528 (1996)
CND (approx figures)	×	27-32,000	25-30,000	*no previous figures*
Stonewall	×	6,000	5,000	*no previous figures*
RSPB	1.19m	1.11m	1.4m	925,000 (1996)
RSPCA	×	49,760	54,000	29,504 (1996)
National Trust	2.8m	2.7m	×	2.29m (1996)

This table shows the membership of political parties in recent years, compared to that of selected pressure groups.

In January 2002, Labour's General Secretary, David Triesman, admitted that disengagement of young people from party politics was threatening the lifeblood of democracy. Triesman said that Labour Party membership had fallen by 10% since January 2001, down to 280,000. The Tories claim a higher membership - over 300,000. The Liberal Democrats admit falling from a peak of 100,000 to 71,000 in 2000, but they rose to 74,000 in January 2001 and 76,000 in January 2002. The Labour Party's all-time low was in 1991 (261,000 members). At the time of the 1997 general election, it had 401,000 members. The drop in numbers in 2002, Triesman claimed, was, in part, the result of an administrative change - the party was terminating any membership more than five months in subscription arrears. This led to a drop of 13,000 members at a stroke. But Triesman acknowledged that there was a move away from political organisations, especially by younger voters. Labour's average membership age was creeping up to between 40 and 45, he said. In a move that will be welcomed by party activists, Triesman said that, after an era of central control, Labour had to take more risks by opening up debate inside the party.

Source: The *Guardian*, 29 January 2002.

Item C The role of political parties

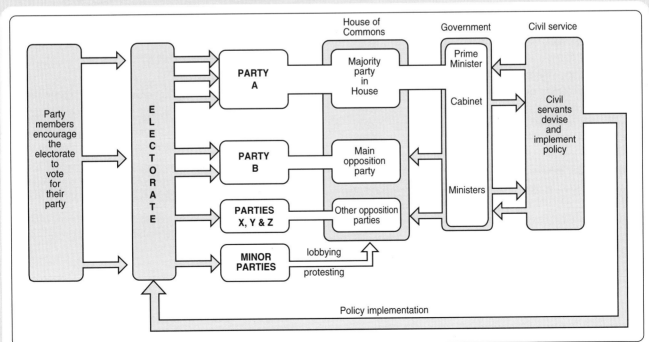

This diagram shows the role of political parties in the British political system.

Questions

1. a) What do Items A and B tell us about the state of the three main parties in 2002?

   b) Why are the membership levels of the main political parties important?

   c) How might low membership levels make it difficult for the main political parties to perform their functions?

2. Use Item C to explain how parties 'provide the means for peaceful resolutions of political tensions'.

8.5 Classifying party systems

Most political scientists (see, for example, Simpson 1998) would accept that party systems can be divided into four categories: the single-party system; the dominant-party system; the two-party system; and, the multi-party system.

A. The single-party system

In a single-party system only one party puts up candidates for election. Other parties are banned. The single-party system is usually, therefore, undemocratic and authoritarian (ruled by a dictator). Nazi Germany and the Soviet Union under Communism are two examples of the single-party system.

B. The dominant-party system

The dominant-party system is a system where many parties may exist and fight elections but only one party tends to win power - either on its own or as the dominant member of a coalition. Political scientists have often cited Japan as the classic example of the dominant-party system. Japan's Liberal Democratic Party (LDP) remained in government from its foundation in 1955 until August 1993.

3. The two-party system

In a two-party system, two parties compete for power on an equal or near equal basis. Other parties may stand against the two dominant parties, but in a two-party system these other parties win few seats and exercise little power. It has often been argued that Britain has a two-party system. But some political scientists deny that this is the case.

4. The multi-party system

A multi-party system is one in which more than two parties compete on an equal or near equal basis. In such a system, power may alternate between the various parties or it may be shared in coalitions. Political scientists often used to cite Italy as the classic example of the multi-party system because proportional representation in Italy continually produced multi-party coalition governments. In April 1993, however, a large majority of Italians voted to change their electoral system to a plurality (first-past-the-post) system.

8.6 The debate over the British party system

In 1955, the political scientist Robert McKenzie published a book called *British Political Parties* (McKenzie 1955). This book is still regarded as the classic statement of the argument that Britain has a two-party system. Of the 597 pages of the book, 595 were devoted to the Conservative and Labour Parties.

McKenzie argued that, in the British two-party system, Labour and Conservative compete in general elections for an absolute majority of seats. The winning party forms the government. The party which loses forms the opposition whose role is to scrutinise the work of government critically and to offer itself as an alternative government. At the next election, the voters choose between the two parties, rejecting the government if their performance is seen as poor and installing what was the opposition in their stead.

McKenzie argued that the two-party system is a central part of British democracy. This is because it offers choice to the electorate and makes government accountable. Choice is provided because the voter has two parties to decide between at election time, both of which would be capable of forming a government. Government is held accountable both as a consequence of the work of the opposition party and by the prospect of being replaced at the next election.

Box 8.3 Advantages and disadvantages of the two-party system

Advantages

1. Presents voters with a clear choice between rivals.
2. Voters can decide between alternative programmes.
3. Normally produces stable and strong government.
4. Governments are able to implement their election promises.
5. There is a government-in-waiting ready to take over if the existing government loses its way.

Disadvantages

1. Politics becomes too adversarial (based too much on conflict).
2. Most people do not support either party, but the two parties' dominance means that votes for other parties are wasted.
3. The system produces huge swings in government policy, making long-term planning difficult.
4. The two-party system gives great power to whichever party is in government, making the House of Commons irrelevant.

8.7 Does Britain have a two-party system?

Box 8.4 on page 146 shows the conclusion that Stephen Ingle reached after surveying the historical development of British political parties between 1689 and 1989.

Box 8.4 Ingle's conclusion on the
development of political parties

'Our historical survey indicates that the British political system has been dominated on and off, over the past 300 years, by two parties, but it also shows the nature of this domination and of the parties themselves to have been subject to constant and considerable change. The pattern of party politics, moreover, has changed just as dramatically, with long spells of dominance by one party and with parties constantly breaking up and regrouping.'

Source: Ingle 1992, p.3.

The passage in Box 8.4 shows how important perspective is in considering whether or not Britain has a two-party system. If someone is living through a period in which two parties have been alternating in power for the previous 30 years, then it appears that Britain has a two-party system. On the other hand, if someone is living through a long period of government by a single party, it appears that a dominant-party system has replaced the old two-party system. Similarly, if someone chooses to examine the party system in Britain between 1945 and 1979, that will probably lead them to different conclusions from someone who looks at trends over the last 150 years.

Is a two-party system the norm?

At the time when McKenzie was writing (1955), it did indeed seem that a two-party system had established itself after the Second World War. Labour governed from 1945 to 1951 and then the Conservatives took over. And, for a while after 1955, it seemed that McKenzie's analysis was faultless. Between 1945 and 1979 - a period of 34 years - both Labour and the Conservatives held power for exactly the same number of years.

But, even this period of seeming two-party rule is open to reinterpretation. Between 1951 and 1964, Labour lost three general elections in a row. For those who, by 1964, had lived through 13 years of Conservative rule, it probably did not seem much like a two-party system. And, if a wider perspective is taken, the idea that the two-party system is the norm loses some of its credence. Box 8.5 shows the conclusions that can be reached if the first nine decades of the 20th century are examined as a whole.

Box 8.5 Andrew Heywood's view

'Taking a longer perspective, it could be argued that Britain has had a dominant-party system through much of the 20th century and certainly since the old Liberal-Conservative two-party system collapsed after the First World War. The Conservatives have been in government, either alone or as the dominant member of a coalition, for 51 of the last 70 years. Two-party politics undoubtedly took place during this period but was largely confined to the 1964-79 period when Labour won four out of five general elections. The important point is that Labour has only twice, in 1945 and 1966, recorded decisive election victories and at no time has the party managed to serve two consecutive full terms in office.'

Source: Heywood 1993, pp.86-87.

Following Heywood's argument, then the four Conservative election victories between 1979 and 1992 merely confirmed a trend (that the Conservative Party is the single dominant party) rather than indicating a turning point (from two-party to dominant-party system).

The British party system since 1974

The key election from which the decline of the model of Britain as a two-party system is dated is the first election of 1974. At this election, the first of a number of developments which have undermined the image of Britain as a political system which is dominated by two parties occurred.

The first of these developments was the rise of the Liberal Party. At the two elections of 1974, they secured 14 and 13 seats respectively, a performance which more than doubled their parliamentary representation. Perhaps more importantly, their share of the votes cast rose even more dramatically. In 1970, they gained 7.5% of the votes. In February 1974 they gained 19.3% and in October 1974 18.3%. Such an increase in support, largely sustained and improved upon in subsequent elections, makes a severe dent in the argument that Britain has a two-party system, a point underscored by the success of the Liberal Democrats in 1997 and 2001 when they won 46 and then 52 seats.

The second of these developments was the string of general election victories won by the Conservatives in 1979, 1983, 1987 and in 1992. This extended period of dominance by the Conservatives gave a new perspective on the party system. It looked increasingly as though not a two-party system existed but a dominant-party system. In this system the Conservatives were the dominant party and Labour and the Liberal Democrats minor players, destined to fight about which one of them was to be the bigger opposition party.

Labour's two overwhelming victories in 1997 and 2001 changed the perspective once more. It was clear from these results that Labour would not be confined to steady decline and perpetual opposition. Indeed, divisions within the Conservative Party - three changes of leadership between 1997 and 2003 and persistent failures in reviving support in the opinion polls after the 2001 defeat - have led the Liberal Democrats to state as one of their aims overtaking the Conservatives as the official opposition at the next general election. If Britain's party system is characterised as a dominant-party system it is no longer the Conservatives who dominate. Perhaps, the best way to describe the system is as one which produces periods of dominance for one or other of the Conservative Party and Labour Party - see Box 8.6 on page 147.

Party systems, not party system

A further complication to the party system in Britain is that it may be incorrect to talk of a party system at all. Instead it might be more accurate to talk of party systems. This is because there are different patterns of party system in general elections, in local government, and in the devolved assemblies of Scotland Wales and Northern Ireland.

In English local government three points must be made. First, the Liberal Democrats control a significant number of councils, around 8% in 2003. This compares with around 25% controlled by Labour and 30% controlled by the Conservatives. Second, the Liberal Democrats hold 21% of

Box 8.6 Who's governed Britain since 1945

Date of general election	Party in power
1945	Labour
1950	Labour
1951	Conservatives
1955	Conservatives
1959	Conservatives
1964	Labour
1966	Labour
1970	Conservatives
1974 (Feb)	Labour
1974 (Oct)	Labour
1979	Conservatives
1983	Conservatives
1987	Conservatives
1992	Conservatives
1997	Labour
2001	Labour

seats in local government. In local government, therefore, the Liberal Democrats are a powerful force and a multi-party system must be acknowledged. Third, many local authorities are in a state of no overall control. In other words, no single party has an overall majority. In these councils, the Liberal Democrats often join governing coalitions, strengthening their position and further adding to the difficulties in characterising the party system (Fisher 2003, p.15).

In both the Scottish and Welsh Assemblies, there also exists a multi-party system. In addition to the Labour and Conservative Parties and the Liberal Democrats, the two nationalist parties are important. Indeed, the Scottish National Party and Plaid Cymru are crucial players in Scottish and Welsh politics. In the 1999 Scottish and Welsh Assembly elections, the nationalist parties did especially well. While their performance fell back in the 2003 Assembly elections, they remained, nonetheless, powerful political forces (Fisher 2003, p.14).

Finally, in Northern Ireland a unique party system operates which bears little resemblance to that in the rest of the UK. First, the parties that stand for election are different. The most important are the Ulster Unionist Party (UUP), the Democratic Unionist Party (DUP), the Social and Democratic Labour Party (SDLP) and Sinn Fein. In addition there are numerous smaller parties. Second, the electoral system is different (the Single Transferable Vote system - a system of proportional representation - is used - see Unit 4). And third, the issues which dominate Northern Irish politics revolve around its constitutional status, a fact which makes it unique in British politics.

Britain, therefore does not have a single-party system. It has a number of party systems. Nationally, a point of transition between a two-party and a multi-party system might be close to being reached. In other parts of the UK as new assemblies are established, many with proportional representation (see Unit 4), new party systems distinct to these assemblies emerge.

Main points Sections 8.5 - 8.7

- Most political scientists accept that party systems can be divided into four categories: (1) the single-party system; (2) the dominant-party system; (3) the two-party system; and (4) the multi-party system.
- In a two-party system, two main parties are likely to win a majority of seats. While one party forms the government, the other scrutinises and criticises government policy and develops its own policies, working on the assumption that it will take over the reins of government at the next election.
- There is a debate about whether Britain has a two-party system. Supporters argue that power has been shared by the Conservatives and Labour since 1945. Some opponents argue that the Conservative Party has been the dominant party throughout the 20th century. Others argue that a multi-party system has developed since 1970.
- Before 1997, many commentators argued that a dominant-party system was developing (because the Conservatives won four general elections in a row). The Labour victory in 1997 suggests that the two-party model may be appropriate after all.
- With the advent of new assemblies introduced since 1997 and the strong performance of the Liberal Democrats in English local government it may now be accurate to speak of the party systems of the UK rather than the party system.

Activity 8.2 The party system

Item A General election results 1945-2001

General Election	Seats			Prime Minister
	Lab	Con	Lib/Lib Dem	
1945	393	210	12	C. Attlee (Lab)
1950	315	298	9	C. Attlee (Lab)
1951	295	321	6	W. Churchill (Con)
1955	277	345	6	A. Eden (Con) 1
1959	258	365	6	H. Macmillan (Con) 2
1964	317	304	9	H. Wilson (Lab)
1966	364	253	12	H. Wilson (Lab)
1970	288	330	6	E. Heath (Con)
1974 (Feb)	301	297	14	H. Wilson (Lab)
1974 (Oct)	319	277	13	H. Wilson (Lab) 3
1979	269	339	11	M. Thatcher (Con)
1983	209	397	23	M. Thatcher (Con)
1987	229	376	22	M. Thatcher (Con) 4
1992	271	336	20	J. Major (Con)
1997	418	165	46	T. Blair (Lab)
2001	413	166	52	T. Blair (Lab)

1. Eden resigned Jan. 1957 and replaced by Macmillan
2. Macmillan resigned Oct. 1963 and replaced by Home
3. Wilson resigned Mar. 1976 and replaced by Callaghan
4. Thatcher resigned Nov. 1990 and replaced by Major

Source: Craig 1989, Simpson 1998 and Butler & Kavanagh 2002.

Item B The main parties, 1832-2001

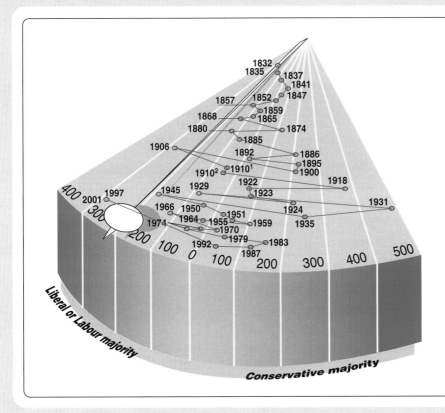

This diagram shows how the pendulum has swung between the Conservative Party and the main parties opposed to it in general elections held between 1832 and 1997. The position of the pendulum has been calculated by subtracting the number of seats won by the Liberal Party/Liberal Democrats and the Labour Party from the number won by the Conservatives. In 1918, 1931 and 1935, the figure for the Conservatives include those allies who joined the coalition government, but the figure does not include those Conservatives who remained outside the coalition.

Source: Craig 1989, Simpson 1998 and Butler & Kavanagh 2002.

Item C The party system in local government

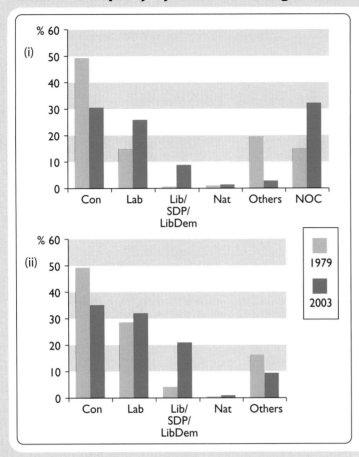

It is worth noting that slightly different party systems exist at both local and European levels. In local government, not only are the Liberal Democrats more prominent than at national level, but many local authorities are under 'no overall control', meaning that parties have to cooperate more than when there is a majority. The electoral system (AMS) used to elect the London Assembly yielded slightly different results from those at the national level - the Greens secured some seats. A similar phenomenon occurred at European level. Labour changed the system for electing MEPs for the 1999 elections to a form of proportional representation (closed-list PR). The result was the election of not only Labour, Conservative and an increased number of Liberal Democrat MEPs, but also Green and UK Independence Party MEPs.

Chart (i) shows the share of council control in Britain in 1979 and 2003. Chart (ii) shows the share of local government seats in Britain in 1979 and 2003. NOC stands for 'no overall control'.

Source: Fisher 2003.

Item D The party system in Scotland

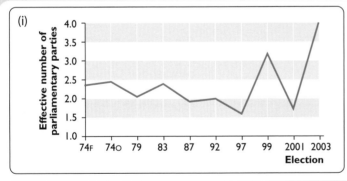

Graph (i) shows the effective number of parliamentary parties in Scotland between 1974 and 2003.
Table (i) shows the results of the election to the Scottish Parliament in 1999 (in brackets) and 2003. Turnout in 2003 was 49.4% - down from 58.7% in 1999.
Note: the first elections to the Scottish Parliament were held in 1999 using a version of the Additional Member voting system, a proportional system (see Unit 4).

(i)	Constituencies		Regional Lists		
SCOTLAND	Share of votes %	Seats won	Share of votes %	Seats won	Total seats
Conservative	16.6 *(15.5)*	3 *(0)*	15.5 *(15.4)*	15 *(18)*	**18 *(18)***
Labour	34.6 *(15.5)*	46 *(0)*	29.3 *(15.4)*	4 *(18)*	**50 *(56)***
LibDem	15.4 *(14.2)*	13 *(12)*	11.8 *(12.4)*	4 *(5)*	**17 *(17)***
Scottish National	23.9 *(18.7)*	9 *(7)*	20.9 *(27.3)*	18 *(28)*	**27 *(35)***
Scottish Socialist	6.2 *(1.1)*	0 *(0)*	6.7 *(2.0)*	6 *(1)*	**6 *(1)***
Greens	0 *(0.0)*	0 *(0)*	6.9 *(3.6)*	7 *(1)*	**7 *(1)***
Others	3.4 *(1.7)*	2 *(1)*	9.0 *(5.7)*	2 *(0)*	**4 *(1)***

Source: Fisher 2003.

Item E **The party system in Wales**

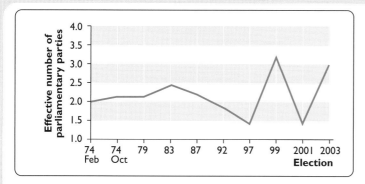

The graph shows the effective number of parliamentary parties in Wales between 1974 and 2003.

The table shows the results of the election to the Welsh Assembly in 1999 *(in brackets)* and 2003. Turnout was 38.2% in 2003 - down from 46.6% in 1999.

Note: the first elections to the Welsh Assembly were held in 1999 using a version of the Additional Member voting system, a proportional system (see Unit 4).

| WALES | Constituencies | | Regional Lists | | |
	Share of votes %	Seats won	Share of votes %	Seats won	Total seats
Conservative	15.9 *(15.8)*	1 *(1)*	16.3 *(6.5)*	8 *(8)*	**9** *(9)*
Labour	37.6 *(37.6)*	27 *(27)*	35.4 *(35.5)*	1 *(1)*	**28** *(28)*
LibDem	13.5 *(13.5)*	3 *(3)*	12.4 *(12.5)*	3 *(3)*	**6** *(17)*
Plaid Cymru	28.4 *(28.4)*	9 *(9)*	30.3 *(30.6)*	8 *(8)*	**17** *(17)*
Others	4.7 *(4.7)*	0 *(0)*	5.6 *(5.1)*	0 *(0)*	**0** *(0)*

Source: Fisher 2003.

Item F **The party system in Northern Ireland**

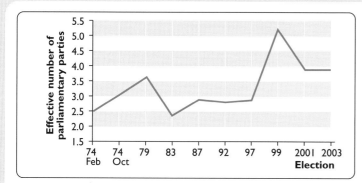

Party	Seats	+/-	Votes	%	+/-
DUP	30	10	177,944	25.71	7.49
Sinn Fein	24	6	162,758	23.52	5.89
UUP	27	-1	156,931	22.67	1.43
SDLP	18	-6	117,547	16.98	-4.98
Alliance	6	0	25,372	3.68	-2.82
Independent	1	1	19,256	2.79	2.22
PUP	1	-1	8,032	1.16	-1.39
NIWC	0	-2	5,785	0.83	-0.77
UKUP	1	-4	5,700	0.82	-3.69

The graph shows the effective number of parliamentary parties in Northern Ireland between 1974 and 2003.

The table shows the results of the first two elections to the Northern Ireland Assembly in 1998 and 2003 (the second and final columns show the change from 1998).

Note: Elections in Northern Ireland are held using the Single Transferable Vote system, a proportional system (see Unit 4).

The party system in Northern Ireland is almost completely different from the rest of the UK. Of the mainland parties, only the Conservatives field candidates, who attract only a small share of the vote. The four principal parties are the Ulster Unionists (UUP), the Democratic Unionists (DUP), the Social and Democratic Labour Party (SDLP) and Sinn Fein (SF). The party system in Northern Ireland revolves around the constitutional status of Ireland, with the UUP and DUP supporting the separate status of Northern Ireland, while the SDLP and Sinn Fein favour a united Ireland. Since the 1970s, all four parties have held parliamentary seats, the UUP being the largest party. In 2001, however, the UUP experienced a significant challenge from the DUP, and the Northern Irish party system appears to have become more fragmented. Elections to the Northern Ireland Assembly use STV – a proportional electoral system designed, in this case, to ensure that both broad communities are represented. As we can see, its use has had an important impact upon the ENPP index.

Source: Fisher 2003 and Norris 2004.

Questions

1. a) Using Items A-F, give arguments for and against the view that Britain has a two-party system.

   b) Why is it important to know whether Britain has a two-party system or some other system?

2. Comparing Item C with Item A, explain the differences between the party systems in national and local government.

3. a) Using Items D and E, describe the main characteristics of the Welsh and Scottish party systems.

   b) Using Item F, describe the main characteristics of the party system in Northern Ireland.

References

Ball (1987) Ball, A., *British Political Parties*, Macmillan, 1987.

Butler & Kavanagh (2002) Butler, D. & Kavanagh, D., *The British General Election of 2001*, Macmillan, 2002.

Craig (1989) Craig F.W.S., British Electoral Facts 1832-1937, Gower Publishing Company, 1989.

Fisher (2003) Fisher, J., 'All change? Party systems in Britain', *Politics Review*, Vol.13.1, September 2003.

Garner & Kelly (1998) Garner, R. & Kelly, R., *British Political Parties Today*, Manchester University Press, 1998.

Heywood (1993) Heywood, A., 'The dominant-party system', *Talking Politics*, Vol.5.2, Winter 1993.

Ingle (1992) Ingle, S., 'The Glorious Revolution and the party system', *Politics Review*, Vol.1.3, February 1992.

Lancaster (2002) Lancaster, S. (ed.), *British Politics Update: 1999-2002*, Causeway Press, 2002.

McKenzie (1955) McKenzie, R., *British Political Parties*, Heinemann, 1955.

McNaughton (2003) McNaughton, N., 'The changing nature of UK Political Parties', *Talking Politics*, Vol. 15.3, April 2003.

Norris (2004) Norris, P., 'The 2003 Northern Ireland Assembly elections', *Talking Politics*, Vol.16.3, April 2004.

Simpson (1998) Simpson, D., *UK Government and Politics in Context*, Hodder and Stoughton, 1998.

9.1 *The origins of the Labour Party*

Electoral reform in the 19th century gave more and more working-class men the vote. At first, this made little difference to the party system. The Conservative Party and the Liberal Party both claimed that they could represent the new voters. It was not until the beginning of the 20th century that a new political party was set up specifically to represent the interests of the newly enfranchised working class in Parliament. This party - the Labour Party - owed its existence to the support of the trade union movement. Links between the Labour Party and the trade unions have remained ever since.

Socialist groups in the 19th century
By 1900, the few socialist groups which existed in Britain had enjoyed little success. In 1900, less than 70% of men and no women had the vote. As a result socialists had little chance of being elected and mainly confined themselves to activity outside the parliamentary system through demonstrations and protests. At this time MPs were not paid and it was therefore difficult for those on poor wages to become MPs as they had no means of supporting themselves. This discouraged socialists from forming parties whose aim was to achieve seats in Parliament.

Trade unions in the 19th century
Although socialist groups had not gained much success by 1900, the same was not true of the trade union movement. In 1850, the trade union movement was of little consequence. By 1900, however, several million workers had joined unions, the TUC (Trades Union Congress - the national body for all trade unions) had been formed, unions had won some legal rights and a number of union leaders had become MPs. The first union leaders to be elected as MPs were elected in 1874. Alexander and Thomas Burt were miners sponsored by their union and recruited to stand for their local Liberal Party (a few local Liberal parties decided to put up working-class candidates after the extension of the vote in 1867 because they realised that working-class people would make up the majority of voters in their constituency). By 1884, there were nine 'Lib-Lab' MPs, as these working-class Liberals became known. The Liberal Prime Minister, Gladstone, promoted one of these Lib-Lab MPs, Henry Broadhurst, to the Cabinet in 1886. Gladstone was convinced that Lib-Lab MPs should be concerned with trade union matters alone. They should not put forward the working-class view on other issues.

The birth of the ILP and LRC
At the 1887 TUC conference, Keir Hardie (see Box 9.1) attacked Broadhurst, arguing that workers should not join a party which supported the employers against the workers. Six years later, he helped to set up the Independent Labour Party (ILP). The ILP pressed the unions to form a working-class parliamentary party. In 1900 a conference was held which was attended by seven unions, a Fabian Society representative, a

representative of the Marxist SDF and a member of the ILP. Although none of the major trade unions attended, the Labour Representation Committee (LRC) was set up with the aim of winning working-class - ie 'labour' - representation in Parliament with its own policies and whip. In effect, the LRC was to be a new political party. The new party won two seats in the 1900 general election.

Box 9.1 Keir Hardie

Keir Hardie (1856-1915) was the son of a servant who worked as a miner before campaigning full time for the creation of a union-backed working-class (ie 'labour') party. He was first elected as an MP in 1892.

Taff Vale
When, in August 1900, workers on the Taff Vale railway went on strike, the company sued the union. In July 1901, Law Lords decided the case in favour of the company. This meant that any union could be sued if it organised a strike - a disaster for unions as they would no longer be able to use their main weapon in disputes. Unions realised that their funds would be in danger unless a new law was passed to protect them. But, the Conservative government refused to intervene and unions could not be sure what priority would be given to this issue by the Liberals. As a result, the LRC began to gain wider support from the unions. By 1904, the number of union members affiliated to the LRC had more than doubled to 956,025 and the unions had agreed to charge members one penny each to raise the funds necessary to pay Labour MPs' salaries. The Taff Vale case, therefore, not only provided the LRC with a clear issue to campaign on (the right to strike) it also brought an increased membership and greater funds.

The Lib-Lab pact, 1903
In 1903, Ramsay MacDonald, Secretary of the LRC, made a secret pact with the Liberal Chief Whip, Herbert Gladstone.

The deal was as follows. After the forthcoming general election, LRC MPs would support the Liberals in Parliament if the Liberals agreed not to put up candidates in a number of constituencies during the election campaign itself. When the 1906 general election was called, no Liberal candidates were put up in 30 constituencies. This allowed LRC candidates in these constituencies to have a clear run against the Conservatives. Of the 50 LRC candidates who stood in the 1906 general election, 29 were successful. Most of these owed their success to the secret Lib-Lab pact. Winning 29 seats was a major achievement. The LRC MPs elected Keir Hardie as their Leader and decided to take a new name - the Labour Party. The gains made in 1906 provided the platform for the new Labour Party to develop into a major party.

9.2 *The Labour Party 1906-79*

Between 1906 and 1916, Labour did not appear to be a great threat to the Liberal Party. The Liberals won a large overall majority in the election of 1906, so the new Labour MPs could make little impact. Between 1906 and 1916, the Labour Party failed to win any new seats. The number of Labour MPs rose to 40 in 1910 because the Miners' Federation joined the Labour Party and its Lib-Lab MPs were instructed to take the Labour whip. It was not until the Liberal Party split in 1916 that Labour's fortunes began to improve. Between 1916 and 1924, four factors combined to change Labour from a small, opposition party into a major party of government. First, the Liberal split in 1916 and its continuation after the war undoubtedly boosted Labour's support. Second, Labour MPs served in Lloyd George's wartime coalition government, providing Labour members with experience of government and bolstering the party's credibility. Third, the Representation of the People's Act of 1918 gave the vote to a huge number of people. Many of the new voters came from the working class. And fourth, in 1918, the Labour Party adopted a new constitution and its structure and organisation were shaken up. This provided it with a political platform and the organisation necessary for it to become a mass party.

The Labour Party in power

It is a measure of the Labour Party's initial success that in 1924, just 21 years after its first two MPs were elected, the Labour Party was able to form a government (see Box 9.2), albeit a minority government which relied on Liberal support to survive. The first Labour government lasted just ten months and is, perhaps, most notable for the way in which Labour ministers tried desperately to convince the public that, whatever their opponents might claim, the Labour Party was a party of moderation and respectability. Since the government relied on Liberal support, there was no chance of implementing a socialist programme even if ministers had wanted to do so.

The same points can be made about the second Labour government of 1929-31. This was also a minority government and it contained many of the same faces - for example, Ramsay MacDonald was Prime Minister and Philip Snowden Chancellor in both administrations. But, the second government ended with the Labour Party in disarray. In August 1931, Ramsay MacDonald, convinced that there was a

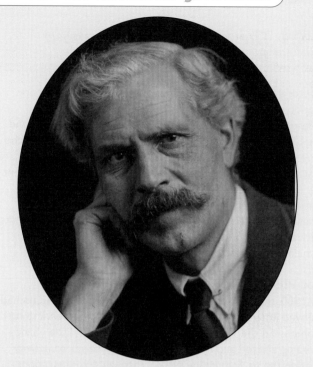

Box 9.2   The first Labour government

The first Labour Prime Minister was Ramsay MacDonald (above). Like Keir Hardie, MacDonald (1866-1937) was Scottish and his mother worked as a servant. Success at school brought him to London. He worked as a clerk and as an agent for a Liberal MP before leaving the Liberal Party and joining the ILP. In 1900, he was Secretary of the LRC. He was elected as MP for the first time in 1906.

major economic crisis, dissolved the Labour government and agreed to form a 'national' government (a coalition government containing members of all three main parties). MacDonald failed to consult with his colleagues before agreeing to this course of action and it is unlikely he would have gained their agreement if he had done so. The result was a split in the party. MacDonald and seven other MPs joined the National Government while the Labour Party went into opposition (in the subsequent election the number of Labour MPs was reduced from 288 to 46). MacDonald and his colleagues were expelled from the party.

The Labour Party since 1931

The Labour Party remained in opposition until it won its first overall majority in 1945. This was the first time that a Labour government had been able to set its own agenda. Despite the economic difficulties facing Britain after the war, the Labour government under Attlee embarked on an ambitious programme of nationalisation and set in place the main elements of the welfare state.

In the 34 years between 1945 and 1979, the Labour Party held power for 17 years - the same number of years as the Conservatives. Between 1979 and 1997, however, the party remained in opposition. Despite doubts (especially in the late 1980s) that Labour could ever win an overall majority again, the party proved doubters wrong by winning its largest ever overall majority in 1997 and, for the first time, won two consecutive terms with an overall majority in 2001.

9.3 Reform in the Labour Party 1979-97

Between 1979 and 1997, there was extensive reform of the structure and organisation of the Labour Party. In part, this was a reflection of the party's failure to win a general election between 1979 and 1997. In part, it was a reflection of an ideological struggle between different factions within the party. There were three distinct phases.

Phase 1. The Bennite challenge 1979-83

Following Labour's 1979 general election defeat, a group of Labour Party activists led by Tony Benn (see Box 9.3) attempted to change the balance of power within the party. These reformers argued that:

> 'By ignoring the wishes of Labour's activists, its parliamentary leaders had lost touch with the wishes of its natural working-class electorate, which paved the way for Mrs Thatcher's victory in 1979. Benn thus contested that organisational reform had become necessary, not just to satisfy abstract theories of party democracy, but to ensure that future Labour governments would not "betray" the socialist ideas developed in opposition.' (Kelly 1994, p.40)

According to Kelly, therefore, the internal party reforms supported by Tony Benn and his colleagues were designed not just to ensure that the Labour Party became electable once again, they were also designed to ensure that a distinct ideological standpoint was reflected in the way in which the party worked.

Box 9.3 Tony Benn

Tony Benn served as a Labour MP for nearly 50 years. He was a minister between 1974 and 1979. Despite his background (his father was a Viscount and Benn had to renounce his seat in the Lords before he could take his seat in the Commons), Benn always remained on the socialist wing of the Labour Party.

Rule changes, 1980

The pressure for reform exerted by Benn and his supporters produced two main changes. First, as a result of a rule change made at the 1980 party conference, it became mandatory (compulsory) for Labour MPs to be reselected by their constituency Labour parties (CLPs) before each general election. And second, the right to elect Labour's Leader and Deputy Leader was no longer the responsibility of the parliamentary party (PLP) alone. From 1981, the Leader and Deputy Leader were to be elected using an 'electoral college'. This electoral college was made up of the PLP (which had 30% of the vote), CLPs (which had 30% of the vote) and trade unions (which had 40% of the vote). For the first time, it became possible to challenge the Leader and Deputy Leader whether they were in government or in opposition. Prior to this, it had not been possible to challenge the Leader and Deputy Leader while they were in government.

The aim of these reforms was to give greater power to Labour activists in the CLPs who (it was assumed) were more radical than the party's leadership and, therefore, more likely to support socialist measures. There is little doubt that these reforms encouraged the damaging split which resulted in the departure of 30 Labour MPs to the SDP (see below). The culmination of this phase was the adoption of a radical manifesto for the 1983 general election.

Phase 2. Modernisation, 1983-94

Labour's poor showing in the 1983 general election resulted in a backlash against the ideas and strategy of Benn and his colleagues. After 1983, the party leadership began to reassert its authority and it introduced organisational reforms which both broadened and centralised the decision-making process within the party.

The leadership reasserts its authority

One way in which the Labour Party leadership tried to reassert its authority was by purging the party of members of the Militant Tendency in the mid-1980s. The Militant Tendency was a Trotskyist group whose members joined the Labour Party in the hope of moving Labour policies to the left. Neil Kinnock's public battle against the Militant Tendency (see Box 9.4) suggested that the party was changing direction and moving away from the hard left.

Box 9.4 Neil Kinnock and the Militant Tendency

It was after Labour's defeat in the 1983 general election that the new Leader, Neil Kinnock, engaged in a public battle with the Militant Tendency.

OMOV

While Tony Benn and his colleagues aimed to extend the power of CLPs because that was where party activists were to be found, after 1983 the Labour leadership aimed to extend power beyond the CLPs to ordinary members. The introduction of 'one member, one vote' (OMOV) became an important part of the party's modernisation programme. OMOV extended democracy within the party by encouraging the participation not just of activists but of every ordinary member.

The Labour Party and the unions

The debate over OMOV also, most importantly, raised the question of the Labour Party's relationship with the trade unions. Traditionally, the Labour Party had been very close to the unions. The unions provided the party with most of its funds and most of its members and, in return, the unions had been given an important part in decision-making within the party. Since the introduction of OMOV for leadership elections and the selection of parliamentary candidates in 1993, the power of the unions within the Labour Party has declined. Significantly, due to the adoption of new fund-raising techniques, the proportion of Labour's income from union sources fell from c.70% in 1987 to c.47% in 1997 to c.30% in 2003 (Kelly 2003).

Phase 3. Blair and New Labour since 1994

The third phase of reform began in 1994 with Tony Blair's election as Labour Leader. Blair and his colleagues began to argue that the modernisation process had not gone far enough for the party to win over enough voters to win the forthcoming general election - particularly those people living in 'Middle England' (people in social group 'C1' - people with junior managerial or administrative posts - who mainly live in the Midlands and South East England). As a result, Blair and his colleagues set about distancing the current Labour Party (New Labour) from the Labour Party of the past (Old Labour). At the first party conference after his election as Leader Tony Blair made a significant attempt to establish a new identity for the Labour Party he was now leading. This involved two crucial changes, one of presentation and one of substance. The presentational change involved referring to the Labour Party after his election as Leader as 'New Labour' The intention was to establish a distance between the party which had last governed in 1974 and had been associated as a result of Conservative propaganda with failure, and the current Labour Party which had changed its leadership and principles in such a way that it was now ready to govern once more. The substantive change involved a change in these principles. The old Clause IV of the Labour Party Constitution was the theoretical basis of policy-making in the party ever since its foundation. Clause IV was the link between Labour and socialism and in particular with its mission to advance the interests of the industrial, manual working class. To change this Clause was to change the fundamental mission of the Labour Party. After a substantial consultation process with Labour members, a new Clause IV was unveiled by the NEC in April 1995. A special conference was held on April 29 at which 90% of constituency members and 55% of affiliated trade unions approved the change (for a comparison of the two versions of Clause IV see Unit 7, Box 7.16).

In addition to these changes in presentation and principle two further sets of changes occurred which were to establish the newness of New Labour. The first set of changes concerned with ideology and policy. Ideologically (see also Unit 7) a shift was made towards the centre and this shift was reflected in policy changes. In particular, there was an acceptance of the free-market economy which had developed during the Thatcher years, and an acceptance of the emphasis Thatcher had placed on freedom and responsibility. After his victory in the 1997 general election, Blair emphasised the importance of the New Labour project by stating that his party had been '…elected as New Labour and would govern as New Labour'. In other words, the changes were of fundamental importance.

Main points   Sections 9.1 - 9.3

- It was not until 1900 that a new political party was set up to represent the interests of the newly enfranchised working class in Parliament.
- This party - the Labour Party - owed its existence to the support of the trade union movement. Links between the Labour Party and the trade unions have remained ever since.
- It is a measure of the Labour Party's initial success that in 1924, just 21 years after its first two MPs were elected, the Labour Party was able to form a government.
- Labour won its first overall majority in 1945. In 2001, it won a second term with an overall majority for the first time.
- Between 1979 and 1997, reform of the structure and organisation of the Labour Party went through three main phases: (1) the Bennite challenge 1979-83; (2) modernisation 1983-94; and (3) changes under Blair since 1994.

Activity 9.1 The Labour Party - change over time

Item A Labour's electoral record

(i) Labour Prime Ministers and general election victories since 1900

1920

J. Ramsay MacDonald
PM 1924, 1929-31
Minority government
1923
Minority government
1929

1940

Clement Attlee
PM 1945-51
1945
(Labour majority of 146)
1950
(Labour majority of 5)

1960

Harold Wilson
PM 1964-70, 1974-76
1964
(Labour majority of 4)
1966
(Labour majority of 96)
Feb 1974
Minority government
Oct 1974
(Labour majority of 3)

1970

James Callaghan
PM 1976-79

Key
General election after which the Labour Party was invited to form the government.

1990

Tony Blair
PM 1997-
May 1997
(Labour majority of 178)
June 2001
(Labour majority of 167)

2000

(ii) The development of the Labour Party

Date	MPs elected	Total votes polled
1900	2	63,304
1906	29	323,195
1910 (Jan)	40	505,657
1910 (Dec)	42	371,772
1918	57	2,244,945
1922	142	4,241,383
1923	191	4,438,508
1924	151	5,489,077
1929	288	8,389,512
1931	46	6,362,561
1935	154	8,325,491
1945	393	11,995,152
1950	315	13,266,592
1951	295	13,948,605
1955	277	12,404,970
1959	258	12,215,538
1964	317	12,205,606
1966	364	13,064,951
1970	288	12,179,341
1974 (Feb)	301	11,639,243
1974 (Oct)	319	11,457,079
1979	269	11,532,148
1983	209	8,457,124
1987	229	10,029,270
1992	271	11,559,735
1997	418	13,516,632
2001	413	10,740,168

Source: Pelling 1991, Curtice 1997 and Dorey 2002.

Item B Tony Blair and New Labour

A British Prime Minister is a Party Leader. Traditionally, the party was a limit on a Labour Prime Minister's freedom of manoeuvre. The trade unions, constituency parties, as well as the conference and National Executive Committee were all significant factors that Harold Wilson and James Callaghan had to consider. Blair has built on the changes to the party made under Neil Kinnock. The policy role of conference and National Executive Committee have been weakened. More power has been given to the party leadership. The Millbank model of party management (the party headquarters were located in Millbank Tower - they have now moved to Old Queen Street) emphasises the Leader's authority, centralised control of communications and the discipline of keeping 'on message'. Blair's reinvention of the party as New Labour has involved a lessening of the importance of trade unionists and party activists, as well as that of backbenchers. Party members' lack of support for the Blair project was seen in response to the leadership's efforts to 'manage' the selection of party candidates for London Mayor and First Minister in Wales. Ultimately, both efforts were unsuccessful. The leadership's favoured candidate for London Mayor - Frank Dobson - came third. The leadership's favoured candidate for First Minister of the Welsh Assembly - Alun Michael - was forced to resign in February 2000 after a vote of no-confidence, spending less than a year in post. What was striking about these two examples was the open relish with which party members rejected the leadership's preferred candidate. As Thatcher found in 1990, the withdrawal of backbench party support can result in consequences the Leader did not intend.

Source: Kavanagh 2001.

Item C **Labour and the unions**

At the heart of New Labour has been an appeal to the middle classes. This brought into question Labour's historic links with the trade unions. Unlike previous Labour Leaders, Tony Blair had a weak emotional attachment to union-party links. As a result, there has been an attempt to weaken those links and even some talk of breaking them altogether. At the 1995 conference, the leadership engineered a 20% reduction in the union share of votes. At the same time, there was a campaign to encourage donations from wealthy individuals. By 1997, only 46% of Labour's income came from the unions. By the end of 1997, there was talk from some union leaders about voluntarily giving up their right to vote. This suggestion drew little complaint from the Labour leadership. But, the leadership should be cautious. Apart from giving the party insider advice from the workplace, the unions have always donated to Labour when others were reluctant to do so. Labour must hope that wealthy backers do not become fair weather friends. Also, Blair, like his predecessors has had to rely on the union block vote during tricky debates at conference. Had it not been for their support in 1996, for example, he could have faced embarrassment over both child benefit and minimum wage policy. Parties made up of individual members only are far harder for Leaders to control.

Source Kelly 1998.

Questions

1. Using Item A assess whether the Labour Party is a 'natural party of government'.

2. Using Item C examine whether New Labour has been right to distance itself from the trade unions.

3. Using Item B, list the main elements in the modernisation process.

4. To what extent is New Labour really 'new'. Use Items A-C in your answer and explain your conclusions.

9.4 The Labour Party - structure and organisation

Labour Party branches

Ordinary members of the Labour Party belong to a local branch (there is a national membership list, so members join via party headquarters and are then assigned to a particular local branch depending on their address). Members are invited to attend branch meetings and can stand for election to the branch's executive committee at the branch's annual general meeting. Individual branches are responsible for looking after their own members and finance. Branches choose candidates for local elections. Branch rules are laid down in the Labour Party constitution.

The Constituency Labour Party (CLP)

Each branch is able to elect a number of delegates to the local CLP's general committee (GC) and to the CLP's executive committee (EC). The number of delegates is determined by the number of paid-up members in the branch. In addition, a number of delegates are appointed to the CLP's GC by trade unions which are affiliated to the Labour Party. Ordinary branch members and union members can attend meetings of the CLP's GC, but only delegates are allowed to vote. Delegates to the CLP can stand for election to the CLP's general management committee. Rules governing the CLP are laid down in the Labour Party constitution.

Until 1987, one of the key functions of the CLP was to select parliamentary candidates. But, since 1993, every ordinary member has been able to vote in the selection process. Local and national election campaigns are organised at constituency level. Delegates are elected by the CLP to attend regional and annual conferences.

The Labour Party's Partnership in Power reforms of 1997 resulted in the setting up of policy forums, enabling CLP members to participate in the policy-making process (see Activity 9.2 Item B below).

The National Executive Committee (NEC)

According to Clause VIII of the Labour Party constitution:

'There shall be a National Executive Committee of the Labour Party (the NEC) which shall, subject to the control and directions of party conference, be the administrative authority of the party.' (Labour 1999, p.8)

In 2003-04 the NEC contained 33 members - see Box 9.5.

Box 9.5 Members of the NEC

- 24 members elected by party conference
- the Leader and Deputy Leader of the party
- the Leader of the European Parliamentary Labour Party
- the party Treasurer
- three frontbench MPs
- one youth member elected at the national Young Labour Conference
- one member elected by the Labour Party Black Socialist Society at its conference.

Source: www.labour.org.uk/nec/

Duties and powers of the NEC

The duties and powers of the NEC are laid down in the constitution and are extensive. Its general responsibility is to ensure that the party machinery runs smoothly at all levels (at constituency, district, county and regional level) and to oversee the work of the party between conferences. In practice, this involves five principal areas of activity. First, it has a policy-making role. It participates in the consideration of reports produced by the policy commissions of the National Policy Forum and in their publication prior to submission to conference. Second, the NEC is the guardian of the constitution and is responsible for ensuring that its rules and procedures are obeyed. Third, the NEC has power to discipline members if rules are breached and can expel members, subject to conference. Fourth, the NEC is responsible for party finances and running the party headquarters. Fifth, the NEC plays an important part in the selection of parliamentary candidates, especially at by-elections.

Labour Party headquarters

In 1997 the Labour Party moved its headquarters from Walworth Road to Millbank Tower, a set of prestigious offices in Central London. This was the culmination of a process of greater professionalisation in the Labour Party which had begun during the leadership of Neil Kinnock. The offices at Millbank were first used in 1995 when the communications and polling operation moved there. This operation played a central part in what was generally acknowledged to be a highly effective Labour campaign in 1997. In an attempt to cut costs, Labour has now abandoned the Millbank offices and has its headquarters at Old Queen Street in London.

The National Policy Forum

The National Policy Forum was set up in 1990 to streamline the party's policy-making process and to produce a rolling programme of policy-making. The Forum appoints various policy commissions. Each commission deals with a specific policy area, producing reports for the NEC and, ultimately, conference to approve. Each commission has around 20 members and is headed by a frontbench MP.

The annual party conference

Labour's annual party conference has a number of functions. First, formally speaking at least, the conference is an important decision-making body. In the past, affiliated organisations were able to submit policy resolutions to conference, sometimes resulting in votes that went against the wishes of the leadership. In 1992, for example, conference supported unilateral nuclear disarmament against the wishes of the leadership. Rule changes agreed in 1997, however, mean that affiliated organisations cannot submit policy resolutions on a subject to annual conference before a National Policy Forum Commission has reported on that subject and that the role of conference is limited to either approving or rejecting the recommendations of each commission. Kelly argues that these rule changes were:

'A clear sign that [conference] was being changed from a serious deliberative assembly into a celebration of new policies initiated by the Leader and his closest advisers.' (Kelly 1998, p.5)

The 1997 rule changes were opposed by 102 CLPs at the 1997 annual conference. Despite this, they were eventually endorsed. Kelly argues that, as a result, party conference has become 'little more than a talking shop':

> 'In September 2002, Labour's conference voted overwhelmingly to reject PFI [the Private Finance Initiative]. However, as when conference defeated the government on pensions two years earlier, Gordon Brown immediately told delegates that he could not accept their decision and would carry on with the original policy. There could be no greater demonstration that the Labour Party conference, once described as "the expression of democratic policy-making" (Minkin 1978), had been reduced by New Labour to little more than a talking shop.' (Kelly 2003, p.63)

The voting system used by conference is described in Box 9.6.

Box 9.6 The voting system

Before 1993, voting was dominated by trade unions which had one conference vote for every registered affiliated member of the Labour Party (an affiliated member is a union member who pays the political levy as part of their union subscription). Each union cast all its votes in a single block (hence the phrase 'block vote'). How the union cast this vote was normally determined by the union's leaders. So, provided that Labour leaders had the support of union leaders, they were able to secure a conference majority without difficulty. In fact, they could quite easily ignore the concerns of constituency delegates at the conference since their votes were relatively so few. In 1993, however, an electoral college was introduced. This divided conference into a union section with 70% of the vote and a constituency section with 30% of the vote. Moreover, for every 30,000 new individual members, the constituency section would gain an extra 1% of the vote (while the union section would lose 1%). In 1995, the proportion of votes in the union section was reduced to 50%, significantly reducing union influence over the party.

The party conference's second function is to provide the opportunity for ordinary members to air their views in public. The third function is to provide a platform for leading members of the party. Cabinet (or shadow Cabinet) ministers use the conference to make set-piece speeches designed to appeal both to party members and the wider public (since they are televised). The reception of these speeches can make (or, occasionally break) the public standing of a minister.

The Leader and the Parliamentary Labour Party (PLP)

Until 1922, the Labour Party's main spokesperson was known as 'Chairman of the Party'. It was only after 1922 that the term 'Leader of the Labour Party' came into common usage.

All MPs who take the Labour whip belong to the Parliamentary Labour Party (PLP). Until 1980, the PLP alone chose the Leader in a series of ballots. The last Labour Leader to be elected in this way was Michael Foot in 1980. He defeated Denis Healey in the second ballot.

Selecting the Leader and Deputy Leader

Nomination

Candidates for the posts of Leader and Deputy Leader of the Labour Party must be MPs. Between 1981 and 1988, candidates had to secure the support of 5% of the PLP before they could be nominated. Following Tony Benn's abortive challenge to Neil Kinnock in 1988, however, the rules were changed.

Since 1989, candidates have had to secure the support of 12.5% of the PLP if there is a vacancy or 20% of the PLP if there is no vacancy to the positions while Labour is in opposition. If Labour is in government then, whether there is a vacancy or not, challengers have to secure the support of 20% of the PLP and they also have to gain the backing of two-thirds of those who can vote at annual conference. Before 1981, challenges to the leadership while the Labour Party was in government were not allowed.

Electoral college

Since 1981, the Labour Leader and Deputy Leader have been chosen by an electoral college. Between 1981 and 1993, this electoral college was split as follows: the trade unions had 40% of the vote; the CLPs had 30% of the vote; and the PLP (including MEPs) had 30% of the vote. Since 1993, this electoral college has been divided equally between trade unions, CLPs and the PLP (including MEPs). Also since 1993, one member, one vote has been introduced. So, every paid up member of the Labour Party is able to vote in the constituency section and every trade union member who pays the political levy and whose trade union is affiliated to the Labour Party is able to vote in the trade union section (the block vote, therefore, no longer has a place in the selection of Labour Leaders).

Electoral procedure

To win, a candidate for the leadership or deputy leadership has to gain more than 50% of the vote. If no candidate wins more than 50% of the vote outright, the candidate with the least number of votes is excluded and their second preference votes redistributed (the Alternative Vote system - see Unit 4).

Under the rules laid down in the constitution, the election for Leader and Deputy Leader should take place at the time of the annual party conference unless for some reason the Leader or Deputy Leader becomes 'unavailable' (ie becomes ill, resigns or dies). If that happens, then the NEC can arrange for a ballot before the next annual conference is held. This happened when John Smith died in May 1994. The results of the leadership election were announced in July 1994, more than two months before the annual party conference was held. The results of the leadership elections in 1976, 1983 and 1994 are summarised in Box 9.7 on page 160.

9.5 The location of power in the Labour Party

McKenzie's thesis, 1955

In his classic analysis of the organisation of the Labour Party, McKenzie (1955) argued that real power in the Labour Party

Box 9.7 The leadership election in 1994

Leader	MPs/MEPs	Ordinary members	Trade unions	Total
Blair	60.5	58.2	52.3	57.0
Prescott	19.6	24.4	28.4	24.1
Beckett	19.9	17.4	19.3	18.9

Deputy leader	MPs/MEPs	Ordinary members	Trade unions	Total
Prescott	53.7	59.4	56.6	56.5
Beckett	46.3	40.6	43.4	43.5

MPs' & MEPs' section = 33.3 %; ordinary members' section = 33.3%; trade union section = 33.3%

rested with the Labour leadership. There was, he argued, a fundamental gap between the party's constitutional theory, which suggested that real power lay with extra-parliamentary bodies such as the annual conference, and party political practice which resulted in the party leadership taking all the key decisions. McKenzie suggested that this was a consequence of the fact that the party leadership always has to perform the role of government or government-in-waiting. The government is accountable to Parliament, not to bodies outside Parliament. Equally, the government is expected to represent the wishes of the people as a whole and not just the wishes of a narrow section. In other words, members of the government have a wider responsibility than to the annual Labour Party conference and, to demonstrate that they are capable of government (ie to win general elections), the Labour leadership has to be prepared to ignore or act against the wishes of the majority of ordinary party members.

The location of power 1955-94

The fact that Labour Leaders continued to ignore or to act against the wishes of the majority of ordinary members in the years after McKenzie wrote his book in 1955 suggests that power remained with the Labour leadership. Indeed, there is good evidence that the moves towards centralisation undertaken by Neil Kinnock after 1983 strengthened the power of the leadership. Nevertheless, the power of the Leader was by no means absolute. It was restricted in two ways. First, starting in the late 1980s, there were attempts to democratise the party (see Section 9.3 above). And second, Leaders were genuinely restricted by the annual party conference. Neil Kinnock could not have abandoned the policy of unilateralism without the support of conference, for example. It may be true that Labour Leaders usually won in the end, but they were always aware that failure to carry the majority of conference with them would lead to a public fight and unsightly shows of disunity.

The location of power under Tony Blair

The relationship between Leader and wider party was given a further twist after Blair became Leader. By 1998, a debate was taking place about whether Blair's reforms had strengthened or weakened democracy in the party. Blair and his supporters argued that the new policy-making process (see Section 9.3 above) provided a more focused and, therefore, effective role for members, allowing them to influence policy during the consultation process and at party conference. Moreover, the decision to hold internal referendums on the revision of Clause IV and on the acceptance of the key principles on which Labour was to fight the 1997 general election can be interpreted as the leadership giving a greater say to ordinary individual members. Opponents place an altogether different interpretation on events. They claim that the changes to policy-making place greater power in the hands of the Leader and the NEC. It is the Leader and NEC, they claim, who shape the policy that is debated at conference. In addition, they say, the two internal party referendums were presented as 'back me or sack me' issues and gave no real choice to ordinary members.

Two examples from 2003 provide further evidence of just how much power is held by the Labour Leader. The first of these is the parliamentary vote on the Labour government's proposals to establish foundation hospitals. The government managed to win a majority in this vote despite considerable opposition from many Labour MPs. That a rebellion capable of defeating the government was avoided demonstrates the power of the Leader to control backbenchers. The second example is Tony Blair's decision to go to war against Iraq. This demonstrates the capacity of the Leader to ignore the views of grass-roots members. Grass-roots members were overwhelmingly opposed to the war but Tony Blair decided to go ahead anyhow and, despite the difficulties which he faced after the conclusion of the war, his position as Leader remained secure.

Main points Sections 9.4 - 9.5

- **The NEC is the administrative authority of the Labour Party. Its duties and powers are extensive. Its general responsibility is to ensure that the party machinery runs smoothly at all levels and to oversee the work of the party between conferences.**
- **The role of annual conference has changed. Although, formally, it is the party's decision-making body, in practice it has lost the power to initiate policy.**

- **Until 1980, the PLP alone chose the Leader in a series of ballots. Since 1981, the Labour Leader and Deputy Leader have been chosen by an electoral college.**
- **Candidates for the posts of Leader and Deputy Leader of the Labour Party must be MPs and must have the support of 12.5% or 20% of the PLP, depending on circumstances.**
- **Traditionally, real power in the Labour Party has rested with the leadership.**

Activity 9.2 *Labour Party - structure and organisation*

Item A **The structure and organisation of the party**

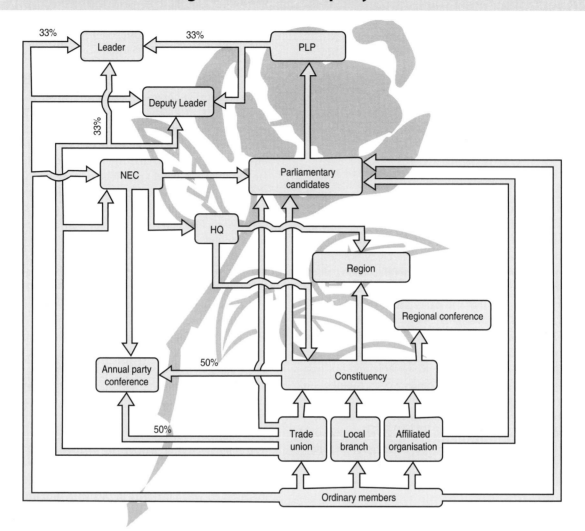

Item B **Policy-making**

Richard Kelly estimates that, between 1997 and 2003, over 40,000 members contributed to policy forum debates at CLP level - a huge increase on the number inclined to attend a Labour conference. He quotes the Chair of Bracknall CLP who wrote: 'The local forums allow us to discuss policy in an informal way, unlike the stifling and rather forbidding conference debates of old'. According to Labour's regional organisers, the government's 'NHS Direct' policy drew on suggestions made at CLP forums, as did 'the wider remit of the Low Pay Commission, the commitment to nursery places for all three-year-olds and the dumping of PR for local elections'. Patrick Seyd is more critical about the introduction of policy forums at CLP level. He argues that the forums: 'allow Labour leaders to gauge activists' views...but are of very limited relevance to Labour's developing programme in government'. Seyd found that some of the party's key manifesto commitments in 2001 - such as the Public Finance Initiative and more selective secondary education - had barely been discussed, let alone supported by the policy forum process. Seyd argues that given that the party conference has been neutered and that the leadership not only sets the forum agenda, it is also free to ignore forum reports if it wants to, the real result of the introduction of the forums has been to keep the traditionally argumentative membership quiet. The drafting of Labour's 2001 manifesto was revealing. In 1996, the party held a ballot of all members, asking them to approve it. Then, there were complaints about the 'all or nothing' nature of the ballot. In 2001, there wasn't even a ballot. When asked about this, the National Policy Forum's national coordinator said that there was no need given the policy input members enjoyed via the policy forums.

Source: Kelly 2003.

Item C **Power in the Labour Party**

(i) The major debate about where power lies in the Labour Party has surrounded the relationship between the PLP leadership and the extra-parliamentary party. The idea that power really does lie with the extra-parliamentary party doesn't fit with the reality. The parliamentary leadership consists of full-time experienced politicians permanently engaged in defining party policy on the national stage and reacting to day-to-day events. In such circumstances, and particularly when Labour is in government, it is impossible to refer every decision to conference or to the NEC and, more often than not, all these bodies can do is pass judgement on decisions which have already been made by parliamentary leaders who, of course, are skilled in the art of defending the decisions they have made. The Labour leadership has, in any case, usually been able to 'manage' the party in such a way that it follows the leadership's broad preferences.

Source: Garner & Kelly 1998.

(ii) Although Blair's government was confident of re-election in 2001, Labour's national officials took few chances during the selection of parliamentary candidates. Candidate had to be on the National Parliamentary Panel, which rejected over 200 applicants between 1999 and 2001. Attempts at the 1999 conference to allow candidates from outside the panel were roundly defeated, thanks largely to opposition from trade unions, which had supplied about a quarter of the panel's candidates. There were many accusations of unfairness. From February 2001 until the general election, central control was tightened again via 'emergency rules' that allowed Labour's Millbank HQ to draw up its own short-lists for seats with candidate vacancies. It was alleged that vacancies were then manufactured so that Millbank could short-circuit local opposition and 'parachute' favoured candidates into surprised CLPs.

Item D **Policy-making in the Labour Party**

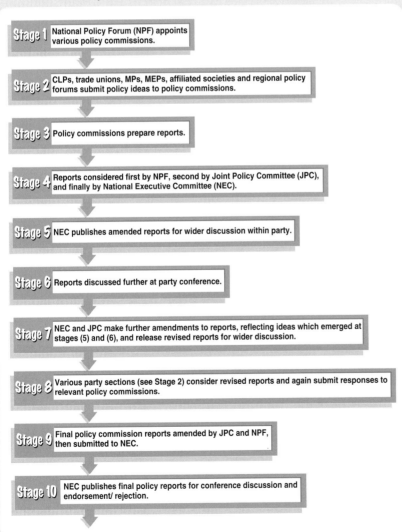

St. Helens South was an example. Just weeks before the general election, sitting MP Gerry Bermingham stunned the CLP by announcing his resignation. This allowed Millbank to construct a short-list which included Blairite convert (and ex-Tory MP) Shaun Woodward while excluding St. Helen's council leader Marie Rimmer - the one local candidate likely to defeat him in a selection battle. But such tactics did not always produce the result Millbank desired. In Birmingham Erdington, for example, Blair's policy 'wonk' Derek Scott was overlooked in favour of a local candidate. The illegality of all-women short-lists also boosted local autonomy, even though it then revived claims of sex discrimination. Whereas 34% of safe seats went to women candidates prior to the 1997 election, only 11% did prior to 2001, resulting in a drop in female MPs from 101 in 1997 to 95. In the first by-election of the new Parliament, at Ogmore, the panel excluded Mark Seddon from the short-list, despite his considerable local support and place on the NEC. Seddon's problem, it was leaked, was his 'failure to toe the government's line on either the Afghan war or the creeping privatisation of public services'.

Source: Kelly 2003.

Stage 1 National Policy Forum (NPF) appoints various policy commissions.

Stage 2 CLPs, trade unions, MPs, MEPs, affiliated societies and regional policy forums submit policy ideas to policy commissions.

Stage 3 Policy commissions prepare reports.

Stage 4 Reports considered first by NPF, second by Joint Policy Committee (JPC), and finally by National Executive Committee (NEC).

Stage 5 NEC publishes amended reports for wider discussion within party.

Stage 6 Reports discussed further at party conference.

Stage 7 NEC and JPC make further amendments to reports, reflecting ideas which emerged at stages (5) and (6), and release revised reports for wider discussion.

Stage 8 Various party sections (see Stage 2) consider revised reports and again submit responses to relevant policy commissions.

Stage 9 Final policy commission reports amended by JPC and NPF, then submitted to NEC.

Stage 10 NEC publishes final policy reports for conference discussion and endorsement/ rejection.

Source: Kelly 1998.

Questions

1. a) What do Items A and D tell us about the structure and organisation of the Labour Party?

   b) How has this structure and organisation changed since 1980?

2. a) Using Items B, D and your own knowledge, describe how the policy-making process works in the Labour Party.

   b) How democratic is the policy-making process?

3. Using Items A-D, explain where power resides in the Labour Party.

9.6 *The origins of the Liberal Democrats*

The Liberal Democrats came into being in March 1988 when the Liberal Party formally merged with the Social Democratic Party (SDP) to form a new party. At first, this new party was known as the Social and Liberal Democrats (SLD) but, after a ballot of the members in October 1989, Liberal Democrats was adopted as the common name of the party. Although the party is, therefore, the youngest of the three main parties, its roots reach back way beyond 1988. While the SDP was formed after a split in the Labour Party in 1981, the foundation of the Liberal Party is generally dated to June 1859.

The rise of the Liberal Party

Like the Conservative Party, the Liberal Party emerged from an existing parliamentary group - the Whigs. Whigs supported free trade, religious tolerance and the power of Parliament over that of the monarch. At first, the Liberal Party was a loose coalition of Whigs, Peelites (Conservatives who had broken from their party in 1846 because they supported free trade) and Radicals (MPs who supported reform, especially religious reform). Support for free trade and individual freedom were the main areas of agreement. But, under the leadership of Gladstone (Prime Minister 1868-74, 1880-85 and 1892-94) the Liberal Party developed into a modern political party with a mass membership and nationwide extra-parliamentary organisation.

Between 1860 and 1914 the Liberal Party was the main alternative to the Conservative Party. The two parties alternated in power and dominated Parliament. But in the early 20th century the Liberal Party went into rapid decline. Although the Liberals won an overall majority in the general election of 1906 and remained the party with the largest number of seats after the general elections in 1910, within 20 years the party was only able to win a handful of seats and it had been replaced as the main party of opposition by the Labour Party.

The Liberal Party 1916-1987

The period 1916 to 1987 saw a deep and long-lasting decline in the fortunes of the Liberal Party. Box 9.8 lists some of the reasons suggested by historians for the decline of the Liberal Party. The only time the number of Liberal MPs reached three figures was in 1923 and in 1935 the number of Liberals in the Commons fell to a low of 21 seats. From 1935 until 1988 (when the Liberal Party was formally disbanded), the Liberals never managed to win more than 23 seats in a general election. The Liberals always managed to maintain a toehold in Parliament, though, and, beginning in the 1950s, managed periodic revivals. From February 1974 when they secured 19% of the vote, a more sustained improvement in their fortunes seemed possible. The nature of the electoral system, however, ensured that they never won the number of seats that their share of the votes might suggest they should have done.

Box 9.8 The decline of the Liberal Party

The following possible reasons for the decline of the Liberals have been suggested:

1. Divisions within the Liberal Party (particularly the split between David Lloyd George and Herbert Asquith) led different factions within the party to compete against each other in the 1918 election.

2. Working-class and female voters - who first won the vote in 1918 - were not greatly attracted to the Liberal Party.

3. Changed social and economic conditions after the First World War made the Liberals less attractive.

4. The Labour Party became established as the party of the working class.

5. Liberal support was evenly spread rather than concentrated and the nature of the electoral system ensured that the party never won the number of seats that their share of the votes might suggest it should have done.

The SDP

In November 1979, shortly after Margaret Thatcher's election victory, Roy Jenkins (a former Labour Home Secretary and Chancellor) delivered the annual Dimbleby lecture. In his speech, he lamented the drift of Conservatives to the right and Labour to the left and called for a realignment of British politics to enable the majority of moderate voters to be represented. Jenkins allowed his Labour Party membership to lapse.

It was the organisational changes won by Tony Benn and his colleagues at the special Labour conference in 1981 (see above, Section 9.3), however, which were the catalyst for the formation of the Social Democratic Party (SDP). Shortly after the conference, three senior Labour MPs, Bill Rodgers, David Owen, Shirley Williams, together with Roy Jenkins, issued the 'Limehouse Declaration'. This was a statement which attacked the Labour Party for heading towards extremism and set up a Council for Social Democracy. Rodgers, Owen, Williams and Jenkins (who became known as the 'gang of four' - see Box 9.9 on page 164) set up the SDP in March 1981 and the following autumn formed a formal alliance with the Liberal Party.

Box 9.9 The gang of four

This photo shows the four founding members of the SDP - Bill Rodgers, David Owen, Shirley Williams and Roy Jenkins soon after their breakaway from the Labour Party. Initially the prospects for the Alliance seemed excellent. By the end of 1981, the SDP was able to claim 27 former Labour MPs and one former Conservative. It received a great deal of money and many offers of support. Opinion polls suggested that the Alliance would win a majority of votes. The findings of these polls seemed to be confirmed when the Alliance won three by-election victories. But, this early enthusiasm was not translated into general election success. In the 1983 general election, although the Alliance came close to pushing Labour into third place in terms of votes cast, it won only 23 seats. Of these 23 seats, 17 were won by Liberals and six by members of the SDP. The general election of 1987 was even more of a disappointment. The number of seats and the percentage of the vote won by the Alliance dropped.

From Alliance to merger

After the 1987 general election, David Steel, the Liberal Leader, called for a complete merger of the two parties. He argued that voters had been confused about the exact nature of the Alliance. The fact that there were two Leaders (David Steel and David Owen) particularly caused problems in the 1987 election campaign. The debate over merger was fierce with both parties divided on the issue. But, after balloting the membership, a merger was agreed.

Within the SDP, however, the Leader, David Owen, and a group of supporters refused to accept this majority decision and they set up a rival party which retained the name SDP. Owen and two other MPs fought on until 1990 when successive electoral defeats demonstrated clearly that the party had little support. Similarly, disenchanted Liberals continued to struggle on under the banner of the Liberal Party.

Record since merger

Since merger, the Liberal Democrats have regularly scored 20% of the vote in local elections and higher in council by-

elections. They have also won some spectacular by-election victories. Until the 1997 general election, however, they failed to win more than 25 seats. In 1992, they won 17.8% of the vote in the UK as a whole (18.3% in Great Britain) and 20 seats. In the 1994 Euro-elections, they won 16% of the vote and two seats.

The Liberal Democrats after 1997

The general election of 1997 was an important breakthrough for the Liberal Democrats. First, they more than doubled the number of seats which they had won in the House of Commons in 1992, returning a total of 46 MPs. This was achieved, in part, because of tactical voting against the Conservatives by voters whose principal aim was to ensure the Conservative candidate lost and who were prepared to support whichever of the two main opposition parties would achieve this goal. Second, the new Labour government made it clear it would cooperate with the Liberal Democrats and this process of cooperation extended to the setting up of a Cabinet Committee on which senior Liberal Democrats sat with Labour ministers.

By the time that Paddy Ashdown resigned as Liberal Democrat Leader in 1999, however, this policy of cooperation was beginning to break down, largely because of the Blair government's lack of progress on electoral reform (see also Unit 13). Despite supporting and raising the possibility of extending such cooperation in his election campaign, the new Leader, Charles Kennedy has adopted a more critical approach to relations with Labour. The results of the 2001 general election strengthened Kennedy's position as the Liberal Democrats increased their support by 2% and won an extra six seats, taking their number of MPs to 52. The Liberal Democrats more critical stance towards the Blair government was particularly apparent in 2003 when the Liberal Democrats were the only one of the three main parties to oppose the war against Iraq.

9.7 Structure and organisation - the Liberal Democrats

A federal structure

When the members of the Liberal Party and the SDP agreed to merge in 1988, one of the key issues that had to be resolved was the structure and organisation of the new party. The result was a compromise between the centralised structure of the SDP and the federal structure of the Liberal Party. This structure is laid down in a written constitution. It is summarised in diagram form in Box 9.10 on page 165.

A federal party is a party in which the central decision-making body of the party (the federal party) is not all-powerful. Power is devolved to area and local parties. The area and local parties remain independent with regard to local and internal affairs. Any matter of national concern is dealt with by the federal party. The federal principle survived the merger of the two parties and, as a result, considerable autonomy is granted to area and local party organisations.

In Wales and Scotland, the party has three tiers. In England, there are four. Nationally, there is the federal party. This is responsible for the preparation of policy for Britain as a whole. It also has overall responsibility for parliamentary

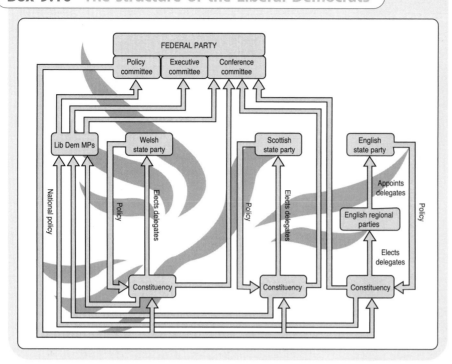

Box 9.10 The structure of the Liberal Democrats

elections and national fund raising. All other matters are delegated to the three 'state' parties - one each for England, Scotland and Wales. Scotland and Wales are then subdivided into constituency parties (known officially as 'local' parties) while England is subdivided into 12 regional parties and then into local parties.

The state parties

The state parties are responsible for the operation of local parties, selection procedures for parliamentary candidates, the arrangements for collecting and renewing party membership and local policy matters. In England, each regional party appoints representatives to the English Council, the state party's governing body. For its own convenience, the English state party has delegated policy-making powers to the federal party. In Scotland and Wales, members of the local parties elect representatives to the Scottish Conference and the Welsh Council, their governing bodies. The Scottish and Welsh state parties have policy-making powers.

Membership

Every member who joins the Liberal Democrats automatically becomes a member of the federal party, the relevant state party and the relevant local party. Their membership fees are divided between these three levels in the way determined by the federal conference and the relevant state conference.

Party headquarters

The Liberal Democrats' federal party headquarters is based in Cowley Street in London - see Box 9.11. In 2004, 68 full-time staff were employed there (up from 24 in 1994 and 40 in 1998). The main tasks carried out by this staff are the organisation of campaigns and elections, the management of the national membership list and national finances and the

organisation of federal conferences. Because of the party's federal structure, party headquarters is not the focal point of the party in the way in which the party headquarters of the Labour Party and Conservative Party are the focal points.

Each state party has its own headquarters and employs its own administrative staff. If ordinary members have a query they would approach their regional party headquarters (in England) and their state party headquarters (in Scotland and Wales) in the first instance.

Advantages and disadvantages of the federal system

The Liberal Democrats' federal structure means that considerable autonomy is given to the party in the English regions, Scotland and Wales. This reflects the Liberal Democrat emphasis on community politics. The party argues that flexibility is needed to respond to the needs of a particular locality and this is best achieved by giving the local party power to respond to local needs as it sees fit.

Box 9.11 Liberal Democrats' federal party headquarters

This photo shows Liberal Democrat Leader, Charles Kennedy, at the Liberal Democrat headquarters in Cowley Street, London.

But, giving such autonomy to local parties can also create difficulties. This can be demonstrated by reference to the actions of the Liberal Democrats in Tower Hamlets, East London. Tower Hamlets hit the headlines in 1993 when a British National Party candidate was elected to the local council. This shocked the major parties and highlighted the racial tension that existed in the area. Following this election, an internal Liberal Democrat inquiry revealed that the local party had issued an election leaflet in 1991 which encouraged racism. The inquiry's report suggested that the local Liberal

Democrats had deliberately contributed to the growth of racist sentiments during the time when they had been the largest party on the local council. In addition to criticising the behaviour of local activists, the report blamed the federal nature of the party. Lack of central control, the report suggested, had resulted in inadequate supervision and discipline in the local party.

The federal conference

Twice a year (in March and September) representatives from every local party are elected on a system of one member, one vote to attend the federal conference (local parties with less than 30 members have to combine with neighbouring parties to obtain representation). The federal conference is the final decision-making body of the party. The party conference in March 2004 is pictured in Box 9.12.

Box 9.12 The Liberal Democrat conference in March 2004

Charles Kennedy, the Liberal Democrat Leader speaking at the conference held in Southport in March 2004.

The federal conference is responsible for making policy decisions at the federal level. In other words, it takes policy decisions which affect the country as a whole. For example, the federal conference would take decisions about foreign policy or about transport in Britain as a whole. It would not take decisions about transport in Scotland. That and other Scottish issues would be decided at the conferences organised by the Scottish Conference. But, since the English state party has delegated policy-making powers to the federal party, the federal conference does make policy decisions which only affect England. The federal conference is also responsible for electing members to the three federal committees (the executive, policy and conference committees).

The three federal committees

Each of the three federal committees contains, in addition to representatives elected by the federal conference, members of the parliamentary party, councillors and representatives from the Scottish and Welsh state parties. At least a third of each committee must be women and at least a third must be men. Details on the three federal committees are given in Box 9.13.

Box 9.13 The three federal committees

1. The federal executive

The federal executive is chaired by the President of the party. The President is elected for a two-year term by all members of the party on a one member, one vote basis. The executive committee has 14 elected members. In addition, the Party Leader, President, three Vice Presidents, two other MPs, one peer, two councillors and one representative from each state party have the right to vote. The executive committee is responsible for overseeing and implementing the decisions made by the federal party. It has the right to initiate a ballot of all members on any issue it considers important.

2. The policy committee

The policy committee contains 29 members: the Party Leader, four MPs, one peer, the President, three councillors, two representatives from the Welsh and two from the Scottish state parties and 15 people elected by federal conference (Liberal Democrat Press Office, January 1999). This committee is responsible for drawing up and developing policy proposals. Most of the policy proposals debated at conference are put forward by the policy committee.

3. The conference committee

The conference committee is responsible for organising the two annual conferences and for drawing up the agenda for the conferences. This committee contains 21 voting members: 12 people elected by the federal conference, two members elected by the federal executive, two elected by the federal policy committee; a representative from each state party, the party's Chief Whip and the Party President.

Source: Liberal Democrat Press Office, January 1999.

Policy-making

It is the federal principle which determines Liberal Democrat policy-making. Policy decisions which affect a particular locality are made locally while those affecting the country as a whole are made by the federal institutions.

In a federal United Kingdom, there would probably be a federal Parliament, a Scottish Parliament, a Welsh Parliament and regional Parliaments in England. While the federal Parliament would make decisions about matters which affected the country as a whole, each of these state and regional Parliaments would be responsible for making decisions about local issues. The Liberal Democrat policy-making system reflects this division of responsibility.

The supreme policy-making body is the federal conference. If conference accepts the motions proposed by the federal policy committee, local, regional and state parties, then they become party policy. But, policy proposals concerning, for example, Scottish affairs would not be put forward to the federal conference. They would be proposed and debated at a conference organised by the Scottish state party and, if the proposals were passed, they would become party policy in Scotland.

Power of the party leadership

Although the federal conference is supposedly the sovereign body and it must give its formal approval to policy, the party leadership retains a great deal of control over the formulation of policy. Most major policy proposals are initiated by the federal policy committee which is dominated by the party leadership. This committee sets up working groups to study subjects in depth and, after consultation, submits these papers to federal conference for approval. Conference can amend these papers. But, if that happens, the policy committee must review them once more before they return to conference. Although representatives at conference are able to propose motions on policy issues for debate, the policy committee has the power to insist that a final decision is postponed. Also, the policy committee, together with the parliamentary party, is responsible for drawing up the party's election manifestos. So, again, the system ensures that the party leadership retains control of the policy-making process. In addition, the federal conference committee determines which motions are debated at conference. As with the policy committee, composition of this committee is such that the party leadership is able to keep a firm grip on its decisions.

Selecting the Liberal Democrat Leader

The system adopted by the Liberal Democrats stipulates that a contest, using the Single Transferable Vote system (see Unit 4) must take place two years after every general election. A leadership election can also be called either when the current Leader resigns or is incapacitated or when a majority of MPs or 75 local parties demand it. Every paid-up member is entitled to vote in the election on a one member, one vote basis. Candidates for the leadership must be MPs, they must be proposed and seconded by other MPs and they must be nominated by no less than 200 members in at least 20 different local parties.

Main points   Sections 9.6 - 9.7

- **The Liberal Democrats came into being in March 1988 when the Liberal Party formally merged with the SDP. The roots of the party, however, reach back way beyond 1988 - to the foundation of the Liberal Party in 1859.**
- **Since merger, the Liberal Democrats have regularly scored 20% of the vote in local elections and have also won several by-elections. Until 1997, the number of MPs remained under 25.**
- **Despite securing a slightly lower percentage of the popular vote than in 1992, the Liberal Democrats won 46 seats - mainly because of a growth in tactical voting. In 2001, six more Liberal Democrats were elected, bringing the total to 52.**
- **The federal structure of the Liberal Democrats is laid down in a written constitution. A federal party is a party in which the central decision-making body of the party is not all-powerful. Power is devolved to area and local parties.**

Activity 9.3 *The Liberal Democrats*

Item A Liberal Prime Ministers and election victories 1900-45

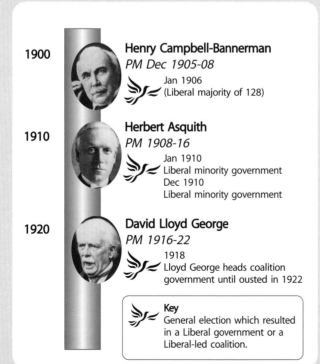

1900

Henry Campbell-Bannerman
PM Dec 1905-08
Jan 1906
(Liberal majority of 128)

1910

Herbert Asquith
PM 1908-16
Jan 1910
Liberal minority government
Dec 1910
Liberal minority government

1920

David Lloyd George
PM 1916-22
1918
Lloyd George heads coalition government until ousted in 1922

Key
General election which resulted in a Liberal government or a Liberal-led coalition.

Item B General election results 1945-2001

Election	No of candidates	MPs elected	Total votes	% of UK total
1945	306	12	2,252,430	9.0
1950	475	9	2,621,487	9.1
1951	109	6	730,546	2.6
1955	110	6	722,402	2.7
1959	216	6	1,640,760	5.9
1964	365	9	3,099,283	11.2
1966	311	12	2,327,457	8.6
1970	332	6	2,117,035	7.5
1974 (Feb)	517	14	6,059,519	19.3
1974 (Oct)	619	13	5,346,704	18.3
1979	577	11	4,313,804	13.8
1983	633	23	7,780,949	25.4
1987	633	22	7,341,633	22.5
1992	632	20	5,998,446	17.8
1997	639	46	5,242,894	16.8
2001	587	52	4,815,249	19.0

Source: Butler & Kavanagh 2001 and Dorey 2002.

Item C Charles Kennedy's election as Leader

When Paddy Ashdown resigned in the summer of 1999, there were no immediate 'heirs-apparent' to succeed him. When candidates formally announced their candidacy at the end of June, there were five contenders - Jackie Ballard, Malcolm Bruce, Simon Hughes, Charles Kennedy and David Rendel. A sixth, Don Foster, withdrew from the contest at the last minute. Despite a reputation for being a 'lightweight'

Candidate	1st Round	2nd Round	3rd Round	4th Round
Charles Kennedy	22,724	+895=23,619	+1,545=25,164	+3,261=28,425
Simon Hughes	16,233	+1,145=17,378	+1,982=19,360	+2,473=21,833
Malcom Bruce	4,643	+598=5,241	+827=6,068	N/A
Jackie Ballard	3,978	+627=4,605	N/A	N/A
David Rendel	3,428	N/A	N/A	N/A

(because he had appeared on light-hearted or satirical TV programmes such as *Have I Got News For You*), Charles Kennedy quickly emerged as the front-runner. He campaigned on a broad range of issues, such as increased public expenditure, joining the single European currency, pensions reform, and greater emphases on environmentalism and social justice. With regard to the relationship between the Liberal Democrats and the Blair government (a key issue for many Liberal Democrats), Kennedy merely made it clear that he supported the principle of cooperation and believed that it might even be extended to other policy areas, such welfare reform. The result of the Liberal Democrats' leadership contest was announced on 9 August 1999, the party's MPs, peers and ordinary members having voted via the Single Transferable Vote method of election (favoured by many Liberal Democrats for general elections). As the table above indicates, Charles Kennedy finally emerged victorious at the fourth stage, having attracted the support of 56.6% of the votes cast, compared to the 43.4% won by Hughes. The turnout, however, was a rather modest 62%, with barely 51,000 of the Liberal Democrats' 83,000 members voting. This was rather ironic for a party which places such a high emphasis on grass-roots political activity and the extension of democracy through greater decentralisation.

Adapted from Alderman & Carter 2000.

Item D The aims of the Liberal Democrats

Key Proposals

Freedom from heavy-handed central government control

* Give local people more power and choice over public services.

Fair taxes not higher taxes

* Scrap tuition fees and top-up fees.
* Scrap the Council Tax.
* Scrap charges for personal care for the elderly.

Beef up the fight against crime

* Make education the new 'tough on crime' to cut reoffending.
* Make criminals payback to victims - not layback in prison - with tougher community sentences.

Place the environment at the heart of government

* Tackle immediate threats from pollution and waste.
* Boost energy conservation and renewable generation.
* Reduce road traffic congestion and pollution.

Source: *Free, Fair, Green* - the Liberal Democrats' alternative Queen's Speech published in November 2003.

Questions

1. a) What is the evidence in Item A that the Liberal Party declined during the inter-war period?

   b) Explain why this happened.

2. a) What does Item B tell us about the performance of the Liberal Party/Liberal Democrats in the period 1945-2001?

   b) Would you say that the Liberal Democrats are a major or a minor party today? Give reasons for your answer.

3. Using Item C and your own knowledge, explain how the election of Charles Kennedy differed from that of the Leaders of the other main parties.

4. What does Item D tell us about the aims of the Liberal Democrats?

9.8 The roots of the modern Conservative Party

Historical background

If a political party is judged by its ability to win elections and form governments then the Conservative Party has been by far the most successful party in Britain throughout the 20th century. The roots of this success were laid in the 19th century. Although there is no firm date to mark the transition from Tory Party to Conservative Party, most commentators date this transition to 1834, the year in which Robert Peel became Leader (see, for example, Garner & Kelly 1998).

Robert Peel's leadership

Robert Peel's great achievement was to develop a political party which could represent the interests of all people of wealth whether that wealth was derived from property, land, industry or the professions. Peel argued that social, economic and political change should not automatically be opposed. It should be welcomed, but only if it occurred slowly and if it built upon established institutions rather than sweeping them away. By encouraging change, Peel appealed to entrepreneurs and those who had become wealthy through the changes brought by the Industrial Revolution. By emphasising respect for established institutions such as the monarchy and the Church, Peel appealed to the ancient traditions of the landed aristocracy. In the short term Peel was successful. The Conservatives won the general election of 1841. In the longer term, however, this new voting alliance was uneasy and, in 1846, the party split. Those who supported free trade were forced to leave the party, while those who supported protectionism remained.

One nation conservatism since 1865

Conservative fortunes were revived by the practical and ideological contribution of Benjamin Disraeli - Conservative Prime Minister in 1868 and between 1874 and 1880. Disraeli's ideological strategy - one nation conservatism (see Unit 7) - was a great success. Between 1830 and 1865, the Conservatives had an effective parliamentary majority for only five years. But, from 1865 to 1900, the Conservatives had overall majorities for 17 years. The one nation strand of conservatism remained a key aspect of Conservative Party ideology and practice in the 20th century. It underpinned, for example, the long period of rule under Harold Macmillan whose governments demonstrated an ability to come to terms with the post-war welfare state and Keynesian economics.

'Liberal' conservatism

Like most political parties the Conservative Party is a broad alliance. Not all Conservatives are one nation conservatives. Indeed, during the 1990s, the one nation Conservatives were in the minority. Since the election of Margaret Thatcher as Conservative Party Leader in 1975, the Conservative Party has been dominated by those who subscribe to a different tradition - 'liberal' conservatism - see Unit 7.

9.9 Factions and tendencies within the Conservative Party

Today, few people would argue that the Conservative Party does not have an ideology. Yet, that used to be the common view. Stephen Ingle argues that the Thatcher governments changed this:

'Thatcherism could be said to have brought ideology into Conservative Party politics and in doing so destroyed the basis of unity, trust and loyalty which had been the party's most reliable weapon. Thus one of the party's abiding myths, that it was not an ideological party, [has] been destroyed.' (Ingle 1993, p.3)

Within the Conservative Party, there are a number of groups or 'factions' (a faction is an organised group within a party which focuses on a particular ideological approach or particular policy). An examination of these factions suggests that the myth that the Conservative Party was not an ideological party is just that. Many of the factions existed before Margaret Thatcher became Leader. Their different aims reflect the different ideological approaches within the Conservative Party (see Box 9.14 for examples).

Box 9.14 Examples of groups within the Conservative Party

Name of group	Date set up	Aims/ideology
Bow Group	1951	Broadly supports liberal conservative policies.
Monday Club	1961	Set up to protect right-wing principles and to oppose one nation conservatism.
Tory Reform Group	1975	Supports one nation conservatism.
No Turning Back Group	1983	Set up to protect and extend Thatcherite policies.
Bruges Group	1988	Set up after Thatcher's anti-European 'Bruges Speech' to oppose moves towards greater European integration.

In addition to the formal groups mentioned above, there are informal groupings of Conservative MPs, also known as 'tendencies'. For example, in the 1980s, Conservatives were divided broadly into 'wets' (opponents of Thatcherism) and 'dries' (Thatcherites). In the 1990s, the key division was between Europhiles and Eurosceptics. Indeed, the split between Europhiles and Eurosceptics became so pronounced in the period 1992-97 that the party's reputation for unity suffered badly. Following the Conservative defeat at the general election of 1997, the division in the party between Europhiles and Eurosceptics has remained central.

9.10 *The structure and organisation of the Conservative Party*

The structure of the party before 1998

Until the 1997 general election, surprisingly little was known about the internal workings of the Conservative Party. This was due, in part, to the fact that Conservative Party had no official constitution:

> 'The arcane nature of Tory organisation owes much to the lack of any grand constitution outlining the powers and functions of its various organs. Indeed, a legal inquiry in 1982, involving Conservative Central Office and the Inland Revenue found that "the Conservative Party" did not even exist as "a compact, legally recognised organisation". It concluded that the party consisted instead of "three separate components" operating mainly on the basis of convention.' (Kelly 1994, p.52)

The three components referred to by Kelly were: the volunteers in the constituency associations (who were represented in the National Union of Conservative Associations); the party professionals at the regional headquarters and at Central Office; and, the parliamentary party (MPs and MEPs).

One reason why the Conservative Party did not exist as a 'compact, legally recognised organisation' was that, historically, the party had only existed in Parliament as a parliamentary group. The extension of the franchise in the 19th century produced the pressure to build up popular support. But, the real power in the party remained with the parliamentary leadership. To a large extent, this remained true until 1998. Writing in 1993, for example, Ingle claimed that:

> 'Properly speaking the Conservative Party is that body of MPs and peers who take the Conservative whips and the function of the constituency associations and regional and national structures is to support and sustain that body.' (Ingle 1993, p.3)

William Hague's reforms 1997-98

Following his election as Leader in June 1997 (a month after the Conservatives won their lowest number of MPs since 1906), William Hague argued that nothing short of a 'cultural revolution' was necessary in the Conservative Party. To achieve this, he made it clear that he intended to change the structure of the party. In autumn 1997, a Green Paper entitled *Blueprint for Change* was published. Following consultation, the proposals in this paper were amended and a fresh set of proposals published in February 1998 under the title *The Fresh Future*. The proposals in this paper were put to a ballot of party members and the results announced at a Special Reform Conference held on 28 March 1998. Of those who voted in the ballot, 96% supported the proposals (though only 33% of the membership voted in the ballot).

As a result of this ballot, the Conservative Party now has a written constitution, a national membership scheme and, for the first time, the party's three separate components have been united within a single party structure. While constituency associations (see below) remain the key organisation at local level, the party structure has four new elements. These are outlined in Box 9.15.

Box 9.15 The structure of the Conservative Party

1. The Board

The Board is the ultimate decision-making body of the Conservative Party. In March 2004, it contained 16 members from all three components of the party - the voluntary, political and professional. It meets once a month and is chaired by the Party Chairman. It is responsible for organising the annual party conference and has taken over the functions which used to be performed by the National Union. It is also responsible for running Conservative Central Office. The Board has a number of sub-committees, including membership, candidates and conferences.

2. The National Convention

The National Convention is made up of national, regional and area officials, officers from constituency associations and members of affiliated organisations. It is supported by a network of 11 Regional Councils and 42 Area Councils. Its function is to channel to the Leader grass-roots views and to advise the Board on extra-parliamentary organisation. It meets twice a year.

3. The National Convention executive

The executive is made up of the six senior officers of the National Convention, five of whom are the Convention's representatives on the Board. It has day-to-day responsibility for voluntary activity and is accountable to the Board.

4. The Policy Forum

The aim of the Policy Forum is to allow ordinary members to play a part in devising policy by making proposals to conference. The Forum is made up of regional policy congresses which coopt experts and parliamentary spokespeople. It is chaired by the minister responsible for policy development. Like the National Convention, the Forum has advisory powers.

Changes under Iain Duncan Smith

Although Iain Duncan Smith didn't make wholesale changes to the structure put in place by Hague, a number of significant developments took place while he was Leader. These are explored in Item C in Activity 9.4 below.

Constituency associations

Like all political parties, the Conservative Party relies on volunteers to work on its behalf locally. These volunteers join their local constituency association, the key organisation at local level. Constituency associations are run by an executive committee which is elected at the annual general meeting (AGM). They are divided into branches which are based on local council polling districts and exist to fight local elections. The executive committee of the constituency association is made up of representatives from the branches. Constituency association meetings are attended by ordinary members rather than delegates.

The functions of constituency associations

Constituency associations have three main functions. First, they provide the local organisation necessary to win elections. Second, they play an important part in the selection of candidates for local and national elections. And third, they provide a place for like-minded people to meet and socialise. Studies have shown that the majority of members of the Conservative Party do not attend party meetings or participate in party activities. They join so that they can use the party's social facilities.

Kelly argues that William Hague's reforms had the unintended consequence of lowering morale in the constituency associations - see Box 9.16.

> ### Box 9.16   The Conservative Party 1998-2001
>
> At the hub of the 1998 reforms was a central Party Board, mainly made up of unelected officials, and responsible for most aspects of extra-parliamentary activity - chiefly the projection of a new Conservative 'image' at constituency level and the subsequent recruitment of new members. However, given that the Conservative Party under Hague seemed to lack any clear 'big picture', the Party Board naturally struggled to make much impact. Once the Party Board's limitations were revealed, the centralisation it embodied looked pointless to rank and file members, who were further 'de-energised' as a result. It is significant that, having estimated the membership to be 400,00 in 1997, Central Office put it at only 318,000 for the leadership contest of 2001. The effects of this flawed centralisation, and the low morale it produced, were all too clear during the 2001 general election. In most of the marginal seats he visited, Hague was seriously short of foot-soldiers, placing an impossible burden on the Leader and his élite 'A-Team'. However, any sympathy for Hague should be limited - for it was a burden he himself invited, via a centralised party structure devoid of any clear political mission.
>
> Source: Kelly 2003.

The impact of Hague's reforms on constituency associations

Until 1998, constituency associations were completely autonomous (free to act as they liked). This meant, for example, that John Major was unable to prevent Tatton Constituency Association from selecting, and refusing to deselect, the disgraced ex-minister Neil Hamilton as their candidate for the 1997 general election. The leadership simply had no power over constituency association candidate selection.

According to Richard Kelly (1998), William Hague's reforms curtailed this freedom in three ways. First, a new Ethics and Integrity Committee (overseen by the new Board) was set up with the power to suspend or expel unsuitable members. This gave the national party some control over candidate selection (it could have forced Neil Hamilton's constituency association to deselect him in the run-up to the 1997 general

election, for example, if it had been in operation then). Second, the Party Board has the power to set efficiency criteria for each individual association. If associations do not meet these criteria, the Board can order an association to be reorganised and force its officers to be replaced. And third, whereas associations had complete control over their local finances before 1998, they now have to submit annual accounts to Central Office. In addition, the introduction of a national membership scheme means that some membership funds automatically go to Central Office (whereas, before, all membership funds were collected and retained locally).

The annual party conference

The annual party conference has no formal powers to make party policy. Decisions made at conference are advisory only. The party leadership may choose to ignore them. It is, therefore, no surprise that the traditional view of the annual party conference is that it has little political importance. Rather, it is usually seen as a rally of the party faithful where dedicated party members meet together, reinforce each others' views and enjoy an exciting social occasion. In support of this view, it should be noted that, until 1965, the Party Leader only attended the conference on the final afternoon. Although Party Leaders have always attended since then (which may suggest that the conference has grown in importance), they are automatically given a standing ovation regardless of their popularity or the content of their speech. This suggests that the purpose of the conference is to rubber stamp the decisions made by the party leadership.

Political significance of conferences

Just because annual party conferences are carefully stage-managed public relations exercises, that does not necessarily mean that they do not have any political importance. It has long been known, for example, that a poor speech from a frontbencher can dash their hopes of promotion or even (in the case of Reginald Maudling in 1965) their hopes of party leadership. Besides, the polite surface often conceals underlying currents. Journalists often make a great deal of the length of time that standing ovations last and they attempt to 'decode' the 'mood' of the conference. A cool response to a senior figure's speech, for example, might be a sign of widespread grass-roots discontent.

Despite the fact that the annual party conference does not have a formal role in policy-making, senior Conservatives often use it as a forum either to 'test the water' before devising concrete proposals or actually to announce new policies. That senior party figures use the conference for this purpose suggests that they consider conference to be an important body.

Regional and sectional conferences

It has been suggested that, in fact, the regional and sectional conferences have a bigger influence over policy development than is generally realised. Richard Kelly (1989) has argued that much of the ground work for the annual party conference is done at these regional and sectional conferences. He notes that debates at these conferences are much more critical and frank than those at the annual party conference, and they are encouraged to be so by senior Conservatives. Kelly suggests that:

'[The annual party conference] is in a sense the climax of an oblique "conference system" where ministers earn their ovations only by showing some accommodation of the advice rendered by Tory activists at previous conferences held that year.' (Kelly 1992, p.27)

Conservative Central Office

The Conservative Party employs a full-time bureaucracy which has its headquarters in Smith Square, London. Conservative Central Office was set up in 1870 by Disraeli as his private office. The Party Chairman (the Conservatives refuse to use the gender-neutral term 'chair') and other party officials are appointed by the Party Leader and are answerable to the Party Leader alone. The Party Chairman is in charge of Central Office. The structure and organisation of Central Office is described in Box 9.17.

Box 9.17 Structure and organisation of Central Office

In the late 1990s, the number of staff employed by Central Office declined, though it does vary according to circumstances (more staff are employed at the time of a general election, for example). In January 1994, around 250 staff were employed by Central Office, in January 1999, the figure was around 100, while in March 2004, the number employed by Central Office had increased to 180 (including field workers). The structure and organisation of Central Office has been altered several times since the general election defeat of 1997. When Michael Howard became Leader in October, he wasted little time in streamlining operations. The number of departments was cut from 11 to three - Press and Broadcasting, Research and Development (covering policy, research and development) and Marketing (taking charge of opinion research, direct marketing, electronic marketing, advertising, party political broadcasting, membership, constituency marketing support and tours and events involving the Leader and shadow Cabinet). Two new appointments were made - Guy Black to head the Press Department and Will Harris to head the Marketing Department. Greg Clark, who was in charge of policy, was put in charge of the Research and Development Department, with David Willetts MP as its Chairman.

Central Office continues to divide the UK into 26 areas, each headed by an Area Campaign Director. The job of the Area Campaign Director is to liaise between the 12 or so constituency associations in their local area and Central Office.

Source: Conservative Party Press Release, 20 November 2003.

The role of Central Office

Central Office is responsible for the party's finances and for membership policy (since 1998, it has been responsible for maintaining the national membership list). It also has a coordinating role at election time. It is responsible for national campaigning, liaising with the media and for ensuring satisfactory resources are available in the constituencies.

Central Office provides an important bridge between ordinary party members and the parliamentary party. It provides constituency associations with information and advice and trains the professional agents employed by constituencies. While candidates for election are selected locally, this takes place under the supervision of Central Office. As noted above, since 1998 Central Office has had some genuine control over candidate selection (control which was lacking before).

The Party Chairman

The Conservative Party Chairman, Deputy Chairman and Vice Chairmen are appointed by the Party Leader. The Party Chairman has a dual role - to run Central Office and to publicise policies which concern the structure and organisation of the party. The Party Chairman is also responsible for running the party's national election campaigns.

Main points   Sections 9.8 - 9.10

- **If a political party is judged by its ability to win elections and form governments then the Conservative Party has been by far the most successful party in Britain throughout the 20th century.**
- **Within the Conservative Party, there are a number factions and tendencies. The split between Europhiles and Eurosceptics became so pronounced in the period 1992-97 that the party's reputation for unity suffered badly.**
- **Before the 1997 general election, the Conservative Party had no written constitution and was not even a legally recognised body.**
- **Since 1997, there have been significant reforms. The party now has a written constitution and the various components have been joined together to make a single party. The extra-parliamentary party is run by the Board and the voice of ordinary members is heard via the National Policy Forum.**
- **The National Policy Forum and party conference have advisory powers only. The Leader can ignore their views.**

Activity 9.4 *The Conservative Party*

Item A Conservative Prime Ministers and general election victories since 1900

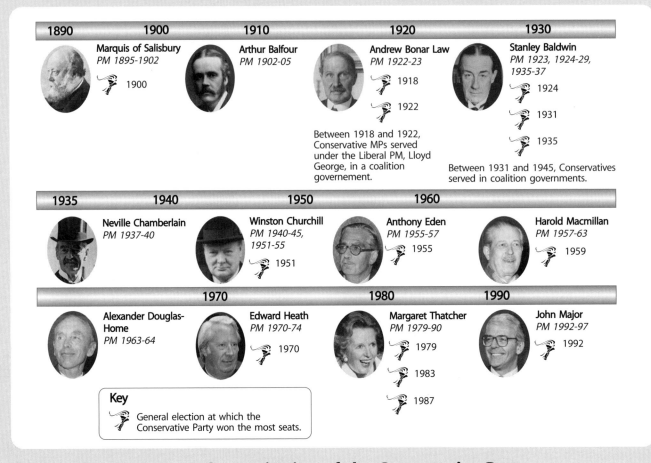

1890	1900	1910	1920	1930

Marquis of Salisbury
PM 1895-1902
1900

Arthur Balfour
PM 1902-05

Andrew Bonar Law
PM 1922-23
1918
1922

Between 1918 and 1922, Conservative MPs served under the Liberal PM, Lloyd George, in a coalition governement.

Stanley Baldwin
PM 1923, 1924-29, 1935-37
1924
1931
1935

Between 1931 and 1945, Conservatives served in coalition governments.

1935	1940	1950	1960

Neville Chamberlain
PM 1937-40

Winston Churchill
PM 1940-45, 1951-55
1951

Anthony Eden
PM 1955-57
1955

Harold Macmillan
PM 1957-63
1959

1970	1980	1990

Alexander Douglas-Home
PM 1963-64

Edward Heath
PM 1970-74
1970

Margaret Thatcher
PM 1979-90
1979
1983
1987

John Major
PM 1992-97
1992

Key

General election at which the Conservative Party won the most seats.

Item B The structure and organisation of the Conservative Party

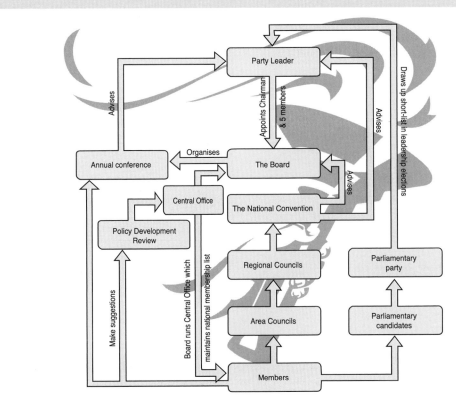

Item C Party organisation under Iain Duncan Smith

(i) Iain Duncan Smith and the Party Board

Richard Kelly argues that, shortly after becoming Leader, Iain Duncan Smith announced that he was 'broadly content' with the 1998 reorganisation. This, says Kelly, was a 'remarkably complacent view given the party's atrocious performance in 2001. Any idea that the Party Board would be given a more democratic appearance was thus discarded, along with the possibility that the Leader selection rules would be cured of the problems seen during Iain Duncan Smith's election.' In an article published after Howard had replaced Duncan Smith, Kelly concludes that Duncan Smith 'showed stark contempt for the Party Board'. He points out that, in February 2003, Duncan Smith replaced the party's Chief Executive, Research Director and Campaigns Director without consulting the Board - even though the appointment of a Chief Executive was the job of the Board. This caused a public row and the new Chief Executive, Barry Legg, eventually resigned. The Legg Affair, says Kelly, was especially damaging since it prompted a public row between Iain Duncan Smith and the Board, it prompted Legg's resignation (which meant paying him a large sum in compensation) and it raised grave doubts about Duncan Smith's ability to work with party officials.

(ii) Iain Duncan Smith and the Policy Forum

Kelly was also concerned about Iain Duncan Smith's reform of the party's Policy Forum. This, he says, had shown signs of being a useful channel for grass-roots policy ideas. But, under Duncan Smith, it was downgraded in favour of a 'Policy Renewal Programme' (PRP). Involvement in the PRP was openly determined by the size of contribution to party funds. A contribution of £500, for example, bought 'Gold Level' engagement, allowing the donor to attend meetings overseen by shadow Cabinet members. A contribution of £100, on the other hand, bought 'Bronze Level' engagement. For this, the donor received 'information' about the 'Gold Level' meetings.

(iii) Iain Duncan Smith and the party conference

Kelly is critical of the restructuring of the party conference. This, he says, has been done in such a way to exclude further the involvement of ordinary members. He quotes one of Iain Duncan Smith's advisers as saying: 'Conference should be less of a bun fight and more of a showcase. Speeches from the floor should be limited so as to allow more time for guest speakers from outside the party' (*Daily Telegraph*, 11 April 2002). Conference arrangements, Kelly notes, were previously controlled by the National Convention (the ordinary members' executive body). Under Duncan Smith they were removed from National Convention control and placed in the Leader's office. The result has been that grass-roots input has been notably reduced.

Source Kelly 2003 and 2004.

Questions

1. Using Items A and B, assess whether the Conservatives are the 'natural party of government'.
2. Describe the functions of the main bodies of the Conservative Party in Item B.

3. How did the structure and organisation of the Conservative Party change under Iain Duncan Smith?

9.11 *The role of the Conservative Leader*

Until the resignation of Margaret Thatcher in November 1990, there was a general consensus among writers that Conservative Leaders enjoyed almost unrestrained power so long as they were able to bring electoral success (see, for example, McKenzie 1955 and Garner & Kelly 1998).

The powers of the Conservative Leader are indeed considerable. First, in theory at least, the Leader alone is responsible for choosing the Cabinet or shadow Cabinet. Second, unlike the Labour Leader, the Conservative Leader does not have to work with an elected Deputy Leader (Conservative Leaders are free to choose or not choose a Deputy Leader). Third, the Conservative Leader has sole responsibility for the formulation of the party's election manifestos. And fourth, the Conservative Leader chooses the

Party Chairman. These powers allow Conservative Leaders to introduce the policies and style of their own choosing. With the adoption of a written constitution in 1998, the Leader's formal role was described in writing for the first time. The wording showed that the Leader was to have a great deal of freedom of movement:

'The Leader shall determine the political direction of the party having regard to the views of party members and the Conservative Policy Forum.' (Conservative 1998, p.6)

Iain Duncan Smith's replacement of the Policy Forum with a Policy Development Review meant that he had even more freedom of manoeuvre than was envisaged in 1998.

Why is the Conservative Leader so powerful?

There are two main reasons why the Conservative Leader has such a powerful position in the party. First, belief in hierarchy and leadership is embodied in Conservative ideology. As Ian Aitken put it, it is a 'top-down' rather than a 'bottom-up' party (*Guardian*, 14 January 1998). And second, the British electorate tends to favour parties which are united behind a strong leader. Since electoral success is judged to be of primary importance to the Conservative Party, that helps to explain why the party encourages strong leadership.

9.12 The selection of the Party Leader

'Emergence'

Until 1965, the Conservative Leader was chosen by what has been called 'emergence'. New Party Leaders were not selected by any formal system. Rather the new Leader would 'emerge' from meetings held between senior party members, influential backbenchers and others considered to be of importance within the Conservative Party. It is, perhaps, no surprise to learn that those senior Conservatives involved in the choice of Leader were known as the 'magic circle'.

After the resignation of Harold Macmillan in 1963 this system proved itself inadequate. There was no clear successor to Macmillan and the 'magic circle' chose Alexander Douglas-Home as Leader (see Box 9.18). Many Conservatives considered Douglas-Home to be an inappropriate choice. This view seemed to be confirmed when Douglas-Home lost the 1964 general election. Before Douglas-Home resigned, however, he set up an inquiry to establish a new way of choosing the Conservative Leader.

Box 9.18 Alex Douglas-Home

Alex Douglas-Home, Conservative Party Leader from November 1963 to August 1965.

New system, 1965

The result of the inquiry was that a new system for electing the Conservative Leader was set up. From 1965, a candidate for the post of Leader needed a nominator and a seconder. There would then be a maximum of three ballots in which Conservative MPs would be allowed to vote. In the first ballot, a successful candidate needed to gain more than 50% of votes cast and to have 15% more votes than any other candidate. Later, this was changed. A successful candidate needed more than 50% of the votes of those entitled to vote and 15% more votes than any other candidate. If the first ballot was inconclusive, a second would be held. In the second ballot, a successful candidate simply needed to win more than 50% of the votes cast. If that did not produce a winner, a third round would be held. In this ballot, the three most popular candidates (according to the results of the second round) would contest the post. The winner was the candidate who had the majority using an Alternative Vote system. Candidates could withdraw from the contest at any stage.

Contests under this system

The first contest to be held under this system took place in 1965. It was won by Edward Heath. Heath failed to gain the required majority in the first round but he led his opponents by such a margin that they all withdrew. Subsequent contests took place in 1975, 1989 and 1990. In 1975, Margaret Thatcher won on the second ballot. In 1989, Margaret Thatcher won on the first ballot. Then, in 1990, despite having a majority, Margaret Thatcher withdrew after the first ballot because she had failed to win an outright victory (and a number of Cabinet colleagues made it clear that she had lost their support). Her withdrawal was followed by the victory of John Major.

New rules, 1991

Following the leadership contest of 1990, changes were made to the leadership election system. The contest had to take place within 14 days of a new Commons session or within three months of a new Parliament. Also, any challenger had to have the backing of 10% of Conservative MPs. These new arrangements were made in response to the 'frivolous' challenge of Anthony Meyer in 1989. Meyer took advantage of a rule change in 1974 which stipulated that there should be a leadership election every year whether or not the Conservatives were in power (Margaret Thatcher was elected unopposed every year between 1975 and 1989). Although Meyer had no hope of winning himself, he hoped that other more serious challengers would come forward. His actions, therefore, put the Leader under pressure. The leadership elections of 1995 (when John Major resigned voluntarily and then won a convincing majority in the first ballot) and 1997 (when John Major resigned following the general election defeat - the first time in the 20th century that a Conservative Leader resigned immediately after a general election defeat) were held under the new rules.

William Hague's reforms

The 1997 Conservative leadership contest was particularly controversial for two reasons. First, the 1997 general election had resulted in just 165 Conservatives being elected as MPs. Under the existing rules, that meant that the new Leader would be chosen by an electorate of just 164. Many within the party (and outside) argued that this was undemocratic and that ordinary party members should have a say. And second, when opinion polls were conducted in constituency associations, it became clear that a large majority of ordinary members favoured Kenneth Clarke and yet it was William

Hague who won the contest. As a result, critics questioned the legitimacy of Hague's position as Leader.

To gain legitimacy, to prevent similar criticisms being made in the future and to improve the Conservative Party's electoral prospects, William Hague announced that he intended to introduce reforms and held a special ballot of ordinary members asking them to endorse his position as Leader and to approve the principles behind the intended reforms (outlined in Section 9.10 above). The support gained in the referendum was sufficient to provide Hague with some legitimacy and paved the way to changes in the way in which the Party Leader was to be elected.

The rules introduced in 1998

The key change introduced in 1998 was the rule allowing ordinary Conservative Party members to have the final say in who should become Party Leader. In a leadership contest where only two candidates stood, there would simply be a ballot of all party members. In a leadership contest where more than two candidates stood, there would be a primary ballot (or series of ballot) of Conservative MPs to whittle down the number standing to just two candidates. Then, there would be a ballot of all party members to choose between the two remaining candidates.

The two leadership 'contests' since 2001

Since the new rules were introduced in 1998, two leadership 'contests' have taken place. In both cases the process has yielded a surprise. In 2001 the first surprise was that one of the most important front-runners for the leadership, Michael Portillo, was eliminated in the ballot of MPs (see Dorey 2004). This left Iain Duncan Smith and Kenneth Clarke to contest the leadership in a ballot of party members. When the votes were counted it was the underdog, Duncan Smith, who was found to have defeated the front-runner, Clarke. The main reason for this was thought to be Clarke's role in ousting Margaret Thatcher while he was a Cabinet minister in

1990 and his passionate pro-Europeanism:

> 'Many on the right of the party jubilantly viewed Iain Duncan Smith's victory as a clear endorsement of Thatcherism and Euro-scepticism.' (Dorey 2004, p.4)

Many commentators have argued that the electoral system chosen by the Conservatives for their Leader, while praiseworthy in its democratic intention, has flaws. Certainly, in the case of Iain Duncan Smith, the system allowed a candidate to win who was not the main choice of MPs. This placed Duncan Smith under pressure from the start:

> 'A few days [before the leadership election result was announced] Lord (Douglas) Hurd warned that, if Iain Duncan Smith did emerge victorious, he could not expect the "automatic loyalty" of pro-European Conservatives, particularly as Duncan Smith himself had not displayed much loyalty to the leadership over Maastricht in the early 1990s. Some Clarke supporters were, in private, going much further, claiming that, if Iain Duncan Smith were elected as Leader, he would be "lethal to the Conservative Party".' (Dorey 2004, p.5)

As the months went on, Duncan Smith proved to be unpopular both with a significant number of colleagues in Parliament and, judging by opinion polls, with the wider electorate. His term in office ended when, on 28 October 2003 Michael Spicer, the Chair of the party's 1922 Committee, received 25 letters from MPs demanding a vote of no-confidence (25 MPs make up just over 15% of the parliamentary party, 15% being the minimum necessary to trigger a vote). The vote was held the following day. To survive, Iain Duncan Smith required at least 83 of the 166 votes. He received just 75 votes and was forced to resign.

The events which followed almost marked a return to the old system of emergence as senior MPs united behind Michael Howard, with some who might have stood against him deciding not to do so. When nominations closed, Howard was the only candidate. As a result, he was not required to hold a ballot of the membership.

Main points   Sections 9.11 - 9.12

- **The 1998 Conservative constitution states that the role of the Leader is to 'determine the political direction of the party having regard to the views of party members and the Conservative Policy Forum'.**
- **Although commentators argued before Thatcher's removal that the power of Conservative Leaders was almost unrestrained, in fact it has always been restricted by the need to retain the support of senior colleagues and backbenchers.**

- **Before 1965, Conservative Leaders 'emerged'. Between 1965 and 1998, Leaders were chosen by a ballot (or series of ballots) of MPs. The rule change in 1998 meant that, for the first time, ordinary members would have the final say on who should become Leader.**
- **The two leadership contests held since 2001 have both yielded a surprise. In 2001 the underdog, Iain Duncan Smith won. In 2003, nobody stood against Michael Howard and so he was elected without a membership ballot.**

Activity 9.5 Conservative Leaders

Item A Leadership elections, 1990-2003

(i) Leadership election, 1990

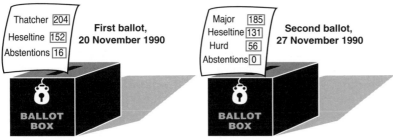

Thatcher 204		Major 185
Heseltine 152	**First ballot,**	Heseltine 131	**Second ballot,**
Abstentions 16	**20 November 1990**	Hurd 56	**27 November 1990**
		Abstentions 0	

Thatcher withdrew as she had not won an outright victory.

Heseltine and Hurd withdrew even though Major had not won an outright victory.

(ii) Leadership election, 1997

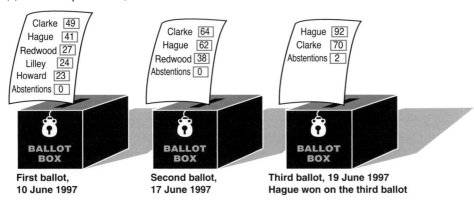

Clarke 49	Clarke 64	Hague 92
Hague 41	Hague 62	Clarke 70
Redwood 27	Redwood 38	Abstentions 2
Lilley 24	Abstentions 0	
Howard 23		
Abstentions 0		

First ballot, 10 June 1997 — **Second ballot, 17 June 1997** — **Third ballot, 19 June 1997** — **Hague won on the third ballot**

(iii) Leadership election, 2001

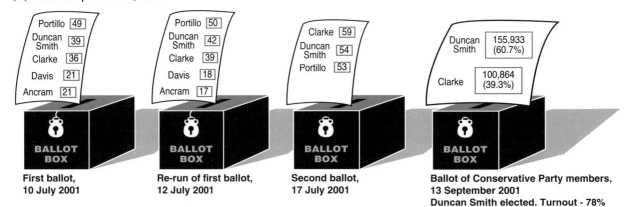

Portillo 49	Portillo 50	Clarke 59	Duncan Smith 155,933 (60.7%)
Duncan Smith 39	Duncan Smith 42	Duncan Smith 54	
Clarke 36	Clarke 39	Portillo 53	Clarke 100,864 (39.3%)
Davis 21	Davis 18		
Ancram 21	Ancram 17		

First ballot, 10 July 2001 — **Re-run of first ballot, 12 July 2001** — **Second ballot, 17 July 2001** — **Ballot of Conservative Party members, 13 September 2001. Duncan Smith elected. Turnout - 78%**

(iv) Leadership election, 2003

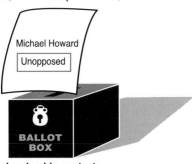

Michael Howard

Unopposed

Leadership contest, 31 October 2003

Source: Lynch & Garnett 2002.

Item B The leadership contest of 2001

The 2001 Conservative leadership contest was the first in the party's history in which the mass membership was granted the final say as to which of two remaining candidates would become Leader. Previously, the Conservative Parliamentary Party had jealously guarded its autonomy from the extra-parliamentary party. Although MPs could, and sometimes were encouraged to, take soundings as to opinions in their constituency parties, the final decision remained with individual MPs. This all changed following William Hague's internal reforms of the Conservative Party. First, though, a series of ballots had to be held to determine which two MPs would be presented to the mass membership for the final decision. The rules stipulated that, when more than three candidates presented themselves, a series of ballots would be held. The candidate polling fewest votes in each ballot would be eliminated from the contest so that, eventually, only two were left. In the first ballot in 200, two candidates tied for last place. This meant holding a rerun two days later. This time, Michael Ancram came last by one vote. However, following the rerun, David Davis announced that he was withdrawing from the contest. This ensured that the second ballot would be between three contenders. The result of the second ballot placed Michael Portillo, previously the front-runner, last, his tally of 53 votes just one fewer than that obtained by Iain Duncan Smith. The winner was Kenneth Clarke. The most notable feature of the campaign preceding the ballot was the lack of detailed or specific policy commitments and, instead, the often personal, acrimonious character of the contest. Animosities were not confined to the candidates. Other senior Conservatives used the leadership campaign to perpetuate existing enmities or settle old scores. The most notable of these attacks came from John Major who declared his support for Clarke and launched an attack against Margaret Thatcher. By encouraging anti-Maastricht rebels such as Iain Duncan Smith, he claimed, Thatcher had undermined his government in 1992-97. Major's allegations provoked a robust response from Norman Tebbit who simultaneously lambasted both Major and Clarke. When the result of the third and final ballot was announced on 13 September (a day later than originally planned, due to the terrorist atrocities in New York and Washington two days previously), Iain Duncan Smith was the clear victor.

Source: Dorey 2004.

Item C The 2003 Conservative leadership election

The end for Iain Duncan Smith's leadership of the Conservative Party came when he faced a motion of no-confidence on 29 October 2003. The rules devised by William Hague stipulated that such a motion could only be triggered if at least 15% of Conservative MPs (at least 25 MPs in 2003) wrote to the Chair of the 1922 Committee calling for a vote. By 28 October, the 25 letters had been received and so the vote was arranged for the following day. Duncan Smith needed 83 votes to gain a majority, but needed at least 100 to have any realistic chance of surviving since any figure below 100 would seriously undermine his credibility, legitimacy and moral authority. But when the result was announced at 6.59 pm on 29 October, it was discovered that only 75 MPs had expressed their confidence in Duncan Smith's leadership. Duncan Smith was, therefore, forced to resign and could not stand in the forthcoming leadership contest. Almost as soon as the result of the no-confidence vote was announced, Michael Howard was being urged to put his name forward by such diverse Conservatives as Stephen Dorrell (a left-ish former minister who had backed Michael Portillo in 2001), Oliver Letwin (a 'moderniser') and Liam Fox (a Conservative on the right of the party). Once he declared his candidacy, Howard received the endorsement of other senior figures, including Portillo. Even Ann Widdecombe whose comments had helped to end Howard's bid for the leadership in 2001 said that she would support him if Ken Clarke did not stand. This early momentum gathered pace until finally, on 31 October, Clarke ruled himself out. By then, at least 100 Conservative MPs had pledged their support. As no other candidates came forward in the 48 hours after Duncan Smith's resignation, Howard, pledging to lead a modernising Conservative Party from the centre, was elected unopposed.

Source: Dorey 2004.

Questions

1. a) Using Item A, explain what procedure was used in each of the leadership contests.

   b) How did the rules differ?

2. Using Items A-C explain how procedures for choosing a new Leader changed after 1998.

3. Why do you think Michael Howard was elected unopposed in 2003? Use Item C in your answer.

9.13 Other political parties

Throughout the 20th century, new parties have been set up in the hope that they would attract sufficient support to break the mould of British politics. But, with the exception of the Labour Party which was itself a minor party in the early years of the 20th century, no party has managed to achieve nationwide success. Since 1918, British politics has been dominated by the three main parties and there is little sign that this will change, certainly while the current electoral system survives.

But, although the three main parties dominate the political arena, that does not mean that the minor parties do not have any significance. In Wales and Scotland, for example, the nationalist parties are an important force and they regularly win seats in Parliament. Despite the small number of MPs from these parties, they can still play a crucial role in certain circumstances. Between 1993-94 and 1997, for example, the Major government's overall majority was eroded through deaths, by-election losses and suspensions. As a result, the government had to rely on the support of the ten Ulster Unionist MPs. This made it difficult for the government to find a peace settlement acceptable to the republicans. Similarly, in the 1974 general election, Labour won an overall majority of three while 11 Scottish National Party (SNP) MPs and three Plaid Cymru (Welsh nationalist) MPs were elected. Once the Labour government's overall majority of three disappeared as a result of by-election losses, it was forced to do a deal with the nationalist parties. In return for their support in Parliament, the government promised to hold referendums on devolution in Scotland and Wales (see Unit 5). This shows that, even within the existing electoral system, it is possible for minor parties to exert influence and to play an important political role. Besides, the setting up of the Scottish Parliament, Welsh Assembly and Northern Ireland Assembly has provided minor parties with new opportunities.

Minor parties and local politics
While parliamentary success is unusual for the minor parties, they have found it easier to make an impact in local politics. The number of Green councillors has grown since the mid-1980s and even the Monster Raving Loony Party has won seats on local councils. It should be noted that success even at local level has been far harder to achieve for minor parties whose politics is located on the extreme right or the extreme left than it has been for the nationalist parties or Greens. The nationalists and Greens are generally perceived as being within the mainstream while the parties on the extreme left and right are generally perceived as being a threat to the system.

Parties outside the mainstream
On the few occasions when groups on the extreme right or left have achieved electoral success (winning a substantial percentage of the vote may be regarded as an electoral success, even if the candidate is not elected), this has been greeted by considerable popular concern. Again, this suggests that minor parties do have a significance even if they are unable to win seats in elections. Their role is, perhaps, as barometers of public opinion. When people are generally content with the existing party system the minor parties do badly, while a significant vote for a minor party can suggest that people are discontented with the existing party system. The ebb and flow of support for minor parties provides a judgement on the party system and provides a legitimate avenue for the expression of views beyond the mainstream.

9.14 The Scottish National Party (SNP)

The SNP (see Box 9.19) was founded in 1934 when two small nationalist parties merged. Its aim is an independent Scotland. At present, there are two distinct viewpoints within the SNP. While the right wing (which has generally maintained control of the party) stresses traditional values and nostalgic nationalism, the left wing has pressed the case for a socialist Scotland as an independent country within the EU (the party's official policy at the time of the 1997 general election). Following the 1997 general election, the party temporarily suspended its demand for an independent Scotland and supported the Yes Yes campaign (which aimed for a Scottish Parliament with tax-varying powers) in the referendum which was held in September 1997. It did this on the grounds that a devolved Parliament would be the first step on the road to independence (see Unit 18 for further information on devolution).

Box 9.19 The SNP

The SNP's electoral record
The SNP won its first seat in Parliament in a by-election in Motherwell in April 1945 but lost the seat in the following general election. It was not until a by-election held in 1967 that the SNP won another seat. But, again, it lost the seat in the next general election in 1970. The 1970 general election was, however, the first general election in which the SNP managed to win a seat. This was a turning point in the party's fortunes. It has won seats in every general election since then.

The SNP's best general election result came in October 1974 when it won 30.4% of the vote in Scotland and 11 seats. Although it was unable to sustain this level of support (especially in the years following the referendum in 1979), the SNP has established itself as the third party in Scotland. Voters who are disaffected with the Conservatives or Labour tend to register their protest with the SNP. The SNP therefore plays a role similar to that played by the Liberal Democrats in England. This was graphically illustrated in the by-election in the constituency of Monklands East which was held on 30 June 1994 following the death of Labour's Leader, John Smith. While Labour won a majority of 15,712 in the 1992 general election, this majority was cut to just 1,640 in the by-election. The SNP vote went up from 6,554 to 15,320, a gain of 27%. This is just the sort of by-election result achieved by the Liberal Democrats in England.

In the 1997 general election, the SNP vote grew by 0.6% compared to 1992 and the party won six seats (compared to three in 1992). In the 2001 general election the SNP vote was down 2% (from 22.15% to 20.1%) and the party won five seats. Box 9.20 compares the SNP's performance in general elections to those in elections to the Scottish Parliament.

Box 9.20 SNP - general and Scottish Parliament elections, 1997-2003

Election	% vote	No. seats
1997 general election	22.1	6
1999 Scottish Parliament election	18.7	35
2001 general election	20.1	5
2003 Scottish Parliament election	23.9	27

9.15 Plaid Cymru

Box 9.21 Plaid Cymru

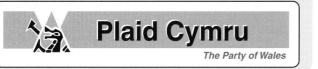

Plaid Cymru
The Party of Wales

Plaid Cymru (see Box 9.21) was founded in 1925. Its aim is an independent Wales. Following the 1997 general election, Plaid Cymru supported the Yes campaign in the referendum held on whether to set up a devolved Welsh Assembly. Like the SNP, it saw a devolved assembly as the first step towards independence. But, Plaid Cymru has always laid more stress on cultural and linguistic identity than the SNP (partly because there are many more Welsh speakers than Gaelic speakers). Plaid Cymru aims for a completely bilingual Wales and it works hard at increasing the use of Welsh in schools, broadcasting and in public administration. The problem that Plaid Cymru faces with insisting on bilingualism is that it does tend to alienate people living in Wales who do not speak Welsh. Most party members are Welsh speaking and most of the party's support comes from areas where Welsh is the first language. Between 1992 and 1997, Plaid Cymru had close links with the Green Party. In 1992, Cynog Dafis was elected as an MP on a joint Plaid Cymru/Green ticket and the Green Party agreed not to put up candidates against Plaid Cymru candidates. During the period 1992-97, however, the Green

Party split over this policy and, in 1997, some Green candidates did stand against Plaid Cymru candidates. Despite this, Plaid Cymru puts the environment high up on its political agenda.

Plaid Cymru's electoral record

Plaid Cymru won its first seat in a by-election in 1966. It lost this seat in the subsequent general election. Its best performance in terms of size of vote then came in the 1970 general election when it won 11.5% of the vote in Wales (175,016 votes). But, it did not win any seats in that election. Like the SNP, Plaid Cymru did well in October 1974. It won 10.8% of the vote and three seats. But, the disappointing referendum result in 1979 led to a decline in votes which continued until the 1992 general election when its share of the vote rose from 7.3% in 1987 to 11.1% and the number of seats captured rose from two to four. In 1997, Plaid Cymru was the second party in terms of seats captured (it retained its four seats). Its share of the vote rose by 1% compared to that in 1992. In the 2001 general election Plaid Cymru substantially increased its percentage of the vote in Wales from 12.45% in 1997 to 14.3% in 2001. The number of seats won remained the same as in 1997 however. Election results between 1997 and 2003 are given in Box 9.22.

Box 9.22 Plaid Cymru election results, 1997-2003

Election	% vote	No. seats
1997 general election	9.9	4
1999 Welsh Assembly election	28.4	17
2001 general election	14.3	4
2003 Welsh Assembly election	28.4	17

9.16 Fringe parties

Box 9.23 The Green Party

Green Party

The Green Party

The Green Party (see Box 9.23) emerged from the protest movements of the 1960s and the growing environmental concerns of the 1970s and 1980s. The party's origins can be traced back to 1973 when an environmental pressure group was formed, named 'People'. As this group began to explore the connections between environmental concerns and began to formulate policies to deal with them, it transformed itself into the Ecology Party. It changed its name to the Green

Party in 1985. The Green Party is committed to the broad aims of other European Green parties, namely the decentralisation of political power and the placing of environmental issues at the top of the political agenda.

Although the Greens have not enjoyed any electoral success in parliamentary elections, they have enjoyed some success in local, regional and European elections. The party's greatest electoral success came in 1999 when it won seats in the London Assembly, Scottish Parliament and European Parliament. The Green Party won the fifth largest number of votes in the 2001 election, polling over 9% of the vote in Brighton.

Fascist groups

Fascist politics emerged in Britain, as in most other West European countries, in the years between the two world wars. After sitting as a Conservative MP between 1918 and 1922 and as a Labour MP between 1926 and 1931, Oswald Mosley opted out of mainstream politics and set up the British Union of Fascists (BUF) in 1932. At its peak in 1934, the BUF had around 35,000 members. It contested elections, but never won a seat. Like other Fascist groups, the BUF was racist, militaristic and violently nationalistic. Modern Fascist groups trace their ancestry back to Mosley's group through a complex web of splits and schisms.

The National Front and BNP

One of the most influential post-war Fascist groups is the National Front (NF), founded in 1967. In the mid-1970s, the NF had a membership of around 20,000. Although the NF contests elections, it also maintains links with neo-Nazi paramilitary groups both at home and abroad. The NF has never won a seat. But, it has polled well in some constituencies. In the London boroughs of Hackney, Newham and Tower Hamlets, for example, it gained 10% of the vote in 1977. Its support dwindled in the late 1970s and had fallen to around 6,000 by 1980. It has been argued that support for the NF fell because Margaret Thatcher's government promoted policies which attracted the support of many who had shown an interest in the far right (Ball 1987).

In the 1980s, the NF split and from this split the British National Party (BNP) emerged. The BNP hit the headlines in September 1993 when a BNP candidate won a local seat in a ward by-election in Tower Hamlets, East London. Although this seat was subsequently won back by Labour in the local elections of May 1994, the support given to the BNP in this part of London was a source of great concern to many people.

In May 2001 serious racial violence broke out in Oldham and Burnley (see Unit 2, Section 2.19). In both areas, these outbreaks, which were characterised by conflict between Asians and whites, were attributed in part to the actions of the BNP. Indeed the rioting in Oldham followed soon after a BNP demonstration had been held to protest against Asian youths attacking whites. The intensity of the feelings which lay at the heart of these events was capitalised upon by the BNP which was trying to re-brand itself as a respectable party. As a consequence, the party did especially well in the 2001 general election in two Oldham seats and in Burnley. In Oldham West the BNP leader Nick Griffin came fourth and won 6,500 votes. In the other Oldham seat, Oldham East and

Saddleworth, the party achieved 11.2% of the votes. A similar percentage was gained by the BNP in Burnley where they secured 4,151 votes. In the 2002 local elections three Burnley wards elected BNP councillors suggesting that in some parts of the country at least the party has a serious following.

Marxist groups

Like the Fascist groups, Marxist groups have, on the whole, been on the periphery of British politics, though there have been periods when their influence has appeared to be growing. In the 1945 general election, for example, the Communist Party of Great Britain (CPGB - see Box 9.24), founded in 1920, won two seats and polled over 100,000 votes. But, since 1950, no Communist MP has been elected and, by 1964, the CPGB won just 0.8% of the vote in the constituencies it contested. Although the CPGB remained an important lobbying group (especially within the trade union movement), it split in the 1980s between those who followed the line laid down by the Communist government in the Soviet Union and the 'Eurocommunists' (who aimed to promote a new, independent and progressive form of Marxism).

Box 9.24 The CPGB

The Trotskyist left

In the 1980s, the Trotskyist left received more publicity than the CPGB. Perhaps, the best known Trotskyist group is Militant Tendency. The activities of Militant Tendency were the subject of considerable media interest in the mid-1980s because it was revealed that members of Militant had joined the Labour Party in the hope of influencing Labour Party policy. This led Neil Kinnock to conduct a purge of Militant members from the Labour Party with the result that there was a wave of expulsions, including several MPs.

Other Trotskyist groups include the Socialist Workers Party (SWP) which was prominent in the anti-Nazi League of the 1970s (set up to combat the NF). The SWP rejects the parliamentary system, though it does sometimes put up candidates for election. Members of the SWP are expert at ensuring that their flags and posters are prominent at any demonstration or protest organised for a left-wing cause - see Box 9.25 on page 182.

Other minor parties

The above survey of minor parties is by no means exhaustive. It does not include, for example, the Monster Raving Loony Party (MRLP) or the Natural Law Party, both of which put up candidates around the country in national and local elections. Those standing for the MRLP are literally joke candidates. Like those who stand for the Natural Law Party, they use

Box 9.25   The SWP

elections to promote their ideas rather than to mount a serious challenge to the main parties. The Natural Law Party is a party which promotes transcendental meditation as a means to right the wrongs of the world.

The UK Independence Party

Box 9.26   The UKIP

The UK Independence Party (UKIP - see Box 9.26) was set up in 1993. Its main aim is to campaign for the withdrawal of the UK from the EU, though it has formulated a complete political programme. It put up 24 candidates in the 1994 Euro-election, winning an average of 3.3% of the vote. Candidates from the party stood in all by-elections held between 1994 and 2003. None won more than 2.9% of the vote. Although, in 1996, the party's Leader, Alan Sked, tried to make an electoral pact with the Referendum Party (a party set up in 1995 by multi-millionaire James Goldsmith to campaign for a referendum on EU membership). The pact did not materialise and Referendum Party candidates stood against UKIP candidates in 165 constituencies. In the 1997 general election, the party put up a total of 194 candidates and won an average of 1.2% of the vote. The party lacked the funds and high media profile of the Referendum Party and was outperformed by it. After the 1997 general election, however, the Referendum Party made the decision not to contest any more elections and, in July 1997, Goldsmith died. A month later, Alan Sked resigned as Leader of the UKIP, shortly after the party had polled just 39 votes in the Uxbridge by-election. In the 2001 election the party won the sixth highest number of votes, capturing 1.5% of the votes cast in the UK. If the votes in England alone are considered, however, the party would have won the fourth highest number of votes - an achievement which might be improved upon if UK membership of the euro-zone rises up the political agenda.

Political parties in Northern Ireland
Between 1972 when direct rule from Britain was imposed on Northern Ireland and 1992, none of the three main political parties fielded any candidates in Northern Ireland. In the general elections of 1992 and 1997, however, the Conservative Party did put up candidates in Northern Ireland. But, none was elected. Since 1972, therefore, the people of Northern Ireland have elected MPs from what, in terms of the UK as a whole, are minor parties. The results of elections held between 1997 and 2003 are shown in Box 9.27.

Box 9.27   Elections in Northern Ireland 1997-2003

(i) Result of 1998 election to the Northern Ireland Assembly

Unionists				Nationalists				Others	
UUP		DUP		SDLP		SF			
%	seats	%	seats	%	seats	%	seats	%	seats
21	28	18	20	22	24	18	18	20	18

(ii) Northern Ireland results in the 2001 election (1997 result in brackets)

Party	Seats	Share of votes	Change from 1997
Ulster Unionist Party	6 (10)	26.8%	-5.9%
DUP	5 (2)	22.5%	+8.9%
SDLP	3 (3)	21.7%	-3.1%
Sinn Fein	4 (2)	21.0%	+5.6%
Other	0 (1)	8.0%	-5.5%

(iii) Result of 2003 election to the Northern Ireland Assembly

Unionists				Nationalists				Others	
UUP		DUP		SDLP		SF			
%	seats	%	seats	%	seats	%	seats	%	seats
22.7	27	25.7	30	17	18	23.5	6	9.3	9

1. UUP stands for Ulster Unionist Party.
2. DUP stands for the Democratic Unionist Party.
3. SDLP stands for the Social Democratic and Labour Party.
4. SF stands for Sinn Fein.

In addition, the Progressive Unionist Party (PUP), the Alliance Party, the Workers Party and the Women's Coalition put up candidates.

Unlike in the rest of the UK most of the political parties in Northern Ireland are clearly divided between those supported by the Protestant community and those supported by Catholics.

The Unionists
The two main Protestant parties in Northern Ireland are the Ulster Unionist Party (UUP) and the Democratic Unionist Party (DUP). Traditionally, both opposed power-sharing with the Catholic community, though the UUP signed up to the

Good Friday Agreement. The UUP was the party which governed Northern Ireland from the time when it was set up as a province in 1922 until direct rule was imposed in 1972. Before 1972, the UUP was closely associated with the Conservative Party. But, it broke with them over direct rule. Despite this, UUP MPs tend to vote with the Conservatives on most issues in Parliament. The same is true of the Democratic Unionist Party (DUP). The DUP is an offshoot of the UUP, founded in 1971 by Ian Paisley. The DUP takes a more extreme position than the UUP on Northern Irish affairs. It refuses any concessions to the Catholic population of Northern Ireland and refused to sign up to the Good Friday Agreement.

The UUP and DUP played an important part in keeping John Major's government in power in the period 1992-97. By voting with the government, the UUP and DUP (with 12 MPs in all) ensured that the government maintained a majority. Since the Major government relied on Unionist votes, it found it difficult to make progress towards a peace settlement after the IRA's first ceasefire was announced in 1994.

Nationalist and republican parties

The main nationalist party in Northern Ireland is the Social Democratic and Labour Party (SDLP), founded in 1970.

Although the SDLP was not set up to represent just Catholics, the vast majority of its support comes from the Catholic community. The SDLP was one of the main architects of the Good Friday Agreement. In the 1980s, the SDLP's grip on the Catholic vote was challenged by Sinn Fein, the republican party whose military wing is the IRA. Before the early 1980s, Sinn Fein boycotted elections, but the popular support for the hunger strikers encouraged the party to put up candidates for election. In the 1983 general election, Gerry Adams won Belfast West for Sinn Fein and he held the seat until 1992. In 1997, Adams was re-elected, together with Martin McGuinness, Sinn Fein's Chief Negotiator. Following the election, Adams and McGuinness were refused access to Parliament because they refused to take the Oath of Loyalty. Like the SDLP, Sinn Fein signed up to the Good Friday Agreement.

The Alliance Party

While almost all political parties in Northern Ireland appeal to either Protestants or Catholics, the Alliance Party, founded in 1970, is an exception. This party manages to gain around 10% of the vote (it won 8% of the vote in 1997) mainly from middle-class people in both communities. The party supports the Good Friday Agreement.

Main points   Sections 9.13 - 9.16

- **Throughout the 20th century, new parties have been set up in the hope that they would attract sufficient support to break the mould of British politics. But, apart from the Labour Party, no party has managed to achieve nationwide success.**
- **Minor parties do have some significance - especially if the government only has a small overall majority in Parliament (as between 1992 and 1997).**

- **Plaid Cymru made gains in 1997 and 2001. The SNP vote in 1997 grew by 0.6% compared to 1992. It fell back by 2% in 2001.**
- **Other minor parties failed to make an impact in the 2001 general election (except in Northern Ireland).**

Activity 9.6 Minor parties

Item A General election result 2001 - the minor parties

Party	Votes	% Share	Av vote %	Candidates	Lost Deposits
UK Independence	390,575	1.5	2.1	428	422
Green	166,487	0.6	2.8	145	135
Scottish Socialist	72,279	0.3	3.3	72	62
Socialist Alliance	60,496	0.2	1.8	98	95
Socialist Labour	57,536	0.2	1.4	114	113
British National	47,129	0.2	3.9	33	28
Liberal	10,920	0.0	3.2	9	8
Pro-Life Alliance	9,453	0.0	0.7	37	37
Independent	127,590	0.5	2.2	139	128

Source: Curtice & Steed 2002.

Item B The SNP and Plaid Cymru in general elections 1945-2001

(i) The SNP's electoral record

Election	MPs	Total votes	% *
1945	0	30,595	1.2
1950	0	9,708	0.4
1951	0	7,299	0.3
1955	0	12,112	0.5
1959	0	21,738	0.8
1964	0	64,044	2.4
1966	0	128,474	5.0
1970	1	306,802	11.4
1974 (Feb)	7	633,180	21.9
1974 (Oct)	11	839,617	30.4
1979	2	504,259	17.3
1983	2	331,975	11.8
1987	3	416,473	14.0
1992	3	629,564	21.5
1997	6	630,263	22.1
2001	5	464,314	20.1

* This column shows the number of votes won by the SNP as a percentage of the total votes cast in Scotland.

(ii) Plaid Cymru's electoral record

Election	MPs	Total votes	%*
1945	0	16,017	1.2
1950	0	17,580	1.2
1951	0	10,920	0.7
1955	0	45,119	3.1
1959	0	77,571	5.2
1964	0	69,507	4.8
1966	0	61,071	4.3
1970	0	175,016	11.5
1974 (Feb)	2	171,374	10.7
1974 (Oct)	3	166,321	10.8
1979	2	132,544	8.1
1983	2	125,309	7.8
1987	3	123,599	7.3
1992	4	156,796	8.9
1997	4	161.030	9.9
2001	4	195,892	14.3

* This column shows the number of votes won by Plaid Cymru as a percentage of the total votes cast in Wales.

Source: Lancaster 2002b.

Item C The Green Party

The biggest single day in the Green Party's history comes on Thursday 10 June 2004 when Greens will, for the first time, defend seats in the European Parliament and London Assembly, as well as contest council elections across the country. The Green Parties in the UK now have more elected representatives in more influential positions than ever before. There are two Members of the European Parliament, seven members of the Scottish Parliament, three Green Party Members in the London Assembly. Jenny Jones is the Deputy Mayor of London.

In addition, 53 Greens sit on 26 different local councils - including district councils, English and Welsh county councils, Metropolitan and London Borough councils - and are part of the ruling administration on two of them. There are also many Green Party Parish, Town and Welsh Community Councillors. Lord Beaumont represents the Green Party in the House of Lords.

Caroline Lucas was one of the two members of the Green Party to be elected as MEP in 1999

Source: www.greenparty.org.uk

Questions

1. 'Disappointing.' To what extent is that a reasonable description of the impact made by the minor parties in the 2001 general election? Use Items A and B in your answer.

2. a) 'The minor parties face problems which the major parties do not have to face.' Explain this statement using Items A-C and your own knowledge.

b) Would you agree that the growth of minor parties is healthy for democracy? Explain your answer.

3. Using Items A-C, describe the prospects for the minor parties in the next five years.

4. 'The Liberal Democrats should be added to the list of minor parties.' Give arguments for and against this view.

References

Alderman & Carter (2000) Alderman, K. & Carter, N., 'The Liberal Democrat leadership election of 1999', *Parliamentary Affairs*, Vol.53.2, April 2000.

Ball (1987) Ball, A., *British Political Parties*, Macmillan, 1987.

Butler & Kavanagh (2002) Butler, J. & Kavanagh, D., *The British General Election of 2001*, Palgrave, 2002.

Conservative (1998) *Constitution of the Conservative Party*, Conservative Central Office, February 1998.

Craig (1989) Craig, F.W.S., *British Electoral Facts 1832-1987*, Gower Publishing Company, 1989.

Curtice (1997) Curtice, J. 'Anatomy of a non-landslide', *Politics Review*, Vol.7.1, 1997.

Curtice & Steed (2002) Curtice, J. & Steed, M., 'An analysis of the results' in *Butler & Kavanagh (2002)*.

Dobson (1998) Dobson, A., 'The 1997 general election - explaining a landslide' in *Lancaster (1998)*.

Dorey (2002) Dorey, P., 'A languid landslide - the 2001 general election' in *Lancaster (2002)*.

Dorey (2004) Dorey, P., The Conservative Party under Iain Duncan Smith' in *Lancaster (2004)*.

Garner & Kelly (1998) Garner, R. & Kelly, R., *British Political Parties Today*, Manchester University Press, 1998.

Ingle (1993) Ingle, S., 'Political parties in the nineties', *Talking Politics*, Vol.6.1, Autumn 1993.

Kavanagh (2001) Kavanagh, D., 'Tony Blair as Prime Minister', *Politics Review*, Vol.11.1, September 2001.

Kelly (1989) Kelly, R., *Conservative Party Conferences*, Manchester University Press, 1989.

Kelly (1992) Kelly, R., 'Power in the Conservative Party', *Politics Review*, Vol.1.4, April 1992.

Kelly (1994) Kelly, R., 'British political parties: organisation, leadership and democracy' in *Wale (1994)*.

Kelly (1998) Kelly, R., 'Power in the Labour Party: the Blair effect', *Politics Review*, Vol.8.2, November 1998.

Kelly (2003) Kelly, R., 'British political parties: developments since 2000' in *Lancaster (2003)*.

Kelly (2004) Kelly R., 'Tough times for the Tories', *Politics Review*, Vol.13.3, February 2004.

Labour (1999) *Labour Party Rule Book*, Labour Party, 1999.

Lancaster (1998) Lancaster, S. (ed.), *Developments in Politics*, Vol.9, Causeway Press, 1998.

Lancaster (2002) Lancaster, S. (ed.), *Developments in Politics*, Vol.13, Causeway Press, 2002.

Lancaster (2002b) Lancaster, S. (ed.), *British Politics Update 1999-2002*, Causeway Press, 2002.

Lancaster (2003) Lancaster, S. (ed.), *Developments in Politics*, Vol.14, Causeway Press, 2003.

Lancaster (2004) Lancaster, S. (ed.), *Developments in Politics*, Vol.15, Causeway Press, 2004.

Lynch & Garnett (2002) Lynch, P. & Garnett, M., 'Conservatives' convictions: 2001 Tory leadership election', *Politics Review*, Vol.11.3, February 2002.

McKenzie (1955) McKenzie, R.T., *British Political Parties*, Heinemann, 1955.

Pelling (1991) Pelling, H., *A Short History of the Labour Party*, Macmillan, 1991.

Wale (1994) Wale, W. (ed.), *Developments in Politics*, Vol.5, Causeway Press, 1994.

10 Pressure groups

10.1 What is a pressure group?

A pressure group is a body which seeks to influence government policy or public opinion, but without actually seeking governmental office itself. Unlike political parties, which offer policies on virtually every issue, pressure groups tend to be concerned with one specific issue, or a narrow range of similar issues, such as animal welfare, environmental protection or tackling poverty. Except in very rare circumstances, pressure groups do not themselves put up candidates in elections. Instead, they seek, directly or indirectly, to influence those who are elected to Parliament. Box 10.1 provides an indication of the diversity of pressure groups in Britain today.

Due to the wide variety of pressure groups, and the almost infinite range of issues they represent, writers have usually sought to classify pressure groups, in order to distinguish between certain types. After all, the Legalise Cannabis Campaign and the Police Federation are both examples of pressure groups, but they clearly have very little in common. One of the earliest distinctions was between 'sectional' and 'cause' groups.

10.2 Sectional pressure groups

Sectional pressure groups was the term applied to pressure groups which represented the interests of a particular section of society, usually on the basis of occupation or profession. As such, their members have a direct, material interest in belonging to the group, for they usually obtain visible, tangible benefits. The most obvious examples of sectional pressure groups are trade unions, often representing workers on the basis of their particular occupation, such as building, nursing or teaching, for example. Another well-known example of a sectional pressure group is the Confederation of British Industry (CBI), which represents companies and employers mainly involved in manufacturing industry (although the CBI is actually a federation or 'peak association' made up of tens of thousands of individual businesses and companies).

Because sectional pressure groups are generally concerned with the interests of a particular section of society, their membership is usually 'closed', meaning that only those people in the relevant occupation, profession or section of society, are eligible to become members. However, membership of such groups is also often high in relation to the number who are eligible to join. For example, about 90% of farmers belong to the National Farmers Union. This enables many sectional pressure groups to claim that they are genuinely representative of those working in a particular industry or profession. Box 10.2 gives some examples of sectional groups.

Box 10.2 Sectional groups

Membership is based on the protection of economic or professional interests.

Professionals
The Law Society
British Medical Association (BMA)

Trade Associations
Society of Motor Manufacturers and Traders

Trade Unions
Transport and General Workers Union (TGWU)
UNISON
National Union of Teachers (NUT)

10.3 Cause pressure groups

Unlike sectional groups, cause groups are usually concerned either with a social or ethical issue - a 'cause' - or with campaigning on behalf of others in society who they perhaps consider are not being treated fairly. Many cause groups, therefore, are concerned with broader issues relating to notions of equality, fairness, justice, human or animal rights. For example, Friends of the Earth and Greenpeace campaign to save the environment from destruction, while the Campaign for Nuclear Disarmament (CND) aims to rid Britain - and, ultimately, the world - of nuclear weapons

Membership of cause groups is generally open. So, anyone who supports the cause can join if they so wish. However, while their total membership may be numerically large, it is invariably small as a proportion of those who could join, which, conceivably, could be everybody in Britain. For example, during the 1980s, CND could claim a membership

Box 10.1 Examples of pressure groups

Age Concern	Confederation of British Industry	Liberty
Association of Chief Police Officers	Country Landowners' Association	MENCAP
Britain in Europe	Countryside Alliance	MIND
British Field Sports Society	English Collective of Prostitutes	National Farmers Union
British Medical Association	Friends of the Earth	National Trust
Business for Sterling	Greenpeace	National Union of Students
Campaign for Nuclear Disarmament	Howard League for Penal Reform	National Union of Teachers
Campaign for Real Ale	Institute of Directors	Royal College of Nursing
Charter 88	League Against Cruel Sports	Royal Society for the Protection of Birds
Child Poverty Action Group	Legalise Cannabis Campaign	World Wildlife Fund for Nature

of 250,000 people, yet its critics could argue that this was just 0.45% of Britain's (56 million) population.

Partly for this reason, cause groups have often found it more difficult than sectional groups to persuade governments to treat them seriously. This is because, unless ministers themselves share the groups' goals or values, they are quite likely to:

- question the group's 'representativeness' (ie claim that it is not representative of the views of the population as a whole)
- argue that the cause is of little overall importance to the rest of the electorate
- allege that the 'cause ' is extreme.

This is certainly not to say that 'cause' groups are always or necessarily unsuccessful. Rather, compared to sectional groups, they tend to encounter greater difficulty in persuading ministers and civil servants to change policies.

In general, governments are usually less reliant on cause groups for advice and assistance in policy-making and implementation. For example, whereas health policies are heavily dependent on the support and cooperation of the British Medical Association (a sectional group), ministers would not, as a matter of course, approach the Child Poverty Action Group (a cause group) before altering social security benefits or reforming the welfare state. This is not to say that cause groups are never consulted by policy-makers. Rather, such consultations are infrequent, not regular and routine.

It is important to be aware that consultation is different from negotiation. Negotiation implies that both sides involved have resources and power, with the result that their discussions involve 'give-and-take'. Consultation, on the other hand, often involves listening to someone's views or concerns without necessarily being obliged to act on them.

Cause groups sometimes feel that they are being consulted mainly as a matter of courtesy, or because policy-makers want to increase the 'legitimacy' of a policy by claiming that they have listened to the views of 'interested parties'. Box 10.3 gives some examples of cause groups.

10.4 Problems with the sectional/cause classification

As Box 10.3 suggests, the sectional/cause classification is not as clear as it might initially appear because some pressure groups straddle the two categories, at least, on particular issues or occasions. For example, the British Medical Association (a sectional group) has regularly supported various causes - for example, endorsing campaigns to tackle the underlying causes of ill-health, such as smoking, alcohol abuse, poor diet or lack of exercise (leading to obesity). Similarly, during the 1990s, the British Dental Association (a sectional group) used much of its energy on a particular cause - the campaign for the fluoridation of domestic water supplies (Baggott 1995, p.15).

Meanwhile, a pressure group concerned with family poverty, such as the Child Poverty Action Group, could be categorised both as a sectional and a cause group because it simultaneously represents a particular section of society (broadly defined as 'the poor'), yet its membership - and

---

Box 10.3 Cause groups

Membership of cause groups is mainly based on altruistic motives (ie because people want to help others), ethical concerns or moral principles. It should be noted that trade unions are in this category because they campaign for causes as well as campaigning to protect the interests of their members.

Ethical concerns
Legalise Cannabis Campaign
Voluntary Euthanasia Society

Animal welfare
Royal Society for the Prevention of Cruelty to Animals
Royal Society for the Protection of Birds

Trade Unions
Transport and General Workers Union (TGWU)
UNISON
National Union of Teachers (NUT)

Help other people
MENCAP
SHELTER
Campaign for Racial Equality

---

perhaps, more so, its leadership - is mainly made up of other, predominantly middle-class, people who feel strongly about the issue, and wish to campaign for fairer treatment on the behalf of families and children living in poverty (Whiteley & Winyard 1987).

Because of this blurring of boundaries between some sectional and cause groups, and the overlap between them, some writers have adopted a different way of categorising pressure groups, focusing, instead, on the way(s) in which they seek to exercise political influence, and campaign for changes in policy.

10.5 Insider groups and outsider groups

Some pressure groups are more important or useful to governments than others, and these groups seem to enjoy a greater input into policy-making. As a result, Wyn Grant (1989 and 2000) has categorised them according to:

- their status
- their position in the political system
- the methods they use to seek influence.

This leads to a distinction between 'insider' and 'outsider' pressure groups.

Insider pressure groups

Insider pressure groups are those which usually enjoy close and regular contacts with the ministers and senior civil servants who formally make policy in Britain. Such pressure groups are often closely linked to the particular government department which is responsible for their policy concerns. For example, the British Roads Federation has a close relationship with the Department of Transport.

Many insider groups are also those who might also be placed in the category of sectional groups because the majority of them represent people on the basis of occupation, profession or socio-economic function.

There are a number of reasons why certain pressure groups enjoy 'insider' status. These are outlined in Box 10.4.

Box 10.4 Reasons why groups enjoy insider status

The main reasons why groups enjoy insider status are as follows:

1. They possess the expertise or specialist advice which governments need for policy-making.

2. Ministers need the cooperation of insider groups if policies are to be implemented. Without that cooperation, the groups might campaign against or obstruct policies with which they disapprove (during the late 1980s and 1990s, for example, the Conservative governments of Margaret Thatcher and John Major found their education reforms being undermined by teaching unions and their NHS reforms by the BMA).

3. The aims of the group are considered - by ministers and civil servants - to be reasonable or realistic. This makes it much easier for discussions and dialogue to take place since there is normally a considerable amount of common ground. To put it another way, it is difficult to imagine ministers or senior civil servants sitting down for meaningful and constructive talks with Hunt Saboteurs or anti-globalisation protestors.

4. Insiders are also considered to be responsible in the way in which they seek to achieve their goals, usually preferring peaceful persuasion and dialogue to confrontation or direct action. They abide by the political 'rules of the game', so that ministers and senior civil servants can 'do business' with them. On the relatively rare occasions when they do resort to demonstrations or public campaigns, this is usually a sign that negotiations have broken down and that a compromise cannot be achieved.

5. Insider groups are considered to be 'representative' in terms of their membership. For example, since the overwhelming majority of police officers belong either to the Association of Chief Police Officers or the Police Federation, these two groups can claim to speak authoritatively on behalf of Britain's police on law-and-order matters, just as the National Farmers Union - with about 90% of farmers belonging to it - has long been able to be the voice of the farming community on agricultural matters. This high percentage of membership means that it is usually in the interests of policy-makers to ensure that the views of such groups are carefully considered in order to prevent them from withdrawing their co-operation when a policy needs to be implemented (ie. put into practice).

'Outsider' groups

There are seven main reasons why some organised interests are consigned to 'outsider' status.

First, the aims or demands of outsider groups are considered to be extreme or excessive. Pressure groups campaigning for the abolition of poverty or low pay, for example, or an end to all experiments on animals, tend to be viewed by policy-makers as unreasonable or unrealistic and, as a result, not taken seriously. Alternatively, an 'outsider' pressure group might be supporting policies at variance with the government's own ideological stance. For example, the Labour government elected in 1997 and 2001 followed the outgoing Conservative government in supporting the maintenance of the UK's nuclear arsenal. As a result, the Campaign for Nuclear Disarmament (CND) which aims to rid Britain - and, ultimately, the world - of nuclear weapons - has continued to be excluded from policy-making because, ideologically, the government does not agree with its stance.

Second, the methods used by outsider groups might be viewed as extreme or irresponsible. For example, pressure groups such as the Animal Liberation Front and Hunt Saboteurs engage in forms of direct action. Invariably, such tactics are criticised and condemned by mainstream politicians and civil servants.

Third, some of the issues which 'outsider' pressure groups promote are not considered important by policy-makers. Politicians might judge that there are few votes to be won - or plenty to be lost - if they were to respond favourably to the issues supported by 'outsider' pressure groups.

Fourth, outsider groups often do not possess the expertise or have access to the information which ministers and civil servants need to make policy - nor is cooperation with such pressure groups needed in order to implement polices.

Fifth, the issues with which many outsiders are concerned are not the responsibility of any one government department. This makes it difficult for groups to target their lobbying effectively. For example, there have always been several pressure groups concerned with the issue of poverty, but no one single department can be considered responsible for tackling poverty, because poverty has a variety of causes which cut across departmental boundaries.

Sixth, it is sometimes difficult for outsider groups to present policy-makers with a clear or coherent set of proposals because of the sheer number of different groups campaigning on the same issue. Instead of persuading policy-makers to treat the issue more seriously, the large number of groups might encourage them to be more dismissive because of the apparently incoherent and inconsistent proposals being put forward. An example is given in Box 10.5.

Box 10.5 Pressure groups and poverty

The issue of poverty is addressed both by SHELTER - which links poverty with homelessness - and Age Concern - which seeks to highlight the scale of poverty among the elderly. At the same time, the National Union of Students attempts to highlight poverty among students (due to the abolition of maintenance grants), while the Child Poverty Action Group (CPAG) focuses on the plight of children living in low-income households. Each of these groups campaigns against poverty from a different angle, allowing policy-makers to claim that there is no single solution to poverty and that the campaign against it is incoherent.

And seventh, some organised interests are 'outsiders' because they are not deemed to be 'representative' of the people they claim to be campaigning on behalf of. According to Whiteley and Winyard, this was a problem experienced by the 'poverty lobby' (quite apart from the other problems identified above). The organised interests campaigning on behalf of the poor have often been taken less seriously by senior civil servants precisely because members of the groups - particularly the senior members or full-time leadership - were not themselves 'poor' or living in poverty (Whiteley & Winyard 1987, p.132).

Occasionally, a pressure group's status might change from 'insider' to 'outsider', or vice versa, either because the issues with which it is concerned become more/less important, or because a change of government leads to a different set of priorities. For example, in the 1970s, trade unions were 'insiders', regularly consulted by Conservative and Labour governments alike on economic and industrial matters, but during the 1980s, under Margaret Thatcher, the trade unions became 'outsiders', viewed with contempt by many Conservative ministers on the grounds that they were at least partly responsible for many of the economic problems which Britain was facing during this time (Dorey 2001, chapter seven; Dorey 2003). Even with the election of a Labour government in 1997, the trade unions have not regained the 'insider' status they once enjoyed. Tony Blair is known to feel much more comfortable meeting people from the business community than talking with trade union leaders (Dorey 1999).

By contrast, during the 1970s and 1980s, the environmental pressure group Friends of the Earth was an 'outsider'. Since the early 1990s, however, it has gradually acquired 'insider' status, partly because environmental issues have become more important generally, but also because Friends of the Earth, and especially its leadership, have become more professional or 'respectable' in their overall approach, and less involved in forms of direct action.

10.6 Think tanks

Think tanks are organisations set up to undertake research and to formulate policy ideas which (they hope) will be adopted by those who have the power to make decisions.

'Think tank' is an American term that was first used in Britain in 1970 when Edward Heath's Conservative government set up the Central Policy Review Staff (CPRS). The CPRS was a small unit in the Cabinet Office (see Unit 16). Its aim was to serve the Cabinet as a whole by providing strategic advice on policy and by promoting inter-departmental cooperation. To achieve this aim, it undertook research and presented papers which were free from a departmental perspective. Although the CPRS survived the downfall of Edward Heath, it fell out of favour with Margaret Thatcher and was disbanded in 1983. Although the term 'think tank' has only been used since 1970, think tanks first came into existence long before this. The Fabian Society, for example, was set up in 1884.

Think tanks and pressure groups
Think tanks are different from other pressure groups in three respects. First, most think tanks aim to influence the policy decisions made by a particular political party (most other

pressure groups are careful not to be too closely tied to a particular political party). Second, think tanks are interested in a whole political programme not just a single issue or narrow policy area. Third, think tanks are openly ideological. Their ideas come from a carefully considered ideological standpoint and there is, usually, little concern with 'balance'. Think tanks often compete with each other to win over the ideological soul of a political party. Sometimes that means that they get involved in public debates about internal party matters.

These differences have led some critics to question whether think tanks are in fact pressure groups at all. But, if the definition of a pressure group is an institution whose aim is to influence political decisions without putting up candidates for election, then think tanks qualify as pressure groups.

The range of think tanks
Think tanks have grown in number since 1970. They now range right across the political spectrum. During the 1980s, it was the New Right's think tanks which gained access to government. For example, the Adam Smith Institute championed the policy of privatisation. Since May 1997, the election of a Labour government has ensured that different think tanks - for example, the Institute of Public Policy Research (IPPR) - have come into favour with ministers.

Main points   Sections 10.1 - 10.6

- **A pressure group is a body which seeks to influence government policy or public opinion, but without actually seeking governmental office itself.**
- **Due to the wide variety of pressure groups, and the almost infinite range of issues they represent, writers have usually sought to classify pressure groups, in order to distinguish between certain types.**
- **One of the earliest distinctions was between 'sectional' and 'cause' groups. Sectional groups represent the interests of a particular section of society, usually on the basis of occupation or profession. Their members are mainly drawn from that particular section of society. Cause groups are usually concerned with a social or ethical issue - a 'cause' - and are open to all.**
- **The sectional/cause classification is not as clear as it might initially appear because some pressure groups straddle the two categories, at least, on particular issues or occasions.**
- **An alternative classification is to distinguish between 'insider' and 'outsider' pressure groups. Insider pressure groups are those which enjoy close and regular contacts with ministers and senior civil servants. Outsider groups do not enjoy such contacts.**
- **Think tanks are different from other pressure groups because: (1) they aim to influence policies made by a particular political party; (2) they are interested in a whole political programme; and (3) they are openly ideological.**

Activity 10.1 Classifying pressure groups

Item A Two pressure groups

(i) The Campaign for Nuclear Disarmament (CND)

CND campaigns non-violently to rid the world of nuclear weapons and other weapons of mass destruction and to create genuine security for future generations.

We aim to...
- Change government policies to bring about the elimination of British nuclear weapons as a major contribution to global abolition.
- Stimulate wide public debate on the need for alternatives both to the nuclear cycle and to military attempts to resolve conflict.
- Empower people to engage actively in the political process and to work for a nuclear-free and peaceful future.
- Cooperate with other groups in the UK and internationally to ensure the development of greater mutual security.

CND is funded entirely by its members and supporters.

Source: www.cnduk.org

(ii) The Royal College of Nursing

We are the voice of nursing.

We are the leading professional union for nursing. As the voice of nursing at home and abroad, we campaign on behalf of the profession. We also lead the way in developing future nursing practice. We safeguard the interests of patients and nurses by lobbying government and other professional bodies to ensure that the views of the profession are heard where it counts. We have a framework that allows members to share expertise of policy issues. Through the specialist nursing forums, members can get involved in the policy-making process, both local and national.

Source: www.rcn.org.uk

Item B The aims and activities of selected pressure groups

Group	Aims and objectives	Regular contact with government?	Uses direct action?
Animal Liberation Front (ALF)	To stop or prevent medical experiments on animals, often by releasing the animals from laboratories.	No	Yes
Anti-Nazi League	To fight racism by opposing the activities of the far-right, particularly the British National Party.	No	Yes
British Medical Association (BMA)	To represent the material and professional interests of doctors.	Yes	No
Confederation of British Industry (CBI)	To defend and advance the interests of companies and employers, mainly in manufacturing industry.	Yes	No
Friends of the Earth	To promote awareness of environmental issues, and campaign for policies to protect the environment.	Yes	Yes
Hunt Saboteurs	To obstruct, sabotage and, ultimately, prevent, blood sport events, particularly fox hunts.	No	Yes
Law Society	To represent the material and professional interests of lawyers.	Yes	No
National Farmers Union	To defend and advance the interests of farmers, and influence agricultural policy.	Yes	No
Outrage!	To promote gay rights and challenge homophobia.	No	Yes
Police Federation	To represent the material and professional interests of police officers.	Yes	No

Questions

1. How would you classify the two pressure groups mentioned in Item A? Give reasons for your answers.

2. Which of the pressure groups in Item B are insider groups, and which are outsider groups? Explain how you know.

3. Which do you find the more useful method of classifying pressure groups: sectional/cause or insider/outsider? Explain your answer.

10.7 Pressure groups and decision-makers

The aim of virtually all pressure groups is to influence public policy (whether at a national or local level) either, directly, by lobbying elected representatives and civil servants who formally take decisions or, indirectly, by 'agenda-setting' - raising awareness of an issue or problem, in the hope that public opinion, or the concern of backbenchers, will then persuade decision-makers to act. Some pressure groups use the media to highlight a particular issue or perceived injustice. A growing number of pressure groups use the legal system, taking a case to court in order to challenge the legality of a particular policy or decision.

Campaigning at governmental level

Most key political decisions in Britain are taken in the 'core executive', involving ministers, senior civil servants, and government departments (see Units 15 and 16). It is at this level, therefore, that pressure groups often hope to persuade policy-makers of their case. However, as noted above, it is only 'insider' pressure groups who normally enjoy regular and close contacts with ministers and senior civil servants, and who can therefore realistically expect to have some input into policy-making. The earlier in the policy-making process that such pressure groups can make their views known, the more likely it is that they will be able to shape the subsequent policy.

The relationship between 'insider' pressure groups and ministers and civil servants is symbiotic - it is a two-way process which is beneficial to both sides. Ministers and civil servants want the specialist advice and expertise which certain pressure groups can provide. Those groups, in turn, expect to have some influence over the policy being pursued. In exchange for the group's advice, therefore, ministers and civil servants will seek to ensure that the policy is generally acceptable to the group concerned. Much policy-making involves such 'trade-offs' and compromises. In addition to wanting the expertise of key pressure groups during the making of policy, ministers and civil servants also often need the cooperation of such groups when the final policy is being implemented.

Many government departments have a close relationship with one or two key pressure groups, as illustrated by Box 10.6.

Under Margaret Thatcher in the period 1979-90, government departments were much less willing to consult with pressure groups during the policy-making process than they had been in the past. But, ministers usually found it necessary to re-establish relations with pressure groups when implementing the policies. For example, although Conservative

Box 10.6 Examples of government departments and their 'client' pressure groups

Department	'Client' groups
Department of Health	British Medical Association Royal College of Nursing
Department of Transport	British Roads Federation Automobile Association (AA) Royal Automobile Club (RAC)
Home Office	Assoc. of Chief Police Officers Police Federation

ministers largely disregarded the British Medical Association and teaching unions when formulating NHS and education reforms respectively during the late 1980s, they found it necessary to consult with these pressure groups when subsequently attempting to implement these reforms. In part, this was because practical problems arose which ministers had not foreseen. Had they consulted the pressure groups to start with, such problems would probably have been avoided. In part also, however, the problems arose because the groups concerned acted in ways which undermined the implementation and effectiveness of the reforms.

Since Margaret Thatcher's downfall in November 1990, governments have, in general, re-established regular contact and consultation with key pressure groups when making policy. However, the trade unions have not regained their pre-Thatcher role in economic and industrial policy-making, and continue to struggle to make themselves heard or be taken seriously by ministers. Similarly, a few previously strong 'insider' pressure groups have experienced some decline in influence, or have had to concede ground to new(er) pressure groups who have entered the policy-making arena. For example, following the BSE ('mad cow disease') crisis in farming during the 1990s, and the 2001 foot-and-mouth epidemic, the National Farmers Union (NFU) lost influence. As a result, it was unable to prevent the Blair government, after it was re-elected in 2001, from abolishing the Ministry of Agriculture, Fisheries and Food (with which the NFU had long enjoyed an extremely close and good working relationship), and setting up, instead, the Department of Food, Rural Affairs and the Environment.

10.8 Lobbying Parliament

There are four main ways in which pressure groups can seek to exercise influence through Parliament (particularly the House of Commons). These are summarised in Box 10.7.

Box 10.7 Lobbying Parliament

The four main ways in which pressure groups can seek to exercise influence through Parliament are:

1. Amending legislation
2. Private Members' Bills
3. Departmental select committees
4. Backbench committees

1. Amending legislation

Pressure groups often seek to influence MPs on standing committees because it is at standing committee stage that a proposed law is debated in detail, clause by clause. Pressure groups approach MPs on standing committees in the hope that they will table amendments to improve the Bill or remove anomalies which may have become apparent during the preceding Second Reading debate on the principles of the Bill. Some pressure groups suggest amendments themselves (although only MPs can actually table them) if they consider particular clauses of a Bill would be detrimental to the section of society or values which they seek to represent.

2. Private Members' Bills

Each November, at the start of the new Parliamentary Session (year), the names of 20 backbench MPs are drawn in a ballot for the right to present a Private Members' Bill, although, in practice, only the first 12 are actually likely to obtain parliamentary time to do so. These 20 MPs are invariably approached by numerous pressure groups, each trying to persuade an MP to introduce a Bill reflecting the groups' cause or benefiting its membership. For example, each year, the MPs successful in the ballot will invariably be approached by anti-abortion pressure groups imploring them to introduce a Private Members' Bill to limit abortion, or outlaw it altogether. Similarly, MPs are also likely to be approached by pressure groups campaigning for the legalisation of euthanasia. These are just two examples of the wide range of issues - many of them social, moral or conscience issues - on which MPs might be lobbied to introduce a Private Members' Bill if they are successful in the parliamentary ballot.

Labour MP, Austin Mitchell, who came sixth in the ballot for the 1983-84 parliamentary ballot said that letters, draft Bills, ideas and invitations poured in. Before too long, Mitchell had 50 suggestions, 20 possible Bills (three in draft) and five front-runners.

Rather more recently, when introducing the Second Reading of her Female Genital Mutilation Bill (to prohibit parents from sending, or taking, their daughters abroad for operations, such as female circumcision which was outlawed in the UK in 1985), Ann Clwyd said that she chose this particular Bill 'over the many hundreds of others that were suggested to me' (House of Commons Debates, 21 March 2003, col.1190).

Of course, not all MPs opt to introduce a Private Members' Bill in response to lobbying from pressure groups, as an MP may well have a particular interest or issue of their own which they wish to address through legislation. Nevertheless, Private Members' Bills are doubtless a very popular target for many pressure groups.

3. Departmental select committees

Departmental select committees, first set up in 1979, have since proved a major focus of pressure group activity in Parliament. The role of departmental select committees is to examine the administration, expenditure and policies of government departments. As a result, the inquiries and investigations undertaken by these committees often involve the presentation of evidence by pressure groups. Much of this evidence is in the form of written submissions or reports presented to a particular select committee. Sometimes, however, in response to written submissions, pressure groups are invited to provide oral evidence. This means that a senior representative of the pressure group appears in front of the select committee to be cross-examined.

Box 10.8 lists some of the pressure groups which submitted evidence to the Home Affairs Select Committee's 2001-02 inquiry into *The Government's Drugs Policy: Is It Working?*

Box 10.8 The government's drugs policy

The following pressure groups submitted evidence to the Home Affairs Select Committee's 2001-02 inquiry into the government's drug policy:

- Action on Hepatitis C
- Addaction
- ADFAM
- Alliance for Cannabis Therapeutics
- Association of Chief Police Officers
- Bristol Drug Action Team
- Centre for Addiction Studies
- Christian Institute
- Church of England Board for Social Responsibility
- Criminal Justice Association
- Dance Drugs Alliance
- Drug Education Forum
- DrugScope
- Liberty
- Local Government Association
- London Drug Policy Forum
- National Children's Bureau
- National Crime Squad
- National Drug Prevention Alliance
- National Schizophrenia Fellowship
- National Treatment Agency
- National Union of Teachers
- Netherlands Drug Policy Foundation
- Positive Prevention Plus
- Quaker Action on Alcohol and Drugs
- Release
- Royal College of Physicians
- Royal College of Psychiatrists
- Royal Pharmaceutical Society of Great Britain
- Transform
- Turning Point
- UK Harm Reduction Alliance

In seeking to persuade the select committee of problems arising from a particular policy or law, pressure groups hope that the committee's final report will draw attention to these and prompt the government or relevant minister to amend the policy or law in question.

As Box 10.9 on page 193 illustrates, a major study into the relationship between Parliament and pressure groups discovered that over two-thirds of groups believed that their evidence had some impact on select committees and their reports, with a further 16.3% believing that their evidence had a significant impact.

Box 10.9   Perceived impact of pressure groups on select committees

Q. What impact do you believe your evidence made upon the committee and its report?

Response	%
Significant	16.3
Some	69.2
Minimal	8.1
None	4.1
Varied	0.6
Don't know	1.7

Source: Rush 1990.

4. Backbench committees

Some pressure groups also seek to exercise indirect influence via the backbench subject committees, of which there are two types:

- party subject committees, usually corresponding to the policy areas covered by government departments
- all-party subject committees - of which there are over 230, covering an extremely wide variety of issues and interests - ranging from adoption and animal welfare to wine and yachting.

Again, some pressure groups hope that, by lobbying the MPs on a particular backbench committee and maybe being invited to give a talk, they can exert an indirect influence in particular policies. Given, however, the limits on the power of backbench MPs to influence governmental policy at all, the key word here is 'indirect'.

Jones (1990) found that most pressure groups had a very favourable impression of the role of backbench committees - as shown in Box 10.10.

Box 10.10   Pressure groups' perceptions about the usefulness of backbench committees

Perception	Party committees %	All-party committees %
Very useful	12.6	21.0
Useful	61.2	47.9
Not very useful	24.3	26.9
Of no use	1.9	4.2

Source: Jones 1990.

10.9   Using the courts

Another avenue sometimes pursued by pressure groups is legal action through Britain's courts. Such action often aims to challenge the legality of a government policy or law, possibly on the grounds that the relevant minister has exceeded their statutory powers (acted 'ultra vires'). Alternatively, a legal case might be pursued by a pressure group on the grounds that a particular policy is discriminatory against the particular section of society which they represent. Such cases are likely to become more frequent now that the European Convention on Human Rights has been incorporated into British law.

One other way in which pressure groups might occasionally use the courts is by seeking an injunction, to prevent another individual or organisation from pursuing a particular course of action. During the 1980s, for example, the National Viewers and Listeners Association, led by the anti-pornography campaigner Mary Whitehouse, pursued a number of court cases like this to prevent the broadcast of certain controversial television programmes, especially those reputed to be of a sexually explicit nature.

More recently, two animal welfare groups, Animal Aid and the National Anti-Vivisection Society, mounted a legal challenge against a decision by John Prescott, the Deputy Prime Minister, to allow Cambridge University to build a £32 million research laboratory which would conduct experiments on monkeys, in an attempt at finding a cure for such diseases as Alzheimer's and Parkinson's. The groups alleged that Prescott's decision was 'perverse and unreasonable', based on limited facts and inaccurate information. It was also claimed that he had made comments which were likely to prejudice the outcome of the planning process for the proposed laboratory. A spokesperson for Animal Aid alleged that:

'John Prescott has dismissed the well-founded case of his own inspector...so this challenge has a solid base in morality, science and the democratic process.' (Guardian, 3 January 2004)

Legal action through the courts, however, is an expensive process and, because of that, is beyond the means of many pressure groups. Legal action tends to be a last resort, when other courses of action available to a particular pressure group have failed.

10.10   Using the media

Environmental groups have become particularly skilful at using the media, not only by pursuing high-profile public campaigns and forms of direct action intended to attract media attention, but also by developing their own internal, media departments. A good example of this is the environmental pressure group Greenpeace:

'Greenpeace Communications...has a full in-house film, video and photographic capability incorporating a small television studio, three editing suites, a digital sound studio and a commercial film and television archive. These facilities also include compressed digital satellite encoders and decoders and three-dimensional computer graphics. The Greenpeace press desk operates on a 24-hour basis to accommodate the deadlines of media organisations around the world.' (Anderson 1997, p. 85)

The media encompasses several forms of communication and transmission of information and so there are various ways in which pressure groups use the media to increase public awareness of an issue. This is demonstrated in Box 10.11 on page 194.

Box 10.11 Pressure group use of the media

Type of media	Types of pressure group activity
Television and radio	1. Attracting news coverage through direct action (particularly for television news broadcasts).
	2. Being interviewed or providing a 'soundbite' as part of a news item on a particular issue.
	3. Issuing a press release on a particular issue or event.
	4. Participating in current affairs documentaries, such as BBC's *Panorama*.
	5. Being represented on the panel of a programme such as television's *Question Time*, or its radio equivalent, *Any Questions*.
	6. Lobbying script-writers to address an issue in a soap opera or other popular serial.
Newspapers and magazines	1. Attracting news coverage through direct action.
	2. Being quoted in a news item or in a feature on a particular topic.
	3. Being invited to write a column or 'opinion piece'.
	4. Writing to the 'readers' letters' page.
	5. Placing an advert.
Publishing	1. Publishing books and leaflets.
	2. Producing pamphlets which may then be inserted in newspapers and magazines.
Advertising	1. Placing an advert on commercial television (eg. Sky or ITV), and/or in a newspaper or magazine.
	2. Hiring advertising billboards on which to paste large posters.
Internet	1. Virtually every pressure group now has a website, giving details about the group itself and the issue it is concerned with and constantly updated to highlight new developments and the group's response to them.
Opinion polls	1. Commissioning an opinion poll on a topic, and then having the results (if favourable to the group's cause) publicised in the media, in the hope of influencing politicians.

Clearly, the forms of media in Box 10.11 are not mutually exclusive, and many pressure groups will use a combination - possibly all - of them over time. However, it is the better-resourced, wealthier, pressure groups which are best able to use the media because advertising in a newspaper or on television, for example, can prove rather expensive, as might commissioning a professional polling company to conduct an opinion poll on an issue.

By contrast, pressure groups which rely heavily on direct action to highlight an issue and attract media attention may have little control over how they are reported or portrayed in the media. Newspapers might ignore (or give little coverage to) a demonstration or rally by pressure groups with which they disagree politically (such as CND, campaigners against fox-hunting, or anti-war protestors) or they might choose to highlight the activities of a tiny number of trouble-makers on a march in an attempt to discredit the group or issue as a whole.

It is a reflection of newspapers' political stance that pro-Conservative (and, therefore, anti-Labour, anti-Blair) newspapers gave several pages of extremely favourable coverage to the September 2000 'fuel protestors' (see Activity 10.3 Item B), and were sympathetic and supportive in their coverage of the various (pro-fox hunting) Countryside Alliance marches held in London since 1998.

Although television has a statutory duty to avoid displaying political bias, it too can effectively weaken a pressure group's case or credibility, by focusing the cameras on a few eccentric or oddly-dressed individuals. Television news coverage of direct action by environmentalists, such as anti-roads campaigners, often shows participants with pink hair, nose-rings, and other facial piercing even though such coverage can trivialise the issue which the groups are highlighting, or deter viewers who might otherwise have identified with and agreed with the protestors.

Furthermore, because the attention span of the media is short, the publicity gained by a pressure group, even when favourable, soon dissipates because the media and, therefore, public attention, moves onto another issue. For this reason, heavy reliance on media coverage can be a risky strategy.

Main points Sections 10.7 - 10.10

- **Pressure groups aim to influence public policy either, directly, by lobbying or, indirectly, by 'agenda-setting' (raising awareness of an issue or problem).**
- **The relationship between 'insider' pressure groups and decision-makers is a two-way process which is beneficial to both sides. Decision-makers want pressure groups' specialist advice and expertise. Groups, in turn, expect to have some influence over the policy being pursued.**
- **The four main ways in which pressure groups can seek to exercise influence through Parliament are: (1) amending legislation; (2) Private Members' Bills; (3) departmental select committees and; (4) backbench committees.**
- **Another avenue sometimes pursued by pressure groups is legal action through Britain's courts - challenging the legality of a government policy or law, arguing that ministers have exceeded their statutory powers. Legal action, however, is expensive.**
- **There are various ways in which pressure groups use the media to increase public awareness of an issue. Many pressure groups use a combination of techniques to gain media attention. But, it is only the better-resourced groups which are best able to use the media because they can afford advertising or to commission polling companies.**

Activity 10.2 Pressure groups and decision-makers

Item A Seeking to influence the government (1)

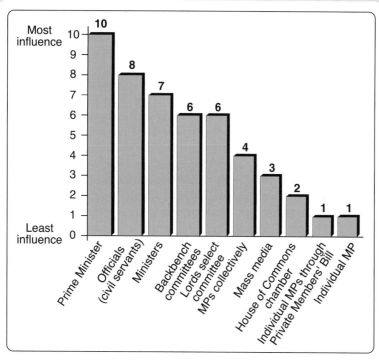

This chart shows how much influence each person or group has in the decision-making process.

Source: Rush 1990.

Item B Seeking to influence the government (2)

Q. Based on your experience, please place the following in order of importance in terms of seeking to influence public policy:

Source of influence	Ranking in terms of importance
Parliament	4
Ministers	2
Civil servants/govt depts	1
Political parties in general	8
One political party in particular	9
Other pressure groups	7
The media generally	3
Public opinion	6
Particular sections of public opinion	5

Source: 'Appendix - Survey Results' in Rush 1990.

Item C Two adverts

Questions

1. What does Item A tell us about (a) the tactics which pressure groups should use and (b) the tactics they actually use?

2. Judging from Items A and B, what is the best way for pressure groups to influence government policy?

3. What does Item C tell us about the sort of tactics that pressure groups use?

10.11 Direct action

The use of direct action usually represents a last resort, implying that other forms of lobbying and campaigning have failed. As a result, direct action can be a risky strategy because it can draw attention to a group's failure to exert influence through normal channels and processes, and stiffen decision-makers' resolve not to give in to the group concerned. By giving in, ministers are likely to claim, they would merely be surrendering to 'mob rule' while also serving to encourage other pressure groups to resort to direct action.

Whether direct action is successful depends partly on the precise form that action takes, partly on the issues involved, partly on which sections of society are involved, and partly on the extent of public sympathy or support.

Wyn Grant has devised a way of classifying direct action. This classification is illustrated in Box 10.12.

Direct action does seem to have become more popular in the UK since the 1980s, perhaps indicating that new concerns and issues are affecting - or angering - more people. Certainly, there has been a great deal of direct action in protest at issues such as environmental damage, road-building in picturesque parts of the countryside or the export of live cattle for slaughter in Europe.

The growth of direct action might also reflect a general decline of deference towards (respect for) the political élite, coupled with a belief that traditional forms of political activity (such as writing to MPs) are often ineffective. For example, the environmental pressure group Earth First! declares that:

'Conventional "green" campaigning is not enough to stop the destruction that is happening. Politicians and companies ignore letters, petitions and public inquiries; they reject overwhelming evidence because it goes against their interests…the only solution is for people to take their future in their hands and physically halt further destruction of nature.' (quoted in Grant 2000, p.145)

It would seem that an increasing number of pressure groups and citizens also believe that direct action is either morally justified, or politically necessary.

Box 10.12 Direct action by pressure groups

Action	Objective	Legality
Protest marches	• Raise public awareness of an issue. • Indicate scale of public concern or support to politicians.	Usually legal
Boycotts	• To inflict commercial punishment on a company or producer.	Legal
Publicity stunts	• Draw public attention to an issue. • Gain media coverage.	Depends on type
Blockades/occupations	• Exert direct pressure on company, producer or supplier. • Prevent continuation of activities.	Blockades might be liable to civil action, often in the form of injunction to cease activity. Occupations are usually illegal, involving criminal offence of trespass, and may also be liable for criminal damage.
Damage to property	• Prevent continuation of activities. • Intimidate or punish those involved in 'immoral' activities.	Illegal
Violence	• Intimidate or punish those involved in 'immoral' activities.	Illegal

Source: Grant 2000, p.140.

Main points Section 10.11

• **Direct action is usually a last resort, implying that other forms of lobbying and campaigning have failed. As a result, it can be a risky strategy.**

• **Whether direct action is successful depends on: (1) the precise form that action takes; (2) the issues involved; (3) which sections of society are involved; and (4) the extent of public sympathy or support.**

• **Direct action does seem to have become more popular in the UK since the 1980s, perhaps indicating that new concerns and issues are affecting - or angering - more people.**

• **The growth of direct action reflects a general decline of deference towards the political élite and a belief that traditional forms of political activity are often ineffective.**

Activity 10.3 Pressure groups and direct action

Item A The Countryside Alliance and the campaign to defend fox-hunting

Left, an official brochure produced to commemorate the Countryside Alliance march through London in March 1998.

The Countryside Alliance was formed in 1998, supposedly to protest against the Blair government's neglect of the problems affecting rural areas and farming communities. The real issue behind the group's formation, though, was the proposed ban on fox-hunting. After all, many of the problems affecting rural areas had existed in the 1980s and 1990s when the Conservatives were in power (and may indeed have been a result, directly or indirectly, of Conservative policies). It was only after a Labour MP introduced a Private Members' Bill to outlaw hunting with hounds that the Countryside Alliance was launched. Since then, the group has organised well-attended and favourably-reported marches and rallies, not only in London, but in other British cities too, while also picketing the Labour Party's annual conferences. Clearly shocked by the support apparently enjoyed by the Countryside Alliance in rural areas - one of its London marches attracted an estimated 400,000 people - and in the extremely favourable coverage it received in anti-Labour daily newspapers - the Labour government held back legislation designed to ban fox-hunting, eventually seeking a compromise - the idea being that fox-hunting would not be banned entirely, but would be subject to strict controls. But a sufficiently large number of Labour MPs was so determined to secure a total ban that, in the spring of 2003, an amendment was tabled calling for an outright ban on hunting (effectively defying Tony Blair). This, in turn, prompted the Countryside Alliance to warn that if the Bill reached the statute book with this amendment intact, the group would embark on a campaign of civil disobedience, involving such activities as refusing to pay council tax, car insurance and TV licence payments, and blockading dairy centres in order to disrupt milk supplies.

Source: The *Sunday Times*, 17 August 2003.

Item B The fuel blockade of September 2000

The photo on the right shows fuel protestors driving in convoy in September 2000. In addition to driving slowly along motorways, causing congestion, they picketed oil refineries, causing many garages to run out of fuel.

In protest against the high levels of tax levied on fuel in Britain (particularly compared to fuel duties elsewhere in Europe), a relatively small group of lorry drivers and farmers instigated, in early September 2000, a 'spontaneous' blockade of Britain's oil refineries. The result was that, within five days, the protestors nearly brought Britain to a standstill as garages ran out of petrol and panic-buying emptied supermarket shelves. In spite of the chaos and inconvenience their action caused, the 'People's Fuel lobby' (the ad-hoc umbrella group set up during the protest) enjoyed substantial support among the British public. The government was portrayed in the tabloid press as being arrogant and out of touch, particularly when ministers made it clear that they would not surrender to those 'holding the country to ransom'.

Within a week, the fuel protestors had called off their action, but issued the Blair government with a 60-day ultimatum - either announce a cut in fuel duty in the November pre-Budget speech, or face renewed blockades. In November, the Chancellor offered just enough concessions and initiatives to avert a repeat performance. There was only a token protest by a handful of disgruntled lorry drivers and farmers when the 60-day deadline expired. Although the taxation adjustments made in November were relatively small, the fact that concessions were made indicates that the government had been shaken by the protest. As a result of the protest, it is likely that the option of collecting additional revenue through higher fuel taxes will be off the agenda for some time. In the immediate aftermath of the fuel protests, the Blair government's popularity plummeted. Several opinion polls conducted during the second half of September showed that the Conservatives had secured a lead over Labour for the first time since September 1992. But, although the Labour government suffered a temporary loss of support, its position in the polls soon recovered and it went on to win a second landslide in the general election of June 2001.

Source: Anderton 2000, Dorey 2001 and McNaughton 2001.

Item C The anti-Iraq War demonstration in London

In February 2003, an estimated 2 million people joined a march through London to demonstrate against the UK's involvement in the forthcoming war with Iraq. This did not prevent the British government joining forces with the USA and invading Iraq in March.

Questions

1. a) Why did the protestors in Items A-C resort to direct action?

   b) How successful were they?

2. a) What other channels could the protestors in Items A-C have used in order to pursue their objectives or express their grievances?

   b) Did any of them actually do so, and if so, which channels did they use?

3. What are the arguments for and against the use of direct action?

10.12 Pressure groups and the European Union

The 1986 Single European Act (SEA)

Like most aspects of British politics, the role of pressure groups has changed since Britain joined the EU. Pressure groups go where the power goes. As more and more power has shifted towards Brussels, pressure groups have begun to place increasing emphasis on lobbying EU decision-makers.

This has particularly been the case since the Single European Act (SEA) was passed in 1986. The SEA resulted in two major changes, both of which have encouraged greater pressure group activity in Brussels (these changes were then extended by the Maastricht Treaty, Amsterdam Treaty and Nice Treaty - see Unit 12).

1. The change in voting procedures

The SEA changed the voting procedure in the Council of Ministers. Whereas a single-member state had previously had the power to veto a proposal, the SEA allowed the introduction of qualified majority voting on some matters. That meant that pressure groups could no longer rely on the veto of a single member to stop any legislation they did not like.

2. Extension of the range of policies

The range of policies covered by the EU has also been extended. Policies which had previously been decided by national governments are now decided by the EU. As a result, pressure groups have been forced to lobby the EU to have any hope of influencing decisions.

Why do pressure groups lobby the EU?

According to Baggott, there are three main reasons why many British pressure groups have increasingly turned towards Europe. These are outlined in Box 10.13 on page 199.

The EU provides pressure groups with four main avenues of (potential) influence.

1. Lobbying the UK's central government

Pressure groups often seek to persuade a minister of their case, in the hope that this will influence the minister's negotiating position in the Council of Ministers, which is the European Union's ultimate decision-making body. This strategy is most readily available to those pressure groups which already enjoy insider status and which can, therefore, seek to influence the relevant minister as part of their routine meetings and discussions. Many authors believe that lobbying through the British government remains a valuable and very worthwhile strategy for many pressure groups and organised interests (see, for example, Greenwood & Jordan 1993, pp.76-78; Hayes-Renshaw & Jordan 1997, p.229; Thairs 1998, p.166).

Box 10.13 **Reasons why pressure groups lobby the EU**

The three main reasons why many British pressure groups have increasingly turned towards Europe are:

1. Recognition that EU institutions have developed increasing influence over various domestic policies - part of a process known as 'Europeanisation'.

2. The realisation that some European institutions are more open and accessible to pressure groups, and also more receptive or responsive to their views and arguments.

3. Certain pressure groups which were marginalised or ignored by the Conservative governments of the 1980s and 1990s - such as trade unions, local authorities, equal opportunities campaigners, for example - have found that the EU offers the possibility of overriding or overturning some of the policies of British government (Baggott 1995, pp.207-08).

Even if a minister refuses to adopt a pressure group's viewpoint at EU level, or does adopt it, but is then outvoted in the Council of Ministers (due to the use of Qualified Majority Voting - see Unit 12), the group concerned might still be able to use its 'inside' status to influence the way in which policy is implemented back in the UK.

2. Setting up an office in Brussels

Although lobbying central government remains a useful strategy, an increasing number of pressure groups have also set up offices in Brussels, employing full-time, professional, staff. Such groups are then able to maintain regular contacts with the European Commission which is also based in Brussels. The Commission is effectively the 'civil service' of the European Union, responsible for drafting policy proposals, and then implementing them once they have been formally approved by the Council of Ministers. Because of this, many pressure groups aim to be in touch with the Commission on a regular basis. Having an office in Brussels enables meetings to be arranged at short notice or for discussions over specific details to be conducted over a working lunch in the Belgian capital. Most pressure groups with an office in Brussels lobby both the EU and the British government. As Mazey and Richardson observe:

> 'A European lobbying strategy becomes essential for a group in addition to the maintenance and strengthening of links with national officials.' (Mazey & Richardson 1993, p.15)

Similarly, Baggott asserts that:

> 'The most successful groups...will be those which have good political contacts at both the national and at the European level.' (Baggott 1995, p.218)

Of course, maintaining a permanent office in Brussels is an option only normally available to well-organised pressure groups with sufficient financial resources. In many cases, it is professional or sectional pressure groups which tend to have such resources, or to put it another way, those groups who tend to be insiders in the UK.

3. Joining a 'Euro-group'

A third means, therefore, by which some British pressure groups seek to influence public policy at EU level is by joining a trans-national 'Euro-group' made up of similar pressure groups from other member states. The number of these Euro-groups has increased significantly, from about 430 in 1980 to over 700 in 2003 (for the full list, see www.europa.eu.int/comm/ civil_society/coneccs). The diversity of such groups is indicated in Box 10.14 on page 200, along with examples of the Euro-groups to which certain British pressure groups belong.

4. The European Court of Justice (ECJ)

The European Court of Justice (ECJ) is the body with primary responsibility for ensuring that EU laws and decisions are implemented. Some pressure groups have successfully taken cases to the ECJ, on the grounds that the British government is in breach of EU law. In a number of cases heard in the 1990s, the ECJ found in favour of various British pressure groups which had claimed that the government, or employers, were not fully or properly applying EU decisions and directives, particularly with regard to part-time and women workers. One survey in the mid-1990s found that about 30% of cases taken to the European Court of Justice concerning equal pay and equal treatment at work had been pursued or funded by the Equal Opportunities Commission (Barnard 1995, p.254).

A mixed approach

Just as pressure groups in the UK often pursue more than one avenue or activity at any one time in order to maximise their chances of exercising influence, they also often pursue a mixed approach at the EU level, with two or more of the strategies outlined above being pursued simultaneously. As Greenwood states:

> 'The multi-level character of the European policy process means that the actors seeking to participate in European public affairs therefore have a number of so-called "routes" of influence...they are seldom mutually exclusive. In practice, interests tend to use a combination of routes simultaneously as a means of accessing European public affairs.' (Greenwood 2003, pp.32-33)

The three laws of Euro-lobbying

Mazey and Richardson (1993) identified three laws of lobbying. It is by observing these laws that pressure groups have the best chance of influencing decisions made by the EU.

1. Discover where the power lies

The first law of Euro-lobbying is to discover exactly where the power lies. Although the Council of Ministers is the ultimate EU decision-making body, much of the power actually lies with the Commission. It is the Commission which draws up policy proposals for the Council of Ministers and it is the Commission which is responsible for policy implementation. As a result, it is the Commission which is targeted by most pressure groups based in Brussels.

2. Be willing to compromise

The second law of Euro-lobbying is to be willing to compromise. Since so many different interests are at stake, it

Box 10.14 Examples of Euro-groups and the British pressure groups which belong to them

Policy sector	British pressure group	'Euro-group'
Agriculture	National Farmers Union	Committee of Professional Agricultural Organisations
Banking & Finance	British Bankers' Association Building Societies Association Council of Mortgage Lenders	European Banking Federation European Federation of Building Societies
Civil Engineering	Institution of Civil Engineering	European Council of Civil Engineers
Construction	Federation of Master Builders	European Builders Confederation
Dentistry	British Dental Hygienists Association	European Liaison Committee for Dental Hygiene
Employment	Trades Union Congress (TUC)	European Trade Union Confederation
Food and drink	Food and Drink Federation Ice Cream Federation Seasoning and Spice Association	Confederation of the Food and Drink Industries of the EU Euroglaces (Association of the Ice Cream Industries of the EEC) European Spice Association
Law	Law Society	International Bar Association
Media	National Union of Journalists	European Federation of Journalists
Paper	Paper Federation of the UK	Confederation of European Paper Industries
Small Businesses	Federation of Small Businesses	European Small Business Alliance
Timber	Timber Trade Federation	European Timber Trade Association
Tobacco	Tobacco Manufactures' Association	Confederation of European Community Cigarette Manufacturers
Transport	Association of Train Operating Companies British Ports Association	Community of European Railways European Sea Ports Association
Veterinary	British Veterinary Association	Federation of Veterinarians of Europe

Source: www.europa.eu.int/comm/civil_society/coneccs

is rare for any single party to achieve its goals completely. Pressure groups need to be willing to make deals. They often have to make a concession over one clause in the hope that the favour will be returned later. Mazey and Richardson say that EU policies are:

'As much peace treaties between competing interests and nations as they are rational decisions.' (Mazey & Richardson 1993, p.21)

3. Intervene as early as possible

The third law of Euro-lobbying is that the most effective time to influence a decision is at the earliest possible stage. Ideally, a pressure group should be there at the start. The further along the road a policy has travelled, the less chance groups have to change it. One EU official told Mazey and Richardson that, in general, probably 80% of the initial proposal remains in a directive's final draft. That indicates just how important it is to be involved in drawing up the initial proposal. It also indicates how important advance information can be. It may be expensive to maintain an office in Brussels, but groups which do so are likely to have earlier access to the decision-making process than other groups.

Main points Section 10.12

- There are three main reasons why many British pressure groups have increasingly turned towards Europe: (1) recognition that EU institutions have developed increasing influence; (2) realisation that some European institutions are more open and accessible to pressure groups; and (3) the possibility for groups marginalised in the UK to overturn government policies.
- The EU provides pressure groups with four main avenues of (potential) influence: (1) lobbying central government; (2) setting up an office in Brussels; (3) joining a Euro-group; and (4) taking cases to the ECJ.
- Pressure groups often pursue a mixed approach at the EU level, pursuing two or more strategies simultaneously.
- The three laws of Euro-lobbying are: (1) discover where the power lies and target it; (2) be willing to compromise; and (3) intervene as early as possible.

Activity 10.4 Pressure groups and the EU

Item A Decision-making in the EU

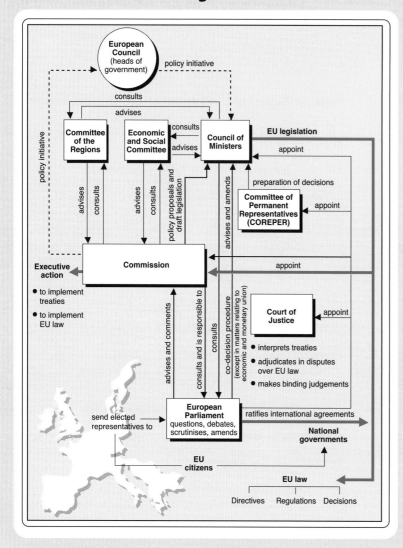

Source: Mazey & Richardson 1993.

Item B The importance of 'multi-channel' lobbying at EU level (1)

Effective European lobbying has always depended on using the full range of methods available in whatever mix appears appropriate to the particular case. Strategy and tactics may change as the particular issue evolves. An interest which is not represented at the European level is not going to be able to cope with the unpredictability of the decision-making process in Brussels where a draft directive may suddenly be taken from the piles of paper on an official's desk and launched on a new stage of its life. There is no substitute for an effective presence in Brussels.

Source: Grant 2000.

Item C The importance of 'multi-channel' lobbying at EU level (2)

With the expansion of EU competence, new routes of influence for pressure groups have opened up. Indeed, in certain areas, such as environmental policies, interest groups have had much more influence at the EU level than they have had domestically. The point about the EU is that it opens up new lines of access for pressure groups. Within the EU, power is much less concentrated than it is within the British state. There are a number of different terrains and points of pressure, and groups can move from one to another if they are unsuccessful. In addition, the EU makes a virtue of its openness to interest groups. The downside is that lobbying the EU is much more complex. It needs a degree of coordination, access, and funds to travel that are not available to certain groups.

Source: Richards & Smith 2002.

Questions

1. Suppose you had been asked to organise a campaign at EU level on an issue you feel strongly about.

   a) Describe the tactics you would use.

   b) Explain which points in the EU decision-making process you would target.

   c) What factors do you think would determine the success or failure of your campaign?

2. a) According to Items B and C, what are the advantages to pressure groups of lobbying at EU level?

   b) What might be some of the difficulties or disadvantages of such lobbying?

3. Why is EU lobbying more feasible or useful for some pressure groups than for others? Give reasons for your answer.

10.13 Pressure groups and democracy

Pressure groups are a vitally important part of Britain's liberal democracy. They can be said to perform a number of valuable roles. These are outlined in Box 10.15.

Box 10.15 The roles played by pressure groups

Pressure groups play the following roles:

1. **Keeping politicians in touch with public opinion between elections**
   For ordinary citizens, they provide a means of influencing politicians in between general elections, and of ensuring that governments are kept aware of the issues that people are most concerned about. People acting in concert with like-minded fellow citizens are much more likely to be listened to than if they acted as isolated individuals.

2. **Providing alternative viewpoints**
   Pressure groups can also be said to provide alternative viewpoints and arguments to those presented by the government or partisan newspapers. Having come across information provided by pressure groups, citizens might see things differently, and come to a different conclusion about a particular issue, than if they had only heard the claims of politicians or the press. Trade unions, for example, can publicly highlight cases of bullying or discrimination in the workplace, which unsympathetic governments or newspapers might otherwise ignore.

3. **Protection for minorities**
   Pressure groups can offer some protection to minorities who might otherwise be overlooked or discriminated against. In this respect, pressure groups can provide a valuable counterweight to what the political philosopher, John Stuart Mill called 'the tyranny of the majority'.

4. **Provide information and advice to decision-makers**
   For governments and civil servants, pressure groups often provide valuable information and advice necessary for the development and implementation of policy. For example, health policies are unlikely to be successful if the government has not discussed them with the British Medical Association (BMA), while measures to tackle crime are unlikely to succeed if the advice of the Association of Chief Police Officers or the Police Federation has not been taken into account.

5. **Provide checks and balances needed in a liberal democracy**
   More generally, pressure groups can be said to provide part of the 'checks and balances' which a liberal democracy requires, in order to prevent political power from becoming concentrated in too few hands. Along with competition between several political parties, the existence of a wide variety of pressure groups can help to ensure that power is dispersed throughout society and that no one individual or closely-knit set of individuals becomes over-mighty.

Criticisms of pressure groups

The points in Box 10.15 need to be qualified. Pressure groups can also be criticised on a number of grounds.

1. Pressure groups do not reflect the views of the majority

Pressure groups often represent well-organised, active or vocal minorities. As a result, they might not reflect the views or wishes of the majority of citizens.

2. Governments listen to powerful groups and ignore others

Some pressure groups are more powerful or influential than others. Some have greater resources - financial or in terms of expertise - than others. Some have greater social or economic importance to society than others. More powerful pressure groups tend to be listened to more carefully and sympathetically by governments, often at the expense of weaker pressure groups with fewer resources. For example, pressure groups representing business interests or employers, such as the Confederation of British Industry (CBI) or the Institute of Directors (IoD), are normally listened to rather more seriously by ministers than trade unions, or pressure groups representing single parents. This was clearly illustrated when the first Blair government pledged to introduce a statutory minimum wage. The CBI wanted such a wage set at no more than £3.50 per hour, while trade unions called for it to be set in the £4.15-£4.50 range. The minimum wage was finally introduced at £3.60 per hour, much closer to the figure urged by the CBI than the trade unions.

3. The strong groups limit government's scope for action

The strength or socio-economic importance of some pressure groups is such that they limit governments' scope for action. Governments feel they have to respond favourably to the demands of such groups. As a result, on certain issues, pressure groups themselves effectively determine policy, rather than elected politicians.

In the 1990s and early 21st century, pressure groups representing employers or business interests have been much more likely than other pressure groups to convince governments of the need to pursue particular policies. In the 1970s, by way of contrast, there was a widespread public perception - encouraged by much of the media - that it was the trade unions who were virtually 'running the country', demanding higher wages and various other favourable employment policies, frequently backed by strike action if and when these demands were not met. Critics then claimed that the trade unions had become too powerful, and were rendering Britain 'ungovernable'.

4. Pressure groups can help to marginalise Parliament

The close and regular involvement of certain pressure groups in policy-making may be said to sit uneasily with Britain's claim to be a parliamentary or representative democracy because it means that various policies are effectively determined through negotiations - often behind closed doors - between ministers, senior civil servants and pressure group leaders, and only afterwards presented to Parliament for approval. Certainly, during the 1970s, some writers and politicians warned that Britain was becoming a 'corporate state' in which economic and industrial policies were being determined jointly by the ministers, the CBI and trade union leaders (Dorey 1991). This, critics claimed, not only eroded the elected government's freedom to manoeuvre, it also further marginalised Parliament. Furthermore, the millions of citizens who did not belong to these particular pressure groups, or who disagreed with them, were, to some extent, 'disenfranchised', either because their political voice was not loud enough to be heard, or because what they were saying was not what policy-makers wanted to hear at that time. If liberal democracy needs constantly to beware the danger of the 'tyranny of the majority', so too does it need to guard against the other extreme, the 'tyranny of the minority' over the less well-organised majority.

5. Pressure groups can undermine the rule of law

Some pressure groups might feel so strongly about their 'cause' that they - or at least some of their members - are prepared to pursue disruptive, even unlawful, action, in an effort to force the government to take their views seriously. While supporters or sympathisers might agree with such action, viewing it as proof that the pressure group has the courage of its convictions, critics point out the dangers to social stability and the rule of law of permitting 'militant minorities' to engage in such forms of direct action, particularly when this involves inflicting harm or inconvenience on other, innocent citizens. For example, it was trade unions' use of direct action, in the form of strikes and picketing, which did so much to turn public (and political) opinion against them in the late 1970s and early 1980s.

As noted above in Section 10.10, direct action became increasingly popular in the 1990s. To their supporters, groups which engage in such campaigns are heroes courageously standing up to over-mighty government or to threats to their traditional way of life. To those who disagree with these groups, though, they are selfish or irresponsible minorities adopting the undemocratic principle that 'might is right', and arrogantly placing themselves above the law. It is certainly interesting to note that whereas most newspapers invariably accuse trade unions and workers who pursue direct action of being selfish, and of 'holding the county to ransom', the same newspapers have, in recent years, portrayed the 2000 'fuel protestors', and the Countryside Alliance, as heroes and as ordinary people who have been brave enough to tell ministers that 'enough is enough'.

Main points   Section 10.13

- **Pressure groups benefit the UK because they: (1) keep politicians in touch with public opinion between elections; (2) provide alternative viewpoints; (3) provide protection for minorities; (4) provide information and advice to decision-makers; and (5) provide checks and balances needed in a liberal democracy.**
- **Pressure groups can also be criticised because: (1) they do not promote the view of the majority; (2) governments listen to powerful groups and ignore others; (3) the strong groups limit government's scope for action; (4) they can help to marginalise Parliament; and (5) they can help to undermine the rule of law.**

Activity 10.5 *Pressure groups and democracy*

Item A **Pressure groups are essential to a democratic society**

1. There is more to democracy than the occasional vote. ✓
2. Pressure groups offer a chance for minorities and disadvantaged groups to argue their case. ✓
3. Pressure groups increase surveillance of government. ✓
4. Pressure groups combat other pressure groups. ✓
5. Community/cause groups offer people the weapons to fight on their own behalf. ✓
6. Pressure groups relieve frustration. ✓

A former prominent campaigner, Des Wilson, once outlined six key reasons why he believed pressure groups were essential to a democratic society and were, therefore, generally 'a good thing'.

Source: Wilson 1984.

Item B **Pressure groups are useful to governments**

Graham Wilson, an expert on pressure groups, has identified four main reasons why governments consult (some) pressure groups:

1. Pressure groups can provide governments with advice, which is useful for identifying problems and making policy. ✓
2. Pressure groups can provide legitimacy to government policies. ✓
3. Pressure groups can assist governments in implementing policies. ✓
4. Some pressure groups might be able to 'veto' policies which they are unhappy with, or have not been consulted about. ✓

Source: Wilson 1990.

Questions

1. Look at Item A.
   a) Briefly explain what Wilson means by each of his six statements in support of pressure groups.
   b) How convincing do you find each of these claims?

2. Look at Item B.
   a) Why do governments find some pressure groups useful?
   b) What kinds of pressure groups are most likely to be consulted by governments?

3. Why are some kinds of pressure groups more influential or successful than others?

References

Anderson (1997) Anderson, A., *Media, Culture and the Environment*, UCL, 1997.

Anderton (2000) Anderton, A., *The Student's Economy in Focus 2000/01*, Causeway Press, 2000.

Baggott (1995) Baggott, R., *Pressure Groups Today*, Manchester University Press, 1995.

Barnard (1995) Barnard, C., 'A European Litigation Strategy: The Case of the Equal Opportunities Commission' in *Shaw & More (1995)*.

Dorey (1991) Dorey, P., 'Corporatism in the UK, *Politics Review*, Vol.1.2, 1991.

Dorey (1999) Dorey, P., 'The Blairite Betrayal: New Labour and the Trade Unions' in *Taylor (1999)*.

Dorey (2001) Dorey, P., *Wage Politics in Britain: The Rise and Fall of Incomes Policies since 1945*, Sussex Academic Press, 2001.

Dorey (2003) Dorey, P., 'Margaret Thatcher's taming of the trade unions' in *Pugliese (2003)*.

Grant (1989) Grant, W., *Pressure Groups, Politics and Democracy in Britain*, Philip Allan, 1989.

Grant (2000) Grant, W., *Pressure Groups and British Politics*, Macmillan, 2000.

Greenwood (2003) Greenwood, J., *Interest Representation in the European Union*, Palgrave, 2003.

Greenwood & Jordan (1993) Greenwood, J. & Jordan, G., 'The United Kingdom: a changing kaleidoscope' in *Schendelen (1993)*.

Hayes-Renshaw & Jordan (1997) Hayes-Renshaw, F. & Jordan, G., *The Council of Ministers*, Macmillan, 1997.

Jones (1990) Jones, J. B., 'Party Committees and All-Party Groups' in *Rush (1990)*.

Lowe & Ward (1990) Lowe, P. & Ward S. (eds), *British Environmental Policy in Europe*, Routledge, 1998.

Mazey & Richardson (1993) Mazey, S. & Richardson J. J., *Lobbying in the European Community*, Oxford University Press, 1993.

McNaughton (2001) McNaughton, N., 'Populist movements - a new development in the politics of pressure', *Talking Politics*, Vol.14.1, September 2001.

Pugliese (2003) Pugliese, S. (ed.), *Margaret Thatcher: The Rebirth of Liberty?*, Politico's, 2003.

Richards & Smith (2002) Richards D. & Smith, M. J., *Governance and Public Policy in the UK*, Oxford University Press, 2002.

Richardson (1993) Richardson, J. J. (ed.), *Pressure Groups*, Oxford University Press, 1993.

Rush (1990) Rush, M. (ed.), *Parliament and Pressure Politics*, Clarendon Press, 1990.

Schendelen (1993) Schendelen, M. van (ed.), *National Public and Private EC Lobbying*, Dartmouth, 1993.

Shaw & More (1995) Shaw, J. & More G. (eds) *New Legal Dynamics of European Integration*, Oxford University Press, 1995.

Taylor (1999) Taylor, G. (ed.), *The Impact of New Labour*, Macmillan, 1999.

Thairs (1998) Thairs, E., *Business Lobbying on the Environment: The Perspective of the Water Sector'* in *Lowe & Ward (1998)*.

Wilson (1984) Wilson, D., *Pressure: The A-Z of Campaigning in Britain*, Heinemann, 1984.

Wilson (1990) Wilson, G. K., *Interest Groups*, Blackwell, 1990.

Whiteley & Winyard (1987) Whiteley, P. & Winyard, S., *Pressure for the Poor*, Methuen, 1987.

11 The UK's constitution

11.1 Constitutions defined

A constitution is a system of rules specifying how a state is governed and which describes:
- the structure and powers of government
- the relationship between different parts of government
- the relationship between government and citizen.

The constitution is, therefore, an essential starting point for uncovering the structure and processes of government and for discovering where power lies in the political system.

11.2 The different parts of government

Government involves three main tasks:
- **the legislative function** - the process of making laws;
- **the executive function** - the role of implementing the law and making sure that legislative requirements are carried out;
- **the judicial function** - the task of law enforcement, of deciding whether laws have been broken and, if they have, of dispensing punishment.

Separation of the powers

Constitutions usually define which people or institutions have the power to carry out these tasks. Some constitutions state that legislative, executive and judicial powers should be exercised by a different person or group. This is known as 'the principle of the separation of the powers'. The purpose of this principle is to avoid the concentration of power into the hands of a single person or group.

11.3 Sources of the UK constitution

In many countries, the constitution has been codified, which means that it is written down in a single document. Copies are often widely available. The constitution of the USA, for example, is inexpensive and relatively short and can be bought in bookshops.

A similar rule book cannot be purchased in the UK, however. This is not because the UK does not have a constitution. It is because the rules which describe the structure and powers of government, and the relationship between government and citizen, are not found in any single document. In other words, the British constitution remains 'uncodified'. The fundamental rules and principles underlying the operation of government in the UK are scattered among a variety of different sources. These are illustrated in Box 11.1 and described below.

A. Statute law

A statute is an Act of Parliament. It is a written law which has been passed (approved) by Parliament and is enforceable in the courts of law. Over time, some statutes have come to be regarded as having special significance because they contain

Box 11.1   The sources of the UK constitution

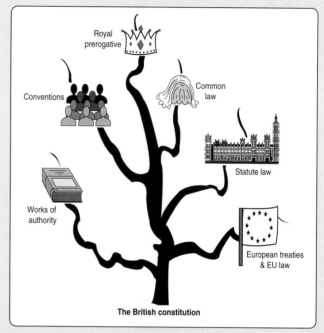

The British constitution

Source: Kingdom 1991.

rules relating to certain rights or duties of the citizen or to how the government of the country should be organised.

The Habeas Corpus Act of 1679

The Habeas Corpus Act of 1679 is an example of a statute of constitutional significance because it gives some protection for the citizen against wrongful imprisonment. The Act enables anyone who has been confined to demand to be brought before a court for a just trial. In the past, this Act was used to free slaves, to free apprentices from cruel owners and to prevent husbands confining their wives without their consent.

Other examples

Other examples of statute law are the Representation of the People Acts, which state the rules under which elections may take place, and the Parliament Acts of 1911 and 1949 which place limits on the powers of the House of Lords.

Because (at least in theory) Parliament can pass any law it wishes, statute law takes precedence over (is seen as more important than) the other sources of the constitution. In other words - in theory at least - the UK has parliamentary sovereignty (see Section 11.7 below).

But that does not mean that Parliament is all-powerful. In 1972, for example, Parliament passed the European Communities Act and the UK joined the European Economic Community (EEC). One of the conditions of membership of the EEC (now called the EU - European Union) is that European law is binding on all member states and, therefore, takes precedence over domestic law. Despite this, because Parliament has the power to repeal (change) the 1972

European Communities Act, it is still possible to argue that parliamentary sovereignty still exists since Parliament could pass a law withdrawing the UK from membership of the EU.

B. Common law

Common law is made by judges. It arises out of the custom that a decision made by one court of law must be followed by other courts facing similar facts. Judges, in this way, are bound by legal precedents. Much of the original law on civil liberties, for example, as well as the procedures to be followed by the courts in reviewing the actions of public bodies, is based on common law.

C. Royal prerogative

The royal prerogative is a set of privileges or powers held by the monarch. The range of powers and who exercises them is outlined in Box 11.2.

Box 11.2 Royal prerogative

The royal prerogative includes the powers to:

- declare war
- make treaties
- take possession of or give up territory
- issue orders to armed forces
- do anything necessary to defend the realm
- in an emergency to confiscate or destroy property and to intern aliens
- make appointments
- control and manage the civil service.

Although these powers are still exercised in the name of the monarch and, on rare occasions, the monarch still has a role to play (for example, appointing the Prime Minister), in practice, they have mainly passed to government ministers. Although government ministers are responsible to Parliament and can be questioned about particular policies, parliamentary authority is not required for the exercise of these powers. However, Parliament could (by passing laws) restrict or abolish them.

Source: HMSO 1994.

A criticism of prerogative powers

Since parliamentary authority is not required for the exercise of prerogative powers, these powers provide the executive (government) with a means of by-passing the legislature (Parliament). Critics argue that this permits profoundly undemocratic government - see Box 11.3.

Box 11.3 No people power

'The prerogative derives from the time when Britain was ruled according to the divine right of kings. Government ministers have inherited its powers which allow them to rule virtually by decree in many areas not covered by statute...The prerogative is all about the power of government over the people and virtually nothing to do with the power of the people over government.'

Source: *Independent on Sunday*, 17 July 1994

D. Conventions

A convention is a practice which, through custom, is considered to be the appropriate or proper behaviour or procedure to follow in given circumstances. Although they are not enforced by the law courts, constitutional conventions are rules related to the exercise of governmental powers which, through precedent, are considered binding by and on those concerned.

Examples of constitutional conventions include the doctrines of individual and collective ministerial responsibility (see Units 15 and 16) and the rule that the assent (agreement) of the monarch is required before Bills passed by the two Houses of Parliament can become law.

E. Works of authority

Certain books written by constitutional theorists are sometimes used to work out appropriate constitutional procedures. Two major sources are Erskine May's *Parliamentary Practice*, first published in 1844, and *An Introduction to the Study of the Law of the Constitution* by A.V. Dicey, first published in 1885. These works have no legal standing but appeals to them can be persuasive in settling disputes or uncertainties arising from interpretations of aspects of the constitution.

F. Treaties and laws of the European Union

As noted above, the treaties and law of the European Union, and the judgements of the European Court of Justice, now form a significant additional source of the UK constitution. The implications of this are explored in Section 11.8 below and in Unit 12.

11.4 Flexible or rigid constitutions?

Since the UK's constitution is uncodified and is derived from sources of varying status (some being more important or influential than others), it can, at least in theory, be easily changed. For example, even those constitutional rules laid down in statute law can be altered by the same processes which apply to any other piece of legislation.

To some people, this flexibility is a major disadvantage. It means, for example, that hard-won civil rights could be abolished overnight by a political party which temporarily wins power. Written, or codified, constitutions, by way of contrast, often contain sections which outline the basic rights of citizens and these usually have a special status preventing easy or quick alterations to them.

Others regard the UK constitution's capacity to change to be an advantage. The constitution can adapt to political developments and changing circumstances and is, therefore, less likely to contain outdated rules and obligations. Written constitutions tend to be much less flexible. They contain special rigid, often lengthy, procedures which must be followed before any constitutional changes can be introduced. As a result, such changes are usually rare. The USA's constitution, for example, has been altered only 26 times and the first ten amendments were made together in 1791, just four years after the constitution had been drawn up.

11.5 *The development of the UK constitution*

One of the reasons why the UK does not have a codified constitution is that British political history over the past three centuries has followed an evolutionary rather than a revolutionary route. In other countries, written constitutions have been introduced following sudden and total changes to their political systems. The French Revolution of 1789 and the Russian Revolution of 1917 both led to the introduction of written constitutions. Similarly, new written constitutions were introduced in Germany after defeat in 1918 and 1945, and India drew up a written constitution when British rule ended in 1947.

Absolute monarchy to constitutional monarchy

Until the 17th century, there was no real separation of powers. Instead, there was a system of absolute monarchy. The monarch could overrule decisions made by Parliament. Ministers were merely personal advisers and judges were appointed and removed by the monarch (see Box 11.4).

It was only after the English Civil War of 1642-52, and the short period of republican government before the monarchy was restored in 1660, that the power of the monarch was curtailed. Attempts by Charles II and James II to reassert royal power resulted in the latter's exile in 1688 (the so-called 'Glorious Revolution') and the introduction of a Bill of Rights which granted Parliament protection against royal absolutism.

From the beginning of the 18th century, therefore, Britain was no longer governed by an absolute monarch. Constitutionally, although monarchs still exercised considerable power, they required the support of Parliament.

The monarch's business was carried out by the Cabinet (the monarch's ministers) which brought matters before Parliament for its approval. This system became known as a constitutional monarchy. Britain remains a constitutional monarchy today, although considerable changes in how it operates in practice have taken place along the way.

Checks, balances and corruption

With the abolition of absolute monarchy, the principal institutions of government provided a set of mutual checks and balances - at least in theory. The idea was that the House of Commons could reject what the nobility (the Lords) had proposed, and vice versa. The monarch could act as a check on both Houses while they, in turn, had sanctions which could be used to check the power of the monarch's ministers.

The theory of checks and balances was only partly borne out in practice. A very small electorate (even by the end of the 18th century, less than 5% of adult men and no women were entitled to vote) allowed patronage and corruption to flourish. The constitution operated essentially in the interests of the aristocracy since power was held primarily by a small group of substantial landowners in the Lords who were 'in loose alliance' with the merchants and the representatives of small towns who sat in the Commons (Dearlove & Saunders 1991, p.24).

With the break-up of the old feudal system and the rapid economic and social changes that accompanied the industrial revolution, this constitutional set-up became unworkable. Industrialisation produced a new class of wealthy factory owners. The economic power of this capitalist class was not matched, however, by political power since this new 'middle class' was not represented in Parliament.

Box 11.4 Absolute monarchy

This produced the principal political division of the 19th century. The large landowners wanted to preserve the status quo. The new industrial capitalists were eager for political representation and power for themselves. Both groups wished to avoid granting any representation or power to the working class (the vast majority of the population). But the middle classes needed the support of working-class reformers to achieve any extension of the franchise and reform of the House of Commons.

The Great Reform Act, 1832

Political conflict culminated in the Great Reform Act of 1832 which extended the vote to the new middle classes and gave parliamentary representation to the new industrial towns. It was now no longer possible for the Lords, through patronage, to control the composition of the House of Commons. In addition, the powers of the monarch were limited further as the choice of senior Cabinet members (the centre of executive power) now passed to the Commons (the centre of legislative power). For a while, these changes produced a 'golden period' of dominance for the Commons, as the power of the Lords waned. This 'golden period' is described in Box 11.5.

The constitution after 1832

The British constitution after 1832 was not democratic. The vast majority of the adult population was denied the vote. As the 19th century progressed, however, those in power grudgingly came to realise that some form of working-class representation in Parliament was necessary in order to avoid threats to the existing political and social order posed by the growth in ideas about equality and socialism. In 1867, the Electoral Reform Act gave the vote to some male workers and began the process of creating a mass electorate. Further extensions of the franchise were introduced in 1884 but women had to wait until the 20th century before they were permitted to vote at general elections (see also Unit 3).

The importance of a mass electorate

The growth of a mass electorate was of great importance constitutionally. It encouraged the development of mass political parties. These parties came to dominate Parliament. The result was a constitutional shift which ended the brief period during which the House of Commons predominated. Power shifted to the Prime Minister and the Cabinet who were chosen from the party with the majority of seats in the Commons. At the same time, the growth of a mass electorate meant that parties could only govern if they gained the support of the electorate at election times. A view of the constitutional implications of these changes is provided in Box 11.6.

Some writers saw the need to consider public opinion as adding a new,

Box 11.5 The British constitution in the post-1832 period

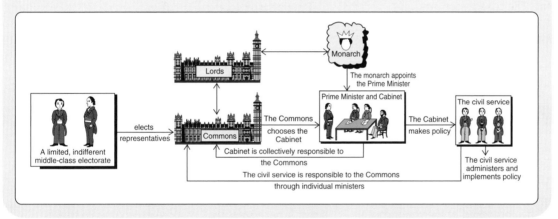

Box 11.6 A view of the constitution of the UK since the development of a mass electorate

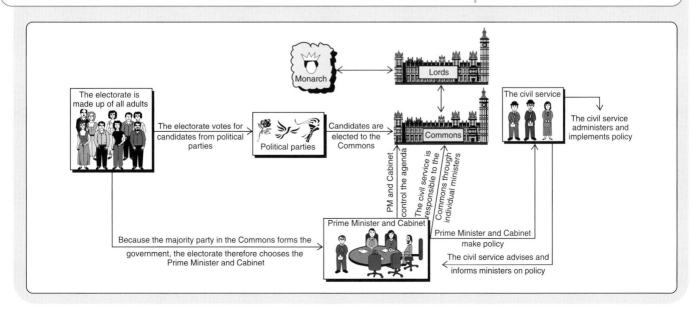

democratic dimension to the constitution. Parliament was the supreme legislative body, the executive (Prime Minister and Cabinet) was accountable to Parliament, and the electorate chose their parliamentary representatives. Political sovereignty, in other words, was now seen as resting with the voters.

To others, however, this represents an idealised view of the constitution. It is based on the assumption of a one-directional flow of power from the electorate to Parliament to government. It ignores the possibility that power also flows in the reverse direction. In general, more recent interpretations of the UK constitution acknowledge the dominant role of the executive in the policy-making process (especially the role of the Prime Minister and the 'core executive' - see Unit 15). Parliament is seen in a much more diminished role and the electorate largely viewed as passive.

An evolved constitution

It can be argued that developments since the late 19th century (the extensions of the franchise and the changes in the balance of power between the legislature and the executive) were achieved without fundamentally altering the structures of power or class in British society. A democratic element (a mass electorate) was added to the existing constitution without altering the dominance of the ruling classes and without threatening the continuation of the capitalist economic system. The constitution gradually evolved and continues to do so.

Main points (Sections 11.1 - 11.5)

- Government involves three main tasks: (1) the legislative function; (2) the executive role; and (3) the judicial task of law enforcement.
- Constitutions define which people or institutions have the power to carry out the three tasks. In some constitutions, each task is carried out by a different person or group - the principle of the separation of the powers.
- The six main sources of the UK's constitution are: statute law, common law, the royal prerogative, constitutional conventions various 'works of authority' and the treaties and laws of the European Union.
- Until the 17th century, Britain was an absolute monarchy. There was no separation of powers. Since the late 17th century, Britain has been a constitutional monarchy.
- Industrialisation was the catalyst for constitutional changes, leading to a period when the House of Commons was dominant.
- The widening of the franchise in the 19th century and the growth of a mass electorate produced a constitutional shift with power moving from Parliament to the executive.

Activity 11.1 The constitution in Britain and the USA

Item A The American constitution

Articles 1-5 (adapted)

All legislative powers herein granted shall be vested in a Congress of the United States which shall consist of a Senate and a House of Representatives. The House of Representatives shall be composed of members chosen every second year by the people. The Senate shall be composed of two senators from each state chosen for six years. All Bills for raising revenue shall originate in the House of Representatives. Every Bill which shall have passed the House of Representatives and the Senate shall, before it becomes law, be presented to the President of the United States. If he approve, he shall sign it, but if not, he shall return it with his objections. If, after reconsideration, two-thirds of the House of Representatives shall agree to pass the Bill, it shall be sent, together with the objections, to the Senate, by which it shall likewise be reconsidered; and, if approved by two-thirds of that house, it shall become a law. The executive power shall be vested in a President of the United States of America. He shall hold his office during the term of four years. The President shall be Commander-in-Chief of the armed forces. He shall, from time to time, give to the Congress information of the state of the Union, and recommend

to their consideration such measures as he shall judge necessary and expedient. The judicial power of the United States shall be vested in the Supreme Court. The Congress, whenever two-thirds of both houses shall deem it necessary, shall propose amendments to this constitution, or, on the application of the legislatures of two-thirds of the several states, shall call a convention for proposing amendments, which in either case shall be valid as part of this constitution when ratified by the legislature of three-fourths of the several states or by conventions in three-fourths thereof.

Amendment 1 (adapted)

Congress shall make no law respecting of religion or prohibiting the free exercise thereof; or abridging the freedom of speech or of the press; or the right of the people peaceably to assemble and to petition the government for a redress of grievances.

Amendment 6 (adapted)

In all criminal proceedings, the accused shall enjoy the right to a speedy trial by an impartial jury of the state and district wherein the crime shall have been committed.

Item B **The UK constitution**

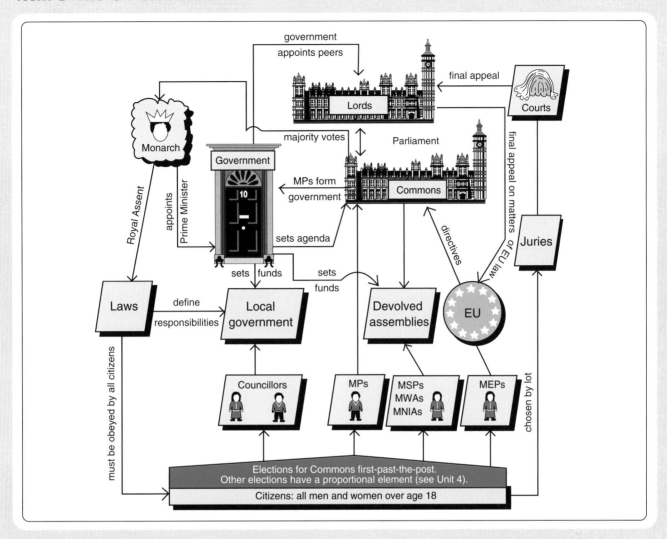

Item C **The British and American constitutions compared**

This cartoon compares the rigidity of the American constitution with the flexibility of the British constitution.

Questions

1. Judging from Items A and B, do you agree with the point being made in Item C?

2. Using Item A, draw a diagram of the American constitution in a style similar to that used in Item B.

3. Judging from Item B, would you say that the principle of separation of the powers is put into practice in the UK? Give reasons for your answer.

4. 'The capacity of the UK's constitution to evolve is its major strength.' Explain and discuss this statement.

11.6 A unitary state

A state is described as 'unitary' when the powers of government are held by a central authority, or set of authorities. Local or regional authorities may exist, but any powers they possess have been granted to them by the central authority and could be withdrawn by that authority. This differs from a federal state, such as the USA, where the constitution guarantees certain powers to regional (ie state) governments and to the central government.

Whether or not it is accurate to describe the UK today as a 'unitary state' is explored in Unit 18 (see Section 18.1).

11.7 What is parliamentary sovereignty?

According to the principle of parliamentary sovereignty, Parliament is the only body that can make law for the UK. No authority can overrule or change the laws which Parliament has made. This principle, therefore gives statute law (Acts of Parliament) precedence over the other sources of the constitution.

The principle of parliamentary sovereignty, however, cannot be found in any Act of Parliament. It is a part of common law which established itself as judicial rule in the late 17th century. Norton (1982 & 1988) points out that, if the principle of parliamentary sovereignty were to be part of statute law, it could not have the pre-eminence claimed for it. This is because parliamentary sovereignty implies that Parliament can pass, change or repeal any law it likes and is not bound by the laws made by previous Parliaments. If the principle of parliamentary sovereignty was found in an Act of Parliament, it would be possible for Parliament to repeal this Act and do away with the principle.

As it stands, the principle of parliamentary sovereignty means that British courts are obliged to enforce any law passed by Parliament. This is very different from the USA, for example, where the Supreme Court can declare a law passed by Congress to be unconstitutional.

11.8 Limits on parliamentary sovereignty

Political developments that have taken place since the late 19th century have ensured that there is good reason to argue that, today, parliamentary sovereignty is limited.

1. The growth of a mass electorate

When the principle of parliamentary sovereignty was established, less than 5% of the adult male population and no women had the right to vote - see Box 11.7. Today, virtually all adults aged 18 and over have this right. As a result, the House of Commons, is now elected by popular vote. So where does sovereignty now lie - with Parliament or with the electorate?

2. The party system

The growth of a mass electorate in the late 19th century led to the development of the party system (see Unit 8). This, in turn, altered the balance of power between Parliament and the executive (in favour of the executive). Since the government is now generally formed from the largest party in the House of Commons, it can usually rely on its majority to secure parliamentary approval for its proposals. Most laws are, therefore, proposed not by Parliament but by government. Parliamentary sovereignty, therefore, is limited.

3. Referendums

It can be argued that the use of referendums limits parliamentary sovereignty since important decisions are made by the electorate and not Parliament. The use of referendums in the UK is described in detail in Unit 5 (Sections 5.19 - 5.23).

4. Extra-parliamentary pressure

There have been occasions when powerful pressure groups outside Parliament have been able to frustrate attempts by Parliament to introduce new laws. In the 1970s, for example, trade unions forced Parliament to amend the 1971 Industrial Relations Act and in the late 1980s extra-parliamentary action forced the government to replace the poll tax with the council tax (see Box 11.8). These examples suggest that, in practice, the principle of parliamentary sovereignty is limited.

Box 11.8 Extra-parliamentary action: the campaign against the poll tax

This photograph shows a demonstration against the poll tax in 1990.

Box 11.7 Growth of a mass electorate

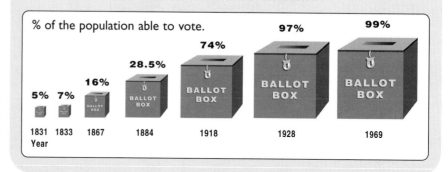

% of the population able to vote.

Year	1831	1833	1867	1884	1918	1928	1969
%	5%	7%	16%	28.5%	74%	97%	99%

5. International agreements and treaties

The UK has, at various times, committed itself to international agreements and treaties which place upon it certain obligations. For example, in 1949 the UK joined NATO and, as a result, handed over some control over defence policy and foreign policy.

Theoretically, of course, commitments like this do not infringe parliamentary sovereignty since Parliament could decide to ignore or cancel its commitments. But, in practice, the political (and often economic) consequences of so doing make such actions unlikely - the more so with the increasingly global nature of political and economic events and relationships.

The possible limits placed on parliamentary sovereignty by external agreements and treaties is thrown into sharpest focus by the UK's membership of the European Union - see below.

6. Membership of the EU

Membership of the European Union continues to raise important questions about the limitations on the sovereignty of the UK Parliament. Under the terms of membership, Britain is a member of the EU 'in perpetuity' (for ever). EU law is binding on all member states and, therefore, takes precedence over British domestic law. The UK Parliament can express its disapproval in the case of amendments to the Treaty of Rome (the founding treaty signed by all members of the EU), but otherwise EU legislation automatically becomes law within the UK, irrespective of what the British Parliament thinks about it. The 1986 Single European Act and the Maastricht Treaty can be seen as reducing UK sovereignty since they extended the range of policy areas on which the EU can legislate (see also Unit 12).

On the face of it, this seems to breach the principle of the sovereignty of Parliament. But (despite the enormous economic and political consequences of doing so), Parliament could agree to repeal previous legislation and withdraw from the EU. By doing so, it would demonstrate that parliamentary sovereignty still exists.

7. The 1998 Human Rights Act

There were concerns that the incorporation of elements of the European Convention on Human Rights into British law with the 1998 Human Rights Act would further erode parliamentary sovereignty. The constitutional significance of this piece of legislation is examined in Unit 13.

11.9 What is the 'rule of law'?

In 1885, the first edition of A.V. Dicey's *An Introduction to the Study of the Law of the Constitution* was published. This book became one of the most influential works of authority on the British constitution. Dicey described the rule of law as one of the 'twin pillars' of the constitution (the other being parliamentary sovereignty - see Sections 11.7 and 11.8 above). He saw the rule (or supremacy) of law as the ultimate source of authority to which all, including the institutions of the state, are subject - see Box 11.9.

According to Dicey in Box 11.9, therefore, rule of law has three main elements:

Box 11.9 Dicey on the rule of law

When we say that the rule of law is characteristic of the English constitution, we generally include under one expression at least three distinct though kindred conceptions. We mean in the first place that no man is punishable or can be lawfully made to suffer in body or goods except for a distinct breach of law established in the ordinary legal manner before the ordinary courts of the land. We mean in the second place not only that no man is above the law but that every man, whatever be his rank or condition, is subject to the ordinary law of the realm and amenable to the jurisdiction of the ordinary tribunals. Third, the general principles of the constitution (as, for example, the right to personal liberty or the right of public meeting) are the result of judicial decisions determining the rights of private persons in particular cases brought before the courts.

Source: Dicey 1885.

1. Nobody should be punished unless they have broken the law.
2. The same laws should apply to officials of the state just as to the ordinary people.
3. The rights of the individual do not stem from decisions made by the executive (government), but from judgements made in individual cases by independent judges.

Writing more than a century later, Moyra Grant described the rule of law as follows:

'Essentially the concept of the rule of law seeks to equate law and justice, ie it seeks to ensure that the law and the legal system are fair and equitable. This is an idea which is hard - perhaps impossible - to achieve in practice.' (Grant 1994, p.51)

While Dicey argued that the rule of law had three main elements, Grant identifies five. By examining these five elements, she suggests, it is possible to see the strengths and weaknesses of a constitution which relies on the rule of law. Box 11.10 on page 213 summarises Grant's findings.

11.10 The rule of law as a constitutional check

Grant concludes that the rule of law is best seen as a set of ideal principles, rather than as a description of what actually happens in practice. As an ideal, the rule of law is seen as a protection against the arbitrary and excessive use of government power. In those societies which have a written, codified constitution, protection against arbitrary government may be built in and overseen by the courts. In the USA, for example, the constitution gives the Supreme Court the power to declare that laws passed by Congress are unconstitutional.

No such check applies in the UK. This explains why Dicey regarded the rule of law as one of the twin pillars of the constitution. He claimed that it acted as a balancing mechanism which kept parliamentary sovereignty in check. So, although the courts in the UK have no power to decide on the content of laws passed by Parliament (because of

Box 11.10   Grant's five elements of the rule of law

Element	Problems
1. Legal equality Everyone, including governments should be equally subject to the same laws, and should have equal access to the law.	In reality, this ideal is not achieved. In general, only the very rich can afford to take legal action in the law courts. Also, some people are exempt from some laws - for example MPs (through parliamentary privilege) are immune from prosecution for slander for what they say in Parliament. The monarch is above the law.
2. The just law There is no such thing as an unjust law (justice and the law are the same thing).	The rule of law can be undermined in the following ways. First, some laws are not seen as just by a majority of people (eg the poll tax, which many people refused to pay on the grounds that it was unjust). Second, judges are not always consistent in their sentencing practices. Third, miscarriages of justice are known to have occurred.
3. Legal certainty The law should amount to a clear statement of rights, obligations and limits to power, especially the power of the state and government. It should not be uncertain, arbitrary, ambiguous or contradictory.	The law is often uncertain because, in enforcing it, it has to be interpreted, and interpretations can differ. Also, if the government is found in court to have broken the law, it may then choose to change the law rather than to follow the court ruling.
4. Innocent until proved guilty Everyone is innocent until proven guilty.	This element is compromised by: (1) the 1994 Criminal Justice Act which eroded an accused person's right to remain silent; and (2) media coverage which can prejudice jurors' attitudes before a trial takes place.
5. Independence of the judiciary Judges are free from personal bias and external political pressure (to ensure that justice is an end in itself and not merely a political tool).	This element may not be fully achieved. Senior judges, as members of the House of Lords, are also part of the legislature. Also, the Lord Chancellor (the most senior judge) is a member of all three branches of government (judiciary, legislature and executive) and therefore potentially open to conflicts of interest (but see Unit 13 for impending constitutional changes).

Source: Grant 1994.

parliamentary sovereignty), they may be called upon to review allegations that government ministers or officials have acted illegally.

The practice

Some constitutional analysts have raised doubts about the practical effectiveness of the rule of law as a check. McAulsan & McEldowney (1985), for example, argue that parliamentary sovereignty has now taken precedence over the political and legal constraints embodied in constitutional conventions and the rule of law. This is partly because, in practice, 'parliamentary sovereignty' has come to mean the wishes of the government of the day. A similar argument was made in a lecture given by Lord Hailsham - see Box 11.11.

McAulsan & McEldowney argue that, particularly since the Conservative Party came to power in 1979, governments have taken the rule of law less seriously. These authors provide a list of examples of ministerial actions which, they allege, amount to 'abuse and excess power'. In short, they argue that there has been:

> 'A general pattern of contempt for...the constraints on power imposed by the checks and balances...involved in a constitution based upon the concept of limited government.' (McAulsan & McEldowney 1985, p.32)

Similar criticisms have been made of Labour governments since 1997.

Box 11.11   Elective dictatorship

In a lecture delivered in 1976, Lord Hailsham claimed that the British system of government had become an 'elective dictatorship'. He argued that, because governments in the UK are usually formed from the largest party represented in the House of Commons, the power arising from parliamentary sovereignty had come, effectively, to rest with the government. At the same time, the checks on this power, such as the rule of law, had become weak. Britain had become a 'dictatorship' in the sense that one body - the government - monopolised power, but it was an 'elective dictatorship' because most members of the government were elected representatives.

There are others, however, who argue that the rule of law can still be seen as an effective check on the actions of modern governments. Jowell (1989), for example, argued that the courts have become more prepared to uphold the rule of law against executive actions which appear either to exceed the powers granted by legislation or to bypass appropriate legal procedures. He sees the rule of law as providing limits and restricting the abuses of power which can occur under any government in modern times.

Main points   Sections 11.6 - 11.10

- According to the principle of parliamentary sovereignty, Parliament is the only body that can make law for the UK. This gives statute law precedence over other sources of the constitution.
- The principle of parliamentary sovereignty has been modified as a result of: (1) the growth of a mass electorate; (2) the development of a party system; (3) the use of referendums; (4) extra-parliamentary pressure; and (5) signing international agreements.
- EU law is binding on all member states and therefore takes precedence over British domestic law. Parliament could repeal previous legislation and withdraw from the EU but, in practice, this is unlikely.
- Dicey argued that the rule of law has three main elements: (1) nobody can be punished unless convicted by a court; (2) the law applies equally to everyone; and (3) the general principles of the constitution arise out of decisions made by an independent judiciary.
- Grant (1994) argued that the rule of law has five main elements: (1) legal equality; (2) just law; (3) legal certainty; (4) innocent until proven guilty; and (5) the independence of the judiciary.
- There is a debate about the effectiveness of the rule of law as a check on parliamentary sovereignty.

Activity 11.2 Parliamentary sovereignty

Item A The EU and sovereignty

Membership of the EU has brought a new role for the British courts. Under the terms of EU membership, if there is a clash between the provisions of European law and domestic UK law, then the European law must win out. Under the provisions of the Treaty of Rome, cases which reach the highest domestic court of appeal (in Britain, the House of Lords) must be referred to the European Court of Justice. In 1990, the European Court of Justice (ECJ) in the Factortame case ruled that courts in the UK had the power to suspend an Act of Parliament which appeared to breach an EU law. The House of Lords then restrained the minister from enforcing the Act. The effect of this was to challenge the principle of parliamentary sovereignty because it challenged the idea that the decisions of Parliament are binding and can be set aside by no body other than Parliament. The ECJ's ruling meant that British courts could now set aside Acts passed by Parliament. This does not mean, however, that the principle of parliamentary sovereignty is dead. Parliament retains the power to repeal the 1972 European Communities Act. Furthermore, if Parliament passed an Act explicitly overriding European law, it is likely that the British courts would enforce the Act. While the principle of parliamentary sovereignty may not be dead, it is clearly under challenge. The power of government is no longer concentrated in the Cabinet, but is shared with the European institutions. As a result, the constitution is not what it used to be.

Adapted from Norton 1994.

Item B Two horses

'The UK government has seated Parliament on two horses, one straining towards the preservation of parliamentary sovereignty, the other galloping in the general direction of Community [EU] law supremacy.'

Source: De Smith in Street & Brazier 1981, p.91.

Item C The UK constitution

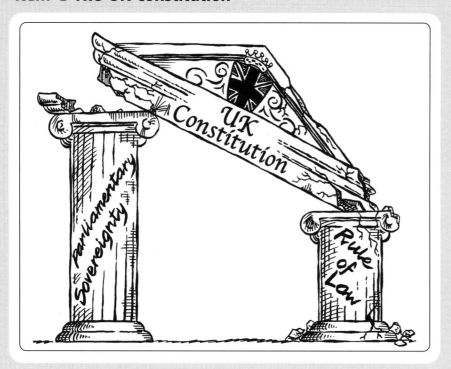

Questions

1. To what extent did the developments described in Item A erode the principle of parliamentary sovereignty?

2. At the time you are reading this unit, which horse appears to be gaining the most ground? Explain your answer.

3. How accurate is the view of the UK constitution presented in Item C?

4. Has the principle of parliamentary sovereignty outlived its usefulness? Give arguments for and against.

11.11 *The role of the monarchy*

The formal way of describing the British government is to say that the UK has a parliamentary government under a constitutional monarchy. Norton (1992) points out that this has resulted in the development of a whole series of institutions whose relationships are governed by convention rather than statute - see Box 11.12.

Box 11.12 A constitutional monarchy

'Parliamentary government under a constitutional monarchy...refers to government through rather than by Parliament, with the system being presided over by a largely ceremonial monarch. Government is elected through Parliament and is expected to formulate - to 'make' - public policy. The role of Parliament is to scrutinise and, if necessary, modify that policy before giving its assent. The monarch - as a neutral figure representing the unity of the nation - then formally gives the final seal of approval.'

Norton 1992, pp.30-31.

The official view of the monarch's constitutional position is given in Box 11.13.

The monarchy and political power

Although, as Box 11.13 indicates, the monarch does have an important political role to play, in practice, power has been substantially removed from the personal control of the monarch. A formal link remains and is reflected in official titles such as 'Her Majesty's government', but executive power has come to be employed by ministers or their agents. As

Box 11.13 The 'official' view

'The Queen personifies the state. In law, she is head of the executive, an integral part of the legislature, head of the judiciary, the commander-in-chief of the armed forces of the Crown and the "supreme governor" of the established Church of England. As a result of a long process of evolution during which the monarchy's absolute power has been progressively reduced, the Queen acts on the advice of her ministers. Britain is governed by Her Majesty's government in the name of the Queen. Within this framework, and despite of a trend during the past 100 years towards giving powers directly to ministers, the Queen still takes part in some important acts of government. These include summoning, proroguing (discontinuing until the next session without dissolution) and dissolving Parliament; and giving royal assent to Bills passed by Parliament. The Queen also formally appoints many important office holders.'

Source: HMSO 1994, p.8.

Norton puts it:

'Ministers remain legally responsible to the Queen for their actions, but, by convention, are responsible to Parliament.' (Norton 1982, p.14)

In addition, membership of the EU has had an impact. Since EU law takes precedence over UK law, it is, therefore, no longer the case that all laws effective in the UK receive Royal Assent.

There are, however, two areas where there is at least the potential for the monarch personally to exercise power. These two areas are outlined in Box 11.14 on page 216.

Box 11.14 Areas where the monarch might exercise power

1. The power to appoint the Prime Minister

By convention, the monarch invites the Leader of the largest party in the House of Commons to form a new government after a general election has been held. There is, however, always the possibility of a 'hung' Parliament - a Parliament in which no single party has an overall majority of seats in the Commons. If this were to happen, the choice of Prime Minister and, therefore, the choice of party or parties from which the government could be drawn, might not be obvious. In such a case, the monarch would play a decisive role in determining the nature of the government.

2. The power to dissolve Parliament

The power of the monarch to dissolve Parliament could also lead to the monarch's personal involvement in politics. Suppose, for example, that a newly formed minority government wished to call a general election in an attempt to strengthen its position. The monarch could decide not to dissolve Parliament and invite the Leader of another party to form a coalition government (a government made up of politicians from more than one party). Constitutional precedents offer no clear guidance in such a case.

11.12 Is the monarchy under threat?

There is evidence to suggest that attitudes towards the monarchy have been changing. Today, it would be difficult to claim, for example, that members of the royal family are just as popular or as well-respected as they were in the1950s. In the 1950s, the monarchy appeared to be above criticism. When the broadcaster and journalist Malcolm Muggeridge wrote an article which asked whether Britain really needed a Queen, he was sacked by a Sunday newspaper and by the BBC. Not only does this indicate the strength of support for the monarchy at the time, it also suggests how deferential people were towards the royal family. Even in the 1980s, over 85% of people told opinion pollsters that they supported the monarchy.

By the mid-1990s, however, opinion had shifted significantly. A survey carried out in 1994, for example, found that 66% of those questioned thought that the monarchy should continue indefinitely and 26% wanted the monarchy to be abolished at some point (*Guardian*, 19 September 1994). The same poll showed that support for the monarchy varied according to age. Among the over-55s, 74% were in favour but among the under-35s only 48% were. In a poll taken a few days before the death of Diana (Prince Charles' ex-wife) in 1997, only 48% of all respondents agreed that the country would be worse off without a royal family (*Guardian*, 12 August 1997). Following Diana's death, however, attitudes towards the monarchy became more ambiguous. Polls indicated that although support for the institution had increased, a large majority wanted the monarchy to be modernised. This trend has continued. In a poll taken in 2000, for example, although 70% of people were in favour of retaining the monarchy in the short term, only a minority of people felt sure that it would exist in 50 or 100 years time.

There are two main reasons for the longer-term decline in the monarchy's popularity, at least in its present form. First, the behaviour of individual members of the royal family has failed to meet the standards expected of prominent public figures. The well-publicised break-up of a number of marriages, including that of the heir to the throne, and other personal scandals and rumours have given the impression that the royal family is in crisis. Second, the cost of supporting the monarchy, and of maintaining a royal family, has been criticised.

The arguments for and against the monarchy are outlined in Box 11.15.

Box 11.15 Arguments for and against the monarchy

For	Against
The main arguments in support of the monarchy are the following:	The main arguments against the monarchy are as follows:
• despite the bad publicity, it is still a popular public institution	• the hereditary principle is not acceptable in a democratic society - people should gain positions on merit not because they are born into a particular family
• the monarchy symbolises national unity and purpose both to people living in Britain (helping to integrate society) and to the outside world	• far from uniting the nation, the privileges enjoyed by the extended royal family emphasise to ordinary people just how great a divide there is from top to bottom in British society
• through its maintenance of British traditions, the monarchy provides continuity in an otherwise rapidly changing society	• the popularity of the monarchy has declined and no longer commands universal respect or support
• the cost of sustaining the monarchy is less than the income from tourism and trade which the monarchy generates (it is also a great deal less than supporting a presidency in some countries - for example, the USA)	• because of the behaviour of individual members of the royal family, the monarchy no longer provides a model of idealised family life
• the hereditary principle keeps the royal family above party politics (a disassociation from party politics would be essential in the event of a hung Parliament since the monarch would need to make decisions about the formation of a new government - any alternative - such as a presidency - would automatically introduce a party political element).	• the cost of maintaining a monarchy is too great - it is an unnecessary burden on the taxpayer since income generated by tourism does not directly feed back into public finances and, in any case, abolishing the monarchy would not necessarily reduce tourism
	• there is no reason why the function of the Head of State could not be performed by an elected president or even by the holder of an existing post (former MP Tony Benn, for example, has suggested that the Speaker of the House of Commons could be given the power to dissolve Parliament and to choose the Prime Minister - see Unit 14 for a description of the Speaker's role).

11.13 Republicanism and modernisation

Since the 1990s, here has been increasing speculation about what would happen if the UK was to become a republic (a republic is a state whose head is not a monarch). Most British republicans argue that the monarchy should be replaced by an elected president with limited powers rather than a strong executive president like that in the USA or France:

> 'A British President would be a figurehead and honest broker, chosen by a college of politicians, as in Germany, or elected directly by the people, as in Ireland. Members of the royal family would be free to stay in Britain, just as members of the Hapsburg royal family are free to live in the Republic of Austria. But the wealth and buildings they held in the public name would be taken away.'
> (*Independent on Sunday*, 28 October 1994)

Traditionally, republicanism in Britain has been associated with those on the political left. Since the 1990s, however, calls for a major re-think on the future of the monarchy have come from the political right, too.

Modernising the monarchy

As an alternative to outright abolition, some writers have suggested that the monarchy should be significantly modernised. A report published by the Fabian Society in 2003 argues that the monarchy's constitutional position needs clarifying and that the role of the monarchy should be 'depoliticised' (Fabian Commission 2003). The report recommended reform of the royal prerogative powers exercised by the Prime Minister and the government. Instead, it argues, these powers should be put on a statutory basis, with Parliament deciding who should carry them out.

The Fabian report also believes that, to maintain public support, the private lives of the royal family should be separated from their public duties. It therefore recommends a reduction in the number of royals receiving public funding and taxing the royal family on their private income and wealth (including levying inheritance tax on private properties such as Balmoral and Sandringham).

Item B of Activity 11.3 below gives details of another set of proposals to modernise the monarchy.

Main points   Sections 11.11 - 11.13

- **The UK has a parliamentary government under a constitutional monarchy. Although the monarch's duties are mainly ceremonial, some important powers remain notably: (1) appointing the Prime Minister; and (2) dissolving Parliament.**
- **By the 1990s, attitudes to the monarchy were changing. A major reason for this has been the behaviour of members of the royal family which has failed to meet the standards expected of prominent public figures.**
- **Supporters of the monarchy argue that: (1) it is still popular; (2) it symbolises national unity; (3) it provides continuity in a rapidly changing society; (4) it is cost effective; and (5) the hereditary principle keeps the royal family above party politics.**
- **Opponents of the monarchy argue that: (1) its privileges emphasise the divide in British society; (2) its popularity has declined; (3) it no longer provides an ideal model of family life; (4) its cost is too great; (5) an elected representative could perform its functions; and (6) the hereditary principle is not acceptable in a democracy.**
- **There are three options for the future of the monarchy: (1) it could be retained in its present form; (2) it could be abolished (the UK would become a republic); or (3) it could be modernised.**

Activity 11.3 *The role of the monarchy*

Item A **Monarchy in the UK?**

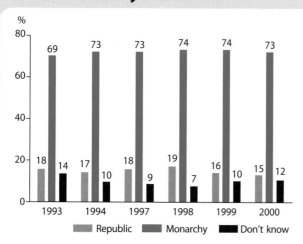

(i) This chart shows the percentage of people supporting the monarchy between 1993 and 2000.

The data for both charts was collected by MORI in 2000.

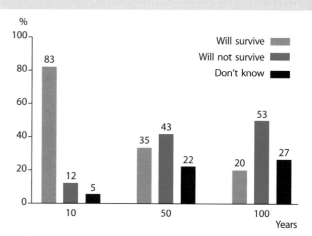

(ii) This chart shows the percentage of people who believe that the monarchy will still exist in ten years, 50 years and 100 years.

Item B Modernising the monarchy

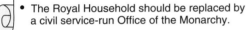

Demos' report on the monarchy - main points

- Automatic right of succession of the heir to the throne should be abolished and the public should have the right of veto over a new monarch.

- Royals should receive state education and be treated on the NHS.

- The monarch should not automatically be head of the Church of England.

- The monarch should become a roving ambassador to 'heal bitterness about Britain's past around the world'.

- The Speaker of the Commons should take responsibility for appointing the Prime Minister and dissolving Parliament.

- The need for Royal Assent allowing Bills to become law should be abolished.

- A Minister of Justice should take responsibility for appointing judges.

- The Royal Household should be replaced by a civil service-run Office of the Monarchy.

In September 1998, the think tank Demos published a report which argued that the monarchy required dramatic reform if it was to match public expectations. The report ruled out a republic. Instead, it aimed to modernise the monarchy by allowing it to keep its ceremonial role, but removing its political and religious functions. The Queen would lose her power to dissolve Parliament, appoint Prime Ministers or give the Royal Assent to Bills. Church and Crown would be separated. The report also called for a democratic monarch whose legitimacy is drawn from the will of the people. There would be no automatic right of succession. Rather, the people would be asked whether they support the heir to the throne in a referendum. If the heir was rejected, a second referendum would be held. If the next in line was also rejected, there would be a third referendum. The report also suggested regular referendums throughout a reign to ensure the monarch retains the support of the people. Other ideas in the report include: abolishing the civil list, replacing royal courtiers with civil servants and setting up an independent honours commission. In a poll published on 6 September 1998, 60% of people thought the monarchy should be modernised and 49% thought the Queen should give up her political role.

Source: The *Guardian*, 7 September 1998.

Questions

1. How could the information in Item A be used to support
   a) retaining the monarchy in its present form?
   b) abolishing the monarchy?
   c) modernising the monarchy?

2. a) How would the role of the monarch change if the proposals outlined in Item B were put into practice?
   b) What are the benefits and drawbacks of these proposals?

References

Dearlove & Saunders (1991) Dearlove, J. & Saunders, P., *Introduction to British Politics: Analysing a Capitalist Democracy*, Polity Press, 1991.

Dicey (1885) Dicey, A.V., *An Introduction to the Study of the Law of the Constitution*, Macmillan, 1959.

Dunleavy et al. (2003) Dunleavy, P., Gamble A., Heffernan, R. & Peele, G. (eds), *Developments in British Politics 7*, Palgrave Macmillan, 2003.

Fabian Commission (2003) The Fabian Commission, *The Future of the Monarchy*, Fabian Society, 2003.

Gamble (2003) Gamble, A., 'Remaking the constitution' in *Dunleavy et al. (2003)*.

Grant (1994) Grant, M., 'The rule of law - theory and practice', *Talking Politics*, Vol.7.1, Autumn 1994.

HMSO (1994) Central Office of Information, *The British System of Government*, HMSO, 1994.

Jowell (1989) Jowell, J., 'The rule of law today' in *Jowell & Oliver (1989)*.

Jowell & Oliver (1989) Jowell, J. & Oliver, D. (eds), *The Changing Constitution*, Clarendon Press, 1989.

Kingdom (1991) Kingdom, J., *Government and Politics in Britain: an Introduction*, Polity Press, 1991.

McAulsan & McEldowney (1985) McAulsan, P. & McEldowney, J.F. (eds), *Law, Legitimacy and the Constitution*, Sweet & Maxwell, 1985.

Norton (1982) Norton, P., *The Constitution in Flux*, Martin Robertson, 1982.

Norton (1988) Norton, P., 'The changing constitution - part 2', *Talking Politics*, Vol.1.1, Autumn 1988.

Norton (1992) Norton, P., 'The constitution' in *Wale (1992)*.

Norton (1994) Norton, P., 'The constitution in question', *Politics Review*, Vol.3.4, April 1994.

Politics Review (2003) 'The future of the monarchy', *Politics Review*, Vol.13.2, November 2003.

Street & Brazier (1981) Street, H. & Brazier, R. (eds), *Constitutional and Administrative Law*, Penguin 1981.

Wale (1992) Wale, W. (ed.), *Developments in Politics*, Vol.3, Causeway Press, 1992.

12.1 Supranational and intergovernmental institutions

An important characteristic of the EU is its mixture of 'supranational' and 'intergovernmental' institutions. A supranational organisation is one in which institutions are created which have powers above that of any individual nation's government. An intergovernmental organisation, on the other hand, is one in which each member state has the right to veto any measure to protect its national interests. The way in which the EU works is that, regarding some issues, member states are able to veto proposals which they feel are disadvantageous. Regarding other issues, however, decisions are made at the European level and must be implemented by members regardless of their reservations.

Decisions in the EU are made by four main institutions - the Council of Ministers, the European Commission, the European Parliament and the European Court of Justice. Two consultative bodies also make an impact on some decisions - the Economic and Social Committee and the Committee of the Regions.

12.2 The Council of Ministers

The Council of Ministers (now often referred to as the Council of the European Union) is the EU's ultimate decision-making body. Its job is to discuss and approve (or reject) proposals drawn up by the Commission. Unlike other EU institutions, members of the Council of Ministers directly represent the interests of their member state. The Council of Ministers has the power to issue regulations, directives, decisions, recommendations or resolutions:

> 'The Council has the power to make regulations (or Community laws) which are binding on member states and directly applicable. Directives are equally binding as to the aims to be achieved, but leave national authorities to decide on the methods of carrying them out. In addition, the Council can issue decisions binding those to whom they are addressed, whether member states, firms or private individuals. Recommendations and opinions are not binding. The Council can also indicate a general policy direction through resolutions.' (HMSO 1992, pp.17-18)

A revolving council

The Council of Ministers is, in reality, not a single council. It is a series of councils. The ministers responsible for the matter under discussion attend. So, if, for example, an environmental matter is under discussion, then the environment minister from each member state attends. The member state holding the presidency of the Council of Ministers chairs its meetings. The presidency is held by each member state for six months on a rota basis. The three areas most commonly discussed by the Council are foreign affairs, economics and finance, and agriculture. The Council of Foreign Ministers has a coordinating role, though there is a tendency to refer matters to the twice-yearly summits of heads of government (see below).

Voting procedure

The voting procedure used by the Council of Ministers depends on the matter under discussion. There are three different kinds of votes. Some matters require unanimity - ie all the ministers must be in agreement. Other matters require a simple majority. Many EU issues and policies, however, are determined by 'qualified majority' voting. Under this system, each member state is allocated a certain number of votes, with roughly one vote allocated for every four million people in its population (the allocation of votes is designed to favour the smaller states to prevent their views always being swamped). No single member state can block a proposal. At least three member states (including two of the big states) must vote against a proposal for it to fail. The number of matters decided by the qualified voting system increased after the passing of the Single European Act in 1986 and was further extended after the Amsterdam Treaty was signed in 1997. The accession of ten new member states in May 2004 has also led to a change - with effect from November 2004, as illustrated by Box 12.1 on page 220.

COREPER

Before proposals are put before the Council, they are considered by the Committee of Permanent Representatives (COREPER) which is made up of senior civil servants from the member states. This committee is able to resolve many of the issues under discussion and often the meeting of the Council of Ministers which follows acts merely as a rubber stamp. The Council of Ministers has its own staff of 2,000.

The European Council

Established in 1974, the European Council was set up to try to break the log-jam in Community policy-making. The European Council brings together all the heads of member governments, their foreign ministers and the President of the Commission. Meetings are held twice a year (though extra meetings may be called in exceptional circumstances). They are always held in the country of the member state holding the presidency of the Council of Ministers. The aim of these meetings is to discuss major policy issues:

> 'The growing dominance of the European Council...is one of the biggest EU changes since its inception. When it began in the early 1970s, the idea was that heads of government should meet informally for a fireside chat. Now each presidency works towards a climax of decisions at summits normally held in June and December. And the conclusions from each summit tend to map out the agenda for the whole EU.' (Economist, 8 March 1997)

Box 12.1 Allocation of votes in Council of Ministers before and after November 2004

Country	Votes prior to November 2004	Votes from November 2004
Austria	4	10
Belgium	5	12
Cyprus	N/A	4
Czech Republic	N/A	12
Denmark	3	7
Estonia	N/A	4
Finland	3	7
France	10	29
Germany	10	29
Greece	5	12
Hungary	N/A	12
Ireland	3	7
Italy	10	29
Latvia	N/A	4
Lithuania	N/A	7
Luxembourg	2	4
Malta	N/A	3
Netherlands	5	13
Poland	N/A	27
Portugal	5	12
Slovakia	N/A	7
Slovenia	N/A	4
Spain	8	27
Sweden	4	10
United Kingdom	10	29

Under the pre-November 2004 allocation of votes, the minimum number of votes required to secure a 'qualified majority' in the Council of Ministers was 62 (71%) out of the total of 87 votes.

From November 2004, a minimum of 232 (72%) votes out of a new total of 321 will be necessary for a 'qualified majority' to be attained. Furthermore, a majority (sometimes two thirds) of member states must approve a decision.

12.3 The European Commission

The Commission is the permanent bureaucracy of the EU. The President of the Commission is chosen by the European Council but is also subject to the European Parliament's formal approval. The Commission is headed by a college of commissioners, or 'executive', whose members are nominated by the member states in consultation with the President.

The number of commissioners appointed from January 1995 was 20 (two each from the five largest members, namely Britain, Germany, France, Italy and Spain, and one each from the ten other member states). However, following the May 2004 enlargement of the EU, there will be just one commissioner for each member state.

The Commission's role

The Commission's primary responsibility is to initiate European legislation. Each commissioner has responsibility for a particular sector which is allocated by the President of the Commission. In March 2004, for example, the two British commissioners were Chris Patten (External Relations) and Neil Kinnock (Vice President). Patten was appointed in 1995.

Kinnock was a commissioner responsible for transport policy between 1995 and 1999. In 1999, he became Vice President. Commissioners have to abandon any national allegiance. Since 1995, the length of tenure of office has been set at five years. The role of the Commission is outlined in Box 12.2.

Box 12.2 The role of the EU Commission

The European Commission is the executive organ of the Community, ensuring that Community rules and provisions of the treaties are implemented and observed correctly. It puts forward policy proposals and executes the decisions taken by the Council [of Ministers]. It attends all Council meetings, where it participates in discussions as an equal partner. The Commission administers the structural funds established by the Community, prepares a draft Budget which must be approved by the Council and the European Parliament and negotiates international agreements on behalf of the Community.

Source: HMSO 1992, p.18.

The work of the Commission is organised through 36 'Directorates-General', each of which corresponds to a particular policy or set of related policies.

The bureaucracy

The Commission has a large administrative staff of around 20,000 people, based in both Brussels and Luxembourg. The Commission works, in theory, in all the members' languages, though, in practice, English and French predominate. Around 15% of the Commission's staff are employed in linguistic work (translating and interpreting). It should be noted that, although the Commission is often criticised for being over-bureaucratic, in fact:

> 'The Commission employs fewer people than the French Ministry of Culture and the British Lord Chancellor's office, neither of which is a major department of state. It is smaller than the governments of cities like Amsterdam and Madrid.' (Geddes 1993, pp.43-44)

Civil servants working for the Commission must be completely neutral and objective. They must act in the interests of the EU as a whole, rather than for their individual member states.

Powers

The Commission can investigate any complaint that the principles laid down in the treaties signed by member states have been breached and impose fines if it finds that rules have been broken or disregarded. When requested by an individual state, it can consider whether there is a case for a temporary waiving of rules. If a member state does not fulfil its obligations, the Commission can take it to the European Court of Justice (see below).

12.4 The European Parliament

The European Parliament (EP) is located in Strasbourg (see Box 12.3 on page 221), although its committees are normally held in Brussels. Since 1979, its members (Members of the

European Parliament - MEPS) have been directly elected every five years. The number of MEPs has risen from 518 in 1989 to 626 in 2004. This reflects the growth of the EU (in 1990, for example, East and West Germany were unified and in 1995 three new member states joined the EU).

Box 12.3 The EU Parliament in Strasbourg

This photo shows the EU Parliament in Strasbourg.

Following the enlargement of the EU in May 2004, the total number of MEPs will be increased, in stages, to 786 by 2009. Some existing member states, however, will see their representation reduced slightly. For example, Britain, France and Italy will each see their number of MEPs reduced from 87 to 78.

The powers of the EP have been restricted by the fact that the final decision on legislation remains with the Council of Ministers. For this reason, the EP has often been accused of being little more than a talking shop. Since the late 1980s, however, the EP's formal and informal influence has been growing.

Cooperation procedure

When the Single European Act came into operation in 1987, the so-called 'cooperation procedure' gave the EP new powers. The cooperation procedure allows the EP to become involved in the decision-making process at a number of different stages:

'Under the cooperation procedure, there is a second reading process. On first reading, the Council is confined to adopting 'common positions' which must be referred back to the EP. In making the reference back, the Council is obliged to provide the EP with explanations for common positions - including giving reasons for any EP amendments which have been rejected - and, if the EP is dissatisfied, it can exert further pressure at its second reading by amending or rejecting common positions by votes that include an absolute majority of its members.' (Nugent 1994, pp.176-77)

Although, under the cooperation procedure, the EP cannot veto measures outright, it can put considerable pressure on the Commission and the Council:

'If the Parliament rejects the Council's position, then unanimity by the Council is required for the proposal to come into force as Community law. If the Parliament proposes amendments, the Council votes by qualified majority where the Commission endorses them and unanimously where the Commission has been unable to do so.' (HMSO 1992, p.21)

Co-decision procedure

The Maastricht Treaty gave the European Parliament further powers by introducing the co-decision procedure. This works as follows:

'[The co-decision procedure] is similar to the cooperation procedure up to the point when the EP issues its second reading position. The procedure then changes, for if the Council cannot accept the EP's position as indicated by a vote of the majority of its component members, and if the differences between the two institutions cannot be resolved in a Conciliation Committee composed of an equal number of representatives from both the Council and the Parliament, the EP can prevent the text from being adopted (again by a vote of an absolute majority of its members) if the Council seeks to press ahead. In other words, the EP has a potential veto on legislative proposals which are subject to this procedure.' (Nugent 1994, p.177)

The 1997 Amsterdam Treaty extended the use of the co-decision procedure. It removed the old cooperation procedure and replaced it with the co-decision procedure in all cases except those dealing with economic and monetary union. The aim was to provide the European Parliament with a greater role in decision-making and to make decision-making more transparent. It was also intended to reduce the 'democratic deficit' in the European Union.

MEPs sit in the European Parliament on the basis of party group, rather than according to country. Box 12.4 shows the political groups which the UK's MEPs sit with in the European Parliament.

Box 12.4 Political groups to which the UK's MEPs belong, 2003

Party label in the UK	Number*	Party group in the EP
Conservative	36	European People's Party
Democratic Unionist (NI)	1	N/A
Green	2	Greens and Radicals
Labour	29	European Socialists
Liberal Democrat	10	European Liberal, Democratic Reform
Plaid Cymru	2	Greens and Radicals
Scottish National Party	2	Greens and Radicals
UK Independence (UKIP)	3	Europe of Democracies and Diversities
Social Democratic and Labour Party	1	European Socialists
Ulster Unionist	1	European People's Party

* Based on result of the 1999 European Parliament election.

12.5 The European Court of Justice

In April 2004, the European Court of Justice (ECJ) had 15 judges - one from each member state. Judges are appointed by member states for a period of six years. There are six advocates general who assist the judges by analysing the arguments of those in dispute. The Court sits in Luxembourg, its role being to interpret European law and to make decisions which are binding on member states. It rules on the interpretation and application of EU laws and sorts out disputes between member states. Given the scope of the treaties, a very wide range of matters can be brought before the Court. It is, in effect, the Supreme Court of the European Union.

Due to the increasing workload of the Court of Justice, the Single European Act provided for a Court of First Instance to be set up. This court listens to and makes judgements on points of law only. There is the right of appeal from this court to the ECJ.

Norton points out that the ECJ is the court of last resort in the EU:

'Under the terms of EU membership, if there is a conflict between the provisions of European law and domestic UK law, then the European law is to prevail. The 1972 European Communities Act provided that any dispute over the interpretation of community treaties (and the laws made under them) was to be treated as a matter of law. Under the provisions of the Treaty of Rome, cases which reach the highest domestic court of appeal (in the case of the UK, that means the House of Lords) must be referred to the Court of Justice...for a definitive ruling. Lower courts may also request a ruling from the Court of Justice on the meaning and interpretation of the treaties. There is no appeal from a decision of the Court of Justice.' (Norton 1995, p.30)

The European Court of Justice should not be confused with the European Court of Human Rights. The European Court of Human Rights was established by the Council of Europe which has twice as many members as the EU. The European Court of Human Rights examines violations of the 1950 European Convention on Human Rights.

12.6 The Economic and Social Committee

The Economic and Social Committee (ESC) is based in Brussels. Lists of nominees are put forward by each member country and the 222 members of the committee are appointed from these lists by the Council of Ministers. To ensure that a broad spectrum of interests is represented, membership is divided into three equally sized groups -

employers, workers and interest groups. Each member state's list of nominees is supposed to reflect this division.

The ESC is a consultative body, but, since 1972, it has been able to deliver opinions without being consulted. Numerous articles in treaties require the Council of Ministers to consult the ESC, but its opinions are not binding. Despite this, Nugent argues, the committee plays an important role:

'First, it provides a useful forum in which representatives of sectional interests can come together on a largely cooperative basis to exchange views and ideas. Second, it is a consultative organ that gives some limited - but in most cases only very limited - opportunities for interests to influence Community policy and decision making.' (Nugent 1994, p.217)

12.7 The Committee of the Regions

Established by the Maastricht Treaty, the Committee of the Regions is a consultative body which is meant to be the guardian of the principle of subsidiarity - the principle that decisions should be taken at the lowest appropriate level. The membership and structure of the Committee of the Regions is similar to that of the ESC. Under the terms of the Maastricht Treaty, the committee must be consulted by the Council of Ministers and Commission whenever the ESC is consulted. Also, when the committee considers that specific regional interests are involved, it can issue an opinion on the matter.

Main points   Sections 12.1 - 12.7

- **The EU has a mixture of intergovernmental and supranational institutions, with decisions ultimately made by four bodies.**
- **The Council of Ministers takes the final decision on most policies, its precise membership depending on the policy under discussion.**
- **The European Commission is the bureaucracy of the EU, whose primary role is to prepare policies and legislation and to oversee their implementation by member states.**
- **The European Parliament used to be widely viewed as little more than a talking shop, but its formal powers and involvement in decision-making have steadily been increased.**
- **The role of the European Court of Justice is to interpret European law, and adjudicate when disputes arise.**
- **Two consultative bodies have an input into various EU decisions - the Economic and Social Committee and the Committee of the Regions.**

Activity 12.1 Decision-making in the EU

Item A The EU decision-making process

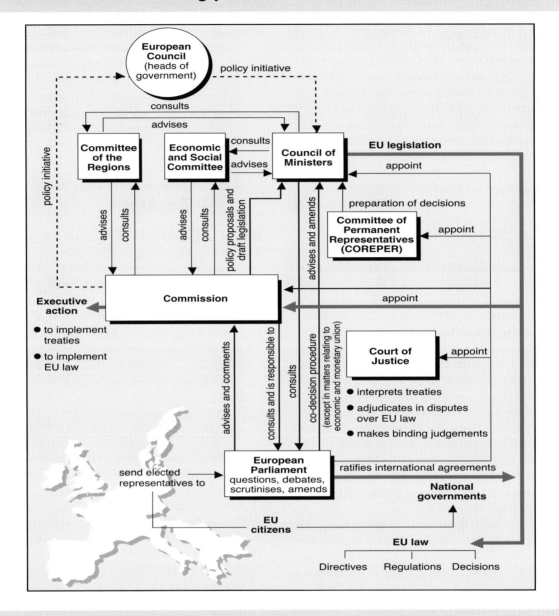

Source: Mazey & Richardson 1993.

Item B The qualified majority voting system (1)

Before 1995, the 12 members of the EU had a total of 76 votes in the Council and a measure could be blocked by 23 (or more) votes - a minimum of two large states and one small state voting against the measure. In March 1994, the British government proposed that the blocking threshold remain at 23 votes even after the new members joined the EU in January 1995. The main argument was that this was a question of protecting national sovereignty, especially as the number of decisions which required qualified majority voting had grown and was likely to grow. Most other members argued against this on the grounds that retaining the 23 vote blocking mechanism would make it too easy to reject proposals and EU business would grind to a halt. The 1997 Amsterdam Treaty extended qualified majority voting to 11 new areas of policy. In 1998, a qualified majority required 62 votes. A measure could be blocked, therefore, by 26 (or more) votes - a minimum of two large states and either Spain or two small states.

Source: The *Guardian*, 20 March 1994 and 30 January 1995, and the *Independent*, 16 June 1997.

Item C The qualified majority voting system (2)

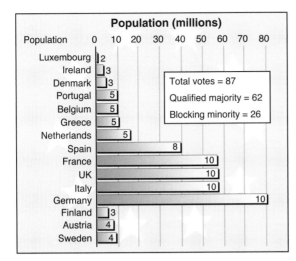

Population (millions)

Population	0	10	20	30	40	50	60	70	80	votes
Luxembourg										2
Ireland										3
Denmark										3
Portugal										5
Belgium										5
Greece										5
Netherlands										5
Spain										8
France										10
UK										10
Italy										10
Germany										10
Finland										3
Austria										4
Sweden										4

Total votes = 87
Qualified majority = 62
Blocking minority = 26

This chart shows the population of each member state of the EU and the number of votes each member state has in the Council of Ministers.

Source: The *Guardian*, 16 March 1994 and *Observer*, 14 September 1997.

Item E The Council of Ministers

The output of the Council of Ministers is comparable to that of a government. Every working day, hundreds of officials from the member states meet in Brussels to discuss texts drawn up by the Commission. National interests are then promoted and defended as negotiation and bargaining takes place. The outcome is an agreed text which is adopted by the Council at one of its 100 or so sessions each year. In about 70% of cases, the agreement is reached at the level of experts meeting in working groups; 15-20% is decided upon by senior national officials meeting in COREPER; 10-15% is discussed and decided by the ministers in Council. The

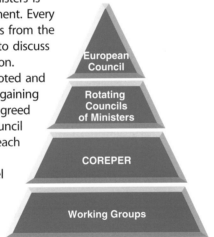

The structure of the Council of Ministers

final adoption of measures is always and only done by the ministers meeting in Council. The lower levels of the pyramid act as a filter. Agreement is reached on as many issues as possible, allowing ministers to concentrate on the most controversial areas. In all, the whole process takes about 18 months from the initial proposal. Internal disputes are increasingly referred to the European Council. This causes problems. Heads of government are not close enough to most issues and so they often rubber-stamp agreements reached by officials. Pushing so much onto summit meetings encourages a 'package' approach which ends in compromise. Ministers at lower levels are often reluctant to concede anything, leaving it to the summit. The initiative of the Commission has been eroded.

Source: Hayes-Renshaw 1998 and the *Economist*, 8 March 1997.

Item D The European Parliament

Criticisms of the European Parliament (EP)

- The EP is not a truly representative body. In the 1994 European elections, for example, only 36% of people bothered to vote. This suggests that most people do not believe that participation in such elections is worthwhile. It also means that MEPs cannot claim with any justification to have a mandate for their vision of Europe.

- The EP is expensive. In 1994, it cost over £500 million to run it. The cost of maintaining an MEP is much greater than maintaining an MP.

- The EP is not a proper Parliament. MEPs from different countries belong to different political parties which are only linked by a system of weak alliances. Parliamentary democracy cannot function properly without political parties being organised on a Europe-wide basis.

- The continued existence of the EP only makes sense if there are plans for its power to continue to evolve. This assumes that an EP with greater powers is desirable. If it is not, then the EP should be abolished immediately.

- British MEPs are in a minority in the EP and, therefore, cannot protect Britain's interests.

Recommendation

The work of the EP should be confined to consultation and MEPs should be nominated or elected from national Parliaments.

Source: The *Times*, 13 April 1995.

Questions

1. a) Using Items A and E, describe the different stages that a proposal has to go through before becoming law.

   b) Where is power located in the EU?

   c) Isolate the intergovernmental and supranational elements in the decision-making process. Would you say that the balance is right? Give reasons for your answer.

   d) What evidence is there of a 'democratic deficit'?

2. Using Items B and C, give arguments for and against the view that qualified voting should be extended.

3. 'The European Parliament plays an important role now and it should play an even more important role in the future.' Do you agree with this statement? Use Item D in your answer.

4. 'It is the EU's chief decision-maker but it lacks accountability.' Is that an accurate description of the Council of Ministers? Use Item E in your answer.

12.8 The formation of the European Economic Community

The term 'European Union' has evolved as the organisation has evolved. At first, the organisation was known as the 'European Economic Community' (EEC) or 'Common Market', but after the Single European Act was passed in 1986, the name changed to 'European Community' (EC). In 1993, after the ratification of the Maastricht Treaty, the name changed again from European Community to 'European Union' (EU). The evolution of the name reflects changes in the structure and nature of the organisation.

It is a great irony of British politics that the idea of a 'United States of Europe' was first put forward by the Conservative Leader, Winston Churchill, in September 1946. The irony is that when other Western European countries did move together during the 1950s, Britain remained aloof, adopting a stance of semi-isolation. Indeed, even after joining the European Community in 1973, Britain often displayed considerable scepticism towards various European initiatives, ensuring that Britain gained the reputation for being an 'awkward partner'.

The first moves towards European union

The first step towards what has become the European Union occurred in January 1948, when the 'Benelux' countries - Belgium, Netherlands and Luxembourg - joined together to form a customs union.

This was soon followed by the establishment of the Organisation for European Economic Cooperation (OEEC), set up to administer the $13 billion Marshall Aid provided by the USA to assist post-war reconstruction. Named after the American Secretary of State, George Marshall, the aid package was offered to the countries of Eastern Europe, but they refused it on the grounds that acceptance would lead to American interference in their domestic affairs. Consequently, the members of the OEEC, and therefore the beneficiaries of Marshall Aid, were countries from Western Europe.

The Schuman Plan

The next important step on the road to European integration came in 1950, when Jean Monnet, a French civil servant, and Robert Schuman, the French Foreign Secretary, devised what subsequently became known as the Schuman Plan. This had two aims. First, it sought to promote economic recovery in France and West Germany by pooling both countries' coal and steel industries. Second, it aimed to place other key industries under joint sovereignty, with a view to making war between France and West Germany virtually impossible.

The European Coal and Steel Community

The Schuman Plan was announced in 1950 and led to the formation of the European Coal and Steel Community (ECSC) which was officially launched in 1952. Following the signing of the Treaty of Paris the previous year (1951), the ECSC had six members: Belgium, France, Italy, Luxembourg, Netherlands and West Germany. The declared aim of the ECSC was to:

'Establish a common market for coal and steel, to ensure supplies, to promote expansion and modernisation of production, and to provide better employment conditions.' (HMSO 1992, p.3)

The next key step came in June 1955 when the Foreign Ministers of the six founder members of the ECSC met in Messina, Italy to discuss further cooperation and integration. Box 12.5 shows the declaration that was made at that meeting.

Box 12.5 Declaration at the Messina Conference

The governments of Belgium, France, the Federal Republic of West Germany, Italy, Luxembourg and the Netherlands consider that the moment has arrived to initiate a new phase on the path of constructing Europe. They believe that this has to be done principally in the economic sphere and regard it as necessary to continue the creation of a united Europe through an expansion of joint institutions, the gradual fusion of national economies, the creation of a common market, and the gradual co-ordination of social policies. Such a policy seems to be indispensable if Europe is to maintain her position in the world, regain her influence, and achieve a steady increase in the living standards of her population.

Source: Pilkington 2001.

Two years after the Messina Conference, in March 1957, the Treaty of Rome was signed. This set up the European Economic Community (EEC), which was officially launched on 1 January 1958. The signing of the Treaty of Rome was the first major step towards establishing a free-trade zone (between member states) within Western Europe. It set in motion the process towards ever closer European union, which continues today.

12.9 Britain and the EEC, 1958-79

Britain's early relations with Europe
Although the British government was invited to join the negotiations which led to the foundation of the EEC, it refused to become involved on the grounds that joining a supranational organisation would endanger national sovereignty. It was argued that if Britain joined the EEC, it would lose the right to follow independent economic and defence policies. There were a number of reasons for Britain's decision not to join. Britain was geographically separate from mainland Europe and, unlike its neighbours, had not been subject to conquest in recent times. In addition, Britain still had strong ties with countries outside Europe. Although the British Empire broke up after 1945, Britain still retained trading links with former colonies, especially those in the British Commonwealth. And third, the British government believed that it had a 'special relationship' with the USA.

EFTA
In response to the creation of the EEC, Britain attempted to establish a free-trade area which covered all members of the OEEC (including the six members of the EEC). France, however, rejected this idea and negotiations failed. Instead, Britain and six countries which belonged to the OEEC but not to the EEC (Austria, Norway, Sweden, Denmark, Portugal and Switzerland) formed the European Free Trade Association (EFTA) in 1960. The aim of EFTA was to dismantle barriers to trade between members (so that trade would increase among members) and to provide a base from which to negotiate with the EEC over the creation of a single European market. During the 1960s, however, it became apparent that Britain's trade was growing faster with the EEC than it was with EFTA.

Britain's attempts to join the EEC
When the British government realised that the EEC was becoming a powerful trading bloc, it applied to join the EEC. Britain's first application was made in 1961. Negotiations continued until 1963 when the French President, Charles de Gaulle, vetoed Britain's application. Britain reapplied in 1967, but again this application was vetoed by de Gaulle. It was only after de Gaulle retired in 1969 that the British government was able to negotiate its entry into the EEC. In 1971 the Prime Minister, Edward Heath, held talks with de Gaulle's successor Pompidou. The following year, Heath signed the Treaty of Accession and on 1 January 1973, Britain became a member of the EEC (together with two other new members - Ireland and Denmark).

The EEC referendum, 1975
When Britain joined the EEC in 1973, it was confronted by a number of problems. These are outlined in Box 12.6.

> **Box 12.6** Problems facing the UK, 1973-75
>
> The problems facing the UK over its membership of the EEC were as follows:
> - Most British politicians did not share the vision of those Euro-enthusiasts who looked forward to the creation of a European superstate. Although the British government, by joining the EEC, had accepted the EEC's supranational structure, many politicians accepted this only reluctantly.
> - Friction arose because Britain had not been a member from the start. As a result, Britain had to accept existing policies and regulations which it had played no part in developing.
> - There was a price to pay for membership, in the short term at least. Since Britain had substantial trading links with non-EEC countries (especially Commonwealth countries) its contribution to EEC funds was particularly high (trading with non-EEC countries was penalised). On the other hand, because Britain's agricultural sector was highly efficient, it did not benefit from the EEC's Common Agricultural Policy (CAP) as much as other member states.

Rather than addressing each of the problems outlined in Box 12.6 and tackling them head-on:

> 'British membership of the EC was advocated on pragmatic economic grounds. Britain thought it was joining a common market - an economic organisation - and played down the political consequences of membership.' (Geddes 1993, p.33)

Concern about membership of the EEC came to a head after the second general election of 1974. The new Labour government came to office with the pledge to renegotiate Britain's terms of membership and to hold a referendum. This referendum was held in June 1975. There was a 64% turnout and 67% voted in favour of remaining in the EEC.

12.10 Margaret Thatcher and the EEC

On becoming Prime Minister in 1979, Margaret Thatcher launched an attack on the EEC because Britain's contribution to the EEC budget was too high (Britain was the second largest contributor to the EEC budget even though it had the third lowest GDP per capita of all members). The result was a long and acrimonious battle over Britain's contribution. The issue was not settled until 1984 when a rebate was agreed.

The Single European Act 1986
The second major development in the Thatcher years was the passing of the Single European Act in 1986. This Act was supported by Thatcher and her allies on the grounds that a

free, single market would mean greater deregulation and less governmental intervention (and therefore greater economic growth), but it was also supported by the President of the European Commission, Jacques Delors, on the grounds that it would restart the move towards greater European integration. The result has been an ongoing debate about the future direction of Europe. This debate has yet to be resolved.

Margaret Thatcher's increasing hostility towards Europe

Having signed the Single European Act, Margaret Thatcher became increasingly critical of apparent plans for greater social and political integration. This, she maintained, was entirely different to the proposals for a free, internal, market within Europe, based on deregulation and competition within and between sovereign member states.

Many other European leaders, however, interpreted the Single European Act rather differently. They assumed and readily accepted that creating a free-trade zone between members states would also entail 'harmonisation' of various other economic aspects, such as currencies, and - ultimately - maybe taxes. These European leaders also anticipated common social policies, as well as a strengthening of the EEC's institutions to achieve these objectives. Certainly, as George notes, for France and (West) Germany especially:

'The emergence of a single European currency was an essential complement to the freeing of the internal market. They argued that that EMS [European Monetary System] needed to be strengthened by the creation of a European central bank, and by moves to establish...[a] common currency of the Community.' (George 1998, p.191)

Margaret Thatcher rejected this vision - see Box 12.7.

Box 12.7 Extract from a speech made by Thatcher in 1988

I neither want nor expect to see such a [European central] bank in my lifetime, nor, if I am twanging a harp, for quite a long time afterwards...A European central bank in the only true meaning of the term means surrendering your economic policy to that banking system that is in charge of the maintenance of the value of the currency, and must therefore be in charge of the necessary economic policy to achieve that.

Source: *Independent*, 22 October 1988.

In 1988, the President of the European Commission, Jacques Delors, made it clear that he believed the EC should have a 'social dimension'. Having declared, in a 1988 speech to the European Parliament, that: 'In ten years, 80% of economic legislation - and perhaps tax, and social legislation - will be directed from the Community', Delores then spoke as guest at the TUC's 1988 annual conference. Here, he outlined his vision for Europe. A key passage in his speech is given in Box 12.8.

Box 12.8 Part of Delors' speech to the TUC in 1988

It is impossible to build Europe only on deregulation... 1992 is much more than the creation of an internal market abolishing barriers to the free movement of goods, services and investment...The internal market should be designed to benefit each and every citizen of the Community. It is therefore necessary to improve workers' living and working conditions, and to provide better protection for their health and safety at work.

Source: *Independent*, 9 September 1988.

This prompted a strong response from Margaret Thatcher. Just a couple of weeks later, she made a speech warning that her vision for the EC 'is under attack from those who see European unity as a vehicle for spreading socialism. She argued that:

'We haven't worked all these years to free Britain from the paralysis of socialism only to see it creep through the back door of central control and bureaucracy in Brussels.' (quoted in the *Independent*, 15 October 1988)

Thatcher's ideas on Europe were not shared by a number of her Cabinet colleagues, notably Geoffrey Howe and Michael Heseltine. It was Howe's resignation in November 1990 (prompted largely by disillusion with Thatcher's stance on Europe) which led to a leadership contest which, in turn, led to Thatcher's downfall.

Main points   Sections 12.8 - 12.10

- **The Treaty of Rome was signed in 1957, and the EEC officially launched on 1 January 1958.**
- **The founder members of the EEC were Belgium, France, Italy, Luxembourg, Netherlands and West Germany.**
- **The UK decided not to join the EEC at first, believing itself still to be a world power, politically and militarily, and enjoying special trade links with the Commonwealth, as well as a 'special relationship' with the United States.**
- **The UK applied to join the EEC, in 1961 and 1967, but both applications were vetoed by de Gaulle, who doubted Britain's commitment and motives. The UK finally joined the EEC on 1 January 1973.**
- **During Margaret Thatcher's premiership, Britain's relationship with the EEC became increasingly strained. She successfully fought for a reduction in Britain's contributions to the EEC budget and signed the Single European Act.**
- **Having signed the Single European Act, Thatcher became increasingly critical of the 'social dimension' being promoted within the EEC.**

Activity 12.2 *The development of the EEC*

Item A **The evolution of the EEC**

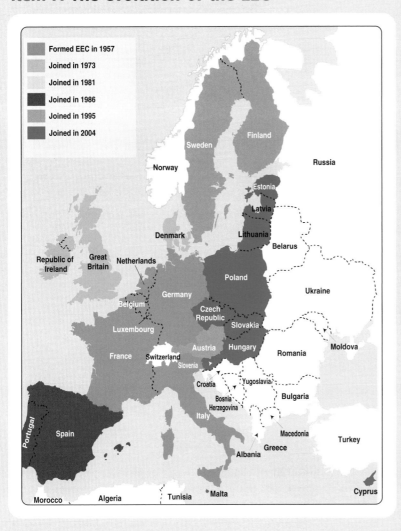

Formed EEC in 1957
Joined in 1973
Joined in 1981
Joined in 1986
Joined in 1995
Joined in 2004

Item B **De Gaulle's veto**

(i) After refusing to join the community we are building, after creating a free-trade area with six other states (EFTA), and after trying to prevent a real beginning for the Common Market, Britain has now applied for membership - on its own terms. But, Britain is insular, maritime, linked by trade, markets and food supply to very different and often very distant lands. How can Britain be brought into this system? How far is it possible for Britain to accept a truly common tariff? For this would involve giving up all Commonwealth preferences and treating as null and void obligations entered into with the free-trade area. It is possible that one day Britain might manage to transform itself sufficiently to become part of the EEC. In that case, the Six would open their door and France would raise no obstacle.

Adapted from a speech made by President de Gaulle in January 1963.

(ii) To tell the truth Britain's attitude is easy to explain. Having seen more clearly the great changes sweeping the world - the enormous power of the USA, the growing power of the Soviet Union, the revitalised power of the EEC, the new power of China and the growing independence of Commonwealth countries, its future is at stake. Moreover, financial difficulties and social problems force Britain to seek a framework both to safeguard itself and to play a leading role in the world.

Source: A speech made by President de Gaulle in September 1967.

Item C **A common tariff**

Trade between the EEC and the rest of the world was regulated so that every EEC member charged the same tariff (tax on imported goods) when trading with non-members. This had two advantages. It encouraged trade within the EEC and it prevented non-members from selling goods to the member with the lowest tariff on the understanding that this member would then sell on the goods to the other members. This common external tariff had been achieved by 1968.

Item D Britain and the EEC

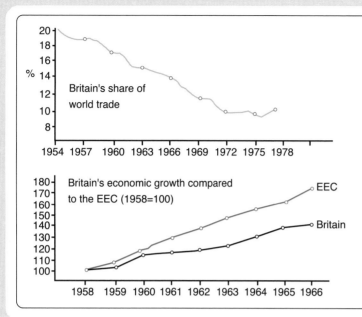

Industrial production 1959-67			
	1959	**1963**	**1967**
Britain	105	119	133
W. Germany	107	137	158
France	101	129	155
Italy	112	166	212
USA	113	133	168
Japan	120	212	347

This table gives comparisons with industrial production in 1958 (=100).

Source: Coates 1994.

Questions

1. Suppose Items A and C were used to illustrate an article entitled: 'The evolution of the EEC, 1958-98'. Write the article to accompany the pictures.

2. Judging from Item B, why did President de Gaulle veto Britain's two applications to join the EEC in the 1960s?

3. Using Items B and D, explain why Britain was not one of the founding members of the EEC and why it applied to join the EEC in the 1960s.

12.11 The Major government and the Maastricht Treaty

There was a widespread expectation that John Major's election would bring a more constructive and conciliatory stance towards Europe after the 'megaphone diplomacy' of the Thatcher years. However, developments at both European level, and in British politics, were to confound such expectations.

Following the general election of 1992, the Major government had a small majority and this placed considerable power into the hands of a hard core of 'Eurosceptics' on the Conservative backbenches and in the Cabinet.

At European level, meanwhile, the next stage of European integration was agreed at a summit attended by the heads of the 12 member states, in the Dutch city of Maastricht, at the end of 1991. This summit produced the Treaty on European Union (more popularly known as the Maastricht Treaty) which both amended, and added to, the provisions and commitments in the 1957 Treaty of Rome. These are outlined in Box 12.9.

Box 12.9 Main provisions of the Maastricht Treaty

- The Treaty provides for moves towards economic and monetary union, including the establishment of a European central bank.

- The Treaty endorses a commitment to strengthening intergovernmental cooperation on issues such as asylum and immigration, tacking international crime, drug trafficking and terrorism.

- The Treaty provides for the establishment of a common foreign and security policy, conducted on an intergovernmental basis.

- The Treaty strengthens control of the European Community's budget.

- The Treaty introduces measures of institutional reform, most notably new powers for the European Parliament (granting it a co-decision-making role), some extension of Qualified Majority Voting in the Council of Ministers, and the creation of an advisory Committee of the Regions.

- The Treaty embodies the concept of subsidiarity, meaning that action should only be taken at Community level if the objectives cannot be sufficiently achieved by the member states acting alone.

- The Treaty introduces the concept of (European) Union citizenship - it confers certain rights on the citizens of the member states.

Source: HMSO 1992.

In ratifying the Maastricht Treaty, member states established a European Union (this explains the change of name from EEC or EC to EU). In fact this new European Union comprised three pillars. The European Community forms one pillar, foreign and security policy forms a second pillar and justice and home affairs forms the third pillar. While the European Community functions by means of a mix of supranational and intergovernmental institutions, members agreed that in the spheres of foreign affairs, defence, home affairs and justice they should proceed through intergovernmental cooperation.

Although some member states wanted a commitment to greater federalism to be explicitly stated in the text of the Treaty, the British government vehemently opposed the use of the word 'federal'. Instead, the text of the Treaty uses the term 'ever closer union':

> 'This Treaty marks a new stage in the process of creating an ever closer union among the peoples of Europe, in which decisions are taken as closely as possible to the citizen.' (quoted in Nugent 1994, p.65)

12.12 Controversies

A. Federalism
The issue of federalism was central to the future direction and development of the European Union. Federalism, as Box 12.10 indicates, is a system of political rule in which different levels of government have different powers and responsibilities.

Box 12.10 Federal political systems

Federal systems of government have the following five features:

1. Two levels of government, a general/central, and a regional level.

2. Formal distribution of law-making and executive authority and sources of revenue between the two levels.

3. A written constitution.

4. An 'umpire' - a supreme or constitutional court - to make judgements in disputes between the two levels.

5. Central institutions, including a two-chamber Parliament, each chamber having a different level of representation and/or having a different basis for election.

Source: Geddes 1993.

The aim of a federal political system is to ensure that decisions are taken at the most appropriate level, so that policies affecting everyone are taken by the national government, while matters only affecting a particular region are determined by the regional government.

The opposite to a federal system of government is a unitary system of government, as operated in pre-devolution Britain. Although there is also an extensive system of local government in Britain, its powers and responsibilities are ultimately determined by central government, so that they cannot be said to enjoy genuine freedom of action.

To its supporters, a federal system is about decentralising decision-making and policy-making to the lowest possible level, nearest to the people most affected (this aspect is also known as 'subsidiarity').

Opponents focus on the extent to which major decisions and policies - particularly those relating to economic affairs, foreign affairs and defence - are determined at the higher level in the federal system. For Eurosceptics, 'a "federal Europe" means a European super-state with a huge, centralised Brussels bureaucracy limiting the sovereign authority of member states' (Geddes 1993, p.13). Concern that this would be the result of ratifying the Maastricht Treaty was so strong in the early 1990s that John Major insisted that the word 'federal' be entirely omitted from the Maastricht Treaty.

B. Economic and Monetary Union (EMU)
The Maastricht Treaty made clear the objective of developing a common currency among member states - the euro - which would replace their individual currencies. It was also proposed that this would be accompanied by the establishment of a European Central Bank, which would be empowered to set interest rates for all member states.

The proposal for a single European currency was bitterly opposed by most Conservatives and John Major negotiated an opt-out, ensuring that Britain would not participate in economic and monetary union for the foreseeable future.

For many Conservatives (and some Labour MPs too), adopting the euro would represent the ultimate loss of sovereignty, namely loss of formal control over economic policy since interest rates would be set at European level. Many opponents of British membership of the euro believe that a nation no longer in control of its own currency or economic affairs is hardly a nation at all.

C. The Social Chapter
John Major also secured an opt-out for Britain from the protocol (Social Chapter) which implemented the Social Charter originally agreed by the political heads of member states in 1989. The Social Chapter aimed to harmonise laws concerning the rights of workers, in an effort to prevent unfair competition between member states through the exploitation of employees. Health and safety regulations, a common minimum wage and an agreed maximum number of working hours were the most notable features of the Social Chapter. However, John Major secured an opt-out for Britain on the grounds that it would impose unacceptable costs and bureaucratic burdens on British employers and, ultimately, result in higher unemployment - which would harm the very workers it was intended to protect.

Even the opt-outs and the removal of any reference to federalism were not sufficient to prevent John Major's government from encountering serious problems in securing parliamentary ratification of the Maastricht Treaty. Indeed, Major was compelled to make ratification of the Maastricht Treaty a matter of confidence. In other words, he made it clear that, if the Conservative rebels persisted in their opposition and defeated the government by voting with the opposition parties, he would call a general election (see Baker, Gamble & Ludlam 1993 and 1994, Jones 1994 and Cowley 1999).

Main points **Sections 12.11 - 12.12**

- After Margaret Thatcher had been replaced by John Major, Britain signed the Maastricht Treaty, which changed, and added to, some of the provisions of the Treaty of Rome. The Maastricht Treaty formally established the European Union.
- Some Conservatives were strongly opposed to aspects of the Maastricht Treaty, and John Major therefore insisted that Britain be permitted to

opt out of the Social Chapter, and the final stage of Economic and Monetary Union (the adoption of a single European currency).
- In spite of these opt-outs, John Major was only able to secure parliamentary ratification of the Maastricht Treaty by making it a vote of confidence in his government.

Activity 12.3 *Maastricht and its consequences*

Item A **The Maastricht Treaty and federalism (1)**

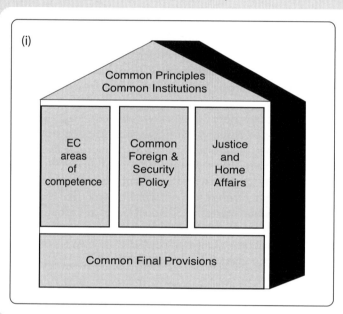

(i)
- Common Principles
- Common Institutions
- EC areas of competence
- Common Foreign & Security Policy
- Justice and Home Affairs
- Common Final Provisions

(ii) The negotiation of the Maastricht Treaty was marked by a clash between two rival views of the future of the EU. One shared by Germany and the federalist smaller states saw the EU as a tree with all its activities brought together in one set of institutions, eventually creating a single federal state. According to this view, the EU is a single, growing, living organism with one trunk, its roots sunk in the rich European soil. The rival metaphor, backed by France and Britain, was that of the temple. Supporters of this view wanted different policy areas split off from each other in separate pillars. Unity was provided by the 'pediment' - the part of the Treaty which covered policy areas common to all members. It was this architectural version which won out.

Item B **The Maastricht Treaty and federalism (2)**

The Maastricht Treaty was criticised by its opponents for bringing a federal superstate. Like the Single European Act, however, it simply amends, refines and extends key provisions of the existing treaties. It is paradoxical that the most centralised of the EU member states, the UK, should have drawn this conclusion from a treaty geared towards decentralised, devolved and regionalised decision-making. Indeed, it is the provisions for decisions to be taken at levels lower than that of national governments which annoyed the British government. The Maastricht Treaty set up a new Committee of the Regions to achieve this. Only the British government wanted to appoint national government nominees to this new body. The federal and non-federal characteristics of the EU post-Maastricht can be listed as follows:

Federal characteristics	Non-federal characteristics
1. Important policy responsibilities are exercised at both the central (EU) and the regional (member state) levels.	1. Although the power of the centre (EU) has grown, the balance between the two levels is tipped very much in favour of the regional (member state) level.
2. Well-developed institutions exist at both levels.	2. Control of financial resources remains with the regional level. The EU budget is just 3% of total national budgets.
3. The Court of Justice is a central judicial body with the authority to rule on disputes between the two levels.	3. The EU's political structure is not well ordered or based on established and shared principles.
4. There is common citizenship.	4. The rights of EU citizenship are extremely limited.

Source: Lodge 1993 and Nugent 1994.

Item C Subsidiarity

The subsidiarity principle means that decisions made by Parliaments, governments and other authorities are to be taken as close as possible to the citizen. In other words, decisions are taken at the lowest possible level (preferably by the local or regional authority). Decisions are taken at a higher level only if there is a good reason. Article 3b of the Maastricht Treaty defines subsidiarity as follows: 'The Community shall act within the limits of the powers conferred upon it by this Treaty and of the objectives assigned to it therein. In areas which do not fall within its exclusive competence, the Community shall take action, in accordance with the principle of subsidiarity, only if and in so far as the objectives of the proposed action cannot be sufficiently achieved by the member states and can, therefore, by reason of the scale or effects of the proposed action, be better achieved by the Community. Any action of the Community shall not go beyond what is necessary to achieve the objectives of this Treaty.' But subsidiarity does not just apply to legislative powers. The Treaty claims to mark: 'A new stage in the process of creating an ever closer union among the peoples of Europe, in which decisions are taken as closely as possible to the citizen'. Subsidiarity is, therefore, one of the fundamental characteristics of the EU and expresses the principle that member states preserve their individual identities.

Source: OOPEC 1992.

Questions

1. Why was the ratification of the Maastricht Treaty such an important event in the history of the European Community? Use Items A and B in your answer.
2. 'The aim of the Maastricht Treaty was to produce a federal Europe.' Using Items A-C, give arguments for and against this view.

3. Using Item C, explain why the principle of subsidiarity is supported by (a) politicians who support a federal Europe and (b) politicians who oppose a federal Europe. Given that the principle is supported by these different groups, how useful is it?

12.13 The Amsterdam Treaty

After becoming Labour Party Leader in 1994, Tony Blair expressed positive and constructive views about the European Union and, within days of election in May 1997, the opt-out from the Social Chapter was reversed and, for the first time, a Minister for Europe was appointed.

Since then, the government's Euro-enthusiasm has cooled somewhat - in part reacting to new moves towards European integration which have been proposed and in part reacting to the hostile coverage in anti-European, pro-Conservative newspapers which portray moves towards further integration as a surrender of British sovereignty and betrayal of British interests.

The 1997 Amsterdam Treaty

Although the Maastricht Treaty was finally ratified by all member states, the ratification process revealed widespread popular discontent with the European project. In Denmark, for example, the Treaty was actually rejected in a referendum (held in June 1992) before being ratified after a second referendum (in May 1993). In France there were mass demonstrations against the Treaty. Polls held throughout the 1990s suggested that developments in Europe were failing to capture the popular imagination in many EU member states - see Box 12.11.

By the time that the 1997 Amsterdam Treaty was agreed, the optimistic mood which had been prevalent among federalists in the early 1990s had changed. The grand vision of a federalist future had receded. The new key word was 'flexibility' - member states were to be allowed to integrate at their own pace, opting out when they disagreed with

Box 12.11 Support for EU membership in 1998

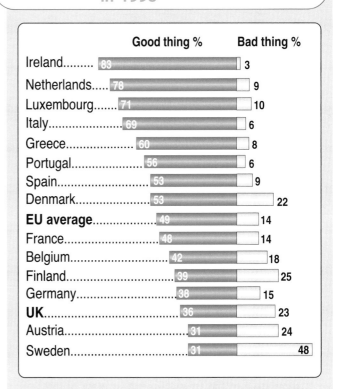

This graph shows the results of a survey conducted by the European Commission in March 1998. Respondents were asked whether they thought membership of the EU was a 'good thing' or a 'bad thing'.

measures acceptable to the majority of states. It should be noted that, by 1997, the main priority of many officials was to ensure that economic and monetary union went ahead as planned. To safeguard this project, they were prepared to make compromises or postpone controversial decisions. The provisions of the Amsterdam Treaty are outlined in Box 12.12.

Box 12.12 Provisions of the Amsterdam Treaty

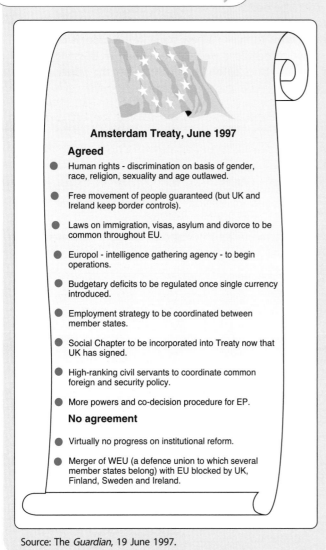

Amsterdam Treaty, June 1997

Agreed

- Human rights - discrimination on basis of gender, race, religion, sexuality and age outlawed.

- Free movement of people guaranteed (but UK and Ireland keep border controls).

- Laws on immigration, visas, asylum and divorce to be common throughout EU.

- Europol - intelligence gathering agency - to begin operations.

- Budgetary deficits to be regulated once single currency introduced.

- Employment strategy to be coordinated between member states.

- Social Chapter to be incorporated into Treaty now that UK has signed.

- High-ranking civil servants to coordinate common foreign and security policy.

- More powers and co-decision procedure for EP.

No agreement

- Virtually no progress on institutional reform.

- Merger of WEU (a defence union to which several member states belong) with EU blocked by UK, Finland, Sweden and Ireland.

Source: The *Guardian*, 19 June 1997.

12.14 *The Treaty of Nice*

The Treaty of Nice was finalised in December 2000. The central element of the Treaty was an agreement to expand the European Union by admitting new countries. Critics argue that the Treaty was a missed opportunity because members failed to review the workings of the institutions of the European Union. The governments of all member states were committed to the Treaty. The government of the Republic of Ireland, however, was, at first, prevented from signing because, in June 2001, 46% of Irish voters voted against signing the Treaty and only 35% voted in favour. A second referendum, held in October 2002, reversed that decision, with 63% in favour of signing and 48% voting against.

Changes to qualified majority voting in the Council of Ministers

Under the system operating until 2004, each member had a number of votes proportional to the population of their member state and at least 62 out of the 87 possible votes are necessary for a proposal to be carried. The Treaty of Nice agreed to the changes listed in Box 12.13. They are to be introduced from January 2005 when new member states join the EU. In addition, to be successful, a proposal will have to be supported by a majority of member states and those states in favour will have to represent at least 62% of the population of the EU. Although, under the Nice Treaty, policy areas where qualified majority voting applies will increase, national governments will still be able to veto decisions in key areas such as taxation.

Box 12.13 Qualified majority voting under the Nice Treaty

Member state	Current votes	Current number of citizens per vote (millions)	Reallocation of votes under Nice Treaty	Number of citizens per vote (millions)
Germany	10	8.21	29	2.83
UK	10	5.95	29	2.05
France	10	5.86	29	2.02
Italy	10	5.76	29	1.99
Spain	8	4.92	27	1.46
Netherlands	5	3.16	13	1.22
Greece	5	2.10	12	0.88
Belgium	5	2.04	12	0.85
Portugal	5	2.00	12	0.83
Sweden	4	2.22	10	0.89
Austria	4	2.02	10	0.81
Denmark	3	1.77	7	0.76
Finland	3	1.73	7	0.74
Ireland	3	1.23	7	0.53
Luxembourg	2	0.20	4	0.10
Total	**87**	**4.31***	**237**	**1.58***

* Average

Votes for new member states will be:

Poland	27	Romania	14
Czech Republic & Hungary	12	Bulgaria	10
Lithuania & Slovakia	7	Latvia, Estonia,	
Malta	3	Slovenia & Cyprus	4

Source: McCormick 2002.

12.15 *The launch of the euro in 2002*

In January 2002, 12 members of the EU relinquished their national currencies, and introduced the euro, a single European currency. Only Britain, Denmark and Sweden, opted out of joining the euro.

The launch of the euro fuelled the debate over whether Britain should join (the debate is explored in Kettle et al. 1997 and Browne 2001).

The Blair government's position since 1997 has been that it is in favour Britain joining the euro in principle, but only when the time is right, and certain economic conditions have been met. At such a point, the British people would be asked to give the consent via a referendum. The five economic conditions or 'tests' are shown in Box 12.14.

> **Box 12.14 The five conditions to be met for British membership of the euro**
>
> 1. Sustainable convergence between Britain and the economies of those countries which have already adopted the euro.
> 2. Sufficient flexibility to cope with economic change.
> 3. Likely to encourage investment.
> 4. Likely beneficial impact on Britain's financial services sector.
> 5. Likely beneficial impact on employment in Britain.

Cynics could be forgiven for suspecting that the 'five economic tests' - which the Chancellor of the Exchequer, Gordon Brown has referred to repeatedly after October 1997 - are little more than a means of enabling the Labour government to avoid holding a referendum while public opinion remains strongly opposed to British membership of the euro. In other words, determining whether the five conditions have been met will probably be a political, rather than purely economic, decision. The five conditions will probably only be seen to have been 'met' when - and if - public opinion becomes more favourable to the euro. In his March 2004 Budget speech, Gordon Brown asserted that no decision, about whether the five conditions had been met, would be taken until 2005 - the likely year of a general election (the implication being that this too will not be found to be the right moment for a decision).

While New Labour is generally considered to be much more pro-European - and pro-euro - than the Conservatives,

it is important to note that some Labour MPs are opposed to British membership of the euro. Like many Conservatives they are concerned about issues of sovereignty and national identity, and resent the idea of unelected and unaccountable European bankers determining British economic policy.

12.16 *Enlargement of the EU*

Since its official launch on 1 January 1958, the EEC/EU has steadily expanded, with additional countries joining in periodic waves, as indicated by Box 12.15.

In order to be eligible for membership of the European Union, countries have to meet certain conditions:

> 'Politically, these include guarantees of democracy, human rights and protection of minorities. Economically, they require a functioning market economy, the capacity to cope with the single market, and acceptance of the goal of EMU [Economic and Monetary Union].' (*Economist*, 19 July 1997)

A further expansion is scheduled for 2007 or 2008, when Bulgaria, Romania and Turkey are expected to join the EU.

One consequence of this enlargement has been a modification of decision-making in the EU - as indicated in Sections 12.13 and 12.14 above.

> **Main points Sections 12.13 - 12.16**
>
> - **Although the Maastricht Treaty was finally ratified by all member states, the ratification process revealed widespread popular discontent with the European project.**
> - **The Amsterdam Treaty of 1997 and the Nice Treaty of 2000 secured agreement on the next phase of EU enlargement, paving the way for ten new countries, most of them from Eastern Europe, to join the EU on 1 May 2004.**
> - **A single European currency (the euro) was introduced in 2002. The Blair government has ruled out Britain's membership until five specific economic conditions have been met, and a referendum has been held.**

Box 12.15 The expansion of the EU

Year of joining	Countries	Year of joining	Countries	Year of joining	Countries
1958	Belgium	1981	Greece	2004	Czech Republic
	France				Cyprus
	Italy	1986	Portugal		Estonia
	Luxembourg		Spain		Hungary
	Netherlands				Latvia
	West Germany	1995	Austria		Lithuania
			Finland		Malta
1973	United Kingdom		Sweden		Poland
	Denmark				Slovakia
	Ireland				Slovenia

Activity 12.4 Further enlargement of the EU

Item A Expansion to the East

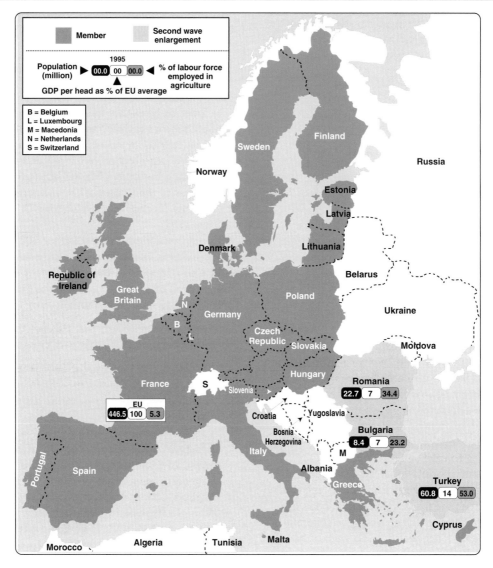

This map shows the members of the EU after May 2004 - after the first wave of expansion to the East was completed. The countries who aim to join in the second wave of expansion are highlighted.

Source: www.europarl.eu.int.

Item B Arguments against enlargement

Take the simple matter of everyday business. First, with an EU of even 21, far less legislation will be passed. In the Council of Ministers, it already takes three hours to go round the table letting each minister have a say. Second, the Commission acts by consensus but, with more commissioners, consensus will be harder to reach. Third, the need to translate into additional languages can only slow procedures down. And fourth, the new Parliament building in Strasbourg is not big enough to house greater numbers. The first wave of enlargement is to be carried out without increasing members' financial contributions. That means cutting the same cake 21 different ways and so less will be done. Expansion would bring 100 million new consumers, but with only a third of the purchasing powers of existing EU consumers. Price differences are staggering. Poland alone could destroy the carefully designed 'fortress Europe' policy aimed at keeping out unwanted immigrants and criminals. And, with over 25% of Poles working on the land, fundamental reform of the Common Agricultural Policy is necessary or massive subsidies will have to be paid to Polish smallholders.

Source: The *Independent on Sunday*, 20 July 1997.

Item C Arguments in favour of enlargement

For those who support a European single market but fear monetary and political union, enlargement is the answer. Enlargement will vastly increase the size of the single market while, at the same time, making political or economic integration difficult, if not impossible because of institutional difficulties. Like John Major's government, the Blair government supports enlargement on the grounds that it will weaken the commitment of the Franco-German centre to integration and federalism. One of the aims of the British presidency in 1998 was to make serious progress on the enlargement issue. To the extent that the Cardiff summit recognised the firm commitment to membership of 11 applicant countries, this was done (though a great deal of fine detail was left to the Austrian presidency). As a result, it is clear that Europe is moving at five speeds at least. The fastest lane is that of the 11 who are entering the single currency. Then come Britain, Sweden, Denmark and Greece which will stay out of the euro at first. Trailing them are the five-plus-one fast-track applicants; then the other five; then Turkey. The challenge will be to keep the convoy moving forward without breaking up.

Source: The *Economist*, 20 December 1997 and Pilkington 2001.

Item D An enlarged EU

This cartoon shows a body builder (an enlarged EU) kicking sand in the face of Uncle Sam (the USA) as he runs past him.

Questions

1. a) Judging from Items A-C. what are the likely consequences of enlargement?
   b) What reforms will the EU need to make if enlargement is to be a success?

2. Using Item B, explain why many federalists are opposed to enlargement.

3. What point is being made by Item D? How accurate a prediction is it? Explain your answer.

12.17 Europe as a divisive issue in British politics

Divisions over Europe are nothing new. Ever since the formation of the EEC, British politicians have been divided about the extent to which Britain should become involved in the European project. Indeed, the positions adopted by the two main parties have fluctuated so much that, at different times, both have been predominantly pro-European and predominantly anti-European. With the exception, perhaps, of the Heath government which negotiated Britain's entry into the EEC, no British government has adopted an unreservedly pro-European stance. As a result, the UK has earned the reputation of being a semi-detached member of the EU.

Factors shaping attitudes towards the EU

Ashford (1992) claims that three factors affect the attitudes towards the EU adopted by the main parties. These are outlined in Box 12.16 on page 237.

12.18 The Conservative Party and Europe, 1945-97

With hindsight, it is possible to see mainstream Conservative thinking over Europe going through four distinct phases in the period from 1945 to 1997.

Phase 1 - Detached from Europe (1945-61)

The first phase was dominated by Churchill's view of what Britain's relationship with Europe should be. In one sense, Churchill was a supporter of European integration - see Box 12.17 on page 237.

However, Churchill's 'United States of Europe' did not include Britain. Britain was to encourage its European neighbours to unite, but it was to remain aloof. This reflected Churchill's view that Britain was still a great power with world-wide obligations (to the Empire, for example). Britain, in other words, was not just geographically detached from Europe, it should remain politically detached as well. When

Box 12.16 Ashford on attitudes towards the EU

First, Ashford contrasts the adversarial nature of the British system with that of other European countries, such as Germany, which have a more consensual style of politics. Regardless of which party has been in power in Britain, criticism has been made of the government's stance on Europe by the opposition parties. This has led governments to be reluctant to accept moves towards greater integration and, in turn, it has led to a lack of enthusiasm towards the EU among the British electorate.

Second, due to divisions within parties, Ashford claims, there have never been clear-cut proposals over Britain's future role in Europe.

Third, both main parties are concerned that their ideological self-image is under threat from further European integration. Many Conservative supporters can see the advantage of a single market, for example, but oppose giving up economic sovereignty to achieve this. Similarly, although most Labour supporters agree with the provisions of the Social Chapter, some - particularly left-wingers like Dennis Skinner - regard the EU as a capitalist club which is incompatible with socialism.

Anthony Eden became Prime Minister in April 1955, the decision was taken not to participate in the Messina Conference in June (see above, Box 12.5). Although Britain was invited to become a founder member of the EEC, the invitation was turned down.

Box 12.17 Churchill on European integration

'If Europe is to be saved from infinite misery and indeed from final doom, there must be an act of faith in the European family. We must build a kind of United States of Europe.'
Source: Lipgens 1981, p.319.

Phase 2 - Pro-Europeanism (1961-75)

The second phase began when Harold Macmillan, Conservative Prime Minister, applied to the EEC for entry in 1961. This phase lasted from 1961 to 1975. It is characterised by the pro-European stance adopted by the Conservative leadership.

Box 12.18 shows how Macmillan justified his U-turn.

Box 12.18 Macmillan's U-turn

Justifying his party's apparent U-turn, Macmillan said in 1961: 'Most of us recognise that, in a changing world, if we are not to be left behind and to drop out of the mainstream of the world's life, we must be prepared to change and adapt our methods. All through history, this has been one of the main sources of our strength.'
Source: House of Commons Debates, 2 August 1961.

Macmillan, therefore, supported membership of the EEC on the grounds of pragmatism. Although Britain's application to join the EEC was vetoed in 1963 and again in 1967, the Conservative leadership continued to press for membership. Edward Heath, a pro-European, became Leader of the Conservative Party in 1965 and it was he who finally signed the Treaty of Accession in 1972. Having negotiated Britain's entry into the EEC, the Conservative leadership then supported continued membership when the referendum on this issue was held in 1975.

Phase 3 - Transition (1975-87)

The third phase began in 1975 when Margaret Thatcher was elected Leader of the Conservative Party cnd lasted until 1987. While in opposition between 1975 and 1979, Thatcher began to criticise the over-bureaucratisation of the EEC and she complained about the amount Britain contributed to the EEC budget. When she became Prime Minister in 1979, her attitude was markedly different from that of Edward Heath. Although she remained committed to membership of the EEC, she made it clear that her aim was to get the best deal for Britain (regardless of what that meant for the other members). Between 1979 and 1984 the EEC agenda was dominated by the question of how much members (especially Britain) should contribute to the EEC Budget. This was finally resolved when it was agreed that Britain should receive a rebate. Then, between 1984 and 1987 the British government was at the heart of plans to create a single market in Europe. This idea clearly reflected the deregulatory policies which the Thatcher government pursued in the UK. Ironically, however, it was the Single European Act which became the root of conflict in the Conservative Party.

Phase 4 - Division (from 1987)

The fourth phase began after the Single European Act came into operation in 1987 and still continues. While the majority of Conservatives approved the idea of a single European market, the full implications of the Single European Act took many of them by surprise and alienated them. By 1988, Margaret Thatcher had joined the ranks of the disaffected. In her Bruges Speech of September 1988, she criticised what she saw as growing federalism - see Box 12.19.

Box 12.19 Thatcher's Bruges Speech

'My first guiding principle is this: willing and active cooperation between independent and sovereign states is the best way to build a European Community.'

Source: Thatcher 1988.

The Bruges Speech was a turning point since Thatcher's Euroscepticism was not shared by some of her Cabinet colleagues. Divisions over Europe were then instrumental in Thatcher's downfall. And, they soon reappeared when John Major became Prime Minister.

Although, in the run-up to the Maastricht Treaty, Major's negotiation of opt-outs appeased the majority of Conservatives, hard-line Eurosceptics began to emerge. After the 1992 general election, the Major government's forced departure from the Exchange Rate Mechanism (ERM) increased antagonism to the whole European project and the government's small majority ensured that backbench rebellion could have serious consequences. The Eurosceptics took advantage of this and put pressure on the government. This culminated in the withdrawal of the whip from eight backbench MPs in November 1994. Although the whip was restored in April 1995, the Conservative Party remained deeply divided on Europe.

This division within the party deeply affected government policy. John Peterson notes that once Britain had left the ERM:

'Over the next four years, Major and members of his Cabinet often seemed content to scorn the EU just to occupy a middle ground within the Conservative Party.' (Peterson 1997, p.24)

Perhaps the best example of this is the policy of non-cooperation which was adopted by the British government after the EU imposed a ban on the export of British beef. In response to this ban:

'The UK vetoed all proposed EU measures which required a unanimous vote whether they related to beef or not, while demanding that a timetable be agreed for lifting the ban.' (Peterson 1997, p.25)

This policy of non-cooperation (which ended in June 1996) not only ensured that relations between Britain and other EU members deteriorated, it also enabled the Labour Party to claim that the Conservatives were failing to provide the lead which Britain needed in Europe.

12.19 The Conservative Party and Europe since 1997

Europe remained a divisive issue in the Conservative Party during the run-up to the 1997 general election and remained one after the party's defeat. Following that defeat, William Hague was elected Party Leader. As Robert Leach points out, there were four reasons why Hague could take his time before making a firm commitment about the party's position on Europe. These are outlined in Box 12.20

Box 12.20 Hague and the EU

There were four reasons why William Hague could take his time before making a firm commitment about the party's position on Europe

- because the election defeat brought a strong will to unite
- because some leading pro- and anti-Europeans had failed to be re-elected and the others were marginalised by the parliamentary arithmetic
- because the fear that the Conservative Party would be outflanked by rival anti-European parties had vanished with the failure of the Referendum Party and others
- because parties in opposition can wait on events before making major policy statements.

Source: Leach 1998.

Despite this, within weeks of the 1997 Conservative Party conference, Hague made a firm pledge against joining the single currency for the following ten years. He then consolidated this strong anti-European stance with a number of speeches which made his opposition to further integration very plain. In a speech made in France in May 1998, for example, he argued that the original idea of economic, strategic and political integration was outdated in a globalised high-tech world and he defended 'diversity, pluralism and the nation state' (*Independent*, 20 May 1998). In the autumn of 1998, Hague held a ballot of all Conservative Party members, asking them whether they supported his policy on Europe. A majority (84% of votes cast) backed the policy on a turnout of 60%.

Hague's successors as Conservative Leader, Iain Duncan Smith from September 2001 until November 2003 and Michael Howard, have maintained the Conservative Party's Eurosceptic stance, continuing to rule out British membership of the euro for the lifetime of a Parliament and opposing proposals for an EU constitution or for a 'Euro-army' (the proposed Rapid Response Force) which, Conservative critics claim, would pose problems for Britain's membership of NATO, along with the 'special relationship' with the United States.

Conservative Eurosceptics view these proposals with alarm because constitutions and armies are characteristics of nation states, the implication being that these are the latest manifestations of an emerging European superstate. They argue that an EU constitution and a Euro-army have nothing whatsoever to do with the economic objective of the Treaty of Rome - namely the setting up of a free-trade zone within Europe. The EU, they claim, is developing political and military aspirations which ought to be beyond its remit.

The EU has proved a less divisive issue for the Conservative Party since 2001, largely because the prospect of the Blair government holding a referendum on the euro before the 2005 general election has steadily receded. The party also recognises that divisions and in-fighting over Europe alienated voters. Since 2001, there seems to have been a tacit agreement to avoid further public arguments over Europe as far as possible. There has, in other words, been a 'cessation of hostilities' in the Conservative Party (Dorey 2004).

12.20 *The Labour Party and Europe, 1945-97*

The Labour Party has also gone through four discrete phases with regard to its stance vis-à-vis Europe from 1945 to 1997.

Phase 1 - Labour and Europe 1945-75

As with the Conservative Party, mainstream Labour thinking was hostile towards the EEC at first. It was not until Labour won power in 1964 that the pro-European wing of the party managed to gain an ascendancy. The party voted in support of an application to join the EEC in 1967, but 36 Labour backbenchers voted against their party. The split in the party between pro- and anti-Europeans remained, festering, until Labour formed the government again in 1974. Most commentators agree that the split was the main reason why Harold Wilson (see Box 12.21) agreed to a referendum in 1975.

Box 12.21 Harold Wilson

Harold Wilson used the referendum on the EEC in 1975 as a means of healing divisions within the Labour Party.

Phase 2 - Labour and Europe 1975-83

Although the electorate voted in the 1975 referendum by a substantial majority to remain in the EEC, a significant minority of Labour MPs and supporters remained opposed to membership on the grounds that the EEC was a capitalist club which would hinder rather than foster socialism. For example, 'socialist' measures, such as public ownership and import controls (to keep out foreign goods, in order to protect British industry and jobs), were clearly incompatible with the free-trade objectives and principles laid out in the Treaty of Rome.

The Labour left also - rather like the Conservative right - strongly criticised the loss of parliamentary sovereignty and national autonomy that EEC membership entailed, and complained that decisions directly affecting ordinary British people were increasingly taken by 'faceless bureaucrats' in Brussels, and unelected, unaccountable bankers who had no concern for the well-being and welfare of ordinary working people.

After Labour's general election defeat in 1979, it was this faction which gained the upper hand in the Labour Party. The anti-European direction in which the Labour Party thus moved at this time was one reason why several senior Labour MPs and former Cabinet ministers - most notably Roy Jenkins, David Owen, Bill Rodgers and Shirley Williams - left the party to form the SDP in 1981 (the SDP subsequently merging with the Liberal Party to become today's Liberal Democrats, arguably Britain's most pro-European political party - see Unit 9).

Consequently, the Labour Party contested the 1983 general election on an anti-European platform - its 1983 manifesto committing a Labour government to withdraw from the EEC. The scale of the defeat, however, was so great that the party was forced to re-evaluate its policies.

Phase 3 - Transformation after 1983

Under the leadership of Neil Kinnock (1983-92), the Labour Party was transformed into an overwhelmingly pro-European party. This transformation came about for reasons listed in Box 12.22.

Box 12.22 Reasons why Labour became pro-EEC

The Labour Party was transformed into an overwhelmingly pro-European party for the following reasons:

1. The Labour Party remained in opposition throughout the 1980s. This frustrated the party's supporters who felt helpless in the face of the Thatcher 'revolution'. Many began to look to Europe to offset the worst excesses of Thatcherism.

2. The pro-European Liberal/SDP Alliance took away votes from Labour in the 1983 general election.

3. The Social Charter and the social dimension of changes agreed by the EC in the late 1980s appealed ideologically to Labour supporters.

4. A pro-European stance made sense tactically in the late 1980s since it became clear that the Conservative Party was moving gradually towards an anti-European position.

Phase 4 - Labour and Europe 1992-97

Although divisions over Europe in the Labour Party remained at the time of the party's defeat in the 1992 general election, they were much less obvious than those in the Conservative Party and they remained so throughout John Major's second term in office. Labour's strategy remained consistent:

- to present a united front (in contrast to the open divisions within the Conservative Party)

- to criticise the Conservative government's obstructionist tactics and its Eurosceptic rhetoric
- to argue that a Labour government would take a positive lead in Europe while still managing to protect Britain's national interests.

When Tony Blair and John Prescott were elected as Leader and Deputy Leader in 1994, this was widely regarded as a victory for the pro-Europeans. But, any hopes of movement towards the federalist camp were quickly dashed. Faced by a Europhobic press and opinion polls which showed that most British people were lukewarm about moves towards further integration, the Labour leadership (like the Conservative leadership) argued that its main priority was to protect British interests within the EU. In a speech delivered in Bonn in June 1996, for example, Tony Blair outlined his viewpoint. A key extract from the speech is given in Box 12.23.

Box 12.23 Blair speech in 1996

'[I am aiming for] relations based on national interest, which demands that we are a leading player in Europe; succeeding in Europe, not failing; winning, not losing; walking tall in Europe, not skulking on the sidelines; constructive and engaged, not simply because the interests of Europe demand it, but above all because the interests of Britain demand it.'

Source: *Independent*, 19 June 1996.

Significantly, the Labour Party followed the Conservative lead and made a commitment to hold a referendum before joining the single currency.

In the run-up to the 1997 general election, the Labour Party was able to make a great deal of political capital out of its stance on Europe. During the election campaign, Conservative divisions on Europe re-emerged. As Dobson notes:

'Europe worked wholeheartedly against the Conservatives and, without doubt, its continued prominence as an issue contributed mightily to the Labour landslide.' (Dobson 1998, p. 21)

12.21 Labour and Europe since May 1997

The new Labour government acted quickly to signal a change in approach and attitude. Within days of the election, the Foreign Secretary, Robin Cook, announced that Britain would sign the Social Chapter and, within a month, Cook had appointed an MEP to be his European parliamentary private secretary - to handle liaison with the European Parliament (no MEP had been appointed to such a post before). At the same time, Doug Henderson began work as the first Minister for Europe, bringing Britain into line with other EU members. Previously a civil servant, not a minister, had been sent to represent Britain in intergovernmental talks.

A change in style, but not substance

These moves suggested a change of style and attitude and that has persisted. There is, however, rather less evidence of a change in substance - see Box 12.24.

Box 12.24 A change in style but not substance

Although the Labour government has been far more willing to negotiate and accept compromises rather than to seek confrontation, there is still a big divide between those member states who, ultimately, have a federalist agenda and the British position - where the fundamental aim remains the building of a loose alliance of nation states. This divide was apparent during the negotiations over the 1997 Amsterdam Treaty when Britain blocked the merging of the WEU (a defence union) with the EU and when Tony Blair argued that no further institutional reform would be needed for successful enlargement (a claim that many other members would hotly dispute). And, it was apparent in 1998 when it was agreed that 11 member states would be going ahead with the single currency in January 1999, leaving Britain (and three other member states) on the sidelines. The Labour government had already announced (in October 1997) that it would not join the single currency until 2002 at the earliest.

By the spring of 2004, it had become clear that there would be no referendum on membership of the euro before the next general election, widely expected to be held in 2005. Recognising that public opinion was still overwhelmingly opposed to British membership of the euro, the government continued to maintain that the time was not yet right because the five economic conditions had not been met.

Blair and labour market flexibility

In spite of his pro-European rhetoric, Blair has resisted proposals, particularly in the sphere of employment protection and workers' rights, which he maintains would undermine labour market flexibility in Britain and inhibit the global competitiveness of the British economy. Indeed, Blair - in a manner which Margaret Thatcher or Norman Tebbit might admire - has lectured other EU leaders, particularly those of France and Germany, about the need for them to liberalise and deregulate their economies, reform their welfare states, and render their labour markets more flexible. In other words, he has urged them to follow the British path to economic renewal and welfare modernisation.

Britain's support for the USA's spring 2003 bombing of Iraq also strained Tony Blair's relationship with some of his EU counterparts, and served to strengthen the Franco-German axis.

12.22 The other parties

The Liberal Democrats

The Liberal Democrats are enthusiastic supporters of greater European integration. As early as 1951, Liberals were arguing that Britain should join the European Coal and Steel Community and the Liberal Party was the only mainstream party to support Britain's entry into the EEC in 1957. The Liberal Democrats can, therefore, claim to have a long tradition of pro-Europeanism. Their long-term aim is for a federal Britain within a federal Europe.

Although the Liberal Democrats remain the most pro-European of the main parties, in recent years they have adopted a 'Euro-realist' approach and accept the need for some reforms. In a policy paper published in 1996, for example, they attacked EU decision-making as 'unnecessarily secretive and largely unaccountable'. They back an extension of qualified majority voting in an enlarged EU and call for more open government.

The nationalist parties

Both the Scottish National Party (SNP) and Plaid Cymru (the Welsh nationalists) were originally opposed to Britain's entry into the EEC. They were concerned that smaller nations, like Scotland and Wales, would lose much of their identity and distinctiveness in the EEC, and that most of the apparent benefits of membership would be enjoyed mainly by the people and businesses in England. After all, one of the reasons for the rise of Scottish and Welsh nationalism from the 1960s onwards, was a perception that Westminster and Whitehall failed to pay sufficient attention to the particular needs and concerns of Scotland and Wales. It was feared that EEC membership would represent a transfer of power even further away from Edinburgh and Cardiff. As a result, in the 1975 referendum on whether Britain should remain in the EEC, the SNP campaigned for a No vote, favouring British withdrawal.

Since the 1980s, however, the SNP has adopted a pro-European stance. Ironically, this was partly a response to the centralisation of power by central government at Westminster during Margaret Thatcher's premiership (in spite of her rhetoric about 'rolling back the state'). The SNP's changed attitude towards Europe also reflects developments in the EU itself, most notably the recognition of regional interests and problems (for which there are specific EU funds), and the principle of subsidiarity enshrined in the Maastricht Treaty (which also established the Committee of the Regions). Indeed, the SNP now calls for an independent Scotland within a federal EU.

For the same reasons as the SNP, Plaid Cymru has become more positive in its attitude towards the EU. Plaid Cymru now aims for an independent Wales in a federal EU.

The Green Party

The Green Party (see also Unit 9, Section 9.16) is sceptical about the European Union because it sees it as an organisation whose goal is to encourage economic growth and 'modernisation'. Greens believe that Western rates of growth have not only become unsustainable, but are largely responsible for most environmental problems (such as global warming and climate change) and the depletion of the earth's natural resources.

Ironically, perhaps, the system of proportional representation used for the 1999 Euro-election enabled Britain's Green Party to obtain two seats in the European Parliament.

The UK Independence Party (UKIP)

The UK Independence Party (UKIP - see also Unit 9, Section 9.16) seeks Britain's withdrawal from the European Union in order to regain parliamentary sovereignty and national autonomy. The UKIP insists that it is not anti-European. Rather, it argues that the UK's independence is being destroyed by the ever-increasing number and scope of directives from Brussels.

Ironically, the UKIP won three seats in the 1999 Euro-elections, making it Britain's fourth largest party in the European Parliament. However, this relative success has been undermined somewhat by a succession of leadership resignations, and allegations by a former leadership contender, Rodney Atkinson, that the UKIP was being 'infiltrated by extremists'.

Main points   Sections 12.17 - 12.22

- Europe has consistently been a divisive issue in British politics, not only causing disagreement between the Labour and Conservative Parties, but also within them.
- The Conservative Party has moved from being a broadly pro-European party in the 1960s and 1970s to an increasingly Eurosceptic party since the 1980s, although some senior or well-known Conservatives remain committed pro-Europeans.
- The Labour Party supported withdrawal from the EEC in the 1983 general election, but has steadily become more pro-European - although left-wingers are still hostile to this 'capitalist club'.
- Britain's only consistently pro-European party is the Liberal Democrats.
- The party most strongly opposed to British membership of the European Union is the UK Independence Party.

Activity 12.5 British political parties and the EU

Item A Labour Party manifesto 1983

Labour wants to see Europe safe and prosperous. But the EEC was never devised to suit us, and our experience as a member of it has made it more difficult for us to deal with our economic and industrial problems. The next Labour government, committed to radical, socialist policies for reviving the British economy, is bound to find continued membership a most serious obstacle to the fulfilment of those policies. British withdrawal is the right policy for Britain. We are not 'withdrawing from Europe'. We are seeking to extricate ourselves from the Treaty of Rome and other Community treaties which place political burdens on Britain.

Michael Foot was Leader of the Labour Party in 1983.

Item B Labour Party manifesto 2001

We face a very simple question. Do we want to be part of the change, influencing its direction? Or do we want to opt out? We have spent 50 years on the margins. It is time to make the most of our membership. We have seen the alternative. In the last four years, we have seen the benefits of engagement. Labour believes that Europe brings benefits for Britain, and a Europe reformed by British ideas, working with our MEPs, will be even better for Britain. We want to take Europe forward, to meet British needs. Europe is a crucial market, accounting for more than half of our trade. Our argument is that if Britain is stronger in Europe, it will be stronger in the rest of the world.

Tony Blair was Leader of the Labour Party in 2001.

Item C Conservative Party manifesto 1983

The creation of the European Community has been vital in cementing lasting peace in Europe and ending centuries of hostility. We came to office determined to make a success of British membership of the Community. This we have done. The European Community is the world's largest trading group. It is by far our most important export market. Withdrawal would be a catastrophe for this country. As many as two million jobs would be at risk. We would lose the great export advantages and the attraction to overseas investors which membership now gives us. It would be a fateful step towards isolation, at which only the Soviet Union and her allies would rejoice.

Margaret Thatcher was Leader of the Conservative Party in 1983.

Item D Conservative Party manifesto 2001

> The guiding principle of Conservative policy towards the EU is to be in Europe, but not run by Europe. The EU has, with the prospect of enlargement, reached a fork in the road. Down one route lies a fully integrated superstate with nation states and the national veto disappearing. The Blair government is taking us down this route. The alternative is a Europe of nations coming together in different combinations for different purposes and to differing extents. In other words, a network Europe. We will insist on a Treaty 'flexibility' provision, so that outside the areas of the single market and core elements of an open, free-trading and competitive EU, countries need only participate in new legislative actions at a European level if they see this as in their national interest. The next Conservative government will keep the pound. We will maintain our national veto on European legislation.

William Hague was Leader of the Conservative Party in 2001.

Item E Liberal Democrats' manifesto 2001

> Liberal Democrats are firm supporters of the European Union, but as critical members of the European family, we are also firm on its failings. We believe that the EU offers the best means of promoting Britain's interests in Europe and in the wider world. Nations acting together can achieve more. The EU must have the resources and powers to act in areas where problems cannot be solved at a national level. But it should stay clear when European action is not necessary. We favour the application of majority voting in the Council where necessary to ensure that the EU functions effectively. But we will maintain a veto on the constitution, defence, budgetary and tax matters and regulations on pay and social security.

Charles Kennedy was Liberal Democrat Leader in 2001.

Questions

1. Using Items A-D, explain how the Labour and Conservative Parties have changed their attitudes and policies towards the EU since 1983.

2. Why are the Liberal Democrats so strongly committed towards the EU? Use Item E in your answer.

12.23 British public opinion, the EU and the euro

As noted above, the result of the referendum held on membership of the EEC in 1975 suggested that support for Britain's continued membership of the EEC was 'unenthusiastic - wide, but not deep'. If the British people have never been enthusiastic Europeans, then their support has certainly declined since the 1990s, as illustrated by a wide range of opinion polls and attitude surveys.

Box 12.25 shows that the British people have the least favourable view of the European Union compared to the citizens of other member states.

Box 12.25 Citizens' attitudes towards their country's membership of the EU (%)
(Don't knows not included)

Country	Benefited	Not benefited	Good thing	Bad thing
Ireland	82	9	73	6
Greece	75	17	62	7
Luxembourg	69	21	77	6
Denmark	67	21	57	22
Spain	66	19	62	7
Portugal	65	22	55	11
Belgium	57	31	56	12
Netherlands	54	34	62	12
Italy	49	35	58	10
France	48	33	44	17
Austria	40	45	35	20
Finland	40	47	39	22
Germany	37	37	46	10
Sweden	31	50	40	32
UK	30	45	28	29

Source: European Commission 2004.

A sizeable minority of British people regularly express support for withdrawal from the EU, although there is still usually a small majority favouring continued British membership of the EU. This is illustrated in Box 12.26.

Yet even this small majority in favour can sometimes swing in favour of withdrawal from the EU, as it did temporarily during the September 2000 fuel protests.

Perhaps, though, it is somewhat surprising that support for Britain's withdrawal from the EU is not even higher, given the constant barrage of anti-EU propaganda published by many of Britain's newspapers, particularly some of the tabloids.

The British public and the euro
The aspect of the EU about which British people are most sceptical is membership of the single European currency. British public opinion has, by at least a 2:1 majority, consistently been opposed to Britain joining the euro, as illustrated by Figure 12.27.

Box 12.26 Support for British withdrawal from/remaining in the EU

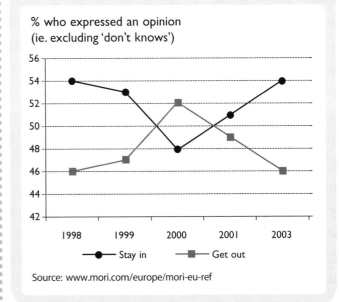

% who expressed an opinion (ie. excluding 'don't knows')

Source: www.mori.com/europe/mori-eu-ref

Box 12.27 Lack of support for Britain joining the euro

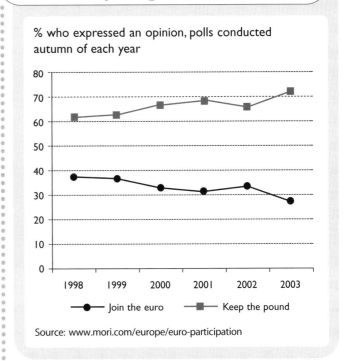

% who expressed an opinion, polls conducted autumn of each year

Source: www.mori.com/europe/euro-participation

There are several reasons why the British people are generally lukewarm, or even sceptical, in their attitudes towards the EU, and clearly opposed to adopting the euro:

First, national pride is particularly pronounced in Britain - often bordering on the xenophobic - so that European integration and/or joining the euro are perceived as the death knell of 'Britishness' and national identity.

Second, this feeling of national pride and independence has been greatly bolstered by Britain's role in the two world wars of the 20th century, and also the fact that Britain used to have an Empire spanning one-third of the globe. Britain was seen - and saw itself - as a world superpower, both politically and militarily, and the legacy of this image is still strong today.

Third, many British people feel isolated from Europe, not merely in a physical or geographic sense, but culturally, socially, and linguistically too. Many people in Britain like having their summer holidays in Europe, and some even buy a cottage in France, but they still do not feel themselves to be European.

Fourth, many British people feel a close affinity with the United States, a country where the values of capitalism, individualism and liberal democracy are deeply entrenched. Indeed, there have occasionally been opinion polls which have revealed that more people in Britain 'identify' with the United States more than with Europe. This, of course, partly reflects the frequency with which British politicians talk about 'the special relationship' with the United States, as they did in their attempts at justifying the military attacks on Iraq.

Fifth, some Euroscepticism is a consequence of ignorance about the EU, which is reinforced by a lack of interest. People who know or care little about EU politics and developments are more likely to accept what they read in the newspapers and much of the coverage of EU affairs in the British press is extremely negative. The 2003 British Social Attitudes Survey, for example, found that 'people who intend to vote "no" in a referendum are less knowledgeable about the euro than those who would vote yes', a finding which strongly suggested that 'public antipathy towards the euro reflects a continued ignorance of the fact and a corresponding susceptibility to anti-European "scare stories"'. It was also discovered that 52% of readers of broadsheet newspapers were in favour of British membership of the euro, compared to only 28% of tabloid readers (Park et al. 2003).

Perhaps not surprisingly, this British Euroscepticism is reflected in turnout to elections to the European Parliament. As Box 12.28 illustrates, turnout in the UK in the 1999 Euro-election was the lowest of any member state in the European Union. Further disillusion with, or disinterest in the EU, coupled with the more general rise in voter apathy, led to concern that turnout in Britain for the 2004 European Parliament election might fall below 20%.

Box 12.28 Turnout in European Parliament elections, by country (%)

Country	1994	1999
Austria	67.7*	49.0
Belgium	90.7	90.0
Denmark	52.9	50.4
Finland	60.3*	30.1
France	52.7	47.0
Germany	60.2	45.2
Greece	71.2	70.2
Ireland	44.0	50.5
Italy	74.8	70.8
Luxembourg	88.5	85.8
Netherlands	35.6	29.9
Portugal	35.5	40.4
Spain	59.6	64.4
Sweden	41.6*	38.3
United Kingdom	36.4	24.0

* First European elections after joining EU in 1996.

Source: Pilkington 2001, p.216.

Britain's low turnout in European Parliament elections partly reflects a general lack of interest or understanding of EU politics, but it also derives from a common perception that the European Parliament is relatively weak or ineffectual compared to other decision-making institutions, such as the Commission. Certainly, few British people seem to feel that the European Parliament has much of an impact on their day-to-day life, and this reinforces the sense that the European Parliament is 'remote', not just geographically, but politically. This does, though, beg the question as to why the citizens of most other EU member states seem to vote in much higher numbers in Euro-elections, and generally have a more positive perception of the European Union.

Main points Section 12.23

- If the British people have never been enthusiastic Europeans, then their support has certainly declined since the 1990s.
- A sizeable minority of British people regularly express support for withdrawal from the EU, although there is still usually a small majority favouring continued British membership of the EU.
- The aspect of the EU about which British people are most sceptical is membership of the single European currency. British public opinion has, by at least a 2:1 majority, consistently been opposed to Britain joining the euro.
- British people are generally lukewarm or sceptical because: (1) national pride is particularly pronounced in Britain; (2) the image of the UK as a world leader is strong; (3) people feel isolated from Europe; (4) many British people identify with the USA; (5) people are ignorant about the EU.
- Turnout in Euro-elections is the lowest in the EU.

Activity 12.6 British public opinion, EU membership and the euro

Item A Attitudes towards the euro by social background, (1) (%)

Class/occupation	Join	Not join	Don't know
Managerial/professional	47	48	6
Intermediate occupations	30	63	7
Small business/self-employed	36	57	7
Lower supervisory/technical	26	67	8
Semi-skilled/routine	25	67	8

Education	Join	Not join	Don't know
Degree	56	37	7
HE below degree level	41	54	5
A level (or equivalent)	36	60	4
GCSE (or equivalent)	30	65	5
CSE (or equivalent)	26	66	9
No qualification	23	67	10

Source: Park et al. 2003, p.221.

Item B Attitudes towards the euro by social background, (2) (%)

(%, difference between saying euro would be a 'good thing' and saying a euro would be 'bad thing', for Britain)

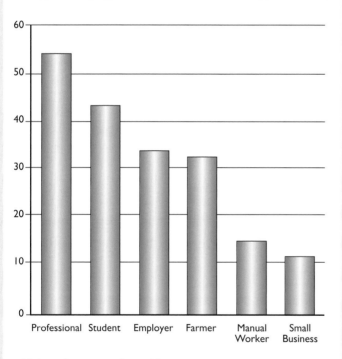

This poll was conducted in autumn 1996.

Source: Hix 2000, p.57 .

Item C Result of the 2001 general election

Party	Vote received	% of vote	Seats won
Labour	10,740,168	42	413
Conservative	8,352,845	33	166
Lib Dems	4,815,249	19	52
UKIP	390,563	1.5	0

Item D Issue saliency in the 2001 election

Issue	Voters citing it as important in deciding how to vote:
1. NHS	89%
2. Law-and-order	82%
3. Education	81%
4. Economy	74%
5. Employment	70%
6. Pensions	65%
7. Taxation	64%
8. Transport	64%
9. Asylum/immigration	52%
10. EU membership	43%
11. Joining the euro	40%

Source: ICM/The Guardian, 30 May 2001.

Questions

1. What do Items A and B indicate about social background and attitudes towards the EU and the euro?

2. Using Items C and D, explain why, given their stance on Europe, the Conservative Party and the UKIP did not receive more support in the 2001 general election.

References

Ashford (1992) Ashford, N., 'The political parties' in *George (1992)*.

Baker, Gamble & Ludlam (1993) Baker, D., Gamble, A. & Ludlam, S., 'Whips or scorpions?: the Maastricht vote and Conservative MPs', *Parliamentary Affairs*, Vol.46.2, 1993.

Baker, Gamble & Ludlam (1994) Baker, D., Gamble, A. & Ludlam, S., 'The parliamentary siege of Maastricht 1993: Conservative division and British ratification', *Parliamentary Affairs*, Vol. 47.1, 1994.

Browne (2001) Browne, A., *The Euro: Should Britain Join? Yes or No? The Intelligent Guide to the Euro Debate*, Icon Books, 2001.

Coates (1994) Coates, D., *The Question of UK Decline*, Harvester Wheatsheaf, 1994.

Cowley (1999) Cowley, P., 'Chaos or cohesion?: Major and the parliamentary Conservative Party' in *Dorey (1999)*.

Dobson (1998) Dobson, A., 'The 1997 general election: explaining a landslide' in *Lancaster (1998)*.

Dorey (1999) Dorey, P. (ed.), *The Major Premiership: Politics and Policies under John Major, 1990-1997*, Macmillan, 1999.

Dorey (2002) Dorey, P., 'A lethargic landslide: the 2001 general election' in *Lancaster (2002)*.

Dorey (2004) Dorey, P., 'The Conservatives under Iain Duncan Smith' in *Lancaster (2004)*.

Dunleavy et al. (1997) Dunleavy, P., Gamble, A., Holliday, I. & Peele, G. (eds), *Developments in British Politics 5*, Macmillan (now Palgrave), 1997.

Dunleavy et al. (2000) Dunleavy, P., Gamble, A., Holliday, I. & Peele, G. (eds) *Developments in British Politics 6*, Macmillan (now Palgrave), 2000.

European Commission (2004) European Commission, *Eurobarometer 60: Public Opinion in the European Union, Autumn 2003*, European Commission, 2004.

Geddes (1993) Geddes, A., *Britain in the European Community*, Baseline, 1993.

George (1992) George, S. (Ed.), *Britain in the European Community*, Baseline Books, 1992.

George (1998) George, S., *An Awkward Partner: Britain in the European Community* (3rd edn), Oxford University Press, 1998.

Hayes-Renshaw (1998) Hayes-Renshaw, F., 'Council of Ministers, *Politics Review*, Vol.7.3, February 1998.

Hix (2000) Hix. S., 'Britain, Europe and the Euro' in *Dunleavy et al. (2000)*.

HMSO (1992) HMSO, Central Office of Information, *Britain in the European Community*, HMSO, 1992.

Jones (1994) Jones, A., 'Parties, ideologies and issues: the case of the European Community' in *Robins, Blackmore & Pyper (1994)*.

Kettle et al (1997) Kettle, M., Palmer, J., Elliott, L. and Keegan, V., *The Single Currency: Should Britain Join? A Guardian Debate*, Vintage, 1997.

Lancaster (1995) Lancaster, S. (ed.) *Developments in Politics: an Annual Review*, Vol.6, Causeway Press, 1995.

Lancaster (1998) Lancaster, S. (ed.) *Developments in Politics: an Annual Review*, Vol.9, Causeway Press, 1998.

Lancaster (2002) Lancaster, S. (ed.) *Developments in Politics: an Annual Review*, Vol.13, Causeway Press, 2002.

Lancaster (2004) Lancaster, S. (ed.) *Developments in Politics: an Annual Review*, Vol.15, Causeway Press, 2004.

Leach (1998) Leach, R., 'Political Ideas' in *Lancaster (1998)*.

Lipgens (1981) Lipgens, W., *European Intergration*, Vol.1, Oxford University Press, 1981.

Lodge (1993) Lodge, J., 'Europe' in *Wale (1993)*.

Mazey & Richardson (1993) Mazey, S. & Richardson, J., 'Pressure groups and the EC', *Politics Review*, Vol.3.1, September 1993.

McCormick (2002) McCormick, J., *Understanding the European Union* (2nd edn), Palgrave, 2002.

Norton (1995) Norton, P., 'The Constitution' in *Lancaster (1995)*.

Nugent (1994) Nugent, N., *The Government and Politics of the European Union*, Macmillan, 1994.

OOPEC (1992) Office for the official Publications of the European Communities (OOPEC), *From Single Market to European Union*, (part of series *Europe on the Move*), 1992.

Park et al (2003) Park, A., Curtice, J., Thomson, K., Jarvis, L. & Bromley, C., *British Social Attitudes: The 20th Report*, Sage/National Centre for Social Research, 2003.

Peterson (1997) Peterson, J., 'Britain, Europe and the world' in *Dunleavy et al. (1997)*.

Pilkington (2001) Pilkington, C., *Britain in the European Community Today* (2nd edn), Manchester University Press, 2001.

Robins, Blackmore & Pyper (1994) Robins, L., Blackmore, H. & Pyper, R. (eds) *Britain's Changing Party System*, Leicester University Press, 1994.

Thatcher (1988) Thatcher, M., *Britain in the European Community*, Conservative Political Centre, 1988.

Wale (1993) Wale, W. (ed.), *Developments in Politics*, Vol.4, Causeway Press, 1993.

13.1 Pressures for constitutional reform

According to Norton, the British constitution:

'Used to be a subject of praise, but little discussion. Today, it is a subject of discussion, but little praise.'
(Norton 1989, p.10)

Norton argues that debate about constitutional reform has only developed since the 1960s. It was during the 1960s and 1970s that governments first appeared ineffectual in the face of rising unemployment and inflation. This apparent weakness, he suggests, led not just to criticism of individual politicians but to criticism of the system of government itself.

At first, the call for constitutional reform came from a small number of outspoken critics. Lord Hailsham's warning in 1976 that Britain was becoming an elective dictatorship (see page 213), for example, received attention because it was a view not often heard in public.

Calls for reform in the late 1980s

It was only in the late 1980s, however, that support for constitutional reform began to reach the political mainstream. This was due to three main factors:

- the Conservative Party's electoral success between 1979 and 1997
- a growth in interest in constitutional reform in the Labour Party
- the formation of the constitutional reform group Charter 88 in 1988.

These three factors are interlinked. By the late 1980s, the Conservative Party had won three general elections in succession. At the 1987 election, just 32% of the electorate voted Conservative - 68% either voted for another party or did not vote at all. Frustration with the Conservatives' monopoly on power raised a number of questions about the constitutional arrangements of the UK, such as:

1. Should there be electoral reform to prevent a single minority party dominating?
2. Should there be devolution of power so that regions could be governed by local people?
3. Should the unelected institutions of the House of Lords and the monarchy be democratised?

Frustration with the Conservatives' monopoly on power also sparked an interest in constitutional reform within the Labour Party - see Box 13.1.

Charter 88 was set up in 1988 to press for a series of linked constitutional reforms. Its members were able to play on Labour's new interest in constitutional reform and lobbied hard in an attempt to shape the party's policies.

A changing landscape

Frustration is not in itself enough to explain why constitutional reform rose up the political agenda. By the time the Conservatives were voted out of office in 1997, there had been a number of significant developments with constitutional implications. These are outlined in Box 13.2.

Box 13.1 Labour's conversion to the cause of constitutional reform

'Labour's conversion to the cause of constitutional reform is a relatively recent one. Up until the late 1980s, the dominant view within the party was that constitutional reform was a waste of time. There were more important matters for a Labour government to address, such as poverty and unemployment. But Neil Kinnock's Policy Review from 1987 began to change Labour's approach to the constitution.'

Source: Driver & Martell 1998, p.121.

Box 13.2 Constitutional developments 1992-97

1. The ratifying of the Maastricht Treaty raised questions about Britain's sovereignty.
2. What many saw as an erosion of civil liberties suggested the advantages of a Bill of Rights.
3. The centralisation of power (the reduction of the powers of local government, for example) and the increasing use of unelected quangos led to calls for greater democracy and accountability.
4. The uncovering of miscarriages of justice led to calls for judicial reform.
5. Corruption in the House of Commons and criticisms of its unrepresentative make-up led to calls for the modernisation of parliamentary procedures.

13.2 Labour's reform proposals

In its 1997 general election manifesto, the Labour Party promised to make a number of constitutional reforms if it won the election. These pledges are outlined in Box 13.3.

Box 13.3 Labour's pledges

In its 1997 general election manifesto, the Labour Party promised to:

- abolish the right of hereditary peers to sit and vote in the House of Lords
- set up a special select committee in the Commons to review its procedures
- hold a referendum on the voting system for elections to the House of Commons
- draw up a Freedom of Information Act
- hold referendums and, if they supported the idea, to set up assemblies in Scotland and Wales
- hold a referendum and, if it supported the idea, to set up a directly elected strategic authority and mayor for London
- incorporate the European Convention on Human Rights into British law
- hold a referendum on whether to join a single European currency.

Compared to constitutional reform programmes of other post-war governments, the pledges made in Box 13.3 on page 248 amounted to a formidable and radical package of reform. The following sections assess how far the promised reforms have been translated into practice.

13.3 Labour's constitutional reforms in action

Labour won the 1997 election and began to put its reform programme into practice. By 2004, the Labour Party had won a second general election (in 2001) and had been in office for seven years. The constitutional reforms passed between 1997 and 2004 are summarised in Box 13.4.

Box 13.4 New Labour's constitutional reforms 1997-2004

By 2004:

1. There had been devolution of power to the Scottish Parliament and Welsh Assembly (see Unit 18).

2. A mayor and a new assembly had been elected in London (see also Unit 18).

3. Changes had been made to parliamentary procedures (see Unit 14).

4. Elements of the European Convention on Human Rights had been incorporated into British law with the passing of the 1998 Human Rights Act (see Section 13.5 below).

5. A Freedom of Information Act had been passed (see Section 13.6 below).

6. All but 92 of the hereditary peers no longer sat in the House of Lords and the days were numbered for those who remained (see Unit 14).

7. Steps had been taken to abolish the post of Lord Chancellor (see Section 13.7 below).

On other intended reforms, progress was slower. The Jenkins Commission produced recommendations on voting reform for elections to the House of Commons. But, the government, in effect, ignored them and the promised referendum on the issue did not materialise. Also, no referendum was held on whether the UK should join the single European currency.

13.4 Criticisms of Labour's programme

The following criticisms have been levelled at Labour's programme of constitutional reform - some from the political right, but some from the left, too.

1. The reforms do not go far enough

Some critics of Labour's programme of constitutional reform have argued that it has not gone far enough. With a majority of 179 following the 1997 election victory (and 167 after

2001 general election), it is argued, the government has been in a position to do what it likes. Rather than proceeding in relatively small steps, it could have taken advantage of its strong position and brought forward its longer-term aims. For example, rather than tinkering with the House of Lords by ending hereditary peers' rights to vote and reducing their numbers (see Unit 14), the government could have taken immediate steps to replace the Lords with an elected second chamber.

2. The reform pledges have been watered down

Some critics argue that some of the reforms pledged were later watered down because some leading ministers lacked enthusiasm for them. In 1998, for example, it became clear that this was the case with the promised Freedom of Information Bill (see 13.6 below). Although a radical Bill was drawn up by David Clark, opposition from the then Home Secretary, Jack Straw, ensured that it was delayed. Then, in July 1998, Clark was sacked in Tony Blair's first reshuffle and Straw drew up another Bill which lacked Clark's radical edge.

3. The reforms lack coherence

Some critics argue that the Labour Party has not really looked at the constitutional reform package as a whole. As a result, it has lacked coherence. For example, devolution for Scotland and Wales went ahead without fully considering the knock-on effects for England. Similarly, removing hereditary peers from the House of Lords on the grounds that they were undemocratic begged the question of what to do about the monarchy since monarchs are chosen by blood-line (as were the hereditary peers).

4. Piecemeal legislation often doesn't work

As early as 1994, it was pointed out that introducing piecemeal legislation had ended up achieving little in the past and what was needed was a new, integrated approach to constitutional reform. This point is explored in Box 13.5.

Box 13.5 How to achieve a new constitutional settlement

Past efforts at constitutional reform show that officials will be obstructive and little will be achieved if a new government attempts reform by introducing piecemeal legislation. This is what happened in Harold Wilson's first government. A Bill was introduced to reform the House of Lords. But, the Commons was divided between those who wanted abolition, those who wanted other changes, or no change, and those who supported the Bill. Eventually the Bill had to be abandoned. To bring about a new constitutional settlement, it is necessary to introduce a new way of law-making. Rather than introducing separate laws for each area of change, a new government should set up a non-partisan Constitutional Convention. This would draw up a package of measures which would then be submitted to the people in a referendum.

Source: The *Observer*, 20 November 1994.

Box 13.6 Reasons why Labour's reform programme is dangerous

The main arguments in support of the view that the Labour government's constitutional reform programme is dangerous are:

1. **Devolution will break up the UK**
   Devolution will lead sooner or later to the break up of the Union and a revival of English nationalism. This could lead to great hostility and bitterness between the various nations which made up the United Kingdom.

2. **A new electoral system will lead to weak government**
   Any major change to the electoral system will lead to weak, coalition government which will cause uncertainty and instability.

3. **House of Lords reform will damage the balance of power**
   Moves to make the House of Lords more democratic will only strengthen the Upper House and cause rivalry between the two legislative chambers.

4. **Changes have been rushed through**
   Changes, such as the abolition of the traditional office of Lord Chancellor, were rushed through without proper thought of all the constitutional implications.

5. **The government will manipulate a euro referendum**
   Eurosceptics are worried that the government will manipulate the eventual referendum on the single currency to ensure that a Yes vote is secured. If that happens, they claim, Britain's sovereignty will be fatally undermined.

5. The reforms are dangerous

Some critics (mainly from the right) have argued that Labour's reform programme is dangerous and will lead to further problems in the future. A number of reasons are given for this accusation. These are outlined in Box 13.6.

6. The reforms are unnecessary

Some critics (mainly Conservative) argue that the constitution of the UK is working satisfactorily and should be left alone.

Main points   Sections 13.1 - 13.4

- **The debate about constitutional reform has only developed since the 1960s and it only reached the mainstream in the late 1980s. This was largely due to frustration with the political system and a changing political landscape.**
- **In its 1997 election manifesto, the Labour Party made a series of pledges on constitutional reform.**
- **Since 1997, Labour has introduced reforms in some areas but not others.**
- **Critics of Labour's package of reforms have argued that: the reforms (1) do not go far enough; (2) have been watered down; (3) lack coherence; (4) have been introduced piecemeal; (5) are dangerous; and (6) are unnecessary.**

Activity 13.1 *Labour's pledges in 1997*

Item A **Comments on Labour's 1997 pledges on constitutional reform**

(i) 'The most important constitutional changes proposed by a major political party this century.' (Rush 1997, p.39)

(ii) 'The most important programme of constitutional reform ever introduced in the UK.' (Magee & Lynch 2003)

(iii) 'A programme of change more radical than any previous set of constitutional proposals.' (Dunleavy et al. 2003b, p.9)

(iv) 'Labour's constitutional revolution …the most far-reaching programme of constitutional reform since 1832 and, some argue, since 1688.' (Gamble 2003b, p.18)

Item B **The Labour government's progress on constitutional reform**

Pledge	Action
To abolish the right of hereditary peers to sit and vote in the House of Lords.	The House of Lords Act 1999 removed the right of all but 92 hereditary peers to sit and vote in the House of Lords. Since then, plans for Stage 2 reforms stalled because of lack of agreement on the way ahead.
To set up a special select committee in the Commons to review its procedures.	This select committee was set up by the government in 2001 and some reforms to House of Commons procedures were some reforms to House of Commons procedures were introduced in 2002.
To hold a referendum on the voting system for elections to the House of Commons	Such a referendum has not been held, although new voting systems are used for the devolved assemblies and European Parliament.
To draw up a Freedom of Information Act.	A watered-down Freedom of Information Act was passed in 1999, but the government delayed its introduction until 2005 (see Section 13.6 below).
To hold referendums and, if they supported the idea, to set up assemblies in Scotland and Wales.	Referendums were held in 1997. The Scottish Parliament and Welsh Assembly have been in operation since 1999.
To hold a referendum and, if it supported the idea, to set up a strategic authority and mayor for London.	The referendum was held in 1998. The first elections for the Greater London Assembly and mayor were held in 2000. Some other cities and towns now also have directly elected mayors.
To incorporate the European Convention on Human Rights into UK law.	The 1998 Human Rights Act incorporated elements of the Convention (see 13.5 below).
To hold a referendum on whether to join a single European currency.	To be held 'when the time is ripe'.

Item C **A step nearer to a modern state**

It increasingly looks as if New Labour's enduring legacy will be a 21st-century constitution. The announcement that Lord Irvine's resignation as Lord Chancellor is to pave the way for a transition to an independent Supreme Court, along with an independent commission for the appointment of judges, opens up the prospect of a reformed judicial and legal system to join the rest of New Labour's constitutional reforms. If the withdrawal of the Law Lords from the legislature also triggers, as it should, a new look at the case for an elected House of Lords, progress will have been made. Britain would then have an independent Supreme Court and Central Bank, an elected second chamber, devolved Parliaments in Scotland and Wales, entrenchment of freedom of information and incorporation of the European Convention on Human Rights into British law. No government in modern times has such a remarkable record. You might almost believe New Labour was a great reforming government. Why, though, has there been little attempt by the government to show how the various initiatives hang together and how they will improve British government, justice and democracy? Each initiative is rolled out piecemeal, almost in the hope that nobody will notice the cumulative ambition.

Source: The *Observer*, 15 June 2003.

Item D **Half-baked and half-hearted**

If the Blair governments' constitutional reform measures were a student essay, they would probably be awarded a borderline D+/C-, on the grounds that some potentially promising and valuable features had been seriously undermined by a failure to think them through properly, and place them in a proper structure. The tutor's comments would also point out that there was a lack of clarity and/or coherence in what had been produced, and a corresponding lack of direction, all leading, ultimately, to a messy and uncertain conclusion. In large part, this is the result of disagreements within the Labour Party and the Blair government itself, for while some MPs and ministers are passionately in favour of certain aspects of constitutional reform, others believe that 'bread and butter' issues (education, health, employment, pensions and transport) are what really matter, and that too much time is being devoted to constitutional matters which are of little interest or direct relevance to ordinary people. However welcome and overdue many of the reforms might be in themselves, they seem to lack an overall 'narrative' and sense of trajectory. It is often said that half-a-loaf is better than no loaf, but if that half-loaf is also half-baked, then people are left with an unpleasant taste in their mouth.

Source: Dorey 2003.

Questions

1. Judging from Items B-D, would you say that the Labour government has lived up to the expectations of those quoted in Item A?

2. Using Items B-D, explain whether there has been significant constitutional reform since 1997.

3. Identify which of the six criticisms outlined in Section 3.4 above are being used in Items C and D.

13.5 *Human Rights Act 1998*

In November 1998, the Human Rights Act received Royal Assent, giving citizens of the UK a Bill of Rights of the kind taken for granted in virtually every other Western democracy. The new Act incorporated parts of the European Convention on Human Rights (ECHR) into UK law and came into effect in 2000 - see Box 13.7.

Box 13.7 The Human Rights Act 1998

The main provisions of the Human Rights Act 1998 were:

1. It became unlawful for a public authority - a government department, local authority or the police - to breach rights laid down by the European Convention on Human Rights (ECHR), unless an existing Act of Parliament meant that the authority was unable to have acted differently.

2. The Act allowed anyone who felt that their rights under the Convention had been breached to take their case to a UK court or tribunal, rather than waiting to go to the European Court of Human Rights in Strasbourg.

3. All UK legislation must be given a meaning that fits with the rights laid down by the ECHR, if that is possible. If a court says that it is not possible, it is up to Parliament to decide what to do.

Source: Home Office 2000.

The Human Rights Act and parliamentary sovereignty

Some commentators welcomed the Human Rights Act as a major development because, unlike most other democracies, the UK had never had a rights-based culture. Previously, under UK law, anything was permitted unless specifically prohibited. Parliament had traditionally been all-powerful, able to pass any law it wanted, with no concern for the rights of minorities.

Yet, before the introduction of the Human Rights Bill, it was precisely this aspect which opponents of the Bill saw as a threat. There were concerns that the incorporation of the ECHR into UK law would erode parliamentary sovereignty (see Unit 11) because, it was feared, judges would be given the power to strike down laws that breached the ECHR. In effect, this would mean that judges, not Parliament, would have the power to decide what the law should be in certain circumstances. In the event, the 1998 Act did not give judges this power. Instead, it limited their powers to declaring laws to be 'incompatible' with the convention. It is then left to Parliament to amend any laws so affected.

Because of this, it is suggested that parliamentary sovereignty has been preserved. Judges will not be drawn into political controversy by being asked (as judges are in Canada, for example) to strike down laws voted for by the people's elected representatives. If a particular piece of legislation is unclear, judges are obliged to interpret it so as to conform to the ECHR. But, in those cases where the meaning is clear, judges have to follow the law even if it breaches the ECHR, their only power being able to declare the law 'incompatible'. The passing of the Human Rights Act, it is argued, does not therefore undermine the sovereignty of Parliament since:

'The ultimate decision, in a case of conflict lies with
Parliament not the courts.' (Peele 2001, p.23)
Under the Act, however, judges are able to override most
secondary legislation - statutory instruments and regulations
put out by government departments.

Some commentators do not agree that parliamentary
sovereignty has not been breached. Richards & Smith (2001),
for example, take a broader political, rather than a legal, view.
They argue that the 1998 Act should be seen in conjunction
with other developments, such as Scottish and Welsh
devolution and the granting of independence to the Bank of
England. Together, such developments represent a significant
series of 'structural constraints' on parliamentary sovereignty.
These authors provide a specific example which is outlined in
Box 13.8.

Box 13.8 The ECHR and parliamentary sovereignty

On 27 January 1999, the Home Secretary, Jack Straw,
signed the Sixth Protocol of the European Convention
on Human Rights, part of which abolishes the death
penalty in the United Kingdom. This was a significant act
because the implication for Parliament was that future
governments would not be in a position to reopen the
debate on the death penalty without first overturning the
entire European Convention on Human Rights. As a
result, although the Labour Cabinet claims that
parliamentary sovereignty has not been affected by
signing up to the ECHR, the reality is that, now,
Parliament's scope for action is clearly limited by the
terms of the ECHR.

Source: Richards & Smith 2001.

Other criticisms of the Human Rights Act

Some critics of the Human Rights Act believe it does not go
far enough in guaranteeing civil rights and have argued that
parliamentary sovereignty is a myth used to prevent
meaningful constitutional change. This was the position
adopted, for example, by the political journalist Hugo Young
(*Guardian*, 8 July 1997). He argued that the way in which the
1998 Act incorporates the ECHR is feeble and little more
than tokenism because judges in the UK do not have the
same powers as European judges sitting in Strasbourg. He
claimed that a new order of freedoms and rights cannot be
properly installed unless Parliament's sovereign power to
override the ECHR is reduced as close as possible to zero.

13.6 Freedom of information

Governments claim that they represent the national interest.
If they do indeed represent the national interest and they
argue that secrecy is a crucial means of defending the state,
then (logically speaking) secrecy must be in the interest of
everybody living in the nation. This, in effect, was the
argument made by the government of the UK during the
Cold War period. Secrecy, so the argument went, was
necessary to protect British citizens from the threat posed by
communism, especially Soviet communism.

While this argument was used to justify 'closed' (secretive)
government, some people argued for 'open' government
which minimises the areas for secrecy and maximises the
availability of information. According to the former Labour
MP Tony Benn, an open government is a more participatory
and a more democratic system of government. His arguments
are outlined in Box 13.9.

Box 13.9 Government control of information

'If we accept that the control of information about
decisions and how they are arrived at is a prerogative of
the government, then we are accepting that democracy
cannot be mature enough to allow people to share even
the thinking that precedes these decisions.'

Source: Benn 1979, p.129.

As a result of the collapse of communism in Eastern Europe
in the early 1990s, the perceived threat to national security
from foreign states reduced. This resulted in new interest in
and new demands for open government.

The Campaign for Freedom of Information

The Campaign for Freedom of Information is a pressure
group set up in 1984. Since then, this group has managed to
win the support of many leading politicians and ex-civil
servants. The group plays a watchdog role, checking on the
proposals made by government in areas which might involve
secrecy. All-party support and the backing of senior civil
servants have helped to give the group legitimacy. Supporters
of the Campaign for Freedom of Information aim to give the
public the right of access to official information with very few
exceptions. Their case has been strengthened by comparing
the position in the UK with examples of freedom of
information legislation in other countries. The USA, for
example, has had a Freedom of Information Act since 1966
and, in Sweden, it has been a legal right to inspect
government documents (apart from those covered by a
Secrecy Act) since 1809.

Margaret Thatcher and freedom of information

The Campaign for Freedom of Information was set up when
Margaret Thatcher was Prime Minister. It aimed to put
pressure on a government which appeared reluctant to
reduce the degree of state secrecy. Indeed, Thatcher argued
against freedom of information on constitutional grounds. In a
letter to the Campaign for Freedom of Information she
wrote:

'Under our constitution, ministers are accountable to
Parliament for the work of their departments and that
includes the provision of information…A statutory
right of access would remove this enormously
important area of decision making from ministers
and Parliament.' (quoted in Wilson 1984, pp.134-35)

John Major and freedom of information

While Margaret Thatcher refused to consider more open
government, her successor as Prime Minister, John Major,
claimed to take a different view. His government began to

promote the idea that the process of government should be more open. This new approach was connected with the development of the Citizen's Charter which, it was claimed, would make available more information on the services provided by government. This idea was taken up in the 1992 Conservative election manifesto which admitted that 'government has traditionally been far too reluctant to provide information' and promised 'we will be less secretive about the workings of government' (Conservative 1992, p.16).

Following the Conservative Party victory at the 1992 general election, these manifesto promises were developed into a new Whitehall code of practice which came into force in 1994. The government issued a code of practice which claimed that the three themes outlined in Box 13.10 would underlie its approach to open government.

Box 13.10 The Major government's code of practice

The three themes the Major government claimed would underlie its approach to open government were:

1. The government would handle information in a way which informed policy-making and debate.

2. The government would provide timely and accessible information to the citizen to explain the government's policies, actions and decisions.

3. The government would restrict access to information only when there were good reasons for doing so.

Criticisms of the Major government's approach

Critics - particularly the Campaign for Freedom of Information - argued that the code of practice introduced by the Major government was too weak and allowed ministers too much discretion. The policy-making process, internal opinion, discussion and advice, all still remained secret. Crucially, the government gave people the right of access to information, but not the right to see correspondence, documents or reports.

In addition, the credibility of John Major's government's support for open government was undermined by the three developments outlined in Box 3.11.

The developments outlined in Box 13.11 led critics to argue that the Major government's claims to support more open government were largely rhetorical - a change of style rather than substance.

The Labour government's first freedom of information proposals

The Labour Party's 1997 general election manifesto contained the following pledge:

'Unnecessary secrecy in government leads to arrogance in government and defective policy decisions...We are pledged to a Freedom of Information Act, leading to more open government.' (Labour 1997, p.33)

Following Labour's general election success, the minister given the job of drafting a Freedom of Information Bill was David Clark. He was responsible for the White Paper which was published in December 1997. The proposals made in the White Paper are outlined in Box 13.12.

Box 13.11 Three key developments under Major

Three key developments were as follows:

1. The Minster for Open Government, William Waldegrave, stated that in exceptional circumstances it was necessary for ministers to tell lies in the House of Commons. He also vigorously defended the use of blocking answers by ministers - the device where half truths or half answers are used in Parliament to avoid spelling out the true picture.

2. Evidence given by ministers at the Scott Inquiry (set up in 1992 to investigate the Arms to Iraq scandal) revealed just how secretive the working of government was. It became clear that much crucial information had not been disclosed to the House of Commons.

3. The response of the government to European plans for more open government suggested a continuing desire for secrecy. In 1994, for example, a new information code drawn up by the European Council of Ministers called for the widest possible access to documents. Attempts to make use of this code, however, were blocked (*Guardian*, 18 April 1994).

Box 13.12 The White Paper on freedom of information, December 1997

- Everyone will have the legal right to see information held by national, regional and local government and some other organisations working on behalf of government - including government agencies, the NHS, quangos, privatised utilities, and private sector organisations working for government.

- Information about the security and intelligence services and the special forces, personnel files, and information vital to crime prevention will be exempt from the Act.

- Information will be withheld if documents have a bearing on: (1) national security, defence and international relations; (2) internal discussion of government policy; (3) law enforcement; (4) personal privacy; (5) commercial confidentiality; (6) the safety of individuals; and (7) the public and the environment.

- In each case, there would need to be the risk of 'substantial harm' for information not to be released.

- In the case of civil service advice to ministers, a simple test of 'harm' will be applied.

- Members of the public will be able to contact the relevant public body for information and a fee will be charged for the service.

- If access to information is denied, there will be the right to appeal to an Information Commissioner who will decide whether or not to grant access.

Source: HMSO 1997.

Although this White Paper was welcomed by the Campaign for Freedom of Information, in July 1998 David Clark was sacked and responsibility for the proposed legislation handed to the Home Secretary, Jack Straw. It was then announced that Straw intended to delay introducing the Bill and that he was fighting for changes in some of the provisions contained in the White Paper.

The Freedom of Information Act 2000

The Labour government eventually published its revised Freedom of Information Bill in May 1999. It contained many changes from the earlier White Paper. The main changes are outlined in Box 13.13.

Box 13.13 Main changes from the White Paper

The Freedom of Information Bill differed from the White Paper as follows:

1. The White Paper's requirement that ministers should demonstrate that 'substantial harm' would come from publication had been replaced by the far weaker test of 'prejudice'.

2. The Security and Intelligence Services were subject to a complete exemption from the terms of the Bill.

3. Information that related to government policy was also exempted, whereas the White Paper had proposed that such information could only be withheld if ministers could show that substantial harm to the public interest would result.

Pressure groups, including the Campaign for Freedom of Information, argued strongly that the Bill was a deep disappointment as it would do little to improve openness in government departments. When Jack Straw presented the final version to Parliament in October 1999, he made minor concessions. But Maurice Frankel of the Campaign for Freedom of Information claimed:

'an overriding defect [of the Bill is] the several blanket exemptions which allow authorities to withhold information without evidence of harm.'

As the Bill passed through the House of Lords, the government made further concessions, namely:

- acceptance that, if the public interest for and against disclosure was equally balanced, the information would be disclosed
- the placing of a statutory obligation on public authorities to help applicants seeking information.

MPs, from all parties, tabled 118 last-minute amendments in an attempt to improve the legislation, but the Home Secretary imposed a guillotine to force the measure through and the Bill received the Royal Assent on 30 November 2000.

Delay in implementation

The Freedom of Information Act was expected to come into operation in 2002. Elizabeth France, who was appointed Information Commissioner with responsibility for enforcing the legislation, argued in a leaked letter that it would be 'sensible and realistic' to implement it in 2002, as first planned. She had wanted the government to introduce a

phased implementation, starting with government departments, from October 2001, followed by local councils from April 2003, NHS bodies by October 2003 and schools and universities from April 2004. Tony Blair, however, argued that all 70,000 public bodies affected by the Act should be ready to implement it at the same time. The result was that the Act will not come into force until January 2005, more than four years after Parliament approved it.

13.7 Abolition of the post of Lord Chancellor

In June 2003, without warning and, according to the *Observer*, without the Prime Minister consulting or even informing the Cabinet (*Observer*, 15 June 2003), the government announced the abolition of the office of Lord Chancellor. The intention to abolish one of the oldest posts in government was announced as a 'by-product' of a Cabinet reshuffle (Gamble 2003). Constitutionally, the position of Lord Chancellor has long been criticised. The holder of the office is a member of all three branches of government:

- as a Cabinet member, the Lord Chancellor is part of the executive
- as Speaker in the House of Lords, the Lord Chancellor is part of the legislature
- as the most senior judge, the Lord Chancellor is part of the judiciary.

The position of Lord Chancellor, therefore, goes against the principle of separation of the powers.

Shortly after the announcement that the post of Lord Chancellor would be abolished, it was realised that this could only be done if new legislation was passed. As a result, the new Minister for Constitutional Affairs, Lord Falconer kept the title of Lord Chancellor and continued to head the judiciary and to act as Speaker of the House of Lords.

Although the post of Lord Chancellor is to be abolished, the details of what will replace it are less clear.

Main points Sections 13.5 - 13.7

- **The 1998 Human Rights Act incorporated parts of the European Convention on Human Rights into UK law.**
- **There is some debate about whether incorporation has eroded parliamentary sovereignty. Critics have argued that preserving parliamentary sovereignty is an excuse to limit the constitutional significance of the Human Rights Act.**
- **Supporters of open government were dissatisfied with the lack of progress during the period of Conservative governments and disappointed with Labour's diluted Freedom of Information Act. The implementation of this Act was delayed until 2005.**
- **In 2003, the government announced the abolition of the office of Lord Chancellor, a post which is constitutionally controversial since the holder is a member of the executive, legislature and judiciary.**

Activity 13.2 Constitutional reforms under New Labour

Item A **The Human Rights Act 1998**

The 1998 Human Rights Act sets up a legal framework which will be hard to change or remove. It creates a space beyond Westminster in which judges can operate, giving them a set of criteria by which they can hold ministers and their departments to account. In the past, the main weapon open to judges was the common law. But judgements made in the light of common law could always be overturned by Parliament passing a new statute. The Human Rights Act cannot be overturned in this way. It gives judges a new power they may well exploit in the future. Indeed, there are signs that judges are beginning to do just that.

Source: Gamble 2003b.

Item B **Tony Blair and freedom of information**

The cartoon (left) was published in February 2002, shortly after the Enron scandal broke in the USA. Freedom of information is enshrined in the American constitution.

In opposition in 1996, Tony Blair claimed that freedom of information was fundamental to bringing about a new relationship between the government and the people who would be 'stakeholders in running the country'. In July 2002, it became known that Tony Blair created a precedent for secrecy in Whitehall by refusing for the first time to accept the findings of the parliamentary Ombudsman on release of information under the 'open government' code. Richard Wilson, the Cabinet Secretary, told the Commons Public Relations Committee that a political decision at the highest level of government had been made to block the release of information on ministers' declarations under the Prime Minister's Code of Conduct. Wilson defended the government, saying:

'Even an insignificant piece of information can be highly damaging. The concern that the government has is that it is very important not to constrain the relationship which exists between ministers, permanent secretaries and their colleagues. You would find ministers feeling that everything they did might become the subject of public speculation.'

Source: Gore 1999 and the *Guardian*, 12 July 2002.

Item C **The Lord Chancellor**

Lord Falconer (right) is the Lord Chancellor charged with the task of abolishing himself.

Constitutional traditionalists claimed that the post of Lord Chancellor as it had evolved over centuries was the best way of guaranteeing the independence of the judiciary because the holders of the office were sufficiently senior and independent to resist direction from the Prime Minister and to ensure that the appointment of judges was not influenced by party political considerations. They feared that any move to separate the functions of the Lord Chancellor would actually politicise the judiciary by putting the spotlight directly on the appointment process for judges. In the USA, it was argued, the judiciary is highly politicised. The President nominates new judges to the Supreme Court and the Senate holds hearings to confirm their appointment. These hearings are intensely partisan. Having a political Lord Chancellor who is trusted to be impartial avoids a politicised appointment process.

Source: Gamble 2003.

Questions

1. 'The Human Rights Act 1998 affects the sovereignty of Parliament.' Using Item A and your own knowledge, give arguments for and against this statement.

2. a) Why do you think the Campaign for Freedom of Information has been disappointed with the Labour government's record on freedom of information? Use Item B in your answer.

b) Why is freedom of information seen as being of constitutional importance?

3. Why might the abolition of the office of Lord Chancellor lead to the difficulties outlined in Item C?

13.8 Should the UK have a written constitution?

Supporters of the UK constitution in its current form argue that its great strength is its capacity for evolution. The constitution should not be written down in a single document, they argue, because it is constantly changing. Written, codified constitutions lack flexibility.

Against this, a growing number of people argue for constitutional reform. They claim that the constitution of the UK is out-of-date and undemocratic. These drawbacks could be remedied by producing a new written constitution.

A written constitution - arguments against

When people talk of a 'written constitution' what they mean more precisely is a constitution that has been codified (drawn up in a single document). Although part of the UK constitution is written (statute law, for example), part is not. Supporters of the current system argue that this is its strength. Since the constitution is not cast in stone, it is able to evolve and develop according to circumstances. It has a flexibility which codified constitutions do not have.

Norton (1988) points to three main arguments that are used against the introduction of a written constitution. These are outlined in Box 13.14.

A written constitution - arguments for

Four arguments can be put forward to support the idea that the UK should have a written constitution.

1. To protect against arbitrary government

According to Norton (1988), the main argument in favour of a written constitution is that it would keep in check the power of the executive. People who support this line tend to argue that power in Britain has become too centralised. They claim that the old checks and balances have been eroded and the executive is able to push through Parliament whatever measures it wants to push through. A written constitution would describe and entrench (firmly establish):

- the structure and powers of government
- the relationship between different parts of government
- the relationship between government and the citizen.

It would, therefore, prevent arbitrary government since any disputes would be solved by (new) constitutional judicial procedures. The argument is similar to that made by Lord Hailsham in 1976 - namely, that Britain has, in effect, become an elective dictatorship and the only way to curb the power of the executive is to write down precisely where its powers lie.

Box 13.14 Arguments against the introduction of a written constitution

1. A written constitution is unnecessary

Not only is the current system flexible, it has a number of checks and balances built into it. For example, there is a degree of balance between the executive, legislature and judiciary. The executive does not always manage to get its own way. Opposition from within Parliament or from outside sometimes forces the government's hand (as, for example, over the poll tax). Also, judgements in the courts may curb government excesses.

2. A written constitution is undesirable

A written constitution would mean that any dispute over the powers of government, the relationship between parts of the government and the relationship between government and the citizen would be settled by a court. Power would, therefore, be transferred from the executive (which is an elected body) to the judiciary (which is not). In addition, the judiciary would have the power to declare laws and actions unconstitutional. In other words, judges would have to make political decisions. Political decisions, supporters of this view argue, should be left to politicians.

3. A written constitution is unachievable

There are two main reasons why a written constitution is unachievable. First, it would be difficult to gain a consensus about what exactly should be written down in the constitution. And second, under the existing constitution, there is no body that can authorise or legitimise a new constitution. The one thing that Parliament cannot do is to use its power under the doctrine of parliamentary sovereignty to destroy that doctrine, because its legitimacy to do so derives from the very power which it seeks to destroy. To create a new, written constitution, it would be necessary to start from scratch - which would cause constitutional and political turmoil that would not be worth enduring.

Adapted from Norton 1988.

2. To protect citizens' rights

Linked to the above argument is the idea that citizens' rights can only be protected properly if they are entrenched in a written constitution. Without this, a government with an overall majority can too easily remove civil rights simply by introducing a Bill and relying on its parliamentary majority to pass it. For example, since the attack on the Twin Towers in the United States on 11 September 2001, the government has been able to persuade Parliament to pass pieces of anti-terrorist legislation which curtail certain rights - despite the passing of the 1998 Human Rights Act. As a result, for example, a number of asylum seekers have been detained without trial. Under a written constitution, the government would not be able to introduce legislation targeting minorities in this way or restricting people's rights. The only way to do this would be to amend the constitution - which would be a deliberately difficult and lengthy process, involving a procedure different from that of passing ordinary laws.

3. To bring the constitution up-to-date
It was noted in Unit 11 that parliamentary sovereignty has been profoundly affected by Britain's membership of the European Union. Also, since 1997, power has been devolved to Scotland, Wales and Northern Ireland (see Unit 18). Since parliamentary sovereignty is no longer fully intact and since the relationship between the centre and the regions has significantly changed, it could be argued that there is the need for a new constitutional settlement.

4. To move into line with the rest of the EU
The UK is the only country in the EU without a written constitution. If a written constitution was adopted in the UK, it would bring it into line with its European partners.

13.9 Prospects for further constitutional change

There are two main schools of thought on the prospects for further constitutional change. On the one hand, according to Andrew Gamble, the constitutional reforms introduced by the post-1997 Labour governments have set in motion a trend that makes further reforms almost inevitable:

'The breach with past precedent has gradually assumed major proportions, and created a new context within which British politics is conducted. Pressure for further major changes will build in the years ahead - over freedom of information, the voting system for Westminster, the composition of the second chamber, the powers of the devolved administrations and their relationship with the centre, and the prerogative powers wielded by the Prime Minister. For all the disappointment of some constitutional radicals that change has not been faster, the distance already travelled is by past British standards remarkable.' (Gamble 2003)

On the other hand, despite the changes that have been introduced, doubts continue over whether the Labour government has the genuine inclination to make further or fundamental changes to the constitution. As Dunleavy pointed out in 1997, there is a strong incentive for a government of either main party to preserve both the two-party system and a flexible, unfixed constitution. This argument is explored in Box 13.15.

According to Dunleavy, these vested interests make it unlikely that a government will want to push the reforms too far:

Box 13.15 Pressures against further constitutional reform

The existing constitutional set-up gives the following advantages to the two main parties:

● an electoral system which protects Labour and Conservatives from third-party competition and bolsters the two parties' internal unity

● permanent control of Parliament through the whip systems and the 'usual channels' which guarantees the government passage of its Bills and allows the main opposition the scope to debate, criticise and question

● great freedom for the executive (which the opposition can later enjoy in its turn)

● extensive protection from judicial interference or controls

● scope for the two main party élites to rearrange the constitution, administrative arrangements, the rights of citizens or the provisions of the law.

Adapted from Dunleavy 1997.

'Constitutional reforms that seriously enhance the checks and balances on the executive do not find favour with Labour... At the Westminster centre, Britain retains a centralised government [and]...the executive form remains a single party government.' (Dunleavy et al. 2003b, pp.11,12)

As Gamble has recognised, one significant area of the constitution for which the Labour government has no reform proposals is the monarchy. Yet, since the monarch is still the head of state, this institution remains at the centre of the UK's constitutional arrangements. Gamble argues that it is difficult to reform other areas of the constitution without reviewing the constitutional position of the monarchy (Gamble 2003). He suggests that one reason why governments are reluctant to reform the monarchy in any fundamental way is that to do so would also mean a considerable reduction in the powers of the office of Prime Minister - because of its use of prerogative powers (Gamble 2003b).

13.10 The other major parties and constitutional reform

Constitutional reform has always been a central plank in the Liberal Democrats' policy programme (they are particularly interested in securing reform of the electoral system - for party and ideological reasons). It is no surprise, therefore, that the Liberal Democrats broadly supported Labour's commitment to constitutional reform during the run-up to the 1997 general election. Two months after that election, the new Labour government announced the setting up of a Joint Cabinet Consultative Committee which included leading Liberal Democrat politicians. Initially, the purpose of the committee was to consider constitutional reform. Later, it was revealed that this was part of 'the Project' devised by Tony Blair and the then Leader of the Liberal Democrats, Paddy Ashdown, in 1994 when the two politicians privately agreed to work together to realign progressive forces in British politics and to bring the Liberal Democrats into government alongside New Labour (Rathbone 2002).

In 1999, however, Ashdown resigned as Leader of the Liberal Democrats and was replaced by Charles Kennedy. Two years later, no doubt frustrated by the lack of progress, Kennedy announced that his party would no longer participate in the joint Cabinet committee. In the four years of its existence, the committee had met only twice. Kennedy perhaps recognised that it was merely

> 'a way of making the Liberal Democrats feel that they were being consulted, without actually giving them any real power.' (Rathbone 2002)

The Conservative Party has been far less interested in pursuing major aspects of constitutional reform. Many Conservatives believe that the strength of the UK's constitution is its capacity to evolve gradually to deal with changing circumstances. Conservatives tend to believe that, by and large, existing constitutional arrangements work satisfactorily and do not require the sort of changes introduced by the Labour government since 1997.

Main points   Sections 13.8 - 13.10

- Those opposed to a written constitution argue that it is: (1) unnecessary; (2) undesirable; and (3) unachievable.
- Those in favour of a written constitution say it is needed in order to: (1) protect against arbitrary government; (2) protect citizens' rights; (3) bring the constitution up to date; and (4) move into line with the rest of the EU.
- Some believe that the extent of Labour's constitutional reforms make further reforms likely. Others doubt Labour's continued commitment to reform particularly for measures that would threaten single-party government or the flexibility of the constitution or which would strengthen checks on executive dominance.
- The Liberal Democrats remain strongly committed to constitutional reform. The Conservatives remain sceptical, believing that Labour's reforms are unnecessary or even dangerous.

Activity 13.3 The Conservatives and Liberal Democrats and constitutional reform

Item A The Conservative Party and constitutional reform

Britain's constitution has never been set in stone, but has evolved and adapted to cope with the changing circumstances of different centuries. Because the Labour government did not understand how the stability of our democratic structures have underpinned our national life, it altered them in a crude, unthinking way, often for narrow party advantage. We will work to ensure devolution is a success. But we will restore balance to our vandalised democracy. We will strengthen the independence of the House of Lords as an effective revising chamber by requiring new members to be approved by an independent appointments commission. We will set up a Joint Committee of both Houses of Parliament in order to seek consensus on lasting reform in the House of Lords. We would like to see a stronger House of Lords in the future including a substantial elected element. Conservatives will support reforms of the House of Commons to make ministers more accountable. We reaffirm our commitment to keeping Britain's voting system for general elections. We want to return to people responsibility for their own lives by reducing the level of political interference and regulation. And that involves reducing the number of politicians. We will abandon the government's plans for a new tier of regional politicians in England. We will cut the number of government ministers and, once we have strengthened parliamentary scrutiny, we will reduce the size of the House of Commons. And we will cut the number of political advisers and spin doctors employed, at the taxpayer's expense, to serve government ministers.

time for **common sense**

Conservatives

Source: The Conservatives' 2001 general election manifesto.

Item B The Liberal Democrats and constitutional reform

Liberal Democrats have long been at the forefront of the constitutional reform agenda in the United Kingdom. While recent constitutional reforms have been significant, they have been piecemeal and lacked coherence. Much remains to be done in fields as varied as English regional devolution, freedom of information, reform of the Upper House, and proper financial accountability of the government to the House of Commons. Above all, there is an urgent need to re-connect citizens and government. Liberal Democrats would re-connect citizens with government by supporting a referendum on the recommendations of the Jenkins Commission on electoral reform as a first step towards our ultimate goal of the Single Transferable Vote system. Liberal Democrats would make government more politically accountable by:

- replacing the House of Lords with an elected Senate
- enacting meaningful freedom of information legislation for England and Wales, with exclusions limited to material that could cause substantial harm if released, and the final decision on exclusions lying with an Information Commissioner, not ministers
- cutting the number of MPs in the House of Commons to around 450
- cutting the number of ministers
- moving towards a written constitution for the UK.

Liberal Democrats would empower the nations and regions of the United Kingdom by:

- further strengthening the devolution settlement in Scotland and Wales
- creating the option for devolution to the English regions by legislating for referenda on regional assemblies.

Extracts from 'Reforming governance in the UK: policies for constitutional reform', *Policy Paper 40*, Liberal Democrats, 2000.

Questions

1. Using Items A and B and other information in this unit, outline similarities and differences on constitutional reform between: (a) the Conservatives and Liberal Democrats; (b) the Conservatives and Labour; and (c) the Liberal Democrats and Labour.

2. Judging from Items A and B, how would the prospects for future constitutional reform be affected if (a) the Conservatives and (b) the Liberal Democrats won the next general election?

References

Benn (1979) Benn, T., *Arguments for Socialism*, Penguin, 1979.

Conservative (1992) *The Conservative Manifesto 1992*, Conservative Central Office, 1992.

Dorey (2003) Dorey, P., 'Half-baked and half-hearted: the Blair governments and constitutional reform' in *Lancaster (2003)*.

Driver & Martell (1998) Driver, S. & Martell, L., *New Labour: Politics after Thatcherism*, Polity Press, 1998.

Dunleavy (1997) Dunleavy, P., 'The constitution' in *Dunleavy et al. (1997)*.

Dunleavy et al. (1997) Dunleavy, P., Gamble, A., Holliday, I. & Peele, G., *Developments in British Politics 5*, Macmillan, 1997.

Dunleavy et al. (2003a) Dunleavy, P., Gamble, A., Heffernan, R. & Peele, G. (eds), *Developments in British Politics 7*, Palgrave Macmillan, 2003.

Dunleavy et al. (2003b) Dunleavy P., Gamble, A., Heffernan, R. & Peele, G., 'Introduction: transformations in British politics' in *Dunleavy et al. (2003a)*.

Gamble (2003) Gamble, A., 'After the Lord Chancellor? The continuing remaking of the British constitution', http://www.palgrave.com/politics/dunleavy/update1.htm.

Gamble (2003b) Gamble, A. 'Remaking the constitution' in *Dunleavy et al. (2003a)*.

Gore (1999) Gore, P., 'Freedom of Information under Blair', *Talking Politics*, Vol.12.1, Summer 1999.

HMSO (1997) Freedom of Information White Paper, *Your Right to Know*, HMSO, Cmnd 3818, 1997.

Home Office (2000) *Human Rights Act: An Introduction*, Home Office Communication Directorate, October 2000.

Labour (1997) Labour Party general election manifesto, *New Labour- Because Britain Deserves Better*, Labour Party, 1997.

Lancaster (1997) Lancaster, S. (ed.), *Developments in Politics*, Vol.8, Causeway Press, 1997.

Lancaster (ed.) (2003) Lancaster, S. (ed.), *Developments in Politics*, Vol.14, Causeway Press, 2003.

Ludlam & Smith (2001) Ludlam, S. & Smith, M.J. (eds.), *New Labour in Government*, Palgrave, 2001.

Magee & Lynch (2003) Magee, E. & Lynch, P., 'The changing British constitution', *Politics Review*, Vol.13.2, November 2003.

Norton (1988) Norton, P., 'Should Britain have a written constitution?', *Talking Politics*, Vol.1.1, Autumn 1988.

Norton (1989) Norton, P., 'The changing constitution - part 2', *Contemporary Record*, Vol.3.2, November 1989.

Peele (2001) Peele, G., 'The Human Rights Act', *Talking Politics*, Vol.14.1, September 2001.

Rathbone (2002) Rathbone, M., 'Labour and the Liberal Democrats', *Talking Politics*, Vol.14.3, April 2002.

Richards & Smith (2001) Richards, D. & Smith, M.J., 'New Labour, the constitution and reforming the state' in *Ludlam & Smith (2001)*.

Rush (1997) Rush, M., 'Thinking about the constitution' in *Lancaster (1997)*.

Wilson (1984) Wilson, D., *The Secrets File: the Case for Freedom of Information in Britain Today*, Heinemann, 1984.

14 Parliament

14.1 Parliamentary and presidential systems

Systems of government can be classified as either parliamentary or presidential. The terms refer to the type of relationship between the executive and the legislature.

In parliamentary systems, the executive and the legislature are interconnected. There is no strict separation of powers. The government (executive) is normally chosen from the representatives of the majority party (or coalition group, if no single party has a majority) elected to the legislature (the Parliament or assembly). The government is accountable for its actions to the legislature and it is dependent upon the continued support of the legislature to remain in office.

In presidential systems the legislature and executive are distinct (a clear separation of powers). The head of the executive, the President, is chosen by the electorate rather than by the legislature. Presidents do not sit in, and cannot normally be removed by, the legislature. The President acts as head of government and as ceremonial head of state (Leeds 1981, p.23).

Most European countries have parliamentary systems whereas the USA has the best known example of a presidential system. Presidential systems can also be found in Latin American states and in some Asian and African countries. Describing a system of government as 'presidential', however, does not necessarily mean that a country has a president rather than a monarch as its head of state. Ireland and Germany, for example, both have presidents as heads of state but they both operate parliamentary systems of government.

The UK's system is contrasted with that in the USA in Box 14.1.

14.2 Changing functions of Parliament

Parliament is perhaps the most visible of the UK's political institutions. Its proceedings are reported in the press and broadcast on radio and television. Whether or not Parliament is the focal point of political power in the UK, however, is far more debatable. Some commentators argue that the work done by the Commons and the Lords makes an important contribution to the shaping of legislation. Others argue that, in reality, Parliament is little more than a talking shop where ambitious politicians polish their egos and their public speaking skills.

But Philip Norton notes that:

'The functions ascribed to Parliaments...are not static. The form of Parliaments may remain, but what is expected of them will change as political conditions change.' (Norton 1985, pp.1-2)

Political conditions have certainly changed during Parliament's long history. Relations between Parliament and the monarchy and between the House of Commons and the House of Lords are very different from those which existed in the 19th century or earlier.

Perhaps the most important development over the past hundred years or so is the growth in the power of the executive (the government). Today, it is the government which sets the legislative agenda and, since it is formed from the majority party (or parties) in the Commons, it is usually able to gather a majority in favour of its proposed laws, regardless of the strength of feeling of Opposition MPs. But, even if the executive has the upper hand, the House of Commons still performs a number of functions. These are described in Box 14.2 on page 263.

Box 14.1 Parliamentary and presidential systems

The UK

The executive and the legislature are tightly linked. The executive - government ministers - sit in one of the two Houses of Parliament (the Commons or the Lords). Ministers take part in debate and vote together with the other members of Parliament. The executive is not independent of Parliament - the House of Commons can overthrow the government by a vote of no-confidence. On the other hand, the government, through the Prime Minister, can dissolve the legislature and hold a general election. In practice, however, the most important factor is the party system. Normally, the UK government is formed from the party holding a majority of seats in the House of Commons. The government expects its backbench MPs to support it by voting according to party instructions. This means, in effect, that the government brings into law legislation which it has itself proposed. In this sense, the government controls the House of Commons. In the UK, therefore, the executive and the legislature are not two independent branches of government, and legislation and execution are not two disconnected processes.

Source: Berrington 1964, pp.20-22.

The USA

The relationship between the legislature and the executive in the USA presents a sharp contrast to the relationship in the UK. The writers of the United States constitution in 1787 believed that liberty would best be preserved by placing the various powers of government in separate hands. Executive power is invested in a President, elected for a four-year term not by the legislature but, in practice, by the United States electorate. The President can only be dismissed by the legislature for criminal misconduct. The only part Presidents can play in the legislative process lies in their right to veto Acts of Congress (and even this veto can be overridden by a two-thirds majority in each House of Congress). Congress holds the power to legislate and it can refuse to pass the Bills the President wants or refuse to grant the money which the President judges necessary to run the public services. Constitutionally, if Congress is uncooperative, there is little the President can do about it. The President cannot dissolve Congress and Congress cannot overthrow the President. The formal separation between executive and legislature is almost complete and far greater than in the UK.

Box 14.2 Functions of the House of Commons

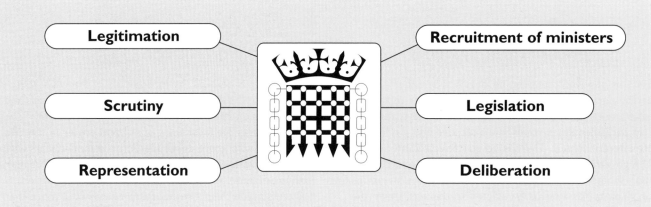

Legitimation

Scrutiny

Representation

Recruitment of ministers

Legislation

Deliberation

1. Legitimation

The House of Commons is the elected part of Parliament. Following a general election, the majority party in the House (or coalition of parties if there is a hung Parliament) forms the government. In supporting the government (by giving their assent to government proposals to change the law and agreeing to public policy in general), MPs of the governing party (or parties) provide the government with legitimacy in its exercise of political power. That is why the government is thrown into crisis if it loses a vote in the Commons - the loss of a vote is a loss of legitimacy which can only be restored if a subsequent vote of confidence in the government is passed.

In addition, since assent to legislative proposals is based on majority voting, a further dimension to the process of legitimacy comes from Parliament as a whole. This is the general agreement from all sides in Parliament that once parliamentary approval has been given to a change in the law, that new law should be obeyed unless and until Parliament agrees to the law being changed again.

2. Scrutiny

The policy proposals, executive actions and expenditure of governments are all legitimate subjects for examination and criticism by Parliament. They are of particular concern to the Opposition parties, but a government's own supporters (whose loyalty is needed by the government) are also involved in the process of scrutiny.

3. Representation

The representative part of Parliament is the House of Commons. Each MP represents a particular geographical area (a constituency) in the UK. Although MPs are almost always elected according to the party they belong to, after the election they are expected to represent the interests of all their constituents, regardless of party affiliation.

One of the functions of MPs, therefore, is to look after the interests of their constituents in Parliament and to take up their grievances. In this sense, Parliament is often seen (realistically or not) as an institution able to give expression to public opinion or feeling.

4. The recruitment of government ministers

Parliament is the recruiting ground for the vast majority of government ministers. Some members of government are still chosen from the House of Lords, but most ministers are selected from among MPs of the governing party in the House of Commons. Many MPs ('career politicians') have ambitions to become government ministers and see their backbench parliamentary role as a preparation for future promotion to office.

The Prime Minister can bring into government individuals from outside Parliament, but they would normally be expected to win a seat in the Commons at a by-election or be given a seat in the House of Lords.

5. Law-making

Much of the work done by Parliament involves the scrutiny of legislative proposals put forward by the government. As far as the government is concerned, it is Parliament's job to give assent to the government's legislative programme. The process of scrutiny leading up to assent, however, can provide MPs in the Commons and members of the House of Lords with the possibility of influencing the content of legislation.

6. Deliberation

Both Houses of Parliament are debating chambers and debates are held on, for example, topical issues or on specific matters of policy.

Main points   Sections 14.1 - 14.2

- In parliamentary systems of government, the executive and the legislature are interconnected, whereas in presidential systems they are clearly separated.
- The functions of Parliament are not fixed. They change over time.
- Today, Parliament has six main functions: (1) to provide the government and political process with legitimacy; (2) to oversee and criticise executive actions and policies; (3) to represent the interests of constituents; (4) to serve as a recruiting ground for ministers; (5) to scrutinise and amend legislative proposals; and (6) to debate key issues and policies.

Activity 14.1 *The role of Parliament*

Item A The MP, the House and the constituency

Item B Baroness Amos and Lord Falconer

At the end of 2003, Baroness Amos (Leader of the House of Lords) and Lord Falconer (Secretary of State for Constitutional Affairs and Lord Chancellor for the transitional period) were the only two members of Tony Blair's Cabinet who were drawn from the House of Lords. (Lord Grocott, the Lords Chief Whip, also attended Cabinet meetings.) The government as a whole (including the Chief Whips in the Commons and the Lords but excluding other government whips) contained 91 ministers, 21 of whom were in the Cabinet. Of the 70 non-Cabinet ministers, 12 were members of the House of Lords.

Source: http://www.cabinet-office.gov.uk/central/2003/ministers.htm, 19 December 2003.

Item C The US Congress and the UK Parliament

The United States Congress is less party-based than the UK Parliament. This is because the doctrine of separation of powers means that no members of the US executive are members of either House (apart from the Vice President who has the right to preside over the Senate). By contrast, all members of the UK government sit in either the House of Commons or the House of Lords and the continuance of the government depends on its maintaining a majority in any vote of confidence in the Commons. When James Callaghan's government lost such a vote in 1979, Callaghan had no option but to call an election. Labour lost the election to the Conservatives and Margaret Thatcher became Prime Minister.

Source: Batchelor 2003.

Item D Newspaper headline, March 1979

LABOUR GOVERNMENT LOSES NO-CONFIDENCE VOTE IN THE COMMONS - GENERAL ELECTION TO BE CALLED

Questions

1. a) To which function of Parliament does Item A refer?
   b) What point is the cartoon making about this function?
2. Using Items A, B and D, explain in what ways and why the House of Commons and the House of Lords have different roles.
3. Item B shows that most ministers in Tony Blair's government were selected from the House of Commons.
   a) Why do you think this is the usual practice?
   b) Give arguments for and against recruiting ministers from the House of Lords.
4. a) To which function of Parliament does Item D refer?
   b) What does Item D tell us about the role of Parliament?
   c) With reference to Item C, why would a similar situation not occur in the US system of government?

14.3 *The legislative process (1)*

Parliament is the UK's legislative authority. Strictly speaking, it has three elements - the monarch, the House of Lords and the House of Commons - and all three elements must be in agreement before a proposal can become law. When a proposed new law is being debated by Parliament, it is called a Bill. Once a Bill has passed successfully through both Houses of Parliament and received Royal Assent, it becomes an Act of Parliament.

The legislative role of the monarch, however, has largely been taken over by government ministers. Usually, therefore, when people talk about 'Parliament', they are referring to the Palace of Westminster where the House of Commons and the House of Lords are located.

Types of Bills
There are various types of parliamentary Bills, the two main types being public Bills and private Bills.

Private Bills
Private Bills play only a minor role in legislation today. They are intended to apply only to a particular area, a specific organisation or a certain section of the population. They are sometimes promoted for large capital projects on behalf of private companies or by public bodies (such as local authorities) as a means of avoiding long and costly public inquiries. Private Bills were popular in the 19th century when local authorities sought means to improve their public facilities or develop large-scale projects. The Transport and Works Act of 1992, however, restricted the scope of private Bills so that such large-scale projects are normally now given legal authority in other ways.

Public Bills
The vast majority of Bills passing through Parliament are public Bills (they are aimed at the public as a whole). Most public Bills are sponsored by the government and therefore referred to as 'government Bills'. But around 10% of Commons' time is spent on a second type of public Bill - the Private Members' Bill. Private Members' Bills are introduced and promoted by backbench MPs.

14.4 *The legislative process (2) Private Members' Bills*

Private Members' Bills encounter special difficulties in their passage through Parliament - only 13 Fridays each parliamentary session are devoted to Private Members' Bills, for example. The vast majority, therefore, fail and do not become law. Out of 2,067 Private Members' Bills introduced between 1983 and 2002, only 256 were successful in the sense that they received Royal Assent (House of Commons Information Office, September 2003). Many of those which were successful were either politically uncontentious or received government support.

There are four ways of introducing a Private Members' Bill into Parliament (see Box 14.3).

Box 14.3 Four ways of introducing a Private Members' Bill into Parliament

1. Ballot Bills
At the start of each parliamentary session, MPs can enter their names in a ballot from which 20 names are drawn. In each session, however, only certain Fridays are set aside for discussion of 'Ballot Bills' and many of these tend to be taken up with the later stages of Bills already in the pipeline. Attendance at the House on Fridays is usually low (many MPs return to their constituencies on Thursday evenings) and the MP promoting a Ballot Bill might well see it delayed or pushed off the Commons timetable because an insufficient number of MPs are present in the chamber for a division (vote) to take place. Even so, the chances of success for a Ballot Bill are much higher than Private Members' Bills introduced in other ways.

2. The Ten Minute Rule
Under the Ten Minute Rule an MP is allowed ten minutes to outline the case for a new piece of legislation. MPs frequently use this procedure to gain publicity for ideas they wish to express rather than in the hope of getting new legislation onto the statute book.

3. Standing Order No.57
Standing Order No.57 allows Members of Parliament to introduce a Bill of their choosing. With this method, the MP does not make a speech when introducing a Bill. Chances of getting the Bill debated are slim since the presentation of Ballot Bills is given priority in terms of Friday time allocation.

4. Bills brought from the House of Lords
On occasions, MPs may introduce into the Commons a Bill which a backbench peer has already steered through the requisite stages in the House of Lords. Such Bills, however, are likely to run out of time because they would not normally reach the Commons until late in the parliamentary session.

Why Private Members' Bills fail or succeed
Overall, the majority of Private Members' Bills fail because the government does not provide the support necessary for their successful passage through Parliament. The main requirement is that of time. Without the provision of extra time by the government, a Bill has little chance of success.

Controversial Private Members' Bills such as the anti-hunting Bill proposed by Michael Foster in 1997 - see Box 14.4 - are especially vulnerable to hostile tactics. For example, filibustering is a common tactic - an opponent of a Bill carries on speaking (often about unrelated matters) simply to use up time and to prevent a vote being taken. Similarly, the tabling of new clauses and amendments can keep a debate going until time runs out (as happened with Michael Foster's Bill).

Some Private Members' Bills do receive government (and even cross-party) support. These Bills are sometimes used as a means of introducing social reforms with which the government does not wish to be directly identified. In the 1960s, for example, reforms to the law on abortion and homosexuality were achieved through Private Members' Bills.

Box 14.4 Michael Foster's Ballot Bill

Pressure groups often target MPs who have been successful in the ballot in the hope that they will introduce a Bill in support of their cause or interest. As soon as it became known that Labour MP Michael Foster had come top of the ballot in 1997, he was approached by a number of anti-hunting pressure groups who wanted him to introduce an anti-hunting Bill. When Foster announced on the radio that he would introduce a Bill which was 'in the best interests of the city of Worcester [his constituency] and the people of this country', one of these pressure groups - the International Fund for Animal Welfare - paid for a MORI opinion poll in Worcester which showed that 70% of his constituents supported a ban on hunting (*Guardian*, 8 June 1997). This poll undoubtedly helped to persuade the MP to choose to introduce an anti-hunting Bill. Having agreed to do so, Foster then consulted closely with a number of pressure groups in drawing up the Bill:
'The Bill has been drawn up by animal welfare groups, including the Royal Society for the Prevention of Cruelty to Animals, the International Fund for Animal Welfare and the League Against Cruel Sports.' (*Times*, 29 November 1997)
Although the Bill was not successful, it passed its second reading in the Commons with a majority of 260 (411 in favour and 151 against) and the Prime Minister, Tony Blair, hinted that the government might take action to ban hunting (*Times*, 29 November 1997).

Similarly, in 1994, the age of consent for homosexuals was lowered to 18 after the government supported a Private Member's Bill.

14.5 *The legislative process (3) government Bills*

Some types of government Bill are introduced in every parliamentary session - for example the Finance Bill containing the provisions of the Budget. Some are brought in to deal with emergencies (wars or civil strife, for example) or in response to pressure. Others are planned as part of the general process of implementing government policy. Often, such Bills relate to manifesto promises.

Pre-parliamentary consultation
Consultation takes place between the sponsoring government department and other departments (especially the Treasury). There may also be consultation with outside organisations. Sometimes the consultation process involves the publication of a Green Paper in which the government outlines its ideas, presents policy options and invites comments. The 1993 Ripon Commission report, however, noted that Green Papers were becoming rare. The trend was to produce less formal 'consultation papers'.

   In addition to, and sometimes instead of, an initial consultation stage, the government publishes a White Paper which states its policy on a particular topic or view. In effect, a White Paper is a statement of intended legislation and may be the subject of parliamentary debate. Once the Cabinet decides to go ahead with the proposals, a date is fixed for their introduction into Parliament and a draft Bill is drawn up.

Passage of a Bill through Parliament
A government Bill is usually given its first reading in the House of Commons, though it can begin in the Lords. It then goes through further stages - second reading, committee stage, report stage, third reading.

The Bill then passes to the other House (for a government Bill, normally the House of Lords) where it goes through the same series of stages. If the Lords accept the Bill, it is passed for Royal Assent, and so becomes law in the form of an Act of Parliament. The process is summarised in Box 14.5.

Box 14.5 Passage of a Bill through Parliament

Bills can begin in the Commons or the Lords, so they can pass through Parliament in one of two ways.

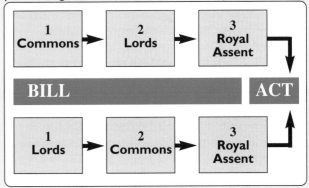

It is rare for the Lords to reject a government Bill outright, but, if they do, the Bill is delayed for a year (which is the only significant power remaining with the House of Lords on legislative matters). A more likely occurrence is for the Lords to seek to amend the Bill. In this case, the Bill goes back to the Commons which can then decide to accept the alterations. If the Commons rejects them, the Lords can continue to consider them (the Bill might go backwards and forwards between the Houses a number of times). Eventually, however, the Lords would be expected to withdraw their amendments (bearing in mind that the Lords' power to delay is limited).

   The legislative functions of Parliament are outlined in Box 14.6 on page 267.

Box 14.6 The legislative functions of Parliament

The functions of Parliament with regard to law-making are:

- to debate the proposed legislation
- to scrutinise it at the committee stage
- to suggest amendments
- to agree on its final shape.

It should be emphasised, however, that it is the government (on the whole) which decides what matters require legislation and the government is normally able to command a majority in any vote taken in the House of Commons. The scope for backbench MPs (of any party) or for individual members of the House of Lords to make an impact on legislation which comes before Parliament is, therefore, limited.

14.6 The role of the whips in the legislative process

Each of the main parties in the House of Commons appoints a Chief Whip and assistant whips. The role of government whips in the legislative process is to ensure that the government maintains its majority in votes taken in the House. The Opposition whips organise their supporters to mount an effective challenge to the government.

MPs receive weekly printed instructions from their party whips indicating when they should attend the House to vote. These instructions are also called 'whips'. A three-line whip means attendance is essential. A one-line whip merely requests the attendance of MPs. A two-line whip means that MPs must attend unless arrangements have been made under the 'pairing' system. 'Pairing' is the term used when government and Opposition whips agree for an MP on each side to 'pair up' and be absent from the House at the same time. When the governing party in the Commons has a large majority, there are insufficient partners in the main Opposition party for the pairing system to work properly. When this happened after the 1997 general election, an alternative system was introduced. Labour backbenchers were organised into groups of around 50. Taking it in turns,

these groups were allowed a 'constituency week' in which they were not obliged to attend the House for one-line or two-line whips.

Applying pressure

Whips can apply pressure on rebellious MPs from within their own parties in a number of ways. Normally a severe talking to is enough to secure the MP's loyalty. But, if an MP votes against the government in a motion with a three-line whip, the whip may be withdrawn from the MP - the equivalent of being expelled from the party. This is what happened to eight Conservative MPs in 1994 when they voted against the government Bill increasing Britain's contributions to the EU. This was the only time in the 20th century that such a large number of Conservative MPs were disciplined in this way at the same time.

Withdrawal of the whip, in practice, is often only a temporary punishment for disloyalty, but permanent exclusion is a possibility. In 1997, the Conservative Party withdrew the whip from one of its MPs - Peter Temple-Morris - after he had opposed his party's line on the single European currency. Temple-Morris's response was to resign from the party but to continue to take his Commons seat for the remainder of the Parliament as an 'independent Conservative'.

If MPs from a particular party vote in large numbers against the party line, however, withdrawal of the party whip becomes less of a realistic sanction. Between 2001 and 2004, there were a number of occasions when a significant number of Labour backbench MPs rebelled' and voted against the government - see Item C in Activity 14.2 below.

Whips in the House of Lords

The main parties in the House of Lords also appoint whips, but the whips in the Lords do not have the same range of sanctions and cannot operate the system as rigorously as in the Commons. There have been occasions when a member of the Lords has had the whip withdrawn. But this weapon has less impact since, unlike MPs in the Commons, members of the House of Lords do not require party support to stand for periodic election. In addition, the House of Lords is not so strictly divided on party lines as the Commons; many peers (the 'crossbenchers') do not formally ally themselves with any particular political party.

Main points Sections 14.3 - 14.6

- **Parliament is the UK's legislative authority, responsible for translating parliamentary Bills into Acts of Parliament. Proposed legislation comes in the form of private Bills or public Bills. Private Bills play only a minor role today.**
- **Public Bills introduced by backbench MPs are called 'Private Members' Bills'. These can be introduced using the ballot, the Ten Minute Rule, through 'ordinary presentation' or by adopting a Bill already steered through the House of Lords by a backbench peer.**

- **Most public Bills are sponsored by the government. Government Bills may follow the publication of a Green Paper and/or a White Paper. They pass through various stages in each House before receiving Royal Assent and becoming law.**
- **The role of government whips is to ensure that the government maintains its majority in votes taken in the House. The role of Opposition whips is to mount an effective challenge to the government. The party whips can apply pressure in various ways to encourage party loyalty.**

Activity 14.2 Legislative machinery

Item A A whip

PRIVATE & CONFIDENTIAL   PARLIAMENTARY LABOUR PARTY

MONDAY, 9th FEBRUARY 2004
- The House will meet at 2.30pm

1. Work and Pensions Questions
   Last tabling date for Education and Skills and Solicitor General.

2. Scottish Parliament (Constituencies) Bill: Second reading
   (Rt. Hon. Alistair Darling and Anne McGuire)

YOUR ATTENDANCE BY 9.00PM FOR 10.00PM IS ESSENTIAL.

PRIVATE & CONFIDENTIAL   PARLIAMENTARY LABOUR PARTY

TUESDAY, 10th FEBRUARY 2004
- The House will meet at 11.30pm

1. Scotland, Advocate General, Constitutional Affairs, Leader of the House and House of Commons Commission Questions.
2. Ten Minute Rule Bill:
   Health and safety at Work (Offences) - Andy Love.
3. Opposition Day (4th allotted day). There will be a debate entitled 'The State of the Environment' followed by a debate 'Local Taxation'. Both debates arise on a motion in the name of the Liberal Democrats.

YOUR ATTENDANCE FROM 3.00PM FOR 4.00PM AND AT 6.00PM FOR 7.00PM IS ESSENTIAL.

Information provided by the House of Commons Information Office.

Item B The Parents' Jury

Poor marketing practices in relation to children's food have drawn the wrath of parents. The Parents' Jury, made up of more than 800 parents, set up by the campaigning group The Food Commission, have given Kraft's Dairylea Lunchables an award for the worst food targeted at children's lunch boxes. The packs contain cheese slices, wheat crackers and processed meats, which are high in fat and salt. One disgruntled parent described the product as 'absolutely vile, over-processed rubbish!'. Football stars who promote products such as crisps, burgers, highly sugared cereals, chocolate bars, sweets and fizzy drinks are also infuriating parents. During the 2002 World Cup, many parents wrote to the UK Food Commission to criticise the use of David Beckham's photo to endorse sugary soft drinks. They claimed that it undermines children's nutrition.

Source: www.epha.org/a/523

David Beckham - undermining children's nutrition?

Item C Labour rebels

Between June 2001 when Labour won a second general election in a row and January 2004, there were a number of rebellions in the House of Commons involving backbench Labour MPs. What was particularly striking was the size of some of these rebellions. A record was set in February 2003 when 121 Labour MPs voted against the government's plans for war against Iraq - only to be broken a month later when 139 Labour MPs voted against the government on the same issue. In each case, however, there was little chance of a government defeat since the Conservatives, as the main Opposition party, supported the government. These occasions, together with some other examples, are listed below. Not all of them involved divisions on a Bill.

Date	Issue	Labour MPs voting against the government	Government majority
February 2003	Iraq	121	195
March 2003	Iraq	139	179
May 2003	Foundation Hospitals	63	74
July 2003	Foundation Hospitals	63	35
November 2003	Foundation Hospitals	62	17
January 2004	University funding ('top-up' fees)	72	5

Source: *Guardian*, 28 January 2004 and Jones 2004, p.32.

Item D The passage of a Bill through Parliament

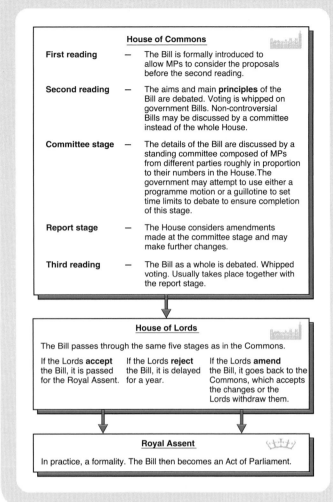

House of Commons

First reading	—	The Bill is formally introduced to allow MPs to consider the proposals before the second reading.
Second reading	—	The aims and main **principles** of the Bill are debated. Voting is whipped on government Bills. Non-controversial Bills may be discussed by a committee instead of the whole House.
Committee stage	—	The details of the Bill are discussed by a standing committee composed of MPs from different parties roughly in proportion to their numbers in the House. The government may attempt to use either a programme motion or a guillotine to set time limits to debate to ensure completion of this stage.
Report stage	—	The House considers amendments made at the committee stage and may make further changes.
Third reading	—	The Bill as a whole is debated. Whipped voting. Usually takes place together with the report stage.

House of Lords

The Bill passes through the same five stages as in the Commons.

If the Lords **accept** the Bill, it is passed for the Royal Assent.	If the Lords **reject** the Bill, it is delayed for a year.	If the Lords **amend** the Bill, it goes back to the Commons, which accepts the changes or the Lords withdraw them.

Royal Assent

In practice, a formality. The Bill then becomes an Act of Parliament.

Questions

1. How does the role of the whips affect the way in which Parliament performs its legislative function? Use Item A in your answer.

2. a) Suppose a minister agreed to meet representatives of the Parents' Jury (Item B) and to sponsor a Bill imposing a 'fat tax' on the advertising of highly processed and fatty foods aimed at children. Using Item D, describe the process to be undertaken before the Bill becomes law.

   b) How much influence would backbench and Opposition MPs have on the final form of the Bill?

   c) Suppose ministers refused to sponsor such a Bill. Advise the Parents' Jury on the best way to proceed to achieve legislation.

3. a) With reference to Item C, why do you think so many Labour MPs have been prepared to vote against their own government?

   b) Why might the Labour whips be reluctant to take action against these MPs?

14.7 Seating arrangements in the House of Commons

The importance of parties, including the division into governing and Opposition parties, is emphasised in the seating arrangements of the House of Commons chamber. Government ministers occupy the front benches on one side of the House. They face the frontbench team of the Opposition party (or parties) on the other side. The seating arrangements, therefore, serve to favour a two-party system and a confrontational (or 'adversarial') style of party debate.

The seating in other Parliaments is organised differently. The European Parliament, for example, is arranged almost in a circle. This makes a symbolic as well as a practical difference to the way in which the proceedings in the European Parliament work.

14.8 House of Commons business

After each general election, a new Parliament begins. This new Parliament has a life of up to five years - the Parliament Act of 1911 states that five years should be the maximum time between general elections.

Each Parliament is divided into sessions with each parliamentary session normally lasting about a year (from November to November). At the start of each session, the Queen's Speech is delivered. The speech is written by the Prime Minister and outlines the legislative proposals which the government intends to put before Parliament during the year ahead. There are annual breaks, when the House is in recess - for example at Christmas, Easter, Spring Bank Holiday, Summer and during the party conference season.

Daily business

Since the mid-1990s there has been a number of changes to the timetable in operation for the House of Commons. Until 1995, the daily business of the House started at 2.30 pm on Mondays to Thursdays and 9.30 am on Fridays. The amount of business to be covered, however, meant that the House frequently sat past its official closing time of 10.30 pm. There were complaints of unsociable working hours (all-night sittings were not uncommon) and members whose constituencies were distant from London had little time to spend in their constituencies.

Growing demands from some MPs for reforms to working practices led to a series of changes designed to reduce the number of late-night sittings and, generally, to rationalise the hours of business. Box 14.7 on page 270 outlines the Commons timetable and organisation of business following changes introduced in January 2003. It also shows the normal order of business.

Box 14.7 Business in the Commons

(i) Sitting times of the House of Commons

Monday	2.30 pm - 10.30 pm
Tuesday	11.30 am - 7.30 pm
Wednesday	11.30 am - 7.30 pm
Thursday	11.30 am - 6.30 pm
Friday	9.30 am - 3.00 pm

The House only sits on Fridays when Private Members' Bills are debated.

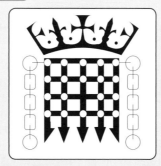

(iii) Westminster Hall

Since 1999, the House also sits in an additional chamber in the Commons called Westminster Hall. 'Non-controversial' issues are debated. Since January 2003, the timetable for these sittings has been:

Tuesday & Wednesday	9.30 am - 11.30 am
	2.00 pm - 4.30 pm
Thursday	2.30 pm - 5.30 pm

(ii) Organisation of business

The normal order of daily business in the House is as follows (NB. Not all types of business occur on every day):

- Prayers
- Petitions (Fridays only)
- Private business (except Fridays)
- Oral questions (except Fridays)

  Prime Minister's Question Time 12.00 noon - 12.30 pm on Wednesdays; Questions to ministers start 2.30 pm on Mondays, and 11.30 am Tuesdays, Wednesdays & Thursdays.

- Urgent questions/statements (statements at 11.00 am on Fridays)

- Presentation of Bills
- Ten Minute Rule Bills (Tuesdays & Wednesdays)
- Main business
- Moment of Interruption - 10.00 pm Mondays, 7.00 pm Tuesdays & Wednesdays, 6.00 pm Thursdays, 2.30 pm Fridays. At this point, business comes to an end except for the half-hour adjournment debate. In certain circumstances, business may continue beyond the normal sitting times.
- Exempted business
- Petitions (except Fridays)
- Adjournment debate

Source: House of Commons information office, December 2003.

When the changes described in Box 14.7 were introduced, it was announced that they were experimental until the end of that Parliament. In January 2004, however, more than 250 MPs signed a motion asking that the hours for Commons sittings be reviewed again. Peter Hain, the Leader of the House of Commons, agreed to this (BBC Radio 4, 11 January 2004).

The usual channels

The weekly business of the House is arranged by the government and Opposition Chief Whips. The Speaker is informed about which leading speakers from each party would like to address the House during debates. This is termed 'arranging business through the usual channels'. The business for the two weeks ahead is announced each Thursday by the Leader of the House. The Leader of the House also arranges the Commons' programme for the entire parliamentary session.

14.9 The Speaker of the House of Commons

The proceedings in the chamber of the House of Commons are chaired by the Speaker or one of the Deputy Speakers. Speakers are chosen by their fellow MPs at the start of each new Parliament or when the previous Speaker retires or dies.

Although Speakers are elected MPs, they are not permitted to speak on behalf of their constituents in the Commons and they do not take part in debates since they are supposed to be impartial. The Speaker votes in the House only in the event of a tie and, even then, is guided by precedent - by the decisions of Speakers in similar previous cases.

As well as representing the House of Commons on ceremonial and formal occasions, it is the Speaker's job to see that the procedural rules of the House (contained in the Standing Orders) are followed and to decide which MPs are called upon to speak. In attempting to preserve order, there are a number of sanctions at the Speaker's disposal. First, MPs can be directed to withdraw remarks made in 'unparliamentary language'. Second, if these instructions are ignored, MPs can be suspended from the House. Third, in the event of a serious general disorder in the chamber, the Speaker can suspend the entire proceedings.

In 1985, the Speaker of the House of Commons, Bernard Weatherill, suspended proceedings for 20 minutes following continued protests from a group of Opposition Labour MPs against the government's refusal to agree to a debate on the dispute in the coal industry.

Main points Sections 14.7 - 14.9

- **The layout of the Commons favours a two-party system and an adversarial style of debate.**
- **A Queen's Speech is delivered at the start of each parliamentary session. Written by the Prime Minister, it outlines the government's programme.**
- **Complaints about the Commons' working hours have led to a number of changes since 1995.**
- **The weekly business of the House is arranged 'through the usual channels'.**
- **Proceedings in the Commons are chaired by the Speaker or Deputy Speakers. It is their job to ensure that the procedural rules of the House are followed and order is maintained.**

Activity 14.3 Commons business

Item A Changes to House of Commons sittings and business

The first parliamentary reform introduced after New Labour's 1997 election victory was that of Prime Minister's Question Time. The traditional 15-minute slots on Tuesday and Thursday afternoons were replaced with a 30-minute appearance on Wednesdays only. Tony Blair justified this reform by claiming that it would facilitate in-depth questioning and would, therefore, allow more effective scrutiny of the Prime Minister by the House of Commons. Sceptics, on the other hand, argued that Blair was simply ensuring he would only need to answer parliamentary questions once, rather than twice, each week, allowing him to reduce the time he spent in the Commons. Another reform in the Labour government's first term was to allow 'parallel sittings' in a room off Westminster Hall. The aim was that MPs would be able to debate certain matters away from the floor of the House. This, it was suggested, would allow backbench MPs to have a greater opportunity to become involved in parliamentary business. Sceptics, however, pointed out that 'parallel sittings' provided the government with more time for its business and legislation in the main chamber. Reforms introduced with effect from January 2003 were mainly concerned with the House of Commons' hours of sitting. Although ministers and sympathetic MPs justify these reforms in terms of 'modernisation', family-friendly hours and enhancing parliamentary scrutiny of 'the executive', many other MPs, including some Labour backbenchers, suspect that the overall effect - whether by accident or design, and probably the latter - has been to make life somewhat easier for ministers.

Source: Dorey 2003, pp.156-58.

Item B The layout of the House of Commons chamber

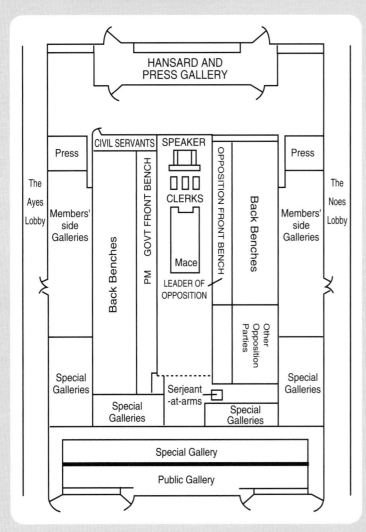

Item C The Speaker

When Betty Boothroyd was elected as Speaker of the House of Commons in 1992 (a position she held until retiring in 2000), Prime Minister, John Major, spoke of the qualities needed to carry out the job effectively:

> 'The holder of the office of Speaker must know when to turn a blind eye and when not. She needs a quick mind and a ready wit. She must be unfailing in her impartiality. She will sometimes need the wisdom of Solomon and, if I am strictly honest, she will sometimes need the patience of Job.'

Quoted in the *Guardian*, 28 April 1992.

Questions

1. Why have the Blair governments introduced changes to the sitting hours and procedures of the House of Commons (Item A)?

2. Judging from Item C, what are the qualities required by the Speaker of the House of Commons? Which qualities are most important?

3. What are the arguments for and against moving the House of Commons to a new, purpose-built, semi-circular chamber outside London? Use Item B in your answer.

14.10 House of Commons committees

Official and unofficial committees

Philip Norton explains that:

'Within the House of Commons there are basically two types of committee: official and unofficial. Each can be further subdivided. The two principal types of official committees are the standing and select committees, though the House also makes use of a form of hybrid, known as special standing committees. Unofficial committees comprise essentially party committees and all-party groups. The official committees are established by the House under its Standing Orders. They are subordinate bodies: the House retains the final say on all matters. Unofficial committees are, as the name indicates, not bodies established formally by the House: they are created within the parliamentary parties or by groups of Members.' (Norton 1991, p.5)

Norton points out that although the use of committees can be traced back to the 14th century, extensive use of committees in the House of Commons is a recent development. Since 1907, the sending of Bills to standing committees has been normal practice. It is only since 1979, however, that select committees have been appointed to investigate the activities of government departments.

Standing committees

When a Bill has received its second reading, it reaches its committee stage. The Bill is then usually sent to standing committee for consideration - unless the House decides otherwise (the committee stage of uncontentious Bills or Bills of constitutional importance, such as the 1998/99 House of Lords Bill, are taken on the floor of the House). Standing committees examine the details of a Bill within the confines of a Bill's general principles which were approved at the second reading. The job of standing committees is to debate and consider amendments to the Bill.

Despite their name, standing committees are ad hoc committees. They are set up specifically to examine a particular Bill and are then disbanded. No collective identity (which might lead to a stronger, more investigative role) is, therefore, likely to develop among a committee's members.

Membership

Standing committees are referred to as Standing Committee A, B, C and so on. Members come from different parties in rough proportion to the party political make-up of the House as a whole. A government with a secure majority can, therefore, normally expect to secure acceptance of its proposals, although during the detailed consideration of a Bill it may wish to make minor amendments.

The Committee of Selection, composed of senior MPs, decides which MPs should sit on each standing committee (after consulting party whips). The relevant minister and Opposition spokesperson are included as a matter of course and members with a special interest or expertise in the subject of the Bill are normally considered. The total number of members on a committee can vary between 16 and 50. It is up to the Committee of Selection to decide exactly how many should serve on each committee but most have about 18 members. A standing committee's work is presided over by a senior backbencher appointed by the Speaker from the 'Chairman's panel' (they are supposed to be impartial).

Meetings of standing committees are adversarial, with MPs of the governing party and Opposition members sitting on opposite sides of the room.

Procedure

Standing committees consider each clause in a Bill in turn. Amendments can be put forward but, unless they are moved by the minister, they usually fail (clauses of government Bills which are voted on tend to be whipped).

In order to reduce the time a committee spends on a Bill, the government may seek to apply the guillotine. This involves setting a time limit for debate on each clause. Its use is not restricted to the committee stage and it is used particularly for those occasions when it has not been possible to reach agreement with the Opposition 'through the usual channels'.

There are two main criticisms of standing committees:

- that they take excessive time to carry out their work
- that they are adversarial.

In addition, it is argued that these committees have inadequate information at their disposal since they are not permitted to take evidence from outside bodies or individuals.

Possible reforms

In response to these criticisms, Norton (1995) identified four possible reforms - see Box 14.8 on page 273.

Box 14.8 shows that there have been some, relatively minor, changes to the way in which standing committees work, but the idea that the work of standing committees is amalgamated with that of select committees (Downs 1985) has not been acted upon. Select committees are responsible for scrutinising and reviewing the work of government departments. An amalgamation would result in the committee reviewing the work of a particular department, including the draft legislation produced by that department.

Select committees

According to a government pamphlet:

'Select committees are generally set up to help Parliament with the control of the executive by examining aspects of public policy and administration. They may also undertake more specific responsibilities related to the internal procedures of Parliament. They examine subjects by taking written and oral evidence and, after private deliberation, present a report to the House.' (HMSO 1994, p.80)

Drewry (1989) explains that select committees were used a great deal before the mid-19th century, but the development of a disciplined party system in Parliament and greater control by the executive led to their decline. A number of non-departmental select committees have a long history, but it is only since 1979 that departmental select committees have been in operation.

Non-departmental select committees

Perhaps the most important non-departmental select

Box 14.8 Possible reforms to standing committees

I. Fixed timetable

A fixed timetable for the passage of Bills would prevent or reduce the need for the imposition of the guillotine. It would also allow more balance since each part of the Bill would be given a certain amount of time for scrutiny. Since 2000, government Bills can be given a timetable by setting out how long will be available for each of the Bill's stages.

2. Permanent committees

A recommendation of the Hansard Society Commission is that standing committees should be set up on a permanent basis. A core of permanent members would be supplemented by the co-option of extra members for each Bill. This would allow a body of knowledge to develop and help to reduce the partisan nature of the committees.

3. Earlier stage

Norton (1992) has suggested that the committee stage of the passage of a Bill should precede the Bill's second reading. This would allow the committee to consider wider issues since the principles upon which the Bill is based would not have been established. Among the proposals of the cross-party Commons modernisation committee which came into effect in 2003 was support for the principle of

using pre-legislative committees to examine draft Bills before they are formally presented to Parliament. It has been pointed out, however, that:

> 'This will only happen if ministers are prepared to take the extra time to publish Bills in draft.'
> (Cowley & Stuart 2003).

4. Special standing committees

In 1993, the Ripon Commission recommended that, where appropriate, standing committees should be able to take on the powers of 'special standing committees' (a cross between standing and select committees) which can question witnesses and consider particular aspects of a Bill before carrying out clause-by-clause examination. Committees would, therefore, be able to obtain adequate information to scrutinise the Bill properly. In addition, outside groups would be able to make representations in an open environment, rather than relying on the secret or private contacts that are normally made with government departments. Special standing committees have been used for some uncontentious Bills which involve 'complex or novel questions of policy'.

Source: House of Commons Information Factsheet L6, September 2003.

committee is the Public Accounts Committee, first set up in 1861. This committee has a large staff of auditors working under the Comptroller and Auditor General. It checks the government accounts, attempts to ensure that money has been spent in properly authorised ways, and also assesses whether value for money has been achieved.

Other non-departmental select committees include the Public Administration Committee (which supervises the work of the Parliamentary Commissioner for Administration - the Ombudsman) and the European Scrutiny Committee (which reviews the legal developments and documents of the European Union).

There are also non-departmental select committees which deal with the House's internal affairs (such as the Select Committee on Standards and Privileges) and ad hoc committees set up to investigate particular issues.

Departmental select committees

In 1979, despite ministerial reluctance, MPs voted to set up a number of departmental select committees whose task would be to examine the expenditure, administration and policy of individual government departments and to report back to the House. Initially, 14 departmental select committees were set up. By the end of 2003, there were 18 - see Box 14.9).

Departmental select committees each have 11 members (except for the Committee on Northern Ireland Affairs which has 13 and the Committee on Environment, Food & Rural Affairs with 17). Members are chosen by the Committee of Selection, but party whips are influential in determining membership. Apart from the Committee on Northern Ireland Affairs (which includes five MPs from Northern Irish parties), membership of select committees (as with standing committees) roughly reflects the relative party sizes in the Commons as a whole. Unlike standing committees, however, no government ministers or frontbench Opposition members are included and no whips attend.

Box 14.9 Departmental select committees in 2003

This table shows the departmental select committees in existence in September 2003.

Constitutional Affairs	Office of the Deputy Prime Minister (Housing, Planning, Local Government & the Regions)
Culture, Media & Sport	
Defence	
Education & Skills	Science & Technology
Environment, Food & Rural Affairs	Scottish Affairs
Foreign Affairs	Trade & Industry
Health	Transport
Home Affairs	Treasury
International Development	Welsh Affairs
Northern Ireland Affairs	Work & Pensions

Select committees do not tend to operate on the adversarial party lines of standing committees. Party-based differences may still occur, but select committees, generally, aim to produce unanimous reports at the end of their investigations.

Powers

Most departmental select committees meet once a week. In theory, they can investigate any issue within the scope of the work of the relevant department, but time places severe limits on what a small group of backbench MPs (who have the support of only a small administrative staff) can achieve. The committees do have, however, the power to send for 'persons, papers and records'. Witnesses can be interviewed (in public unless confidential or security matters are discussed), evidence taken and specialist advisers appointed.

Limitations

Despite such powers, however, the committees may not obtain the information they require. The tradition of government secrecy can make it difficult to obtain information from ministers and civil servants. Without the express permission of the House as a whole, committees cannot compel ministers or other MPs to attend, although they generally do.

More important is the difficulty some committees face in persuading ministers and other witnesses to give straight answers to direct questions. Committees do not have automatic recourse to departmental papers - though concern is normally expressed in the House and increasingly by the media if evidence is refused on unreasonable grounds. Norton (1995a) notes the pressures of time on individual members. Although each committee typically meets once a week for up to two hours, preparation time can add an estimated eight hours per week to a committee member's already busy schedule. This has led to criticisms that select committees lack the necessary expertise to examine complex issues effectively Box 14.10 gives an example.

Box 14.10 The Foreign Affairs Select Committee inquiry into the decision to go to war with Iraq

In 2003 an investigation by the Select Committee on Foreign Affairs into the government's decision to invade Iraq became a major item in the print and broadcasting media. According to Anthony Sampson, the media coverage revealed the limitations of select committees. It demonstrated, he said, their lack of legal assistance, the inability to carry out proper research, and the tendency of the committee's members to make party-political points.

Source: *Observer*, 17 August 2003.

The government is not obliged to act upon the recommendations of select committees, and there is no guarantee that their reports will even be debated in the House. Government departments, however, are normally expected to reply within 60 days, the response usually being in the form of a detailed memorandum.

Reasons for popularity

Membership of select committees is more popular with MPs than membership of standing committees. In part, this is because MPs believe that the work done by select committees is important (if nothing else, ministers and civil servants are aware that a select committee can investigate any aspect of a department's work and so the committee acts as a deterrent against arbitrary government). In part, it also reflects the media attention which is sometimes given to the work of select committees. Select committees allow backbenchers to engage in investigative work and, in some cases, this is a substitute for ministerial office.

Reform of departmental select committees

Since 1999, demands to strengthen the effectiveness of departmental select committees have been made in a series of reports from the Liaison Committee (comprising the Chairs of all select committees) and the House of Commons Modernisation Committee. Not all of these demands have been met. For example, recommendations to reduce the influence of party whips on the selection of committee members and to introduce the opportunity for the full House to ask questions about each committee report were rejected by the government. It was agreed, however, to allocate extra resources to help the committees in their work and to consider paying an additional salary for the committee Chairs.

Main points **Section 14.10**

- **Standing committees are ad hoc committees which examine a Bill clause-by-clause within the confines of the Bill's general principles (as approved at second reading).**
- **Members of standing committees are taken from parties in rough proportion to the size of each party in the House as a whole, so the government has an in-built majority. Proceedings are adversarial and often whipped.**
- **Select committees are set up to help Parliament to control the executive by examining aspects of public policy and administration.**
- **Non-departmental select committees include the Public Accounts Committee which checks that the government has spent money in properly authorised ways.**
- **Proceedings in departmental select committees are not normally adversarial and the committees can call for 'persons, papers and records'.**

Activity 14.4 Committees in the House of Commons

Item A Liaison Committee

Every so often the Chairs of all select committees meet together as the Liaison Committee to consider matters affecting committees generally. In 2002, the Prime Minister agreed to appear before the Liaison Committee twice a year to discuss 'international and domestic affairs'. The first session occurred in July 2002 (the first time a Prime Minister had ever agreed to be questioned by an investigative committee of the House) with further sessions planned for each January and July. A transcript of the evidence is made public on the internet after the meeting.

Source: HoC 2003.

Item B Select committees

Select committees scrutinise each government department's policies, activities and spending. They generally conduct inquiries on specific departmental issues and publish reports. They are attracting growing media attention. Absenteeism is low and they are often independent minded. A critical report on the privatisation of air traffic control in 2000 is a good example. The government also sometimes has acted on their recommendations. For example, in 1999 the government took up a suggestion by the Home Affairs Committee to use tagging and other community-based sentences to reduce prison overcrowding. In July 2001 the attempted removal of two feisty Labour select committee Chairs (Gwyneth Dunwoody on Transport and Donald Anderson on Foreign Affairs) was defeated by the Commons - the only real government defeat yet). Nevertheless, the committees lack the time, resources, staff, expertise, power and, perhaps above all, the will to be more than merely an irritant to the government. Moreover, the balance of party power on the committees reflects that of the Commons as a whole - and most backbenchers want to be frontbenchers - and their membership is heavily influenced by the whips. The government has explicitly rejected recent suggestions from the Liaison Committee for strengthening the committees' powers. A more recent proposal to offer the Chairs of select committees an additional salary (£12,500 above an MP's normal salary) may help to raise the prestige of the committees. It would offer an alternative career structure for MPs.

Source: Grant 2004.

Item C Departmental committees and draft legislation

Since Labour returned to power in 1997, departmental committees have been able to consider a number of draft Bills (ie before they enter the formal parliamentary procedures for the passage of legislation). Although the committees cannot make changes to a draft Bill, they can suggest amendments. This can lead to more thorough debate once the Bill enters Parliament should the government not accept the committee's amendments.

Source: HoC 2003.

Item E The standing committee on the Social Security Bill in the 1997-98 parliamentary session

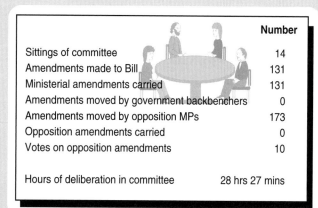

	Number
Sittings of committee	14
Amendments made to Bill	131
Ministerial amendments carried	131
Amendments moved by government backbenchers	0
Amendments moved by opposition MPs	173
Opposition amendments carried	0
Votes on opposition amendments	10
Hours of deliberation in committee	28 hrs 27 mins

Information from the House of Commons Information Office, 5 November 1998.

Item D The record of standing committees

The most shocking thing about the Commons is the way in which laws are made. If you want to see what it is like, sit on a standing committee. A Bill is produced and that Bill has to be defended. At the same time, it has to go through the committee stage. The government has a majority on that committee and it selects the members of the committee. It doesn't pick people who are going to be difficult - it picks a tame majority which can be relied on to defend the measure and uncritically see it through the process. And then, ministers will say, 'Parliament has decided'. I'm not easily shocked, but I was in respect of what became the 1993 Education Act. Members of the government party on that Bill spent their committee time writing their Christmas cards. This is the reality of how legislation is scrutinised in standing committee. People stay out of the room, except for crucial votes. Government MPs are told to say nothing so that a Bill can go through as quickly as possible. The opposition simply engages in a tactic called 'delay' - talking about anything remotely connected to the Bill in the vain hope of extracting some political benefit. David Butler has described the committee stage as a 'futile marathon'. He cites a standing committee which met for two months in 35 separate sessions for a total of 120 hours. Yet, no fewer than 35 hours were spent on the first two clauses and, when only 17 of the 129 clauses had been examined, a guillotine was applied, depriving most of the details of the Bill from any scrutiny at all. There were 173 votes on the committee stage and, surprise surprise, the government won them all. You could replay the same story for any major piece of legislation. This is why we have such bad legislation. It is a shocking state of affairs.

Source: Wright 1997 (at the time of writing, Tony Wright was Labour MP for Cannock and Burntwood).

Questions

1. To what extent and in what ways is the select committee system able to act as a check on the executive? Use Items A and B in your answer.

2. What evidence is there in Items A-C that the powers of select committees have increased in recent years?

3. Judging from Items D and E, why do you think standing committee work is unpopular with

   a) Opposition MPs

   b) government backbenchers?

4. What are the drawbacks of the standing committee system? Use Items D and E in your answer.

14.11 *Debates in the House of Commons*

The House of Commons is a debating chamber, and an elaborate set of rules for the conduct of debates has developed over time. Some of the rules are laid down in Standing Orders (the regulations governing the House of Commons' procedures). Others operate by convention - see Box 14.11.

Box 14.11 Debating conventions in the House of Commons

The subject for debate starts off as a proposal or 'motion' made by a member. When a motion has been moved, the Speaker proposes the question (in the same terms as the motion) as the subject for debate. In both Houses, members speak from wherever they have been sitting and not from a rostrum (although frontbench members usually stand at one of the dispatch boxes on the Table of the House)... Generally, no member may speak twice to the same motion, except to clarify some part of a speech that has been misunderstood, or by leave of the House.

Source: HMSO 1994, pp.60-61.

Procedure

Major debates are normally opened and closed either by government ministers or members of the Opposition front-bench. Frontbenchers are generally given more time than backbenchers to make their speeches.

MPs wishing to make contributions to a debate must first 'catch the Speaker's eye', although this is usually done by notifying the Speaker before the beginning of the debate. Until 1998, Privy Councillors were given priority in debates (Privy Councillors are mainly existing and former Cabinet ministers or leading members of the Opposition parties). Unlike ordinary MPs who are referred to as 'honourable members', Privy Councillors are referred to as 'right honourable members'.

Although the purpose of debates is, in theory, to decide upon government policy and administration, a government can usually rely on its majority in the House to gain approval for its actions (see Box 14.12 for the range of debates). The 'division' (vote) at the end of the debate is, therefore, generally a foregone conclusion. It is called a 'division' because the normal method of voting involves MPs dividing into those going into the 'ayes' lobby and those going into the 'noes' lobby. Since 2001, however, that has not been the only method of voting - see Box 14.13 on page 277. Commons debates are perhaps more accurately seen as a device for expressing government, Opposition and dissenting views.

Box 14.12 Debates in the Commons

1. **Debates on White Papers**
2. **Debates on Bills**
3. **Debates on ministerial statements**
4. **Debates on reports of parliamentary committees**
5. **Debates on the Queen's Speech**
   The Queen's Speech is the annual address to Parliament, written by the Prime Minister, outlining the government's legislative programme for the forthcoming session. The subsequent debate takes place over a number of days and is one of the few occasions during the year when a major Commons speech is delivered by the Prime Minister.
6. **Daily adjournment debates**
   These take place during the final half hour of each day's sitting when an MP can raise almost any subject. These debates are often used to air constituents' grievances or draw attention to matters in which individual backbenchers are personally interested.
7. **Government motions**
   About 20 days per session are devoted to debates on government motions.
8. **Opposition days**
   There are 20 days per session for debates on subjects chosen by the opposition.
9. **Motions of no-confidence (in the government)**
   No-confidence debates are more likely to be called for by the opposition when the government's majority is small. If defeated, the government must resign or call a general election, but this occurred only once in the 20th century - James Callaghan's Labour government was defeated on a no-confidence vote in March 1979.
10. **Private Members' motions**
    About 10 days per session are reserved for debates on these motions, together with the final day before each recess (holiday). These debates are usually poorly attended.
11. **Emergency debates**
    Requests for emergency debates are rarely granted by the Speaker, but opposition requests for them can secure media attention.

Quality of debates

Debates vary in quality, but are frequently little more than a series of speeches during which party political points are made to a sparsely attended chamber. Unless the government has a small majority, most debates make little impact on government policy. Even if the government only has a small majority, it is not often the quality of points made in a debate which result in government action. For example, in 2004, the government made a series of concessions over its plans for university 'top-up' fees. These concessions were made, however, in response to threats of a large number of Labour

Box 14.13 Deferred divisions

Traditionally, votes in Parliament involve MPs walking through one of two division lobbies. The introduction of deferred divisions in 2001 allows less significant votes - those that would normally be taken at the end of the day's business - to be deferred to the following Wednesday, when MPs vote by filling in ballot papers rather than using the division lobbies. Supporters argue that this is a more sensible use of time. Opponents say that it divorces the debate from the vote (the delay can be up to a week) and that it can reduce attendance in the chamber. Since their introduction, however, there have been relatively few deferred divisions.

Source: Cowley & Stuart 2003.

MPs to vote against the government rather than because of the content or quality of debates in the House.

Media coverage of debates

Lengthy sections of debates on important issues are sometimes covered live on radio and television, bringing the views expressed to a much wider audience. Yet the broadcasting of the proceedings of the House is of fairly recent origin. Regular radio coverage began in 1978 and television cameras were first allowed into the Commons in 1989.

Importance of debates

Performance in debates can help to determine the direction of an MP's career. A reputation as a poor performer in the Commons does not help an MP to gain promotion to the front-bench, nor does it make it easy for an MP to retain such a position.

In general, as a means of scrutinising the executive or of influencing policy, debates have their limitations. But, they may have some effect in forcing the government to explain its policies and to justify its actions. They also bring conflicting political views to the attention of the electorate.

14.12 Parliamentary Questions

Question Time in the House of Commons is held each weekday (except Fridays). The Prime Minister now answers questions in a single session lasting for half an hour from 12 noon every Wednesday when Parliament is in session. Other government ministers answer questions from 2.30 pm on Mondays and from 11.30 am Tuesdays, Wednesdays and Thursdays. They take turns to answer questions (a rota system is used to determine which minister answers at which time). Overall, Question Time lasts for about one hour, four days a week. Box 14.14 outlines the system for MPs wishing to 'table' a question.

The Table Office

The Table Office (which consists of four clerks under the control of the Principal Clerk) scrutinises proposed questions to ensure that they conform to the parliamentary rules. The admissibility of questions is determined by whether they conform to principles established by rulings made by successive Speakers. For example, a question:

Box 14.14 Tabling questions

Questions are usually handed in at or sent to the Table Office in writing. Most questions are answered in writing but if an oral answer is required, at least three days' notice must usually be given to allow time for an answer to be prepared. An MP may ask up to two oral questions and any number of written questions a day, but may ask only one oral question of any one minister on any day.

Source: HMSO 1994, p.88 and House of Commons Information Office Factsheet P1, January 2004.

- must be framed as a genuine question and not as a statement or speech;
- must not seek expressions of opinion on a question of law (as this is a matter for the courts);
- must not seek information that is readily available elsewhere or for confirmation of a rumour or press report for which the minister is not responsible;
- must not be 'tendentious, controversial, ironic, vague, frivolous or repetitive';
- must relate to a matter for which the minister is officially responsible.

Supplementaries

Before each Question Time, ministers work with their civil servants to prepare their responses. In particular, they try to anticipate the supplementary questions which follow each initial answer. Each questioner is permitted to ask one supplementary question and the Speaker may then allow further supplementaries from other MPs. Supplementaries from Opposition MPs are often, therefore, designed to test the ability and efficiency of the minister. The purposes behind questions (particularly those designed for oral answers) are summarised in Box 14.15 on page 278.

Prime Minister's Questions

Supplementary questions must be confined to matters for which the answering minister has responsibility. Since the Prime Minister is in charge of no department in particular, during the last two decades of the 20th century the convention developed of tabling 'open' questions at Prime Minister's Questions (PMQs). Usually these took the form of each questioner asking the Prime Minister to list their engagements for the day. Having asked the open question, questioners could then ask what they really wanted to ask in the form of a supplementary question - the intention being to introduce an element of surprise by asking the Prime Minister a question on any aspect of government policy.

Despite some streamlining of this process in 1997 (normally it is now only the first questioner who needs to ask about the Prime Minister's engagements for the day), the whole process of PMQs is still open to the criticism that it has become a ritualistic session of set pieces in which the Leaders of the main parties attempt to score points against each other (the Leader of the main Opposition party is allowed three or four supplementary questions, the Leader of the next largest party, two). The result is that PMQs often deteriorate into rowdy slanging matches. The fact that clips from these confrontations are often shown on prime time television news causes concern that the reputation of Parliament has suffered.

Box 14.15 Why are questions asked at Question Time?

1. To gain information (but more effective ways, such as writing to the appropriate government department, are usually available).
2. To press for action on an issue.
3. To raise a grievance on behalf of a constituent or group.
4. To give publicity to the aims or interests of a pressure group.
5. To impress constituents, constituency party or party managers.
6. To embarrass the government (particularly the Leader of the Opposition's questions to the Prime Minister).
7. To attempt to show government policy or actions in a favourable light.

The importance of Question Time

For Opposition members, Question Time is an opportunity for political point scoring while government ministers and their civil servants tend to regard it as an exercise in damage limitation and reveal as little as possible. Ministers are not obliged to answer questions. If they refuse to answer a question, they do not even have to supply a reason, although they usually do. Referring to the carefully prepared responses of ministers which are provided by civil servants, one backbench MP declared:

> 'Most of the words they say haven't even passed through their own brains.' (quoted in Jordan & Richardson 1987, p.72)

Yet, despite the criticisms, MPs on both sides of the House tend to agree that Question Time has its place in scrutinising the work of the government. It may not be a mechanism for obtaining detailed, informative and open answers to searching political questions. It can help, though, to publicise party political positions and conflicts and, as with debates, it has a part to play in securing a degree of ministerial accountability to Parliament - see Box 14.16.

Box 14.16 Question Time and ministerial responsibility

At the despatch box, ministers are without the official support they enjoy during select committee appearances. Question Time therefore provides an undiluted form of ministerial responsibility under the public and media gaze, in which any significant ministerial omission or admission will be seized upon.

Source: Flinders 2003.

Written questions

In addition to oral questions, MPs can also put questions to ministers for written answers. Indeed, any question written by an MP and directed to a minister must be answered (so long as it meets the criteria laid down by the Table Office). These written questions and answers are published in *Hansard* and there are normally now over 50,000 written questions per year.

14.13 Informal processes

Sections 14.11 and 14.12 above examined the formal ways by which the House of Commons can attempt to scrutinise or influence the executive. They showed that there are a number of limitations which restrict the effectiveness of the House's scrutiny role. A focus on the formal mechanisms, however, can lead to other forms of influence being overlooked. Matthew Flinders (2003) argues that informal processes of influence and constraint can be significant, but by their very nature tend not to be recorded.

These informal processes include those that take place within the parliamentary parties, particularly those within the party from which the government is formed. Labour governments cannot afford to ignore totally the views of the Parliamentary Labour Party. Conservative governments cannot afford to ignore totally the views of the 1922 Committee. And it is here that the non-disciplinary role of the party whips can be crucial. The whips act as a two-way communications channel. On the one hand, they work to ensure that the government maintains its majority in the Commons. On the other hand, they bring backbench views and feelings on particular issues to the attention of the executive.

There is evidence, for example, that, since 1997, in response to backbench pressure, the Labour government has, on occasion, made concessions to head off potential rebellions in the division lobbies (Cowley & Stuart 2002). Such concessions are often the outcome of behind-the-scenes negotiations on proposed legislation before the Bill is introduced formally into Parliament.

Main points Sections 14.11 - 14.13

- An elaborate set of rules for the conduct of debates in the House of Commons has developed over time. Some of the rules are laid down in Standing Orders. Others operate by convention.
- Although the purpose of debates is, in theory, to decide upon government policy and administration, a government can usually rely on its majority in the House to gain approval for its actions.
- It is only on rare occasions that debates make an impact on government policy. They do sometimes force the government to explain and justify its actions and bring issues to the attention of the public.
- Government ministers take it in turns to answer questions in the Commons at Question Time each weekday (except Friday). PMQs now take place on Wednesdays (12.00 noon -12.30 pm).
- MPs on both sides agree that Question Time can be an important means of scrutinising the work of government and in securing a degree of ministerial accountability to Parliament.
- The government can also be influenced through more informal processes. Behind-the-scenes negotiations can result in government concessions to backbench opinion.

Activity 14.5 Debates and informal processes

Item A **Debates (1)**

The Commons debates endlessly into the night. After all, politicians' only qualification is being able to talk. The Commons is supposed to be the great meeting place of the nation where ideas and issues are thrashed out and, in some sense, that is what happens. But, debates in the Commons do not necessarily reveal what the public needs to hear. It is fair to say that an exchange on *Newsnight* is far more revealing and important than an exchange in the House. The House is an echo chamber. It used to be the other way round - the media used to reflect issues raised in the Commons. I remember when those of us who were elected in 1992 had a celebration after the first year. John Smith (Leader of the Labour Party until his death in 1994) came to cut the cake and made a speech in which he said: 'I know some of you think this place is not very effective, but what you must remember is that this place is an intimate theatre'. I like that phrase. It is about play-acting.

Adapted from Wright 1997.

Item C **Informal processes**

The executive and the majority party are not the same thing. The executive is always a minority in the House, which means that it must retain the respect and confidence of the party from which it is drawn. Backbench members of the government's party often play a major role in moulding government policy and controlling the executive. For example, Eurosceptic Conservative backbenchers significantly affected the governments of Margaret Thatcher and John Major. Since 1997, dissident Labour backbenchers have similarly influenced the government over matters ranging from state disability payments, pensions, part-privatisation of air traffic control, financing of London transport and the war with Iraq. Other informal processes are not party-related. Unofficial meetings with ministers and civil servants, letters, telephone calls and even chance meetings in the corridors of the Palace of Westminster can all be useful mechanisms through which backbenchers can make their feelings known on a specific issue.

Source: Flinders 2003.

Item B **Debates (2)**

As a new backbench MP, you will probably only have three and possibly four chances to speak in a debate each year - and then, not in the great debates. Despite the abundance of lackwits in Parliament, you should always prepare your speech on the assumption that there will be at least one person present who, unlike yourself, is a real expert on the discussion. You must also get used to speaking in an empty chamber - as a newcomer you will probably be called to speak at a time when most MPs are engaged in other activities such as attending meetings that mean far more to them than what you have to say. Finally, you should remember that your purpose in speaking is not to convince anyone to act other than they would have done anyway. Still less can you hope to change people's minds. Your purpose is to let those who count know you exist. Once the debate is over, you will be in the corridors conspiring to move upwards. The corridors are far more important these days than the chamber itself. Private words in ears, accompanied by promises and threats, are far more effective than grand public gestures in helping you climb the greasy pole.

Source: Sedgemore 1995.

Item D **Informal processes and party cohesion**

Party cohesion does not necessarily indicate a lack of backbone on the part of MPs. For example, when party cohesion has existed among Labour MPs since the party's return to power in 1997, it has been due to the following factors:
- a shift rightwards in the beliefs of its MPs in recent years
- a broad agreement among Labour MPs with much of the government's programme
- no significant factional opposition within the Parliamentary Labour Party
- a conscious desire among Labour MPs not to appear disunited
- government willingness to consult, negotiate and do deals with its backbenchers over most issues.

Source Cowley & Stuart 2002.

Questions

1. What are the main purposes of debates in the House of Commons? Use Items A and B in your answer.
2. Using Items C and D, explain why informal processes are important.
3. Using Items A-D, discuss the relative importance of formal and informal processes through which backbench MPs can attempt to influence the work of governments.

14.14 *The socio-economic background of MPs*

After each general election, a significant number of new faces appear in the House of Commons. These new faces, however, tend to look very much like those which they have replaced. MPs are predominantly white, male and middle class.

The fact that most MPs come from a relatively narrow stratum of society is a cause of concern for those who argue that the House of Commons should be a microcosm of the nation. It patently is not. MPs are, on the whole, older and more highly educated than the general population. If the House of Commons was truly representative, there would be three times the number of black and Asian MPs than the 12 (all Labour) elected in 2001 and almost three times the number of women MPs (118 in 2001).

The class background of MPs

In class terms (as judged by occupation), MPs are generally drawn from a narrow segment of society, regardless of the party in power. This is illustrated by Item A in Activity 14.6 below. Of the 629 MPs from the three main parties, only 52 have a manual working background (all but one of these are Labour MPs). That makes just 8.2% of the total in a Parliament dominated by the party originally set up to provide representation for the working class.

Indeed, in the 19th century, one of the major criticisms of Parliament was that the House of Commons was made up entirely of people from the middle and upper classes. In the early part of the 20th century, this began to change as the franchise was extended and the Labour Party grew in popularity. Before the Second World War, a high proportion of Labour MPs had working-class backgrounds. This is clearly no longer the case.

Since much of the work of an MP requires communication skills, it is perhaps little surprise that middle-class occupations such as barrister, solicitor, teacher and lecturer are often seen as suitable training.

The educational background of MPs

MPs' educational experiences are also not typical of the electorate as a whole (see Item B in Activity 14.6). For example, 449 MPs from the three main parties went to university which is a much higher proportion than in the population as a whole. Similarly, at 31%, the proportion of MPs from the three main parties who went to public schools is about four times higher than for the population in general. Box 14.17 gives more details about recent changes in the educational background of MPs.

A university education is often regarded as a sign of a trained mind and is, therefore, taken as an indication that a person would be capable of handling the complexities of an MP's work.

The age of MPs

Generally, MPs are middle-aged. The proportion of MPs over 60 has fallen as the work of MPs has increased. Although the voting age was reduced from 21 to 18 in 1969, the minimum age at which a person can stand as a candidate for election to the House of Commons remains 21.

Box 14.17 Trends in the educational backgrounds of MPs

The following trends have developed over recent years:

- more and more MPs attend university
- the percentage of Labour MPs who attended university has never been higher - 67% of those elected in 2001 compared to 57% when Labour won a general election in 1974
- the percentage of Conservative MPs who attended university has never been higher (83%)
- the 2001 and 1997 general elections saw the lowest ever number of Old Etonians elected (18, mainly Conservatives)
- just 8.4% of Conservative MPs elected in 2001 were Old Etonians compared to 29% in 1945.

In 2001, only five MPs under the age of 30 were elected. In comparison, ten MPs under the age of 30 were elected in 1997 but just one in 1992. It seems, from these relatively small numbers, that parties are generally reluctant to put up young candidates in winnable seats. Perhaps as a result, many young people feel very remote from the typical MP who is a white male in his late 40s.

In addition, previous political experience (service as a local councillor or previous nominations as a parliamentary candidate) is often a prerequisite. Young candidates have little chance of competing against more experienced colleagues.

Why are many MPs middle-aged, white, middle-class men?

The selection process is likely to lead to the selection of candidates who are replicas of the selectorate (those party members responsible for selecting candidates). If most of those involved in the selection process are middle-aged, white, middle-class men, then it is likely that they will choose people like themselves.

Besides, the selectorate is often reluctant to choose candidates who do not conform to the stereotype supposedly popular with the voters. There are fears, often not openly expressed, that such candidates will be electoral liabilities. This can be the case in particular with women and black and Asian candidates. It is no surprise, therefore, that potential candidates who are untypical in some way often do not feel that it is worth pursuing their candidature.

The selection of women candidates

Box 14.18 on page 281 shows the number and percentage of women candidates and MPs in 1997 and 2001. Since the 2001 general election, both Labour and the Conservatives have changed their approach to the selection of women candidates. The Labour Party has reduced its target of having women as half the party's MPs. While this proportion is still regarded as desirable, the target has been reduced to 35%.

The 2002 Sex Discrimination (Election of Candidates) Act means that parties are now allowed to discriminate positively in favour of women, for example, by permitting all-women short-lists of candidates. After this Act was passed, it was reported that Labour's NEC had drawn up plans to impose

Box 14.18 Women candidates and MPs in the three main parties

1997	Candidates	MPs
Labour	155 (24%)	101
Conservative	66 (10%)	13
Lib Dem	139 (21%)	3
Total	360	117

2001	Candidates	MPs
Labour	148 (23%)	95
Conservative	93 (15%)	14
Lib Dem	140 (22%)	5
Total	381	114

all-women short-lists on at least half of the vacant winnable seats for the next election (*Guardian*, 10 July 2002). Any seat where an MP announced retirement plans after December 2002 would automatically have an all-women short-list imposed on it.

It was also reported that Conservative Central Office was planning to impose short-lists of candidates in the most winnable seats before the next general election. The short-lists of 15 to 20 names would consist of a high number of women and black and Asian candidates. These proposals, however, provide no guarantees that the patterns of candidate selection will change significantly, and are likely to be resisted by local Conservative associations which traditionally guard their independence jealously.

The Liberal Democrats have opted for a 40% target for female candidates but decided not to take advantage of the change in the law to allow women-only short-lists.

Black and Asian candidates

Box 14.19 shows that there was an increase in the number of black and Asian candidates at the 2001 general election. Most of the new candidates were selected in unwinnable seats, however. All of the 12 black or Asian MPs following the election are in the Labour Party. But this number amounts to only 2% of the Parliamentary Labour Party which means that black and Asian people continue to be under-represented in the House of Commons.

Box 14.19 Black and Asian candidates

	Total	Lab	Con	Lib Dem
1997	42	13	10	19
2001	66	22	16	28

This chart shows the number of black and Asian candidates in the general elections held in 1997 and 2001.

Main points Section 14.14

- After the 2001 general election, only 52 of the 629 MPs from the three main parties were from a working-class background.
- More than two-thirds of MPs from the three main parties are university educated and almost one-third attended public school.
- Only five MPs elected in 2001 were under 30.
- The selection process is likely to lead to the selection of candidates who are replicas of the selectorate. If most people involved in the selection process are middle-aged, white, middle-class men, then it is likely that they will choose people like themselves.

Activity 14.6 MPs elected in 2001

Item A Occupational background of MPs elected in 2001

Occupation	Lab	Con	Lib Dem
Professions:	**179**	**64**	**27**
Lawyer	31	31	6
Civil servant/local government	30	2	3
Teaching (all levels)	98	7	12
Other professions	20	24	6
Business	**33**	**60**	**14**
Manual worker	**51**	**1**	**0**
Miscellaneous:	**149**	**41**	**10**
White collar	73	2	1
Politics	44	18	4
Publisher/journalist	32	14	4
Other	0	7	1

Item B Educational background of MPs elected in 2001

Education	Lab	Con	Lib Dem
State school	48	3	4
State school & degree	296	57	30
Public school	2	6	1
Public school & degree	66	100	17
Total	**412**	**166**	**52**
Oxford or Cambridge	65	79	14
Other universities	210	59	22
All universities	**275**	**138**	**36**
%	67	83	70
Eton	2	14	2
Other public schools	66	92	16
All public schools	**68**	**106**	**18**
%	17	64	35

Item C Age of MPs elected in 2001

Age	Labour	Conservative	Lib Dem
21-29	4	I	-
30-39	39	25	14
40-49	152	64	14
50-59	165	57	23
60-69	44	18	1
70-79	8	I	-
Median age	50	48	47

Source: Butler & Kavanagh 2002, p.199.

Questions

1. 'It is misleading to list MPs' characteristics as if they are a single species because the members from the main parties differ significantly along most dimensions.' Judging from Items A-C, would you agree with this statement?

2. 'In social, if not in political, terms, Conservative and Labour MPs have more in common with each other than with the voters who elected them.' Is there evidence in Items A-C to support this view?

3. a) Would you describe Colin Pickthall (Item D) as a typical Labour MP? Explain why.

   b) How would you expect his profile to differ if he was (i) a Liberal Democrat MP or (ii) a Conservative MP?

Item D Profile of a Labour MP

Name: Colin Pickthall

Date of birth: 13 September 1944

Party: Labour

First elected: April 1992

Constituency: Lancashire West

Schools: Broughton Road County Primary 1952-56 (State School)
Ulverston Grammar 1956-63 (State School)

University: University of Wales 1963-66 (BA-English & History)
University of Lancaster 1966-67 (MA-Socialism and English poetry in the 1930s &1950s)

Former employment: Labourer in Shipyards
Teacher at Ruffwood Comprehensive School, Kirkby 1967-70
Lecturer Edge Hill College 1970-92

Previous political experience: County Councillor 1989-93
Chair of Governers, Skelmersdale College of Further Education

Parents: Father worked in shipyards in Barrow-in-Furness
Mother was a housewife

Adapted from interviews held in November 1994 and July 1998.

14.15 How accountable are MPs?

Section 14.14 above showed that MPs are not representative of their constituents in terms of their class, gender, ethnicity and age. But this does not mean that MPs cannot represent their constituents in some other way. There are three main theories of representation.

1. Trustee model

The trustee model is associated with the 18th-century MP Edmund Burke. In a speech to his Bristol constituents in 1774, Burke argued that if they elected him as their MP, they should expect not a slavish concern to please them but the exercise of his own judgement and conscience.

According to this theory of representation, although MPs have a duty to consult and to take into account the opinions of their constituents, their primary duty is to act according to their own consciences. In other words, voters hand responsibility for decision-making to trustees (their representatives). The acceptance of this view by most MPs today explains why, for example, the House of Commons has consistently voted against the reintroduction of the death

penalty even though surveys show that a majority of voters supports it.

2. Delegate model

The second theory is that MPs are the voters' delegates and it is an MP's job to act as a mouthpiece through which the voters' concerns are voiced. The MP's personal views on an issue are not relevant. If MPs subscribe to this theory, therefore, they will vote according to the wishes of their constituents rather than their conscience.

In practice, it is difficult for MPs to put this idea into practice because issues arise where constituents are split and it is unclear what the majority view is.

3. Mandate model

A third theory is that MPs are not elected on their own individual merits but because they are members of a particular political party. Once elected, MPs have a popular mandate to ensure that the policies outlined in the party's manifesto are put into effect. It is, therefore, their job to support their party at all times (unless the party is failing to deliver its manifesto promises). Since loyalty to party comes first, at times it will be necessary to suppress personal views or to disregard the views of constituents.

Accountability

Accountability means explaining why a particular course of action has been taken and being open to criticism about that course of action. The three contradictory views of the role of a representative described above ensure that there are different views about to whom an MP should be accountable.

MPs who support the Burkean view of representation do not have to account for their actions other than to explain that they voted according to their conscience. Of course, if they choose to ignore the views of their constituents completely, there is the chance that they will not be elected next time. Also, there is usually great pressure from the party whips to make MPs conform to the party line. If MPs are allowed a free vote, however, there is, in theory, no reason for those who follow the Burkean line to worry about accountability.

MPs who see themselves as delegates are much more accountable. It is their duty to express the wishes of their constituents and to vote accordingly. They must, therefore, be able to convince their constituents that they have exercised their powers and discharged their duties properly.

MPs who believe in the mandate model place party before constituent or conscience. They fulfil their duty by voting for their party and pressing the party leadership to stick to its manifesto commitments. Mandate MPs are unlikely to rebel or vote against their party even if, privately, they do not agree with the decisions made. During Labour's first term after the 1997 general election victory, there was criticism that Labour backbenchers were too loyal to the leadership. Many people thought, for example, that more MPs should have voted according to their conscience over the cutting of benefit for single mothers rather than voting slavishly in line with the wishes of the party leadership. Box 14.20 shows, however, that there is evidence that MPs were not so willing to support the government as the critics claimed.

Box 14.20 Robots and poodles?

A study of the parliamentary voting patterns of Labour MPs during Tony Blair's first term of office, 1997-2001, did not entirely substantiate the perception of Labour backbenchers as robots or as Blair's 'poodles'. While the number of Labour backbench rebellions during the period was relatively small, the numbers involved in each rebellion was relatively high. Blair's first term was not characterised by a particularly high degree of party cohesion when compared with previous Parliaments. And certainly, since the 2001 general election, there have been a number of occasions when very large numbers of Labour MPs have voted against their party or abstained. In January 2004, for example, the government's 161-seat majority in the Commons was reduced to just five votes when MPs voted at the second reading of the Bill on university funding. 'Rebel' Labour MPs believed that the Bill broke manifesto commitments.

Source: Cowley 2002 and the *Guardian*, 28 January 2004.

In practice, politicians veer between the three models, depending on what seems the best thing to do at the time. Understandably, therefore, it is difficult to determine a hard and fast rule about just how accountable MPs are or to whom they are accountable. It could be argued, however, that they are accountable to their constituents, their party and their conscience all at the same time and it is by the way in which they resolve any conflicts which arise from this that they are judged.

Accountability and the work of backbench MPs

The work of backbench MPs has a direct bearing on their accountability. During the course of their work, MPs meet groups from their constituency, have meetings with local and national party officials and pursue their own particular causes and interests. MPs also have access to the media and employ a secretarial staff.

As a result, they are able to explain why a particular course of action has been taken and they provide opportunities for criticism about that course of action. All MPs hold constituency surgeries, for example, where constituents have the opportunity of airing grievances or questioning an MP's behaviour.

A growing workload

To be accountable, MPs have to be seen to be active in their constituency (to maintain the support of party members and their constituents). On average, constituencies cover 150 square miles and their boundaries are set so that each constituency has about 65,000 constituents. It is therefore simply not practical for MPs to meet all or even most of their constituents. Furthermore, most constituencies are a long way from Westminster and so MPs have to spend a lot of time travelling to and from Parliament. This means that the time spent meeting constituents is limited.

In Parliament, the volume of MPs' work has grown as the activities of government have grown. Parliamentary sessions last longer and more legislation is passed than was the case a century ago. In 1900, the average length of a public Act was 200 pages. By the 1970s this had increased to 2,000 pages. Similarly, the average length of a parliamentary session has increased. In addition, the development of select committees has resulted in more work for the 25% of MPs who sit on them. Some MPs spend 20 hours a week preparing for and attending meetings of these committees.

The growth of 'professional' MPs

In 1981, Anthony King wrote an article identifying a new breed of 'professional' or 'career' politicians (King 1981). These were MPs who had entered Parliament at a relatively young age and whose aim was to retain their seats for the whole of their working lives. These MPs, he argued, looked upon their work as a career with the same promotional prospects that could be found in any profession. Each general election results in more MPs whose occupational backgrounds have close connections with the world of politics (such as political researchers and organisers) or who have experience of the civil service or local government. All these MPs can be said to be 'professional' politicians in the sense that it was through paid political work that they were noticed and selected as candidates. Like those MPs identified by King, these MPs hoped for continual re-election and promotion to ministerial posts and the Cabinet. The growth of professional politicians can have a bearing on the question of accountability of MPs - see Box 14.21.

Box 14.21 Professional politicians and accountability

If remaining in office and gaining promotion are prime concerns, then these motives can affect the way they perform their job. It might mean, for example, that MPs are more likely to obey the party whips and never vote according to conscience or to take note of the wishes of their constituents. On the other hand, it might mean that they are prepared to work harder for constituents in the hope of being re-elected.

Source: King 1981.

Accountability and ministers

A large minority of MPs of the governing party achieve ministerial office. Government ministers are obliged to take individual ministerial responsibility for the work of their departments and collective responsibility for the work of government. Being bound by collective responsibility automatically reduces ministers' room for manoeuvre as representatives.

In all matters concerning their ministerial work, ministers are (in theory at least) accountable to Parliament. They must,

therefore, answer questions about the work of their department in the House and they also reply to written questions from MPs.

Ministers work very long hours and experience heavy workloads. As well as their ministerial duties, they also have the normal parliamentary and constituency duties to perform. The sheer volume of work makes it difficult for a minister to be an efficient representative.

Main points Section 14.15

- There are three main theories of representation: (1) the trustee model; (2) the delegate model; (3) the mandate model.
- Accountability means explaining why a particular course of action has been taken and being open to criticism about that course of action.
- There are different views about to whom an MP is or should be accountable. In practice, politicians veer between the trustee model, delegate model and mandate model.
- The type of work done by backbench MPs and their workload has a direct bearing on their accountability.
- There is a debate about whether the growth of professional MPs has made them more or less accountable.
- In all matters concerning their ministerial work, ministers are accountable to Parliament.

Activity 14.7 Party cohesion and the accountability of MPs

Item A Party cohesion 1945-2001

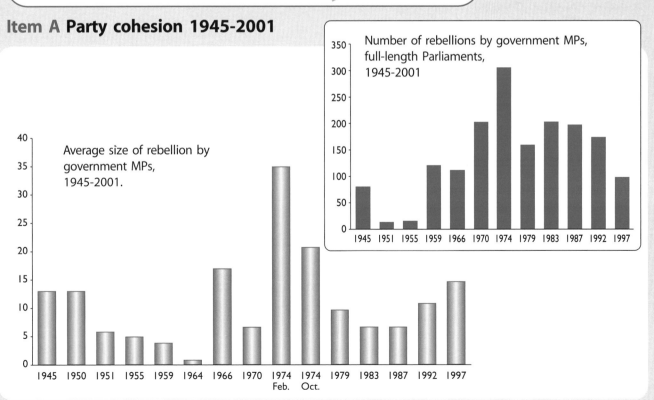

Average size of rebellion by government MPs, 1945-2001.

Number of rebellions by government MPs, full-length Parliaments, 1945-2001

Source Cowley & Stuart 2002.

Item B Diary of a wavering MP

Brian Iddon, Labour MP for Bolton South East, reacted to the debate on the second reading of the government's Bill on university funding as follows:

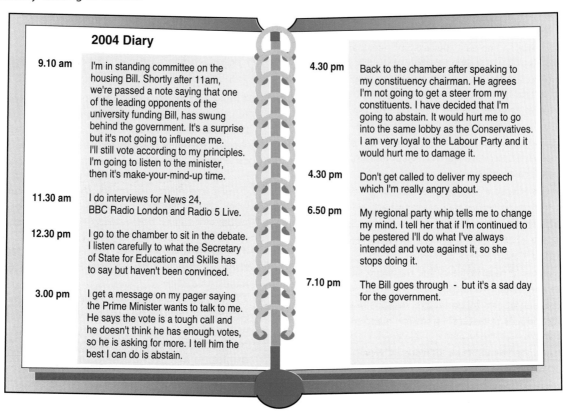

2004 Diary

9.10 am — I'm in standing committee on the housing Bill. Shortly after 11am, we're passed a note saying that one of the leading opponents of the university funding Bill, has swung behind the government. It's a surprise but it's not going to influence me. I'll still vote according to my principles. I'm going to listen to the minister, then it's make-your-mind-up time.

11.30 am — I do interviews for News 24, BBC Radio London and Radio 5 Live.

12.30 pm — I go to the chamber to sit in the debate. I listen carefully to what the Secretary of State for Education and Skills has to say but haven't been convinced.

3.00 pm — I get a message on my pager saying the Prime Minister wants to talk to me. He says the vote is a tough call and he doesn't think he has enough votes, so he is asking for more. I tell him the best I can do is abstain.

4.30 pm — Back to the chamber after speaking to my constituency chairman. He agrees I'm not going to get a steer from my constituents. I have decided that I'm going to abstain. It would hurt me to go into the same lobby as the Conservatives. I am very loyal to the Labour Party and it would hurt me to damage it.

4.30 pm — Don't get called to deliver my speech which I'm really angry about.

6.50 pm — My regional party whip tells me to change my mind. I tell her that if I'm continued to be pestered I'll do what I've always intended and vote against it, so she stops doing it.

7.10 pm — The Bill goes through - but it's a sad day for the government.

Source: *Guardian*, 28 January 2004.

Item C Professional politicians

Critics take the view that it is unhealthy for the House to have MPs whose background is limited to politics. An experience in other spheres ensures a House that is better informed and able to appreciate concerns and problems. A second problem is that the ambition to achieve promotion might ensure slavish obedience to the whips in the House. A third is that constituents might come to see the House as an essentially closed institution, full of career politicians driven by ambition for office rather than by a desire to serve their constituents. This could undermine trust in Parliament. On the other hand, knowledge of the political world ensures that some new members already know how to use parliamentary procedures. Given the demands now made of members by constituents and pressure groups, the capacity to hit the ground running is a valuable one. Also, the rise of the career politician over the past 20 years has coincided with a rise in greater backbench dissension. Most important, however is the fact that, for the career politician, it is essential to be re-elected. Volatility in voting intentions (more pronounced since the mid-1960s) ensures that members are aware of their electoral vulnerability. To try to bolster support, tremendous effort is put into constituency activity and casework.

Source: Norton 1994.

Questions

1. What does the data in Item A suggest about party cohesion among Labour MPs during Tony Blair's first term of office?

2. To whom are MPs accountable and to whom should they be accountable? Use Items A-C in your answer.

3. Using Item C, would you say that the growth of career politicians is likely to result in MPs becoming more or less accountable to: (a) their constituents (b) their local party (c) their parliamentary colleagues? Give reasons for your answers.

14.16 Composition of the House of Lords

The House of Lords (also referred to as the 'Upper' House) is made up of the Lords Temporal and the Lords Spiritual (Lords are also known as 'peers'). The Lords Spiritual are the 26 most senior bishops of the Church of England, including the two archbishops. The vast majority of peers are Lords Temporal and have been created by the monarch on the advice of the Prime Minister. A number of senior judges (known as Law Lords) also sit in the House as Lords Temporal. At the time of writing, none of the peers was elected to the House by the electorate.

Until the passing of the House of Lords Act in 1999, about 60% of peers were 'hereditaries'. Hereditary peers were those who had inherited a title and automatically became members of the House of Lords provided they had reached the age of 21. Most of the remaining members were 'life peers' who, as the name suggests, were appointed as members of the House for life but whose heirs would not succeed to a peerage.

Some life peers have previously been MPs. 'Elevation' to the House of Lords is often a way of rewarding MPs for their previous political service. On occasion, it is politically convenient for the MP's party to elevate them. Some life peers are created in order to bring into politics experienced or distinguished people from other walks of life. Some members of the House of Lords are also known to have made generous donations to one or other of the political parties before they were made peers.

The 1999 Act, intended as the first stage in a process of reform of the Upper House, removed the automatic right of hereditary peers to sit and vote in the House. As the result of negotiations between the Labour government and the Conservative Leader in the Lords, a transitional arrangement allowed 92 hereditaries (about 10%) to remain in the House until the second stage of reform was introduced. A further

ten hereditary peers were given life peerages (Baldwin 2002). Box 14.22 shows the composition of the House of Lords before and after the first stage of reform.

In 2000, an Appointments Commission was set up to recommend the appointment of a small number of members of the public as non-party peers (sometimes referred to as the 'people's peers'). The first 15 people's peers were appointed the following year and it is expected that more will be appointed at regular intervals.

Unlike the House of Commons, there is no fixed number of peers in the House of Lords. In February 2004, there was a total of 679 of whom 113 were women. On a typical day, between 250 and 350 peers are in attendance. Further reform (stage 2) of the House of Lords is currently the subject of a great deal of debate.

14.17 Crossbenchers and party peers

Although there is a party system in the Lords, including party whips, a major difference between the two Houses of Parliament is the significant number of crossbenchers in the Lords (see Box 14.22). Crossbenchers do not take the whip of the main political parties and, in this sense, are independent.

Before the 1999 reforms, about two-thirds of crossbenchers consistently voted with the Conservatives (though crossbenchers did not attend the House as regularly as party peers). Even if, on paper, therefore, there was not a Conservative overall majority, in practice Conservative supporters dominated the House. Consequently, Conservative governments could expect their legislative programmes to have a smoother passage through the Lords than governments formed from other parties. This was one reason for the Labour government's determination to end the right of hereditary peers to sit and vote in the Lords.

Party allegiance for any peer, however, is ultimately a

Box 14.22 Composition of the Lords

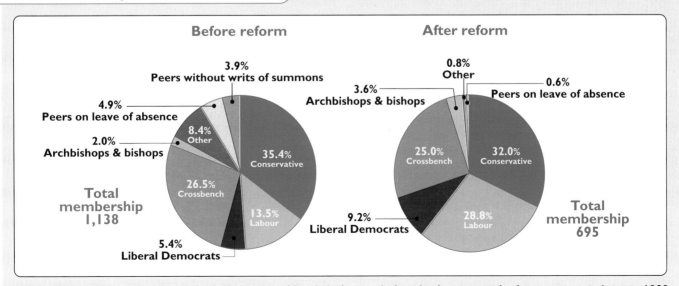

These charts show the composition of the House of Lords before and after the first stage of reform was carried out in 1999.
Source: Baldwin 2002.

voluntary affair. They are not elected and, therefore, do not represent constituents. As a result, the ultimate sanction of withdrawal of the party whip for disloyalty lacks the severity it has in the Commons.

14.18 Organisation and procedures in the House of Lords

There are currently a number of similarities between the way in which the Commons and the Lords are organised. In the chamber of the House of Lords, peers supporting the government sit on benches facing those who support the Opposition parties. There is also the distinction between the front and back-benches which is found in the Commons. At the start of 2004, 14 peers were members of the government. It is their job to explain and defend government policy in the Lords. They are shadowed by Opposition peers who sit on the Opposition front-bench.

Business in the Lords

The business of the House of Lords is arranged by the Party Leaders and party whips 'through the usual channels' (see Section 14.8 above). Traditionally, proceedings have been presided over by the Lord Chancellor who acts as a Speaker. In 2003, however, the government announced its intention to abolish the office of Lord Chancellor and stated that it would consult the House of Lords about who should take over as its Speaker (a select committee on the Speakership of the House was appointed to consider this).

Traditionally, the role played by the Lord Chancellor has been less active than that played by the Speaker in the Commons. Peers are expected to regulate their own proceedings, under the guidance of the Leader of the House of Lords (a government minister of Cabinet rank). They decide themselves who is to speak and when, for example. In the Lords, the Speaker merely 'puts the question' to the House when a decision is required - see Box 14.23.

Box 14.23 The Speaker in the House of Lords

In the House of Lords, the Speaker has no authority to check or curtail debate. Members of the House of Lords do not address themselves to the Speaker during debates, but to all their fellow members in the house. If two peers rise to speak at the same time during a debate, the House itself, not the Speaker, determines who shall speak.

Source: HMSO 1994, p.61.

The activity of the House of Lords grew considerably in the second half of the 20th century. Today, the House normally sits on about 160 days a year, averaging about seven hours a day (compared to just under three hours in 1950). Sittings usually start at 2.30 pm Mondays - Wednesdays, 3.00 pm on Thursdays and at 11.00 am if and when it sits on Fridays. Peers have never received a salary for their parliamentary work, but since 1957 they have been able to claim expenses.

14.19 Powers of the House of Lords

The extension of the franchise through the Reform Acts passed in the 19th century increased the authority of the Commons. The Parliament Act of 1911 removed the Lords' veto over public legislation, replacing it with the weaker power of delaying the passage of a Bill for two years. The 1911 act also effectively removed the Lords' power over money Bills (which give approval for raising taxes, for example). The Parliament Act of 1949 reduced the Lords' power of legislative delay to one parliamentary session. Currently, the House of Lords still has an absolute veto over any proposal to extend the life of a Parliament beyond five years. This gives the Lords some significance as a 'residual guardian of the constitution' (Richards 1988, p.173).

14.20 Functions of the House of Lords

Some of the functions of the House of Lords are similar to those performed by the Commons, but there are differences both in the range of activities and how they are carried out. The role of the House of Lords as it currently operates can be divided into five separate areas.

1. Legislative role

Although some non-controversial Bills are introduced into the Lords first, conventionally the role of the Upper House is to amend and revise Bills sent from the Commons. Almost two-thirds of the time that the House of Lords is in session is spent carrying out this legislative role. The more leisurely pace and less partisan nature of the Lords' proceedings can allow a more detailed examination of a Bill than in the Commons. As a result, peers can point out problems which may not have been foreseen by the government and they can pass amendments to clauses in Bills before returning them to the Commons for reconsideration. When this happens, however, the government can often rely on its overall majority in the Commons to overturn the amendment if it wishes.

The Salisbury Convention

Since it is unelected, the House of Lords rarely rejects a Bill in its entirety. Also, it usually accepts the principle that it should not defeat a government Bill at second or third reading if the proposed legislation is meeting a manifesto commitment of the governing party. This is known as the 'Salisbury doctrine' after the Conservative Leader of the Lords, Lord Salisbury, who, in 1945, suggested such a response to the legislative proposals of the newly elected Labour government. Lord Salisbury argued that, since the new Labour government had a clear mandate to introduce its nationalisation and welfare state measures, the Lords should not oppose them at second reading.

2. Scrutinising role

The House of Lords examines the work of government through questions and select committees. Although the Lords has no structure of departmental select committees on the Commons model, it can and does set up committees to investigate particular policy areas or subjects. Box 14.24 gives three examples.

Box 14.24 Three examples of select committees in the Lords

1. European Union Select Committee

The European Union Select Committee is particularly significant. Through its six sub-committees, it investigates and reports on those European proposals which appear to raise important issues of policy or principle, or other matters to which the committee feel the House should be alerted.

The terms of reference of this committee are wider than for those of its counterpart in the Commons since the Lords' committee can consider the merits of the proposals before it. The committee and its sub-committees have an administrative and secretarial support staff and can employ specialist advisers to assist in their investigations. The work done by the committee is widely admired by European decision-makers and is often cited as a model that other EU members should follow.

2. Constitution Select Committee

This committee was established in 2001. Its tasks are to monitor the working of the constitution and to consider the constitutional implications of Bills passing through the House.

3. Joint Committee on Statutory Instruments

This committee consists of members of both Houses and has a scrutiny role over the type of delegated legislation known as 'statutory instruments'. Some Acts of Parliament lay down broad principles rather than provide detailed laws. The Act allows ministers to make further, more specific laws (secondary legislation). These more specific laws are known as 'statutory instruments' or 'regulations'. For example, an Act might say that fines or fees should be imposed, but it would not set the level of fines or fees. The minister would set the level by drawing up a statutory instrument. The job of the Joint Committee on Statutory Instruments is to draw attention to any instrument it thinks Parliament should be concerned about.

Source: Norton 1995a and House of Lords Information Service April 2004.

Question Time in the Lords

The House of Lords has a daily Question Time but the procedure is different from that in the Commons. Questions are either 'starred' or 'unstarred':

'Starred questions are so-called because they appear on the order paper with an asterisk against them. They are asked in order to obtain specific information, and not with a view to making a speech or raising a debate, although supplementaries may be asked. In addition "unstarred" (debatable) questions may be asked at the end of business on any day, when speeches may be made.' (HMSO 1994, pp.91-92)

Up to four starred questions are answered on Mondays and Thursdays. Five are answered on Tuesdays and Wednesdays (no more than one question tabled by a particular peer). According to Norton (2003), this allows an emphasis on depth rather than breadth. Question Time is also briefer than in the Commons.

3. Deliberative role

Debates are held on specific matters of policy or on topical issues, but, although there are whips, party lines are not so rigidly adhered to as in the Commons. The House of Lords has a reputation for holding high level debates - though some commentators are sceptical about this and claim that such a view is held most strongly by the peers themselves who have a vested interest in maintaining their privileged position.

4. Legitimating role

As an elected body, it is the House of Commons which has the chief legitimating role in Parliament. But, according to Rush (1994), the House of Lords also contributes to legitimacy in the sense that it gives formal approval to Bills which pass through it.

5. Judicial role

Unlike the Commons, the House of Lords currently still has a judicial function. This function, however, is a specialised one, divorced from the main proceedings of the House. It is also a role in which the vast majority of peers can take no part. When the House of Lords sits as the highest court of appeal, only the Law Lords can take part (there were 12 Law Lords in April 2004). In 2003, the government announced its intention to replace the current system of Law Lords with a Supreme Court.

Main points Sections 14.16 - 14.20

- Although there are plans for further reform, the House of Lords is currently an unelected body composed of life peers and some remaining hereditary peers.
- Although there is a party system in the Lords, there are many crossbenchers.

- The layout of the Lords is similar to that of the Commons and business in the Lords is carried out 'through the usual channels'. The Lords has a 'Speaker', but peers are expected to regulate their own proceedings.
- The five main functions of the House of Lords are: (1) legislative; (2) scrutiny; (3) deliberative; (4) legitimating; and (5) judicial.

Activity 14.8 The House of Lords

Item A The House of Lords in session

Item B The functions of Parliament

Function	Performed by House of Commons	Performed by House of Lords
Legitimising	X[a]	x
Representative	X	x
Financial	X	x
Redressing of grievances	X	x
Legislative	X	x
Recruitment of ministers	X	x
Scrutinising and informing	X	x
Judicial		X[b]

a X indicates the more important of the two Houses in performing a particular function, x the less important.
b performed exclusively by Law Lords.

This table shows the functions performed by Parliament as a whole and the relative importance of each House.

Source: Rush 1994.

Item C An independent House of Lords?

The House of Lords has once again been demonstrating its independence and potential power. In October 2002, plans to allow gay couples to adopt children were thrown out by the Lords. Though the decision was later overturned in the Commons, this resistance shows the determination of peers to have their say on important moral and social issues. A month later, the government was defeated in the Lords over its plans to build residential centres for asylum seekers in rural areas. In this case, the amendments remained, forcing ministers to think again if the House of Lords was to accept their proposals. The Lords caused further trouble in its opposition to government plans for foundation hospitals and the curtailment of the use of juries in fraud trials. Although peers gave way on these two issues at the last minute, it is further evidence of a more independent second chamber. This independence was highlighted further in March 2004 when a government Bill to abolish the post of Lord Chancellor and to introduce a Supreme Court was delayed by the House of Lords when it decided to send the Bill to a special select committee. Although it was claimed that this was being done in order to scrutinise the Bill more effectively, the move could mean that the Bill may now not complete its passage through Parliament before the next general election. Particularly when the government has a large majority in the Commons and the official Opposition is weak, the House of Lords is likely to see itself as the effective Opposition, willing to defy the wishes of the elected majority.

Source: News briefing in *Talking Politics* Vol.15.2, January 2003 and Vol.16.2, January 2004, and the *Guardian*, 9 March 2004.

Item D Government defeats in the Lords

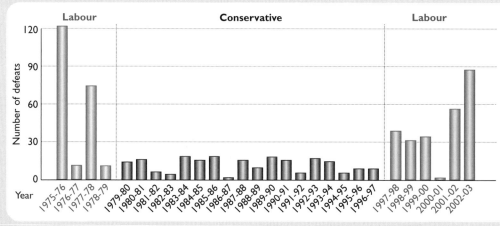

This chart shows the number of government defeats in the House of Lords between 1975 and 2003. It is based on information from http://www.parliament.uk.

Questions

1. How do the powers and procedures of the House of Lords differ from those of the Commons? Use Items A and B in your answer.

2. Using Items A-C, give arguments for and against the view that the House of Lords plays an important role in the British political system.

3. What conclusions can be drawn from Items C and D about Labour's determination to reform the House of Lords?

References

Baldwin (2002) Baldwin, N., 'Reforming the second chamber', *Politics Review*, Vol.11.3, February 2002.

Batchelor (2003) Batchelor, A., 'US Congress & UK Parliament: is there really much of a difference?', *Politics Review*, Vol.13.1, September 2003.

Berrington (1964) Berrington, H., *How Nations are Governed*, Pitman & Sons, 1964.

Butler & Kavanagh (2002) Butler, D. & Kavanagh, D., *The British General Election of 2001*, Palgrave, 2002.

Cowley (2002) Cowley, P., *Revolts and Rebellions: Parliamentary Voting Under Blair*, Politico's, 2002.

Cowley & Stuart (2002) Cowley, P. & Stuart, M., 'New Labour's backbenchers: robots or rebels?', *Talking Politics*, Vol.15.1, September 2002.

Cowley & Stuart (2003) 'Shifting the balance? "Modernising" the House of Commons', *Politics Review*, Vol.12.4, April 2003.

Dorey (2003) Dorey, P., 'Half-baked and half-hearted: the Blair governments and constitutional reform' in *Lancaster (2003)*.

Downs (1985) Downs, S.J., 'Select committees: experiment and establishment' in *Norton (1985)*.

Drewry (1989) Drewry, G., 'The new select committees - nine years on', *Social Studies Review*, Vol.4.4, 1989.

Flinders (2003) Flinders, M., 'Controlling the executive', *Politics Review*, Vol.13.1, September 2003.

Grant (2004) Grant, M., 'The theory and practice of parliamentary government', *Talking Politics*, Vol.16.2, January 2004.

HMSO (1994) Central Office of Information, *Parliament*, HMSO, 1994.

HoC (2003) 'Departmental select committees', *House of Commons Information Office Factsheet P2*, September 2003.

House of Commons (2003) House of Commons Information Office, 'Sittings of the House', *House of Commons Information Office Factsheet No. P7 Ed 3.1*, December 2003.

Jones (2004) Jones, A., *New Politics Pal: 2004 edition*, Leicester, 2004.

Jordan & Richardson (1987) Jordan, A.G. & Richardson, J.J., *British Politics and the Policy Process*, Allen & Unwin, 1987.

King (1981) King, A., 'The rise of the career politician in Britain - and its consequences', *British Journal of Political Science*, Vol.11, 1981.

Lancaster (2003) Lancaster, S. (ed.), *Developments in Politics*, Vol.14, Causeway Press, 2003.

Leeds (1981) Leeds, C.A., *Political Studies*, MacDonald & Evans, 1981.

Norton (1985) Norton, P. (ed.), *Parliament in the 1980s*, Blackwell, 1985.

Norton (1991) Norton, P., 'Committees in the House of Commons', *Politics Review*, Vol.1.1, September 1991.

Norton (1992) Norton, P., 'A reform of Parliament?', *The House Magazine*, 22 June 1992.

Norton (1994) Norton, P., 'A new breed of MP?', *Politics Review*, Vol. 3.3, February 1994.

Norton (1995) Norton, P., 'Standing committees in the House of Commons', *Politics Review*, Vol.4.4, April 1995.

Norton (1995a) Norton, P., 'Resourcing select committees', *Talking Politics*, Vol.8.1, Autumn 1995.

Norton (2003) Norton, P., 'The House of Lords' (address to annual conference of the Politics Association), *Talking Politics*, Vol.15.2, January 2003.

Richards (1988) Richards, P.G., *Mackintosh's The Government and Politics of Britain* (7th edn), Hutchinson, 1988.

Rush (1994) Rush, M., 'The House of Lords, end it or mend it?', in *Wale (1994)*.

Sedgemore (1995) Sedgemore, B., *An Insider's Guide to Parliament*, Icon, 1995.

Wale (1994) Wale, W. (ed.), *Developments in Politics*, Vol.5, Causeway Press, 1994.

Wright (1997) Wright, T., 'Does Parliament work?', *Talking Politics*, Vol.9.3, Spring 1997.

15 The core executive - Prime Minister and Cabinet

15.1 What is the core executive?

Until the 1990s, writers tended to discuss British central government in terms of the Prime Minister and the Cabinet, with much of the debate concerned with where power resided. Indeed, it was often claimed that, as time went on, Prime Ministers acquired more and more power while the Cabinet became weaker and weaker. Eventually, it was claimed, the Cabinet would become so weak that it would be reduced to little more than a 'rubber stamp' or the Prime Minister's 'echo chamber'. For those who believed this, the premierships of Margaret Thatcher and Tony Blair were cited as further evidence of the trend.

Since the 1990s, however, some writers have put forward a new model of political power in central government - that of the 'core executive'. This model insists that the reality is more complex than the old model suggests. Power, according to this model, is dispersed throughout central government. It does not just rest with Prime Minister and the Cabinet, but also with individual ministers and government departments. And further, each is, to a lesser or greater extent, dependent on the others. The pursuit of political goals and policies, it is argued, involves a constant process of consultation and negotiation between various 'actors', and sometimes the creation of alliances on particular issues.

who themselves are 'key actors within the institutions of the core executive' (Smith 1999, p.5). Box 15.1 shows the various elements that make up the core executive.

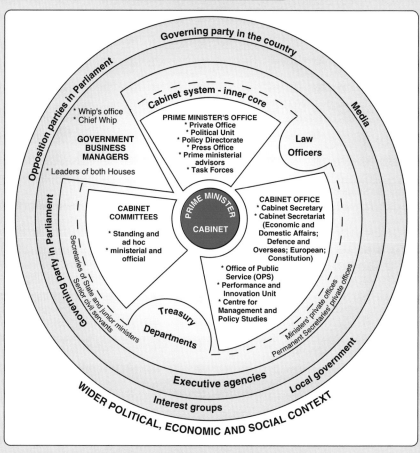

Box 15.1 The core executive in Britain

Source: Pyper & Robins 1995.

The best definition of the 'core executive' is that provided by Rhodes, who describes it as:

'The heart of the machine, covering the complex web of institutions, networks and practices surrounding the Prime Minister, Cabinet, Cabinet committees and their official counterparts, less formalised ministerial "clubs" or meetings, bilateral negotiations and interdepartmental committees. It also includes coordinating departments, chiefly the Cabinet office, the Treasury [and] the Foreign office.' (Rhodes 1995, p.12)

Martin J. Smith suggests that government departments should be added to this definition, not only on the grounds that these are 'the core policy-making units within central government', but also because they are headed by ministers,

The central importance of the core executive in British politics is clearly indicated by the words that Smith uses to open his book on the topic, namely that:

'The core executive is at the heart of British government. It contains the key institutions and actors concerned with developing policy, co-ordinating government activity and providing the necessary resources for delivering public goods.' (Smith 1999, p.1)

The crucial point here is that all parts of the core executive possess, or have access to, resources - knowledge, expertise, legitimacy, political authority and so on - which enable them to exercise political power. No single part of the core executive is able to dominate the others on all issues, all of the time.

15.2 *The role and powers of the Prime Minister*

The formal, constitutional, role and powers of the British Prime Minister suggest an extremely powerful individual, one with the potential to dominate government and the whole political landscape. Box 15.2 shows the formal role and powers of a British Prime Minister.

Box 15.2 Prime Minister's role and powers

- To appoint, promote, demote or dismiss ministers, including junior ministers.
- To chair meetings of the Cabinet, and prepare the agenda (assisted by the Cabinet Secretary).
- To appoint Cabinet committees, and also chair some of them.
- To appoint the most senior civil servants.
- To award peerages (ie, make appointments to the House of Lords).
- To decide when to call a general election.

Any one of these constitutional powers appears formidable. Collectively, they certainly seem to suggest that the modern British Prime Minister is an extremely powerful political figure.

For example, the appointment of ministers (known as the 'power of patronage') provides Prime Ministers with the opportunity to reward loyal supporters and to punish critics in their own party. Since they decide which minister will have a seat in the Cabinet, Prime Ministers could, if they so wished, ensure that the Cabinet was made up entirely of 'Yes-men' and 'Yes-women' who would then be relied upon to endorse their policy proposals and preferences, whatever they might be. Margaret Thatcher was often accused by her critics of replacing ministerial critics on the left of the Conservative Party with ministers who agreed with her particular brand of right-wing Conservatism. More recently, Tony Blair has sometimes been accused of using ministerial reshuffles to remove the last vestiges of Old Labour and, by doing so, creating a predominantly Blairite Cabinet.

It is sometimes argued that two other developments have served to enhance this power of patronage in recent decades.

First, the number of junior ministers has increased, because the responsibilities of government have grown greater and more complex since 1945. As a result, more and more MPs in the governing party either owe their position to the Prime Minister or want to show their loyalty and obedience in order to be rewarded by appointment to a ministerial post in the future.

Second, it is argued that the post-1945 era saw the rise of the 'career politician'. An increasing number of MPs have pursued politics as a full-time, long-term vocation and they aim, therefore, to secure ministerial advancement for themselves when their party is in office (see King 1981 & 1991, Riddell 1993 and Paxman 2003). Again, it has been argued, this effectively boosts further the power of the Prime Minister in whose hands the career prospects of hundreds of MPs now rests.

15.3 *Limitations on Prime Ministerial power*

Yet the formal, constitutional, powers listed in Box 15.2, are subject to a number of constraints in practice, which means that the British Prime Minister is not as powerful as often assumed, or as commonly alleged by critics. The main constraints on Prime Ministerial power are listed in Box 15.3 on page 293.

With regard to the power to appoint the Cabinet, Prime Ministers do not have a free hand in making ministerial appointments. First, they need to ensure that the Cabinet contains a cross-section of opinion as well as a blend of youth on the one hand and political experience or seniority on the other. Even an apparently powerful Prime Minister like Margaret Thatcher felt obliged to include in Cabinet MPs from the one nation or pro-European wing of the Conservative Party, such as Kenneth Clarke, Douglas Hurd, and Chris Patten. She never did appoint a Cabinet full of Thatcherites at any time during her 11 years as Prime Minister. Similarly, Tony Blair has felt obliged to include figures such as John Prescott in his Cabinets since May 1997, even though Prescott is certainly not, either instinctively or ideologically, a 'Blairite'. Second, some MPs simply have to be appointed to the Cabinet by virtue of their popularity and stature in the wider party. Prescott is an example, again. So too is Tony Benn who served in the Cabinet in the late 1970s. Prime Ministers Wilson and Callaghan felt obliged to appoint him because of his widespread popularity, even though they did not agree with his views. Third, Prime Ministers sometimes decide that it is wise to offer a backbench rebel a ministerial appointment to muzzle them. And fourth, on occasion, an attempt to 'punish' an MP by refusing to allocate them a ministerial post can ultimately prove counter-productive. Realising this, a Prime Minister may be reluctant to take such a step.

So, however formidable the Prime Minister's formal, constitutional powers appear to be, they are, in practice, subject to a variety of constraints and - as we shall see shortly - circumstances.

Box 15.3 Constraints on the main political powers of a British Prime Minister

Constraints on the power of patronage

1. If the party has been in Opposition, then the first Cabinet appointed after a general election victory is usually the Shadow Cabinet.

2. Some MPs will have such extensive experience or authority that they can hardly be omitted.

3. Some MPs have sizeable backbench followings. Omitting them from the Cabinet might lead to dissatisfaction on the backbenches, possibly in the form of 'cabals' or factions which might eventually lead to a leadership challenge. At the very least, disgruntled MPs might withhold their support in parliamentary votes ('divisions') on the government's policies and Bills.

4. The Cabinet needs to be reasonably 'balanced', meaning that it must include ministers from the different ideological sections of the parliamentary party.

5. Some MPs are too young and inexperienced to include, while others may be approaching the end of their parliamentary careers or they might indicate that they no longer wish to hold ministerial office.

6. Frequent ministerial reshuffles are likely to alienate those ministers who are demoted or dismissed, while causing resentment among those MPs who feel that they have again been overlooked.

7. Frequent ministerial reshuffles are also likely to reflect poorly on the Prime Minister, suggesting either a sense of panic or raising doubts about their political judgement in appointing ministers who are then rapidly (re)moved.

Constraints on dealings with the Cabinet

1. Certain items always appear on the Cabinet agenda as a formality (for example, a report by the Foreign Secretary and a report on forthcoming parliamentary business and legislation).

2. Some items need to be included due to their urgency.

3. A group of ministers might occasionally insist on the inclusion of a particular item on the Cabinet's agenda. Continued refusal to permit this might lead ministers to wonder what the Prime Minister is afraid of in seeking to avoid discussion of the issue.

4. Although formal votes are not normally taken in Cabinet meetings, Prime Ministers need to be careful in 'summing-up' the overall view of the ministers present. They cannot declare that 'policy A' has been agreed upon if the overwhelming majority of other ministers have expressed - and heard each other express - their preference for 'policy B'.

Constraints on the appointment /chairing of Cabinet committees

1. Membership is usually 'functional', meaning that the ministers serving on a Cabinet committee are usually those whose department has an input into a proposed policy.

2. Prime Ministers' workload is such that they can only chair a few Cabinet committees and, therefore need to delegate the chairing of the rest to other senior ministerial colleagues. For example, during his second term as Prime Minister, Tony Blair chaired six out of 44 Cabinet committees, while the Home Secretary chaired nine, the Deputy Prime Minister chaired eight and the Chancellor chaired four, as did the Lord Chancellor.

Constraints on calling a general election.

1. General elections have to be called at least every five years

2. The threat to call a general election in order to quash backbench unrest would merely serve to draw attention to that unrest, and suggest that a Prime Minister lacked authority over backbenchers.

3. Waiting for the full five years can leave a Prime Minister and government vulnerable to last minute crises or events beyond their control, with insufficient time to put them right.

4. Calling a general election too soon (ie within four years of the previous one) may arouse suspicions that the Prime Minister fears losing popularity during the coming year. People might ask questions like: 'Does the Prime Minister know something we don't know?' or 'Has the Prime Minister been warned about an imminent economic downturn?'

5. A general election campaign is extremely arduous for a Prime Minister, involving constant visits the length and breadth of the country, public speeches, media interviews and so on. Most MPs, by contrast, only need to campaign in their own constituency.

6. A Prime Minister stands to lose a great deal if their government is not re-elected - loss of power, loss of home, likely loss of leadership position. By contrast, even if their party is voted out of office in a general election, many MPs will be re-elected.

Main points Sections 15.1 - 15.3

- **According to the core executive model, power is dispersed throughout central government. It does not just rest with Prime Minister and the Cabinet, but also with individual ministers and government departments.**
- **The Prime Minister has the power to: (1) appoint, promote, demote or dismiss ministers; (2) chair meetings of the Cabinet, and prepare the agenda; (3) appoint and chair Cabinet committees; (4) appoint senior civil servants; (5) award peerages; and (6) decide when to call a general election.**
- **The two arguments in support of the view that**

  the power of patronage has increased in recent decades are that: (1) the number of junior ministers has increased and (2) the post-1945 era has seen the rise of the 'career politician'.
- **In practice, there are constraints on the powers of the Prime Minister.**
- **There are four main constraints on the power to appoint the Cabinet: (1) the need to have a balanced Cabinet; (2) the need to include popular MPs; (3) the need to keep backbench MPs quiet; and (4) realisation that 'punishing' MPs might alienate them.**

Activity 15.1 The debate about Prime Ministerial power

Item A The rise of the British presidency

Blair's premiership has departed so far from traditional Cabinet government that it has been transformed into a presidential form of governance. There have been a large number of developments since New Labour came to power in 1997. As far as executive authority and organisation are concerned, important developments include:

- the infrequency and reduced length of Cabinet meetings
- Blair's regular abandonment of Cabinet agendas
- the Prime Minister's clear preference for informal ad hoc meetings with small numbers of selected ministers and staff around his sofa in the private office.

Three other developments also suggest a strengthening of the premier's position:

- the doubling of the Prime Minister's staff during the first two years of the Blair premiership
- the introduction of New Labour professionals from party positions to strategic posts relating to policy advice and media presentation
- Cabinet Office reforms - the influx of senior advisers with whom Blair had worked closely when he had been Leader of the Opposition.

Blair seems to have placed the Cabinet on the very edge of decision-making. As a result, it seems that the post of Prime Minister has evolved, and is evolving, away from what a Prime Minister used to do and used to be. Blair's premiership is another piece of evidence to support the idea that British politics is gaining a distinctive presidential dimension. The British premiership has become, in essence, a British presidency.

Source: Foley 2000.

Item B Counter-arguments

(i) Prime Ministers, if they are to remain in office, must carry their leading rivals with them. If a backbench revolt were to be led by an MP with leadership calibre - an MP who could win the backing of a large number of colleagues - then the Prime Minister would be in a very insecure position. To avoid this, Prime Ministers must woo and coax their colleagues and their party to support them and their policies. That is why Prime Ministers must be engaged in a continual dialogue with their party. They have no executive powers vested in them. To achieve anything, they must work with and through their ministers - who do have executive powers vested in them. Ministers have powerful and independent departments to brief them, and they possess significant followings in their party. Some will have supporters who hope to see them as Leader, one day. So, to become and remain Prime Minister, an MP must carry these major colleagues, who are their rivals, with them. He cannot dictate to them, but must cooperate, consult, and negotiate with them. At times, even, they should even make it clear that they respect and look up to them. Prime Ministers are not the all-powerful individual which many have recently claimed them to be. They are only as strong as other MPs let them be.

Source: Jones 1985.

Item B **Counter-arguments** (continued)

(ii) Prime Ministers have a set of resources that are partly personal, deriving from their style and authority, and partly structural, deriving from the office. The resources on their own are not sufficient for achieving goals and, therefore, the Prime Minister is involved in processes of exchange, usually with ministers, but also with officials, advisers and, to some extent, MPs. Ministers use strategies to control the Prime Minister - for example:

- building coalitions
- leaking information
- threatening to resign
- offering support to the Prime Minister over controversial issues.

The crucial point is that Prime Ministers operate in structured context. It is structured by:

- the institutions of the core executive
- the networks that relate the Prime Minister to the Cabinet and officials
- the rules of the Whitehall game
- the external political and economic situation.

On their own, Prime Ministers can achieve little. As a result, they are dependent on colleagues and the Cabinet. Meetings of the Cabinet are not about dominance and control, but about building alliances. Consequently, the notion of Prime Ministerial government makes little sense.

Source: Smith 1999.

(iii) In the modern world, no Prime Minister is truly free. The plain fact is that power has drained away - to Europe, to the assemblies in Scotland and Wales, to the law courts. In addition, the British economy is dependent upon international trade. British unemployment depends on decisions taken in boardrooms in America, Japan or South Korea. Much of foreign policy depends on the construction of some laborious lowest-common-denominator form of words which would satisfy the rest of the European Union.

Source: Paxman 2003.

Questions

1. Summarise the debate outlined in Items A and B.
2. Using Item B, identify the kind of constraints and limitations on the exercise of Prime Ministerial power in contemporary Britain.

3. a) Describe the view of Prime Ministerial power given in the pictures in Items A and B.
   b) Do they lend support to the arguments made in Item A or B? Explain your answer.

15.4 *The Prime Minister's support staff*

The Prime Minister's Office

Unlike most of their Cabinet colleagues, Prime Ministers do not have a department of their own to manage and to assist them in policy development and administration. Instead, there is a Prime Minister's Office, which is staffed by a combination of permanent civil servants, civil servants on secondment from government departments, and 'political appointees' - for example, special advisers recruited from outside the core executive.

The Prime Minister's Office is divided into four discrete sections, each performing particular roles and functions, but with some overlap. These four sections are:

- the Private office
- the Political Unit
- the Press office
- the Policy Directorate (previously known as the Policy Unit).

The Private office

The Prime Minister's Private Office is mainly staffed by permanent civil servants on secondment from other government departments. The head of the Private Office is also, usually, the Prime Minister's Principal Private Secretary, one of whose roles is to act as a 'gatekeeper', deciding who has access to the Prime Minister.

The Private Office plays a crucial role in controlling the flow of information, filtering the mass of information which flows to the Prime Minister from other parts of the core executive. As such, the Private Office is a vital link between Ten Downing Street and government departments. As Smith observes:

'[The Private Office is] the centre of the Prime Minister's Whitehall network, ensuring [the Prime Minister] is in touch with all the key actors and institutions within the core executive.' (Smith 1999, p.174)

The Political Unit

The main function of the Political Unit is to deal with the Prime Minister's relations with the wider party, both in Parliament and in the country at large. Due to the party political nature of its work, the main staff in the Political Unit are recruited from the party itself, rather than from the civil service. The Political Unit is also funded, to a large extent, from the governing party's own finances and revenues, rather than from taxation.

The Press Office

The Prime Minister's Press Office oversees relations with the media, often paying close attention to the presentation of policy matters. The Press Office processes the questions submitted to the Prime Minister from the media, and arranges media interviews or press conferences. It also provides regular, usually daily, press briefings and liaises with the press offices located in each of the main government departments, the aim being to coordinate the release of government information or announcements to the media.

The Leader of the Press Office also serves as the Prime Minister's Official Spokesperson or Press Secretary. Tony Blair's first Chief Press Secretary was Alastair Campbell. Campbell was certainly not the first high profile or controversial Prime Ministerial Press Officer. Harold Wilson appointed Joe Haines to the post, while Margaret Thatcher's Press Spokesperson was the pugnacious Bernard Ingham.

The Policy Directorate

Originally established as the Policy Unit by Harold Wilson in 1974, what is now known as the Policy Directorate has become a very important source of policy advice for Prime Ministers. Indeed, it could be said to play two different, but linked roles. First, it enables the Prime Minister to develop policy ideas and preferences, which might then become part of the government's strategy and policy goals. Second, it keeps the Prime Minister closely informed of policy developments and progress in the various government departments.

Consequently, it has been suggested that the Policy Directorate 'is both reactive and proactive' (Smith 1999, p.174), for it is 'sometimes engaging in forward thinking and policy initiative, sometimes in evaluation of initiatives taken by government departments' (Burch & Holliday 1999, p.35).

The staff in the Policy Directorate are changed completely with the arrival of each new Prime Minister, with many of the appointees recruited from beyond the formal civil service.

Taking the Prime Minister's Office as a whole, there has been a marked increase in staff since the 1970s, as Box 15.4 shows.

15.5 Importance of leadership personality and style

Apart from the constraints on Prime Ministerial power described above, the way in which Prime Ministers use their constitutional powers depends partly on their own personality and style. Like all individuals, Prime Ministers have their own personalities, and this means that each adopts a particular style of leadership. For example, Margaret Thatcher and John Major were both Conservative Prime Ministers and, in theory, both had precisely the same constitutional and political powers, yet the way in which each acted as Prime Minister was vastly different, reflecting their different personalities.

Margaret Thatcher sought to 'lead from the front', and expected her ministerial colleagues (and backbench MPs) to follow and support her. She gained the reputation for being a 'conviction politician' - somebody who had strong beliefs, and a clear sense of purpose and direction and somebody who expected colleagues to trust and follow her.

Box 15.4 Expansion and reform of the Prime Minister's support network

(i) There has been a marked increase in the size of the Number Ten staff from 71 in June 1970 to nearly 200 in December 1998. Faced with more pressures, Prime Ministers have little choice but to rely more on the staff around them at Number Ten. A Prime Minister has no more hours in the day available than did Robert Walpole (Britain's first Prime Minister, from 1721 to 1742). No appointment of a Deputy Prime Minister, a 'Cabinet Enforcer' or other such posts can disguise the fact that the Prime Minister's time is finite. This explains the need for a competent and loyal team of officials. In practice, despite the growing number of political appointments and attempts to rationalise Number Ten's structure, there remains an overlap of interests and responsibilities between the Political office, Policy Unit and Press office. These overlaps present opportunities for disputes between staff as well as incentives for coordination.

Source: Kavanagh & Seldon 2000.

(ii) For Blair, creating joined-up government was a mechanism for increasing control by the centre, because it was a way of ensuring that strategies developed in Number Ten were not undermined by the conflicting goals of departments. Since 1997, an important development has been the way in which the resources of the Prime Minister have increased. Initially, when Blair came into power, he expanded the size of the Policy Unit (now the Policy Directorate), almost doubling numbers of personnel. Its role changed too. It has become one not so much of making policy as of ensuring that departments are aware of the Blair agenda and are delivering policy in line with Number Ten's wishes. Since special advisers within Number Ten are overseeing and commenting on the policy proposals coming from departments, Number Ten is developing the capability of being able to direct departments.

Source: Richards and Smith 2004.

By contrast, Thatcher's successor, John Major, was a 'conciliator' he was temperamentally inclined towards a collegial and collective approach to decision-taking, based on discussion and dialogue. Instead of pursuing 'conviction politics', Major wanted, as far as possible, to achieve a consensus among his colleagues.

The importance of 'styles' in the exercise of Prime Ministerial political power has been recognised by Philip Norton. He has identified four particular styles of Prime Ministerial leadership, although he was quick to emphasise that these 'are not mutually exclusive', because Premiers can, and often do, 'exhibit the characteristics of more than one type' (Norton 1987). These four types of Prime Minister are shown in Box 15.5 on page 297.

What Norton meant by these four typologies was as follows.

1. Innovator

Innovators seek office in order to achieve particular policy goals and objectives, which they are personally committed to,

Box 15.5 Prime Ministerial styles of leadership

1. Innovator
Edward Heath (1970-74)
Margaret Thatcher (1979-90)
Tony Blair (1997-)

2. Reformer
Clement Attlee (1945-51)

3. Balancer
Harold Macmillan (1957-63)
Alec Douglas-Home (1963-64)
Harold Wilson (1974-76)
James Callaghan (1976-79)
John Major (1990-97)

4. Egotist
Harold Wilson (1964-70)

Source: Norton 1987, pp.328-29

but which many of their ministerial colleagues and MPs may be less enthusiastic about. Such Prime Ministers tend to risk considerable unpopularity and criticism at times, even from within their own party, which they effectively have to lead, dragging and kicking, behind them.

Margaret Thatcher is the most obvious example of an 'innovator'. As another of Norton's studies indicates, even by 1989 (by which time Thatcher had been Prime Minister for ten years) only about 19% of Conservative MPs and ministers could be categorised as 'Thatcherites'. The rest were either 'one nation' Conservatives (see Unit 7 for a definition), critics of much of Thatcherism, or were 'agnostics' whose support for Thatcher was pragmatic - based largely on her electoral success - rather than ideological (Norton 1990).

A similar style of leadership has been adopted by Tony Blair since he became Prime Minister in May 1997. Indeed, before he came to power, he had already admitted his admiration of Thatcher. He too has often pursued certain policies with which he has personally become identified or associated. Public-Private Partnerships, 'foundation' hospitals, top-up fees for university students, and the pursuit (with the United States) of the March-April 2003 war 'to liberate' Iraq are all examples of policies which many Labour MPs, and some ministers, opposed. Like Thatcher, Blair has relied on a blend of argument, explanation, persuasion, and sheer defiance. Blair has even echoed Thatcher on occasions by insisting that 'there is no alternative', or that 'no change is not an option'.

Not surprisingly, 'innovator' Prime Ministers usually attract considerable controversy, with their supporters viewing them as strong, visionary leaders heroically battling against the 'forces of conservatism' resistant to new ideas and policies, while their critics and opponents accuse them of being arrogant or autocratic.

2. Reformer

Reformers also seek office in order to achieve particular goals and objectives, but these are generally shared and supported by their party. As a result, reformers do not normally become personally associated with their government's policies. Labour's first post-war Leader, Clement

Attlee, can be described as a reformer because the pursuit of full employment and the setting up of the welfare state were policy goals strongly supported throughout the Labour Party. Significantly, nobody talks about 'Attleeism'.

3. Balancer

'Balancers' are Prime Ministers whose main objective is to maintain unity, either within their own party, or in society as a whole. Such Prime Ministers tend to pursue policies which overcome ideological divisions in their own party, or heal social divisions in British society. Balancers place great emphasis on, and devote considerable energy to achieving consensus in order to minimise division and conflict. Although such a leadership style might reflect the personal characteristics and temperament of a particular Prime Minister, it might also be a consequence of being a 'compromise' or 'unity' candidate in a leadership contest (although such a candidate might be elected precisely because they are seen to offer consensus and unity after a period of discord and division).

Norton placed the 1976-79 Labour Prime Minister, James Callaghan, in this category, but Callaghan's 1974-76 predecessor, Harold Wilson could also be added as his final premiership was very different in style to that of the 1960s. For much of the 1974-76 period, Wilson was primarily concerned to hold a divided and quarrelsome Labour government and parliamentary party together, rather than pursuing clear policy goals.

John Major was also a 'balancer' from 1990 to 1997, trying to hold together an increasingly divided and argumentative Conservative Party. Although Britain's relations with the European Union were the most obvious source of division in Major's Conservative Party, there were various other disagreements, both over domestic policies, and the general direction which the party ought to pursue in the post-Thatcher era.

4. Egotist

Egotists are Prime Ministers who seek office for the sake of exercising power, rather than to pursue specific ideological or policy goals. Norton places Harold Wilson's 1964-70 premiership in this category, largely based, it would seem, on some rather unflattering observations about Wilson's leadership in Richard Crossman's subsequent three-volume *Diaries of a Cabinet Minister*.

Norton acknowledges that these four types are not mutually exclusive, and that any Prime Minister might exhibit the characteristics of more than one style, but he maintains that most Prime Ministers do exhibit characteristics from one particular style most of the time.

More recently, a somewhat different classification has been developed by Burch, who classifies Prime Ministers according to the manner in which they approach or treat ministerial colleagues and their departments. He describes them as: 'delegators', 'intervenors' or 'overseers' (Burch 1994, pp.111-13). This classification is outlined in Box 15.6 on page 298.

Margaret Thatcher adopted an 'intervenor' approach, taking a close and active interest in the work of her ministers and their departments, anxious that some of them would lose momentum if not regularly chased-up or cajoled. A similar style seems to have been adopted by Tony Blair. It has been

Box 15.6 Burch's classification

1. Delegators

Delegators tend to trust their ministers to pursue their departmental responsibilities and generally leave them to pursue their tasks with minimal interference.

2. Intervenors

Intervenors are inclined to involve themselves in the work of departments, perhaps feeling the need to push ministerial colleagues towards certain policies, or at least, to seek regular reports on progress, often via 'bilaterals' (face-to-face meetings between the Prime Minister and the minister), but sometimes via the Ten Downing Street Policy Directorate or the Cabinet Office (both of which are discussed below).

4. Overseers

Overseers adopt a more general overview of what their ministers are doing, seeking to ensure that they are all working towards the government's overall objectives.

suggested that 'Tony wants...' have become 'the two most powerful words in Whitehall' (un-named minister quoted in Hennessy 2001, p.747). By contrast, John Major was a delegator, generally content to let his ministers get on with their departmental tasks with minimal interference.

Of course, the approach adopted will largely reflect the personality and style of the Prime Minister. However there will be occasions or circumstances when a Prime Minister adopts one of the other approaches. For example, either the delegator or overseer approaches will be transformed into that of an intervenor if serious problems emerge. This again indicates the extent to which political leadership is affected by circumstances. Prime Ministerial 'power' must always be seen in a wider context.

15.6 The importance of circumstances

Whatever a Prime Minister's constitutional powers, and whatever leadership style Prime Ministers adopt, all have to operate within the context of wider economic and political

factors over which they often have little, if any, control (see Elgie 1995, pp.40-50). A former Conservative Prime Minister, Harold Macmillan, when asked what caused him most anxiety and sleepless nights, replied: 'events, dear boy, events'. So, while all Prime Ministers formally possess the same constitutional powers, how they use those powers - and the extent to which they are able to use them - can vary, not only from one Prime Minister to another, but also within the course of one premiership. Box 15.7 lists the sort of factors which affect the authority of a Prime Minister.

One important factor is the size of the government's majority following a general election. A Prime Minister with a large parliamentary majority is usually in a rather stronger position than one who presides over a small one. For example, Margaret Thatcher, presiding over majorities of 144 and 101 in 1983 and 1987 respectively, was in a much stronger position than her successor, John Major, whose government's majority was just 21 following the 1992 general election. Furthermore, this majority was steadily reduced over the next five years, following by-election defeats and defections. Although, as noted above, John Major's personality and style of leadership were markedly different to those of Margaret Thatcher, he was also constrained by the narrowness of his party's parliamentary majority, which left him very dependent on his ministerial and backbench colleagues. This, in turn, reinforced a widespread perception that he was a weak Prime Minister. Such an image was underpinned by the barbed comment of his former Chancellor, Norman Lamont, that John Major gave the impression of 'being in office, but not in power' and by Tony Blair's Commons jibe that 'I lead my party; he follows his'. Nobody would seriously have made such remarks about Margaret Thatcher.

However, it is also important to emphasise that even 'innovator' or 'intervenor' Prime Ministers find their strength and authority fluctuating during their terms of office, irrespective of their parliamentary majority. For example, economic circumstances or an international crisis can either enhance or undermine a Prime Minister's authority and influence. Margaret Thatcher's 11-year premiership provides a good case study of a Prime Minister whose strength and authority varied in spite of her 'innovator' style and strong personality - see Box 15.8 on page 299.

In contrast, perhaps, to the boost to Margaret Thatcher's

Box 15.7 Factors affecting the authority of Prime Ministers

Enhancing the PM's power	Constraining the PM's power
• Large parliamentary majority	• Small parliamentary majority
• Unified Cabinet	• Divided Cabinet
• Cohesion on backbenches	• Division among backbenchers
• Recent general election victory	• 'Mid-term' blues
• High opinion poll ratings	• Low opinion poll ratings
• Competence and integrity of ministerial colleagues	• Incompetence or scandals involving ministerial colleagues
• Clear objectives and strategy	• Limited grasp of policy detail
• Supportive media	• Media hostility
• Strong, stable economic situation	• Recession/economic crisis
• International crisis, well-handled	• International crisis, poorly-handled
• Weak, ineffective Opposition	• Strong, credible Opposition

Box 15.8 Thatcher's premiership

For the first three years after her general election victory in 1979, Margaret Thatcher's authority was limited. She presided over a major recession (a loss of manufacturing jobs increased unemployment to over three million). There were inner city riots in the summer of 1981 and the Cabinet was divided between 'wets' (one nation Conservatives) and 'dries' (Thatcherites). It was victory in the 1982 Falklands War which transformed her position since it was followed by a landslide majority in the general election held in June 1983. Three years later - in January 1986 - Thatcher's position was weakened again following the 'Westland Affair'. She was even rumoured to have contemplated resignation. In June 1987, however, her authority was restored following another emphatic election victory. Although this gave the impression that Thatcher was unassailable, just two years later events began to unfold which would lead to her downfall. The beginning of the end came in the summer of 1989 when the Chancellor, Nigel Lawson, and the Foreign Secretary, Geoffrey Howe, effectively forced Thatcher to declare Britain's eventual intention to join the European Communities' (it had not yet become the European Union) Exchange Rate Mechanism (ERM), something to which Thatcher was strongly opposed. Lawson and Howe strongly hinted that if Thatcher did not formally announce this intention, at a meeting of the European Council in Madrid, in June 1989, then they would resign. Recognising that a joint resignation by her Chancellor and Foreign Secretary would seriously weaken her own authority and credibility, Thatcher reluctantly concluded that she had to accept their demand on an issue of major economic and diplomatic importance, even though it was against her own views and inclinations. The introduction of the poll tax further weakened Thatcher's position and when Lawson and then Howe did, in fact, resign Thatcher's political capital drained away.

Source: Howe 1995, Lawson 1992, Thatcher 1993.

popularity and authority provided by victory in the Falklands War, apparent Anglo-American victory in Iraq during spring 2003 did not provide Tony Blair with a similar increase in popularity and authority. Although this was partly because - unlike the Falklands War - the Iraq War was not about British sovereignty or territory, the main reason was that, in the months following the war, no weapons of mass destruction (WMDs) were found in Iraq, even though Saddam Hussein's alleged possession of them had been the primary justification for the war. The months following the military victory, merely confirmed the doubts which many people had harboured about the justification for the war, while simultaneously forcing Tony Blair on the defensive. In other words, it was the Prime Minister's authority and credibility which suffered in the aftermath of the Iraq War, raising doubts either about his honesty - 'did he mislead the British people about the alleged military threat posed by Saddam Hussein and Iraq, in order to secure support for war?' - or his judgement - 'had the Prime Minister himself been misled, either by the United States' military and political leadership, or by Britain's own intelligence services?'

This variability of Prime Ministerial power has more recently been confirmed by Sir Richard Wilson, a former Cabinet Secretary, who explained to the House of Commons Select Committee on Public Administration that:

> '[The Prime Minister's] power varies from time to time according to the extent their Cabinet colleagues permit them to have that power, depending on whether the Cabinet is split, depending also on the strength of the government majority in the House of Commons and also popular opinion in the electorate and attitudes in the party.'

Main points Sections 15.4 - 15.6

- Unlike most of their Cabinet colleagues, Prime Ministers do not have a department of their own to manage. Instead, there is a Prime Minister's Office.
- The Prime Minister's Office is divided into: (1) the Private Office; (2) the Political Unit; (3) the Press Office; (4) the Policy Directorate.
- The Private Office controls the flow of information and access to the Prime Minister, the Political Unit liaises with the party; the Press Office liaises with the media. The Policy Directorate devises and monitors policy.

- Norton argues Prime Ministers' leadership styles fall into four categories: (1) innovator; (2) reformer; (3) balancer; and (4) egotist.
- Burch classifies Prime Ministers according to the manner in which they approach or treat ministerial colleagues and their departments. He describes them as: (1) delegators; (2) intervenors; (3) overseers.
- All Prime Ministers have to operate within the context of wider economic and political factors over which they often have little, if any, control.

Activity 15.2 Thatcher, Major and Blair

Item A Margaret Thatcher's leadership style

Changing the orchestra won't affect the tune - they're only there for appearances.

Margaret Thatcher was a bold, innovative, ideological leader, a populist radical who relied on a strong sense of self, a warrior image, self-confidence, determination and conviction. She was an outsider determined to break the post-war consensus (the unwritten agreement between the two main parties that they would not attempt to dismantle the welfare state and that they would run the economy according to Keynesian principles). There was, therefore, a crusading zeal about Thatcher, a strong sense of belief which harboured few doubts and allowed little dissent. On taking office, she said she wanted a conviction government and would not waste time with any internal arguments. In office, she was continually asking of ministers: 'are they one of us?' - in other words, did they share her values and her strength of purpose? This led Thatcher to develop a highly (perhaps overly) personalised and somewhat imperious style of leadership - a warrior style in which she set policy which she knew would be seen as a full-scale attack on her Cabinet, her party or on the political system. She saw governing as adversarial (ie she believed that there were two sides to every issue and that it was her duty to fight hard for the side she supported). She used fear, threat, intimidation and all other means of persuasion to win. This assertive style was essential to Thatcher's success. Not only did she take her Cabinet and party by storm, she also took them by surprise.

Source: Genovese 2003.

Item B John Major's leadership style

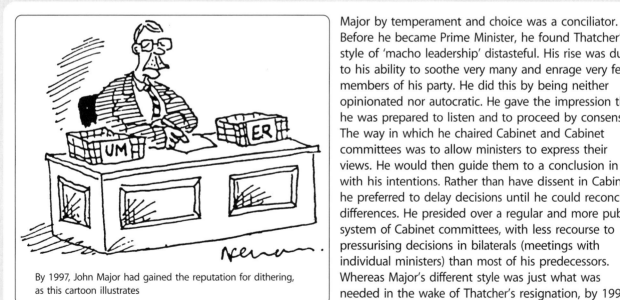

By 1997, John Major had gained the reputation for dithering, as this cartoon illustrates

Major by temperament and choice was a conciliator. Before he became Prime Minister, he found Thatcher's style of 'macho leadership' distasteful. His rise was due to his ability to soothe very many and enrage very few members of his party. He did this by being neither opinionated nor autocratic. He gave the impression that he was prepared to listen and to proceed by consensus. The way in which he chaired Cabinet and Cabinet committees was to allow ministers to express their views. He would then guide them to a conclusion in line with his intentions. Rather than have dissent in Cabinet, he preferred to delay decisions until he could reconcile differences. He presided over a regular and more public system of Cabinet committees, with less recourse to pressurising decisions in bilaterals (meetings with individual ministers) than most of his predecessors. Whereas Major's different style was just what was needed in the wake of Thatcher's resignation, by 1994 it had come to be seen as weak leadership and this reputation for weakness persisted to the 1997 general election. After that election, some of Major's colleagues thought he was a poor general, with no real desire for office, who dithered and was uncertain of his views. It should be noted, however, that Major faced much tougher Labour Leaders than Thatcher had had to face. Major faced Neil Kinnock in his prime, John Smith, and Tony Blair - who was the most effective Labour Leader in Opposition since Ramsay MacDonald.

Source: *Guardian*, 29 April 1994, the *Observer*, 21 September 1997 and Seldon 1997 .

Item C Tony Blair's leadership style

This cartoon was drawn to mark the Blair government's first anniversary in power. The men carrying the throne are spin doctors.

Tony Blair has used the levers of power in both traditional and novel ways - using informal as much as formal power. Cabinet meetings have seldom lasted longer than an hour and are often over in much less time. The agenda at Cabinet meetings is often informal rather than formal. Blair prefers to raise a topic of the moment, as well as to discuss forthcoming announcements and policy initiatives. The really important topics are usually discussed in much smaller groups. In these smaller groups, friends and advisers are sounded out. The Cabinet committee system has remained in place, but its use has been patchy. On many issues, Blair does not use Cabinet committees. Either he works through ad hoc groups, like previous Prime Ministers have done, or he works bilaterally with relevant departmental ministers. For example, he holds a regular series of one-on-one sessions with Secretaries of State to monitor annual work programmes. The picture is not of an all-powerful centre, but of an often beleaguered and isolated Prime Minister.

Source: Riddell 2001.

Item D Changing circumstances

The cartoon on the left was published in the *New Statesman* on 8 October 2001 at the time of the Labour Party conference and shortly after the terrorist attack on the Twin Towers in New York had resulted in the launch of Tony Blair and George W. Bush's 'War on Terrorism'. Opinion polls in October 2001 show that, following the Labour victory at the general election, Tony Blair's rating remained very high. The cartoon on the right was drawn on 29 September 2003 at the time of the Labour Party conference, a few months after British and American troops had invaded Iraq. This war divided the British public and Tony Blair's rating fell. In January 2004, a YouGov poll for Channel 4 News showed that 39% of the respondents thought Tony Blair was generally honest when he first became Prime Minister, but now felt that he had betrayed their trust, 29% felt that he was generally honest and they still trusted him to be generally honest, while 19% did not think Blair was generally honest when he became Prime Minister and they still had a low opinion of his honesty. There were 12% of 'don't knows'.

Questions

1. Judging from Items A-C, how do the Prime Ministerial styles of Thatcher, Major and Blair differ?

2. What do the cartoons in Item D tell us about the importance of changing circumstances on Prime Ministerial authority?

3. Using Items A-D and your own knowledge, explain how external circumstances might make an impact on a Prime Minister's leadership style.

15.7 The Cabinet

Since 1945, the Cabinet has generally consisted of around 20 ministers. The Cabinet is chaired by the Prime Minister. Most Cabinet ministers are the senior minister in charge of government departments, but there are usually one or two non-departmental ministers who can often provide a more objective viewpoint to those ministers primarily concerned with departmental matters. Also attending Cabinet meetings are the government's Chief Whip (who can inform the other ministers about backbench opinion in the party on key issues) and the Cabinet Secretary (the most senior civil servant) who sits immediately to the right of the Prime Minister.

Since 1945, and more particularly since the 1970s, the role of the Cabinet has changed. Cabinet meetings have become fewer in frequency, and shorter in duration. A few decades ago, the regular Thursday meeting starting at 10.00 am lasted for about three hours, and was often accompanied by a second meeting on Tuesdays.

By the 1980s, however, the Cabinet was only usually meeting once each week, on Thursday mornings, albeit still for about three hours. Under Tony Blair's premiership, though, this Thursday morning meeting of the Cabinet often lasts barely an hour (see Hennessy 2000, p.4 and Riddell 2001, p.32).

In one respect, it is deeply ironic that Cabinet meetings should have become fewer and shorter while the complexities of governing Britain have increased. Yet it is precisely because of this complexity that a three-hour meeting has become an inappropriate forum for detailed discussion and decision-making on most issues. Because most Cabinet ministers head departments and are primarily concerned with the policies of their department, they normally have little interest in, or detailed grasp of, the issues concerning their colleagues.

Consequently, an increasing amount of government decision-taking and policy-making takes place in forums below full Cabinet level, most notably in Cabinet committees, and in bilateral or trilateral meetings between specific ministers.

The Cabinet's functions

The full Cabinet has four main functions - confirmation, coordination, arbitration, and information (Burch 1988a; Burch 1988b; Burch and Holliday 1996, p.42). Or as a former Chancellor of the Exchequer expresses it, recalling his time serving in Margaret Thatcher's Cabinet until 1989:

> '[The function of the Cabinet was] to keep all colleagues reasonably informed about what was going on, and to provide a forum for general political discussion if time permitted.' (Lawson 1992, p.125)

The four main functions of the Cabinet are described in more detail in Box 15.9.

General discussion

A fifth function of the Cabinet is that it is a forum in which discussions either about a particular policy initiative or a

---

Box 15.9 The functions of the Cabinet minister

Confirmation

There is little detailed discussion of government policies in the Cabinet, and so the main role of the Cabinet today is to give formal approval to the decisions and proposals which are presented to it. These have usually been determined elsewhere, such as in Cabinet committees (see below).

Coordination

In order to overcome the tendency of Cabinet ministers to become preoccupied with the political affairs and interests of their department, the Cabinet - greatly assisted by the Cabinet Office - can help to ensure that there is coordination between ministers and policies. Meetings of the Cabinet help to ensure that ministers are aware of what their colleagues were doing and what impact this makes on both the government's overall goals and their own departmental objectives. This coordination function aims to ensure greater coherence and consistency of governmental policies and to minimise the scope for conflicts between ministers or their departments and the pursuit of contradictory policies.

Conflict resolution

Very occasionally, the Cabinet might be called upon to resolve a conflict which has arisen elsewhere in the core executive. For example, a Cabinet committee might have been unable to reach an agreement over a particular policy, due to deep divisions among the ministers serving on it. In such a case, the issue may be presented to the full Cabinet for a final decision. Alternatively, a particular minister might be deeply unhappy with a Cabinet committee decision and, therefore, seek to have the issue discussed again in the full Cabinet. Such occurrences are very rare, however, not least because divisions in Cabinet committee would probably lead the Chair to pursue a compromise or possibly a deferral (depending on the urgency of the issue). Certainly, taking disputes to the full Cabinet on a regular basis would rather defeat a major purpose of establishing Cabinet committees in the first place. It would also incur the displeasure of the Prime Minister and their Cabinet colleagues. The Ministerial Code makes it clear that:

> 'If the [Cabinet] committee system is to function effectively, appeals to the Cabinet must be infrequent. Those who chair committees are required to exercise their discretion in advising the Prime Minister whether to allow them…the Prime Minister will entertain appeals to the Cabinet only after consultation with the minister who chairs the Committee concerned.' (Cabinet Office 2001)

Consequently, while 'conflict resolution' is one of the Cabinet's four formal functions, it is one which the Cabinet is only occasionally called upon to perform.

Information

The Cabinet plays an important role in keeping senior ministers informed of the government's programme, including forthcoming legislation, and parliamentary business for the next week. The Cabinet's weekly meetings also include reports on international affairs by the Foreign Secretary, particularly those which have diplomatic, military or security implications for Britain.

more general discussion about the government's general strategy and goals can take place. From time to time, a Prime Minister might allow, or even encourage, a discussion in the Cabinet about a key or controversial policy initiative. Towards the end of 2003, for example, Tony Blair's Cabinet discussed the Home Secretary's proposals for the introduction of compulsory ID cards. Alternatively, there might be a discussion about the government's overall objectives, and what ministers believe should be the government's main tasks and goals in the medium or long term. Such discussions might take place in the context of a 'stock-taking' exercise, reviewing what the government has achieved to date, and deciding what remains to be done. Alternatively, they might take place in the run-up to a general election when the Prime Minister and Cabinet colleagues need to consider what they aim to achieve if they are re-elected at the next general election. This kind of discussion might well prompt policy proposals which are then included in the governing party's election manifesto.

15.8 The shadow Cabinet

Definition and role
Although it is not part of the structure of government, a shadow Cabinet operates in the British political system. In what has long been a predominantly two-party system (in the House of Commons at least), the shadow Cabinet is made up of politicians from the main Opposition party, who sit on the front bench directly opposite government ministers and 'shadow' their Cabinet counterparts. Each member of the shadow Cabinet is normally given a particular policy area to deal with (such as education, foreign affairs, transport and so on), mirroring that of ministers in the Cabinet itself. On becoming Conservative Party Leader in November 2003, however, Michael Howard appointed a much smaller shadow Cabinet in which several of his frontbench team had at least two broad policy responsibilities each, rather than just one.

Although the shadow Cabinet has no formal input into decision-taking and policy-making in British government, it is nonetheless important, because:

- it challenges what the government itself is doing - which contributes to accountability and scrutiny of the executive (a key function of Parliament)
- it develops alternative policies which it hopes will persuade the electorate that it is a credible 'government-in-waiting' which deserves to be voted back into government at the next election.

Not only does the existence of a shadow Cabinet ensure that a frontbench spokesperson can challenge their Cabinet counterpart and put the Opposition's case during parliamentary debates and ministerial Question Time, it also ensures that a team of Opposition politicians can acquire expertise in specific areas of policy, although shadow ministers do not have access to civil servants (which means

that they are often at a disadvantage to government ministers because ministers are armed with an array of information and statistics provided by departmental officials).

An effective shadow Cabinet can expose weaknesses or inconsistencies in what the government is doing and highlight the damaging effects of specific policies, while seeking to show voters how it would do things differently, and more effectively, if in government itself. At the same time, an effective shadow Cabinet, which successfully attacks the government's front bench, can improve the morale of Opposition backbenchers, helping to unify the Opposition party and generating greater confidence.

Although most media attention is on the Cabinet itself and on individual ministers, some Opposition politicians can enhance their reputation - and possible leadership prospects in the future - by performing effectively on the shadow front bench see Box 15.10.

Box 15.10 Thatcher and Blair - successful shadow ministers

In 1974, Margaret Thatcher proved a highly effective shadow Treasury spokesperson for the Conservatives, greatly impressing her party colleagues and media observers by the way in which she skilfully attacked the newly-elected Labour government's Finance Bill (the legislation to implement the budget). Indeed, it has often been suggested that her performance in this role helped to persuade some Conservative MPs to vote for her in the 1975 Conservative leadership contest.

In the early 1990s, meanwhile, while serving as Labour's shadow Home Secretary, Tony Blair boosted his own profile and popularity when he famously declared that a Labour government would be 'tough on crime and tough on the causes of crime', thereby helping the party to shake off its reputation for being 'soft' on crime. Again, it could plausibly be argued that his performance as shadow Home Secretary spokesperson was a significant factor in helping Tony Blair secure the support of enough Labour MPs to win the party's 1994 leadership contest.

One other reason why the shadow Cabinet is important in British politics is that it usually becomes the Cabinet proper when the Opposition wins a general election. This, as noted above, is effectively a constraint on the Prime Minister's power of patronage since the first Cabinet after being returned to government after a spell in Opposition is generally virtually ready-made. For example, it was inconceivable that Tony Blair would have chosen someone other than Gordon Brown to be Chancellor following New Labour's May 1997 election victory, given that Brown had proved such an effective shadow Chancellor in the mid-1990s.

Main points   Sections 15.7 - 15.8

- Since 1945, the Cabinet has generally consisted of around 20 ministers. It is chaired by the Prime Minister. Most Cabinet ministers are the senior minister in charge of government departments, but there are usually one or two non-departmental ministers.
- Since 1945, and more particularly since the 1970s, the role of the Cabinet has changed. Cabinet meetings have become fewer in frequency, and shorter in duration.

- The full Cabinet has four main functions: (1) confirmation; (2) coordination; (3) arbitration; (4) information. A fifth function is that it is a forum in which discussions about policy initiative or general strategy and goals can take place.
- Although it is not part of the structure of government, a shadow Cabinet operates. It is made up of politicians from the main Opposition party, who sit on the front bench in the Commons and 'shadow' their Cabinet counterparts.

Activity 15.3 The Cabinet

Item A The Cabinet at work

Item B The limitations of the Cabinet as a forum for genuine discussion and decision-taking

Criticisms of the Cabinet as an executive body are well known. First, it is too large to deal with a great deal of business. If the officials present are included, there are usually around 30 people in attendance. ISecond, its size and composition are designed to take account of political and representational factors - making it a good place in which to provide information, but not to debate issues at length. Third, since the early 1970s, it has met weekly as a rule (before then it met twice a week), has had fewer papers before it and often rubber-stamps recommendations from other committees. Fourth, on many matters coming to Cabinet, ministers may be inadequately briefed and may not be particularly engaged on some items. Fifth, most ministers are departmentally minded: it is a fact of political life that they make their reputations as departmental ministers, fighting for their budgets and programmes. And sixth, once the Prime Minister and a minister have agreed a course of action, it is difficult for other Cabinet ministers to overturn it. These shortcomings do not detract from the functions of the Cabinet as a sounding-board, occasional court of appeal, or reporting forum.

Source: Kavanagh & Seldon 2000.

Item C Fewer and shorter Cabinet meetings

Tony Blair sitting alone in the Cabinet room.

According to Dennis Kavanagh, it is difficult to think of any other Prime Minister who has shown so little regard for the Cabinet as Blair. Colin Thain talks about 'a lack of drive, energy and debate within the Cabinet' and asks whether this heralds the terminal decline of this institution of government. He also notes that Blair regards the formal Cabinet (that meets weekly on a Thursday) as essentially a reporting body. Blair uses the Cabinet in a very different way from the earlier Labour Prime Minister, Harold Wilson, for whom it was a policy and political debating forum. Jeremy Paxman notes that the decline of government by Cabinet has been a gradual thing. In the Attlee governments of 1945-51, he says, the Cabinet met an average of 87 times a year and considered about 340 papers prepared for it. By the early 1970s, the number of Cabinet meetings had dropped by a third, to about 60 and the number of papers considered had fallen to about 140. By the early 1990s, the number of meetings had slumped to no more than 40 each year, in which fewer than 20 papers were discussed. After the Labour landslide of 1997, Cabinet meetings still took place, with ministers trooping up to Ten Downing Street every Thursday morning. But, argues Paxman, the event had been stripped of any real importance. It frequently lasted not much longer than an edition of the television show *Ready, Steady, Cook*.

Source: Kavanagh 2001, Thain 2002 and Paxman 2003.

Questions

1. a) Using Items A and B and your own knowledge describe the functions of the Cabinet.
   b) Which of its functions is the Cabinet best equipped to perform?

2. Using Item C and your own knowledge explain why Cabinet meetings have steadily become fewer and shorter.

15.9 Collective responsibility

The Ministerial Code

One of the first documents handed to a new minister is the Ministerial Code (until 1997, known as *Questions of Procedure for Ministers*), which contains a section on collective responsibility. This states that:

'Decisions reached by the Cabinet or ministerial committees are binding on all members of the government...Collective responsibility requires that ministers should be able to express their views frankly in the expectation that the they can argue freely in private while maintaining a united front when decisions have been reached...Ministers cannot speak in public for themselves alone. In all cases, they speak as ministers; and the principle of collective responsibility applies. They should ensure that their statements are consistent with collective government policy...Ministers should exercise special care in referring to subjects which are the responsibility of other ministers.' (Cabinet Office 2001)

In other words, within Cabinet and Cabinet committees, ministers are permitted to express their own views and disagree with each other up to the point at which a formal decision is reached, or a policy adopted. After that, however, all ministers - even if they were not participants to the relevant discussion - must publicly endorse the decision or policy and keep their continued doubts private.

The doctrine of collective responsibility is supposed to be beneficial to individual ministers and the government alike. For individual ministers, the doctrine offers an assurance that they can speak freely and frankly in Cabinet and Cabinet committees, safe in the knowledge that what they have said will not (in theory at least) become publicly known. This, in turn, is supposed to enable policy proposals to be subjected to detailed consideration and robust exchanges of views between ministers before overall agreement is reached or a policy finally and formally adopted. In theory, this should have the effect of improving the quality of decisions taken and policies adopted.

For the government, the doctrine of collective responsibility is supposed to maintain an image of public unity, with ministers publicly bound together by a shared sense of purpose. The authority of any government would be grievously weakened if ministers could publicly distance themselves from decisions and policies which they had argued against in Cabinet or Cabinet committee and with which they still privately disagreed. Indeed, without the doctrine of collective responsibility, an unpopular or failing policy would probably prompt a rapid succession of ministers publicly insisting that 'I argued against this policy in Cabinet (committee), and knew from the outset that it would not work, but minister x and minister y refused to listen - so, don't blame me'.

This too, in principle, should result in better decisions being taken because ministers know that, if a policy subsequently fails or proves deeply unpopular, they will all be held responsible by Parliament and the electorate.

There is evidence that the application of collective responsibility has widened over the years. This development is described in Box 15.11.

Box 15.11 The widening application of collective responsibility

Originally, until the end of the 19th century, collective responsibility only really applied to Cabinet ministers. However, during the 20th century, as the number of ministers - particularly junior ministers - has increased, so the doctrine of collective responsibility has been applied more widely, to the extent that it now applies to all ministers, of whatever rank. It also now applies to the shadow Cabinet, in the sense that all shadow ministers and frontbench spokespersons are expected publicly to endorse the Opposition's policies. If they did not do so, then divisions and disagreements in the shadow Cabinet would become publicly aired - which would prevent the Opposition from presenting itself to the electorate as a credible 'government-in-waiting'.

Collective responsibility and ministerial resignations

In principle, all ministers whose opposition to a Cabinet or Cabinet committee decision is so strong that they find it completely unacceptable and publicly indefensible are required to resign from the government and return to the backbenches. This is the only way that ministers can disassociate themselves from a government policy with which they totally disagree. A minister cannot speak out against a particular policy while continuing to hold ministerial office. To do so would be to invite dismissal by the Prime Minister anyway. Of course, some ministers remain in post while making subtle criticisms of a particular policy - or even the government's overall direction - through 'coded' speeches. A reading-between-the-lines of such speeches reveals the minister's doubts and disagreements, but the speeches fall short of the outright criticism - which would probably lead to dismissal.

Sometimes, even when ministers have resigned on the grounds that they could no longer publicly support government policy on a specific issue, there appears to have been deeper, or more subtle, motives. One such example is given in Box 15.12.

Geoffrey Howe and Europe

A second example of a resignation that may have had deeper and more subtle motives than simply disagreeing with a specific government policy was that of Geoffrey Howe. Howe had been a senior figure in the Thatcher governments, serving as Chancellor of the Exchequer, from 1979 to 1983, and then as Foreign Secretary from 1983 to 1989. In July 1989, however, Howe was rather humiliatingly moved, in a Cabinet reshuffle, to the less prestigious post of Leader of the House of Commons, although also given the somewhat tokenistic title of Deputy Prime Minister. Howe did consider resigning,

Box 15.12 Michael Heseltine and the Westland Affair

This cartoon shows Michael Heseltine storming out of the Cabinet room after failing to convince the Prime Minister and the rest of the Cabinet to follow his line. It was first published in the *Guardian* on 10 January 1986.

One of the most dramatic and intriguing political events of the 1980s was the 'Westland Affair', which resulted in the resignation of two Cabinet ministers, and threatened to undermine Margaret Thatcher's own position as Prime Minister. In January 1986, Michael Heseltine, the Secretary of State for Defence, stormed out of a Cabinet meeting, claiming that he was unable to support the government's policy concerning the Westland helicopter company in Yeovil, Dorset. This company was a supplier of helicopters to Britain's armed forces, but was in acute financial difficulties. Heseltine wanted a European consortium to be allowed to rescue Westland, in order to prevent the company going out of business completely, whereas Margaret Thatcher, along with Leon Brittan, the Secretary of State for Trade and Industry, favoured a take-over by Sikorsky, an American company. When the Cabinet backed the Sikorsky option, and Margaret Thatcher stipulated that all future statements on Westland had to be 'cleared' by Ten Downing Street, Heseltine dramatically walked out, claiming that he could not support the government's policy on this issue.

However, a sceptic would ask whether a senior Cabinet minister would really resign over an issue such as the future ownership of a previously unheard of (by the vast majority of the British people) helicopter company in the West Country. Many people suspected that Heseltine's real motivation was to return to the backbenches in order to develop alternative (non-Thatcherite) policy proposals, and cultivate support among Conservative MPs, in preparation for a future leadership challenge. Given that Heseltine did indeed stand (unsuccessfully) as a candidate for the leadership of the Conservative Party in November 1990, some writers believe that this interpretation correctly explains why the Westland Affair blew up.

and even drafted a resignation letter to Thatcher in which he referred to 'differences in our approach' to Europe, but he eventually decided to accept the new post offered to him since it would enable him to continue putting forward his views from within the government rather than from the backbenches.

In November 1990, though, Howe did resign, increasingly exasperated by both Margaret Thatcher's increasingly hostile stance towards Europe and her overall style of leadership. Howe's resignation speech to the House of Commons was dramatic. He explained the frustrations and humiliations which had been inflicted upon him by Thatcher, particularly in his attempts at dealing constructively with his counterparts in Europe. Using a cricketing analogy (as Margaret Thatcher herself had done in a speech the previous evening), he informed astonished MPs that it was 'rather like sending your opening batsmen to the crease, only for them to find, the moment the first balls are bowled, that their bats have been broken before the game by the team captain'. Howe's speech concluded with a barely concealed call for someone to launch a leadership challenge, claiming that: 'The time has come for others to consider their own response to the tragic conflict of loyalties with which I have myself wrestled for perhaps too long' (quoted in Howe 1994, pp.666-67).

While Geoffrey Howe was undoubtedly unhappy at the government's (or more particularly Margaret Thatcher's) stance towards Europe, and may well have felt that he could no longer publicly support this line, it also seems that the real reason for his resignation was less to do with collective responsibility and more to do with prompting a leadership challenge, in the hope that Thatcher would finally be replaced. In other words, on this occasion, invoking the doctrine of collective responsibility appeared 'convenient, rather than convincing' (Dorey 1994-95, p.105).

The resignation of Robin Cook and Clare Short

Tony Blair's decision to join the USA in sending troops to depose Saddam Hussein in Iraq resulted in the resignation of two Cabinet ministers - Robin Cook (in March 2003) and Clare Short (in May 2003). According to Rathbone:

'The resignation of Cook, along with a number of junior members of the government provoked the most difficult crisis which Blair had faced as Prime Minister.' (Rathbone 2003, p.39)

Although few commentators doubted that Cook's opposition to the war against Iraq was genuine, a number pointed out that he had, in effect, been demoted when, after the general election in June 2001, Tony Blair replaced him as Foreign Secretary, offering him the post of Leader of the House of Commons instead (a position he accepted). The implication was that Cook was discontented anyway before the war issue came up and was looking for an opportunity to enhance his reputation with non-Blairite Labour MPs and supporters by making a principled stand. The war issue, in other words, came at a convenient time for him.

Clare Short chose not to resign at the same time as Robin Cook. But, she did openly criticise the line being taken by Tony Blair, describing it as 'reckless'. Despite such open criticism, Blair did not sack Short. Instead, he persuaded her to vote for the government in the crucial vote on the war. Short publicly declared that she had been satisfied by Blair's reassurances and would indeed vote with the government. The government won the vote with a small majority, helped in part by Short's change of heart - a change of heart that ensured that she lost a great deal of credibility with politicians and the public alike. Two months later, Short finally resigned after failing to vote with the government in an important vote on foundation hospitals and then failing to turn up at the weekly Cabinet meeting, claiming that she had a 'competing engagement'. In an interview with the *Guardian* just hours after resigning, Short said that:

'She was leaving over the US-UK mishandling of post-war Iraq. Mr Blair had broken his promises to her...The trigger which prompted Ms Short to quit, two months after she wobbled back into office after attacking Mr Blair's "reckless" conduct was the draft resolution which Britain and America are now promoting at the UN. Negotiated in secrecy, it does not give the UN the "vital role" that London and Washington promised. It left the occupation of Iraq illegal, she said' (*Guardian*, 13 May 2003)

In her resignation speech in the Commons and subsequent media interviews, Short was highly critical of Blair's leadership style, suggesting that there was more to her resignation than the particular issue she cited.

Main points   Section 15.9

- **Ministers are permitted to express their own views and disagree with each other up to the point at which a formal decision is reached. After that, all ministers - even if they did not participate in the discussion - must publicly endorse the decision and keep any doubts private.**
- **The doctrine of collective responsibility allows ministers to speak freely and frankly, knowing that what they say will not become publicly known. This allows robust exchanges of views, ensuring the quality of decisions taken and policies approved is improved.**

- **The doctrine of collective responsibility allows the government to maintain an image of public unity. The authority of a government would be weakened if ministers could publicly distance themselves from decisions and policies which they had argued against and with which they still privately disagreed.**
- **The application of the principle of collective responsibility has widened over the years and now includes all ministers, not just the Cabinet.**
- **In principle, all ministers whose opposition to a Cabinet decision is so strong that they find it completely unacceptable and publicly indefensible are required to resign from the government and return to the backbenches.**

Activity 15.4 Resignation issues

Item A The resignation of Robin Cook

Robin Cook served as Foreign Secretary from May 1997 to June 2001. In June 2001, he was appointed Leader of the House of Commons.

'I have chosen to address the House first on why I cannot support a war without international agreement or domestic support…The reality is that Britain has been asked to embark without agreement in any of the international bodies of which we are a leading partner - not NATO, not the European Union and now, not the Security Council…The US can afford to go it alone, but Britain is not a superpower. Our interests are best protected not by unilateral action but by multilateral agreement and a world order governed by rules…Iraq probably has no weapons of mass destruction in the commonly understood sense of the term…Why is it now so urgent that we take military action against Iraq to disarm a military capacity which has been there for 20 years, and which we helped to create?…What has come to trouble me most over the past weeks is the suspicion that if the hanging chads in Florida had gone the other way and Al Gore had been elected, we would not now be about to commit British troops…I intend to join those tomorrow night who will vote against military action now. It is for that reason, and that reason alone, and with a heavy heart, that I resign from the government.'

Extract from a speech made by Robin Cook in the House of Commons on 17 March 2003.

Item B The resignation of Clare Short

As soon as Clare Short had publicly described Tony Blair's policy on Iraq as 'reckless', the press began to compare what she said with the speech made by Geoffrey Howe in November 1990. Howe's speech triggered Thatcher's downfall and there was speculation that Short's would do the same. The fact that Short was a serving Cabinet minister, rather than an ex-minister as Howe had been, not only made the attack more damaging, but also suggested that the principle of collective responsibility was breaking down. The fact that Blair did not immediately sack her appeared to show that, far from being a presidential figure dominating his Cabinet, the Prime Minister was too politically weak either to keep his ministers in line or to sack one who had publicly attacked him. But Blair survived the crisis. Short's decision not to resign but to vote with the government made her look foolish and unprincipled. When she finally did resign in May, her loss of credibility reduced the damage that might have been inflicted by her resignation speech. Also, the rapid fall of Saddam Hussein's regime seemed to vindicate Blair's determination to go to war. Nevertheless, the resignations of Cook and Short raised for Blair uncomfortable parallels with the resignations of Heseltine, Lawson and Howe which undermined Thatcher's premiership in the late 1980s. These resignations can be seen as the Cabinet biting back against its 'presidential' treatment by the Prime Minister. They show that Cabinet government is not yet dead.

Source: Rathbone 2003.

Item C When ministers do and don't resign

If ministers really did stick to the principle of collective responsibility, the number of resignations in recent years would have been much higher than it actually has been. One spectacular example stands out. In 1992, the UK was forced to leave the European exchange rate mechanism, even though the Prime Minister, John Major, had made membership the central plank of his government's economic policy. Major did not resign, nor did his Chancellor, Norman Lamont. Nowadays, it is far more likely that ministers will resign because they have lost the support of the Prime Minister or because of a publicised lapse in private conduct. David Mellor, Secretary of State for National Heritage, did so in September 1992 after publicity about an extra-marital affair. In short, ministers seem to be responsible for their morals rather than their political conduct. Tony Blair was reluctant to accept the resignation of Secretary of State for Trade, Peter Mandelson, after revelations concerning his personal finances in December 1998. Within a year, Mandelson was back in the Cabinet again, as Secretary of State for Northern Ireland - only to be forced to resign again after a second scandal in January 2001. Since ministerial resignations are embarrassing to a government, every attempt is made to suggest that the departure has been voluntary. This makes it difficult to be sure whether the convention of collective responsibility has played any role in forcing the change. So, for example, when Alan Milburn resigned as Health Secretary in June 2003, citing family reasons, commentators tried to uncover a political motive.

Source: Garnett 2004.

Questions

1. Using Items A-C and your own knowledge explain what collective responsibility is in theory and how it works in practice.

2. 'The principle of collective responsibility explains the resignations of Robin Cook and Clare Short.' Using Items A and B give arguments in support of and against this statement.

3. a) What problems might arise if there was no doctrine of collective responsibility?

   b) What impact has the principle of collective responsibility made in recent years on the relationship between Prime Minister and Cabinet?

15.10 Cabinet committees

Since 1945, Cabinet committees have become the most common forum for detailed discussions of government business. There are three types of Cabinet committee - standing, ad hoc and consultative. Standing committees are referred to by code names or letters. They deal with a specific policy area and are relatively permanent. Ad hoc committees are set up to deal with specific short-term problems and issues or are committees which meet irregularly. For example, Dorey (1991) notes that while Margaret Thatcher was Prime Minister, ad hoc committees were set up to prepare for the 1984 miners' strike, to prepare for the abolition of the Greater London Council and to investigate the replacement of Polaris nuclear submarines by Trident. By their nature, ad hoc committees are not formal structures and it is, perhaps, no surprise that the Cabinet Office refuses to reveal details about the number of ad hoc committees in existence under Tony Blair. There is also a third type of Cabinet committee - the consultative committee. In consultative committees, matters are discussed with politicians outside the UK government - for example, joint ministerial committees include ministers from the devolved assemblies.

Some Cabinet committees have sub-committees. They do not normally take final decisions on policy, but they enable the collective discussion of issues ranging across several department's responsibilities.

Composition of Cabinet committees

The Prime Minister appoints the ministers who serve on Cabinet committees. Critics argue that this is another way in which Prime Ministers can bypass Cabinet. But this is a rather cynical view as membership is usually 'functional'. In other words, the ministers serving on the committee will usually be those who have a departmental interest in the issue or policy under consideration (see Catterall & Brady 1998, p.74, Dorey 1991 and James 1999, p.67). Indeed, the Cabinet Office (see below) explains that:

'Cabinet committees relieve the pressure on the Cabinet itself by settling business in a smaller forum or at a lower level. Committees enable decisions to be fully considered by those Ministers most closely concerned.' (www.cabinet-office.gov.uk/cabsec/ 2003/guide/cabcom)

This means that many Cabinet committees include junior ministers as members, because junior ministers deal with specific, specialised aspects of policy within their department (see Unit 16). So, while junior ministers do not normally attend meetings of the full Cabinet, it is quite common for them to serve on Cabinet committees - see Box 15.13 pn page 310.

The decisions taken, and the policies agreed, by Cabinet committees, have the same authority and status as a decision of the full Cabinet (the committee having been delegated to act on the Cabinet's behalf). Usually, decisions taken by committees are reported back to the full Cabinet as a formality, with little further detailed discussion. After all, if the ministers most concerned with a particular aspect of policy

Box 15.13 Cabinet Committee on Drugs Policy

The composition of the Cabinet Committee on Drugs Policy is as follows:

- Home Secretary (Chair)
- Secretary of State for Health
- Secretary of State for Education and Skills
- Chief Secretary to the Treasury
- Minister of State, office of the Deputy Prime Minister*
- Parliamentary Under-Secretary of State, Foreign and Commonwealth Office*
- Parliamentary Under Secretary of State, Home Office*

* junior ministers

have already discussed it in detail in a Cabinet committee, then the other ministers around the full Cabinet table will not normally feel qualified, or sufficiently interested, to challenge the decision.

The extent to which Cabinet committees are used

The composition and even the existence of Cabinet committees was supposed to be secret until 1992 when, for the first time, a list of all Cabinet standing committees (together with their membership and terms of reference) was made public. Before 1992, editions of *Questions of Procedure for Ministers* argued that such secrecy was a necessary part of collective responsibility. Despite the secrecy, however, the evidence suggests a great deal of variation under different Prime Ministers - see Box 15.14.

Box 15.14 Thatcher and Major's use of Cabinet committees

From the information available, it seems that Margaret Thatcher made less use of the formal Cabinet committee system than did her predecessors. For example, Burch (1994) notes that 941 meetings of Cabinet committees were recorded in 1978, compared to 340 in 1989. Similarly, he notes that, although Thatcher was Prime Minister for much longer than Attlee, she set up less than half the number of ad hoc Cabinet committees and only one sixth of the standing committees he set up in the immediate post-war era. According to Burch & Holliday (1996, p.45), Thatcher cut Cabinet committee meetings by a third between 1979 and 1990. Instead, she organised informal meetings with ministers.

There seems to be a consensus that, although the number of Cabinet committees declined from 26 to 19 in the period 1992-96, John Major made more use of the Cabinet committee system than Thatcher (see, for example, Burch & Holliday 1996, p.280 and Hood & James 1997, p.181). Burch (1994) claims that Major streamlined the system and gave committees a more strategic, wide-ranging remit. For example, whereas Thatcher had chaired four substantive domestic committees, Major chaired just one - a new overarching committee which covered the whole range of domestic policy (known as 'EDP').

Cabinet committees under Blair

Tony Blair's first list of Cabinet committees was published in June 1997. The list revealed that there were 20 committees and a change in emphasis:

> 'The list of Cabinet committees signals a number of changes of emphasis within government, with the scrapping of four committees from John Major's premiership. Committees on nuclear defence policy, competitiveness and on the coordination and presentation of government policies have been disbanded, together with the ministerial sub-committee on terrorism.' (*Times*, 10 June 1997)

Blair set up new committees on devolution, constitutional reform, the incorporation of the European Convention on Human Rights and food safety. Blair himself chaired four committees - constitutional reform, Northern Ireland, defence and overseas policy, and intelligence (Thatcher and Major also chaired the latter two).

By July 1998, the number of Cabinet committees had grown to 26 (committees were set up to deal with matters such as reform of the House of Lords, freedom of information and the 'millennium bug'. By 2004, the number of committees and sub-committees had grown to as many as 54.

The role of the Prime Minister

The shape - and even the use - of the Cabinet committee system depends on the particular style of the Prime Minister. It is the Prime Minister who decides which committees should be set up, what their terms of reference should be, who should chair them and who should sit on them. There may be practical and political restrictions on the Prime Minister's choice - the nature of an issue may require the inclusion of ministers from certain departments, for example. But there is still considerable room for manoeuvre.

The Joint Cabinet Consultative Committee

Two months after the 1997 general election, Tony Blair announced the setting up of a Cabinet consultative committee which would take the unusual step of including leading members of another party. In addition to Blair (who would chair the meetings), the committee was to be composed of five other Labour ministers and five leading Liberal Democrats. The Cabinet Secretary would also attend. It was agreed that the committee would meet at least once every two months. The first meeting was held on 17 September 1997. In September 2001, it was announced that the committee would be suspended because the Liberal Democrats, under the leadership of Charles Kennedy (who took over from Paddy Ashdown in 1999), decided to boycott the committee in protest at what they saw as the government's lack of commitment to constitutional reform.

15.11 The Cabinet Office

Located mainly at 70 Whitehall, but with a few other offices located in nearby streets, and with a direct internal door to Ten Downing Street, the Cabinet Office has been described as 'something of a corporate headquarters overseeing government strategy' (Kavanagh & Seldon 2000, p.70). The Cabinet Office actually contains two sections:

- the Cabinet Secretariat
- a number of special units concerned with particular issues or aspects of policy.

The Cabinet Secretariat

The main role of the Cabinet Secretariat is to aid the Prime Minister and Cabinet ministers in the performance of their duties. It also plays a vital role in servicing Cabinet committees:

'The sole objective of the Cabinet Office Secretariat is to provide an effective, efficient and impartial service to the Cabinet and its committees, and coordinating departmental contributions to the government's work. The Office ensures that decisions are cgnsistent with overall government policy, and where appropriate, coordinates effective follow-up decisions.' (Cabinet Office 1997, pp.5, 15)

The Cabinet Secretariat has four particular responsibilities:

- it prepares and distributes (to the ministers concerned) the agenda and relevant papers for meetings of the Cabinet and Cabinet committees
- it records the minutes of these meetings, and notes the decisions taken - these too are then circulated to the relevant ministers, as well as to the Prime Minster
- it checks the subsequent progress of policy decisions by, and between, government departments
- it coordinates the work of government departments in the case of cross-cutting or inter-departmental policies.

Reflecting New Labour's emphasis on 'delivery', particularly with regard to reform of public services, since July 1998 a succession of Ministers without Portfolio (ie ministers with no specific departmental responsibilities) have been appointed as 'Minister for the Cabinet Office', quickly dubbed 'Cabinet enforcer' by many commentators.

The Cabinet Secretariat is actually divided into seven smaller secretariats, as illustrated in Box 15.15.

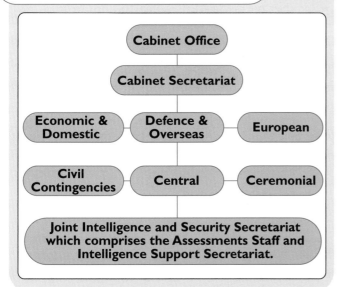

Box 15.15 The structure of the Cabinet Secretariat

Cabinet Office

Cabinet Secretariat

Economic & Domestic — Defence & Overseas — European

Civil Contingencies — Central — Ceremonial

Joint Intelligence and Security Secretariat which comprises the Assessments Staff and Intelligence Support Secretariat.

The responsibilities of the Economic and Domestic Secretariat include legislative and parliamentary affairs, while the Constitutional Secretariat focuses on 'machinery of government' issues, as well as the Blair governments' constitutional reform measures and proposals. The European Secretariat ensures that the work of government departments is in accordance with European Union obligations and directives (see Unit 12). The Ceremonial Secretariat is concerned with the award of official honours, such as the New Year Honours List and the monarch's Birthday Honours List.

Special units

In addition to these individual secretariats, the Cabinet Office also houses a four special units:

- Strategy Unit
- Social Exclusion Unit
- Regulatory Impact Unit
- Delivery Unit.

This reflects the Blair governments' determination:

- to secure effective implementation of policy objectives and public sector reform
- to achieve 'joined-up government'.

With regard to joined-up government, these units represent a conscious attempt to overcome the innate trend towards 'departmentalism' within the core executive (ie the tendency of ministers and departments to become preoccupied with their own policy goals and interests and to lose sight of the wider political picture or government strategy). The special units seek to tackle those 'wicked issues' which are either complex or multi-causal in origin and require the active cooperation of several ministers and departments in order to be effectively tackled - see Box 15.16 on page 312.

15.12 Informal groups

While the Cabinet, its committees and the Cabinet Office make up the Cabinet system in formal terms, the core executive also involves many meetings and groups of a less formal character. Three types in particular have become more numerous since the 1980s, namely bilaterals, trilaterals and task forces.

Bilaterals

Like Margaret Thatcher in the 1980s, Tony Blair has shown a particular liking for bilaterals. Bilaterals are meetings between just two ministers, often either the Prime Minister or the Chancellor and one other minister, although other ministers will also meet in pairs from time to time, if and when their departments have a shared interest in a particular problem or policy proposal. There are also frequent meetings between the Prime Minister and the Chancellor, facilitated, in part, by their proximity to each other in Ten and Eleven Downing Street respectively, and an internal connecting door between the two buildings.

Trilaterals

Trilaterals are meetings of three ministers, often the Prime Minister, the Chancellor, and one other minister. They have become more frequent since 1997, due largely to the shared commitment of Tony Blair and Gordon Brown to pursuing public sector reforms. As a result of this, the Prime Minister and the Chancellor have both taken a close interest in how

Box 15.16 Special units

The Social Exclusion Unit

The Social Exclusion Unit, established in December 1997, aims to develop and coordinate policies which will integrate socio-economically deprived and marginalised sections of the population back into society. Its creation is a recognition that social exclusion is caused by a range of factors - low educational attainment, homelessness, teenage pregnancies and so on - which, in turn, means that a multi-departmental, joined-up government approach is required.

The Strategy Unit

The Strategy Unit, meanwhile, was created in July 2002, and is also intended to promote joined-up government and forward-thinking. It is involved both in reviews of existing policies, to gauge their progress and success to date, and in identifying emerging issues or problems which require new policies or initiatives. In this respect, the Strategy Unit is both reactive and proactive.

For example, during 2003, the Strategy Unit investigated the growing problem of 'binge-drinking' among young adults, particularly among young women, and produced an interim report in September 2003 which warned that alcohol abuse, and accidents or injuries arising from excessive drinking, cost the NHS more than £1.5 billion per year, and caused the British economy more than £6 billion annually through lost production. It was also estimated that the cost of drink-related crime and public disorder was in the region of £7 billion (Asthana 2003, p.13). The Strategy Unit was expected to publish a full report, along with a range of policy proposals to combat the problem of 'binge-drinking' and alcohol abuse, sometime in 2004.

Regulatory Impact Unit

The role of the Regulatory Impact Unit (RIU) is to work with other government departments, agencies and regulators to help ensure that regulations are fair and effective. In addition to taking an overview of regulations which make an impact on business, the RIU also examines the impact on the voluntary sector, charities and the public sector.

The Delivery Unit

The main role of the Delivery Unit, which was set up in June 2001, is to oversee the implementation of government policies, particularly those concerned with the modernisation of public services. Reflecting Tony Blair's emphasis on the vital importance of 'delivery', this section of the Cabinet Office plays a key role in monitoring the work of the various government departments, with a view to ensuring that they are meeting, or are on course to meet, their performance targets.

certain Secretaries of State are proceeding with 'modernisation' of their department's provision of public services, and the extent to which additional funds are being matched by the attainment of specified targets. The result has been an increase in the number of 'trilateral' meetings, involving the Prime Minister, Chancellor, and a particular Secretary of State.

Task forces, working groups and ad hoc advisory groups

While 'task forces', 'working groups' and ad hoc advisory groups are not in themselves new or novel, the period since the election of the first Blair government, in May 1997 has witnessed a considerable increase in the number of such bodies. For example, during the first 18 months of the first Blair government, 295 task forces, and ad hoc advisory groups were created (Barker, Byrne & Veall 1999, p.12), while in 2001-02, there were 41 task forces and 133 ad hoc advisory groups, as well as 32 departmental policy reviews in progress (Cabinet Office 2003, p.xvi). Examples of those set up since 1997 are given in Box 15.17.

Box 15.17 Task forces, working groups and ad hoc advisory groups set up since 1997

Task forces and working groups

- Alternatives to Tobacco Sponsorship
- Britain Abroad
- Child Protection on the Internet
- Creative industries
- Football
- Inequalities and Public Health
- Intellectual Property Rights
- Livestock Farming
- National Crime Reduction
- School Standards
- Shipping
- Tackling Overindebtedness
- Work and Parents
- Youth Justice
- All-Wales Agri-Environnment scheme
- Chronic Fatigue Syndrome
- Cowboy Builders
- Diversity in (Scottish) Agriculture
- Financing of High Technology Business
- Leylandii
- Mobile Homes
- Pensions Education

Ad hoc advisory groups set up since 1997

- Advisory Group on Nanotechnology
- Air Quality Forum
- Gifted and Talented Advisory Group
- Hedgerows Regulations Review Group
- Integrated Sexual Health and HIV Strategy Steering Group
- Literacy and Numeracy Strategy Group
- Ministerial Advisory Group on Retail Crime
- Music Industry Forum
- Partnerships Against Poverty
- Property Crime Reduction Action Team
- Road Safety Advisory Panel
- School Libraries Advisory Group
- Vehicle Crime Reduction Action Team
- Welsh Transport Advisory Group

Source: Barker, Byrne and Veall 1999, Cabinet Office 2003, pp.169-224.

The main role of task forces, working groups and ad hoc advisory groups is either 'to investigate and recommend new policies and practices or, in some cases, practical means of implementing policies on which Labour had already settled' (Barker, Byrne & Veall 1999, p.11).

Main points **Sections 15.10 - 15.12**

- Since 1945, Cabinet committees have become the most common forum for detailed discussions of government business.
- There are three types of Cabinet committee - standing, ad hoc and consultative.

- The Cabinet Office contains two sections - the Cabinet Secretariat and a number of special units.
- While the Cabinet, its committees and the Cabinet Office make up the Cabinet system, the core executive also involves many meetings and groups of a less formal character.

Activity 15.5 Cabinet committees

Item A A selection of Cabinet committees, March 2004

Economic and Domestic Affairs Secretariat
Ministerial Committee on the Criminal Justice System (CJS)
Ministerial Sub-Committee on Crime Reduction (CJS(CR))
Ministerial Sub-Committee on Criminal Justice System Information Technology (CJS(IT))
Ministerial Committee on Constitutional Reform Policy (CRP)
Ministerial Sub-Committee on House of Lords Reform (CRP(HL))
Ministerial Committee on Domestic Affairs (DA)
Ministerial Sub-Committee on Adult Basic Skills (DA(ABS))
Ministerial Sub-Committee on Active Communities and Community Cohesion (DA(AC))
Ministerial Sub-Committee on Drugs Policy (DA(D))
Ministerial Sub-Committee on Equality (DA(EQ))
Ministerial Sub-Committee on Energy Policy (DA(N))
Ministerial Sub-Committee on Older People (DA(OP))
Ministerial Sub-Committee on Rural Renewal (DA(RR))
Ministerial Sub-Committee on Social Exclusion and Regeneration (DA(SER))
Ministerial Committee on Economic Affairs, Productivity and Competitiveness (EAPC)
Ministerial Sub-Committee on Employment (EAPC(E))
Ministerial Committee on the Environment (ENV)

Ministerial Sub-Committee on Green Ministers (ENV(G))
Ministerial Committee on English Regional Policy (ERP)
Ministerial Committee on European Union Strategy (EUS)

Defence and Overseas Secretariat
Ministerial Committee on Defence and Overseas Policy (DOP)
Ministerial Sub-Committee on Conflict Prevention in Sub-Saharan Africa (DOP(A))
Ministerial Sub-Committee on Conflict Prevention outside Sub-Saharan Africa (DOP(OA))
Ministerial Sub-Committee on International Terrorism (DOP(IT))
Ministerial Sub-Committee on Protective and Preventive Security (DOP(IT)(T))
Ministerial Sub-Committee on Consequence Management and Resilience (DOP(IT)(R))
Ministerial Sub-Committee on London Resilience (DOP(IT)(LR))
Ministerial Committee on Northern Ireland (IN)
Ministerial Committee on Intelligence Services (CSI)
Ministerial Group on the Restructuring of the European Aerospace and Defence Industry (MISC5)

European Secretariat
Ministerial Sub-Committee on European Issues (EP)

Item B Cabinet committees - for and against

(i) Cabinet committees are the most private and well protected parts of our democracy. Power ought to reside where the public can see it in Parliament, but in fact it hides in these committees. The Prime Minister appoints their members and is therefore able to pack them to achieve a desired result. Cabinet committees often present the full Cabinet with a fait accompli.

Source: Cockerell et al. 1984.

(ii) Some critics have argued that Cabinet committees enhance the power of the Prime Minister, but, to Harold Wilson, this was a facile view - Cabinet committees

make government more effective and prevent the Cabinet being bogged down in detail. Wilson claimed that the role of the Prime Minister is to ensure that the Cabinet committee system works smoothly by delegating authority to the committees and by being sufficiently sensitive to know when to respond to an appeal by a dissatisfied minority or to spot a case which should go straight to Cabinet. He said that it did not increase Prime Ministerial power since it would be difficult even for a megalomaniac Prime Minister to ignore a decision made by a committee of Cabinet colleagues.

Source: Wilson 1976.

Item B Cabinet committees - for and against (continued)

(iii) The new regime has been impatient with the traditional structure of Cabinet committees which, Mr Mandelson (Minister without Portfolio, based in the Cabinet Office) has said, had 'sometimes been allowed to become excessively slow moving and bureaucratic, and a recipe for delays and non-decision as they failed sufficiently to confront powerful departmental vested interests'. One result has been an increased use in task forces involving a mixture of civil servants and outsiders on issues crossing departments such as welfare-to-work, standards in schools, youth justice and, now, skill shortages.

Source: *Times*, 10 November 1997.

(iv) As the workload of the government increased after 1945, a network of Cabinet committees grew up. It was in these committees that policies were developed and decisions made. It was not long before the rule emerged that, if a Cabinet committee reached a decision, that decision was presented to full Cabinet for approval without further discussion. Only if a Cabinet committee failed to reach a decision might the matter be resolved by the full Cabinet. Since Prime Ministers summed up the discussion, they had a decisive say in determining the collective Cabinet line. On controversial matters, a minister with strong dissenting views would either have to accept the Prime Minister's line or resign.

Source: Magee and Garnett 2002.

Questions

1. What does Item A tell us about the Blair government's priorities?
2. a) Judging from Item B, what are the benefits and drawbacks of the use of a system of Cabinet committees?
   b) What problems would the full Cabinet face if a Cabinet committee system did not exist?
3. a) What do Items A and B tell us about the way in which the core executive operates?
   b) Where is power located within this system?

References

Asthana (2003) Asthana, A., 'Binge drinking: do they mean us?', *Observer*, 21 December 2003.

Barker, Byrne & Veall (1999) Barker, T., with Byrne, I. & Veall, A., *Ruling by Task Force*, Politico's/Democratic Audit, 1999.

Blondel & Muller-Rommel (1988) Blondel, J. & Muller-Rommel, F. (eds), *Cabinets in Western Europe*, Macmillan, 1988.

Burch (1988a) Burch, M., 'The British Cabinet: a residual executive', *Parliamentary Affairs*, Vol.41.1, 1988.

Burch (1988b) Burch, M., 'The United Kingdom' in *Blondel & Muller-Rommel (1988)*.

Burch (1994) Burch, M., 'The Prime Minister and Cabinet from Thatcher to Major', *Talking Politics*, Vol.7.1, autumn 1994.

Burch & Holliday (1996) Burch, M. & Holliday, I., *The British Cabinet System*, Harvester Wheatsheaf, 1996.

Burch & Holliday (1999) Burch, M., & Holliday, I., 'The Prime Minister's and Cabinet Offices: an executive office in all but name', *Parliamentary Affairs*, Vol.52.1, 1999.

Cabinet Office (1997) Cabinet Office, *Ministerial Code: a Code of Conduct and Guidance on Procedures for Ministers*, July 1997.

Cabinet Office (2001) Cabinet Office, *Ministerial Code: A Code of Conduct and Guidance on Procedures for Ministers*, 2001 (www.cabinet-office.gov.uk/central).

Cabinet Office (2003) Cabinet Office, *Public Bodies 2002*, The Stationery Office, 2003.

Catterall & Brady (1998) Catterall, P. and Brady, C., 'Cabinet committees in British governance', *Public Policy and Administration*, Vol.13.4, Winter 1998.

Cockerell et al. (1984) Cockerell, M., Hennessy, P. & Walker, D., *Sources close to the Prime Minister*, Macmillan, 1984.

Cook (2003) Cook, R., *The Point of Departure*, Simon and Schuster, 2003.

Crossman (1963) Crossman, R. H. S, *Introduction to Walter Bagehot's The English Constitution*, Fontana, 1963.

Dorey (1991) Dorey, P., 'The Cabinet committee system in British government', *Talking Politics*, Vol.4.1, Autumn 1991.

Dorey (1994/95) Dorey, P., 'Widened, yet weakened: the changing character of collective responsibility', *Talking Politics*, Vol.7.2, Winter 1994/95.

Dunleavy et al. (1997) Dunleavy, P., Gamble, A., Holliday, I. & Peele, G., *Developments in British Politics 5*, Macmillan, 1997.

Dunleavy et al. (2003) Dunleavy, P., Gamble, A., Heffernan, R. & Peele, G. (eds), *Developments in Politics 7*, Palgrave, 2003.

Elgie (1995) Elgie, R., *Political Leadership in Liberal Democracies*, Macmillan, 1995.

Foley (2000) Foley, M., *The British Presidency*, Manchester University Press, 2001.

Garnett (2004) Garnett, M., 'A feeling of resignation', *Politics Review*, Vol.13.3, February 2004.

Genovese (2003) Genovese, M., 'Margaret Thatcher: revised, revisited, re-examined and reappraised' in *Pugliese (2003)*.

Hennessy (2000) Hennessy, P., *The Blair Revolution in Government*, Leeds University Institute for Politics and International Studies, 2000.

Hennessy (2001) Hennessy, P., *Whitehall*, Pimlico Publishers, 2001.

Hood & James (1997) Hood, C. & James, O., 'The central executive' in *Dunleavy et al. (1997)*.

Howe (1994) Howe, G., *Conflict of Loyalty*, Macmillan, 1994.

James (1999) James, S., *British Cabinet Government* (2nd edn), Routledge, 1999.

Jones (1985) Jones, G. W., 'The Prime Minister's power' in *King (1985)*.

Kavanagh (2001) Kavanagh, D., 'Tony Blair as Prime Minister', *Politics Review*, Vol.11.1, September 2001.

Kavanagh & Seldon (2000) Kavanagh, D. and Seldon, A., *The Powers Behind the Prime Minister: the Hidden Influence of Number Ten*, HarperCollins, 2002.

King (1981) King, A., 'The rise of the career politician in Britain - and its consequences', *British Journal of Political Science*, Vol.11, 1981.

King (1985) King, A. (ed.), *The British Prime Minister* (2nd edn), Macmillan, 1985.

King (1991) King, A., 'The British prime ministership in the age of the career politician', *West European Politics*, Vol.14.2, 1991.

Lancaster (2002) Lancaster, S. (ed.), *Developments in Politics*, Vol.13, Causeway Press, 2002.

Lawson (1992) Lawson, N., *The View From No.11*, Bantam Press, 1992.

Ludlam & Smith (2004) Ludlam, S. & Smith, M.J. (eds), *Governing as New Labour*, Palgrave, 2004.

Magee & Garnett (2002) Magee, E. & Garnett, M., 'Is Cabinet government dead?', *Politics Review*, Vol.12.1, September 2002.

Norton (1987) Norton, P., 'Prime Ministerial power: a framework for analysis', *Teaching Politics*, Vol.16.3, September 1987.

Norton (1990) Norton, P., '"The lady's not for turning": but what about the rest? Margaret Thatcher and the Conservative Party 1979-89', *Parliamntary Affairs*, Vol.43.1, 1990.

Paxman (2003) Paxman, J., *The Political Animal*, Penguin, 2003.

Pugliese (2003) Pugliese, S. (ed.), *The Political Legacy of Margaret Thatcher*, Politico's, 2003.

Pyper & Robins (1987) Pyper, R. & Robins, L. (eds), *Governing the UK in the 1990s*, Macmillan, 1995.

Rathbone (2003) Rathbone, M. 'The British Cabinet today', *Talking Politics*, Vol.16.1, September 2003.

Rhodes (1995) Rhodes, R. A. W., 'Introducing the Core Executive' in *Rhodes & Dunleavy (1995)*.

Rhodes & Dunleavy (1995) Rhodes, R.A.W & Dunleavy, P. (eds), *Prime Minister, Cabinet and Core Executive*, Macmillan, 1995.

Richards & Smith (2004) Richards, D & Smith, M. J., 'The "Hybrid State"?: Labour's response to the challenge of governance' in *Ludlam & Smith (2004)*.

Riddell (1993) Riddell, P., *Honest Opportunism*, Hamish Hamilton, 1993.

Riddell (2001) Riddell, P., 'Blair as Prime Minister' in *Seldon (2001)*.

Seldon (1997) Seldon, A., *Major: A Political Life*, Weidenfeld and Nicolson, 1997.

Seldon (2001) Seldon, A. (ed.), *The Blair Effect: The Blair Government, 1997-2001*, Little, Brown and Co., 2001.

Smith (1999) Smith, M. J., *The Core Executive in Britain*, Macmillan, 1999.

Smith (2003) Smith, M. J., 'The core executive and the modernization of central government' in *Dunleavy et al. (2003)*.

Thain (2002) Thain, C., 'The core executive under Blair: the first term' in *Lancaster (2002)*.

Thatcher (1993) Thatcher, M., *The Downing Street Years*, HarperCollins, 1993.

Wilson (1976) Wilson, H., *The Governance of Britain*, Michael Jospeh and Weidenfield & Nicholson, 1976.

16 The core executive - ministers and civil servants

16.1 Ministers and civil servants

According to one of Britain's leading experts on the civil service:

> 'The relationship between ministers and civil servants is the central hinge of the system of government in Britain - the point where the democratically-elected and the permanent elements in Whitehall come together, the vital connecting link between decision and action, accountability and expertise, change and continuity.' (Theakston 2000, p.39)

Given that the majority of detailed policy decisions are taken within government departments, before being reported - for formal approval - to the Cabinet, the role played by senior civil servants, and the relationship between them and government ministers, is a key (and sometimes controversial) feature of British politics.

16.2 The ministerial hierarchy

Each government department is normally headed by a Secretary of State (although the Treasury is headed by the Chancellor of the Exchequer) who is also a Cabinet minister. These, in turn, are served by Secretaries of State, and, below them in the ministerial hierarchy, Parliamentary Under-Secretaries.

Also formally serving the Secretary of State in running their department are senior civil servants, whose official role is to provide ministers with advice and information relevant to policy proposals, and then faithfully to supervise the implementation of policies once they have been agreed, and then approved by Cabinet (and possibly Parliament if legislation is involved).

This hierarchy is illustrated in Box 16.1.

16.3 Government departments

Most policy-making in Britain takes place within government departments, with each department responsible for a particular set of policies. For example, the Home Office is responsible for policies concerning law-and-order, prisons, criminal justice and so on while the Treasury is concerned with economic policies, public expenditure, and taxation.

It is within the departments that most policies originate. The details are then worked out before they are presented to the Cabinet for approval, and introduced to Parliament in the form of a Bill if legislation is required. Of course, as noted in Unit 15, when the work or policies of one department have implications for those of another, ministers and/or civil

Box 16.1 Ministerial hierarchy

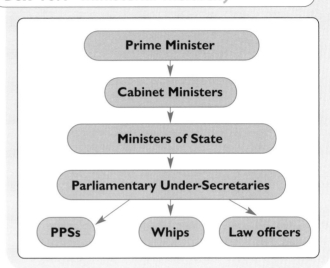

servants in the relevant departments will meet via bilaterals, trilaterals, Cabinet committees or (in the case of the civil servants) official committees.

There is an unofficial hierarchy amongst departments, with the Treasury, and the Foreign (and Commonwealth) Office being the 'élite' ministries. Madgwick once described the Treasury as a 'super department', partly because of its political responsibility for overall economic policy and taxation, but also because other ministers depend upon the Treasury for the allocation of their annual budgets (Madgwick 1991, pp.25-26 - see also Thain & Wright 1995). This makes the Chancellor of the Exchequer the most powerful minister in the core executive - apart from the Prime Minister, and even then, on certain issues, the Chancellor's view may prevail over a Prime Minister who does not possess the same grasp of economic detail. Also, for the same reason, the Chancellor may sometimes be the most unpopular minister because other ministers may resent the Chancellor's refusal to grant all of the monies they have requested for their departmental expenditure.

Departmental 'philosophies'

Several government departments have been characterised by a prevailing philosophy or ethos. This shapes their approach to particular issues and, as a result, influences the type of policies pursued. A number of inter-related factors have shaped these departmental philosophies. The main factors are outlined in Box 16.2 on page 317.

Departmentalitis

In some departments, the prevaaling philosophy or ethos has

Box 16.2 Factors shaping departmental philosophies

The following factors play a part in shaping departmental philosophies:

- The effectiveness or practicability of the approach, as judged by the senior civil servants in the department.
- The manner in which the senior civil servants in a department have been socialised into adopting a particular set of views and values during their 20-40 years in the department.
- The way that new entrants to the department are, in turn, taught that 'this is how things are done'. They will be keen to display their acceptance of their department's values and practices, in order to 'fit in', and impress their superiors for career and promotion purposes.
- The extent to which a department has a close working relationship with one or two key pressure groups (sometimes known as 'policy communities') - where such a close relationship exists, there will often be scepticism or resistance to radical change imposed from above because change would disrupt the 'custom and practice' which senior civil servants and pressure group leaders have developed over many years.

Source: Marsh, Richards & Smith 2001.

been so strongly ingrained, that ministers appointed to head those departments have found it difficult to introduce significant reforms. Indeed, many ministers have ended up 'going native', because they too become persuaded to view things from their department's point of view, and then feel obliged to adopt this departmental approach in their discussions with ministerial colleagues or the Treasury.

A former Labour minister, Gerald Kaufman, referred to this 'departmentalitis', describing it as:

'[A] kind of disease, which…stems from a preoccupation with the department to which the minister is assigned, to the exclusion of all other considerations, including the fortunes of the government as a whole…If you contract departmentalitis, you will ruthlessly pursue your own department's interests, even if another department has a better case: quite simply, your department must win. You will often not even be interested in, let alone care, whether your department's activities impinge adversely on those of a colleague…If you contract departmentalitis, you will go along to a Cabinet committee determined to win…You will forget that you are part of a government, that the fortunes of the government are more important than the fortunes of your own department, that the fortunes of the government may well require that your own department's interests be subordinated to those of another.' (Kaufman 1997a, pp.14-15)

Certainly, just a few months after New Labour's May 1997 election victory, Tony Blair was expressing concern about the trend towards departmentalism which was already becoming apparent among some of his ministerial colleagues. In November 1997, he said:

'One of the things we have lost from Opposition is that shared sense of purpose and strategy. Some ministers have become preoccupied by their departmental brief and we need to draw them back more.' (Observer, 23 November 1997)

Changing the organisation of departments

From time to time, changes are made to the organisation and structure of government departments. For example, the Department of National Heritage, which was created by John Major in 1992, became the Department of Culture, Media and Sport when the first Blair government was elected in 1997. More recently, 2001 saw the creation of the Department of the Environment, Food and Rural Affairs (DEFRA), which replaced the Ministry of Agriculture, Fisheries and Food. DEFRA also incorporated the Environment branch of what had been the Department of the Environment, Transport and the Regions (itself only established in 1997).

There are three main reasons why new departments are created. These are outlined in Box 16.3.

Box 16.3 Reasons why new departments are created

The three main reasons why new departments might be created are as follows:

1. The emergence of a new issue (or the increased importance of an existing issue). For example, the new constitutional landscape created by the first Blair government led to the creation, in 2003, of a new Department of Constitutional Affairs.

2. The high priority which a government or Prime Minister might want to give to a particular issue or policy. For example, Tony Blair's emphasis on the importance of education as a means of providing Britain with a more skilled and (internationally) competitive work-force, resulted in the Department of Education and Employment being transformed into the Department of Education and Skills.

3. Dissatisfaction with the structure or operation of existing departments sometimes results in the creation of new departments. For example, the creation of DEFRA in 2001 was prompted, in large part, by ministerial concern that the Ministry of Agriculture, Fisheries and Food was not in itself appropriate to the tackling of more general problems affecting rural areas and the countryside in Britain, not least because many of these problems were not directly to do with farming itself.

Of course, the creation of a new government department, or the amalgamation of existing ones, usually results in a modified title being given to the relevant Cabinet minister. After the creation of DEFRA in 2001, for example, Margaret Beckett became the Secretary of State for the Environment, Food and Rural Affairs. Similarly, the creation of a new Department for Constitutional Affairs resulted in the new post of Secretary of State for Constitutional Affairs.

16.4 Secretaries of State

Apart from the Chancellor, ministers in charge of government departments usually have the title Secretary of State: Secretary of State for Education and Skills, Secretary of State for Transport and so on. Each Secretary of State is formally responsible for the policies and administration of their department (see the section on Individual Ministerial Responsibility below). These policies and the administration of the department must also be in accordance with the overall strategy and objectives of the government, as confirmed via the Cabinet.

As with Prime Ministers (see Unit 15, Box 15.5), different Secretaries of State have different styles. Indeed, Norton has identified seven main styles (Norton 2000, pp.109-10). These are outlined in Box 16.4 below.

Norton acknowledges that the types described in Box 16.4 are 'ideal types'. In reality, many Secretaries of State display most of the features of one particular ministerial style but it is also possible to identify elements of another style or styles. Indeed, there might be an overlap between certain styles, such as when the personal conviction of a 'commander' is itself derived from their ideological beliefs and goals. Overall, though, Norton suggests that most Secretaries of State are either commanders or managers.

Box 16.4 Different types of Secretary of State

1. Commanders

Commanders are Secretaries of State who pursue a particular policy (or set of related policies) which reflects their personal beliefs and commitments. They may have formed a clear view of what they believe should be done, based, perhaps, on their experiences elsewhere (perhaps having worked in the 'real world' before entering politics). Alternatively, their ideas might have come from their own thinking on a particular set of issues. Norton suggests that, under Blair, David Blunkett and Jack Straw have variously adopted a 'commander' role.

2. Ideologues

Ideologues seek to pursue policies which are linked to a clear and strongly-held political philosophy or set of values. They are determined to pursue policies, via their department, which are based upon a set of strong political principles - their ideology - and which they are determined to put into practice. Such ministers became most notable during the Thatcher-Major years when ideology was an important driving force. Those who were committed to (and closely identified with) Thatcherism and who could therefore be classified as 'ideologues', included Keith Joseph, John Redwood, Nicholas Ridley and Norman Tebbit. 'Ideologues' will often adopt a 'proactive' approach to pursuing policies, attempting to seize the initiative and, quite often, identifying or looking for problems to be solved (as opposed to waiting for problems to force themselves onto the agenda, and then hurriedly responding to them). In pursuing policies based on ideological beliefs, of course, some may also adopt a 'commander' role to some degree. After all, a personal belief about how something should be done, or what sort of reforms ought to be pursued often come from their ideological stance.

3. Managers

Managers are generally content to take policy decisions on a practical, pragmatic basis, according to necessity and circumstances. They are not strongly driven by personal or ideological beliefs, but tend to 'take issue as it comes', adopting a predominantly reactive, responsive role. Furthermore, unlike 'ideologues' and 'commanders', they tend to be much more willing to consult others (senior civil servants, ministerial colleagues via bilaterals, special advisers and so on) and listen to advice, prior to making a decision. In effect, the question they ask themselves when making a decision is: 'Is this likely to work and prove effective?', rather than 'Is this ideologically consistent?'

4. Agents

Agents are political heads of departments who ultimately act on behalf of others individuals or bodies, namely the Prime Minister, the civil service or the European Union.

5. Prime Ministerial

Prime Ministerial Secretaries of State are those appointed to make sure that the Prime Minister's wishes and policy preferences are pursued, although, of course, the Prime Minister might simply opt to appoint a fellow 'ideologue' to secure this objective. On the other hand, the number of ministers willing to act as the Prime Minister's 'agent' might be limited, so a Prime Minister might appoint junior ministers to 'keep an eye' on particular senior ministers, instructing them to report back (Margaret Thatcher allegedly adopted this tactic, particularly with regard to One Nation ministers who were known to be critical of Thatcherite ideology, and who, therefore, she did not trust).

6. Civil service

Senior ministers who generally accept the arguments and views of their senior civil servants and who, therefore, tend to adopt 'the departmental line' in Cabinet or Cabinet committee meetings fit into this category. These ministers may genuinely be persuaded by their civil servants or they may, perhaps, simply want a quiet life, reasoning that as they are likely to be reshuffled in a couple of years, there is little point in expending unnecessary time and energy. A former Labour minister, Gerald Kaufman, has even suggested that some ministers, occasionally, attend Cabinet or Cabinet committee meetings and simply read from the briefing paper prepared for them by their civil servants (Kaufman 1997a, p.57).

7. Team players

Team players are Secretaries of State who see decision-taking as a collective endeavour and, as a result, seek to secure the agreement of their Cabinet colleagues as far and as often as possible. However, as noted in Unit 15, time constraints and organisational factors prevent the Cabinet from routinely taking part in detailed discussions and decision-taking, while many ministers become preoccupied with the work of their particular department. Consequently, Norton acknowledges that very few Cabinet ministers can be classified as 'team players'.

Source: Norton 2000.

Main points Sections 16.1 - 16.4

- Much government activity and policy-making takes place within departments.
- Many government departments develop a particular 'philosophy' or approach to issues, which ministers often find difficult to change, at least in the short-term.
- Government departments are sometimes

restructured or merged in response to new issues or government objectives.
- The main government departments are headed by a Cabinet minister, usually with the title of Secretary of State.
- Different Cabinet ministers display different styles in running their departments.

Activity 16.1 What makes a successful Cabinet minister?

Item A Advice to ministers

How to be a good minister

1. Beware of 'departmentalitis' - ministers are split up and isolated.
2. Don't become big-headed (tempting though that might be after 18 years in opposition).
3. Remember you are still an MP - treat backbenchers courteously and pay attention to what they say.
4. Remember you are a Labour Party member - talk to and listen to other party members (sometimes they have ideas worth taking up).
5. Remember your constituents - do not take them for granted or you'll be out at the next election.
6. Stand up for yourself - always listen to advice, but do not always follow it.
7. Never take no for an answer - the official machinery is capable of stitching ministers up.
8. Control your diary - time is of the essence in ministerial work.
9. Don't sign documents unless they are exactly as you want them.
10. Do your boxes and know your stuff.
11. Remember you are politically mortal - the day will inevitably come when you are no longer a minister.

Source: Kaufman 1996 and 1997.

Item B Mo Mowlam

Mo Mowlam was first elected to Parliament in 1987. In 1988, she was given a junior job on the team shadowing Northern Ireland. A year later she moved to Trade and Industry. She then achieved a rare double by being elected to both the shadow Cabinet and the NEC, a demonstration of her popularity in the party. She used a good memory to political effect. One Labour activist commented: 'Whenever I meet Mo she knows who I am, what I do and when we first met. There are other members of the Cabinet to whom I have to introduce myself each time we meet.' The most common criticism of Mowlam is that she tends to be all things to all people. She does not surround herself with cronies from any particular group and she is difficult to place within the party. One party worker described her as a 'moderniser' and another as 'an ally of the left'. In fact, she encourages such uncertainty, admitting: 'People say that I stuck close to Kinnock, then Smith, then Blair and that I can switch my personality to suit whatever audience I'm with. There's an element of truth in that.' Through hard work and shrewd positioning, Mowlam assembled a strong hand in difficult circumstances. She wooed the unionists without alienating the republicans and maintained good relations with Dublin and the USA. Throughout the negotiations on Northern Ireland in the spring of 1998, she managed to keep the parties talking. The result was the Good Friday Agreement. Just how much party members appreciate her was demonstrated at the 1998 party conference. At the mention of her name in Tony Blair's keynote speech, she was given a standing ovation - the first time that a Leader's speech had ever been interrupted by a standing ovation for a colleague.

Source: The *Independent on Sunday*, 6 July 1997 and the *Guardian*, 30 September 1998.

Item C Alan Clark, Minister of Trade

In his diaries, Alan Clark (who was Minister for Trade between 1986 and 1989) complained about the time ministers waste meeting delegations because there are so few occasions when a minister's mind is altered during a discussion. Despite this complaint, however, he reveals that a delegation from the charity Lynx convinced him to draft legislation which would force fur traders to label garments made of the skins of animals that had been caught in leg-hold traps. Clark felt so strongly about this measure that he spent enormous time and energy on it. He even admitted that: 'Sometimes I think that all I want is to stay in office here long enough to get my fur legislation on to the statute book'. To prepare the path for the legislation, Clark met, threatened and cajoled all sorts of people - such as lawyers, ambassadors, senior civil servants from several departments, eskimos, furriers and small shopkeepers. By June 1988, it seemed that the legislation would be adopted. On 14 June, however, Clark was summoned to see Prime Minister Thatcher. She wanted Clark to drop the scheme. After four and a half minutes, Clark realised he had lost. The meeting was scheduled for 15 minutes, but lasted 55. About three-quarters of the way through the meeting Clark said: 'Well, if that's what you want, I will obey you'.

Source: Clark 1993.

Item D Pressures on ministers

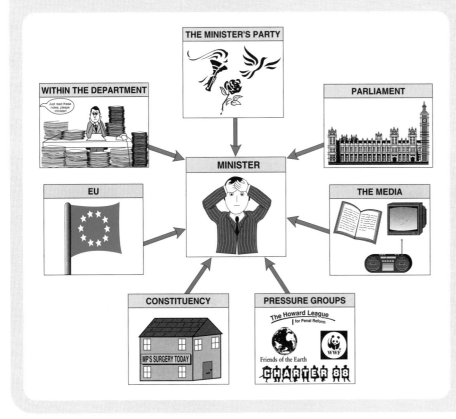

Questions

1. Judging from the criteria in Item A, would you say that Mo Mowlam (Item B) and Alan Clark (Item C) have the sort of qualities necessary to make a successful minister? Explain your answer.

2. Suppose you had been asked to give advice to a minister who complained that there were too many pressures pulling in different directions. What advice would you give? Use Items A, C and D in your answer.

3. Which of Philip Norton's seven ministerial categories (see Box 16.4 above) best describes (a) Mo Mowlam (Item B) and (b) Alan Clark (Item C)? Explain how you reached this conclusion.

16.5 *Ministers without Portfolio*

Most Cabinets also include two or three Ministers without Portfolio, which means that they do not have specific departmental responsibilities, but are nonetheless senior enough to warrant a seat at the Cabinet table. Ministers without Portfolio are usually given titles, such as:

- Lord President of the Council
- Chancellor of the Duchy of Lancaster
- Lord Privy Seal.

Irrespective of which of these titles they are formally given, Ministers without Portfolio are normally given a particular non-departmental responsibility by the Prime Minister. For example, in 2003, Peter Hain was appointed Lord Privy Seal and Leader of the House of Commons, while Douglas Alexander served both as Chancellor of the Duchy of Lancaster, and as a minister for the Cabinet Office. At the same time, Baroness Amos was appointed Lord President of the Council and Leader of the House of Lords.

16.6 *Junior ministers*

Secretaries of State are supported by junior ministers, their numbers having increased significantly during the 20th century - from 15 in 1914 to 32 in 1945 (Theakston 1987, pp.5, 43) to 66 by 2004. This increase reflects the vastly increased workload of government departments.

Being appointed a junior minister is often the first step on the road to becoming a full member of the Cabinet. Junior ministers are 'authorised to supervise the day-to-day administration of a defined range of subjects' (Cabinet Office 2001a, paragraph 41).

There are two types of junior minister - Minister of State (the higher rank) and Parliamentary Under-Secretary of State (the lower rank). Both are answerable to their Secretary of State and neither have formal control or authority over civil servants.

Minister of State

Most government departments have between two and four Ministers of State - see Box 16.5 on page 321.

The precise roles played by each Minister of State is determined by the Secretary of State, although the Prime Minister may also issue guidance. Often, the Minister of State's full title indicates their primary policy responsibility in the department. As Theakston notes, their role and authority are 'essentially informal and indeterminate, depending upon personal and political, not statutory, factors'. This means that the actual role and duties of Ministers of State partly depend upon their relationship with the Secretary of State. Where there is a good professional relationship between a Minister of State and a Secretary of State, it is likely that the Minister of State will be permitted - and trusted - to play a more extensive policy role in the department. Where the relationship is less cordial, however, the Minister of State is likely to be given a very limited role in policy development. They might even be confined to administrative tasks or to replying to correspondence sent to the department by MPs, outside bodies or members of the public (Theakston 1987, pp.93-94 and Theakston 1999, pp.235-36).

There is a certain ambiguity concerning the relationship between junior ministers and senior civil servants. While 'the Permanent Secretary (the most senior civil servant in a department) is not subject to the direction of junior ministers, junior ministers are not subject to the directions of

Box 16.5 Ministers of State, April 2004

Department for Education and Skills

Minister of State for Children and Young People - Margaret Hodge - responsibilities include:

- children and family policy - children's social services, child protection, children in care, Family Policy Unit, Family and Parenting Law, parental responsibility, role of parents in supporting learning
- young people - connexions service and card, careers service, youth service, neighbourhood support fund, Children's and Young People's Unit, young people at risk, homelessness, social inclusion.

Minister of State for School Standards - David Miliband - responsibilities include:

- taking an overview of all schools strategy
- transforming secondary schools - Key Stage 3 strategy, raising attainment at 14-19, curriculum and testing
- school organisation and funding
- transforming the school workforce and the secondary school curriculum
- overview of 5-16 admissions.

Minister of State (Universities) - Alan Johnson - responsibilities include:

- higher education
- raising standards in further education
- Learning and Skills Council
- European Union and overview of international relations
- science and technology policy.

Source: www.number-10.gov.uk, 2 April 2004.

the Permanent Secretary. Instead:

'Civil Servants observe the balance of forces and operate accordingly. They gauge whether the junior minister has [their] boss's confidence.' (James 1999, pp.20-21)

Parliamentary Under-Secretaries of State

Parliamentary Under-Secretaries of State are the most junior in the ministerial hierarchy, and are often allocated very specific tasks, often technically specialised or concerned with administrative minutiae (but still important nonetheless) - see Box 16.6.

16.7 The appointment of ministers

All ministers are appointed by the Prime Minister. The vast majority are MPs in the House of Commons, although some are appointed from the House of Lords. This reflects the constitutional requirement that all ministers are parliamentary figures, either as Members of Parliament (in the House of Commons) or peers (in the House of Lords). This ensures that they are accountable and answerable to Parliament - an important part of the convention of Individual Ministerial Responsibility (discussed below).

If a Prime Minister wanted to appoint an 'outsider' to a ministerial post, then they would either need to give them a

Box 16.6 Parliamentary Under-Secretaries of State

Department for Education and Skills

Parliamentary Under-Secretary of State for Sure Start - Baroness Catherine Ashton.

Baroness Ashton works with Minister of State Margaret Hodge on all children's issues. Her responsibilities include:

- Sure Start, early years and childcare
- special educational needs
- Lords business - all children's business in the Lords and DfES legislation in the Lords.

Parliamentary Under-Secretary of State for Adult Learning - Ivan Lewis.

Ivan Lewis works with Alan Johnson on lifelong learning issues. He has a specific focus on skills and vocational education. His responsibilities include:

- raising attainment at 14-19 (supporting David Miliband)
- adult skills and vocational education
- Learning and Skills Council
- International strategy post-16 (other than EU business)
- behaviour and discipline (working with Margaret Hodge).

Parliamentary Under-Secretary of State for Young People and Learning - Stephen Twigg.

Stephen Twigg works with David Miliband on schools issues. His responsibilities include:

- raising standards in London schools
- raising standards in primary schools
- the school curriculum
- drug and alcohol education, teenage pregnancy, PSHE (working with Margaret Hodge)
- equality issues
- rural schools
- departmental efficiency
- international issues (excluding EU business) in schools (with Alan Johnson).

Source: www.number-10.gov.uk, 2 April 2004.

Life Peerage, so that they could then sit in the House of Lords, or find a safe seat in which they could be elected via a by-election. Such a by-election might be imminent anyway, or it might, very occasionally, be created by the government itself, through offering the sitting MP a peerage in order to create a vacancy.

16.8 Ministers' Policy Advisers

Although Cabinet ministers have junior ministers and senior civil servants to assist them in their departmental and policy-making responsibilities, they (like the Prime Minister) have been making increasing use of Special Advisers (Blick 2004). According to *The Ministerial Code* (which replaced *Questions of Procedure for Ministers* in 1997), each Cabinet minister is entitled to appoint two Special Advisers, subject to the approval of the Prime Minister. In departments with a wider policy remit, however, such as the Treasury, more than two

Special Advisers can be appointed, although again, Prime Ministerial approval is required.

Some Special Advisers and Cabinet ministers develop such a good working relationship that when the minister is moved to another department in a reshuffle, the Special Adviser accompanies them to their new department.

The precise roles performed by Special Advisers vary from minister to minister and department to department. Usually, they are expected to 'bring a more adventurous cast of mind...to suggest things that officials [civil servants] might dismiss as outlandish'. In general, a Special Adviser 'acts as counsellor, confidant and political ally to a minister surrounded by officials who are - quite correctly - non-political' (James 1999, pp.223, 224).

Perhaps not surprisingly, the increased number and activity of Special Advisers under the Blair government has prompted a corresponding increase in concern about their role. In particular, there are concerns that the traditional responsibilities of senior civil servants are being undermined. In response to criticism, a Code of Conduct for Special Advisers was drawn up. This outlines their role, claiming that they 'are an additional resource for the minister, providing advice from a standpoint that is more politically committed and politically aware than would be available to a minister from the civil service' (Cabinet Office 2001b, paragraph 2).

This Code of Conduct has not removed the concerns of those civil servants and political commentators who believe that 'ministers are looking more and more to their Special Advisers for advice at the expense of the civil service' (Jones 2002, p.17).

16.9 *Individual Ministerial Responsibility*

A constant theme in British politics concerns the doctrine of Individual Ministerial Responsibility. This is defined in Box 16.7.

Box 16.7 Individual Ministerial Responsibility

The individual responsibility of ministers for the work of their departments means that they are answerable to Parliament for all their department's activities. They bear the consequence of any failure in administration, any injustice to an individual or any aspect of a policy which may be criticised in Parliament, whether personally responsible or not. Since most ministers are members of the House of Commons, they must answer questions, and defend themselves against criticism in person. Departmental ministers in the House of Lords are represented in the Commons by someone qualified to speak on their behalf, usually a junior minister.

Source: HMSO 1994, p.42.

Individual Ministerial Responsibility has three discrete main elements.

First, ministers are answerable and accountable to Parliament for the work of their department. It is minister who must defend the policies and decisions of their departments, both through ministerial Question Time, which is organised on a four-weekly rota and by appearing before departmental select committees when invited to do so. These forums are therefore the main means by which ministers are made accountable to Parliament, and compelled to explain and justify what they and their departments are doing, or have done. As Rush has noted:

> 'The fact that, almost without exception, all ministers are members of either the House of Commons or the House of Lords clearly facilitates Parliament's ability to render them accountable to the legislature, but it is the doctrine of ministerial responsibility that is the constitutional basis of parliamentary scrutiny...ministers are answerable to Parliament for their conduct of public policy and administration. The doctrine therefore underpins all debates, all parliamentary questions, all committee activity - the means by which Parliament seeks to exercise its scrutiny.' (Rush 2000, pp.107, 108)

Second, it is ministers, not their civil servants, who are held accountable for policies, and, therefore, for policy failure. It is assumed that civil servants act according to the decisions and instructions of their minister, so that ultimate responsibility for decisions and policies rests entirely with the minister. If something goes wrong, the minister should accept full responsibility, and not blame their civil servants.

Third, when a major policy error occurs, it is the minister in charge of the relevant government department who should resign, not the civil servants implementing the policy. The assumption is that the civil servants were simply administering policy as laid down by their minister, and so the minister should accept the blame for deciding on a poor policy.

This model of Individual Ministerial Responsibility has long been a key constitutional convention of British politics, yet it needs to be qualified in three ways.

First, the doctrine assumes that the making of policy and its implementation are distinct. In fact, they are closely linked. Policies are still being 'made' even while they are being implemented. The creation of agencies as a result of the Next Steps reforms (see below) has blurred the distinction between the making of policy and its implementation, resulting in some bitter public disputes between ministers and officials over who is to blame when problems occur. In such circumstances, it is not necessarily the minister who resigns.

Second, the 1979 introduction of departmental select committees somewhat weakened the convention that only ministers should be held publicly responsible for policies. Since 1979, civil servants have themselves often been called for cross-examination by MPs on select committees.

Third, ministers rarely resign as a direct consequence of policy failure. On the relatively rare occasions when such resignations do occur, it is often due to a lack of support in the minister from the Prime Minister, Cabinet or parliamentary colleagues. To express it another way, ministers who have the support of the Prime Minister, the Cabinet and backbenchers are likely to be able to 'ride out' the controversy caused by a policy failure or case of departmental maladministration.

Main points Sections 16.5 - 16.9

- Most senior ministers are supported by junior ministers - Ministers of State or Parliamentary Under Secretaries.
- All ministers are appointed by the Prime Minister.
- Most senior ministers now appoint Special Advisers to provide an alternative or additional source of advice.
- Constitutionally, ministers are responsible for the activities and policies of their particular department.
- In practice, however, it is widely accepted that no minister can really know absolutely everything

that goes on inside their department and that much of the routine work has to be delegated to officials (senior civil servants).
- The doctrine or convention of Individual Ministerial Responsibility has been further weakened by the post-1988 establishment of 'executive agencies'.
- When ministers do resign, ostensibly on the grounds of Individual Ministerial Responsibility, there may be other factors and forces at play. The minister may have lost the political support of their colleagues, for example.

Activity 16.2 Individual Ministerial Responsibility

Item A The parliamentary rota for ministers' Question Time

1st MONDAY	1st TUESDAY	1st WEDNESDAY	1st THURSDAY
Culture, Media & Sport (2.30 - 3.00)	Transport (11.30 - 12.00)	Office of the Deputy Prime Minister (11.30 - 12.00)	Environment, Food & Rural Affairs (11.30 - 12.00)
Church Commissioners	Cabinet Office	Prime Minister (12.00 - 12.30)	
2nd MONDAY	**2nd TUESDAY**	**2nd WEDNESDAY**	**2nd THURSDAY**
Work and Pensions (2.30 - 3.00)	Scotland (11.30 - 12.00)	Northern Ireland (11.30 - 12.00)	Education and Skills (11.30 - 12.00)
	Lord Chancellor's Department	Prime Minister (12.00 - 12.30)	Solicitor General
	President of the Council/Leader of the House of Commons		
3rd MONDAY	**3rd TUESDAY**	**3rd WEDNESDAY**	**3rd THURSDAY**
Home Office (2.30 - 3.00)	Health (11.30 - 12.00)	Wales (11.30 - 12.00)	Trade and Industry (11.30 - 12.00)
		Prime Minister (12.00 - 12.30)	Minister for Women
4th MONDAY	**4th TUESDAY**	**4th WEDNESDAY**	**4th THURSDAY**
Defence (2.30 - 3.00)	Foreign & Commonwealth Office (11.30 - 12.00)	International Development (11.30 - 12.00)	Treasury (11.30 - 12.00)
		Prime Minister (12.00 - 12.30)	

Item B Factors weakening Individual Ministerial Responsibility

Garnett has identified four main factors which have increasingly operated against the convention of ministerial responsibility:

1. The workload of departments is far heavier than in the first half of the 20th century, and issues tend to be more complex. No-one seriously expects an individual to be personally responsible for every decision taken inside a department.

2. Much of the work of departments has now been delegated to semi-autonomous agencies, which are responsible for day-to-day management and delivery of services. Their chief executives are in charge of such operational matters.

3. The governing party in the House of Commons is likely to rally round a minister under attack by the Opposition or the media for an alleged policy failure.

4. A ministerial resignation is likely to reflect badly on the government, and may also imply that the Prime Minister's judgement was awry in appointing the minister in the first place.

Source: Garnett 2004, pp.29-31.

Item C Selected ministerial resignations since 1982

1982
Lord Carrington (Foreign Secretary)
Failure to foresee Argentina's plans to invade the Falklands

2003
Robin Cook (Leader of the House of Commons)
Disagreement with government policy over Iraq

1985
Cecil Parkinson (Trade and Industry Secretary)
Revelations about private life (pregnancy of Sarah Keyes, his mistress)

2002
Estelle Morris (Secretary of State for Education)
Problems concerning aspects of education policy

1986
Michael Heseltine (Defence Secretary)
Disagreement with Cabinet policy over sale of Westland company

2002
Stephen Byers (Secretary of State for Transport)
Strong criticism of transport policies and strategy by Commons' transport select committee

1986
Leon Brittan (Trade and Industry Secretary)
Role in the leaking of confidential documents to damage Michael Heseltine over Westland

RESIGNATION

2000
Peter Kilfoyle (Minister of State for Defence)
Disagreement with direction of government policy

1988
Edwina Currie (Minister of State for Health)
Controversy over her comments about salmonella in eggs

1998
Peter Mandelson (Minister without Portfolio)
Failure to declare personal loan from Paymaster-General

1994
Neil Hamilton
(Minister of State for Trade and Industry)
Accepting 'cash for questions' in Parliament

1998
Ron Davies (Welsh Secretary)
Private life -'moment of madness' on Clapham Common

1995
Charles Wardle (Minister of State for Energy)
Disagreement with government policy over immigration

Source: Budge, Crewe, McKay & Newton 2004, p.146; Pyper 1991, pp.247-48.

Questions

1. Using Item A, explain why Question Time might not be a very effective or efficient means of scrutinising ministers, and holding them to account.

2. In Item C, which resignations are in accordance with the doctrine of Individual Ministerial Responsibility? Explain why.

3. a) In reality, what factors determine whether or not a minister actually resigns? Use Item B in your answer.

   b) What does Item B suggest about the relevance of the doctrine of Individual Ministerial Responsibility today?

16.10 *The Senior Civil Service*

Although there are about 500,000 civil servants in Britain, employed in government departments and agencies throughout the country, the term 'Senior Civil Service' refers specifically to the top 3-4,000 posts (less than 1% of all civil servants). The post of Permanent Secretary is the most senior of all. The Permanent Secretary is in charge of all civil servants in a government department.

It is the 'Senior Civil Service' which has traditionally been most closely and routinely involved with Cabinet ministers and policy advice, although reforms of the civil service since 1979 have placed a much greater emphasis on policy delivery and management by civil servants, with ministers relying less than they used to on senior civil servants for policy ideas. Even so, senior civil servants do still play a significant role in assisting Cabinet ministers in information-gathering and policy development, even if this role has been reduced somewhat since 1979.

16.11 *The formal role of civil servants*

Most of the work done in a government department is never seen by the minister in charge. It is carried out by the department's civil servants. In theory at least, the British civil service is apolitical (not political). Appointments are supposedly not made on political grounds, for example, and promotional prospects are not supposed to be affected by a change in government. As Ridley (1986) notes, this is in contrast to some other European countries where key officials are appointed because they are sympathetic to their government's policies.

The traditional role of civil servants

Traditionally, the job of senior civil servants is to provide advice to ministers, regardless of which party is in power:

> 'All civil servants are bound by the civil service pay and conditions service code which demands that they deliver duties of confidentiality and loyal service "for all practical purposes" to the minister of the day. An individual's duty to the courts, Parliament and the public is subsumed in [secondary to] their primary duty to their minister.'
> (Elizabeth Symons, leader of the top civil servants' union writing in the *Guardian*, 2 April 1993)

There are three main elements in the traditional role played by civil servants. These are described in Box 16.8.

Box 16.8 Three elements in the role played by civil servants

1. Impartiality
Civil servants are expected to be impartial - that is, they must not be seen to be politically active in any way. It is the role of the government to take decisions and the role of civil servants to implement policy loyally regardless which party is in power.

2. Neutrality
Civil servants must remain neutral - even if they personally disagree with a particular government policy. Senior civil servants who wish to participate in national politics or stand for a party must resign. Civil servants must not express their own opinions in the media or before parliamentary committees.

3. Anonymity
Civil servants should remain anonymous. They work behind the scenes and must not discuss what takes place in their department with outside agencies or with the media. In addition, they must not reveal written information. If something is in an official file, it is an official secret (all civil servants working in government departments sign the Official Secrets Act).

Maintaining confidentiality

It can be argued that the preservation of the confidentiality of discussions and documents is a crucial part of the preservation of a neutral civil service. In theory at least, it is for ministers to decide what the public should or should not know and civil servants to remain silent and neutral, even if they do not agree. The reasoning behind this view is that ministers are held responsible for any errors of judgement that take place in their departments and it is they who take the blame, not the civil servants.

Has the traditional role changed since 1979?

In a review of recent reforms affecting the Senior Civil Service, Bayliss & Dargie argue that the role of senior civil servants has begun to change. In 1979, they argue, senior civil servants were 'traditional public administrators' fulfilling (in theory at least) the traditional role described above. By 1998, however, there was a trend towards a new role - that of the 'new public manager':

> 'The development of the new public manager is part of a worldwide change in the organisation and management of public services. The new public manager adopts... management skills that can be used to manage any organisation or service, rather than particular public service skills. This new type of civil servant asks what is to be done, why, and how much it costs...The new public manager also requires training in specific management skills, mobility in careers with flexible labour markets, and competition for recruitment, promotion and retention.'
> (Bayliss & Dargie 1998, p.76)

In other words, new public managers run public services in much the same way that managers in the private sector run businesses.

16.12 *Historical background*

The earliest recorded civil service existed in China 2,000 years ago under the Ch'in dynasty (221-206 BC). It consisted of a centralised bureaucracy of talented people whose role was to serve the state. Entry into the civil service was by examination. Officials were called 'mandarins', a term still used to describe the small élite at the top of the British civil service today.

Before the 19th century, a civil service in the modern sense did not exist. The state's administrative system was not regarded as a single service and the number of full-time staff was small (in the 1820s, for example, the total number of civil servants employed by the Home Office was just 17). What appointments there were, were made by nepotism or patronage rather than on merit. Ministers tended to look after their own departmental affairs while officials performed tasks which today would be considered political. It was not until the mid-19th century that an attempt was made to establish an efficient and organised civil service.

The Northcote-Trevelyan Report (1854)

The impetus for civil service reform came from the Treasury. The Chancellor, Gladstone, set up an inquiry in April 1853 under Northcote and Trevelyan. Trevelyan had served in the Indian civil service (set up by the East India Company) and he aimed to bring the British civil service up to the high standard of administration for which the Indian civil service was known. The Northcote-Trevelyan Report was published in 1854. Its five main recommendations are outlined in Box 16.9 on page 326.

Box 16.9 Main recommendations of the 1854 Northcote-Trevelyan Report

1. Civil service posts should be divided and ranked according to function, with a distinction between intellectual and mechanical tasks.

2. Entrants should normally be young men who would receive 'in-house' training.

3. Recruitment should be through open, competitive examination.

4. Entrance examinations should be in liberal arts, rather than on professional or technical subjects.

5. Promotion and career development should be on the basis of merit, not favouritism or nepotism.

Source: Drewry & Butcher 1991, p.43.

The report was welcomed by Gladstone but was opposed by his colleagues and by top civil servants who saw it as a threat to the system of patronage. Although entrance examinations were conducted by the Civil Service Commission set up in May 1855, open competition was not fully established until the Playfair Report was published in 1875.

Nonetheless, the Northcote-Trevelyan reforms have been described by one Whitehall expert as 'the greatest single transformation the British civil service has ever undergone' (Hennessy 2001, p.31).

The Fulton Report (1968)

Although there were a few small inquiries and adjustments to the civil service after 1875, its structure remained virtually unchanged until 1968 when the Fulton Report, commissioned by Prime Minister Harold Wilson, was published. This report was commissioned in response to growing concern over the continuing tradition of employing recruits with a generalist rather than a specialist background. The main findings and recommendations of the Fulton Report are illustrated in Box 16.10.

Changes following the Fulton Report

The report made a number of recommendations, but only a few were implemented, the main ones being:

- the setting up of a Civil Service College, although most training continued to be done in departments
- a Civil Service Department was also established (but abolished in 1981)
- a new unified grading structure was established, but remained very hierarchical
- a scheme was set up to allow civil servants to gain outside experience by working in industry.

That the Fulton Report's recommendations were only partially implemented was due to two main reasons. First, a number of Labour MPs and ministers were not especially interested in the issue of civil service reform. According to one former Labour politician, John Garrett, the Fulton Report's recommendations 'were thwarted by the lack of political interest in fundamental change. Ministers would not devote the time and attention to what most of them saw as peripheral and boringly technical questions' (Garrett 1980, p.191).

Second, the civil service itself was widely viewed as contemptuous of most of Fulton's recommendations, and skilfully - yet with characteristic civil service discretion and subtlety - pursued a process of dilution and delay (for details of how they did this, see Kellner and Crowther-Hunt 1980, Chapter four and Ponting 1986, Chapter seven). Peter Hennessy recalls un-named civil servants boasting that:

'Fulton was a joke. The civil service is much too smart to worry about Fulton. They accepted everything he said, then did what they wanted to do…Oh, there have been loads of changes. We have renamed everything.' (quoted in Hennessy 2001, p.205)

16.13 Reforms since 1979

By the time that the first Thatcher government was elected in 1979 it was clear that the Fulton reforms had largely failed. Soon after her election, Margaret Thatcher began to argue that the civil service was too large, wasteful of resources and did not provide value for money. The result was a new attempt to reform the service.

Box 16.10 The main criticisms and recommendations of the Fulton Report

Fulton's main criticisms	Fulton's main recommendations
Too many 'gentleman amateurs' or generalists.	Recruit candidates with more relevant degrees.
Too many divisions and grades.	Unified grading structure.
Too few civil servants trained in management.	Civil Service College to provide management training courses.
Not enough contact between civil service and wider society it is there to serve.	Greater 'two-way' mobilty, secondments, and short-term contracts for 'outsiders'.
Too much secrecy.	Inquiry into the Official Secrets Act.
Socially and educationally 'exclusive' (ie, Oxbridge 'over-graduates represented').	More socially 'representative' recruitment and appointments.
Staff management, training and career development inadequate.	Civil Service Department to be established, and promotion criteria modified.

Source: Hennessy 2001, pp.195-98 and Drewry & Butcher 1991, pp.52-55.

Certainly the civil service had grown. In 1961, it employed 640,000 people, but, by 1979, this had grown to 732,000. On taking up office, Thatcher froze civil service recruitment (compulsory redundancies were avoided by not replacing those who retired). She notes that this policy was not readily accepted by civil servants themselves: 'Departments came up with a range of ingenious reasons why this principle should not apply to them. But, one by one they were overruled' (Thatcher 1993, p.94).

The work of the Efficiency Unit

The drive for reform was managed from Downing Street. Derek Rayner (a leading businessman brought in from the private sector) was given a small unit within the Cabinet Office (the Efficiency Unit) whose job was to scrutinise the civil service from within. As a result of this initiative, the Management Information System for Ministers (MINIS) was introduced into the Department of the Environment in 1980 and this led to the introduction of the Financial Management Initiative (FMI) in 1982. The FMI covered all departments and was the first real attempt at streamlining the civil service. Its aim was to improve efficiency by initiating a change of attitude and introducing new management practices. Civil servants were to become the equivalent of line managers in business by being held directly responsible for particular policies in their departments. They were to be given a clear view of their objectives and encouraged to use their initiative to make the best use of resources available to them.

The Ibbs Report (1988)

The Rayner reforms were intended to produce long-term changes, but, by 1987, many of the supporters of the new managerialism remained disappointed. Three main criticisms were made:

- Experimentation with budgeting and performance related pay had not gone far enough.
- Devolution of responsibility had not been achieved in practice.
- Promotion to the top continued to be from too narrow a base.

These concerns led to the setting up of a new efficiency scrutiny, carried out by Robert Ibbs. Ibbs began work under Thatcher and continued when Major became Prime Minister. The Ibbs Report *Improving Management in Government: the Next Steps* was first presented to Margaret Thatcher before the 1987 general election. The document's contents were so sensitive, however, that it was kept secret until after that election. It was finally published in February 1988.

The Ibbs Report made the three main observations outlined in Box 16.11.

Next Steps agencies

The Ibbs Report recommended a 'Next Steps' programme which would lead to substantial changes in the structure of the civil service. This 'Next Steps' programme made the four main recommendations outlined in Box 16.12.

According to Greer, a core principle of the Next Steps programme was that the 'agencies' were to be granted the day-to-day freedom and autonomy to pursue their 'business' and ensure service delivery, but in return they were required to meet certain standards and targets laid down by central

government (Greer 1994, p.60). The agencies retained links with their government department, but they gained a degree of autonomy. Next Steps agencies are now located within government departments and staffed by civil servants. They operate under 'framework agreements' which delegate authority and responsibilities to the Chief Executive, who is then accountable to the minister (Simpson 1998, p.64).

Although the recommendations of the Ibbs Report were accepted in February 1988, the implementation of them was initially rather slow, to the extent that by April 1990, just 12 'executive agencies' had been established (see Flynn, Gray & Jenkins 1990, for a fuller discussion of the launch of the Next Steps agencies). By 1993, however, a total of 97 agencies had been created, and since then, their numbers have continued to increase. By the time Labour came into power in 1997, three-quarters of all permanent civil servants worked for agencies (which were renamed 'executive agencies'). Some examples of these executive agencies and their 'parent' department are provided in Box 16.13 on page 328.

Box 16.11 The Ibbs Report

The Ibbs Report made three main observations:

1. The civil service was deemed too vast both in scale and in size to carry out its role in an efficient manner: 'A single organisation of this size which attempts to provide a detailed structure within which to carry out functions as diverse as driver licensing, fisheries protection, the catching of drug smugglers and the processing of parliamentary questions is bound to develop in a way which fits no single operation effectively' (HMSO 1988, para. 10).
2. Civil servants were said to 'play safe', rather than taking an enterprising outlook.
3. The civil service was criticised for still spending too much, and failing to provide value for money.

Box 16.12 The Next Steps programme

Four main recommendations were made:

1. There was a need to separate policy advice from policy delivery as far as possible, so that more civil servants could focus on delivery.
2. Policy delivery was to be provided by semi-autonomous 'agencies' (made up of civil servants) whose Chief Executive would ultimately be answerable to the relevant departmental minister, who in turn, remained answerable to Parliament.
3. Each agency would have its roles and responsibilities specified in a 'business contract' with the government, and staff would be rewarded on the basis of their performance and success in meeting targets or delivering 'quality services'.
4. Each agency was to enjoy relative autonomy - albeit within the context of the 'business contract' - with regard to setting the terms and conditions of employment (including pay), and recruitment.

Box 16.13 Next Steps agencies and their 'parent' department

Government Department	Executive Agencies
Department of the Environment, Food and Rural Affairs (DEFRA)	Countryside Agency Food Standards Agency Rural Payments Agency
Home Office	Prisons Agency UK Passport Service
Transport	Driver & Vehicle Licensing Agency Driving Standards Agency Highways Agency
Work and Pensions	Benefits Agency Child Support Agency

Contracting-out and privatisation

In the same way that many of the services in local government were contracted-out to private contractors in the late 1980s and early 1990s, steps were taken under the Conservatives to introduce market forces into the civil service. This took two main forms - contracting-out services to the private sector and selling them off (privatising them). The selling off of services proved relatively straightforward (for example, to cut running costs in departments, the Major government sold off departments' information technology (IT) services to private companies). Contracting-out was less straightforward. There was an initiative in 1991, for example, aimed to introduce 'market testing' by opening up civil service work to outside contractors. Although the Major government required government departments to identify 30% of their work for market testing, there was little take-up by departments and the scheme was dropped in 1994 (Hood & James 1997). Similarly, the 1992 Private Finance Initiative (designed to enable private companies to carry out public sector work by putting in place a flow of payments) did not achieve its targets (*Times*, 10 March 1998).

The Citizen's Charter

In accordance with the Conservatives' objective of improving the quality of services provided to the public, 1991 saw John Major launch the 'Citizen's Charter'. The idea was that, because many civil servants are in contact with the general public (for example, issuing passports, dealing with benefit claims or collecting income tax), charters could be drawn up which describe the sort of service which the public is entitled to. By setting targets, the government would make civil servants more accountable to members of the public and improve standards of service provision.

Main points Sections 16.10 - 16.13

- **Although the civil service has a total of about 500,000 staff, it is the top 3-4,000 who belong to the Senior Civil Service.**
- **There are three main elements in the traditional role played by civil servants: (1) impartiality; (2) neutrality; and (3) anonymity.**
- **There are three key dates for civil service reform - 1854 when the Northcote-Trevelyan Report was published, 1968 when the Fulton Report was** published and 1988 when the Next Steps initiative started.
- **From 1979, the civil service was subject to various initiatives intended to improve efficiency, cut costs, and place much greater emphasis on the management and delivery of services. These initiatives culminated in the Next Steps reforms and the Citizen's Charter.**

Activity 16.3 The Conservatives' civil service reforms

Item A Next Steps

The Next Steps initiative is the most far-reaching reform of the civil service in the 20th century. The term 'Next Steps' is used because it is the successor to a whole range of other changes in the management and financial control of government departments that have taken place since 1979. The creation of agencies which are responsible to ministers for the execution of policy will transform public administration and public policy in the UK. The first agency was the Vehicle Inspectorate launched in August 1988. The largest agency is the Social Security Benefits Agency which employs 63,000 staff and the smallest is Wilton Park, employing 30 staff. The aim of the Next Steps initiative is to improve the efficiency and quality of service delivered by public agencies. Agencies do not decide what these services should be. The Vehicle Inspectorate, for example, performs tests, but only has an advisory role in deciding what the structure and parameters of the tests should be. Transport policy, road safety and the links between vehicle testing, driver licensing, vehicle registration and motorway design all remain the responsibility of the Department of Transport. Similarly, although the Benefits Agency costs £2 billion to run and distributes over £50 billion in benefits, the structure and levels of benefits and the agency's objectives are set by the Department of Social Security - the agency is one adviser among many.

Source: Thain 1993.

Item C Brick's view

Item B Setting up a Next Steps agency

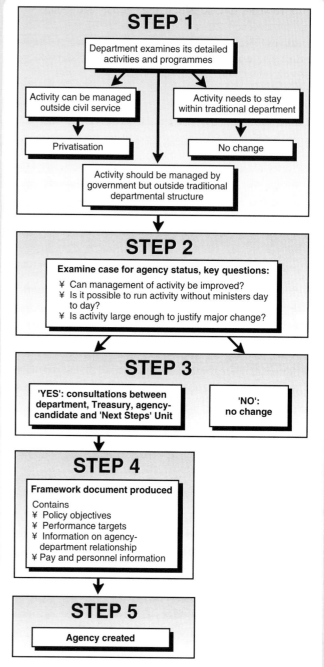

Source: Pyper 1992.

Questions

1. a) Judging from Items A and B: (i) what is the Next Steps initiative; (ii) how does it work; and (iii) what are its benefits and drawbacks?
   b) Explain why the Next Steps initiative has been described as 'the most far-reaching reform of the civil service in the 20th century'.
2. What does Item C tell us about the way in which the civil service has changed since 1979?

16.14 The Labour government and civil service reform since 1997

During its 18 years in Opposition, the Labour leadership criticised the civil service reforms introduced by the Conservatives. There were complaints that constant change and cost-cutting was destroying morale in the civil service. Commercial values and private sector practices, it was argued, were undermining the public service ethos.

Although there was some concern that the civil service was being 'politicised', civil servants were expected to serve a Labour government loyally, if such a government was elected:

'The main issue is not that they have given partisan advice to suit Tory ministers' prejudices but that, very often, they have not been asked for their advice at all…there is no evidence that they will be unenthusiastic servants of a Labour government - quite the contrary. It would therefore be wrong and unjust for new ministers to come into office with a hit list of senior civil servants they want to remove…good civil servants will be useful to Labour ministers…in asking frank questions about new policies, seeking clear departmental goals, clarifying the precise aims of a policy…and drawing up the criteria for its success.' (Mandelson and Liddle 1996, p.247-48)

Some Labour politicians predicted that senior civil servants would actually be relieved to see a change of government in 1997. According to Drewry, this prediction was accurate. Following the 1997 election, 'the sense of relief throughout Whitehall was almost palpable', even if formal neutrality 'meant that any celebrations had to be private and muted' (Drewry 1999, p.156).

Despite the criticism before the 1997 general election, the Blair government has not just maintained and consolidated the Conservatives' civil service reforms, it has extended them - see Box 16.14.

Box 16.14 The Labour government and civil service reforms

Once in office, Labour continued the managerial changes launched by its Conservative predecessors, as well as putting its own stamp on the structure and management of the civil service. The new government made it clear that Next Steps agencies - relabelled as 'executive agencies' - were a key part of the government machine, although there was to be a greater emphasis on target setting and performance. The Blair government continued to show the Major government's commitment to market testing and contracting-out, as long as these could show best value for money. It also accepted the Major government's policy of selling central government assets to the private sector. For example, the Department of Social Security's property estate (including 700 local benefit offices), 740 computer systems and the Benefits Agency Medical Services were sold off to the private sector in August 1997. The Major government's Private Finance Initiative was relaunched and used to finance a number of government department projects - for example the computerisation of the Passport Agency.

Source: *Guardian*, 1 August 1997 and Butcher 2004.

Special Advisers

Just a few months after the 1997 general election, some ministers began to complain about the quality of advice being provided by senior civil servants:

'After an initial honeymoon with the civil service, Labour ministers have begun questioning the quality of the briefings they are being given by officials. Some have criticised "Tory holdovers" and have complained that officials have not adjusted to Labour ways of thinking.' (*Independent on Sunday*, 14 September 1997)

It was partly because of dissatisfaction with the nature or quality of advice that they were receiving that the appointment of Special Advisers became more commonplace under the Blair governments. Ministers viewed Special Advisers as an additional or alternative source of ideas and policy advice, believing that they might prove more creative or original in their thinking than long-serving senior civil servants, who might be wedded to a particular departmental philosophy.

This influx of Special Advisers, however, has raised concerns that senior civil servants are sometimes being bypassed by ministers, and that policy decisions are sometimes being taken without the impartial or expert advice traditionally provided by senior civil servants.

From Citizen's Charter to 'Service First'

Although the Citizen's Charter had been criticised at the time of its launch, by the time that Labour came to power in 1997 elements of the scheme had proved highly popular. In particular, the awarding of Charter Marks for the provision of high quality public services gained public support (nominations from the public rose from 4,000 in 1995, the year the scheme was launched, to 25,000 in 1997).

In June 1998, however, the government announced that the Citizen's Charter programme would be replaced by the 'Service First' programme. The new scheme would differ from the old in that: 'The success of each organisation will be judged on the views of those who use it rather than on how fast it can answer the telephone or reply to letters' (*Times*, 30 June 1998). Yet this still meant that the emphasis was on the quality of service provided, for only if they felt that they were receiving a good standard of service or response would the public express favourable views about the delivery of public services.

Freedom of information

Before the 1997 general election, concerns about Labour's proposed constitutional reforms were raised both by members of the Labour leadership and by senior civil servants. Shadow ministers were worried that senior officials would block the reforms or try to water them down. Senior civil servants, on the other hand, were worried that a Freedom of Information Act might affect their traditional anonymity (if the public gained access to ministerial papers, for example). By the autumn of 1998, this matter had been resolved - see Box 16.15 on page 331.

The 1999 White Paper *Modernising Government*

The publication, in March 1998, of a White Paper entitled *Modernising Government* showed that the Labour government

Box 16.15 The watering down of the Freedom of Information Bill

In the reshuffle of July 1998, the minister responsible for the Freedom of Information Bill, David Clark, was sacked and responsibility for the Bill was handed over to the Home Office. Then, on 30 September 1998, it was announced that freedom of information legislation would not be included in the next Queen's Speech because David Clark's draft Bill needed more work on it. This was widely interpreted as a victory for senior officials reluctant to open up the machinery of state to public scrutiny. Certainly, one 'Whitehall correspondent' reported that anxious senior civil servants in the Home Office were determined to water down the Labour Party's original proposals. It was not only civil servants who were concerned, however. A number of Cabinet ministers were worried about the implications for their own departments of having to make publicly available information which had previously been kept secret. It has also been suggested that the decision to water down the legislation was taken by Tony Blair. After the Freedom of Information Act was passed in 2000, it was announced that it would not be fully implemented until 2005. The wording of the Act ensured that a wide range of government activities would remain secret and confidential.

Source: Hencke 1999, Rawnsley 2000 and Dorey 2003.

was determined to continue with the reform of the civil service:

'The White Paper promised to develop a civil service for the 21st century, stating that the civil service needed incentives to provide innovation and excellent service delivery. There was a need to create a less risk-averse culture. The White Paper pledged to bring in more outsiders to the civil service and to make greater use of short-term contracts.' (Butcher 2004, p.88)

The Wilson Report (1999)

The civil service's response to the *Modernising Government* White Paper was provided by the then Cabinet Secretary and Head of the Home Civil Service, Richard Wilson, who wrote a report published in 1999. The 'Wilson Report' (as it became known) contained the six main themes outlined in Box 16.16.

While some people welcomed the Wilson Report on the grounds that it would transform the civil service. Others were critical:

'Critics expressed anxieties about the further injection of business-oriented values, arguing that the Civil Service Reform Programme's concern with greater efficiency and value for money took insufficient account of the public service ethos. There were also fears that the traditional characteristics of civil service permanence and unity would be eroded.' (Butcher 2004, pp.88-89)

Within a year of the Wilson Report's publication, there had been an increase of almost 50% in the number of appointments to the Senior Civil Service from 'open competition', with nearly 66% of the posts subsequently filled

Box 16.16 The six main themes in the Wilson Report

1. Stronger leadership with a clear sense of purpose.
2. Better business planning from top to bottom.
3. Sharper performance management.
4. A dramatic improvement in diversity (ie recruiting and promoting more women, black and Asian people, and people with disabilities).
5. A service more open to people and ideas, which brings on talent.
6. A better deal for staff.

by outsiders (Butcher 2002, p.30). It should be noted, however, that these percentages start from a low base point and that resistance to change remained commonplace. Shortly before the 2001 general election, Wilson reported that good progress was being made with reform, but there was no room for complacency:

'The number of senior management posts going out to open competition had increased by nearly a half, with almost two-thirds of those posts being filled by outsiders. A new pay and performance management system for officials in the Senior Civil Service, which would enable the best-performing officials at the top to be given significant bonuses was being introduced...Despite these and other developments, however, Wilson admitted that there was still "a lot to do".'

According to Butcher (2004), the government agreed with Wilson was there was 'a lot to do'. Indeed, Butcher claims, the government was becoming increasingly frustrated at the slow pace of reform. A turning point was the outbreak of the foot-and-mouth epidemic in early 2001 - see Box 16.17.

Box 16.17 The foot-and-mouth epidemic

A major factor in Labour's resolve to give civil service reform higher priority was the inadequacies of the civil service revealed in the run-up to the 2001 general election by the failure of senior officials at the Ministry of Agriculture, Food and Fisheries (MAFF) to deal with the foot-and-mouth outbreak. The first case of the disease had been confirmed in February 2001 and it was not until January 2002 that the UK was declared free of the disease. The handling of the epidemic revealed a government department - MAFF - suffering from incompetence as an institution as a whole. It also revealed a fragmented civil service incapable (at least in the early stages) of providing a joined-up response to match the scale of the crisis. There was a series of bureaucratic failures which not only reduced the UK's capacity to deal with the crisis, it actually made the crisis worse than it should have been.

Source: Butcher 2004.

Andrew Turnbull succeeds Sir Richard Wilson

Richard Wilson retired as Cabinet Secretary in September 2002. Before retiring, he expressed concern that the Senior Civil Service was being politicised, and that the influx of Special Advisers was causing confusion between the roles and responsibilities of these advisers and those of the civil servants they worked alongside. He called for a Civil Service Act which would provide a statutory definition of the role and responsibilities of civil servants. Such an Act, he claimed, would 'clarify the grey boundaries between what is and what is not acceptable, as well as the boundaries between government and party'.

Richard Wilson was replaced by Andrew Turnbull who had been a civil servant since 1970 (the post was not externally advertised). Turnbull immediately made clear his intention of continuing with the programme of civil service reform and modernisation, emphasising that the primary focus would continue to be on the efficient administration, management and delivery of public services. To this end, he announced the creation of a special 'reform and delivery team' of senior civil servants to be located within the Cabinet Office, whose role would be to oversee the delivery of the government's public service reforms, and possibly cut the bonuses paid to Permanent Secretaries who failed to meet their particular targets.

In a letter (www.civil-service.net/sirandrewturnbull) to civil servants, Turnbull emphasised that his priority in the years 2002-05 would be to accelerate the pace of reform in the civil service, so that the civil service of 2005 would have the qualities outlined in Box 16.18.

Box 16.18 Turnbull's goals for 2005

The civil service will:

- be respected as much for its ability to deliver as for its policy skills
- be able to develop long-term plans, and then make sure they worked
- be a civil service which young people, and people who were successful in other walks of life, would want to join and work in
- be valued by the public for:
  * the quality of the services it delivered
  * its integrity and trust
  * its impartiality, and readiness to serve all governments and citizens
  * its use of merit as the criterion of recruitment and promotion
  * the extent to which its social composition reflected that of the society which it served.

Modernisation momentum maintained

In a letter to civil service staff written in 2003, Andrew Turnbull outlined four particular objectives which the civil service needed to pursue in order to maintain the momentum of modernisation and improve public service delivery (Cabinet Office, 2003). Civil service staff were told to:

- put customers first
- improve and develop a wider range of delivery skills

- continue to develop the relationships with local public services, and devolve more decision-making powers to local-level managers, while also increasing the incentives for improved performances
- develop strong leadership through the improvement of training or/and the identification of talent and relevant experience.

To maintain the momentum of this modernisation programme, a seminar on civil service reform was held in February 2004, at which senior civil servants (along with other people and bodies - from the private, public and voluntary sectors - involved in public service delivery) were addressed by both Turnbull and Tony Blair. In his address to the seminar, Tony Blair outlined what he believed were 'seven

Box 16.19 Tony Blair's 'seven keys' to civil service modernisation

1. A smaller, strategic centre.
2. A civil service with professional and specialist skills.
3. A civil service open to the public, private and voluntary sectors, and encouraging interaction and interchange between them.
4. More rapid promotion within the civil service, as well as more fixed-term contracts for senior posts.
5. Improved leadership skills and strategic management.
6. A more strategic and innovative approach to policy.
7. Government organised around problems, not problems around government.

keys to the transformation of the Civil Service' (Blair, 2004). These are listed in Box 16.19.

After the seminar, it was announced that, as a step towards 'a smaller, strategic centre', 80,000 civil service jobs would be cut. The aim was to yield financial savings which could then be devoted to the direct delivery of front-line public services (*Times*, 24 February 2004). This move was also probably partly prompted by an announcement by the Conservatives, the previous week, that a future Conservative government would slash spending on state bureaucracy in order to release billions of pounds for investment in public services such as health and education (*Independent on Sunday*, 15 February 2004).

The commitment to reducing bureaucracy was also a theme in Gordon Brown's 2004 Budget. In that Budget, it was announced that some government departments would be obliged to secure a 5% reduction in staff levels to free-up resources for key public services, most notably education and health. The idea was that money saved on civil servants' salaries could then be spent on more 'front-line staff', such as teachers, nurses and doctors, with the result that a real improvement in 'service delivery' would seen and experienced by members of the public.

Main points **Section 16.14**

- Although the Labour leadership criticised the Conservatives' reforms in Opposition , they retained and extended them after the Labour election victory in May 1997.
- The emphasis has remained on increasing efficiency and improving service delivery.
- There has also been a continued shift in the role of senior civil servants, with greater emphasis being placed on the management and delivery of

public services, rather than providing policy advice for ministers (although they do still do this as well).
- Attempts have been made to widen recruitment to the Senior Civil Service (through open competition, for example), in the hope of making it more socially representative, while also exposing the Senior Civil Service to a wider range of ideas and experiences from the 'real world'.

Activity 16.4 New Labour's civil service reforms

Item A Performance-related government

Tough new standards are to be imposed on Britain's public services in what the government is describing as 'performance related government'. In December 1998, the Treasury will announce more than 100 separate annual targets for individual Whitehall ministries, agencies and cross-departmental initiatives. Ministers believe that an electorate opposed to higher taxes can be persuaded to support funds for public services such as health and education if there is this new form of public accountability. Departments will be expected to meet their targets by April 2002, the end of the three-year period for which Treasury funding is guaranteed. Meanwhile, they will be expected to measure annual progress towards targets and publish a report setting out the relevant statistics. Ministers believe that this process will raise standards across the public sector. While extra cash will be given to departments which perform well, the Treasury will provide managerial advice on improving performance to those which fail. The Chief Secretary to the Treasury, Stephen Byers, will require independent government agencies (eg Inland Revenue and the Forestry Commission) to publish their own targets. Expected targets include a Foreign Office requirement to secure 250,000 extra jobs through inward investment, a Home Office goal of cutting car crime by a third in three years, and a Health Department objective of reducing cancer. Controversially, the Department of Social Security may be required to cut relative poverty.

Source: The *Observer*, 8 November 1998.

Item B Contrasts in civil service career profiles and qualities

Yesterday's success story	Tomorrow's equivalent
• Joined straight from university for life	• Joined at a variety of entry points, moving easily between different sectors
• Committed to the civil service	• Committed to public service
• Core values of integrity and impartiality	• Core values of integrity, impartiality and delivery
• Fast stream training	• Career-long development and learning
• Deployed ad hoc where talent needed	• Deployed around a career anchor, using and building talent
• Almost exclusively working in policy and ministerial support roles	• Varying roles between operations, policy, specialist skills and ministerial support
• Follows precedent	• Creates precedents
• Widens experience by short secondment within public sector	• Widens experience by taking a private sector role
• Scholarship to study social policy in US	• Career break to look after elderly parents
• Aims to lead the development of a major policy area	• Aims to deliver the outcomes of a major policy area
• Permanent Secretary - the minister's senior policy adviser	• Permanent Secretary - the minister's senior delivery agent and policy adviser

Source: Cabinet Office 2004, p.28.

Questions

1. Does Item A provide evidence of continuity with or change from the previous Conservative government? Explain your answer.

2. Judging from Item B, how does the 'new' civil service differ from the 'old' civil service?

16.15 The relationship between ministers and civil servants

According to Norton, the civil service is a:

'Well-oiled machine, manned by public servants of integrity and serving loyally successive governments of whatever political persuasion.' (Norton 1989, p.82)

The role of the minister is to determine the policies of the government. The role of civil servants is to advise ministers on how best to implement those policies which they wish to introduce.

In principle, therefore, both ministers and civil servants are motivated by a sense of public duty and a genuine desire to act in the public interest. Both ministers and civil servants know their place and the role they should play. Civil servants brief ministers impartially and objectively. Ministers listen carefully to what their civil servants have to say and make decisions after weighing up this advice. Civil servants expect the minister in charge of their department to fight courageously for funds and to defend the actions of the department in public. Ministers expect to be kept informed of what is happening in the department and they expect civil servants to implement, with a good grace, decisions with which they disagree. Although ministers are members of a political party, they would never dream of asking their civil servants to undertake party political matters. Similarly, whatever their personal views, civil servants would never act in a partisan manner.

In practice, a number of factors affect the relationship between ministers and their civil servants, and often imply that senior civil servants have the upper hand. These factors are described in Box 16.20.

Box 16.20 Factors suggesting civil servants have the upper hand

A. Ministers have limited information

Ministers may have little knowledge of the area covered by their departments. On taking up their new post, they do not see the papers of their predecessors, but are supplied with a briefing document by their officials. From the outset, therefore, there is the chance for civil servants to shape the way in which ministers view their job.

B. Ministers have other commitments

Ministers have other commitments - in Parliament and in their constituencies, for example. They, therefore, have less time to devote to decision-making than their full-time officials. For this reason, they rely on the experience and administrative expertise of their civil servants. Often, this advice is shaped by the internal culture of the department. Senior civil servants will often have been steeped in this internal culture for many years. Headey quotes one Permanent Secretary who said:

'In effect, it was just a question of getting my ministers to take on board policies that we had in hand anyway. Of the six ministers I worked with closely, it would be hard to say that any of them made even a minor contribution to policy.' (Headey 1974, p.109)

It should be noted, however, that this quote comes from the 1970s, before the civil service reforms instigated by Margaret Thatcher (and continued by Tony Blair) had been enacted. Since the late 1970s, more Cabinet ministers seem to have adopted a more activist, innovator or 'commander' role with regard to policy development.

C. Civil servants outnumber ministers

Civil servants outnumber ministers. There are about ten civil servants for every one minister in the top policy-making grades and 40 civil servants to every one minister if all civil servants who make an input into policy-making are included. If all these officials take a similar line, this adds weight to the line taken.

D. Top civil servants meet by themselves

Although civil servants outnumber ministers, there is still a sufficiently small number of permanent secretaries at the top of the hierarchy (about 40 in all) for them to meet together often both formally and socially. A permanent secretary having 'problems' with a minister might, therefore, be able to persuade a colleague in another government department to persuade a more compliant minister to put pressure on the minister causing the 'problems'. In this way, top civil servants might be able to agree upon and engineer certain policies.

E. Time spent with civil servants

Ministers spend more time with civil servants than they do with other politicians. There is time, therefore, for civil servants to apply pressure.

F. Avoidance tactics

Civil servants often outlast ministers and can use various tactics to avoid having to implement a policy they do not like. According to Norton (1989), there are three ways in which civil servants can reverse a minister's decision. First, they can wait for a change of ministers - new ministers may be open to the advice they are offering. Second, they can brief officials in other departments to ensure that their ministers are primed to oppose the minister's decision (as suggested above). Or third, they can leak a document to the media in the hope that this will undermine the minister's credibility.

16.16 Accounts of civil service power

Political scientists and politicians themselves have traditionally held one of three views about the power and operation of the Senior Civil Service in Britain.

A. The orthodox view

The orthodox approach is to accept that civil servants work impartially, conscientiously and professionally, serving ministers irrespective of the political complexion of the government. Moderate Labour and Conservative politicians have generally supported this benign view of Britain's civil service, seeing mandarins overall as faithful public servants, providing their political masters with advice and information, but then loyally carrying out the instructions of their political masters when ministers have finally made up their mind.

The orthodox approach sees the civil service as faithfully serving any government which has democratically secured a parliamentary majority through the ballot box in a free and fair general election. In this respect, they really are civil servants, faithfully serving their political masters (ministers), who are themselves answerable to Parliament, which in turn - via the House of Commons - is answerable to the British people via general elections.

Not surprisingly, this is precisely the view of the civil service which senior civil servants themselves generally express. The views of three former ministers and a Permanent Secretary who support the orthodox approach are given in Box 16.21.

Box 16.21 The orthodox approach

1. **Former Conservative Prime Minister, Edward Heath**
'Civil servants like to be under ministerial control. There is nothing they dislike more than to have a minister whom they feel is weak, who does not know his mind and who wants to leave it all to them…What they like is to have a minister who knows a policy he wants to pursue.' (quoted in Barberis 1996, p.83)

2. **Former Labour Cabinet minister, Denis Healey**
'The minister who complains that his civil servants are too powerful is either a weak minister or an incompetent one.' (quoted in Barberis 1996, p.81)

3. **Former Labour minister, Gerald Kaufman**
'Only bad ministers blame the civil service, because only bad ministers let themselves be dominated by the civil service.' (Kaufman 1997a, p.13)

4. **Former Permanent Secretary, Brian Hayes**
'Power stems from the people and flows through Parliament to the minister responsible to Parliament. The civil servant has no power of his own. He is there to help a minister and to be the minister's agent…I think the job of the civil servant is to make sure that his minister is informed; that he has all the facts; that he's made aware of all the options…It is then for the minister to take the decision. That is how the system ought to operate and that is how…in the vast majority of cases it does operate.' (quoted in Young and Sloman 1982, pp.20-21)

B. The Left's view

Left-wingers tend to view the civil service as a conservative institution. They suggest that, as a result, civil servants have tended to be sceptical about Labour governments and mandarins have sometimes been hostile towards some of their policies. Left-wingers complain about the secrecy which the Senior Civil Service usually insists upon - on the grounds that it is at odds with Britain's claim to be a democratic society. They also complain about the narrow social and educational background of most senior civil servants. With many, if not most, of them having traditionally received an Oxbridge education (and quite possibly having attended a public school prior to this), left-wingers accuse the Senior Civil Service of being unrepresentative of the British people whom it is supposed to serve because it is overwhelmingly white, male, late-middle-aged, upper-middle class and élite-educated. This socio-educational background is alleged both to reflect and reinforce the apparent conservatism of the Senior Civil Service.

This perspective underpins a more general complaint by the Left, namely that the Senior Civil Service in Britain has often enjoyed too much power, particularly in its ability to obstruct or undermine the policies of 'democratically-elected governments' - particularly when these happen to be Labour governments.

Views from the Left are given in Box 16.22.

Box 16.22 Views from the Left

1. **Marcia Williams (Political Secretary to the former Labour Prime Minister Harold Wilson)**
'While politically, [senior civil servants] are said to have no direct affiliation to a political party, their whole background is so conservative in origin that their inclinations must be more to the Right than to the Left.' (Williams 1972, p.353)

2. **Tony Benn, a former Labour Cabinet minister during the 1970s**
'[Because] most senior civil servants come from a very narrow class base, [they are invariably] broadly ignorant of, and unsympathetic to, the aspirations of socialism.' (Benn 1989, p.135)

3. **Professor Ralph Miliband**
'The majority of them are the products of middle- and upper-class homes, with a public school and Oxford or Cambridge education. [They are invariably] socialised into conformity by their careers in the civil service, and would not get very far if they did not…acquire, if they did not have already, the right kind of ideas and attitudes.' (Miliband 1984, p.103)

For left-wingers, this alleged conservatism of senior civil servants partly accounts for the failure of Labour governments historically to implement socialist policies. Labour's more radical policies have, it is claimed, either been watered down by the civil service, or abandoned altogether in the face of civil service opposition.

C. The New Right's view

From the 1970s onwards, the New Right developed its own criticisms of Britain's civil service, and these subsequently shaped the reforms implemented by the Thatcher-Major governments from 1979 to 1997. A key concern of the New Right was that the civil service was a self-serving bureaucracy which had an inherent interest in maximising its budgets and programmes.

This particular objection was part of the 'public choice' school which informed parts of the New Right's politics from the 1970s onwards. As one academic expert on the New Right explains, public choice theorists hold that:

> 'The very essence of bureaucrats is that they are self-interested budget-maximisers, and the pursuit of this self-interest results in the expansion of government... Bureaucrats attempt to maximise the budget of their bureau or department.' (King 1987, p.102-3)

Following on from this, the New Right viewed the civil service as both a cause and a consequence of the expansion of the state in post-war Britain. Successive governments, they argue, intervened - 'interfered' - in more and more areas of economic and social life, resulting in an ever-expanding bureaucracy. With the New Right and Margaret Thatcher committed to 'rolling back the state', the civil service clearly became a prime target for cuts and reforms.

The New Right was also critical of the civil service's alleged 'conservatism' and lack of innovation, characterising it as 'risk-averse'. Intellectually and organisationally, they argued, it was ill-equipped to provide solutions to the economic and social problems affecting Britain in the 1970s and 1980s. Arguments like these were used by those surrounding Margaret Thatcher, and they helped to shape the economic and social reforms which Thatcherites wanted to implement during the 1980s - see Box 16.23.

Box 16.23   John Hoskyns

One of Margaret Thatcher's closest advisers and, for a time, Head of the Policy Unit in Ten Downing Street was John Hoskyns. In his biography of Margaret Thatcher, Hugo Young wrote:

> '[John Hoskyns'] early contacts with the [civil service] machine...did nothing to make him reassess his expectations...Officials were just as negative, pessimistic and failure-bound as he had always thought: A fearsome picture was soon summoned in his mind. He saw the phalanxes of officials like American footballers, heavy-weight line-blockers, [dressed up] in their padding and helmets to withstand every attack. Every positive proposal which shook the conventional wisdom...was likely, Hosykns and his Leader thought, to meet with an instinctive strategy of obstruction from the blinkered asses of Whitehall...There was a genuine clash of cultures between a political leadership fired by an...impatience with the status quo, and the mandarin world of Whitehall, in which scepticism and rumination were more highly rated habits of mind than zeal or blind conviction.' (Young 1989, pp.155 & 157-58)

16.17   *Power as relational and variable*

Recently, though, a number of political scientists have developed a more subtle or nuanced view of the relationship

between senior civil servants and ministers. Instead of seeing power as somehow fixed or 'zero-sum' (where more for one means correspondingly less for the other), the power relationship is seen as one which not only varies according to the people and issues involved, but also entails mutual dependency. In other words, ministers and senior civil servants need each other. Each has certain resources (expertise, political authority, support networks, alliances, contacts, objectives) which need to be shared or exchanged in order for policies to be successfully pursued. According to this view, while not denying the scope for occasional conflict or disagreement, the relationship between ministers and senior civil servants should be seen, not as adversarial, but as symbiotic:

> 'Power has to be seen as fluid and relational, not static. In that sense, power does not lie anywhere within the system because it is everywhere - all actors have resources, and outcomes need to be negotiated.' (Smith 1999, p.14)

This view is supported by former civil servant, Clive Ponting:

> 'The question of where power lies between ministers and civil servants inside Whitehall can never be answered satisfactorily. The dividing line depends on so many things: the political strength and intellect of the individual minister, the type of decisions being taken, the amount of administrative detail involved, the level of political interest in the outcome of the decision, and the personal relationships between the individuals. All these factors mean that boundaries of power are fluctuating continuously.' (Ponting 1986, p.14)

Main points   Sections 16.15 - 16.17

- **The relationship between ministers and civil servants has always been a subject of debate and disagreement, with many writers and politicians complaining about the alleged power of the civil service.**
- **It has often been argued that civil servants have advantages which give them the upper hand in their relationship with ministers.**
- **The Left has often complained that the élitist background of many senior civil servants ensures that they are conservative and therefore unsympathetic to the aims of Labour governments, as well as unable to relate to the lives of ordinary people.**
- **The New Right has also complained about the conservatism of the Senior Civil Service, claiming that it lacks the innovation and creativity found in the private sector. It is also said to be a self-serving, budget-maximising institution, which needs to be exposed to 'market principles'.**
- **Recent 'core executive' studies have advanced a more subtle theory of the relationship between ministers and civil servants, arguing that power is not fixed in the sense that ministers dominate civil servants or vice versa, but is shared and exchanged. Ministers and civil servants, therefore have a symbiotic relationship.**

Activity 16.5 The relationship between ministers and civil servants

Item A Civil service power vs ministerial power

Civil service power	Ministerial power
Numbers - about 1,000 senior civil servants directly involved in policy-making, compared to less than 100 ministers and junior ministers.	Authority - ministers take final decision, in accordance with government's objectives, and ultimately have political authority.
Time - civil servants devote their whole working-week to their departments; ministers have to divide their time between several roles and places.	Time - a good minister can often grasp the key policy issues relatively quickly. Also, time spent on other political duties can give ministers a broader view: they can see the wood for the trees, which civil servants might lose sight of.
Permanence and experience - senior civil servants are often permanent, having spent their professional lives in a department, and acquiring immense expertise. Ministers are temporary, and not usually policy experts.	Political support - ministers often have the support of the Prime Minister, Cabinet colleagues, and their party's MPs. They may also be able to cite public opinion in support of particular policy proposals.
Monopoly of advice & information - ministers are heavily dependent on the advice and expertise of their senior civil servants in developing policies.	Independent advice & information - ministers can (and increasingly do) seek advice from other sources: Special Advisers, pressure groups, party and Cabinet colleagues, for example.
Professionalism and education - senior civil servants are professionals, most of whom have received a university education, and then been trained for their career.	Professionalism and education - ministers are also professionals, with virtually all of them now university-educated. Their years spent in their party at constituency and parliamentary levels is itself a form of training, and perhaps provides political knowledge which civil servants do not possess.
Departmental support - senior civil servants normally have the backing of their department vis-à-vis a minister.	Political longevity and experience - ministers may well have served many years, or even decades, as an MP and minister, and have a greater understanding of the 'real world' outside Whitehall.

Source: Budge, Crewe, McKay & Newton 2004, p.151.

Item B Interdependency between ministers and senior civil servants

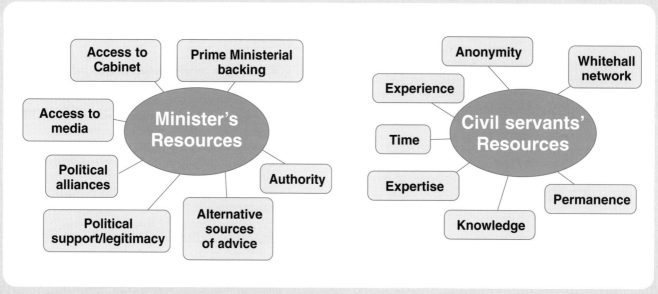

Source: Smith 1999, p.118 and Smith 2003, p.63.

Item C The minister's workload

Questions

1. a) Using Items A and B describe what powers and resources are available to senior civil servants and ministers respectively.

   b) Do you think that the relationship between senior civil servants and ministers is one of dominance or mutual dependency? Give reasons for your answer.

2. 'Civil servants have too much power.' Using Items A-C give arguments for and against this view.

3. Using Items A-C and your own knowledge, explain why the relationships between ministers and senior civil servants vary, with some enjoying a more constructive or harmonious relationship than others.

References

Bayliss & Dargie (1998) Bayliss, R., & Dargie, C., 'The Senior Civil Service in the 1990s' in *Lancaster (1998)*.

Barberis (1996) Barberis, P. (ed.), *The Whitehall Reader*, Open University Press, 1996.

Benn (1989) Benn, T., 'Obstacles to reform in Britain' in *Miliband, Panitch & Saville (1989)*.

Blackburn & Plant (1999) Blackburn, R. & Plant R. (eds) *Constitutional Reform: the Labour Government's Constitutional Reform Agenda*, Longman, 1999.

Blair (2004) Blair, T., Speech at seminar on civil service reform, 24 February 2004, Cabinet Office, www.civil-service.gov.uk/reform, 2004.

Blick (2004) Blick, A., *People Who Live in the Dark: the History of the Special Adviser in British Politics*, Politico's. 2004.

Budge, Crewe, McKay & Newton (2004) Budge, I., Crewe, I., McKay, D. & Newton, K., *The New British Politics*, third edition, Pearson Longman, 2004.

Butcher (2002) Butcher, T., 'The civil service under New Labour', *Politics Review*, Vol.11.3, 2002.

Butcher (2004) Butcher, T., 'The Civil Service under the Blair Government' in *Lancaster (2004)*.

Cabinet Office (2001a) Cabinet Office, *Ministerial Code: a Code of Conduct and Guidance on Procedures for Ministers*, Cabinet Office, 2003.

Cabinet Office (2001b) Cabinet Office, *Code of Conduct for Special Advisers*, Cabinet Office, 2001.

Cabinet Office (2003) Cabinet Office, *Letter to Staff from Sir Andrew Turnbull*, September, Cabinet Office, 2003.

Cabinet Office (2004) Cabinet Office, *Civil Service Reform: Delivery and Values*, Cabinet Office, 2004.

Clark (1993) Clark, A., *Diaries*, Wiedenfeld & Nicholson, 1993.

Dorey (2003) Dorey, P., 'Half-baked and Half-hearted: The Blair governments and Constitutional Reform' in *Lancaster (2003)*.

Drewry (1999) Drewry, G., 'The civil service' in *Blackburn & Plant (1999)*.

Drewry & Butcher (1991) Drewry, G. & Butcher, T., *The Civil Service Today*, second edition, Blackwell, 1991.

Dunleavy et al. (1997) Dunleavy, P., Gamble, A., Holliday, I. & Peele, G., *Developments in British Politics 5*, Macmillan, 1997.

Dunleavy et al. (2003) Dunleavy, P., Gamble, A., Heffernan, R. & Peele, G. (eds), *Developments in Politics 7*, Palgrave, 2003.

Flynn, Gray & Jenkins (1990) Flynn, A., Gray, A., and Jenkins, W., 'Taking the Next Steps: the changing management of government', *Parliamentary Affairs*, 43.2, 1990.

Garnett (2004) Garnett, M., 'A feeling of resignation', *Politics Review*, February, 2004.

Garrett (1980) Garrett, J., *Managing the Civil Service*, Heinemann, 1980.

Greer (1994) Greer, P., *Transforming Central Government: the Next Steps Initiative*, Open University Press, 1994.

Headey (1974) Headey, B., *British Cabinet Ministers*, Allen and Unwin, 1974.

Hencke (1999) Hencke, D., 'House of straw that Jack built', *Guardian* 21 June, 1999.

Hennessy (2001) Hennessy, P., *Whitehall*, Pimlico, 2001.

HMSO (1988) Efficiency Unit, *Improving Management in Government: the Next Steps* (Report to the Prime Minister), HMSO, 1988.

HMSO (1994) Central Office of Information, *The British System of Government*, HMSO, 1994.

HMSO (1999) HMSO, *Modernising Government*, Cm 4310, 1999.

Hood & James (1997) Hood, C. & James, O., 'The Central Executive' in *Dunleavy et al. (1997)*.

James (1999) James, S., *British Cabinet Government*, second edition, Routledge, 1999.

Jones (2002) Jones, A., 'Special Advisers and the demise of Sir Humphrey?', *Talking Politics*, September, 2002.

Kaufman (1996) Kaufman, G., 'Master of arts', *Talking Politics*, Vol.8.3, 1996.

Kaufman (1997a) Kaufman, G., *How to be a Minister*, Faber, 1997.

Kaufman (1997b) Kaufman, G., 'How to be a minister', *Politics Review*, Vol.7.1, 1997.

Kavanagh & Seldon (1994) Kavanagh, D, & Seldon, A., *The Major Effect*, Macmillan, 1994.

Kellner & Crowther-Hunt (1980) Kellner, P. & Crowther-Hunt, Lord, *The Civil Servants: An Inquiry into Britain's Ruling Class*, Macdonald, 1980.

King (1987) King, D., *The New Right: Politics, Markets and Citizenship*, Macmillan, 1987.

Lancaster (1998) Lancaster, S. (ed.), *Developments in Politics: an Annual Review*, Vol.9, Causeway Press, 1998.

Lancaster (2003) Lancaster, S. (ed.), *Developments in Politics: an Annual Review*, Vol.14, Causeway Press, 2003.

Lancaster (2004) Lancaster, S. (ed.), *Developments in Politics: an Annual Review*, Vol.15, Causeway Press, 2004.

Madgwick (1991) Madgwick, P., *British Government: The Central Executive Territory*, Philip Allan, 1991.

Mandelson & Liddle (1996) Mandelson, P. & Liddle, R., *The Blair Revolution: Can New Labour Deliver?*, Faber, 1996.

Marsh, Richards & Smith (2001) Marsh, D., Richards, D. & Smith, M. J., *Changing Patterns of Governance in the United Kingdom*, Palgrave, 2001.

Miliband (1984) Miliband, R., *Capitalist Democracy in Britain*, Oxford University Press, 1984.

Miliband, Panitch & Saville (1989) Miliband, R., Panitch, L. & Saville, J. (eds.), *Socialist Register 1989*, Merlin, 1989.

Norton (1989) Norton, P., *The Constitution in Flux*, Blackwell, 1989.

Norton (2000) Norton, P. 'Barons in a Shrinking Kingdom' in *Rhodes (2000)*.

Plowden (1994) Plowden, W., *Ministers and Mandarins*, Institute for Public Policy Research, 1994.

Ponting (1986) Ponting, C., *Whitehall: Tragedy and Farce*, Sphere, 1986.

Pyper (1991) Pyper, R., 'Ministerial departures from British governments, 1964-90: a survey', *Contemporary Record*, Vol.5.2, 1991.

Pyper (1992) Pyper, R., 'A new model civil service?', *Politics Review*, Vol.2.2, November 1992.

Pyper (1995) Pyper, R., *The British Civil Service*, Prentice Hall/Harvester Wheatsheaf, 1995.

Pyper & Robins (2000) Pyper, R. & Robins, L. (eds), *United Kingdom Governance*, Macmillan, 2000.

Rawnsley (2000) Rawnsley, A., *Servants of the People: The Inside Story of New Labour*, Hamish Hamilton, 2000.

Rhodes (2000) Rhodes, R.A.W. (ed.), *Transforming British Government: Volume Two: Changing Roles and Relationships*, Macmillan, 2000.

Ridley (1986) Ridley, F., 'Political neutrality in the civil service', *Social Studies Review*, Vol.1.4, March 1986.

Rush (2000) Rush, M. 'Parliamentary Scrutiny' in R. Pyper and L. Robins (eds), *United Kingdom Governance*, Macmillan, 2000.

Simpson (1998) Simpson, D., *UK Government and Politics in Context*, Hodder and Stoughton, 1998.

Smith (1999) Smith, M. J., *The Core Executive in Britain*, Macmillan, 1999.

Smith (2003) Smith, M. J., 'The core executive and the modernization of central government' in *Dunleavy et al (2003)*.

Thain (1993) Thain, C., 'The core executive and central government under John Major' in *Wale (1993)*.

Thain & Wright (1995) Thain, C. & Wright, M., *The Treasury and Whitehall*, Oxford University Press, 1995.

Thatcher (1993) Thatcher, M., *The Downing Street Years*, Harper Collins, 1993.

Theakston (1987) Theakston, K., *Junior Ministers in British Government*, Blackwell, 1987.

Theakston (1999) Theakston, K., 'Junior ministers in the 1990s', *Parliamentary Affairs*, Vol.52.2, 1999.

Theakston (2000) Theakston, K., 'Ministers and Civil Servants' in *Pyper & Robins (2000)*.

Wale (1993) Wale, W. (ed.), *Developments in Politics*, Vol.4, Causeway Press, 1993.

Williams (1972) Williams, M., *Inside No.10*, Weidenfeld & Nicolson, 1972.

Willman (1994) Willman, J., 'The Civil Service' in *Kavanagh & Seldon (1994)*.

Young (1989) Young, H., *One of Us: A Biography of Margaret Thatcher*, Pan/Macmillan, 1989.

Young & Sloman (1982) Young, H. & Sloman, A., *No, minister: An Inquiry into the Civil Service*, BBC, 1982.

17 The courts and the judiciary

17.1 The legal system in the UK

An unusual characteristic of the legal system in the UK is that it is not one system but three. The laws and procedures which operate are different in England and Wales, Scotland and Northern Ireland. There is, however, one characteristic which is common to all three legal systems - namely, the distinction between criminal law and civil law. The distinction between criminal and civil law is made in Box 17.1.

Box 17.1 The distinction between civil and criminal law

Criminal law

Criminal law is concerned with behaviour which is disapproved of by the state and has, therefore, been made illegal by statute. Since criminal offences are regarded as offences against the state, most cases in England and Wales are brought by the Crown Prosecution Service on the state's behalf. People accused of theft or murder, for example, are tried in criminal courts. Those found guilty may be punished in a variety of ways, depending on their past behaviour and the seriousness of the offence. Punishment ranges from fines and community service to long-term imprisonment.

Civil law

Civil law, on the other hand, is concerned with the relationships between individuals and groups. It deals with disputes which arise over matters such as the making of contracts or wills, accusations of libel and slander or the custody of children after divorce. Individuals (or organisations) who lose a case in a civil court are not punished in the same way as in a criminal case. Rather, they are ordered to recompense the other party in some way - for example, by paying damages or by handing over the rights to property or the custody of children. As a consequence of their different objectives, the criminal and civil systems operate within different court structures, though these structures come together at the highest level.

17.2 The legal system in England and Wales

A hierarchical system

The legal system in England and Wales is organised hierarchically. Superior courts hear more serious cases and re-examine on appeal cases which were first brought to the lower courts.

The civil courts

At the bottom of the civil court hierarchy are the 270 County Courts. These deal with relatively minor civil actions and, therefore, deal with the majority of civil actions. County Courts are able to make judgements about disputes over contracts to the value of less than £5,000, repossessions of property by building societies, disputes between tenants and landlords, most cases involving wills and legacies and most matrimonial matters (especially divorce cases). County Courts are presided over by Circuit Judges (in December 2002, there were 617 Circuit Judges in total) or by District Judges (in May 2002, there were 415 District Judges).

The High Court

The next step up the hierarchy is the High Court. Confusingly, the High Court is not one court, but three. It is made up of three divisions which have jurisdiction over separate, though occasionally overlapping, areas of law. The three divisions of the High Court are described in Box 17.2.

Box 17.2 The three divisions of the High Court

1. The Divisional Court of the Queen's Bench Division

The Divisional Court of the Queen's Bench Division (the King's Bench when the monarch is male) is the largest division. This division hears cases which are referred from County Courts either because the amount of money involved is too large or because the dispute involves a complex point of law. In addition, it plays the important role of judging writs of Habeas Corpus (deciding whether a person has been unlawfully detained). This court is also responsible for reviewing administrative decisions made by public bodies such as local authorities, government departments and health authorities.

2. The Family Division

The Family Division is the second largest division. This has responsibility for adjudicating on all matters relating to the family and the legal side of people's personal relations.

3. The Chancery Division

The Chancery Division is the smallest division. This is responsible for considering issues involving taxation and wills, issues which are often complex and involve large sums of money. Proceedings in the High Court are presided over by one or more High Court Judges (in December 2002, there were 109 High Court Judges in total). High Court Judges are officially responsible to the Crown.

The Civil Division of the Court of Appeal

Above the High Court is the Civil Division of the Court of Appeal. This court is responsible for adjudicating when the High Court gives permission for a case to go to appeal or when those in dispute successfully request such a right from the Appeal Court itself. The Master of the Rolls presides over this court. Judgements are made by the Lord Justices of Appeal (in December 2002, there were 36 Lord Justices of Appeal in total). They do not hear witnesses except in exceptional circumstances. The three judges who preside over each appeal make their decisions on the basis of documents and the arguments of barristers. Their interpretations of law set precedents which the lower courts must follow.

The House of Lords
The House of Lords is the highest court of appeal in the UK (though judgements in the European Court of Justice can overrule judgements of the House of Lords in civil cases). Cases which reach the House of Lords are heard by Law Lords or Lords of Appeal in Ordinary as they are properly known.

> 'The Law Lords consist of…senior judges made life peers and salaried with a duty to sit on the appeals committees of the House of Lords.' (Davis 1995, p.64)

Normally, two Scottish members are included. Current and past Lord Chancellors may sit in judgement in the House of Lords. The Law Lords only accept cases referred to them by the Court of Appeal. They sit in judgement in a House of Lords committee room, without wigs or robes, and deliver their decision not as a judgement, but after a vote on whether the appeal should be accepted or dismissed. Each appeal, of which there are around 1,500 a year, is normally heard by five Law Lords.

A number of controversies have surrounded the role of the House of Lords as the highest court in the English and Welsh legal systems. The main controversies are listed in Box 17.3.

Box 17.3 The main controversies concerning the legal system in England and Wales

The main controversies concerning the legal system in England and Wales are as follows:

- the unrepresentative social and gender characteristics of the court's membership (see below)
- the manner in which its membership is appointed (also see below)
- the antiquated image of the House of Lords
- the contravention of the principle of the separation of powers which arises because the members of the highest court in the UK are also members of the upper legislative chamber.

Labour's announcement on 12 June 2003
On 12 June 2003, the Labour government announced a radical proposal to abolish the judicial role of the House of Lords and to replace it with a Supreme Court. This would be independent of the House of Lords but would fulfil a broadly similar judicial function. Initially any Supreme Court would be made up of the 12 Law Lords, though the government may consider increasing the number of Supreme Court Judges

from 12 to 14 or 15. The proposals were embodied in a Constitutional Reform Bill introduced by the government in the House of Lords on 24 February 2004.

The Bill also proposed the abolition of the post of Lord Chancellor. The political functions of the Lord Chancellor would be transferred to a Minister for Constitutional Affairs and the legal responsibilities would be the preserve of the Lord Chief Justice.

The government clearly hopes that a Supreme Court will have a more modern image. In addition, giving the members of the highest court a function which is only judicial will remove problems with the separation of powers (as will the abolition of the triple role of Lord Chancellor who is a member of the executive as a Cabinet minister, the legislature as a member of the House of Lords and Head of the Judiciary).

The criminal courts
At the bottom of the criminal court hierarchy lie the Magistrates' Courts. These courts have two roles. First, they pass judgement on the 98% of criminal cases which are not 'indictable' (ie not serious enough to be tried in a Crown Court). Second, they are responsible for the committal proceedings of those cases which are indictable and will go to the Crown Court if the magistrate decides that the evidence appears strong enough. There are around 700 Magistrates' Courts in England and Wales. They are presided over by lay magistrates or 'JPs' (Justices of the Peace) as they are also known. JPs are members of the public who are trained, but not legally qualified. They sit in court part time. In May 2004, there were 28,500 JPs, 49% of whom were women. In areas with a heavy workload, legally qualified, full-time District Judges (Magistrates' Court) provide lay magistrates with assistance. In May 2004, there were 103 District Judges (Magistrates' Court). Of this 103, just 20 were women. There were also 173 Deputy District Judges (Magistrates' Court) of whom 38 were women. District Judges (Magistrates' Court) used to be called stipendiary magistrates. The post of stipendiary magistrate was created in the late 18th century to give a professional gloss to the magistracy at a time when it was falling into disrepute.

The work done by magistrates is described in Box 17.4 on page 342.

Crown Court
All serious crimes are tried in a Crown Court. The Crown Courts were established in 1972 to replace the outdated quarter sessions and assize courts. Offences such as murder, rape, manslaughter and robbery are tried in the Crown Court. Where defendants plead not guilty, they are entitled to a jury trial. In this case, the role of the judge is confined to advising the jury on points of law and providing a summing up of the evidence presented and the legal situation relating to it. If the jury finds a defendant guilty, it is the responsibility of the judge to pass sentence.

Less serious cases are heard by a Recorder. Recorders are part-time judges drawn from the ranks of the barristers. In May 2002, there were 1,324 Recorders. More serious offences are heard in front of a Circuit Judge and the most serious offences are heard in front of a High Court Judge. In December 2002, there were 617 Circuit Judges and 109 High

Box 17.4 The work done by magistrates

The main responsibility of magistrates is to pass sentence on minor offences. Most people brought before Magistrates' Courts plead guilty. In cases where a not guilty plea is registered, three magistrates have to weigh the evidence and make a decision. Occasionally, a Magistrates' Court will refer a case to the Crown Court for sentence because Crown Courts are able to impose stiffer sentences than Magistrates' Courts. As well as committal, trial and sentencing, magistrates are also responsible for remanding or bailing defendants and for granting or withholding licences from pubs, betting shops and casinos.

Court Judges. There are 94 Crown Court centres in England and Wales. The best known is the Central Criminal Court or Old Bailey in London. Like most other Crown Court centres, the Old Bailey contains several court rooms.

Appeals

Appeals against both sentences and convictions in the Magistrates' Court go to the Crown Court. Appeals against Crown Court decisions go to the Criminal Division of the Court of Appeal and then, with the permission of the Appeal Court to the House of Lords.

Behind this apparently simple procedure lies a process for criminal appeals which has been much criticised because of the string of miscarriages of justice which have been revealed since the late 1980s.

There are three categories of appeals which are referred back to the Court of Appeal as a matter of course. These are outlined in Box 17.5.

Box 17.5   Appeals referred to the
Court of Appeal as a matter
of course

Cases where the evidence is flawed or tainted (regardless of whether the accused is guilty or not guilty of the crime).

Cases where the accused is innocent of the specific offence but guilty of other, similar offences.

Cases where the accused is innocent of the charge for which they were found guilty.

Source: *Guardian*, 19 August 1998.

Until 1997, it was the responsibility of the Home Office to decide whether cases should go back to the Court of Appeal. Since 1997, however, the Criminal Cases Review Commission (CCRC) has taken over this responsibility (see below).

If an appeal is allowed, the Appeal Court can either order a retrial or acquit the accused. Acquittal does not have to come via the Court of Appeal, however. The Home Secretary can recommend to the monarch that a pardon be granted or that part or all of a sentence be removed.

17.3 The legal system in Scotland

Unlike Wales, Scotland did not become part of the United Kingdom through conquest. As a result, it was able to preserve a degree of independence from the rest of the UK. One example of this independence is its legal system. The system of criminal justice in Scotland differs in organisation and procedure from the English system.

Prosecutions in Scotland

For legal purposes, Scotland is divided into districts. All criminal investigations in a particular district are overseen by an officer called the procurator fiscal. The procurator fiscal can request the police to make further enquiries before allowing a prosecution to go ahead and has the right to interview witnesses. Procurators fiscal make the final decision about whether a case should go to court. They perform, therefore, the same function as that performed by the Crown Prosecution Service in England and Wales. In overall charge of the procurators fiscal is the Crown Agent, based in Edinburgh. The Crown Agent oversees the work of procurators fiscal and helps them to decide whether to prosecute in difficult cases. The Crown Agent is responsible to the Lord Advocate, the senior criminal lawyer in Scotland.

Scottish courts

Minor criminal cases in Scotland are tried in District or Sheriff Courts (the name varies). More serious cases are tried at the High Court of Justiciary. There is, in other words, no intermediate level of court, equivalent to the Crown Court. In Scotland, all appeals are heard by the High Court of Justiciary in front of three judges. No further appeal to the House of Lords is permitted.

Juries in Scotland

The relationship between judge and jury in Scotland is different from that in England and Wales. The judge decides on questions of law, while the jury decides on matters of fact. Juries in Scotland contain 15 people (compared to 12 in England and Wales). At the conclusion of trials, juries in Scotland are able to give the verdict of 'not proven' as well as that of 'guilty' or 'not guilty'.

The civil system in Scotland

The civil court system in Scotland is described in Box 17.6 on page 343.

The two systems compared

Despite differences in organisation and procedure, the two systems are not that far apart. Madgwick & Woodhouse (1995) noted, for example, that under John Major the Lord Chancellor was a Scottish lawyer, Lord MacKay. They also pointed out that the House of Lords is the final court of appeal for the UK as a whole, creating precedents which have a general application.

Labour's proposals

Under the Labour government's proposals for a new Supreme Court, the final court of appeal in Scottish criminal cases will continue to be the High Court of Justiciary. The final Court of Appeal in civil cases will however, be the new Supreme Court.

Box 17.6 The civil court system in Scotland

The civil court system in Scotland also differs in organisation and procedure from the English system. Most civil litigation in Scotland is dealt with by the sheriff courts (the same courts which also deal with criminal litigation). With very few exceptions, there is no upper limit on the value of contracts dealt with by the sheriff courts. There is the right to appeal in some cases from the sheriff to the sheriff principal (the head of the judiciary in each sheriffdom) and in other cases from the sheriff to the Court of Session.

The Court of Session is the supreme civil court in Scotland. There is, however, the right of appeal from the Court of Session to the House of Lords. A leading principle of the Court of Session is that cases are first decided by judges sitting alone and are then reviewed by several judges. The total number of judges is 25, of whom 17 (the Lords Ordinary) mainly decide cases in the first instance. This branch is called the Outer House. The eight other judges are divided into two divisions of four judges each. This branch is called the Inner House. The main business of each division of the Inner House is to review the decisions of the Lords Ordinary or inferior courts which have appealed to it.

17.4 The European dimension

Two courts outside the UK now play an important part in its legal system. They have entirely distinct functions, but are frequently confused.

A. The European Court of Justice

The European Court of Justice is the highest court of the European Union and sits in Luxembourg (see also Unit 12). In matters relating to EU law, the European Court of Justice is the most senior court and, in its areas of competence, its judgements override even judgements of the House of Lords.

B. The European Court of Human Rights

The European Court of Human Rights sits in Strasbourg. This court was established by the European Convention on Human Rights. Appeals can be made to this court if people believe their rights under the European Convention have been violated. Two conditions, however, are placed on such appeals. First, the appellant (the person making the appeal) must have exhausted all the procedures for justice in their own country. Second, appeals cannot be made directly. They go to court via the Commission of Human Rights. The Commission first decides whether the case is admissible and, if it is, tries to achieve an agreed settlement before referring it to court. It was partly because of concerns at the number of times that the British government had been judged to have been in breach of the European Convention on Human Rights that the Human Rights Act 1998 was passed. This Act incorporated the European Convention on Human Rights into UK law. It is now no longer necessary to apply to the European Court of Human Rights to enforce the rights provided in the convention.

Main points Sections 17.1 - 17.4

- In the UK three separate legal systems are in operation, but they all distinguish between criminal law and civil law.
- Criminal law is concerned with behaviour which has been made illegal by statute. Civil law is concerned with disputes between individuals and groups.
- The three legal systems are organised hierarchically. Superior courts hear more serious cases and re-examine on appeal cases which were first brought to the lower courts.
- Two courts outside the UK now play an important part in its legal system - the European Court of Justice and the European Court of Human Rights.

Activity 17.1 The British legal system

Item A The new Supreme Court

On 12 June 2003, the government announced the intention to abolish the post of Lord Chancellor, replacing it with a new independent Supreme Court and a new Judicial Appointments Commission which would take from ministers the responsibility for appointing judges. The aims were:

- to bring more transparency
- to ensure that the judiciary is fully independent from political influence
- to ensure that, at the same time, there is a robust working relationship between the judiciary and the executive.

The government carried out a consultation exercise.

Consultation papers on the Supreme Court and Judicial Review Commission were published in July 2003. A further consultation on the abolition of the Lord Chancellor was published in September 2003. In January 2004, the Secretary of State for Constitutional Affairs made a detailed statement to Parliament about the government's proposals. The Constitutional Reform Bill was introduced in February 2004. It contains proposals for the abolition of the post of Lord Chancellor, the creation of a Supreme Court and reform of the judicial appointments process. The Bill is careful to lay out the different responsibilities to be held by the Secretary of State for Constitutional Affairs and the Lord Chief Justice (who is to be Head of the Judiciary).

Source: Report of the Select Committee on Constitutional Affairs published in 2004.

Item B The legal system in England and Wales

(i) The criminal courts in 1998

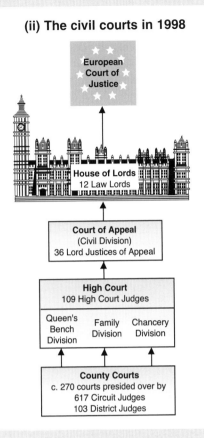

House of Lords
12 Law Lords

↑

Court of Appeal
(Criminal Division)
36 Lord Justices of Appeal

↑

Crown Courts
94 Crown Court centres (cases
heard by High Court Judges,
Circuit Judges, Recorders or
Assistant Recorders)

↑

Magistrates' Courts
c. 700 Magistrates' Courts
(Over 30,000 JPs and
88 stipendiary magistrates)

(ii) The civil courts in 1998

European Court of Justice

↑

House of Lords
12 Law Lords

↑

Court of Appeal
(Civil Division)
36 Lord Justices of Appeal

↑

High Court
109 High Court Judges

| Queen's Bench Division | Family Division | Chancery Division |

↑

County Courts
c. 270 courts presided over by
617 Circuit Judges
103 District Judges

Item C The jury system

"The jury will ignore that last remark..."

Questions

1. What factors might determine whether justice is done in the legal system in England and Wales? Use Items A-C in your answer.

2. a) Using Item B write a paragraph explaining the principles which lie behind the legal system in England and Wales.

   b) Using Item B as a model, draw a diagram of the Scottish legal system.

3. a) Using Item A explain in your own words why the government claims it is important to create a new Supreme Court.

   b) What arguments might an opponent of the creation of a Supreme Court use to support their case?

17.5 The development of rights and liberties in the UK

People living in the UK are both citizens and subjects. They are citizens because they have certain defined rights and liberties, but they are also subjects of the monarch. Unlike in the USA and many other states, the rights and liberties of British citizens are not set out in a single constitutional document. Rather, they are part of the British uncodified constitution (see Unit 11). Some of these rights and liberties are the product of custom and convention. Others are contained in written documents, namely Acts of Parliament. The rights and liberties contained in these Acts are the result of struggles waged by people and their representatives against the absolute power of their rulers. The key events are outlined in Box 17.7.

Box 17.7 The development of rights and liberties

Magna Carta, 1215

In 1215, King John was forced to sign the Magna Carta. This was the first time in the UK that the power of an absolute ruler had been limited by law. The Magna Carta established that laws made by the monarch were to be within the common law, the monarch could only levy certain taxes with the permission of the council and no person could be imprisoned except by a process of law involving the lawful judgement of their peers.

Habeas Corpus, 1679

In 1679, the Habeas Corpus Act was passed. This Act insisted that people should be told the reason for their arrest and should be informed of the charges against them. A person who was arrested had to be brought before a court and charged with a specific offence within three days. This Act was particularly important since it limited the arbitrary power of rulers.

Bill of Rights, 1689

In 1689, the Bill of Rights was passed. Unlike such Bills in other countries, the British Bill of Rights had no special status - it was an ordinary Act of Parliament. Nonetheless, it did increase the rights enjoyed by citizens. The Bill guaranteed the supremacy of Parliament over the monarch and prevented the monarch from imposing taxation unless this was agreed by the House of Commons. The Bill also guaranteed freedom of speech and the right of citizens to petition both the monarch and Parliament.

Further Acts

Subsequently, a number of Acts were passed extending the rights and liberties of British citizens. The right to worship freely, for example, was established by a number of Acts such as the Catholic Emancipation Act of 1829 (which allowed Catholics to stand for Parliament for the first time). Slavery was abolished in 1833. Sex discrimination Acts were passed in 1975 and 1987. A Race Relations Act was passed in 1976. The Data Protection Act was passed in 1984. The Human Rights Act was passed in 1998 (with effect from 2000).

International agreements

In addition to these pieces of domestic legislation, three international agreements have a bearing on rights in the UK. The first is the United Nations Declaration of Human Rights, agreed in 1948. The Declaration sets out a number of general rights which governments are meant to grant to their citizens and more detailed guidelines stipulating specific rights and types of treatment. The second is the European Convention on Human Rights, signed in 1950. This treaty not only set out the rights which all citizens in Europe could expect, it also established a Commission of Human Rights and a European Court of Human Rights to enforce the treaty. The passing of the Human Rights Act in 1998 enables judges in the UK to look at legislation and the acts of public authorities in light of the European Convention on Human Rights. The third international agreement to have a bearing on rights in the UK is the Maastricht Treaty which had been ratified by all member states by the end of 1993. This gave citizenship a new dimension since workers' rights and voting rights were guaranteed throughout the EU.

As a result of the above developments, British citizens enjoy the rights and liberties described in Box 17.8.

Box 17.8 Rights and liberties

1. Freedom of movement.
2. Freedom from arbitrary arrest or unjustified police searches.
3. Freedom of conscience in matters of religion and politics.
4. Freedom of expression.
5. Freedom of association, including the right to protest peacefully.
6. Social freedoms - such as the right to marry, divorce, procure abortions or enjoy homosexual relations.
7. The right to vote and to stand for election.
8. The right to a fair trial.
9. The right not to be coerced or tortured by agents of the state.
10. The right not to be subjected to surveillance without due legal process.
11. The right to own property.

17.6 The Ombudsman

The Ombudsman or Parliamentary Commissioner for Administration (PCA) was first appointed in 1967. It is the job of the PCA to investigate complaints of maladministration which occur in the departments of central government. In 1987, the range of bodies included within the PCA's jurisdiction was extended to include the Equal Opportunities Commission, Sports Council, Legal Aid Board, Charity Commission, Royal Mint and Scottish Tourist Board.

Since 1967, Ombudsmen have been established for Northern Ireland (1969), the health service (1973), local government (1974), Scottish local government (1975), housing association tenants (1993) and, the prison service (1994).

Some sectors of private industry have also established Ombudsmen schemes, but these should not be confused with the statutory schemes.

Procedure

Members of the public cannot refer cases directly to the PCA. They must be passed on through an MP. Since 1988, however, the Local Government Ombudsman has been directly accessible to members of the public. This direct access is also available to those with complaints for the Health, Housing and Prisons Ombudsmen.

Once a complaint is received, it is acted upon only if there is no other way of dealing with it and if the complaint satisfies the provisions of the 1967 Act - which states that a person must have good reason to claim 'to have sustained injustice in consequence of maladministration' (Section 5.1). A major problem is that 'maladministration' is not defined in the Act. Box 17.9, however, provides a definition.

Box 17.9 Definition of the term 'maladministration'

Maladministration can be defined as corruption, bias, unfair discrimination, harshness, misleading a member of the public as to their rights, failing to notify them properly of their rights or to explain the reasons for a decision, general high-handedness, using powers for a wrong purpose, failing to consider relevant materials, taking irrelevant material into account, losing or failing to reply to correspondence, delaying unreasonably before making a tax refund or presenting a tax demand or dealing with an application for a grant or licence and so on.

Source: De Smith & Brazier 1989, p.649.

Powers

Once an investigation does begin, Ombudsmen have wide powers. Although hearings are in private, they can compel witnesses to attend and can inspect relevant files and papers. After the investigation, a report is submitted to a House of Commons select committee. The report is also published. If maladministration has taken place, the Ombudsman recommends an appropriate remedy. Although the government department found to be guilty of maladministration is not obliged to accept the Ombudsman's recommendation, it is under strong pressure to do so. In most cases, an apology or financial compensation are offered. In some cases, changes to administrative procedures are implemented.

Criticisms

A number of criticisms have been made of the way in which the Ombudsman system works. First, it is claimed that Ombudsmen are under-used - for three reasons:

- complaints for the PCA have to be channelled through MPs
- all complaints must be placed in writing
- the system is not well publicised.

Second, the large number of rejected complaints is a cause for concern. Ombudsmen have to be satisfied that both maladministration and injustice have occurred before a

complaint is considered. Some critics argue that this should be considered in the course of an investigation, not as a condition of its beginning. Third, the passive nature of the system has been criticised - Ombudsmen must await complaints, they cannot make inquiries themselves. Fourth, the background of those appointed as Ombudsmen is a cause of concern. Most have civil service or local government backgrounds and there is a concern that, consequently, their sympathies are with those being investigated. Fifth, there is often a long delay before a decision is reached - investigations by the PCA take, on average, over 70 weeks (Pyper 1998). And sixth, critics argue that Ombudsmen ought to be given powers to enforce the recommendations made in reports. Although the recommendations are usually adopted, the gravity of the investigation is reduced because the recommendations are not enforceable. Two examples illustrate why this is of particular importance. In both the Barlow Clowes case of 1989 and the Channel Tunnel Rail Link case of 1995, the government publicly rejected the Ombudsman's conclusion that maladministration had taken place. In the Barlow Clowes case (which involved the collapse of an investment company), the government nonetheless compensated investors. In the Channel Tunnel Rail Link case (concerning property prices along the proposed route), the government refused to pay compensation.

Advantages

Despite these criticisms, the system has its advantages. These are outlined in Box 17.10.

Box 17.10 Advantages of the Ombudsman system

- Ombudsmen reach parts of the system other mechanisms do not reach and they cover a wide range of public bodies
- they are cheap to use
- there is no need for legal advice
- the process is conciliatory not adversarial
- recommendations are largely implemented
- the finding in one case may affect others.

Source: Pyper 1998.

17.7 The Criminal Cases Review Commission (CCRC)

In October 1989, the Court of Appeal overturned the convictions of the 'Guildford Four' (three men and a woman who had been jailed in 1975 after being found guilty of bombing a pub in Guildford). These convictions were overturned on the grounds that the evidence against them had been based on police lies and false confessions. The release of the Guildford Four was of great importance. In the words of Paul Foot:

'The Guildford case broke the dam. Month after month, wrongful convictions were set aside: the Birmingham Six, the Broadwater Three, the Cardiff Three, the Swansea

Two, the East Ham Two, Judy Ward, Stefan Kisko, the Taylor sisters, Eddie Browning. All had been convicted of murder and all were, in the proper sense, victims of miscarriages of justice - they didn't do it.' (*Guardian*, 4 July 1994)

This steady stream of miscarriages of justice in the 1990s severely shook the public's faith in the judicial system and led to demands for change. Until 1997, it was the responsibility of the Home Office to decide whether cases should go back to the Court of Appeal. Since March 1997, however, the Criminal Cases Review Commission (CCRC) has taken over this responsibility. The CCRC is based in Birmingham. To have a case heard by the CCRC, the appeals procedure must have been exhausted and it is necessary to present new evidence which was not available at the time of the trial or was not disclosed to the defence.

By March 2004, there had been 6,647 applications to the CCRC. Of these 6,017 had been completed and 178 had been heard by the Court of Appeal. Of the cases heard by the Court of Appeal, 121 original judgements were quashed, 55 were upheld and two were reserved. This suggests that it is difficult to get a case through the CCRC to the Court of Appeal. Once this hurdle is overcome, however, the chances of securing a reversal of the original judgement are quite good.

17.8 Judicial review

British courts are not only responsible for interpreting the precise meaning of an Act of Parliament, they are also responsible for reviewing the actions of public agents (including ministers) to find out whether their actions are 'ultra vires' (beyond their powers). The government can be brought to court on the same grounds as an ordinary person or organisation. So, when a person or organisation feels aggrieved at the actions of some ministerial, government department or local authority action, they can then apply for a judicial review. Since a judicial review requires judges to make a judgement about decisions made by politicians, the political views of the judges may have a bearing on whether the review should be granted and what verdict should be delivered:

> 'Judicial review is a direct challenge to the lawfulness of the government's action and clearly involves the courts in judgements which have political fall-out.' (Davis 1995, p.66)

Procedure

For a judicial review to take place, the aggrieved individual or organisation must apply for a judicial review at the High Court. The right to judicial review is not automatic. Only when leave to proceed has been granted, can a case be heard in front of two or three judges in the Divisional Court of the Queen's Bench Division. Leave is granted on three grounds. These are outlined in Box 17.11.

Remedies

If leave to apply for judicial review is granted and the judges find against the public agent, five possible remedies are available to the court. First, the court can quash decisions made by public agents who have been acting outside their

---

Box 17.11 Grounds for being granted leave to proceed

1. Ultra vires

A judicial review is granted if it seems that there is sufficient evidence to suggest that a public authority may have exceeded its statutory power (ie an act performed by a public agent may have been ultra vires).

2. Procedural impropriety

A judicial review is granted when there appears to have been procedural impropriety (where actions taken by a public body have contravened 'natural justice'). A public body acts according to 'natural justice' if it has acted in a way that is fair and free from bias (Griffith 1991, p.125).

3. An action was 'irrational'

A judicial review is allowed if it appears that a public body has acted 'irrationally' (in a highly 'unreasonable' way). Clearly, these three grounds give judges a great deal of discretion. Different judges interpret 'fair and free from bias' and 'acting irrationally' in different ways.

---

lawful jurisdiction. A planning authority, for example, which had rejected a planning application for reasons not specified in the legislation which gave it the authority to act, could be ordered to change its decision. Second, a tribunal can be prevented from considering matters outside its authority. Third, a public body can be compelled to perform a specified function by law - for example, a local authority can be compelled to provide schooling. Fourth, any public body can be ordered not to carry out or to stop carrying out an action which the court decides is unlawful. In other words, the court can issue an injunction. Injunctions played a major part in the miners' strike of 1984-85, for example - judges ruled that the strike was illegal as no ballot had been held and issued injunctions against the NUM. And fifth, the judges can choose to clarify the legal position in a particular case. This is a stronger remedy than it might appear since any public body acting against a newly clarified legal position would certainly have judgement made against them in future legal action.

Box 17.12 Problems with judicial review

First, the growing number of cases means there is an increasing willingness on the part of the judiciary to intervene in the day-to-day business of government. Second, some critics have questioned whether unelected judges from an élite social background should be responsible for scrutinising and ruling upon the legality of the actions of elected governments and local authorities. And third, the question has been raised as to whether judges, regardless of their background, are sufficiently well trained to take legal decisions in a highly politicised environment and whether the principles valid in court are appropriate.

Problems with judicial review

Pyper (1998) argues that citizens using judicial review to redress grievances face a number of problems:

- access to the system is limited
- only one-third of actions reach a final hearing
- some judges are more likely to grant leave for cases than others (some grant leave to 80% of applicants while others only grant leave to 20%)
- only one in six cases results in a ruling against the public agent.

Other problems are outlined in Box 17.12 on page 347.

What cannot be doubted is that the process of judicial review necessarily involves judges in decisions of a political nature. The greater use of judicial review may be evidence that people are making greater use of the legal remedies available to them when they feel that their rights are being infringed or it may be that there has been a growth of the abuse of rights by public bodies.

Main points   Sections 17.5 - 17.8

- In the UK, some rights and liberties are the product of custom and convention and others are granted by Acts of Parliament.
- The job of the Ombudsman (PCA) is to deal with complaints of maladministration. Other Ombudsmen are responsible for specific areas of government work.
- The Ombudsman system is under-used, passive and slow, with a low success rate and lacking in teeth. But, it does cover a wide range of public bodies, is cheap and conciliatory, and its recommendations are usually implemented.
- The job of the Criminal Cases Review Commission is to decide whether cases should be referred back to the Court of Appeal.
- Since judicial reviews require judges to judge decisions made by politicians, the political views of the judges may have a bearing on cases.

Activity 17.2 *Gaining redress*

Item A Complaints received and investigations completed by the PCA

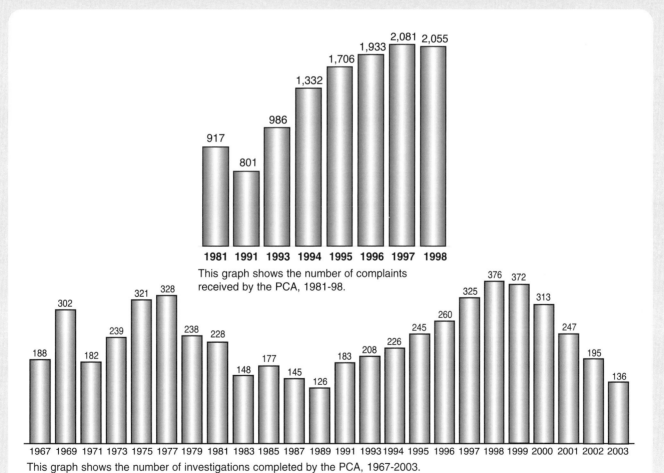

This graph shows the number of complaints received by the PCA, 1981-98.

This graph shows the number of investigations completed by the PCA, 1967-2003.

According to the PCA, the significant increase in cases since 1993 is largely due to two new factors - the impact of the Child Support Agency (25% of all cases in 1995) and civil service staff cuts which have resulted in a lower quality of service.

Item B The Criminal Cases Review Commission

Introducing the Commission

- The Criminal Cases Review Commission is an independent body responsible for investigating suspected miscarriages of criminal justice in England, Wales and Northern Ireland.

- Its jurisdiction does not extend to Scotland, the Channel Islands or the Isle of Man.

- Investigations into suspected miscarriages of justice in Scotland are carried out by the Scottish Criminal Cases Review Commission.

Figures to 31 March 2004	
Total applications	: 6,647
Open	: 212
Actively being worked on	: 418
Completed	: 6,017 (including ineligible) 226 referrals
Heard by Court of Appeal	: 178 (121 quashed; 55 upheld, 2 reserved)

- The Commission has at least eleven Members appointed by Her Majesty the Queen, on the recommendation of the Prime Minister. They are supported by caseworkers and administrative staff.

- The Commission's principal role is to review the convictions of those who believe they have either been wrongly found guilty of a criminal offence, or wrongly sentenced.

- The Commission can seek further information relating to a case and carry out its own investigations, or arrange for others to do so.

- Once the investigations have been completed to the Commission's satisfaction, it decides whether or not to refer the case to the appropriate appeal court.

Item C Judicial review

Judicial review

- It concerns the power of judges to check and control the activities and decisions of governmental bodies, tribunals, inferior courts, and even some private bodies that affect the public.

- Notice: Parliament is not included.

In dealing with judicial review a court may order

- Certiorari or quashing order:
  - *It will quash or nullify the decision in question.*
- Mandamus or mandatory order:
  - *It compels a decision-maker to carry out a duty.*
- Prohibition or prohibiting order:
  - *It prevents a decision-maker from engaging in unlawful activities.*
- Declaration:
  - *It is a statement by the court affirming a particular legal position.*

- Injunction:
  - *It can be either a mandamus or a prohibition.*
- Damages:
  - *Rarely applicable.*

Preliminary Hurdles

- Leave to apply
  - *Is the decision in question subject to judicial review?*

  In essence only public law issues are subject to juicial review (eg. decision of public body)

  Private bodies may be subject to judicial review, as long as its powers are:

  - *Governmental in nature*

  - *Those affected are not in a contractual relationship with the decision-making body*

Leave to apply

- Has the right to judicial review been expressly excluded, say in a statute?

- Lord Denning stated that:
  - *'the remedy by certiorari is never to be taken away by statute except by the most clear and explicit words'*
  R v Medical Appeal Tribunal, ex parte Gilmore (1957) 1 QB 574

Leave to appeal

- Has the applicant sufficient interest in the issue?
- Has the applicant sought review within three months of the actual reason for bringing the application?
- Do the specific grounds for judicial review exist?

Specific grounds for review

- Lord Diplock in Council of Civil Service Union v Minister for Civil Service (1985) AC 374 (HL) provided three grounds, the existence of any of them will render the decision unlawful:
  - *Illegality*
  - *Irrationality*
  - *Procedural impropriety*

Questions

1. What does Item A suggest about people's view of the effectiveness of government.

2. a) Using Item B, summarise in your own words the purpose of the CCRC.

   b) What do the figures in Item B suggest about the effectiveness of the CCRC?

3. Using Item C suggest the advantages and disadvantages of judicial review as a means of securing redress of grievance.

4. Give arguments for and against the idea that it is easy for people in England and Wales to gain redress if they have a grievance.

17.9 *The role of the judiciary*

The role of the judiciary

According to the principle of the separation of powers (see Unit 11), the judicial task of law enforcement (of deciding whether laws have been broken and, if they have, of dispensing punishment) is separate from the executive and legislative tasks of devising and making laws. It is, therefore, the role of judges (known collectively as 'the judiciary') to examine cases where citizens or organisations are accused of breaking the law and to make judgements about whether or not they have done so. In theory at least, the principle of the separation of powers means that the judiciary is quite independent of the executive. Its judgements are not subject, for example, to ministerial direction or control. Equally, it is the role of the judiciary to interpret the law as it stands, not to determine what the law should be.

The role of the judiciary in practice

How far this theory is carried out in practice, however, depends upon a number of factors.

First, it is the job of judges to interpret general laws in specific instances:

> 'The law consists of general rules (rules which relate to all persons or to wide categories of persons). These general rules (laws) are laid down by the legislature. Laws are then given effect through policies chosen and enforced by the executive. Like the laws to which they relate, such policies apply in general, rather than specific, terms.' (Davis 1995, p.63)

By applying the general rule or policy to a particular case, judges decide on the meaning of the law in a particular instance. When an interpretation is made in a senior court, all lower courts are then bound by that interpretation in future similar cases (this is known as the 'principle of precedent'). In essence, therefore, judges in senior courts are actually making the law through their interpretations of what Parliament has laid down. Law made by judges is known as 'common law' (see Unit 11).

Second, judges play an explicitly political role in that they are asked, through the process of judicial review (see Section 17.8 above), to consider whether local or national government has acted lawfully.

Third, senior judges play a formal role in the other two branches of government (at least until the Labour government's constitutional reform proposals become law). At the time of writing, Law Lords can participate in debates and votes when the Lords sits as the legislature and the Lord Chancellor straddles all three branches of the government as a member of the Cabinet (part of the executive), a member of the House of Lords (part of the legislature) and head of the judiciary.

Fourth:

> 'Senior judges make public speeches or publish articles which contribute to the debate on controversial government policies, particularly those which affect them directly…Similarly, it is common practice to appoint judges to lead inquiries into controversial or difficult matters and for their conclusions to be taken into account in legislation.' (Davis 1995, p.64)

And fifth, the incorporation of the European Convention of Human Rights into UK law means that, for the first time in British history, judges will have the right to reverse legislation and Parliament's wishes if they conflict with the aims of the Convention.

How should judges interpret the law?

Given the political dimension to the making of judgements, should a judge interpret the law to ensure that the law reflects current public thinking or should the judgement go beyond current thinking in the hope of altering the consensus? This is the question that leading judicial practitioners and thinkers have asked and three schools of thought have developed from their answers. These are described in Box 17.13 on page 351.

Judicial appointments

Before September 1994, all judicial appointments were made secretly by the Lord Chancellor and the Lord Chancellor's staff. Decisions were made on the basis of 'soundings' taken from other judges and senior lawyers (the Lord Chancellor's Office described them as 'extensive consultations' rather than 'soundings'). According to a pamphlet produced by the Lord Chancellor's Department in 1986, the following selection criteria were used:

> 'The Lord Chancellor's policy is to appoint to every judicial post the candidate who appears best qualified to fill and perform its duties, regardless of party, sex, religion or ethnic origin. Professional ability, experience, standing and integrity alone are the criteria, with the requirements that the candidate must be physically capable of carrying out the duties, and not disqualified by any personal unsuitability.' (LCD 1996)

Clearly, such criteria allow for a wide range of interpretations and, by 1994 when the system was changed, it was accepted that this system was flawed for the reasons outlined in Box 17.14 on page 351.

Box 17.13 Three schools of thought on interpreting the law

1. A creative judiciary

According to Lord Devlin, the judiciary should be creative but not dynamic. It is, in other words, not the role of the judge to make what is effectively new law, nor should judges act as social reformers.

2. A dynamic judiciary

Lord Denning argued that it is the role of the judge to achieve justice. If this means overturning precedent or interpreting legislation very widely, that indeed is the proper role of the senior judge. Supporters of this 'dynamic' judicial role argue that, if the law is not clear, then what Parliament intended to do should be taken into account. Intention, however, is difficult to establish and this perspective gives the senior judiciary a vastly extended role in shaping laws.

3. A moral judiciary

According to Griffith, whether or not judges choose to adopt a dynamic role is not that important:

> 'More important are their reactions to the moral, political and social issues in the cases that come before them.' (Griffith 1991, p.261)

If this is the case, then the factors which determine how senior judges apply the law depend heavily on who is appointed to be a judge and how they are appointed.

Box 17.14 Problems with the judicial appointment system

1. Secrecy

Secrecy meant that the system was open to abuse by those with personal agendas.

2. Lack of objectivity and openness

The system lacked objectivity and openness, a particular problem given that, by 1994, the Conservatives had been in power for 15 years and were under suspicion of appointing supporters to judicial posts.

3. Narrow band of people appointed

Since the system was based on soundings taken from other judges, it was no surprise that those appointed were usually people with similar backgrounds and interests to those who recommended them. In other words, the system ensured that judges were selected from only a narrow band of people.

4. Potential judges unable to apply

The system did not allow those who might be interested in promotion to apply for a position. They had to hope that their ambitions would be noticed by those taking the soundings.

Changes since 1994

A new system for junior judicial appointments (those below the level of High Court Judge) was introduced in September 1994. Since then, junior judicial posts have been advertised, all those with appropriate qualifications have been encouraged to apply, and non-lawyers have taken part in the selection process (short-listed applicants are interviewed by a panel of three comprising a Circuit Judge, a non-lawyer and a senior civil servant from the Lord Chancellor's Office). It should be noted, however, that only barristers and solicitors with ten year's experience are eligible and they must have experience as Recorders. Since Recorders are appointed by the Lord Chancellor's Office in the first place, competition for appointment at the level of junior judge is still by no means open to all who work in the legal professions.

In February 1998 the Lord Chancellor, Derry Irvine, announced that the system used for junior judicial appointments would be broadened to include High Court Judges. Yet, while posts for the High Court are, therefore, advertised and short-listed applicants are interviewed by a panel of three (a High Court Judge sits on the interview panel rather than a Circuit Judge), the Lord Chancellor does not have to select those chosen by the panel. The system of soundings remains in place and the Lord Chancellor reserves the right to appoint people even if they have not applied for the post. Furthermore, the most senior judicial posts are not advertised. Senior judges continue to be appointed using the old system.

In June 2003, it was announced that the government plans to create a new Judicial Appointments Commission which will ensure a much greater degree of impartiality and accountability in the appointment of judges. The Judicial Appointments Commission is likely to contain 15 members - five judges, five lawyers and five people unconnected with the legal profession. It is unclear at present whether (subject to Royal approval) the Commission:

- will make all judicial appointments
- will only make junior appointments itself and make recommendations to more senior posts
- will only make recommendations, leaving the final decisions with ministers or the Prime Minister.

If the third option is adopted, this will severely undermine the radical nature of these proposals (see the Department of Constitutional Affairs' website for the latest news on this).

17.10 Who are the judges?

When you picture in your mind a judge, what do you see? Do you see a young, black woman who speaks with a strong regional accent or an old, white male whose accent suggests an expensive public school and a university education at Oxford or Cambridge? If your mind conjures up the latter image, then, according to a survey published by *Labour Research* in December 2002, that image is not far from the truth. *Labour Research* examined the background of 774 senior judges (Circuit Judges and above) and found that:

- the UK's judiciary remains overwhelmingly élitist, white, male and aged
- in terms of educational background, 67% went to public school and 60% went to Oxford or Cambridge universities
- under Labour, those in the senior courts are more likely to have been public school educated
- the average age is over 60
- only 8% of judges are women.

(*Labour Research*, December 2002, pp.13-14)

The social background of judges

Senior judges are drawn from the ranks of barristers. Traditionally, those training to become barristers have required a private income to survive the first few years of practice. Becoming a barrister is an expensive process. As a result, large sections of the population are excluded. The result is that most barristers and, therefore, most judges come from a small section of society, move in rarefied circles, and share the values of the privileged few. While the 2002 *Labour Research* survey found that just 8% of senior judges were female and only seven (1%) were black, it found that 67% had attended a public school and 60% went to Oxford or Cambridge Universities (over 90% of Law Lords). It also found that a significant minority of judges were involved in party politics and 26 had stood for parliamentary election at some time in their careers. A further ten judges were identified as freemasons. Some judges are notoriously out of touch with ordinary people. The High Court Judge, Mr Justice Harman, for example, had never heard of the footballer Paul Gascoigne, the band Oasis and the singer Bruce Springsteen (*Guardian*, 25 February 1998). It is no surprise, therefore, that according to the 1996 British Crime Survey (which interviewed 16,438 people) four out of five people believe that judges are out of touch with what ordinary people think.

As an example of the slow progress made in creating a more representative judiciary it is remarkable to note that it was only in 2003 that the first female Law Lord, Brenda Hale, was appointed (see Activity 17.3, Item D, below).

Main points Sections 17.9 - 17.10

- In theory, the principle of the separation of powers means that the judiciary is quite independent of the executive. In practice, judges do have to make political decisions.
- There is a debate about whether judges should interpret the law dynamically or not.
- Before September 1994, all judicial appointments were made secretly by the Lord Chancellor on the basis of 'soundings' taken from other judges and senior lawyers.

- Since September 1994, junior judicial posts have been advertised, all those with appropriate qualifications have been encouraged to apply, and non-lawyers have taken part in the selection process. In 1998, this process was extended to High Court Judges.
- In 2003, the Labour government proposed setting up a Judicial Appointments Commission.
- Most judges are old, white males with a privileged background. Some people argue that this affects the judgements they make.

Activity 17.3 *The judiciary*

Item A **A *Labour Research* survey, December 2002**

Proportion of judges who went to Oxbridge universities		
	All	Those appointed since '97
House of Lords	92%	100%
Court of Appeal	91%	95%
High Court (Queen's Bench)	82%	81%
(Chancery)	94%	100%
(Family)	57%	20%
Circuit	53%	46%
All	60%	60%

Item B **Who are the judges?**

Hello. I'm white, elderly, bigoted – and male. What are you going to do about it?

Item C Can we trust the judges?

The Lord Chief Justice, Thomas Bingham, was appointed by John Major's Lord Chancellor, Lord Mackay. Educated at public school and fitting comfortably in the privileged world of the Bar, Bingham was 65 in 1998. According to one lawyer, Geoffrey Bindman who represents the *New Statesman* (a pro-Labour magazine), Bingham has a liberal and humanitarian outlook. The journalist Nick Cohen, however, dismisses the idea that Bingham is in any way progressive. He cites three pieces of evidence. First, during the Gulf War, Bingham allowed 90 Arabs to be imprisoned without trial on the strength of rumours from MI5. He was unapologetic when the Home Office later revealed that all 90 were completely innocent. Second, he protected the security services from public scrutiny by dismissing the charges made by MI5 whistleblowers that MI5 agents bugged government opponents. And third, in October 1998, Bingham threw the case in favour of General Pinochet's extradition out of the Court of Appeal. Nick Cohen points out that the Law Lords are all commercial lawyers trained in dealing with wills, corporations and trusts. None has knowledge of human rights law. They are so conservative, he claims, that a desperate legal profession can only hail one senior judge as a great 'liberal'. That judge, of course, is Lord Bingham.

Source: The *New Statesman*, 21 November 1997 and the *Observer*, 1 November 1998.

Item D The First Female Law Lord

The everyday lives of High Court Judges are ruled by seniority - that is, the order in which a judge was appointed to the bench. This governs the allocation of rooms, the order in which judges appear in the daily lists, who decides on the menus and dress code in judges' lodgings, even the timing of appointments for flu jabs. Judicial appointments have traditionally been dominated by the assumption that those best fitted for the appointment are those who have done best in independent practice as barristers. This has excluded large numbers of very able lawyers and limits selection to a small group - most of whom are white males from a narrow range of social and educational backgrounds But times have changed and, above all, the nature of the judicial task has changed. The European Communities Act, the development of judicial review and, above all, the Human Rights Act have clearly increased the social and political content of the judging task. In this changed world, it matters more who the judges are. There are four reasons, for example, why there should be more female senior judges. First, it would give greater public confidence in the judicial system because it would make the system less alien and more relevant to the female half of the population. Second, it is important symbolically since one of the functions of the judiciary is to promote equality and fairness. Third, it would be sound use of

Brenda Hale, the first female Law Lord.

human resources. And fourth, the most important reason - women would bring a different perspective to judging. Women would not make a difference in the sense that they would make different judgements than men. Women are as diverse as men. The difference is more subtle. For cultural, biological, social and historic reasons, women do have different experiences than men. They lead women's lives and this would be reflected. For example, in one of Brenda Hale's judgements, she tried to put into words the experience of bearing and rearing a child from the woman's point of view. A colleague paid her the compliment of saying it could not have been written by a man. So, when it comes to appointment, the new Judicial Appointments Commission must be strong and forward-looking. This means opening the field to all qualified lawyers and taking active steps to encourage people who might not see themselves as candidates to apply.

Source: Brenda Hale writing in the *Guardian* in 2003.

Questions

1. Is there any evidence in Item A to support the point made in Item B? Explain your answer.

2. Using Items C and D explain why the process of selecting judges is important.

3. Assess the reasons given in Item D for having a more representative senior judiciary.

4. 'Who the judges are and what background they come from is unimportant. All that is important is that that they are good judges.' Using Items A-D and your own knowledge, discuss the arguments for and against this viewpoint.

References

Davis (1995) Davis, H., 'The Judiciary' in *Lancaster (1995)*.

De Smith & Brazier (1989) De Smith, S. & Brazier, R., *Constitutional and Administrative Law*, Penguin, 1989.

Griffith (1991) Griffith, J. A. G., *The Politics of the Judiciary*, Fontana, 1991.

Lancaster (1995) Lancaster, S. (ed.), *Developments in Politics*, Causeway Press, 1995.

LCD (1996) *Judicial Appointments*, Lord Chancellors Department, 1996.

Madgwick & Woodhouse (1995) Madgwick, P. & Woodhouse, D., *The Law and Politics of the Constitution*, Harvester Wheatsheaf, 1995.

Pyper (1998) Pyper, R., 'Redress of grievances', *Politics Review*, Vol.7.3, February 1998.

18 Devolution and sub-national government

18.1 A unitary state

The United Kingdom (UK) is a union of England, Wales, Scotland and Northern Ireland. Traditionally, the UK has been described as a unitary state (see Unit 11, Section 11.6) because regional and local government cannot legally do anything unless it has been empowered to do so by Acts of Parliament. Parliamentary sovereignty also means that any such powers could be limited or removed by future statutes.

In the UK, politics tends to be seen and understood in national political terms. The focus is on the world of Westminster and Whitehall and the centre is seen as London. However, the various agencies of sub-national government (whether local authorities or other bodies) and the devolved national Parliament in Scotland, the Assemblies in Wales and Northern Ireland also affect the lives of ordinary citizens. The services provided by these bodies range from education to refuse collection and from roads to housing. They are, therefore, services which are of vital importance to the whole population. In addition, there is a political principle to consider - the extent to which, in a parliamentary democracy, there is a need for a system of local democracy to counterbalance the power of a centralising state. It is the balance between the demands of centralised power and the needs of local autonomy which is at the heart of a discussion of the role and functions of devolved and sub-national government.

In recent years, major changes have taken place in devolved and sub-national government. Local government structure has changed, for example. The arrival of devolved government in Scotland, Wales and Northern Ireland has also changed the political landscape giving more autonomy to the different nations that make up the UK. There are prospects for further changes, with regional government planned for England. It can be argued that the UK now experiences 'multi-level governance' rather than Westminster government (Pierre & Stoker 2000).

18.2 Local government in England

The structure of local government in England is something of a 'patchwork quilt' of different types of local authority. The three basic units of local government today date back to the 15th century:
- the parish (the area served by the local church)
- the county (or shire)
- the town (also known as the borough or burgh).

Between 1974 and the mid-1990s, the organisation of local government was that shown in Box 18.1.

Box 18.1 Local government in England

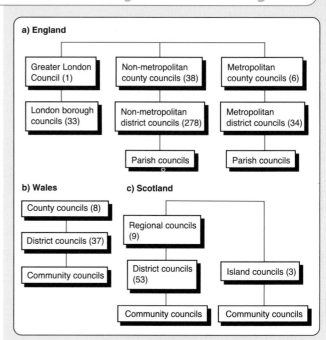

This diagram shows the organisation and structure of local government in England, Wales and Scotland after the Local Government Acts of 1972 and 1973 were passed. The numbers of each type of council are shown in brackets.

Unitary authorities

In 1991, the Conservative government argued that a unitary structure was the best system for organising local government. A unitary system would mean that all functions of local government would be delivered from a single body. In practice, this would mean the abolition of county councils and the transfer of their responsibilities to reformed district councils. The idea of a uniform unitary structure was dropped, however, after warnings of civil war within the Conservative Party. Instead, the government decided that the pattern of local government in each county in England should be decided locally. This would be achieved by local groups (local councils, voluntary associations and local businesses) and national groups (professional associations) making representations to a Local Government Commission.

The Local Government Commission for England

The Local Government Commission (LGC) was set up in 1992 under John Banham and was instructed to issue reports county by county. The LGC's first report proposed a unitary authority for the Isle of Wight. While this report was uncontroversial, that was not the case with the next three reports for Humberside, Avon and Cleveland. Most district councillors were hoping that a unitary authority would mean the same district boundaries but greater powers. The reports, however, recommended the amalgamation of several district councils into a single unitary authority (and the abolition of the county council). Overall, that would mean fewer councillors. As a result, many councillors protested about the recommendations.

In 1993, the appointment of a new Secretary of State for the Environment, John Gummer, put pressure on the LGC to recommend single-tier authorities in all but 'exceptional' cases. But this approach sparked a public outcry and was soon dropped.

The LGC's work 1993-98

Relying heavily on public opinion surveys, the LGC moved away from its earlier support for unitary authorities and began to make recommendations which either allowed the existing two-tier system to remain or proposed new 'hybrid' solutions (a combination of unitary status for one or two parts of a county and the retention of the two-tier system in the rest of the county). Chandler (2001) argues that there was a lack of coherence in the LGC's recommendations.

By the time the LGC had completed its county by county reporting, 46 new unitary authorities had been created in England, covering about a quarter of the non-metropolitan population. Four out of 39 counties had been abolished completely (Avon, Cleveland, Humberside and Berkshire) and the Isle of Wight had become a unitary authority. In the remaining 34 counties, the two-tier system was retained and the old county of Rutland (which had been abolished in 1974) was restored. The result of the Commission's work, therefore, was to create a mixed system of local government in England. In general, rural areas still tend to have two-tier systems while unitary authorities are more common in urban areas. These changes had been implemented by the end of 1998. The current position is illustrated in Box 18.2.

Future structural changes

The Labour government announced in August 2003 that the Strategy Unit at Downing Street will, over the next decade, conduct a review of local government structure because piecemeal reforms 'including foundation hospitals, elected police boards and school funding reform are changing the

relationship between central and local government' (*Guardian*, 6 August 2003). In addition, any future introduction of regional government would change the structure further (see below).

18.3 Local government in Wales and Scotland

In Scotland and Wales, the process of reform was swifter and did not involve a Local Government Commission. Consultation, therefore, was minimal.

The Welsh Secretary, David Hunt, made a statement on 3 March 1993 announcing that 21 unitary authorities would replace the existing district and county councils in Wales.

Similarly, the Scottish Secretary, Ian Lang, announced that the existing regional and district councils would be abolished and replaced by 25 unitary authorities (the three existing island councils would remain as unitary authorities, making a total of 28 in Scotland as a whole) - see Box 18.3 on page 357.

In both Wales and Scotland, there would be joint boards to cover areas such as policing, water supply and tourism. These plans came into effect on 1 April 1996.

18.4 Local government in London

Following the abolition of the GLC in 1985, there was no London-wide authority. Yet, according to the Joseph Rowntree Foundation (1997), there were four good reasons why such an authority should be set up:

- to provide a voice for London as a whole
- to introduce local democratic control to a number of public services that were being provided by government agencies, joint boards and departments
- to increase the capacity of local government in London to achieve particular policy objectives
- to override local parochial interests for the good of the capital as a whole.

In its 1997 general election manifesto, the Labour Party promised to hold a referendum proposing an elected Mayor and London-wide authority. The referendum was held in May 1998 and it supported the government's proposals, though the turnout was low. In 2000, Ken Livingstone was elected as Mayor (the voting system and election results are outlined in Unit 4). A Greater London Assembly, made up of 25 members, was also elected (see also Unit 4). The position of the 33 London borough councils remained unaffected by the changes.

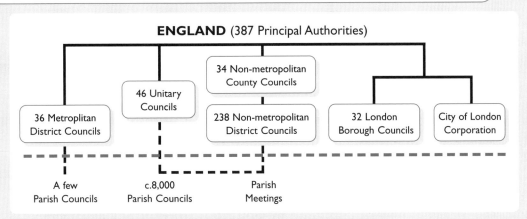

Box 18.2 Local government organisation in England since 1998

ENGLAND (387 Principal Authorities)

- 36 Metropolitan District Councils
- 46 Unitary Councils
- 34 Non-metropolitan County Councils
- 238 Non-metropolitan District Councils
- 32 London Borough Councils
- City of London Corporation

A few Parish Councils — c.8,000 Parish Councils — Parish Meetings

This chart shows local government organisation in England after 1998.

Source: Wilson & Game 1998.

Box 18.3 Local government organisation in Wales and Scotland

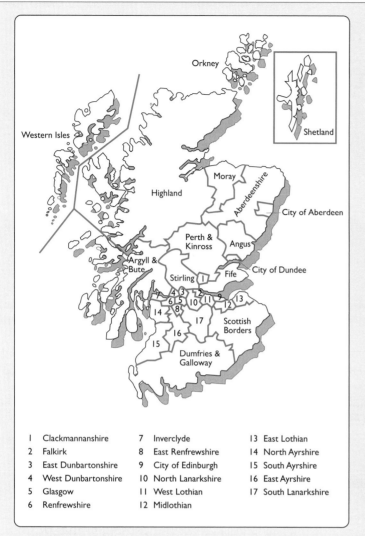

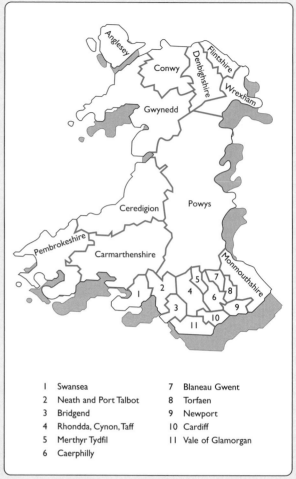

1	Clackmannanshire	7	Inverclyde
2	Falkirk	8	East Renfrewshire
3	East Dunbartonshire	9	City of Edinburgh
4	West Dunbartonshire	10	North Lanarkshire
5	Glasgow	11	West Lothian
6	Renfrewshire	12	Midlothian
		13	East Lothian
		14	North Ayrshire
		15	South Ayrshire
		16	East Ayrshire
		17	South Lanarkshire

1	Swansea	7	Blaneau Gwent
2	Neath and Port Talbot	8	Torfaen
3	Bridgend	9	Newport
4	Rhondda, Cynon, Taff	10	Cardiff
5	Merthyr Tydfil	11	Vale of Glamorgan
6	Caerphilly		

These maps show local government organisation in Wales and Scotland since 1996.

Source: Wilson & Game 1998.

After being elected, the most significant reform introduced by Ken Livingstone was the introduction of congestion charges for parts of central London, yielding an annual revenue of around £65 million.

18.5 *The 2000 Local Government Act*

Before the Local Government Act was passed in 2000, local government was run by councillors who themselves elected the leadership of the council, with the majority party usually taking the senior positions. Much of the work of the council was undertaken in committees and sub-committees made up of councillors from the different political parties.

The Local Government Act of 2000 signalled a change in direction. The key change was the requirement for local authorities with a population of over 85,000 to change their policy-making machinery. Local authorities were given the choice of one of the three management structures outlined in Box 18.4.

A decision by any local authority to opt for the directly elected Mayor has to be ratified first by a local referendum.

Box 18.4 The three management structures on offer

1. A Cabinet of not more than ten councillors with a Council Leader.
2. A directly elected mayor working with a Cabinet of not more than ten senior councillors, selected by the mayor.
3. A directly elected mayor who appoints a council manager to run the council services.

Also, a local authority is required to hold a referendum to decide whether to opt for a directly elected mayor if more than 5% of the local electorate petitions for the change.

How the new system works

The new structures involve a separation of powers between the executive and the rest of the council. The whole council ceases to have a role in policy-making. Instead, its main function is to monitor the executive. As a result, the role played by many councillors has been reduced to that of 'backbencher'. Key decisions are taken by the executive. Under the old arrangements, council decisions were taken either at full council or delegated to sub-committees whose composition had to reflect the political balance of the council. Under the new arrangements, it is possible for the executive to be dominated by one party, though, given the number of 'hung' councils, many executives are made up of councillors from more than one party. The full council still has to approve the budget and the overall plans for the year, but does not become involved in detailed policy decisions. The full council is, however, able to create scrutiny committees which can require the executive to explain their actions.

The response of the local authorities

Most local authorities have chosen the first option - Council Leader working with a Cabinet. By 2002, 316 councils had chosen this option. This involves least change as it is the system closest to that which existed before. In a small minority of local authorities, there has been support for the mayoral concept and the issue has been put to the voters in local referendums.

Mayoral referendums

In total, 30 referendums had been held by the end of 2002 (Game 2003). The outcomes of these referendums were mixed. For example, in Middlesborough, 84% of the voters were in favour of a directly elected mayor whereas 62% of people in Brighton voted against. Turnout in the referendums has also varied, with only 18% voting in Lewisham while 36% voted in North Tyneside. By the end of December 2002, 19 of the referendum results had been against directly elected mayors and only 11 had been in favour. Ten councils opted for an executive made up of Mayor and Cabinet, one opted for an executive made up of Mayor and council manager.

Mayoral elections

The first mayoral elections outside London were held in May 2002. Seven new mayors were elected - three Labour Party candidates, two independents, one Conservative and one Liberal Democrat. In some local authority areas, there was a grass-roots campaign to win support for a referendum against the wishes of the local council and, in some cases, the government has threatened reluctant councils that it would use reserve powers to force referendums. It is clear, however, that government ministers are divided on the issue and, following the experience in London (where the Labour candidate was defeated) and the Labour Party's failure to win the mayoral contests in Hartlepool and Middlesborough in 2002 (independent candidates beat the Labour candidates), there may be a reluctance to push the concept, especially if it was likely to lead to a loss of political control in an area. Game sums up the problem:

'After more than five years in office, the government has on its hands a politically embarrassing initiative apparently run out of steam. Too unpopular to be easily re-energised, but too visible to be quietly and unnoticeably abandoned, mayoral policy poses ministers with a genuine dilemma.' (Game 2003, p.144)

18.6 Councillors

Box 18.5 Councillors

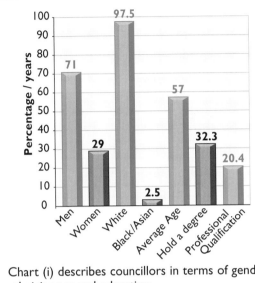

Chart (i) describes councillors in terms of gender, ethnicity, age and education.

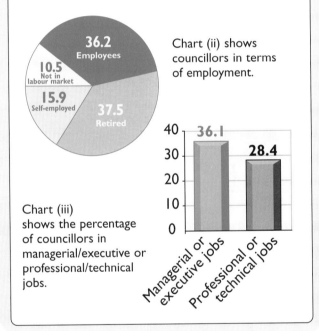

Chart (ii) shows councillors in terms of employment.

Chart (iii) shows the percentage of councillors in managerial/executive or professional/technical jobs.

The other main participants in local decision-making are the local councillors who are elected to all the different types of local authority which have been described (for a description of the election procedure see Unit 5). For the vast majority of councillors the work they undertake is part-time and unpaid, though they can claim expenses for attendance at meetings. The National Census of Local Authority Councillors in 2001 covering nearly all of the 410 town halls in England and Wales, found that local government was run by white, male councillors nearly half of whom were retired or not in the labour market. The survey was based on replies from 374 of the 410 local authorities in England and Wales and from 12,013 of the 21,268 councillors in office after the May 2001 local elections. The findings are shown in Box 18.5.

Main points   Sections 18.1 - 18.6

- In 1992, a Local Government Commission was set up to review the structure of local government in England. Although the government hoped that it would recommend unitary authorities, in some counties it favoured no change or a hybrid system.

- By 1998, 46 new unitary authorities had been created. Four of the 39 counties had been abolished completely and the Isle of Wight had become a unitary authority. In the remaining 34 counties, the two-tier system was retained. Rutland was restored.

- In Scotland and Wales, unitary authorities were imposed by central government. They came into effect on 1 April 1996.

- In London, a mayor and Greater London Authority were introduced, following a referendum.

- Plans for wider introduction of mayors have stalled.

- Elected councillors are untypical of the electorate they serve.

Activity 18.1 *The structure of local government*

Item A **Local government structure today**

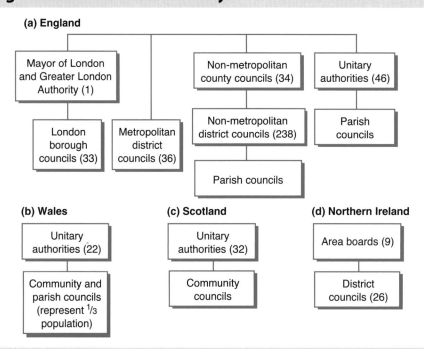

Source: Wilson & Game 1998.

Item B **In support of unitary authorities**

In 1991, the Conservative government published a document outlining its reasons for reviewing local government organisation. This document admitted that changing the structure of local government would not solve all the problems. Nevertheless, it suggested, unitary authorities would bring improvements. First, the document argued, it was important that people should be able to identify a single authority responsible for providing services for their area. Second, a single tier would reduce bureaucracy and improve the coordination of services, increasing quality and reducing costs - even if the county council and district councils in a county were efficient already. Third, a single tier would bring proper financial accountability. People must know who is responsible for setting a budget and achieving value for money in services in their area. Fourth, introducing unitary authorities would also offer the opportunity of relating the structure of local government more closely to communities with which people identify. This should increase interest in local affairs and make for more responsive and representative local government. The document made it clear that the government did not intend that county or district councils be abolished wholesale. In some places, it suggested, it might be best for existing authorities to be merged. In others, the best approach might be to create or recreate quite different authorities. In some areas, there could be a case for two tiers.

Source: HMSO 1991.

Item C **Decision-making in Oxford City Council**

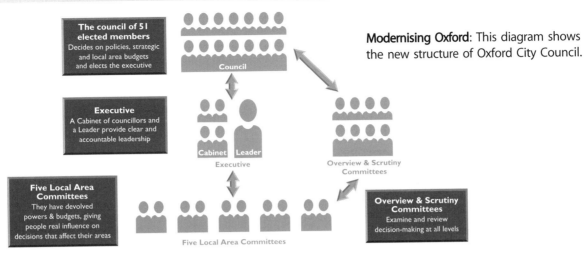

Modernising Oxford: This diagram shows the new structure of Oxford City Council.

In May 2002, Labour regained political control of Oxford City Council by winning 29 of the 48 seats. As part of the government plans for local government reorganisation, Oxford City Council had decided to opt for an executive (a Cabinet of councillors with a Council Leader). Labour took all the seats on the executive, with each of the members of the executive being given a specific area of responsibility (for example, the Council Leader took responsibility for strategic finance). At the same time, scrutiny panels (made up of councillors not on the executive) were set up to examine the decisions made by the executive. If there is a disagreement on a budget or a policy decision, the executive can be overruled by a meeting of all councillors. This, however, is unlikely to happen as Labour has a majority in the council.

Source: Oxford City Council.

Questions

1. a) Using Item A, explain how the organisation of local government has changed since the 1970s.
   b) Would you say that the organisation of local government has been improved? Explain your answer.
2. 'Unitary authorities will result in better local government.' Using Item B and your own knowledge, give arguments for and against this view.

3. a) Using Item C, explain how decisions are made by Oxford City Council.
   b) How does Oxford City Council's decision-making system differ from that in some other councils?
   c) Draw a diagram like that in Item C to show how the other decision-making systems work.

18.7 *The functions of local government*

Local government has two main functions:
- a political or representative function
- an administrative or executive function.

As a result of performing these functions, local authorities provide a wide range of services. The amount spent by local government in 2002 was around £66 billion. This amounted to about a quarter of all public expenditure and a tenth of the UK's gross domestic product. Local government is a major employer, employing about one in ten of the working population.

A. The political function of local authorities

Local authorities are democratically elected bodies. They provide an opportunity for people to stand for political office as councillors. One of the functions of local authorities, therefore, is to provide a forum in which elected representatives can determine how local affairs should be run. Equally, because the local authority is a democratically

elected body, it is (in theory at least) directly accountable to local people.

B. The administrative function of local authorities

The range of activities carried out by local authorities is determined by law and, therefore, ultimately by Parliament. A number of Acts of Parliament, some of which are specific to local government and some of which are more general, lay down the parameters within which local government can operate. It is the function of local authorities to implement and to administer the decisions made by central government.

The precise function of each type of local authority varies and there is a division of responsibility depending on whether the authority is a single tier or two tier. For example, metropolitan district councils and unitary authorities have the responsibility for nearly all the services in their area whereas county councils only control some services (for example, education) and district councils control other services (for example, housing). For a full list of services for each type of authority see Item B in Activity 18.2 below.

18.8 Party politics and local government

There is good evidence to suggest that party politics has grown in importance in local authorities since 1970. The Maud Report of 1967 found that 50% of local authorities were under independent control whereas the Widdicombe Report of 1986 found that just 16% of local councils (mainly in rural areas) were dominated by independent councillors.

As the number of independent councillors has declined, so the number of councillors standing on a party ticket has increased. According to the Widdicombe Report, 83% of councillors in 1985 stood on a party ticket. The result of this is an inevitable growth in party discipline and party voting.

This trend has continued since the Widdicombe Report with the result that local government is increasingly conducted on party lines. Today, most councils are controlled by one of the three main parties and most councillors belong to one of the three main parties.

Following the local elections in 2003, Labour lost ground, leaving the Conservatives in control of the largest number of councils. On a national basis, Labour received 31% of the vote, the Liberal Democrats 30% and the Conservatives 35% but on a low turnout of 32%. In 2003, however, there was a small growth in the number of independents and minor party councillors elected.

The benefits and drawbacks of party control are outlined in Box 18.6.

18.9 The 'nationalisation' of local politics

In addition to the growth of party politics, it is claimed that there has been a growing 'nationalisation' of local politics.

This means that local government is perceived less in local terms and more in terms of national government and national political issues. In other words, local elections are seen as judgements on the performance of parties nationally rather than as a test of local opinion or as a judgement on the performance of local politicians.

Some doubts, however, have been expressed about the extent of the 'nationalisation' of local politics. Rallings & Thrasher, for example, have claimed that:

'We have long suspected, using evidence from the annual local elections, that, for many voters, making a choice of party at local level is something to be done independently of, and even in contradiction to, their national party preference. We now know this to be true.' (Rallings & Thrasher 1997, p.182)

18.10 New ways of involving ordinary people

Concern about the dominance of party groups of councillors and the declining level of voter turnout has led to consideration of new ways of involving ordinary people in their local communities. This was encouraged by a government paper *Local Democracy and Community Leadership* (published in 1997) which suggested a large range of ways of seeking and responding to the views of the citizen. In addition to the use of local referendums (see Unit 5), the paper suggested the use of:

- citizens' juries (groups of c.12 people brought together to study an issue in depth over three to five days)
- focus groups (groups of varying size which meet at length or regularly to discuss issues)
- visioning conferences (conferences where new ideas are floated)

Box 18.6 The benefits and drawbacks of party control

The benefits of party involvement

Greater party involvement in local government is supported on the following grounds:

1. It helps to define the issues placed before the electorate. Parties stand on a manifesto which clearly distinguishes their different policies.
2. Policies tend to be based on principles rather than personalities. This leads to greater consistency.
3. There is greater coherence because of party discipline.
4. More seats are contested and there is a slightly higher turnout at elections.
5. There is greater accountability because the electorate is able to comment on a party's performance by re-electing it or voting it out of office.
6. There is better coordination between local and national politics.
7. The democratic structure of parties allows party members to participate in decision-making. So, as a result, political participation increases.

The drawbacks of party involvement

Greater party involvement in local government has been criticised for the following reasons:

1. Party involvement is not desirable because most local issues are not party political. Local issues are neglected because party concerns predominate.
2. Real decisions are no longer taken in council chambers but in party meetings. Decisions are made by party activists behind the scenes rather than by democratically elected councillors.
3. The electorate votes on party lines rather than on the quality of candidates.
4. Council decisions are made in an adversarial climate (two hostile groups debate angrily). This is neither the most effective nor the most efficient way to make decisions.
5. Wholesale reversal of policies takes place when party control changes hands.
6. Independent councillors find it much harder to be elected because they do not have a party machine behind them.

- deliberative opinion polls (like citizens' juries only larger and more statistically representative)
- citizens panels (statistically representative samples of residents)

- community forums or area-based neighbourhood committees (groups set up to consider policies or proposals which affect their particular community)
- interest and user group forums (groups made up of people who have a vested interest in a particular policy or proposal).

Main points (Sections 18.7 - 18.10

- **Local government has two main functions: (1) a political or representative function; (2) an administrative or executive function.**
- **There is good evidence to suggest that party politics has grown in importance in local authorities since 1970.**
- **Greater party involvement is an advantage because: (1) it helps to define the issues placed before the electorate; (2) policies are based on principles not personalities; (3) there is greater coherence; (4) more seats are contested and turnout is higher; (5) there is greater accountability; (6) better coordination; (7) there is greater participation.**

- **Greater party involvement is a disadvantage because: (1) most local issues are not party political; (2) real decisions are taken behind the scenes; (3) the electorate votes on party lines not on the quality of candidates; (4) decision-making is not effective or efficient; (5) policies are reversed when party control changes; (6) independent councillors find it difficult to be elected.**
- **In addition to the growth of party politics, it is claimed that there has been a growing 'nationalisation' of local politics.**
- **Concern about the dominance of party groups and declining turnout has led to consideration of new ways of involving ordinary people in their local communities.**

Activity 18.2 Local government - services and party politics

Item A Decentralisation of decision-making

The government has emphasised the need to increase public participation in local government. One way in which it hopes to achieve this is through greater decentralisation of decision-making in local government. An example of greater decentralisation can be seen in Oxford. Five area committees have been set up to serve different parts of the city. The committees are designed to provide a forum for local people and community groups to debate issues and form partnerships and contribute to the debate on the council's plans for the future. The area committees meet in public. They are made up of ward councillors. Meetings allow members of the public to speak on issues which concern them, ask questions and suggest agenda items. Area committees have been given powers set out by the executive to take some day-to-day decisions in their local area. In addition, each area committee has its own budget to implement. The intention is to devolve power and budgets, giving ordinary members of the public real influence on decisions. However, the area committees have been criticised on a number of counts:

1. They have power over very few decisions and have a very limited budget.

2. There is a fear that local pressure groups, rather than members of the public, will dominate them.

3. Their decisions can be challenged if four councillors ask for a particular decision to be looked at again. If this happens, the full council or the executive can overrule the original decision.

Source: information provided by Oxford City Council and Oxford County Council.

Item B Local authorities' areas of responsibility

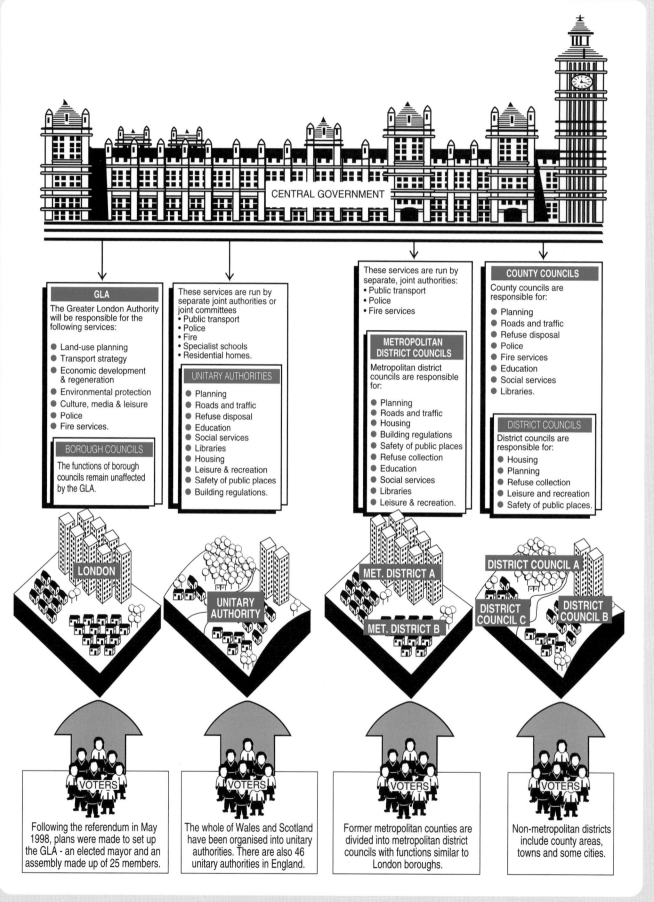

CENTRAL GOVERNMENT

GLA

The Greater London Authority will be responsible for the following services:

- Land-use planning
- Transport strategy
- Economic development & regeneration
- Environmental protection
- Culture, media & leisure
- Police
- Fire services.

BOROUGH COUNCILS

The functions of borough councils remain unaffected by the GLA.

These services are run by separate joint authorities or joint committees
- Public transport
- Police
- Fire
- Specialist schools
- Residential homes.

UNITARY AUTHORITIES

- Planning
- Roads and traffic
- Refuse disposal
- Education
- Social services
- Libraries
- Housing
- Leisure & recreation
- Safety of public places
- Building regulations.

These services are run by separate, joint authorities:
- Public transport
- Police
- Fire services

METROPOLITAN DISTRICT COUNCILS

Metropolitan district councils are responsible for:

- Planning
- Roads and traffic
- Housing
- Building regulations
- Safety of public places
- Refuse collection
- Education
- Social services
- Libraries
- Leisure & recreation.

COUNTY COUNCILS

County councils are responsible for:

- Planning
- Roads and traffic
- Refuse disposal
- Police
- Fire services
- Education
- Social services
- Libraries.

DISTRICT COUNCILS

District councils are responsible for:

- Housing
- Planning
- Refuse collection
- Leisure and recreation
- Safety of public places.

LONDON

UNITARY AUTHORITY

MET. DISTRICT A

MET. DISTRICT B

DISTRICT COUNCIL A

DISTRICT COUNCIL C

DISTRICT COUNCIL B

VOTERS

VOTERS

VOTERS

VOTERS

Following the referendum in May 1998, plans were made to set up the GLA - an elected mayor and an assembly made up of 25 members.

The whole of Wales and Scotland have been organised into unitary authorities. There are also 46 unitary authorities in England.

Former metropolitan counties are divided into metropolitan district councils with functions similar to London boroughs.

Non-metropolitan districts include county areas, towns and some cities.

Source: The *Guardian*, 5 March 1991, Wilson & Game 1998 and McNaughton 1998.

Item C Local election results 2003

	Councils			Councillors		
	+/-	Total			+/-	Total
Labour	-28	66		Labour	-833	3,001
Conservative	+31	110		Conservative	+566	4,423
LibDem	+5	28		LibDem	+193	2,624
SNP	-1	1		SNP	-21	182
Independent	-2	10		Independent	-42	1,142
Other	0	2		Other	-9	254
NOC	-5	123		NOC	n/a	n/a

This table shows the results of the local elections in May 2003. 'NOC' stands for 'no overall control'. In a council where no overall control exists, effective party discipline is essential if alliances are to be forged between parties which seek to share power.

Source: Tonge 2003b.

Item D Local election results 1973-2003

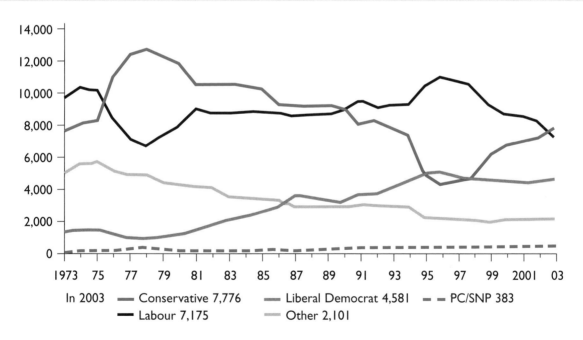

In 2003 — Conservative 7,776   — Liberal Democrat 4,581   - - PC/SNP 383
— Labour 7,175   — Other 2,101

This graph shows the total number of councillors, by party, in all local authorities in Britain between 1973 and 2003.

Source: House of Commons Library

Questions

1. Using Item A, explain what might be the advantages and disadvantages of decentralisation of decision-making.

2. Judging from Item B what are the main difference between the four types of local authority?

3. a) What evidence is there in Items C and D of party political control of local government?

   b) Has the development of party political control been beneficial? Explain your answer.

18.11 *Local finance*

Providing local services costs local government a great deal of money. This money comes from a number of sources - see Box 18.7. First, fees and charges are made for some local authority services. Car parking charges or swimming pool entrance fees are examples. Second, councils also raise money to pay for local services through local taxation. Since 1993, this local taxation has been the council tax - a tax based on property. Third, councils receive money from business rates paid by the owners of offices, shops and factories in the area. Fourth, councils receive central government grants which are earmarked for specific services. And fifth, councils can acquire money by borrowing (for example, to build schools or houses). Local government found itself operating under tighter financial constraints after the mid-1970s. Governments reduced the grants to local authorities and restricted the opportunities for local councils to increase their own revenues.

Box 18.7 Sources of revenue for local government

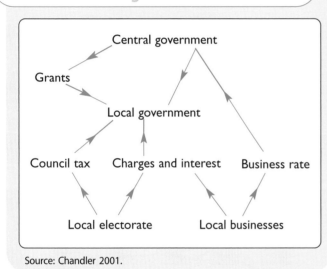

Source: Chandler 2001.

The council tax

Since March 1993, the local taxation levied by local authorities has been called the council tax. The title of the tax was carefully chosen so that those facing new bills would be conscious that they were paying for local authority services. The council tax raised £16.6 billion in 2002-03 which amounted to 25% of local government spending (*Guardian*, 13th August 2003).

It should be noted that business rates are still set, collected and distributed by central government. All the money raised from businesses is collected into a national pool. Central government then decides how much each local authority should receive from that pool. The Labour government has announced, however, that it is considering allowing local authorities to collect some of the money (*Guardian*, 4 July 2003).

Developments since May 1997

Like its predecessor, the Labour government has been wary of giving local authorities greater financial freedom. Nick

Raynsford, the Minister for Local Government, has indicated that he would be willing to use his powers to cap spending (ie to stop councils increasing council tax) (*Guardian*, 1 March 2003). In the longer term, Raynsford is conducting a review of local government finance with the aim of reducing local councils' dependence on national funding. This stood at 75% of total council income in 2003, making UK local government the most dependent on central government in Europe. Options for change include introducing local income taxes, green taxes and congestion charges and increasing the amount of money that councils can raise locally. The hope is that this 'will increase local political accountability, local autonomy, voter turnout and reduce pressures on some councils to raise council tax excessively' (*Guardian*, 6 August 2003).

18.12 *The privatisation of local government*

Until the election of the first Thatcher government in 1979, it was taken for granted that local authorities were themselves responsible for providing services. From 1979, however, there was increasing pressure on local authorities to 'privatise' their services. The long-term aim was for local authorities no longer to be responsible for providing and managing services. Instead, they would be 'enabling authorities' - bodies which regulated the services provided by outside organisations. So, for example, instead of a council employing its own workforce to collect dustbins, an outside contractor would do the work. The council's job would be to check that standards were being met. To achieve this aim, the Conservative government brought in Compulsory Competitive Tendering (CCT). Councils were forced to set their workforce up as free-standing companies ('direct service organisations') and allow private companies to bid against these direct service organisations for contracts.

Best Value

Following the 1997 general election, the Labour government set up a pilot scheme designed to replace CCT with 'Best Value'. The pilot scheme was regarded as a success and the Local Government Act 1999 abolished CCT altogether, replacing it with a national Best Value scheme - see Box 18.8 on page 366. Under this Act, by 2005, all local authorities must have reviewed all their services to make sure they are providing cost-effective, high-quality services which are focused on the needs of local people.

The government's aim in introducing Best Value was to ensure that, within five years, all council services achieved performance levels that were only achieved by the top 25% of councils at the start of the five years. Inspections are carried out by the Audit Commission and published. A star rating is provided, ranging from no stars for poor performance to three stars for excellent performance. If performance does not improve, the government has the power to switch control of a service away from the poorly-performing council.

The Audit Commission

The Audit Commission has provided a bleak picture of some local council services, calling into question the speed at which

Best Value can boost performance. In a review of the 150 largest councils, over half were either good or excellent but 35 were graded weak or poor (*Guardian*, 12 December 2002). Sources within the Labour Party have described Best Value as the last chance for local government. While this may be an exaggeration, if Best Value fails, other patterns of delivery of local services may be introduced.

18.13 Is there a need for local government?

In theory, of course, there is no absolute need to have a system of local government. Services could be delivered locally, but administered and controlled by central government. This happens today with social security. Social security is delivered locally through offices located all over the country. Control, however, rests with the Department of Social Security in London. All services provided by local government could be organised in this way. Some critics of local government favour this approach. They point out that there is a great deal of variation in the standard, range and

quality of services which are offered by local authorities. If all services were controlled from the centre, they argue, then provision would be uniform throughout the country.

Other reasons for and against doing away with local government are given in Box 18.9 on page 367.

18.14 The powers of central and local government

1. Legislative power

From a constitutional point of view, local government is entirely at the mercy of central government. Parliament has the power to reform or reduce the functions performed by local government and it could even pass a law abolishing all local authorities outright. In practice, both Labour and Conservative governments have passed laws affecting the responsibilities of local authorities, without the agreement of the local authorities concerned.

2. Inspections

In addition to wielding the powers described above, some

Box 18.8 Best Value

BV's key purpose - to make a real and positive difference to the services that people receive from their local authority.

How? By requiring councils to make arrangements - in the form of an annual BV Performance Plan (BVPP) and regular service-specific and cross-cutting Reviews - to secure *continuous improvement* in the way they undertake *all their service responsibilities*, having regard to their economy, efficiency and effectiveness. Councils must review all their services every five years to ensure they are applying continuous improvement principles.

BV Performance Plans - assess existing performance, set future targets, and outline the authority's programme of BV Reviews; the principal means by which an authority is held to account for the efficiency and effectiveness of its services and for its plans for the future.

BV Reviews - in reviewing all services on a five-year cycle, an authority should follow the '**four Cs**':

- **Challenge** why, how, and by whom a service is being provided and be able to show that alternative approaches to service delivery have been considered.

- **Compare** its performance with that of similar authorities across a range of relevant national and local indicators, taking into account the views of both service users and potential suppliers.

- **Consult** local taxpayers, service users, external partners and the wider community in setting new and demanding performance targets and an action plan that will deliver continuous improvements.

- **Compete**, wherever practicable, in order to secure efficient and effective services.

Source: Game 2003.

Review questions would typically include:

- **What** does the service do now?
- **How** well does it do it, and for what cost?
- **What** do its customers want of it?
- **How** well does it do it in comparison with others?
- **Could** the benefits of the service be obtained in some other way?
- **Could** some other organisation provide it better and/or cheaper than the council?
- **Can** we do the job better (and by how much)?
- **Can** we make customers happier (and by how much)?
- **How** can we get the same benefits to the people while spending significantly less?
- **Should** we be providing the service at all?

Inspection - all functions of an authority are subject to inspection at least once every five years by either an existing special inspectorate - eg Ofsted, the Social Services Inspectorate, the Benefit Fraud Inspectorate - or by the Audit Commission's Best Value Inspectorate. All inspection reports are published, some 2,000 by the end of 2002.

Failing services - the minister (the Deputy Prime Minister, following the Prime Minister's reorganisation of government departments in May 2002) has wide-ranging powers to intervene where an authority is judged by inspectors not to be delivering a BV service. Ultimately the minister has the power to remove responsibility for the 'failing' service from the authority altogether.

Box 18.9 Reasons for and against doing away with local government

Local government should be abolished because:

1. Inefficiency
Some local authorities are inefficient. The services they provide cost more than the same services provided by other local authorities. Abolition of local government would increase efficiency.

2. Cost
Local government itself is a cost. Meetings of councillors and the full range of support services they require does not come cheap.

3. Narrowness of outlook
Local government can be narrow and introspective. Local authorities are often concerned only with local issues. How these local issues fit into the national picture, or even how they relate to what is happening just over the authority's border, is simply ignored. Central government is better able to plan.

4. Party self-interest dominates
Since local government has become dominated by political parties, narrow party self-interest has come to dominate policy decisions.

5. Lack of interest in local government
There is a marked lack of interest in local democracy. This is reflected in the low turnout in local elections and in the public's lack of knowledge about councils' functions. The public only cares about the efficient delivery of services; it does not care about local democratic control.

6. Run by amateurs
Local councillors are amateur politicians who lack the detailed knowledge to run complex modern bureaucracies.

7. Central government dominates anyway
There is such wide central government control that the scope for local autonomy is so small that it is hardly worth bothering with a system of local government.

8. Remoteness
Local government has become remote to many people.

Local government should not be abolished because:

1. It exists elsewhere
All but the smallest democratic states have systems of local government. The tendency elsewhere is to increase not to erode the powers of local government.

2. It is efficient
Local government is an efficient method of administering certain services since local authorities are run by local people who know local needs. Control exerted from the centre tends to be rigid and inflexible.

3. It is not expensive
There is no indisputable evidence to suggest that services could be provided more cheaply without local government.

4. Policy can be coordinated
Local authorities are multi-purpose bodies and can, therefore, ensure policy coordination across a range of departments. They are not necessarily narrow or introspective.

5. It has independence
Local authorities can experiment with ideas because they have a degree of independence. An individual authority can introduce a pilot scheme, which, if successful, may be adopted elsewhere.

6. It encourages democracy
Local government encourages democracy because local representatives run councils and local people are given the opportunity to vote in local elections. Low turnout is not a good reason for doing away with local democracy. It could be a sign that people are generally happy with the way local affairs are run. Also, local government reflects the different political balance of different parts of the country.

7. It is a defence against central government
Local authorities can be seen as a barrier or defence against an all-powerful central government.

8. It holds local public servants to account
An important function of local government is to hold local public servants accountable. The conduct and misconduct of local authority staff is best left to elected local politicians.

9. It is part of our heritage
Local government is part of our heritage and culture. It ensures that the important principle of 'no taxation without representation' is maintained.

---

ministers are responsible for appointing Chief Inspectors and responding to the work of inspectorates. For example, the Education Secretary is responsible for appointing the Chief Inspector of the Office for Standards in Education (Ofsted) and may take action if an Ofsted report shows that a school is failing. In addition, the Audit Commission monitors the work of local authorities.

3. The doctrine of *ultra vires*
It is not only by legislation that central government can control local authorities. The freedom of local authorities is also restricted by the doctrine of *ultra vires*. Whereas individuals are free to do anything which is not illegal, local authorities are only allowed to do what is specifically allowed by law. Anything else may be judged to be *ultra vires* (beyond their legitimate powers). Government departments circulate advice and guidance to local authorities to help them fulfil their responsibilities within the law.

4. Default powers
Some legislation provides ministers with 'default powers' - a minister who is dissatisfied with the performance of a local authority can, as a last resort, step in and take over the running of a service or transfer it to another body. This happened in July 1995, for example, when a government 'hit squad' (as the media termed it) was sent in to run Hackney Downs Comprehensive School, following a highly critical Ofsted report.

A complex network

It is clear that, constitutionally, central government has the dominant hand. But that does not mean that central-local relations are straightforward. It is not just a question of central government issuing instructions directly to local authorities which must be met, though during the Conservative period of office from 1979 to 1997 there was a strong tendency in that direction.

18.15 *Local government and the Labour government*

The election of a Labour government in 1997 was welcomed by those who favoured a revitalisation of local government, not least because, in its general election manifesto, the Labour Party promised to lean less heavily on local government:

'Local decision making should be less constrained by central government, and also more accountable to local people.' (Labour 1997, p.34)

While this suggested that the government was prepared to restore some independence to local authorities, significant controls remained in place and the introduction of the Best Value scheme (see above) was criticised on the grounds that central government was continuing to interfere excessively in local affairs. It was in response to this criticism that, following its re-election in June 2001, the Labour government produced a White Paper entitled *Strong Local Leadership - Quality Public Services*. This White Paper stated:

'Over the course of this Parliament, we will give councils more space to innovate, to respond in ways that are appropriate to local circumstances, and to provide more effective leadership. We will provide greater freedom for councils to borrow, invest, trade, charge and set spending priorities.' (*Strong Local Leadership - Quality Public Services paragraphs 4.6 - 4.7*)

Chris Game points out that:

'This "space", however, and the new "freedoms and flexibilities" would not come unconditionally. On the contrary, they would be incorporated into the latest refinement of the "carrots and sticks" strategy.' (Game 2003, p.127)

This strategy is examined in Item C in Activity 18.3.

Main points   Sections 18.11 - 18.15

- **Since the mid-1970s, local government found itself operating under tighter financial constraints.**
- **During the 1980s, opponents of local government argued that it was inefficient and unrepresentative while supporters complained that its powers were being eroded by central government.**
- **Constitutionally, local government is entirely at the mercy of central government - Parliament has the power to reform or reduce local government functions.**
- **Although central government has the upper hand, central-local relations are not straightforward. There is a complex network of relationships.**
- **The Labour Party has promised to give more control back to local councils that are performing well.**

Activity 18.3 *Central-local government relations*

Item A **A changing role**

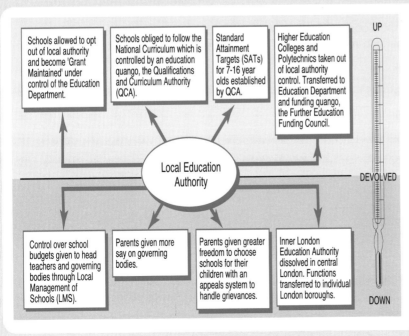

Since 1980, services which used to be provided by local authorities have been devolved either upwards to government departments, quangos or regional bodies or down to lower tier authorities or voluntary bodies (see diagram left). Similar processes have occurred for other services such as housing, transport, the police, urban development, road maintenance and environmental services. At the same time, however, local authorities have been asked to take on some new responsibilities - for example, the Childrens Act 1989 increased local authorities' responsibility for the protection of children in special need. These new responsibilities do not balance the loss of other services. Also, they are generally regarded as 'Cinderella' services - they are not glamorous and are not wanted by other bodies.

Source: McNaughton 1998.

Item B **Central-local government relations**

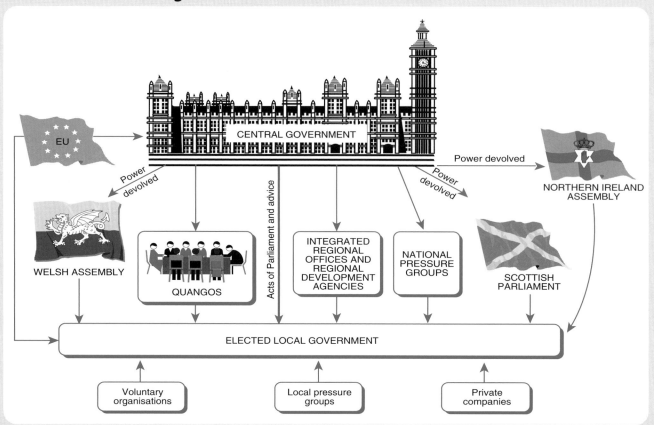

Source: Wilson & Game 1998.

Item C **The CPA process**

The White Paper *Strong Local Leadership - Quality Public Services* resulted in the introduction of the so-called CPA process. 'CPA' stands for Comprehensive Performance Assessment. The idea was that all local authorities would be comprehensively assessed and then rated as Excellent, Good, Fair, Weak or Poor. In mid-December 2002, the Audit Commission produced the first list, rating 22 councils as Excellent and 54 as Good. These 'high performing' councils would be rewarded with fewer inspections, fewer policy plans to be submitted for ministerial approval and some loosening of constraints over their spending. The 76 councils rated Excellent or Good amounted to 51% of the 150 councils on the list. A total of 13 (9%) of councils were rated as Poor and a further 22 (15%) as weak. These councils could expect few of the freedoms offered to the Good or Excellent. With ministerial and civil service oversight, they would be assisted in drawing up and implementing recovery plans. The message was clear. If you are judged - not by your own voters but by external assessors from the Audit Commission - to be failing, you are likely to see your service responsibilities transferred to other providers and, ultimately, your council placed in the hands of government-appointed administrators. Best Value operated on a service-by-service basis. The CPA process uses a similar scale but rates the council as a whole. The trouble is that everybody knows that even the worst managed councils have their areas of strength, just as the best have their weaknesses. So, it was particularly frustrating for those working in services which Best Value had rated Good or Excellent to find that their CPA rating was Weak or Poor. Building as they do on Best Value - which was itself the successor of CCT - CPAs would appear to embody very much the kind of 'command and control' approach to local government adopted by national governments of both parties over the past 20 years.

Source: Game 2003.

Questions

1. Using Items A-C, describe the relationship between central government and local government.

2. a) How does the CPA process described in Item C differ from Best Value?

b) Give arguments for and against the view that the Labour government has given local authorities greater freedom.

18.16 *What is devolution?*

Devolution means the transfer of power from a superior to an inferior political body. According to Bogdanor (1979), devolution has three elements:

- it involves the transfer of power to a subordinate elected body
- it involves the transfer of power on a geographical basis
- it involves the transfer of functions at present exercised by Parliament.

Since Parliament retains the power to suspend the devolved Parliament or assembly, parliamentary supremacy remains intact:

> 'Devolution is the delegation of central government powers without the giving up of sovereignty.' (Simpson 1998, p.7)

In practical terms, therefore, devolution involves the setting up of an elected regional assembly whose powers and responsibilities are carefully defined. Normally, these powers would not include the control of defence or foreign policy (areas which would still be dealt with by the central government). The new elected regional assembly may or may not have tax-varying powers. Whether it does or not, a devolved assembly is by no means independent. It is still bound by decisions made by central government. However, the precise form that devolution takes can vary. In the case of the UK, devolution has produced four different ways of governing the component parts:

> 'Three of the component parts - Scotland, Wales and Northern Ireland - have devolved bodies, while England does not. Scotland, Wales and Northern Ireland, moreover have devolved bodies of quite different types.' (Bogdanor 2003, p.222)

Devolution is different from federalism and separatism. Federalism involves the division of sovereignty between two levels of government which then become (in theory at least) autonomous (ie. completely free to look after their own areas of responsibility). Separatism means the creation of a self-governing independent state with complete control over its internal and external affairs.

Arguments for devolution

Supporters of devolution have argued that it disperses power more fairly, makes government more efficient and better serves people's loyalties. This argument is explored in Box 18.10.

It was also argued that, when pressures for some degree of decentralisation have reached a stage where they can no longer be ignored, then:

> 'Britain can only be held together if some power concentrations at the centre are dispersed.' (Holliday 1997, p.237)

Arguments against devolution

Arguments against devolution have tended to emphasise the cost of establishing a new tier of government and the difficulties of administering this extra tier - see Box 18.11.

Opponents of devolution also argued that devolution would be the first step on the road to complete independence and to the break-up of the United Kingdom. The 1992

Box 18.10 Arguments in support of devolution

Giving power to new assemblies would relieve a major burden on central government. By allowing decisions to be taken close to the local area affected by them, they would also be more efficient because they would be targeted on the area's needs and probably taken more quickly than at national level. By being closer to the people and being seen to be closer, the assemblies would engage the attention and loyalties of citizens. They would be 'their' assemblies. That support would also be an important dynamic in encouraging cooperation and support in the implementation of policies.

Adapted from Norton 1994.

Box 18.11 Arguments against devolution

By setting up a new layer between central and local government, the potential for delay would be increased, as would the potential for clashes between central and regional government. Another layer of government may also produce greater confusion as to the responsibilities of the different layers. Who should the citizen complain to? Who should be held responsible if the dustbins aren't emptied?

Source: Norton 1994.

Conservative election manifesto, for example, claimed that devolution proposals:

> 'Do not intend to bring about separation, but run that risk. They could feed, not resolve, grievances that arise in different parts of Britain.' (Conservative 1992, p.47)

Fear of the unknown was another argument against devolution:

> 'It is a very radical constitutional reform, creating a form of government hitherto unknown in the United Kingdom.' (Bogdanor 2003, p. 224)

18.17 *Devolution in Wales*

The Welsh language is central to Welsh nationalism:

> 'Many of the modern battles of Welsh nationalism have been around the status of the Welsh language. Wales has an estimated 500,000 Welsh speakers out of a total population of 2.7 million. Much of the effort of Welsh nationalists has been to ensure that the Welsh language is protected and that its official status is recognised... Apart from these expressions of cultural nationalism, Wales has been affected only to a small extent by nationalist movements.' (Gamble 1993, p.82)

Since non-Welsh speakers make up a majority of the population in Wales and since Welsh nationalism centres so closely on the language, its appeal is reduced since many non-Welsh speakers feel excluded.

18.18 Steps towards devolution

The 1979 referendum in Wales (see Unit 5 for an analysis) showed that there was little support for devolution there at that time. Yet, as in Scotland (if to a lesser extent), interest in home rule grew between 1979 and 1997. There were two main reasons for this. The first was the 'democratic deficit' which had grown during the Conservative years in power after 1979. This development is examined in Box 18.12.

Box 18.12 Development of a democratic deficit

Between 1979 and 1997, the Conservative Party was a minority party in Wales. Despite this, Conservatives were appointed to ministerial positions at the Welsh Office. A succession of Englishmen were even appointed to the post of Secretary of State. At the same time during this period, local government, the bastion of the Labour Party, was downgraded and many powers passed to quangos, to which Welsh Conservatives - who could not otherwise get elected to office - were often appointed. As a result, the feeling grew that democracy was lacking in Wales.

Source: Bradbury 1998.

The second reason for growing enthusiasm for devolution was economic. Between 1979 and 1997, Wales' economic links with the British economy weakened and its links with the EU strengthened:

> 'In this context there was concern that the interests of Wales were not well represented by the Welsh Office in comparison to other European regions which had their own Assembly to protect regional interests.' (Bradbury 1998, p.7)

The result of the 1997 general election in Wales are shown in Box 18.13.

Box 18.13 Results of the 1997 general election in Wales

	Lab	Con	Lib Dem	PC
Votes	886,432	317,127	200,020	161,030
Seats	34	-	2	4
% Votes	54.7	19.6	12.4	9.9
% Seats	85.0	-	5.0	10.0

Source: Dobson 1998.

18.19 The 1997 referendum

The result of the referendum held in September 1997 confirmed that support for devolution was far less widespread in Wales than it was in Scotland. On a low turnout of little over 50%, there was a majority of just 0.6% in favour of a Welsh Assembly. In other words, only a quarter of the Welsh electorate positively supported devolution. In

part, this result has been explained by suspicion in North Wales (where more people speak Welsh and support for Plaid Cymru is much stronger) that a Cardiff-based Assembly would increase the power of an English-speaking political élite in South Wales.

As well as a North-South divide, there is also an East-West divide, with most western counties of Wales voting for an Assembly and most of the eastern counties which border England voting against.

18.20 The Welsh Assembly

The elections to the Welsh Assembly in May 1999 redrew the Welsh political map. The electoral system used was the Additional Member system (see Unit 4). Although, it was anticipated that Labour would win an overall majority, in fact, it did not, taking 28 of the 60 available seats. Despite the fact that these were the first Assembly elections, only 46.6% of the electors voted. The results of the election are given in Unit 5 - Activity 5.2, Item B.

Unlike the Scottish Parliament, the Welsh Assembly does not have tax-varying powers. Instead, it operates within a budget set by central government. Also, it does not have the power to pass primary legislation (laws), but only the power to deal with secondary legislation (statutory instruments - see Unit 14, Box 14.24). The powers and make-up of the Welsh Assembly are outlined in Box 18.14 on page 372.

Like the Scottish Parliament, the Welsh Assembly has no powers over defence, foreign affairs, the constitution of the UK, social security and transport safety and regulation. The Assembly, however, has taken over control of some of the activities carried out before by the Welsh Office. The 17 policy areas the Assembly works on are listed in Box 18.15 on page 372.

The Welsh Assembly 1999-2003

At first, Labour opted to operate a minority administration with Alun Michael as Leader of an Executive of ten members. However, among Labour supporters there was a great deal of unease 'about the way in which Michael appeared to have been foisted upon the Welsh Labour Party by the London leadership' (Denver 2001, p.22). In February 2000, Michael resigned, following the tabling of a vote of no-confidence in the Assembly. He was replaced by Rhodri Morgan who formed a coalition with the Liberal Democrats from October 2000. Morgan is regarded as a more traditional Labour figure, supporting 'distinctive Welsh solutions to Welsh problems and thereby distancing Wales from Blair's approach in Westminster' (Bradbury 2000, p.26).

Howard Elcock claims that, in the period 2000-03, the Welsh Assembly developed a distinctive policy agenda:

> 'Despite its more limited powers and weaker claims to public support, the Welsh National Assembly has also developed its own policy agenda and has struck out for greater independence from the centre in a number of ways.' (Elcock 2003, p.9)

Some of the policies which can be described as 'distinctive' are listed in Box 18.16 on page 372.

The Welsh Assembly has also introduced greater use of information technology, more open government and a more informal approach in its proceedings (Rathbone, 2003).

Box 18.14 The Welsh Assembly - powers and responsibilities

The Welsh Assembly has committees dealing with some matters previously handled by the Welsh Office. It has no tax-varying powers, nor is it able to make or amend laws. Rather, it works within an annual budget, currently £7 billion, set by Whitehall. Unlike Scotland which has developed a Parliament on Westminster lines, there are no ministers and the Welsh Assembly is headed by a First Minister. According to the Labour government, however, the ten-member executive in the Welsh Assembly has substantial policy-making powers.

The Assembly has power to:

- Take budgetary decisions: it manages the block grant allocated to Wales by the Treasury. This was £7.456 billion in 1999/2000; £8.354 billion in 2000/2001; £9.7 billion in 2001/2002; £10.4 billion in 2002/2003; £11.21 billion in 2003/2004.
- Pass subordinate legislation.
- Formulate policies relating to Wales.
- Change some Welsh organisations, called quangos.
- Set spending targets for publicly funded bodies in Wales.
- Make recommendations to Europe about European laws which could affect Wales.

The Assembly does not have power to:

- Make primary legislation.
- Raise or lower taxes.

Box 18.15 Welsh Assembly policy areas

The Assembly works on 17 policy areas:

- Agriculture, forestry, fisheries and food
- Ancient monuments and historic buildings
- Culture (including museums, galleries and libraries)
- Economic development
- Education and training
- The environment
- Health and health services
- Highways
- Housing
- Industry
- Local government
- Social services
- Sport and recreation
- Tourism
- Town and country planning
- Transport
- The Welsh language

Box 18.16 Distinctive policies, 2000-03

The following policies mark a departure from the line taken by the Blair government:

- grants have been reintroduced for students from low income families
- prescription charges have been abolished for under-25s and free dental checks introduced
- £50 million has been allocated to help communities affected by cutbacks in the steel industry
- tests for seven-year-olds have been abolished and secondary school league tables have been scrapped
- free bus passes have been introduced for the over 60s
- free school milk has been reintroduced.

However, like its Scottish counterpart there have been ongoing cost, design and construction problems with the new Assembly buildings.

Public support for the Assembly has been high. A survey conducted by the University of Wales, Aberystwyth, in 2002, concluded that '65% of the Welsh electorate would like to keep the Assembly, with most of those (39%) wanting its powers increased to the level of the Scottish parliament' (Rathbone 2003, p.190).

18.21 The Assembly election in 2003

Despite the apparent high level of support for the Assembly

expressed in polls, the turnout in the 2003 Assembly election was down to 38% (the result is given in Unit 5 - Activity 5.2, Item B). Labour emerged as the successful party winning 30 of the seats. The Times commented:

'The success, in which Labour drove out nationalists to reclaim its South Wales valleys heartlands was based on a traditional manifesto far removed from New Labour modernisation.' (Times 3 May, 2003)

Plaid Cymru was the major loser, only holding on to 12 seats, five fewer than in 1999. The party had attacked Labour from the left, arguing for higher taxes and against privatisation. It had also put its demand for independence 'on the backburner, with the new goal of a Scottish style Parliament by 2007' (Guardian, 25 April 2003). The Conservatives gained two seats and the Liberal Democrats remained on six seats.

After the election, Labour decided against coalition and, by selecting the Presiding Officer from one of the opposition parties, ensured it had a 30 to 29 seat majority. The Labour Party in Wales has continued with its radical agenda, announcing that there will be no foundation hospitals in Wales and there will be no tuition fees for Welsh students.

The future

There is some concern that, in the long term, the Welsh Assembly and executive may be seen as nothing more than a Welsh council writ large. This may be confirmed by its having followed a local government rather than the parliamentary model in its procedures. It is also like a local authority in some other respects. For example, its officials are accountable to all members of the Assembly, as local government officers are accountable to all members of their councils. By contrast, Scottish civil servants are accountable to ministers on the Scottish Cabinet, just as civil servants in Whitehall are accountable to particular government ministers. However, the Assembly has appointed Lord Ammanford to conduct an independent review of its powers. According to Peele (2003), this review is likely to conclude that the Welsh Assembly should be given the same powers as the Scottish Parliament.

Main points   Sections 18.16 - 18.21

- **Devolution involves the setting up of an elected regional assembly whose powers and responsibilities are carefully defined. Whether a devolved assembly has tax-varying powers or not, it is still bound by decisions made by central government.**
- **Supporters argue that devolution disperses power more fairly, makes government more efficient and better serves people's loyalties. Opponents emphasise the cost of establishing a new tier of government and the difficulties of administering it. They also argue that devolution is likely to lead to complete independence.**
- **A small majority of those who voted in the referendum held in 1997 supported devolution in Wales.**
- **Unlike the Scottish Parliament, the Welsh Assembly does not have tax-varying powers. Instead, it operates within a budget set by central government. Also, it does not have the power to pass primary legislation (laws), but only the power to deal with secondary legislation.**
- **At first, Labour tried to run the executive in the Welsh Assembly alone. But after the resignation of Alun Michael in March 2000, Rhodri Morgan set up a coalition administration with the Liberal Democrats. After the elections in 2003, Labour was able to govern alone as it had an overall majority.**

Activity 18.4 *The Welsh Assembly*

Item A **A Time Line**

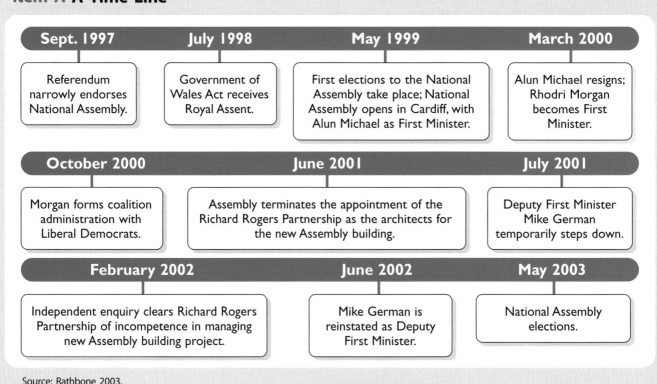

Sept. 1997	July 1998	May 1999	March 2000
Referendum narrowly endorses National Assembly.	Government of Wales Act receives Royal Assent.	First elections to the National Assembly take place; National Assembly opens in Cardiff, with Alun Michael as First Minister.	Alun Michael resigns; Rhodri Morgan becomes First Minister.

October 2000	June 2001	July 2001
Morgan forms coalition administration with Liberal Democrats.	Assembly terminates the appointment of the Richard Rogers Partnership as the architects for the new Assembly building.	Deputy First Minister Mike German temporarily steps down.

February 2002	June 2002	May 2003
Independent enquiry clears Richard Rogers Partnership of incompetence in managing new Assembly building project.	Mike German is reinstated as Deputy First Minister.	National Assembly elections.

Source: Rathbone 2003.

Item B Political rows in Wales

Two key political miscalculations hampered the Assembly in its first few months. First, Tony Blair used all the pressure that Labour HQ could exert to ensure that Alun Michael was chosen as First Minister, rather than Rhodri Morgan (who was independent-minded and had an old Labourish air). Not only did it look as if London was interfering in Welsh affairs, Michael did not have the loyalty of many Labour AMs (Assembly Members) and, after ten months of struggle abruptly resigned. It would have been better if Morgan had been chosen in the first place. And second, Michael chose to rule as a minority administration. It simply didn't work and Morgan negotiated a coalition with the Liberal Democrats as soon as he became First Minister. Two further rows then erupted before the elections of 2003. First, in July 2001, Mike German, Liberal Democrat Leader and Morgan's deputy, faced a police inquiry into his expenses claims in a former job. He denied the charges but temporarily stepped down. Eventually, in June 2002, however, the charges were dropped and German reinstated. Although he was not guilty, his absence was a blow not least because he made it clear that he blamed Labour AMs for a 'witch-hunt'. The second row was longer-lasting. In October 1998, the Richard Rogers Partnership (RRP) won the competition to design a new building for the Assembly. As with many public building projects, costs soon began soaring. Moran put the project on hold for three months while the option of extending the temporary home of the Assembly was explored. The Assembly voted against this idea, though, and building resumed. In June 2001, however, RRP was sacked by the Assembly's Finance Minister and this began a lengthy dispute. In February 2002, RRP were cleared by an independent inquiry. In October 2002, however, the Assembly allowed other companies to bid for the right to construct the building. Critics argue the Assembly handled the project very poorly.

Rhodri Morgan

Mike German holding a baby

Source: Rathbone 2003.

Item C The Assembly's achievements

There are a number of ways in which the Assembly can be said to have pioneered a new approach to politics in the UK. One is the innovative use of information technology. All papers are available on the Assembly's intranet and business - including voting - is conducted electronically. Second, there is a refreshing informality. Members sit in a semicircle and address each other by their first names. There are none of the odd traditions which can make the Commons seem pompous and remote. Since 25 out of the 60 members are women, there is a much better gender balance than in the Commons. Open government is another progressive area. One of Rhodri Morgan's first decisions as First Minister was to publish minutes of Cabinet Meetings on the internet. In addition, the Assembly has made a number of decisions which show that 'One major impact of devolution was simply that Wales need not follow health and education policies being promoted in England'.

Source: Rathbone 2003.

Questions

1. Using Items A-C, give arguments for and against the view that the creation of a Welsh Assembly has been a success.

2. 'Wales doesn't really have self-government.' Using Items A-C and your own knowledge, give arguments for and against this view.

3. Using Items A-C write a short article entitled: 'Wales' bumpy path to devolution'.

18.22 Scottish nationalism

Scottish nationalism arises from the fact that Scotland negotiated the terms of union in 1707:

'As a result, it was able to retain its own distinctive institutions - a separate legal system, church, schools and universities - which have helped to nurture the strong sense of national identity in Scotland. Scots are well aware that they were once an independent nation and could be so again. The union with England which was considered so advantageous at one time could be broken if it ceased to work to Scotland's benefit.' (Gamble 1993, p.75)

Gamble goes on to point out that Britain's economic decline, the development of the EU and the discovery of North Sea oil have all contributed to Scottish discontent with rule from Westminster - as did the fact that four successive general elections between 1979 and 1992 resulted in a Conservative government even though the vast majority of Scottish people did not vote Conservative. These factors combined led to widespread support for some form of 'home rule'.

18.23 Steps towards devolution before 1997

The referendum of 1979

The electoral success of the nationalist parties in the general election of 1974 brought devolution onto the political agenda. The Labour government's weak position in Parliament led to a deal in which referendums in Scotland and Wales were conceded. These referendums were held on 1 March 1979 (see Unit 5). While the result of the Welsh referendum was conclusive (there was very little popular support for devolution), the Scottish result was inconclusive. A majority voted in favour of devolution. The majority, however, was not large enough for devolution to be implemented. In the short term, the result of these referendums was a major blow for the nationalists. But the issue of home rule, especially in Scotland, gradually re-emerged.

Growing support for devolution 1987-97

As in Wales (see Section 18.17 above), there are two main reasons for the growth in support for some degree of home rule after 1979. First, there was an increasingly obvious democratic deficit in Scotland - support for the Conservatives in Scotland fell lower and lower and yet in 1983, 1987 and 1992, the Conservatives won an overall majority in the Commons. This democratic deficit became particularly obvious from 1987 when the Conservatives received their lowest share of the vote in Scotland since universal suffrage was introduced. The second reason for growing enthusiasm for home rule was the a desire for some degree of economic independence. Many Scots believed that the revenue from North Sea oil would have been better invested if it had gone to a Scottish body rather than to the Treasury in London. And, as in Wales between 1979 and 1997, Scotland's economic links with the EU strengthened.

In the 1990s, two main camps emerged. On the one hand, the Scottish National Party (SNP) rejected devolution because it did not go far enough. Instead, it aimed for independence within the EU. On the other hand, the Labour Party and Liberal Democrats were committed to devolution and joined together in the Scottish Constitutional Convention (SCC). The SCC was a forum for all Scottish groups committed to devolution. It was set up in 1989 to reach agreement on how Scotland ought to be governed.

During the 1992 general election campaign, hopes were high among those in favour of devolution that the Conservatives would suffer further losses and the case for devolution would then become irresistible. In fact, the Conservatives gained one seat and an extra 1.7% votes. Although this was a minor gain, it was interpreted by the media as a victory for the unionist cause. Following the election, the Conservative government published a re-evaluation of its position on devolution. This document made it clear that the government did not support change.

The 1997 general election

The 1997 general election result in Scotland (see Box 18.17) suggested that the Conservatives had underestimated support for devolution. For the first time, they failed to return a single MP to Westminster. Over three-quarters of the Scottish seats went to the Labour Party, even though Tony Blair caused controversy by comparing the tax-raising powers of a future Scottish Parliament with those of a parish council and by saying that even after a Scottish Parliament had been set up:

'Sovereignty rests with me as an English MP, and that's the way it will stay.' (quoted in Sell 1998, p.204)

Box 18.17 The 1997 general election result in Scotland

	Lab	Con	Lib Dem	SNP
Votes	1,283,321	493,059	365,359	616,540
Seats	56	-	10	6
% Votes	45.6	17.5	13.0	21.9
% Seats	77.8	-	13.9	8.3

Source: Dobson 1998.

The SNP share of the vote in Scotland in the 1997 general election was 22%, a marginal percentage increase compared to 1992, though on a lower turnout. Although the SNP received a smaller number of actual votes than in 1992, it increased its number of seats from three to six. Following the election, the SNP's official attitude towards devolution changed. The party decided that, tactically, it would support the campaign for a Scottish Parliament in the forthcoming referendum and it would then participate in the Parliament - as a 'stepping stone to independence' (Holliday 1997, p.235). This remains the ultimate goal of the SNP. So, both the SNP and the Conservatives supported the argument that devolution would lead eventually to full independence. The Conservatives feared this, however, while the SNP hoped for it.

18.24 *The 1997 referendum and the creation of the Scottish Parliament*

One of the new Labour government's first steps was to hold referendums on devolution. In September 1997, the Scottish electorate voted convincingly for a devolved Parliament on a turnout of 60.1% (see Unit 5). By a smaller, but still clear, majority, voters also opted for that Parliament to have tax-varying powers. The outcome was, therefore, the 'Yes-Yes' result for which Labour, the Liberal Democrats and the SNP (but not the Conservatives) had been campaigning.

Following the Yes-Yes result in the referendum, the first elections for the Scottish Parliament were held in 1999, using a version of the Additional Member system (see Unit 5). Following each election for the Scottish Parliament, the largest party chooses the First Minister (a sort of Prime Minister for Scotland) and the First Minister chooses an Executive (equivalent to the Cabinet). With the introduction of a proportional element in the electoral system and with four main political parties contesting the seats, some form of coalition government is always likely.

The powers transferred from Westminster to the Scottish Parliament are considerable - see Box 18.18. It has full legislative powers over a wide range of matters and can vary income tax. In addition, the Parliament produces an Executive - in effect the Scottish government - which it then holds to account.

Conflict between Westminster and the Scottish Parliament

The Executive of the Scottish Parliament largely determines the legislative programme and is responsible for implementing policies. Whenever there is a division of powers between different levels of government, there is the potential for disputes over who does what. To avoid this, a joint ministerial committee was set up, comprising UK government and Scottish Executive ministers. The devolution legislation also provided that, in the event of a conflict, the Judicial Committee of the Privy Council would make a binding decision.

The 1999 election for the Scottish Parliament

On 6 May 1999, Scottish voters returned 129 MSPs, but no party had an overall majority (see Box 18.19 on page 377). Labour was nine short of an overall majority while the SNP formed the largest opposition party. The Conservatives failed to win any of the constituency seats, but won 18 of the top-up seats. Despite being the main party with the smallest number of seats, the Liberal Democrats became part of the government through coalition. Three other MSPs were also elected representing minor parties and an independent.

The low turnout rate of 58.7% meant that the hoped-for increased level of political engagement did not materialise. Labour's Donald Dewar was appointed Scotland's first First Minister. Following his death in October 2000, he was succeeded by Henry McLeish. McLeish resigned in November 2001 after a row over office expenses. He was replaced by Jack McConnell.

Box 18.18 The powers of the Scottish Parliament

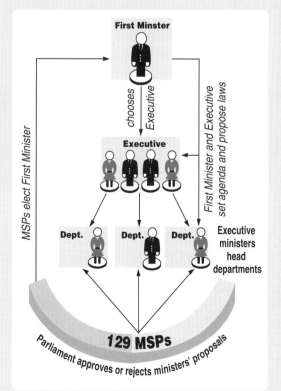

Reserved powers *(not devolved)*	Areas not reserved *(responsibility of Scottish Parliament)*
Common market for UK goods and services	Agriculture, fisheries and forestry
Constitution of the UK	Economic development
Defence and national security	Education
Employment legislation	Environment
Fiscal, economic and monetary system	Health
Foreign policy, including Europe	Housing
Health (in some areas); medicine	Law and home affairs
Media and culture	Local government
Professional regulations (in certain cases)	Research and statistics
Protection of borders	Social work
Social security	Training
Transport safety and regulation	Transport

(i) This diagram shows the way in which the Scottish Parliament is set up.

(ii) This table shows the powers that have been devolved to the Scottish Parliament and those that have not.

Box 18.19 The 1999 election to the Scottish Parliament

Party	Constituencies		Regional lists		Total seats	
	% vote	Seats won	% vote	Seats won	Seats won	% seats
Labour	38.8	53	33.6	3	56	43.4
Scottish National Party	28.7	7	27.3	28	35	27.1
Liberal Democrats	14.2	12	12.4	5	17	13.2
Conservatives	15.5	0	15.4	18	18	14.0
Scottish Green Party	0.0	0	3.6	1	1	0.8
Scottish Socialist Party	1.1	0	2.0	1	1	0.8
Member for Falkirk West	0.8	1	1.2	0	1	0.8
Others	0.9	0	4.5	0	0	0
Totals		73		56	129	

This table shows the results of the election to the Scottish Parliament held in May 1999.

spend has been determined by the Treasury in London. This limits the options available to the Scottish Executive.

The Scottish Nationalist Party (SNP)

After the election to the Scottish Parliament in 1999, the Scottish Nationalist Party found itself in opposition to the coalition government. Having originally opposed devolution, the SNP concentrated its efforts on making devolution work.

Post-election opinion polls suggested that support for an independent Scotland had peaked at around 30%. In 2000, this new reality led the SNP to sideline its demand for independence, the aim being to pick up support from disillusioned Labour voters who might vote SNP but 'who would be nervous of the prospect of an independent Scotland' (*Guardian*, 14 January 2003). This policy shift was confirmed in the 2003 election campaign for the Scottish Parliament when the demand for independence was reduced to a pledge that, if the SNP gained power, a referendum on the issue would be held within four years.

Scottish Parliament elections 2003

The Scottish Parliament elections in 2003 gave Scots the opportunity to express a verdict both on devolution in general and on the performance of the various political parties in particular. The result is summarised in Box 18.21 on page 378. Turnout fell to 49.4% of the electorate, suggesting a lack of enthusiasm for the Parliament. The major

Coalition government

Following the May 1999 election, a formal coalition was arranged between Labour and the Liberal Democrats - despite the fact that the Liberal Democrats had won only 17 seats, coming fourth behind Labour, the Scottish Nationalists (SNP) and the Conservatives. The coalition agreement gave the Liberal Democrats two out of the 11 Cabinet posts and two junior ministerial positions. More significantly, the formal coalition entailed political compromises enshrined in the coalition document *Partnership for Scotland*, designed to last for the four years up to the next election. The document included compromises over spending plans for education and health, replacement of student tuition fees, a rural affairs policy, land reform and freedom of information. On all these issues, the policies were not exactly what either Labour or Liberal Democrat electors had voted for.

18.25 *The work of the Scottish Parliament 1999-2003*

Following the election in 1999, the coalition of Labour and Liberal Democrats began governing Scotland and, despite predictions that it would fall apart, survived policy disagreements in a number of areas, including over student tuition fees (Lynch 2001). A number of laws were then passed in the period 1999 to 2003 that show the Labour Executive in the Scottish Parliament was prepared to go down a different path from that taken by the Labour government in Westminster. These new laws are summarised in Box 18.20.

Yet, the Scottish Parliament and the Executive has also come under heavy criticism from the Scottish media (Bort 2001). One area of considerable concern has been the escalating cost of the new Parliament building originally estimated to cost £40 million pounds and now expected to cost £400 million.

Finance

There has been no attempt made by the Scottish Executive to use its power to increase or decrease the basic rate of income tax by up to 3 pence in the pound. As a result, the amount of money that the Scottish Parliament has had to

Box 18.20 Measures passed by the Scottish Parliament 1999-2003

The following measures were taken in the period 1999-2003:

- a law was passed in Scotland allowing Scottish students not to have to pay tuition fees before starting university courses (it was compulsory for them to pay in England) and maintenance grants were restored in Scotland but not in England

- Section 28 - which prohibits the promotion of homosexuality in schools - was repealed in Scotland but not in England

- fox hunting was banned in Scotland but not in England

- a law was passed in Scotland allowing elderly people to receive greater help in paying the costs of nursing homes than they could obtain in England

- a more liberal Freedom of Information Act was passed in Scotland than that passed at Westminster.

parties did badly, especially the SNP which saw its vote slump and the loss of eight seats. Labour lost six seats but the Liberal Democrats and Conservatives achieved the same number of seats as in the 1999 elections.

Box 18.21 Scottish Parliament elections 2003

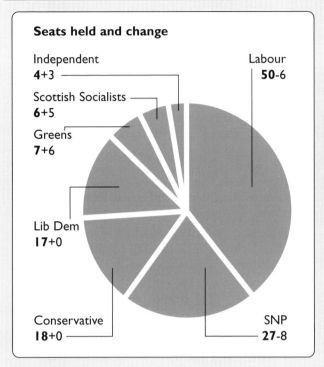

Seats held and change

Independent
4+3

Labour
50-6

Scottish Socialists
6+5

Greens
7+6

Lib Dem
17+0

Conservative
18+0

SNP
27-8

Source: *Guardian*, 3 May 2003.

As in 1999, Labour was the largest party (this time with 50 seats) but it lacked an overall majority. The *Guardian* commented that:

> 'The minority parties and the mavericks were the biggest winners, with the Scottish Green Party and the Scottish Socialist Party substantially increasing their share of the vote and a clutch of independents dislodging the main parties across the country.' (*Guardian*, 3 May 2003)

Owing to the PR system of voting, elections in Scotland are very different from those to the Commons since minority party candidates and independents have a much greater chance of success. The *Times* concluded:

> 'The Scottish electorate has expressed its grave dissatisfaction. It is unhappy about the way it has been governed, it has little confidence in its principal political parties, it is underwhelmed by the impact of its new Parliament.' (*Times*, 3 May 2003)

Following the election, a coalition of Labour and Liberal Democrats formed the Executive but with increased representation for the Liberal Democrats at Cabinet level. Of the 11 Cabinet ministers, three are Liberal Democrats and they also have another two ministers in the total ministerial team of 18 (*Guardian*, 21 May 2003). Both parties have had to compromise on their programmes in order to achieve a working coalition. Labour made an important concession by agreeing to support the Liberal Democrats' policy of introducing a system of proportional representation for elections to local government. At the same time, the Liberal Democrats compromised by supporting Labour's youth crime proposals.

Main points Sections 18.22 - 18.25

- **The development of a democratic deficit and the desire for greater economic independence led to the growth in support for some form of home rule in the late 1980s.**
- **Two camps emerged - the SNP supported independence, the Scottish Constitutional Convention supported devolution.**
- **In September 1997, the Scottish electorate voted convincingly for a devolved Parliament with tax-varying powers.**
- **The Scottish Parliament's powers are considerable. It has full legislative powers over a wide range of matters and can vary income tax. In addition, the Parliament produces an Executive which it then holds to account.**

- **To avoid disputes, a joint ministerial committee was set up, comprising UK government and Scottish Executive ministers. In the event of a major conflict, the Judicial Committee of the Privy Council makes a binding decision.**
- **Following the May 1999 election, a formal coalition was arranged between Labour and the Liberal Democrats. This coalition was renewed after the election in 2003.**
- **A number of laws passed after 1999 show that the Labour Executive in the Scottish Parliament was prepared to go down a different path from that taken by the Labour government in Westminster.**

Activity 18.5 *The Scottish Parliament*

Item A **The Scottish Parliament in operation**

This photo shows the Scottish Parliament in operation in 2002.

Item C **The Parliament at work (1)**

Although the coalition has faced a number of disputes and disagreements, it has survived. Because it has an agreed programme, it has managed to provide stable government. The convention of collective ministerial responsibility has been an important factor. As at Westminster, ministers have been bound by collective decisions and have generally operated in a spirit of partnership. There have been some backbench rebellions by Liberal Democrat MSPs, but few lasted for long - though one did lead to the temporary defeat of the Executive's fisheries policy in 2001. The existence of a coalition government is of importance because it has a bearing on Labour-Liberal Democrat relationships at Westminster. A number of questions arise. Does involvement in coalition government at Scottish Parliament level affect campaigning in general elections? Do the coalition arrangements affect relations between Labour and Liberal Democrat MPs at Westminster? Have the election results dampened down the Blair government's enthusiasm for electoral reform? At some point, it is likely that the SNP will be part of a coalition. How will that affect relations with Westminster? Even now, there is the difficulty of parties being in government and opposition in different parts of the UK simultaneously (ie the Liberal Democrats).

Source: Lynch 2001.

Item B **Twelve differences between the Scottish Parliament and the Commons**

David Steel, Presiding Officer of the Scottish Parliament (the equivalent of Commons Speaker) set out the following 12 differences between the Scottish Parliament and the Commons in a speech made in 2001.

1. The Parliament has a fixed term of four years.

2. There are no annual sessions and legislation can continue through all four years of Parliament.

3. Parliament is elected by a proportional electoral system making it unlikely that a single party will be able to form an Executive on its own.

4. Parliament is laid out differently - in a semicircle with government and opposition benches next to each other rather than facing each other.

5. Sittings rarely go on after 6 pm.

6. Parliament has a high proportion of women MSPs.

7. Bills are scrutinised by committees and evidence taken from interested parties before they are debated in Parliament.

8. A Petitions Committee receives public petitions.

9. A weekly public 'time for reflection' led by different faiths is held instead of Anglican prayers before the opening of parliamentary business.

10. Proceedings are webcast.

11. The Parliament attempts to be more accessible to the public.

12. A new Parliament building is being built in Edinburgh*.

*As in Wales, the cost of this building soared, causing discontent both within Parliament and outside.

Source: Mitchell 2003a.

Item D The Parliament at work (2)

Jack McConnell (right) became First Minster after his predecessor, Henry McLeish resigned in November 2001 following a row over office expenses. McCleish had become First Minster following Donald Dewar's death in October 2000.

In its first three years, the Scottish Parliament enacted over 40 pieces of legislation. Most of this would have been supported by Labour in Westminster had devolution not existed, but some exclusively Scottish legislation would not have been passed for lack of parliamentary time. A few measures passed by the Scottish Parliament would not have by Westminster and these measures did meet opposition from Westminster - notably arrangements over tuition fees and the reintroduction of free care for the elderly. The passing of these measures led to pressure in England and Wales for Westminster to follow Scotland. As in the past, however, there are very real political and constitutional constraints on Scottish policy-making. Finance remains a major issue. Although, in theory, the Scottish Parliament has power over areas such as health and education, there is, in reality, a great deal of overlap between the responsibilities between Westminster and Edinburgh. Devolution has not resulted in separate institutions making policy separately for Scotland, but it has meant that Scottish institutions share some power and responsibility with Westminster-based institutions.

Source: Mitchell 2003b.

Questions

1. Item A shows the Scottish Parliament in operation. Write a paragraph explaining the key developments which made this possible.

2. Using Items A-D, give arguments for and against the view that the creation of a Scottish Parliament has been a success.

3. Judging from Items B-D, how has the political system changed in Scotland since devolution?

18.26 Relations between the devolved assemblies and central government

Between 1999 and 2003, relations between the devolved assemblies and central government remained relatively trouble-free as the political position of all has been largely the same. If, however, a Conservative central government was to be elected, the position might change significantly. An indication of what might happen in these circumstances came in 1999. A national decision by the UK Agriculture Minister to end a ban on beef sold on the bone (following the foot-and-mouth crisis) was not initially accepted by Scotland, Wales and Northern Ireland, with the result that the ban remained in force. Elcock & Parks make the point that 'the relative status of the four administrations in determining when to end the ban appeared curiously indeterminate' (Elcock & Parks, 2000 p. 90).

Issue 1 - finance

The majority of the funding for the Scottish Parliament, and all of it for the Welsh Assembly, comes from Westminster. The actual amounts are worked out according to the 'Barnett formula' which has ensured that per capita expenditure is higher in Scotland and Wales than in England. This has led to accusations that the people living in the devolved areas continue to be subsidised by English taxpayers. Any attempt to redress the balance, however, is likely to cause an outcry since the formula has been applied for over 20 years.

Issue 2 - the West Lothian question

When the debate over devolution began in the 1970s, the Labour MP for West Lothian, Tam Dalyell, pointed out that, if devolution went ahead, there would be an imbalance in terms of power. While a devolved Scottish Parliament would allow the Scots alone to legislate on matters such as health and education, Scottish MPs would still sit at Westminster. Since health and education legislation for England would be decided at Westminster, Scottish MPs would have a say over English health and education legislation while English MPs would not have a say over Scottish health and education legislation. This problem was highlighted in 2003 when Labour only survived a backbench rebellion on the creation of 'foundation hospitals' because of the votes of non-English Labour MPs. In other words, the creation of these hospitals depended upon votes from Scottish and Welsh MPs even though the Scottish Parliament and Welsh Assembly had decided against these proposals.

Peter Lynch suggests that there are five main responses which could be made to the West Lothian question. These are outlined in Box 18.22.

Box 18.22 Five responses to the West Lothian question

Peter Lynch suggests that the problems posed by the West Lothian question could be solved by the following means.

1. Devolving power to the English regions.
2. Reducing the number of Scottish and Welsh MPs.
3. Restricting the voting rights of Scottish MPs so they cannot vote on matters affecting the rest of the UK (the so-called 'in-out' arrangements).
4. Setting up a federal structure.
5. Ignoring the West Lothian question on the grounds that the British constitution has many inconsistencies.

Source: Lynch 1998.

Dorey suggests that the West Lothian question will be partly answered by the planned reduction in the number of Scottish MPs at Westminster and possibly by a few English Regional Assemblies. He concludes that:

'Overall though, answers to the West Lothian question appear either to be too complex, in terms of further constitutional problems, or lacking in widespread support, both among politicians at Westminster and amongst much of the electorate particularly in England...As such, "the West Lothian question" looks as though it will not be answered for some time yet. Indeed, it may never be fully answered at all.' (Dorey 2002 p. 21)

Issue 3 - Scottish over-representation

Closely related to the West Lothian question is the fact that Scotland is over-represented in the House of Commons:

'Scotland has been over-represented in the House of Commons since 1918, gaining 11% of the UK's seats despite having only 8.8% of the UK's population and also being over-represented in terms of the size of Scotland's electorate compared to the UK's electorate.' (Lynch 1998, p.47)

Between 1948 and 1997, the over-representation of Scottish MPs was guaranteed by law. The creation of a Scottish Parliament, however, made it difficult to justify this over-representation and, in July 1997, the government announced that this law would be repealed:

'Scotland has had a privileged position because it joined England as an equal in the Treaty of Union in 1707. The figure of 72 MPs was enshrined in legislation and it is that section of the Act that is to be repealed.' (Guardian, 24 July 1997)

Box 18.23 outlines the plans.

The reduction in the number of Scottish MPs at Westminster will affect the composition of the Commons. In party terms, it is likely that the Labour Party will lose out (in 2001, Labour won 56 of the 72 seats). In regional terms, fewer Scottish MPs will mean a smaller Scottish bloc and what Lynch (1998) calls the 'Englishing' of the House.

Box 18.23 The reduction of the number of Scottish MPs

Unlike the devolution measures drawn up in 1978-79, the 1998 Scotland Act made provisions to reduce the number of Scottish MPs. A clause provided for future reduction in the number of Scottish MPs sitting at Westminster, this is to occur when the Boundary Commissioners next redraw constituency boundaries - probably during 2004 or 2005.

If the Boundary Commission uses the same guidelines as it uses for drawing up English constituencies (each constituency having an average of 70,000 voters), the number of MPs from Scotland will drop from 72 to 59.

Source: Dorey 2002.

Issue 4 - coordination with the centre

Although following the Scottish and Welsh elections in 2003 and the UK general election in 2001, Labour remained the largest party in all three assemblies, conflict between the two tiers of government could be significant if and when this situation changes. The Judicial Committee of the Privy Council would be the arbitrator for unresolved disputes, and this committee's involvement would mean entry into uncharted constitutional waters.

Issue 5 - intra-UK differences

The Scottish Parliament has the power to create legislation and its executive has the power to make policies which apply only to Scotland. This, indeed, is a fundamental reason for devolution. But this degree of autonomy can conflict (and has already done so on a number of issues) with the principle of equal treatment for all UK citizens, irrespective of where they live. For example, students in Scotland, Wales and England now have quite different arrangements for tuition fees and grants so creating a 'post-code lottery'. Some commentators argue that this undermines the idea that Britain is a unitary state.

Issue 6 - changes in the Commons

Devolution has important constitutional implications when it comes to the role of MPs at Westminster. Since devolution, MPs representing constituencies in Scotland and Wales have been barred from sitting on the select committees on education and employment, health and home affairs. In addition, since the role of Scottish MPs, and Welsh MPs to some extent, is restricted (because certain areas are dealt with by the Scottish Parliament), there is an issue about the appointment of ministers at Westminster who are Scottish. This came to the fore in the summer of 2003 with the appointment of John Reid, who sits for a Scottish constituency, as Health Secretary. Despite having overall responsibility for health policy in the government, health policies in his own constituency were outside the minister's control as they were the responsibility of the Scottish Parliament. Procedural changes are outlined in Box 18.24 on page 382.

Issue 7 - devolution and the Cabinet

Although the government made it clear that a Secretary of State for Scotland and a Secretary of State for Wales would

Box 18.24 Procedural changes since devolution

Oral Questions

Oral questions to both the Secretaries of State for Scotland and Wales take place approximately every four weeks. Until devolution the Scottish Office had an hour of questions, and the Welsh Office had thirty minutes. Since devolution, the time available for the Scottish Office has been reduced to thirty minutes. Questions to both departments may be asked by any MPs with constituencies, but they must now relate to the Secretary of State's responsibilities following devolution.

Grand Committees

Another of the main ways in which Scottish and Welsh business is discussed in the Commons is through the work of the Grand Committees. Although the Procedure Select Committee argued in 1999 that the Grand Committees would be found unnecessary after devolution, the government's response was that, although some adjustment to the procedures of those Committees would be necessary, it was reluctant at this early stage to dispense with them.

Source: Fact Sheet P8 - see: www.parliament.uk

---

continue to be members of the Cabinet after devolution was implemented, it is unlikely that these posts will survive in the long term. Once the transitional phase is completed, there will be little for them to do and they will have little legitimacy. The downgrading of these posts was indicated in the Cabinet reshuffle in 2003 when ministers with other posts were given responsibility for Scottish and Welsh affairs. Peter Hain became Leader of the House of Commons and Welsh Secretary, while Alistair Darling became Secretary of State for Transport and Secretary of State for Scotland. In effect, therefore, the posts of Secretary of State for Wales and Secretary of State for Scotland became part-time jobs. The London-based Scottish Office and Welsh Office were integrated into the new Department for Constitutional Affairs run by Lord Falconer.

Issue 8 - devolution to the English regions

The devolution of powers to Scotland, Wales and Northern Ireland raises the question of similar developments in the English regions. In May 2002, the government announced that English regions will have the opportunity to decide whether they want their own regional assembly. Another idea is to set up an English Parliament - see Box 18.25.

Issue 9 - reduced parliamentary sovereignty

As a result of devolution, ministers in Westminster will not answer questions on devolved matters for Scotland and Wales. Equally, by convention, Westminster will not legislate on Scottish devolved issues without the agreement of the Scottish Parliament. This means that the sovereignty of Parliament has been limited by devolution:

> 'The term "devolution", is highly misleading. It seems to imply a mere delegation of powers. But, in practice, it does far more than delegate powers. It divides the power to legislate for Scotland between Westminster and Edinburgh, creating a quasi-federal relationship between the two Parliaments.' (Bogdanor 2003 p. 228)

Box 18.25 An English Parliament

An alternative to the proposal to create English regional government is to create an English Parliament. England is the largest component of the UK with 85% of the population, yet has no devolved body to promote its interests. Opinion polls, however, suggest that only 18% of people support the idea of an English Parliament. Some opponents of the idea of an English Parliament argue that, since devolution, Westminster has been operating, to some extent, with a sharper territorial focus on England. For example, only English MPs now sit on the select committees on education and employment, health and home affairs. As a result, there is no need for an English Parliament.

Source: Bogdanor 2003 and the *Guardian*, 3 January 2001.

By 'quasi-federal', Bogdanor means that, in reality if not in theory, a federal system has been created because the Scottish Parliament is completely free to deal with those areas which are its responsibility.

Conclusion

It is possible to exaggerate the impact which Scottish and Welsh devolution has made. Some commentators argue that Scotland, in particular, has always had a strong degree of autonomy and that devolution provides legitimacy for something that was happening anyway (see, for example, Mitchell 2003b). Also, it is important to point out that the Scottish Parliament and Welsh Assembly are still in their infancy and, in the words of Ron Davies, former Secretary of State for Wales at Westminster, 'devolution is a process, not an event'. The way the process will unfold is uncertain. It will depend on the experience of governments at central and devolved levels, on the way the parties behave and on the reactions of voters.

Main points Section 18.26

- **The West Lothian question asks whether it is fair that Scottish MPs at Westminster have a say in legislation affecting, for example, education in England, when English MPs will have no say in legislation affecting education in Scotland.**

- **The five main responses to the West Lothian question are: (1) devolve power to the English regions; (2) reduce the number of Scottish and Welsh MPs; (3) 'in-out' arrangements; (4) set up a federal structure; and (5) ignore the question.**

- **The number of Scottish MPs is due to be reduced. The role of Scottish MPs will change.**

- **In addition to the West Lothian question and Scottish over-representation, devolution has raised seven other issues: (1) finance; (2) coordination with the centre; (3) intra-UK differences; (4) changes in the Commons; (5) the Cabinet; (6) English regions; and (7) reduced parliamentary sovereignty.**

Activity 18.6 Issues raised by devolution

Item A A comrade in Cardiff

In Wales as well as Scotland, democratic socialism survives and thanks to devolution, there is nothing that the thought police in 10 Downing Street can do about it. Once upon a time, Blairites used to argue that because Labour policy had not been devolved, New Labour principles had to be applied in Edinburgh and Cardiff as well as Whitehall. The need to govern by coalition put an end to all that nonsense. The Welsh Assembly's only duty is to do what is best for Wales. Rhodri Morgan, First Minister and member of the Labour Party, judges that the needs of Wales can best be met by the creation of a society 'held together by a powerful glue of social solidarity' - not a bad working definition of socialism. 'But will that noble sentiment win elections?', the New Labour enthusiast will ask. Of course, it will in Wales. Fortunately, Morgan believes in the policies he espouses. If he hopes to win a second term as First Minister he has no choice but to argue for them. The Welsh reject Blairism. What a delight it will be to watch the Prime Minister campaigning for the Welsh socialists.

Source: The *Guardian*, 30 December 2002.

Item B Diary of a Welsh Assembly Member (AM)

National Assembly of Wales

Monday

09:00 - 10:30 Constituency office.
11:00 - 12:30 University of Merthyr Steering Group meeting.
14:00 - 15:00 Meeting with Director of Education about further and higher education issues and Objective 1 funding.
18:00 - 20:30 National Assembly political party group meeting.

Tuesday

10:00 - 12:00 Legislation Committee meeting, National Assembly building, Cardiff.
14:00 - 17:30 Plenary session, National Assembly building, Cardiff.
17:30 - 18:30 Pre-meeting for the Pre-16 Education Committee at 9:30am tomorrow.

Wednesday

09:30 - 11:30 Pre-16 Education Committee, National Assembly building, Cardiff.
14:00 - 17:30 Wales Co-operative Council inaugural meeting, National Assembly building, Cardiff.

Thursday

09:00 - 13:00 Plenary session, National Assembly building, Cardiff.
15:00 - 16:30 Lapwing Conservation Project - site meeting with representatives of the Royal Society for the Protection of Birds, Rhymney Valley.

Thursday

17:00 - 18:00 Constituency office financial meeting.
18:30 - 20:00 Visit to Quakers Yard to discuss concerns of residents.

Friday

08:30 - 09:00 Video conference facility being fitted in constituency office.
09:00 - 10:00 Receiving a petition at constituency post office re closure of post offices, with local councillor and constituency MP.
10:30 - 13:30 Upper Rhymney Valley Partnership meeting, Ael y Bryn community centre, followed by buffet lunch.
15:00 - 16:30 Meeting with Sure Start, Caerphilly in Ystrad Mynach.
17:30 - 18:00 Constituency surgery, Bedlinog.
18:00 - 18:30 Constituency surgery, Trelewis.
18:30 - 19:00 Constituency surgery, Treharris.
19:00 - 21:30 Constituency political party annual general meeting, Dowlais.

Saturday

10:00 - 12:30 Surgery constituency office.

Sunday

09:30 - 12:30 Catch up with paperwork in constituency office.

Source: www.wales.gov.uk

Item C **An English Parliament**

If devolution is good for Scotland, then why not throughout the UK? We should be thinking about the position of England in a renegotiated and looser union. One idea is a federal system for the whole of the UK with regional assemblies in England taking the same role as those in Northern Ireland, Scotland and Wales. Supporters point to the popular demand for regionalism in the North and in London. They also point out that there is a growing regional dimension to public policy and argue it should be made accountable through elected assemblies. The federal system is neat but flawed. There would be little support for different health service laws or systems of student finance in different regions of England. Even if there was, the victims would be local authorities which would have to play second fiddle to regional bosses. A more effective alternative would be to create an English Parliament made up of the MPs elected from English constituencies. This would have full powers over legislation affecting only England. One of its jobs would be to decentralise central government functions within England and to make regional bureaucracies accountable. If this Parliament was drawn from a House of Commons elected by proportional representation, it would be sensitive to opinion in all parts of England. Regional interests could be articulated in a new democratic second chamber elected on a system of regional PR. For this to work, local government would need to be strengthened. That would be the best way to ensure proper decentralisation.

Source: Leaman 1998.

Item D **The Scottish executive**

This photo shows the Scottish Executive in 2003.

Questions

1. a) Judging Items A-D and your own knowledge, what are the likely consequences of devolution?
   b) 'Devolution has meant the end of the unitary state'. Give arguments for and against this view.
2. What point is being made by Item A?
3. Identify the different roles of a Welsh Assembly member in Item B.
4. Judging from Item C, what are the key arguments for and against an English Parliament?
5. The Scottish Executive in Item D was a coalition. What does this mean and what have been the consequences of government by coalition in Scotland?

18.27 *Northern Ireland - the problem of legitimacy*

From the standpoint of the Westminster government, the problem of legitimacy - of maintaining consent to the central authority of the British state - has been at its most critical in the case of Northern Ireland.

Britain's relations with Ireland have been troubled ever since the first English landing in 1169. The roots of the recent 'Troubles' lie in the 17th century when, after a period of conquest, some 170,000 settlers (Protestants, mainly from Scotland) made the journey to Ireland and were given parcels of land which had been snatched from the Catholics who lived there. From this time onwards, the population of Ireland has been politically divided along religious lines.

It is this division which has given rise to the constitutional problem of securing consent from all sections of the population. Put simply, following the partition (separation -

see below) of Ireland, a majority in Northern Ireland (mainly Protestant and unionist) remained loyal to Britain while a substantial minority (mainly Catholic and nationalist) did not willingly give consent to rule by Westminster. For British governments, the long-term problem has been how to achieve a constitutional settlement which is acceptable to both communities.

18.28 *Civil war and partition*

From 1801 (following the passing of the Act of Union, 1800) until 1921, the whole of Ireland was part of the UK although a significant number of Irish people never accepted the legitimacy of the Union. Between 1919 and 1921, a war was fought between Irish and British troops which resulted in the signing of a compromise treaty. Southern Ireland became a self-governing dominion (the Irish Free State), while six of the nine counties of Ulster (Northern Ireland) remained part of the UK. Ireland was, therefore, partitioned.

Over the years, the Irish Free State gradually loosened its remaining ties with the UK and, in 1949, became a republic. Although the British Parliament retained overall control of Northern Ireland, between 1921 and 1972 the British government did not interfere in the day-to-day running of the province - this was left to the Northern Irish Parliament, set up in 1921. Despite there being a large Catholic minority in Northern Ireland (about a third of its population in 1921), Protestants dominated successive Northern Ireland Parliaments and Cabinets and ensured that their privileged position was maintained. Northern Ireland's Catholics were not only under-represented politically, but under-represented throughout the main institutions of the province: the police force, higher grades of the civil service and the universities, for example. This under-representation of the Catholic population produced social disadvantage and a general lack of opportunities.

18.29 The 'Troubles'

In 1967 the Civil Rights Association (CRA) was set up with the aim of securing civil rights for Catholics through peaceful mass demonstration - see Box 18.26. CRA marches, however, became subject to heavy-handed police tactics. Tensions increased and violent clashes between Catholics and Protestants broke out. These clashes culminated in 1969 when British troops were sent to Northern Ireland to restore order. The British army soon lost the support of the Catholic community and, by 1971, paramilitary groups on

Box 18.26 The civil rights marches

The Civil Rights Association aimed to secure rights for Catholics through peaceful mass demonstrations. In January 1972, 13 civil rights marchers were killed by British troops.

both sides of the conflict had embarked on campaigns of bombing and shooting. Shortly after the killing of 13 civil rights marchers by British troops on 20 January 1972 ('Bloody Sunday'), the British government suspended the Northern Ireland Parliament and direct rule from Britain began. Over the next 30 years, over 3,500 people were killed in violent incidents in Northern Ireland.

Peace initiatives 1969-98
Between 1969 and 1998, the response of the British government to events in Northern Ireland moved through a number of phases. Generally there has been agreement between Labour and the Conservatives and so policies have reflected different approaches rather than party political divisions.

1. Crisis management 1969-75
Between 1969 and 1975, British policy has been described as incoherent and at the level of crisis management (McCullagh & O'Dowd 1986).

2. Criminalisation 1975-85
From 1975 to 1985, containment and stabilisation became paramount and the British government pursued a policy of 'criminalisation' - those convicted of 'terrorist' offences were to be treated as ordinary criminals and denied the special category status of 'political prisoners'. The idea was to portray the violence in Northern Ireland as an extreme crime wave rather than politically motivated.

3. The search for a new constitutional settlement 1985-98
The policy of criminalisation meant that a political solution to the problems of Northern Ireland came no nearer. Although the policy remained in place, a new phase began in 1985 with the signing of the Anglo-Irish Agreement.

The Anglo-Irish Agreement and the Downing Street Declaration
Crucially, the Anglo-Irish Agreement established that the Republic of Ireland had the right to be consulted over policy formulation in Northern Ireland, although executive responsibility remained with Westminster. This development involved the first change in the constitutional status of Northern Ireland since 1921. The Agreement, however, met with opposition from both sides of the political divide in Northern Ireland and was suspended in 1991 to allow further talks to take place.

Although these talks broke down, in 1993 the British and Irish governments issued what became known as the 'Downing Street Declaration' which was an attempt to pull together the different positions. Initially rejected by unionist and Sinn Fein politicians, the declaration did pave the way for political discussions with the different parties and interest groups. Various initiatives during John Major's premiership (including elections to a Northern Ireland Assembly, proposed in the 'Framework Document' of 1995) followed. It was only after the 1997 general election, however, that all-party talks were held. The result was the Good Friday Agreement.

Box 18.27 on page 386 describes the key political and paramilitary organisations in Northern Ireland.

Box 18.27 Key political and paramilitary organisations in Northern Ireland

DUP Democratic Unionist Party: leading unionist party following 2003 Assembly elections; anti-Good Friday Agreement.

IRA (Provisional) Irish Republican Army: on ceasefire since 1994 (apart from 1996-97); weapons decommissioning started 2001; represented politically by Sinn Fein.

SDLP Social Democratic and Labour Party: pro-Agreement; main nationalist party 1970-2001; lost Assembly seats to Sinn Fein in 2003 elections.

SF Sinn Fein: pro-Agreement; became largest nationalist party in 2001; still linked to Provisional IRA but now the dominant arm of the republican movement.

UUP Ulster Unionist Party: leading unionist party until 2003; pro-Agreement, but divided on power-sharing with Sinn Fein.

Source: Tonge 2003a, pp.184-85.

18.30 The 1998 Good Friday Peace Agreement

The Blair government elected in May 1997 gave priority to securing an agreement over new constitutional arrangements in Northern Ireland. All-party peace talks began in September 1997 and eventually led to the announcement of a deal on Good Friday, 10 April 1998 - the 'Good Friday Peace Agreement'. This deal was put to the Northern Irish people in a referendum on 23 May 1998 with 71% of those who voted accepting the agreement. A referendum in the Irish Republic also secured a large majority in favour of the new constitutional settlement.

The Good Friday Agreement retains Northern Ireland within the United Kingdom unless and until a majority of the Northern Ireland electorate decides otherwise. The Agreement has three strands. These are outlined in Box 18.28.

One effect of the settlement and the outcome of the referendums was that both the British and Irish governments conceded modifications to their constitutional claims to Northern Ireland. Compromise and concessions were also made by the Northern Irish parties on both sides:

'The Irish government has finally agreed to rescind [cancel] its territorial claim on Northern Ireland enshrined in…its constitution… The new constitutional commitment instead expresses a hope for the unification of the people rather than the soil of Ireland. Britain has agreed to repeal the Government of Ireland Act 1920. And, it has agreed to pass legislation allowing the Secretary of State to be empowered to hold referendums on Northern Ireland every seven years "if it appears likely to him or her that a majority of those voting would express a wish that Northern Ireland should cease to be part of the UK and form part of a united Ireland".' (*Observer*, 12 April 1998)

In June 1998, the first elections for the new Irish Assembly were held. The Social and Democratic Labour Party (SDLP) emerged with the largest number of first preference votes and the Ulster Unionists (UUP) with the largest share of the seats. The UUP Leader, David Trimble, became First Minister with Seamus Mallon of the SDLP as his deputy - see Box 18.29 for details.

Box 18.29 Results of election to the Northern Ireland Assembly, June 1998

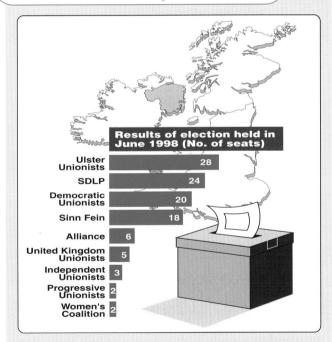

Results of election held in June 1998 (No. of seats)

Ulster Unionists 28
SDLP 24
Democratic Unionists 20
Sinn Fein 18
Alliance 6
United Kingdom Unionists 5
Independent Unionists 3
Progressive Unionists 2
Women's Coalition 2

This chart shows the number of seats won by Northern Irish parties in June 1998.

Box 18.28 The three strands in the Good Friday Agreement

Strand 1 A Northern Ireland executive and Assembly
An executive - consisting of First Minister, Deputy First Minister and ten other ministers - to preside over a 108-member Assembly. Unionists and nationalists to share power in the executive and the Assembly.

Strand 2 A North-South Ministerial Council
To provide an Irish dimension, the North-South Ministerial Council - with the approval of the Northern Ireland

Assembly and the Parliament of the Irish Republic - can implement all-Ireland policies.

Strand 3 A British-Irish Council
The British-Irish Council to provide a forum of representatives from the Dublin and Westminster governments and from the devolved Assemblies of Scotland, Wales and Northern Ireland. No administrative or legislative powers.

Source: Tonge, 2003b.

18.31 Implementing the Good Friday Agreement

The process of implementing the provisions of the Good Friday Agreement, has not been smooth. A series of crises, resolutions and further crises has meant the peace process and the work of the new institutions of devolved government have moved forward haltingly. Between October 2002 and the time of writing (May 2004), the executive and Assembly were suspended and direct rule from Westminster reimposed.

Decommissioning

The key problem was the decommissioning of arms, described as 'the central issue blocking progress' (McDonald 2001). As the journalist Mary Holland has pointed out:

> 'The demand for the handover of guns is hugely symbolic to both sides. The republican movement sees it as a demand for surrender... Unionists...suspect that the IRA is holding on to its weapons for use at some future date.' (Holland 2000)

It was problems over decommissioning which resulted in the setting up of the new power-sharing executive to be postponed by nine months. When the executive and the other institutions of the Good Friday Agreement did eventually start to function, representatives of the IRA and the loyalist paramilitaries were appointed to the Decommissioning Body chaired by General de Chastelain, a Canadian.

18.32 The reimposition of direct rule

Just ten weeks after the various bodies started to function, in February 2000, the Northern Ireland Secretary in the British government introduced legislation suspending the Assembly and power-sharing Executive and reimposing direct rule from Westminster. David Trimble had threatened to resign as First Minister over what he saw as a lack of movement on the decommissioning of arms issue. The unionists in the Executive and Assembly wanted decommissioning to start before the Executive got properly underway, while Sinn Fein's position was that decommissioning couldn't start until the Executive was properly in place.

Following some movement on the part of the IRA on the arms issue, the Assembly and executive were reinstated in May 2000. But this development did not put an end to the difficulties. After two further periods during 2000-01 in which devolved government was suspended, the conflict over decommissioning reached a further crisis point in October 2001. The leaderships of Sinn Fein and the UUP had each been trying to balance moves to sustain and progress the peace process with the need to carry their respective supporters with them against accusations of betrayal. Devolution once again seemed close to collapse when the IRA announced that it had actually decommissioned some of its weapons and that this had been witnessed by members of the disarmament body.

According to press reports, the IRA's decision to start decommissioning in October 2001 was a response to

developments in the USA. Irish republicans had long received financial support from some Irish-Americans. But, following the arrest of three IRA suspects in Columbia for training guerrillas associated with cocaine smuggling, this support came under threat. Then, the al-Qaida attacks in New York and Washington on 11 September 2001 altered the perspective of Americans sympathetic to the republican cause. In response to a changed political landscape, the IRA made its 'historic move'.

Although at the time this start to the decommissioning process was hailed as a major breakthrough, a year later devolved government in Northern Ireland was suspended yet again - and this time there was no speedy resumption. The UUP had already withdrawn from the North-South Ministerial Council and now, amid allegations of a republican spy-ring in the security services, the UUP and the DUP announced its intention to leave the executive. The British government reimposed direct rule in October 2002.

The 2003 Assembly elections

The Northern Ireland Assembly was formally dissolved in April 2003 to make way for elections which were due to take place in May. The elections were postponed, however, partly because the Assembly was under suspension and partly because the IRA had not formally declared an end to war (Tonge 2003b). The Assembly elections were eventually held in November 2003, following further decommissioning of IRA arms (*Observer*, 26 October 2003). Significant gains were made by the DUP (which replaced the UUP as the leading unionist party) and Sinn Fein (which replaced the SDLP as the leading nationalist party). The results are outlined in Box 18.30.

Box 18.30 Elections to the Northern Ireland Assembly, November 2003

Party	First preference votes	%	Seats	Change from 1998
Democratic Unionist	177,944	25.7	30	+10
Sinn Fein	162,758	23.5	24	+6
Ulster Unionist	156,931	22.7	27	-1
SDLP	117,547	17.0	18	-6
Alliance	25,372	3.7	6	-
Independent	19,256	2.8	1	+1
Progressive Unionist	8,032	1.2	1	-1
Others	24,188	3.5	1	-9

Source: Jones 2004, p.57.

The DUP, led by Ian Paisley, is opposed to the Good Friday Agreement and aims to renegotiate its terms, but the British and Irish governments have said they will not do this. The DUP refuses to share power with Sinn Fein until the IRA disbands. Sinn Fein wants the Assembly to be reconvened as soon as possible.

Although some decommissioning of arms has taken place, this has not happened quickly enough or in a sufficiently transparent manner to satisfy unionists (Jones 2004, pp.39, 57).

The British government still hopes for a return to devolved government. But, with the two parties from opposite ends of the political spectrum now being the leading unionist and

nationalist parties, the political situation in Northern Ireland is more polarised than at any time since the Good Friday Agreement was signed. Some commentators find it difficult to envisage the prospect of a power-sharing arrangement involving a DUP First Minister and a Sinn Fein Deputy First Minister (see, for example, Tonge 2003a, pp.189, 201).

Main points   Sections 18.27 - 18.32

- Since Protestant settlers took land from native Catholics in the 17th century, the population of Ireland has been divided along religious lines, making it difficult to secure consent from all sections of the population.
- Following a civil war in 1919-21, Ireland was partitioned. The South became independent and the North continued to be part of the UK.
- Between 1921 and 1972, the British government did not interfere in the running of Northern Ireland. Direct rule began in 1972 after the 'Troubles' broke out.
- Between 1969 and 1998, British attempts to find a peaceful solution in Northern Ireland went through three phases: (1) crisis management 1969-75; (2) criminalisation 1975-85; (3) searching for a new constitutional settlement 1985-98.

- Although several initiatives followed the 1985 Anglo-Irish Agreement, it was not until after the 1997 general election that that all-party talks were held. The result was the Good Friday Agreement, referendums and the new Northern Ireland Assembly.
- Although the new institutions of the Good Friday Agreement started work in 1999, the Assembly has been suspended on a number of occasions. The main issue blocking progress has been the decommissioning of weapons and, since October 2002, there has been direct rule from Westminster.
- Following the 2003 Northern Ireland Assembly elections, political divisions hardened when the DUP became the leading unionist party and Sinn Fein the leading nationalist party.

Activity 18.7   *Northern Ireland*

Item A Terms of the Good Friday Agreement (1)

The Good Friday Agreement creates three interconnecting bodies of government:

Strand 1	Strand 2	Strand 3
Internal arrangements of Northern Ireland	**North/South Ministerial Council**	**Council of the Isles**

Strand 1

Internal arrangements of Northern Ireland

- **Assembly**
  - Made up of 108 members, six from each constituency elected by proportional representation.
  - It has legislative powers. Its first duty is to set up the North-South Ministerial Council.
  - Will be suspended if it does not set up the council within a year.
  - Decisions are made by a weighted majority system to ensure unionists cannot dominate nationalists.

- **Executive Committee**
  - 12 ministers - a First Minister, Deputy First Minister plus heads of departments including:
  - **Health**
  - **Education**
  - **Environment**
  - **Economic Development**
  - **Agriculture**
  - **Finance**

Strand 2

North/South Ministerial Council

A forum for ministers from Dublin and Belfast to promote joint policies.

Can implement all-Ireland policies - but only with the approval of the Belfast Assembly and Dublin Parliament.

Potential areas of responsibility:
- **Agriculture**
- **Transport**
- **Policing**
- **Relations with EU**

Strand 3

Council of the Isles

Representatives from:
- **Dublin government**
- **Belfast Assembly**
- **Westminster**
- **Scottish Parliament**
- **Welsh Assembly**

To meet twice a year for discussions but to have no administrative or legislative powers.

Source: The *Guardian*, 11 April and 29 June 1998.

Item B Terms of the Good Friday Agreement (2)

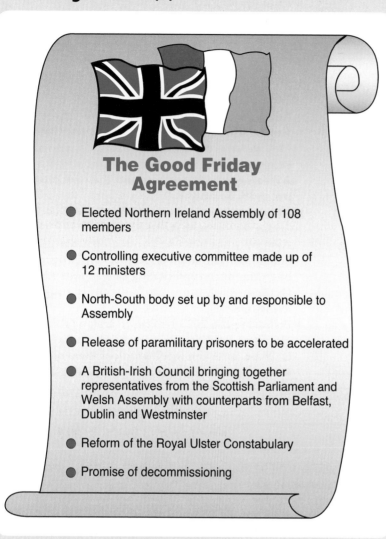

The Good Friday Agreement

● Elected Northern Ireland Assembly of 108 members

● Controlling executive committee made up of 12 ministers

● North-South body set up by and responsible to Assembly

● Release of paramilitary prisoners to be accelerated

● A British-Irish Council bringing together representatives from the Scottish Parliament and Welsh Assembly with counterparts from Belfast, Dublin and Westminster

● Reform of the Royal Ulster Constabulary

● Promise of decommissioning

Source: The *Guardian*, 11 April 1998.

Item C Constitutional implications of the settlement

As part of the Good Friday Agreement, a British-Irish Council (BIC) is to be set up. Law-makers from the Republic will meet regularly with members of the British Parliament, the Northern Ireland Assembly and with representatives of the new Assemblies for Scotland and Wales. The idea is that the BIC will promote the harmonious and mutually beneficial development of relationships between all these people. The BIC will meet in different formats - at summit level twice per year and at ministerial level on a regular basis (with relevant ministers from each institution meeting on a revolving basis - as happens in the EU's Council of Ministers). The aim is that the BIC will exchange information, discuss, consult and try to reach agreement on matters of mutual interest - for example, transport links or environmental issues. This body could, therefore, develop into a body which results in significant constitutional change for the UK. It is possible to see, for example, how a full federal system might evolve in the UK as relations of the various devolved bodies with Westminster is redefined.

Source: The *Guardian*, 11 April 1998.

Item D Devolution in Northern Ireland

Since the Good Friday Agreement, and despite the setbacks and suspensions (four in the first four years), some commentators have been optimistic about the future for Northern Ireland. Implementation of the Agreement saw the introduction of new institutions and practices of devolved government which seemed, at least initially, to attract a high level of public support. Even during the periods of suspension, when there is a return to direct rule from Westminster, devolved power-sharing - even if not always as precisely as defined in the Agreement - is still the goal of all parties.

Others, however, argue that the repeated suspensions of the new devolved institutions have reduced their credibility. They also point to the many issues that remain potential sources of conflict. Unionists demand the disbandment of the Provisional IRA and republicans want a unionist commitment to proper power-sharing before the IRA officially declares its war is ended. Disputes over policing the province continue as does sectarian conflict at street level where violence did not end with the introduction of devolved government.

Constitutionally, one view is that devolution has undermined the principles of parliamentary sovereignty in that the Northern Ireland Assembly, when in operation, is now the prime source of authority as far as the devolved responsibilities are concerned. In addition, the North-South Ministerial Council and the British-Irish Council, also established by the Good Friday Agreement, raise further questions over the notion of territorial sovereignty within the United Kingdom. This is because they bring non-Westminster elements into the policy process.

Source: Lomas 2001, Richards & Smith 2001, Tonge 2003a & 2003b.

Item E Northern Ireland in 2004

Following the 2003 Assembly elections, the situation in Northern Ireland is one of stalemate. The DUP demands changes to the Agreement because that represents the wish of a majority of unionists. Sinn Fein resists change because that represents the wish of nationalists. The Agreement is now technically in review, chaired by the British and Irish governments. The optimistic view is that logic will compel cooperation between Sinn Fein and the DUP. The pessimistic view is that so long as republicans interpret their mandate to mean that they can ignore unionist anxieties about the IRA, and the DUP interpret their mandate to mean they can ignore Sinn Fein, there is little hope of success. An extended period of direct rule seems likely.

Source: Aughey, 2004 & the *Observer* 7 February 2004.

Questions

1. Why do you think (a) nationalists and (b) unionists were able to support the Good Friday Agreement? Use Items A and B in your answer.
2. Judging from Items A-D, to what extent do you think developments in Northern Ireland arising from the Good Friday Agreement affect the UK's position as a unitary state?
3. With the help of Items D and E, give arguments for and against the view that the creation of devolved government in Northern Ireland is unlikely to be successful.

18.33 *The possibility of regional government in England*

It was noted above that one response to the West Lothian question is to devolve power to English regions. If English Regional Assemblies were set up, the argument goes, then they could be responsible for the same policy areas as the Scottish Parliament, leaving MPs responsible for matters which concern the UK as a whole - such as defence and foreign policy. The argument also usually assumes that the Welsh Assembly would be upgraded so that it became responsible for policy-making rather than just administering policy. If these measures were taken, it is concluded, the West Lothian question would become an irrelevance because all MPs would have the same areas of responsibility.

18.34 *Regional government in England before 1997*

In their 1992 election manifesto, the Conservatives pledged to strengthen regional administration. This resulted in the setting up of Integrated Regional Offices (IROs) in April 1994. Although these offices were described as 'integrated', they do not include all government departments:

'Health is not included, nor is the Department of Heritage...Major arms of government like the Employment Service and Highways Agency are left out too.' (Wilson & Game 1998, p.114)

Before 1994, different government departments split England into regions with different boundaries. Since the IROs were set up, however, common regional boundaries have been agreed.

Hogwood (1995) argues that, although the IROs have brought some integration, local authorities in England still have to deal with very many different government bodies and government-funded agencies.

18.35 *Regional government in England 1997-2001*

In 1997, the Labour Party pledged in its manifesto to introduce more local control at regional level and local referendums.

'In time we will introduce legislation to allow the people, region by region, to decide in a referendum whether they want directly elected regional government.' (Labour 1997, pp.34-35)

As the first step towards fulfilling this pledge, the Regional Development Agencies (RDAs) were set up in April 1999 to work with the existing IROs in promoting investment, helping small businesses and coordinating regional economic development.

The establishment of the RDAs was followed by the creation of eight Regional Assemblies, made up of councillors from local authorities (who must make up 70% of the total membership), religious leaders, trade unionists and business leaders. These Regional Assemblies were created to scrutinise each RDA. Each Assembly employs full-time staff and has a budget with grants from central government and subscriptions from local authorities. For example, the North West Assembly is based in Wigan, has a staff of more than 70 and a budget of £1.3 million (*Guardian*, 23 July 2003). The Assemblies are not elected. They have been described as a form of 'administrative devolution for the English regions' (Heppell & McCreanor 2003, p.159).

The 1997 manifesto pledge made clear that the Labour government would not push regionalism. Rather, as Box 18.31 on page 391 shows, it intends to respond to public demand as and when it arises.

Box 18.31   Multi-speed regionalism

Both Labour and the Liberal Democrats talk of a rolling programme of devolution in England, with each region travelling towards its own Chamber, Assembly or Parliament at a speed regulated by public demand. The pattern of devolution in England, therefore, will be uneven and some regions may never decide to create their own tier of regional institutions. Further, nobody is talking about giving regional Parliaments law-making powers or, indeed, tax-raising powers of real significance.

Source: Leaman 1998.

A trend towards regionalism?

Although, in most regions, there is little evidence of a burning desire for regional government, the trend is towards greater regionalism:

'There is a growing regional dimension to public policy, recognised by the Conservatives when they created Government Offices for the regions, by Labour's regional development agencies and by the European Union. Like it or not, public business has to be done at regional level.' (Leaman 1998, p.17)

18.36 Regional government in England since 2001

Labour further developed its ideas on regional government in its 2001 election manifesto. The manifesto stated that where there is no demand for regional government in England, none will be set up. But, where there is a stronger sense of regional identity and a demand for a political voice, referendums can be held and, if positive, directly elected Regional Assemblies set up.

The first timetable for English devolution was announced by Nick Raynsford (the Regions and Local Government Minister) in November 2001. Noting the growing discontent in the North of England because of their proximity to the devolved government in Scotland with its advantages for the country, he said that it was no longer possible to restrict devolution. A White Paper, published in May 2002, gave an indication of the responsibilities that any Regional Assemblies would have when they were set up. These responsibilities are outlined in Box 18.32.

To counter the charge of increased bureaucracy, the government made it clear that, if Regional Assemblies were established, then, in areas where there were already county and district councils, a tier of local government would have to be abolished. Any Regional Assemblies that are established, therefore, are more likely to be in areas where there are unitary local authorities.

Public opinion

A BBC poll in March 2002 suggested high levels of public support for elected Regional Assemblies especially in the North and the West Midlands. However, these figures were contradicted in a British Social Attitudes Survey (2002) which found that 57% of those questioned did not support the creation of Regional Assemblies. There was a higher level of

Box 18.32   Recommendations of the 2002 White Paper

The White Paper published on Regional Assemblies in 2002 made the following recommendations:

- Assemblies would have between 25 and 35 members
- members would be elected by the additional members system of proportional representation
- key powers and responsibilities would include: economic development, planning, housing, health improvement strategies, culture and tourism, skills and employment, waste management and environment
- the budget for each Assembly would vary but a projection suggested that a new North East Assembly would have a budget of c.£350 million per year
- the Assemblies will be funded by central government grants and by part of the council tax collected in the regional area
- the RDAs will continue in existence but will become answerable to the new Assemblies.

support when people were asked about possible economic benefits of the creation of Regional Assemblies. The Conservative Party and the Confederation of British Industry are opposed to the plans while the Liberal Democrats, the Labour Party and most Trade Unions are in favour. Local pressure groups in the regions, pushing for Regional Assemblies, have evolved into a national pressure group - the Campaign for the English Regions. This group hopes that success in a referendum in one region 'may result in a domino effect in which other regions will hold referendums and establish Assemblies' (Elcock 2003, p.26).

Arguments for and against elected Regional Assemblies

The main arguments for and against elected Regional Assemblies are given in Box 18.33 on page 392.

18.37 Next steps

Legislation was passed in 2003 which paved the way for referendums for three regions in England - the North East, North West and Yorkshire and Humberside - to be held during October 2004. However, if the referendums support the idea of creating an Assembly, then there must be only a single tier of local authority beneath them. This means that either county councils or district councils will have to be abolished. Electors will be asked in the referendum to make a choice between these options.

If the choice is for the abolition of the county councils, then district councils will have to merge to create sufficiently large local authorities. Peele points out:

'Consequently, the issue of structure in English local government is once more on the agenda. This is not because of a direct determination to confront the issue, but as a by-product of regional policy.' (Peele 2003 p.208)

Box 18.33 Arguments for and against elected Regional Assemblies

Arguments for elected Regional Assemblies:	Arguments against elected Regional Assemblies:
1. Strengthen the regional economy The Assemblies would strengthen the regional economy by bringing a sharper local focus to key local economic issues. At present, central government overlooks the specific circumstances of each local area.	**1. Lack of natural communities** Most parts of England do not form 'natural communities' with their own distinct regional identities. Attempts to divide England for the purpose of devolved government could, therefore, produce artificially created regions.
2. Create democratic accountability The Assemblies would create democratic accountability. There is already a form of regional government made up of the RDAs, other quangos and Government Regional Offices responsible for a range of services from flood defences to post-16 education, but they are, at present, only accountable upwards to ministers. In addition, these bodies do not work in a transparent way and are hidden from public scrutiny. Regional Assemblies would be elected and accountable to local people.	**2. Little evidence of enthusiasm** With the partial exception of some areas in the north of England, there is little evidence of much enthusiasm for or interest in the prospect of English regional devolution at the present time. **3. Involves major changes in local government organisation** The government announcement in May 2002 made it clear that, if English regions decided on regional assemblies, there would only be a single tier of government beneath the Assemblies so it would mean major changes in local government organisation with considerable disruption.
3. Help to solve the West Lothian question The Assemblies would help solve the West Lothian question as the work of the Assemblies would mirror the work of the devolved government in Scotland, Wales and Northern Ireland. At present, 'England is the largest unit within the European Union without a tier of elected regional governance' (Heppell & McCreanor 2003, p.160).	**4. Cost** There is a cost in establishing the Assemblies and the risk that costs would grow as they have in Scotland and Wales. **5. Might create confusion and conflict** The shift to 'multi-level governance' (local, regional, central and the EU) would create confusion and lack of clarity on the distribution of functions leading to conflict between the different layers.
4. Follow the European trend In Europe, the trend is towards regional government through its social and economic programmes. There is a Committee of the Regions which the Regional Assemblies could lobby.	**6. Could lead to greater EU control** Regional government could lead to greater control by the EU over parts of the UK as giving regions a direct relationship with Brussels would mean that the EU could by-pass Westminster.

Turnout - a potential pitfall

There is concern about the level of turnout in the forthcoming referendums. Ministers have not set a turnout threshold, but the minister in charge, Nick Raynsford, has stated:

> 'If the result is derisorily small, then we will not feel bound to proceed - even if there is a majority in favour.' (*Guardian*, 21 May 2003)

If the government does proceed, then the first elections to the new Assemblies could be expected in 2006 or 2007 (Elcock 2003). Whether the Regional Assemblies are eventually created remains in some doubt as their future will depend upon the level of turnout in the referendums, which are expected to be all-postal ballots as well as which party is then in power at national level.

18.38 *Conclusion*

Governing the UK today is 'a more complex and challenging task than ever before' (Pierre & Stoker 2000, p.29). Multi-level governance means that the government at Westminster can no longer assume the degree of control that it had in the past; it has to contend with devolved and sub-national government. However, a dilemma remains. If devolved assemblies, regional assemblies and local authorities are all given freedom to make their own decisions then it is likely that the decisions made will produce a great variety of levels of service and very varying priorities for the local population. This is already the case without regional government. For example, it has been estimated that spending per head in London is £5,177 compared to £4,825 in the South West (*Guardian*, 12 September 2003). Regional government is likely to increase these differences. In addition, different parts of the country have differing income levels and other resources. Allowing many more local decisions may lead to a further growth of inequality between different parts of the country if the capacity of central government to intervene and redress imbalances is reduced.

Main points Sections 18.33 - 18.38

- One response to the West Lothian question is to devolve power to English regions.
- Integrated Regional Offices (IROs) were set up in April 1994. Regional Development Agencies (RDAs) were set up in April 1999.
- Although, in most regions, there is little evidence of a burning desire for regional government, the trend is towards greater regionalism.

- Since the general election in 2001, the Labour government has taken the first steps towards the setting up of elected regional assemblies.
- Whether these assemblies are set up will depend largely on the level of support and turnout in regional referendums.

Activity 18.8 *The English regions*

Item A The English regions

NORTH EAST

NORTH WEST

YORKSHIRE AND THE HUMBER

EAST MIDLANDS

WEST MIDLANDS

EAST OF ENGLAND

LONDON

SOUTH EAST

SOUTH WEST

Source: Office of the Deputy Prime Minister.

Item B The North East, North West, Yorkshire and Humber

North East

Population	2.5 million
Local councils	Two counties, 18 districts, 10 unitary
MPs	30
Likely size of Assembly	25
Capital	Durham?

North West

Population	6.8 million
Local councils	Three counties, 39 districts, 19 unitary
MPs	76
Likely size of Assembly	35
Capital	Warrington?

Yorkshire and Humber

Population	5 million
Local councils	One county, 9 districts, 14 unitary
MPs	56
Likely size of Assembly	30
Capital	York?

Source: *Guardian*, 17 June 2003.

Item C Regional imbalances

England's less favoured regions need a multi-billion pound boost, with a significant switch of resources from the South and maybe Scotland and Wales - to narrow a widening divide, a cross-party committee of MPs warns today. In a critique of a regional strategy geared to underpinning the success of the South, the Commons' Housing, Planning and Regions Committee also urges ministers to review the funding formula which may favour Northern Ireland, Scotland and Wales at the expense of England. In a lengthy report, the MPs maintain that the gap between the rich and the poor now affects everyone in England. They say that the gap between the English regions is growing, but divisions are not simply a North-South divide. Rather, it is the places in England that are the furthest from the South-East economy that tend to be less prosperous.

Source: The *Guardian*, 4 June 2003.

Item D The wealth gap

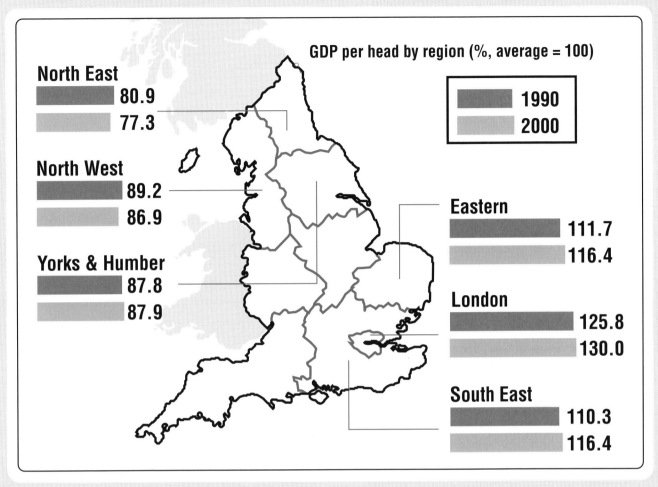

GDP per head by region (%, average = 100)

North East
80.9
77.3

North West
89.2
86.9

Yorks & Humber
87.8
87.9

1990
2000

Eastern
111.7
116.4

London
125.8
130.0

South East
110.3
116.4

Source: Office for National Statistics/*Guardian*, 13 December, 2002.

Questions

1. Look at Item A.
   a) Which region do you live in?
   b) To what extent do you think that there is sense of regional identity in your region?
2. The three regions in Item B are thought to have the strongest sense of regional identity.
   a) Give the arguments for and against each of these regions having elected regional assemblies.

   b) What steps have been taken and what steps need to be taken before such assemblies could be set up?
3. Look at Items C and D.
   a) To what extent do you think that the government should reduce the regional divide?
   b) What effect would you expect any regional assemblies to have?

18.39 *What is quasi government?*

The main characteristic of 'quasi governmental organisations' is that they are run by governmental appointees, not by elected representatives. They are described as 'quasi' governmental organisations because, although they are not actually branches of the government, their role is to perform a specific function or range of functions laid down by central government. The government prefers the term 'Public Bodies' which includes nationalised industries, public corporations, NHS bodies and non-departmental public bodies. Whatever term is used, these bodies are now very important as they spend some £23 billion of public money each year and they are an important component of 'multi-level governance' (Robins 2001).

What are quangos?

According to some commentators, the word 'quango' stands for 'quasi autonomous non-governmental organisation'. Others replace the 'non' with 'national' or argue that the term quango should be replaced with QGA (quasi governmental agency). The government prefers 'NDPB' (non-departmental public body).

The confusion over the term 'quango' reflects a confusion over the precise definition of the term. In general, it is accurate to say that quangos are unelected agencies set up by central government. Their job is to perform functions laid down by central government. They are funded by public money and many are responsible for spending public money.

Since quangos are run by government appointees, they have close ties with central government. But, since ministers have

Box 18.34 Different types of quangos

1. Regulatory
Regulatory quangos tend to be permanent bodies which develop regulations governing aspects of government policy. The Food Standards Agency is an example.

2. Advisory
The function of advisory quangos is to examine specific problems and to make recommendations to government. The Spongiform Encephalopathy Advisory Committee (SEAC) that advises the government on 'mad cow's disease' is an example.

3. Quasi judicial
The function of the third category of quangos - tribunals - is to settle disputes between people who feel aggrieved and government officials. Some tribunals operate on a permanent basis - such as supplementary benefits appeal

tribunals and rent tribunals. Others are set up to address a particular complaint.

4. Spending
The function of this fourth category is to distribute funds on behalf of government. An example would be the Sports Council.

5. Executive
Executive quangos are decision-making bodies often with multi-million pound budgets. An example is the Arts Council.

6. Task Forces
Labour has created many Task Forces. These bring in business people to investigate a wide range of issues. For example, the Football Task Force has investigated ticket prices.

---

no control over their day-to-day running and since those who run them are not elected, they lack accountability. The actions performed by local authorities are the responsibility of elected representatives who are directly accountable to the electorate. Similarly, the actions performed by civil servants are the responsibility of ministers who are accountable to Parliament and ultimately to the electorate. The actions of quangos, however, are the responsibility of those who are appointed to run them. They are accountable neither to an electorate nor to a minister. It is this lack of democratic accountability that is the root cause of criticism of quangos.

Different types of quangos
There are a number of different types of quangos. Most come under the headings in Box 18.34.

18.40 The quango explosion

Despite claims by both Conservative and Labour governments that they wished to reduce the numbers of quangos, their numbers have grown fast and governments have found it hard to resist their development. For example:

- changes in the health service have created some 500 NHS trusts, set up to run local hospitals
- new public bodies have been set up to fund further and higher education
- there has been a growth in regulatory authorities, like Oftel and Ofwat, to monitor services which have been privatised.

Definition and numbers
Confusion over the precise definition of quangos is mirrored in the disagreement about the exact numbers of quangos. The government claimed that the number of public bodies sponsored by UK government departments had fallen to 849 by March 2003 but, by only including national bodies, this figure excluded a number of bodies which would generally be regarded as quangos. The government admits that there are some additional 4,651 Local Public Spending Bodies (Wilson

2003). In total, one estimate suggests some 6,424 quangos in existence.

There is also a disagreement about the number of people running the quangos. The government claims that there are 22,000 people on their national boards. But the total number of public appointments on boards is nearer 35,000 according to the *Guardian* newspaper (*Guardian*, 20 November 2000) or 70,000 according to one academic (Flinders 1999). A comparison can be made here to the total number of elected councillors which stands at around 22,000.

18.41 Appointments

In 1995, the post of Commissioner for Public Appointments was set up to 'regulate, monitor and report on the way in which ministers make appointments to the boards of public bodies' (Cabinet Office 2003, p.iv). However, only about half of all public appointments come within the Commissioner's remit. Concern has been expressed as to how representative the appointments are in terms of gender, age, ethnicity and disability (a majority are white, middle class and male). In addition, there is real concern about the powers of patronage given to ministers because they are free to choose who they wish and some appointments carry significant salaries.

The advantages and disadvantages for central government of setting up quangos are outlined in Box 18.35 on page 396.

18.42 Recent developments

Following the 1997 consultation paper *Opening up Quangos*, Labour has taken some measures to meet these criticisms, but there are no plans to abolish quangos altogether. Rather, it has been argued that quangos have become a permanent part of the political landscape. The main reason for this is that, despite the criticisms that are sometimes voiced, governments find quangos to be very useful instruments. The debate has now shifted away from the existence of quangos to what is perceived as abuses of the patronage system of appointment and lack of accountability to the public.

Box 18.35   Advantages and disadvantages of quangos

Arguments in favour of quangos	Disadvantages of quangos

Arguments in favour of quangos

1. Political advantages for ministers
Often, it is in the interest of ministers not to be directly responsible for performing tasks. By delegating tasks to quangos, they can distance themselves from controversial issues and avoid awkward questions in Parliament. Also, ministers are responsible for appointing people to sit on quangos. They can, therefore, choose people who will support their political objectives and ensure, by this means, that government decisions are implemented in the way in which members of the government desire.

2. Greater efficiency
Quangos may be a more efficient way of administering governmental decisions. Quangos have a free hand. They are not bound by the conventions and ways of work normally followed by civil servants. They have the time and resources to concentrate on tasks which might not gain so much attention in a government department.

3. Provide expert advice
Since specialists rather than generalist civil servants can be appointed to undertake tasks, quangos can provide expert advice to ministers on technical or specialised issues.

4. Role for ordinary people
Quangos bring a large number of ordinary people into public life to play a role on the boards or bodies which run them.

5. Carry out commercial activities
Quangos may carry out commercial activities which need some independence from government ministers.

6. Provide quick and flexible response
Quangos can provide a quick and flexible response to matters of public concern. For example, the Nolan Committee was set up to address concerns about sleaze in public life and it was able to begin work as soon as its members were appointed.

7. Alternative to local government
Quangos provide an alternative to elected local government. By farming out responsibilities to quangos, government increases its control over local affairs from the centre, reducing the powers and responsibilities of local authorities. The creation of quangos, therefore, helps central government to achieve one of its strategic aims.

Disadvantages of quangos

1. Democratic deficit
Quangos are unelected and unaccountable - so there is a democratic deficit.

2. Secretive
Quangos often operate in secretive, closed meetings with limited public discussion of their work.

3. Unresponsive and remote
Quangos are unresponsive and remote from the communities they serve. Women only account for 35% of appointments and the majority are middle aged and middle class.

4. Appointment system unfair
The system of appointment is unfair and dependent on the preferences of ministers. The Commissioner for Appointments has claimed that 'political allegiance' has been the decisive factor in ministers' choice of appointees (*Guardian*, 20 November 2000).

5. Waste and corruption
Some quangos have been accused of waste and corruption.

6. Fragmented policy-making process
The growth of quangos has led to 'increased fragmentation of both government structure and the policy-making process' (Wilson 2003 p.385). Quangos tend to have a single focus and, as such, cannot contribute to the need to have 'joined-up' government.

Main points   Sections 18.39 - 18.42

- **Quango stands for quasi autonomous non-(or national) governmental organisation. There are different definitions, making it difficult to know how many quangos there are.**
- **Quangos are run by governmental appointees, not by elected representatives. They are accountable neither to an electorate nor to a minister. Their job is to perform functions laid down by central government.**

- **The numbers of quangos have tended to grow though official figures show a fall partly because only national bodies are counted and also because the government uses a narrow definition.**
- **There have been complaints about a democratic deficit and abuse of patronage.**

Activity 18.9 Quangos

Item A Government by quango

Neither the local nor the national politicians seem to be in charge as the great machinery of state progressively falls into the hands of unelected, unaccountable quangos. Nothing less than the future of our nation is at stake as a once democratic society is falling into the hands of faceless bureaucracy. It is time our politicians recognised this growing threat and clawed back power from these monsters, restoring it to elected bodies at the lowest level at which decisions can be taken.

Adapted from the *Guardian*, 19 November 1993 and the *Daily Mail*, 25 March 1994.

Item B Quangos and New Labour

This table shows the top five quangos in 2000 by staff numbers and by spending.

In opposition, Labour made hay with the Tories' failure to cull quangos. In power, the Labour government has been an enthusiastic creator of executive and advisory bodies which stand at arm's length from Whitehall departments. The reason is simple. Ministers are, for the most part, executive incompetents and so usually are their senior civil servants. They talk management but have no experience of it. Officially, there are some 1,000 quangos. The top five are shown here. The Higher Education Funding Council dispenses grants to universities. It is thought offensive to the ideal of academic autonomy for the money to be handed out directly by the Department for Education and Skills (DfES).

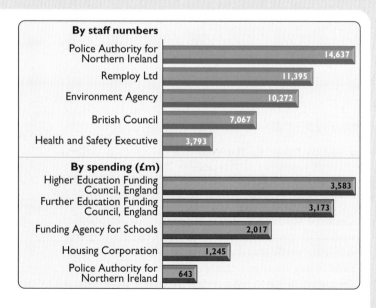

Lower down the list, English Partnerships give grants for the physical regeneration of, for example, former coalfields. There are also c.500 NHS trusts, authorities and boards. Since John Major created the office of Commissioner of Public Appointments, quango jobs have been inspected to ensure successful candidates are deserving. On arriving in power, Labour promised to improve gender balance and diversity. Studies show that it has, mainly by appointing party members onto NHS boards (party members often being black and/or female).

Source: The *Guardian*, 4 September 2000.

Questions

1. 'Quangos should be abolished.' Using Items A and B and your own knowledge, give arguments for and against this statement.
2. What does Item A tell us about quangos? Why do you think the cartoonist chose these images?
3. Are there any signs in Item B that the Labour government has adopted a different approach towards quangos?

References

Aughey (2004) Aughey, A., 'The democratic Troubles', *Prospect*, February 2004.

Bogdanor (1979) Bogdanor, V., *Devolution*, Oxford University Press, 1979.

Bogdanor (2003) Bogdanor, V., 'Asymmetric Devolution: Towards a Quasi-Federal Constitution' in *Dunleavy et al. (2003)*.

Bort (2001) Bort, E., 'Devolution and the end of Britain', *Politics Review*, Vol.10.3, February 2001.

Bradbury (1998) Bradbury, J., 'Yr ie bychan - the little yes: the 1997 Welsh Assembly referendum', *Politics Review*, Vol.7.4, April 1998.

Bradbury (2000) Bradbury, J., 'The Welsh Assembly and the fall of Alun Michael', *Politics Review*, Vol.10.1, September 2000.

British Social Attitudes Survey (2002) *British Social Attitudes Survey: 19th Report*, Sage, 2002.

Cabinet Office (2003) Cabinet Office, *Public Bodies*, HMSO, 2003.

Chandler (2001) Chandler, J., *Local Government Today* (3rd edn), Manchester University Press, 2001.

Conservative (1992) Conservative Party election manifesto, *The Best Future for Britain*, Conservative Central Office, 1992.

Denver (2001) Denver, D., 'The devolution project', *Politics Review*, Vol.11.1, September 2001.

Dobson (1998) Dobson, A., 'The 1997 general election: explaining a landslide' in *Lancaster (1998)*.

Dorey (2002) Dorey, P., 'The West Lothian question in British politics', *Talking Politics*, Vol. 15.1, September 2002.

Dunleavy et al. (1997) Dunleavy, P., Gamble, A., Holliday, I. & Peele, G., *Developments in British Politics 4*, Macmillan, 1997.

Dunleavy et al. (2000) Dunleavy, P., Gamble, A., Holliday, I. & Peele, G., *Developments in British Politics 6*, Macmillan, 2000.

Dunleavy et al. (2003) Dunleavy, P., Gamble, A., Holliday, I. Heffernan, R., & Peele, G., *Developments in British Politics 7*, Palgrave, 2003.

Elcock (2003) Elcock, H., 'Devolution and the English Regions' in *Lancaster (2003)*.

Elcock & Parks (2000) Elcock, H. & Parks, J., 'The English imperium reversed? Devolution sought and (partly) achieved?' in *Lancaster (2000)*.

Fisher et al. (2003) Fisher J., Denver, D., Benyon, J., *Central Debates in British Politics*, Pearson Education, 2003.

Flinders (1999) Flinders, M., 'British quasi-Government: history, diversity and debate', *Talking Politics*, Vol.11.3, 1999.

Gamble (1993) Gamble, A., 'Territorial Politics' in *Dunleavy et al. (1993)*.

Game (2003) Game, C., 'Local government in Labour's second term: Plenty more Modernisation and a few elected Mayors' in *Lancaster (2003)*.

Heppell & McCreanor (2003) Heppell, T. & McCreanor, R., 'English regional governance', *Talking Politics*, Vol.15.3, April 2003.

HMSO (1991) Department of the Environment, *The Structure of Local Government In England*, HMSO, 1991.

Hogwood (1995) Hogwood, B., 'The integrated regional offices and the single regenerational budget', *Commission for Local Democracy Research Report 13*, Municipal Journal Books, 1995.

Holland (2000) Holland, M., 'Trust the key as guns fall silent', *Observer*, 7 May 2000.

Holliday (1997) Holliday, I., 'Territorial Politics' in *Dunleavy et al. (1997)*.

Jones (2004) Jones, A., *New Politics PAL 2004*, Leicester, 2004.

Labour (1997) Labour Party election manifesto, *New Labour - Because Britain Deserves Better*, Labour Party, 1997.

Labour (2001) Labour Party election manifesto, *Ambitions for Britain*, Labour Party, 2001.

Lancaster (1998) Lancaster, S. (ed.), *Developments in Politics*, Vol.9, Causeway Press, 1998.

Lancaster (2000) Lancaster, S. (ed.), *Developments in Politics*, Vol.11, Causeway Press, 2000.

Lancaster (2003) Lancaster, S. (ed.), *Developments in Politics*, Vol.14, Causeway Press, 2003.

Lomas (2001) Lomas, B., 'The Good Friday Agreement: termly report', *Talking Politics*, Vol.14.1, September 2001.

Ludlam & Smith (2001) Ludlam, S. & Smith, M.J. (eds), *New Labour in Government*, Palgrave, 2001.

Lynch (1998) Lynch, P., 'The Scottish devolution referendum 1997: the road to a Scottish Parliament', *Politics Review*, Vol.7.4, April 1998.

Lynch (2000) Lynch, P., 'Devolution and intergovernmental relations in the UK', *Politics Review*, Vol. 9.1, September 2000.

Lynch (2001) Lynch, P., 'Scottish devolution and coalition government', *Politics Review*, Vol. 11.2, November 2002.

McCullagh & O'Dowd (1986) McCullagh, M. & O'Dowd, L., 'Northern Ireland: the search for a solution', *Social Studies Review*, March 1986.

McDonald (2001) McDonald, H., 'Trimble: Good Friday deal is certain to fail', *Observer*, 29 July 2001.

McDonald et al. (2001) McDonald, H., Ahmed, K. & Vulliamy, E., 'How America held the IRA over a barrel', *Observer*, 28 October 2001.

McNaughton (1998) McNaughton, N., *Local and Regional Government in Britain*, Hodder and Stoughton, 1998.

Mitchell (2003a) Mitchell, J., 'Politics in Scotland' in *Dunleavy et al. (2003)*.

Mitchell (2003b) Mitchell J., 'Devolution and the future of the Union' in *Fisher et al. (2003)*.

Norris & Gavin (1997) Norris, P. & Gavin N.T. (eds), *Britain Votes 1997*, Oxford University Press, 1997.

Norton (1994) Norton, P., 'The Constitution in Question', *Politics Review*, Vol.3.4, April 1994.

Peele (2003) Peele, G., 'Politics in England and Wales' in *Dunleavy et al. (2003)*.

Pierre & Stoker (2000) Pierre, J., and Stoker, G., 'Towards Multi-Level Governance' in *Dunleavy et al. (2000)*.

Rallings & Thrasher (1997) Rallings, C. & Thrasher, M., 'The local elections' in *Norris & Gavin (1997)*.

Rathbone (2003) Rathbone, M., 'The National Assembly for Wales' *Talking Politics*, Vol. 15.3, April 2003.

Richards & Smith (2001) Richards, D. & Smith, M.J., 'New Labour, the constitution and reforming the state' in *Ludlam & Smith (2001)*.

Robins (2001) Robins, L., *Politics PAL*, Hyperion Press, 2001.

Rowntree (1997) Joseph Rowntree Foundation, 'The new government of London', *Local and Central Government Relations Research Findings*, No.56, March 1997.

Sell (1998) Sell, G., 'Scottish nationalism in the 1990s', *Talking Politics*, Vol. 10.3, Spring 1998.

Simpson (1998) Simpson, D., *UK Government and Politics in Context*, Hodder and Stoughton, 1998.

Tonge (2003a) Tonge, J., 'Politics in Northern Ireland' in *Dunleavy et al. (2003)*.

Tonge (2003b) Tonge, J., 'The only show in town?', *Politics Review*, Vol.13.1, September 2003.

Totten & Collomb-Robert (2001) Totten, K. & Collomb-Robert, N., *The Northern Ireland Question: Towards a 21st Century Solution?*, Sheffield Halham University Press, 2001.

Wilson (2003) Wilson, D., 'Regulating Society: Quangos' in *Fisher et al. (2003)*.

Wilson & Game (1998) Wilson, D. & Game, C., *Local Government in the United Kingdom*, Macmillan, 1998.

Index